Cricket and the Law

Footbal   of
cricket   1-
cepts es

Crick   of
the gam   1s
and con   of
convent

This   t,
sociolog

David F   ',
Nottingl

Routledge Studies in Law, Society and Popular Culture
Series Editors: Steve Greenfield and Guy Osborn
School of Law, University of Westminster, UK.

Routledge Studies in Law, Society and Popular Culture is an inter-disciplinary series that examines the relationship between the law and all areas of popular culture. Particular foci include the regulation of spheres of popular culture and representations of law within popular culture. 'Popular Culture' is a broad and inclusive church that includes all aspects of leisure and culture, including but not confined to music, sport, film, media, night-time economy, art, literature, the internet etc. Whilst law may well provide a useful vehicle for an analysis of cultural activities within society the absence of law in the field may be just as important and worthy of consideration.

The Series Editors are interested in receiving proposals and manuscripts for this series, please contact Dr Guy Osborn or Steve Greenfield at the University of Westminster (G.Osborn@wmin.ac.uk or S.Greenfield@wmin.ac.uk).

This is the first book in the series.

Cricket and the Law
The Man in White is Always Right

David Fraser

Routledge
Taylor & Francis Group

LONDON AND NEW YORK

First published 2005
by Routledge
2 Park Square, Milton Park, Abingdon, Oxon OX14 4RN

Simultaneously published in the USA and Canada
by Routledge
270 Madison Avenue, New York, NY 10016

Routledge is an imprint of the Taylor & Francis Group

Typeset in Goudy by
Integra Software Services Pvt. Ltd, Pondicherry, India
Printed and bound in Great Britain by
Antony Rowe Ltd, Chippenham, Wiltshire

British Library Cataloguing in Publication Data
A catalogue record for this book is available from the British Library

Library of Congress Cataloging in Publication Data
A catalog record for this book has been requested

ISBN 0–714–65347–0 (hbk)
ISBN 0–714–68285–3 (pbk)

I want to stress again one aspect of the game which is most important. Never argue with an umpire.

– Ian Botham

I don't understand why, in a democratic society, where government and all the accepted standards in every walk of life are being questioned, umpires should be immune.

– Asif Iqbal

Contents

Series editor's preface

Cricket writing has a long and distinguished history, with a breadth and depth of writing that is almost unique within sport. The material ranges from the biographical to the statistical, and the long history of cricket provides a huge wealth of material to draw upon. Cricket as a whole is incredibly well served in terms of its literature, with examples of books reaching beyond the compass of the sport itself and analysing broader social and political concerns.[1] Major issues such as apartheid and, more recently, the human rights record of Zimbabwe and the political relationship between India and Pakistan have been reflected in the playing, or abandonment, of cricket. Down notes the importance of the game to English society thus; 'Cricket surely deserves this special treatment since, more than almost any other sport in England, it is woven deep into the fabric of society, its influence embracing the most noble-born and the most humble'.[2] Evidence of this can be seen for example in the use of cricketing vernacular and metaphor within the English language. That cricket is evocative of something broader than the game itself can be seen in the use of cricket by politicians from Geoffrey Howe to John Major, the latter memorably using cricket as emblematic of all, to him at least, that is great about Britain; 'Fifty years on from now, Britain will still be the country of long shadows on county [cricket] grounds, warm beer, invincible green suburbs, dog lovers and old maids bicycling to Holy Communion through the morning mist'.

Cricket has become subject to increasing regulation at a whole host of levels. Even within some local leagues there are complex player regulations and disciplinary sanctions, whilst the professional game has had to contend with issues such as match-fixing, drug taking and of course the perennial debate that concerns 'chucking'. The increased regulation mirrors other areas of sport and popular culture more generally:

'In recent years the law has increasingly become involved within popular culture on a number of different levels: the law has, in effect, begun to colonise leisure. As the leisure industry has developed it has faced increasing legal regulation. For example, within the music industry we see the increased visibility of the law in contractual problems, disputes about intellectual property and control over the dissemination of material. The media too has been increasingly subject to legal regulation of content. The phenomenon is equally marked within sport'.[3]

Cricket and the Law deals in part with this juridification, but goes further and considers the wider relationship between cricket and the law, and by implication, society itself. As Fraser notes in his preface, '[law] is a social construct, law is not above or separated from the other social practices which govern our lives. Law *is* politics, sociology and literature, and ... it is also cricket'.[4] It is these connections and collisions between two apparently disparate areas of everyday life, and what this relationship tells us about our existence, that lie at the heart of the text. As Allan Hutchinson noted in a review of the first edition of this work; 'Fraser uses cricket as a medium through which to illustrate how issues of legality, ethics and moral judgment inform all person's lives and their daily social practices'.[5]

When we first met David, and saw the first edition of this book, we were delighted that a book of such academic breadth and excellence had been written on the area. Links and ideas that now seem obvious were revealed in a series of perceptive and original chapters. However, its publication on a small imprint emanating from the Institute of Criminology at the University of Sydney meant that few people were able to get hold of the work and the book was deprived of the audience it deserved. When we became series editors of *Studies in Law, Society and Popular Culture* we resolved to not only commission new texts but also to 'reclaim' lost classics. David Fraser's *Cricket and the Law* is a classic, and we are delighted and honoured that we are able to offer this in our series.

Steve Greenfield and Guy Osborn
School of Law
University of Westminster
Series Editors, *Studies in Law, Society and Popular Culture*

Preface

When I first moved to Australia in Dec. 1988, the Pakistani and West Indies cricket teams were touring the country. I knew little, if anything, about cricket and was astounded by the blanket media coverage accorded to the sport. Because of my interest in popular culture and especially in television, and because I am basically quite boring, I soon found myself glued to the TV set watching a game the mysteries and subtleties of which completely escaped me.

One day, as I watched with some Australian friends, there was a unanimous shout from the fielding side and the batter was, or so I was informed, given out LBW. As my friends answered my queries, I suddenly found myself with an anchor, a point of reference from which I could begin to understand this game. The LBW decision bears a strong resemblance to the issues raised in the very problematic area of causation in tort or criminal law, especially when dealing with liability for an omission. How can something which did not occur be said to have 'caused' something which did? How can the umpire be sure the ball would have hit the stumps? What is the factual condition precedent for such a legal adjudication?

While my fascination with cricket and obsession with the game soon found other points of reference and ways of understanding, the connections with Law continue to fascinate. From the case of William Waterfall, the first person convicted of manslaughter on the cricket field at the Derby Assizes of 1775, to the restrictive trade practices litigation of Packer cricket, to continuing controversies over the tax status of benefit proceeds, to debates over ambush marketing and players' sponsorship contracts, cricket provides many useful examples of 'real law'. More importantly, however, cricket offers examples of how legality, ethics and moral judgements inform all our lives and our daily social practices.

The real purpose of writing this work is to explore the interactions of these sometimes competing and contradictory ways of ordering our private and public lives. Traditional 'legal' scholarship has tended to ignore these concerns, mostly by adopting the strictly formalist division of legal positivism between law on the one hand and morality on the other. This leads to the equally disingenuous strategy of defining such concerns as ethics and morality as higher order issues and leaving them to the marginalized area of jurisprudence. My own encounters with these apparently so-called objective categories, through my own work in areas as diverse as law and popular culture and the legal regime of Nazism, as well as the work of others in these and other areas, challenges the cultural and ideological assumptions which inform mainstream legal scholarship.

By focusing here on the ways in which the legal and ethical principles of the game of cricket are formed, constructed and challenged in the daily practice of the game itself, I try to offer concrete examples of law not as an over-arching, objective set of concrete and irreversible rules, but as a social construct, an artifact which is created by us, in society, to serve definite functions. Because it is a social construct, law is not above or separated from the other social practices which govern our lives. Law *is* politics, sociology and literature, and as I hope to show here, it is also cricket.

This means that all of the apparently separate and distinct social phenomena that we encounter in our daily existence are interconnected and together they tell the story of our lives. Not all of them all the time and not always the same story. Out of the complex myriad of factors, we select the elements which narrate our personal and collective existences. This does not mean that I am trying to establish a claim for cricket as a new meta-narrative. Rather, all I am trying to do is to demonstrate that cricket, and all the complexity and contradiction which make up our understanding of that game, can tell us much about the way we live and about the role and function of law in our society. Indeed, one of the main areas of the legal practices of cricket which makes it such a good point for making the broader political point is the very contradictions of the game itself. Cricket is not just obedience to the strict letter of the *Laws* of the game but about appeals to the 'spirit of the game'. Adjudication and law-making in practice deal with, decide, or live with the contradictions of complexity and uncertainty. That is precisely why we watch cricket and it should be why we practise law. This work is concerned with the breaking down of barriers between the parts of our lives. It is an argument against seeing either law or cricket as distinct areas of existence which have nothing to do with one another. It offers support for the contention that it is wrong and counter-factual for us to think, as traditional views of the role and function of 'the law' would have us believe, that there are important and higher things like 'the Law' and unimportant and lower things like cricket. At the same time, I try to offer an examination of the complexities of daily practice which underline the 'fact' that 'the law', like 'cricket' is not one-dimensional or fixed, but that both are informed and constructed by participants in each endeavour. This does not mean that we must not make individual and social orderings and rankings of priorities but it does mean that we must realize that there is nothing pre-ordained or immutable about the orderings we do make. What follows, then, is my own idiosyncratic view of the inter-connections between the various parts of what we might call cricket, law and the meaning of life.

Some of the analogies and metaphors are straightforward – causation and LBW, frequency of appeals and respect for the judicial process, neutral umpires and judicial bias. Others are more complex – walking *versus* the strict respect for the umpire's jurisdiction, *Mankading* and the complex morality which regulates the practice of cricketers indicate an equitable practice which supplements strict legality. Still others involve discussions of broader, traditional meta-constructs, race, class and gender. What they all share is a narrative ability, that is they can all serve as a means to understand and create stories about who we are and how we live.

While most of the examples of moral, legal and ethical problems are taken from first-class cricket, I do not suggest that this is the only source of knowledge we have about the game. Indeed, many of us gain primary experience from village or park cricket rather than from playing in Test matches. There are, of course, differences, or local knowledges within these levels of the game. Neutral umpires are problematic in park cricket where each side provides umpires for its own innings, one factor which may lead to the infrequency of successful LBW appeals. Even the importance of some *Laws* may be exacerbated in park cricket. Thus, while 'timed out' is extremely rare at higher levels of the game, it takes on a certain importance in local matches when wickets fall rapidly and the club has only two or three pairs of pads in the kit. At the same time, however, one is just as likely to find slow over rates, sledging, walking or not walking etc. in village cricket as in a Test. This is, of course, no different from the practice of law where a country solicitor and High Court judge may have little in common at one level of their daily lives but they both work and live in the same legal system.

There may be no meta-narratives or fundamental values as there were in the good old days but our lives and experiences are rich and eventful. Cricket and law, separately and together, are two such events through which we give meaning to our lives.

This book had its origins in Australia where I lived and worked for the past 14 years. Many, but not all, of the examples used to illustrate the issues and questions raised by the intersections of cricket and the law come from the Australian context. The advent of the Internet and World Wide Web have made the study of the game in other parts of the world more accessible and I have benefited enormously from resources made available by *CricInfo*.

Many friends and colleagues have tolerated many discussions about the jurisprudence of cricket over the years. Special mention must be made of Steve Greenfield and Guy Osborn of the Centre for the Study of Law Society and Popular Culture at the University of Westminster. Their work and encouragement have been both inspirational and supportive. Vaughan Black of Dalhousie University and Kathryn McMahon of the University of Warwick have put up with my passion for the game with grace and good humour. Allan Hutchinson of Osgoode Hall Law School has provided the basis for an ongoing and stimulating conversation about the jurisprudence of cricket. The games of life and of law are more interesting for me as a result and this book owes him a debt of gratitude.

Former Australian captains Richie Benaud and Ian Chappell took time to share their thoughts and impressions with me and to them I am grateful.

Professor Mark Findlay of the Institute of Criminology supported and encouraged the publication of a much earlier version of this book and Associate

Professor Chris Cunneen has kindly given permission to reproduce parts of it here.

Finally, a word about language. The *Preamble of the Laws of Cricket* provides that

> The players, umpires and scorers in a game of cricket may be of either gender and the Laws apply equally to both. The use, throughout the text, of pronouns indicating the male gender is purely for brevity. Except where specifically stated otherwise, every provision of the Laws is to be read as applying to women and girls equally as to men and boys.

I have adopted a similar practice in this book. Players and umpires are referred to as 'he' except where indicated. This is done both for the sake of brevity and clarity of language. It is also the case that most of what I discuss in this book involves men doing manly things. Cricket has been predominately male and has always been a highly gendered pursuit. I offer some discussion and analysis of the cult of virility which underpins much of the practice and jurisprudence of cricket throughout the pages which follow.

That being said however, I have also adopted the practice increasingly found in Australian cricket commentary but not so commonly in English or other cricket. I use gender neutral language to describe players – batsmen become batters, fieldsmen become fielders etc. This ambiguity about gender and language found in this book is but one example of the many contradictions and complexities of cricket and law. That is why I love the game and why despite my better inclinations, I may well love the law.

David Fraser

Foreword

Cricket is a unique game. It is the only game in the world where food-breaks such as lunch and tea intervals are built into the game. But perhaps its most unique feature is the way officials who administer the game on the field of play come to decisions. In all other team games, and even individual sports, an official in charge of the game, be he a football referee or a tennis umpire, makes the decision without any reference to what the player may feel about the decision. A tennis player may argue that the ball is out, or a football player may feel that the trip that has seen him go sprawling in the penalty area is worth a penalty to his team. But however much either player appeals to the referee or the umpire it will make no difference to the official's decision. Even without appeals the referee in football could decide to give a penalty, and the umpire in tennis rule the ball out. If the player appeals too excessively he could be penalised, given a red card in football, docked points in tennis. In both sports the player's views about the decisions and whether they were right or wrong are much discussed in the media and by the spectators, but they make no difference to how the officials have arrived at their judgements. An official may occasionally change his mind at the player's request, but he does not have to wait for a player to appeal before giving a decision. But in cricket, in order to get a batsman out the fielding side must appeal to the umpire. True, if the batsman is bowled there is no need for an appeal as everyone can see that the stumps have been disturbed. Also for a clear catch in the outfield an appeal is usually unnecessary, but in other cases such as catches close to the wicket, lbws, run-outs and stumping there has to be an appeal and only then can the official give a decision. If there is no appeal, he has no right to respond. So even if the batsman is out and the umpire knows the batsman is out but for some reason the fielding side does not appeal, the umpire cannot give the batsman out. The batsman carries on.

This unique nature of the game makes the umpire a sort of a judge in an Appeal Court. It is this nature of the game which David Fraser, a lawyer by profession, has examined in such depth.

Fraser is a relative newcomer to cricket. In 1988 while in Australia, he saw Australia play Pakistan and was fascinated by the umpire giving a batsman out lbw after the fielding side had appealed. His curiosity was immediately aroused by the fact that in this case the decision meant the umpire had to judge whether the ball would have hit the stumps, an event that had not occurred but might have had the batsman's legs not got in the way. Putting on his lawyer's hat he thought this was very similar to the problematic area of causation in trot or criminal law, especially when dealing with the liability for an omission.

From this original starting point Fraser goes on to analyse the role of the umpire in the wider question or law-making and provides fascinating material for cricket lovers.

Here you will find some of the game's most memorable and controversial moments but debated and discussed in a very unusual way from a legal perspective.

Fraser highlights how cricket was the last sport to have neutral umpires; in other words, umpires that did not come from countries contesting the match. Now this may seem very obvious. Can you imagine an England–Scotland football match being refereed by an Englishman or a Scotsman but in cricket until the 1990s the home country provided the umpires and it is only in recent years that both umpires in Tests come from a country not involved in the match.

I particularly found the chapter on what the Australians call *Mankading* riveting. This refers to the incident during India's tour of Australia in 1947–48 when Vinoo Mankad, one of the game's greatest all-rounders, ran the Australian batsman Bill Brown out as he wandered out of his crease. Mankad was then running up to bowl, but as he got to the wicket and saw Brown out of his crease he stopped in his delivery stride and whipped off the bails. Under the laws of the game although the ball had not been delivered, the game was live and with Brown out of his crease the umpire had to give him out when Mankad appealed. Although such incidents had happened before in cricket, it was the first time it had happened in Test cricket and it caused a storm. In Australia it has since come to be known as *Mankading*. What Mankad did was perfectly legal but for some in cricket it was not quite ethical, not quite cricket and remains an explosive issue. Fraser gives a fine lawyer's analysis of this issue which provides a new perspective on this subject.

If I have highlighted this chapter it is because it illustrates the unique nature of cricket, as do all the other chapters in this book. Every chapter has some detail or point of interest which makes this a book every cricket lover should have. It will not only reacquaint him with many controversial moments of the game's past, but make him see them in a different light. It will enhance his love of this great game.

Mihir Bose
October 2004
London, UK

1 Introduction

'It's not cricket'. Everyone knows the meaning of these three words. They embody the ideals of fair play, 'gentlemanly' behaviour, and 'good sportsmanship'. What I shall attempt to demonstrate in the rest of this book, however, is that these three words, and all they embody, is in reality, subject to enormous doubt, ambiguity, stress and struggle. While everyone might know what the phrase means at a level of generality, once we turn to the specifics of what might be the actual rules and practices contained in the ideal of 'fair play', in this context, the spirit of the game, or more specifically still, of 'cricket', things become much more complicated. As any good lawyer will tell you, language is full of ambiguity. Indeed, lawyers and judges, to the frustration of the general public, often seem to thrive on making ambiguous that which appears to be perfectly clear.

At some level, that is indeed the project of this book. I want to explore the ambiguities, uncertainties, and contradictions of cricket and of law. The ideal of the uncluttered contest between bat and ball, of willow and leather, which gives to cricket its place in the mythology of England and of Empire, is in fact, and in law, as all of us who love the game in fact must recognize, far from its lived reality. What makes this interesting from a number of perspectives, including perhaps the unexpected angle of legal theory, is that cricket can, and I argue throughout does, offer us exciting lessons about the nature and possibilities inherent in ambiguity and doubt. Indeed, cricket itself, in its laws and practices embodies almost from the beginning these conflicts and contradictions. The *Laws of Cricket* make explicit reference to the 'spirit of the game', which must, at some level at least, be deemed to exceed, or to be outside of, the strict and literal text of the statute.[1] In what follows I will explore in particular contexts three levels of interpretive and practical conflict – the contradictions between and among various readings of the *Laws* themselves; contradictions, real and apparent between the *Laws* and the 'spirit of the game'; and finally, the disagreements about and around the content of our understandings of exactly what constitutes the 'spirit of the game'.

In all of this, I shall attempt to set out the ways in which these interpretive practices and disputes embody and reflect debates within and about law. Law and cricket are, I believe, simply different arenas in which struggles over meanings, interpretations, applications of rules by adjudicators, judges and umpires in these instances, engage us politically, ideologically and socially. For example, debates about LBW decisions are 'the same' as debates about causation in tort or criminal law; debates about dissent on the field are debates about contempt and respect for legal institutions in a democracy. And sometimes, debates around and about cricket are in reality, debates about the very existence of law and democracy. Recent controversies about the existence of corruption and bribery at the highest levels of the game have brought these concerns to the fore of discussions about the rule of law in cricket. Hansie Cronje has provided us with the possibility for some of the greatest jurisprudential inquiries of the new millennium.

The Jurisprudence of Hansie Cronje

My friend and colleague Allan Hutchinson has argued persuasively in his recent book on judging, not just that law is a game of adjudication, but that the core element of all game playing, including law, is 'good faith'. Good faith is at the heart of the game of law and adjudication which is a practice at once free and constrained. It is the understanding and deployment of good faith that we encounter and play with the vital Hutchinsonian distinction between 'anything goes' and 'anything might go' in judging. Thus, 'Accordingly, good faith can be thought of as acting in line with the spirit of the enterprise in which one is engaged and respecting other people's expectations about what is supposed to happen.'[2]

This insight offers us the constraining limit which operates between and among the apparent contradictions of law and the spirit of the game which I discuss in the subsequent chapters of the book. All the conflicts will be, must be, can only be solved, within a framework in which the expectations of the participants in the game – law or cricket – about the definitional content of the game itself, are met. Judges, plaintiffs, defendants, umpires, spectators, players, all share expectations that certain things will occur within certain, yet often unspecified limitations. Judges must decide on the basis of accepted practices and discourses. They must adjudicate, even when in the process of that adjudication, they must call upon some uncertain criteria, for example 'public policy'. They may not, they must not, simply 'flip a coin', they must decide and they must decide as judges. It is when these limitations, however uncertain, on the judicial function, are violated, when good faith ceases to exist, that at some level, we are no longer playing the game. Throughout this book, I want to explore these boundaries at the two levels of playing the game and not playing the game, of law and not law, of the point at which violation of the *Laws* becomes at a true level, not cricket.

This is what happened, perhaps, in South Africa in early 2000, when England met the host country in the fifth Test at Centurion Park. When they visited South Africa for this Test match series, as usual, England lost. But they did not lose everything. In the fifth Test, at Centurion Park in Pretoria, England actually won a game. But this is in reality and in law of secondary importance. What is vital here is the way in which they won, for quite literally, the very existence of cricket and the law hang in the balance.

A normal Test match will be played, if it lasts the distance, over five days. Each team will bat, if required, in each of its two innings until its 10 wickets have fallen. Thus, as we know, the winner is the team which scores more total runs than the other side while managing to take the 20 opposition wickets. The *Laws of Cricket* allow a captain to 'declare' the team's innings closed before all wickets have been lost. Normally this will occur when a team feels it has enough runs to win the game and wishes to leave itself enough time to bowl the other team out in order to win the match. However, this is not what happened at Centurion Park.

There, almost all of the first four days of play had been lost due to rain. In the normal course of events, the batting side, the South Africans in this case, would have batted on day five until it became obvious under the *Laws* that no result was possible and the match would have ended in the typical dull sort of draw for which English cricket in particular has unfortunately been noted. However, the South African captain, Hansie Cronje, met with the England captain Nasser Hussain, at breakfast before the final day's play and proposed a novel, even revolutionary, solution. Cronje would 'declare' his innings closed, after setting a score which England had a reasonable, but far from certain, chance to overcome in its second innings. In return, England would 'declare' their first innings without batting. In other words, the Test would be played to its full in one day instead of five, an exciting run chase would be guaranteed for the fans instead of the predictable batting practice. The 'spirit of the game' would triumph, as the recent trend of captains trying for a 'result', in other words a win or a loss, to go down fighting etc., would be carried out by the two sides here. Hussain agreed. South Africa set a target and England won in the last over of an exciting day's play.

Centurion Park was the first time in the history of Test cricket that a side had 'declared' its innings without batting. For the jurisprudential traditionalists, this constituted a 'forfeiture', rather than a declaration. Under the *Laws* in effect at the time, they had a good point. A strict reading of the *Laws* would indicate that such an act by Hussain was 'illegal'. Under Law 14(1) and (2) of the 1980 *Code*, it appears to be quite clear that

1. Time of Declaration
The Captain of the batting side may declare an innings closed at any time during a match irrespective of its duration.
2. Forfeiture of Second Innings
A Captain may forfeit his second innings, provided his decision to do so is notified to the opposing Captain and Umpires in sufficient time to allow 7 minutes rolling of the pitch.

Law 12 added that a match 'shall be of one or two innings according to the agreement of the sides prior to play' and Law 15 of the 1980 *Code* indicated that

1. Call of Play

At the start of each innings and of each day's play and on the resumption of play after any interval or interruption the Umpire at the Bowler's end shall call 'play'.

Reading these provisions of the *Laws* in force at the time, it would seem clear that Hussain's decision not to bat at all in England's first innings constituted a 'forfeiture', rather than a 'declaration'. An innings can be declared 'closed' under these provisions only 'at any time' during the match. If there is to be a difference between a 'declaration' and a 'forfeiture' on these textual provisions, it must be that a declaration can only take place once play has started by the umpire calling 'play'. Not batting at all, a captain cannot close that which has not already been opened. Since the 'forfeiture' provision of the 1980 *Code* applied only to a second innings, Nasser Hussain acted illegally in forfeiting his first innings. This is the position of former Test umpire Don Oslear who declared therefore that

> As a consequence, the innings in progress at close of play on the final day was England's first innings. Therefore the real result of the match was not a 'victory' for England but a draw.[3]

Oslear was joined by at least two former Test umpires from Australia, Len King and Robin Bailhache in condemning the illegality of the 'declaration'. King referred to the action as a 'farce' and concurred with Oslear that it should not have been possible 'according to the letter of the law'.[4]

For others, in the majority it would appear, the agreement between the captains was cricket at its finest. This was not corruption. This was not tainted by a fundamental illegality. There was no absolute nullity contaminating Hussain's 'declaration'. Instead we must characterize the captains' agreement as competition in the best traditions of the spirit of the game. A result was, if not guaranteed, at least on the cards, but *the* result depended purely on England's ability to score the runs against a South African side bent on preventing them from doing so. In other words, there would be a real game of cricket in which, as Allan Hutchinson would put it, anything might go.

Christopher Martin-Jenkins declared that while there might be some room for 'legal' debate over the distinction between a 'forfeiture' (illegal) and a 'declaration' (legal), the two sides played a game of cricket, the fans saw a game of cricket, and the umpires rendered decisions within the context of a game of Test match cricket. He wrote:

> Traditional sportsmanship often seems to be under threat from the exaggerated aggression of those playing the game for increasingly high financial stakes. The events of yesterday can have only been good for the spirit of the game.[5]

He added

> Initiative and a sense of public responsibility triumphed over the kind of dog-in-the-manger attitude that sometimes gives cricket a bad name. The result was an unexpectedly tense, intense and downright thrilling conclusion to a Test match that had threatened to meander away meaninglessly.[6]

For another commentator, writing with the hyperbole often associated with cricket, the game was a triumph of the human spirit.

> In any case, cricket was treated respectfully by the captains. Nothing untoward occurred. No rubbish was sent down, nor any easy runs given away. They did the right thing. Nature cannot be allowed to dictate terms. Man is not so woefully short of imagination nor Test cricket so insufferably serious that a fair contest cannot be produced when time is tight.[7]

The captains acted in the spirit of the game, for which after all, they were responsible under the *Laws* in force. Law 42(1) stated

> The Captains are responsible at all times for ensuring that play is conducted within the spirit of the game as well as within the Laws.

Law 42(2) added that

> The Umpires are the sole judges of fair and unfair play.[8]

The umpires offered no apparent objection to the deal struck by the captains. Both sides played cricket and England emerged the winners of a tight match. Oslear insists on a close and literal reading of the 1980 *Laws* and the distinction between a declaration and a forfeiture. He and others like King and Bailhache, would argue that the captains' duty to uphold the spirit of the game must be limited and circumscribed by 'as well as within the Laws'. If Hussain had sent out his two opening batters, waited for the umpire to call 'play', and then declared before a ball was bowled, Oslear would have been happy that the *Laws* had been obeyed. Here the umpiring fraternity seems to be adopting a strict rule formalism which ignores any idea that in such circumstances the spirit of the game, obviously shared in these circumstances by almost everyone involved on the day, should have precedence over 'the letter of the law'. As former Australian bowler Geoff Lawson puts it, democracy in the widest sense must be the dominant interpretive norm for determining whether the 'declaration' was or was not 'cricket'.

> Oh, yes, the fans. What a wonderful way to remind us all that the game is not simply played for the players. Fortunately there are still leaders who think the game needs to be relevant to fans as we embark on the 21st century.

...

Now Cronje and Hussain should be praised for their 'innovation', because it reminds us that the game belongs to its followers.[9]

We know from experience of the game of cricket that in many instances, the idea of the spirit of the game is meant not just to supplement the *grundnorm* of the *Laws* but to supersede the technical boundaries of the written regulatory provisions. Instead of an elitist and isolated view that umpires and players should always simply adhere to the formal text of the *Laws*, at some level at least this impulse to allow reference to the spirit of the game as an overarching interpretive norm, seeks to allow not just a greater feeling of democratic involvement in rule-making and rule-application, but to permit the game itself to adapt and grow to changing circumstances, according to the agreement and consent of the participants.

And the matter does not end there. According to the *Laws* of the 1980 *Code* in effect at the time,

> Any decision as to the correctness of the scores shall be the responsibility of the Umpires.[10]

The umpires, in raising no objection to the Hussain 'declaration' and in confirming the England victory, have arguably ratified the legality of the captain's action. Once the score has been approved by the umpires as an England victory, there is legally an England victory. The only way in which Oslear can be correct is if he is arguing that the action by Hussain was what lawyers in the civil law tradition would call an absolute nullity, something which we might call void *ab initio*. In such a case, even the decision of the umpires to confirm the score and the result would be unable to convert an illegal act into a legal one. But this depends not on a literal reading of a clear and unambiguous legal text but on an interpretation which gives supremacy to one legal text about when a declaration may be made over another text which grants power and authority over the score to the umpires alone. The question for resolution will not be decided by some reference to legal formalism or legal positivism since it can be decided only by interpretation. The texts and interpretive strategies and positions compete for preeminence here. The winner will be the most persuasive argument and the most persuasive argument will be determined by one's particular vision of the 'spirit of the game'. 'Cricket' in other words, will decide what 'cricket' is.

Finally, it is perhaps relevant, although in no way strictly binding as matter of the strict technical rules of statutory interpretation, to note that under the current *Laws*, Oslear could have no objections to Hussain's 'declaration' or 'forfeiture'. Law 14(2) now reads

Forfeiture of Innings
A captain may forfeit either of his side's innings. A forfeited innings shall be considered as a completed innings.

Again, this new legal position is not dispositive of the debate over the Centurion Park Test. One might argue that the subsequent legislative change supports Oslear's technical, formal reading of the provision of the 1980 *Code*. In other words, the change indicates that his interpretation of the old provisions was in fact correct and that the legislative body has acted to correct a position which gave rise to a situation in which, arguably, the spirit of the game, as embodied in the captains' agreement, came into conflict with the letter of the law and their duty thereto. On the other hand, one might equally assert that the position adopted by the majority of the people concerned, fans, umpires, players etc. that the decision to bat in only one innings by the England captain was, in fact and in law, appropriate. The subsequent change to the *Laws* could then be seen simply as a clarification by the legislature of a statutory ambiguity. Thus on these possibilities, all based on a reading of the *Laws of Cricket* themselves, Oslear was correct, partly correct, or incorrect, as would be anyone who adopted the view totally opposite to that of the former umpire.

Whatever the position one chooses here, the intriguing questions and techniques of legal interpretation briefly outlined demonstrate that even an argument over the *Laws* themselves cannot be solved unambiguously. When we add the complicating factor of the spirit of the game as a (potential) overriding interpretive referent, life, cricket and law all become intriguing and complex. Both Oslear and Martin-Jenkins are making arguments here about what we mean when we say 'cricket'. They are taking interpretive positions about how we go about defining the content of the game by making adjudicative decisions about the meaning of the law. But, for both, the stakes are not the very existence of the game, of cricket or of the law. They are each acting in good faith as Hutchinson would have it, respecting and acknowledging, while disagreeing with, competing claims to truth and legality. Martin-Jenkins might think that cricket would be the poorer if Oslear's legal formalism were to carry the day, but he would not think that we had stopped playing and watching cricket if the match were declared a draw based on Oslear's reading of the text. We would still almost certainly be talking and arguing about cricket and the law within the parameter of the shared understanding of the fundamental and defining characteristics of both cricket and the law.

Of course, because good faith adjudication takes place within only the limited confines of the contingent possibilities of what may or might happen, it is a limiting concept which has only temporary status at any given time and place. What the requirement of good faith does demand, however, is that whatever interpretation is offered or whatever application is suggested, it must result from a genuine effort to make sense of the rule in hand or to deploy law's argumentative resources in a conscientious way. Understood in this way, the requirement of good faith is more an issue of moral integrity than a matter of analytical accuracy; it is less about legal rightness than it is about political reasonableness.[11]

Allan Hutchinson and all those of us who might for better or for worse fall at some time or another into the non-foundationalist camp, would be proud of Nasser Hussain and Hansie Cronje. Here was a case of democratic rule-making and adjudication in which the possibilities inherent in playing the game, anything might happen, clearly triumphed over those who would offer a narrow and formalist technical reading of the legal text and assert as an apparent epistemological certainty that a 'forfeiture' is not a 'declaration' and can never be one. Anything might and can happen when the players of the game, in good faith, construct a legal practice open to the contingencies of human existence. The Centurion Park Test was non-foundationalist legal practice at its best. Unless, of course, we can demonstrate the absence of good faith.

To 'prove' the assertion that the Centurion Park Test was played in and exemplifies the best spirit of the game or at least to argue for this interpretation in a persuasive and good faith manner, we must place this Test within its context as completely as we can. We must publicly declare our reasoning and our beliefs in order to meet the test (no pun intended) of good faith. We must here turn to the question of bribery, corruption and bad faith.

The world of cricket, from its very beginnings, has been mixed up with gambling and the possibility of corruption. Indeed, the *Laws of Cricket* may well have their origins in an attempt to give some certainty to the limits in which betting and gambling on games could occur. In the past few years, with the rise of global telecommunications, more and more international cricket, particularly of the one-day variety, and the existence of a sub-continental diaspora, allegations of bribery and corruption in cricket have come to the fore. The law, history, politics and other contingencies of cricket bribery and match-fixing allegations are complex and I will not go into them here.[12] It is sufficient for the purposes of playing the game at hand, and introducing the issues of legal theory and practice which inform this book, to note simply that Hansie Cronje was a crook. The King Commission in South Africa detailed his connections with illegal bookmakers and match-fixing. After his original declaration of complete innocence, Cronje admitted to receiving money from bookmakers to provide pre-match information, allegedly limited to weather forecasts, pitch conditions and possibly to the make up of his side.

Several aspects of the Cronje case are interesting for the development of an understanding of the vital and essential connections between cricket and law. The first brings us back to the Centurion Park Test match. As a result of ongoing revelations about Cronje's involvement in match-fixing a reexamination of the result from Pretoria is required. The idea that the match was played as the result of a democratic agreement between the captains and that it was in fact, 'good cricket' played in a state of the ludic interpretive triumph of possibilities, has now been replaced by the idea that the game was fixed by Cronje. In other words, he made a 'sporting declaration' not out of some dedication to 'playing the game' but because his bookmaker friends stood to make lots of money out of an entirely unexpected and unforeseeable England victory, or even out of a South African win, neither of which would have been possible if the normal course of a boring draw had eventuated.[13] In other words, a new, unexpected element can alter the context in which our moral, political and legal decision-making process occurs. History is, like all else, interpretation and interpretation is contingent. This reinforces the idea that all judgement and all judgements occur in a contingent world. Anything might happen. A match which took place and was judged to be in the finest spirit of the game can now, in a matter of months, in a changing human, legal, political and moral landscape, become, 'not cricket'. An apparent apotheosis of good faith comes to epitomize the contingent possibility of bad faith.

Thus

> Defeat ended South Africa's unbeaten sequence of 14 Tests since Headingley 1998, and some traditionalists held up their hands in horror at the 'cheapening' of the five-day game. But most agreed, including match referee Barry Jarman and the travelling England supporters who had endured three miserable days without play, that Cronje's enterprise was to be applauded. What subsequently emerged at the King Commission hearing was that Cronje's initiative had been motivated by a Johannesburg bookmaker, Marlon Aronstam, who rewarded the South African captain with 53,000 rand (around £5,000) and a woman's leather jacket. As the odds favoured a draw, a win by either side was the most satisfactory result for the bookmakers.[14]

This brings me to a second point about Hansie Cronje's impact on current legal theory and practice. It has now emerged, although there is still some doubt about the exact circumstances of the events, that during a previous tour by South Africa to India, Cronje passed on an offer to his entire team from an illegal bookmaker for them to lose a game in return for a large sum of money, rumoured to be US$250,000. There are several elements of interpretive and jurisprudential significance here. There is the fact of bribery, and the possibility of mass corruption in the playing of the game. Of equal interpretive significance is the fact that three team meetings were apparently required before Cronje was told that the offer was rejected.[15]

Cronje approached several members of his side individually and then also apparently put the offer to the team as a whole.[16] A simple assertion of a good faith versus a bad faith test, the fundamental criterion for understanding what 'cricket' and 'law' should mean, will not, I fear, be of much assistance to us here. What the Cronje case, and the series of meetings involved before the South African team decided not to take a bribe to throw a match, indicate is that playing the game is always a problematic political, moral and legal issue. In effect, I think that the Hansie Cronje case again reaffirms the basic thrust of the argument in favour of interpretive and legal ambiguity by demonstrating the contingency of what it even means to play the game.

One of the central allegations in the current match-fixing imbroglio surrounds the bribery of players for so-called side betting. Here, the bettor does not wager on the outcome of the game, or even on the more familiar winning/losing margin or the spread. Instead, bets are placed on all aspects of the contingent occurrences within the playing of the game. Thus, one might bet that a particular batter will score fewer than 20 runs. If a player has been bribed, he might have chosen to play a 'bad' shot after scoring 19 runs. Those watching, judging and playing will in all likelihood be unable to tell whether what happened was in fact simply a careless shot or a deliberate attempt to get out. The basic question posed by this sort of bad faith is whether one is still playing the game. How can we tell if bad faith is present when and if the formal aspects of rule adhesion appear to have been fulfilled?

Naturally one might begin by asserting here that the batter is not playing the game since he is participating in a conspiracy to score fewer than 20 runs. Playing the game requires the batter to do the best they can and to score as many runs as possible. But a fuller understanding of the complexities of the game will demonstrate that this is not a universally simple verifiable truth of what it means to play the game. A batter may get out for less than an optimum score for any number of reasons. They might be batting when the captain chooses to declare. They might have been instructed to pick up the scoring rate and as a result have played a shot they might otherwise not have attempted. They might have believed the umpire made a mistake in a prior decision to give them not out, and as a result have played a shot deliberately intended to right that wrong by giving up their wicket. Many would view this last example not as 'not playing the game' but rather as the actual embodiment of playing the game in true adherence to the spirit and best traditions of cricket. The possibilities are endless, anything might happen. And any of those things would still be cricket. The batter would still be playing the game. Good faith and bad faith have become not bright lines of adjudicative demarcation but rather never-fixed points of reference about what it means to talk about playing the game, and about making legal decisions.[17] Two other examples embody the complexities of our understandings of the law and ethics of 'bad faith' and 'cricket'.

In the World Cup in 1999, for example, Australia deliberately slowed down the run rate in a game against the West Indies in an attempt, under the rules and mathematical calculations in force during the tournament, to prevent New Zealand from advancing to the next stage. Australia had a history of exploiting legal technicalities against New Zealand. The 'underarm bowling' controversy has informed legal and cricket relations between the two countries for decades.[18] Many observers saw this as a yet another cynical attempt, in the great Australian tradition, to use legal formalism in the ethics-less search for victory which for them characterizes Australian cricket.[19] Rule formalism, while not in the spirit of the game, is nonetheless still 'cricket' in the strict sense. In 2002, New Zealand and South Africa used the mathematics of run rates and victory margins under the bonus point system to deny the home side a place in the finals of the triangular One-Day International series played in Australia.[20] In each case we find international cricket captains instructing their players not to score more runs, or to score them more slowly, in order to achieve a result not in the game being played but in relation to other considerations, such as who the opponent would be in the finals. Quite clearly there is some understanding that this is close to, but probably does not constitute, 'collusion' or 'match-fixing', even though it is 'not cricket'.[21] At the same time however, the actions by New Zealand captain Stephen Fleming were passed under the legal and ethical microscope. Some in his own country accused him of cheating and indeed of 'match-fixing'. He was charged by his critics with violating the captain's duty to uphold the spirit of the game at all times and with a breach of Para. C, Section 10 of the *ICC Code of Conduct*, in other words, match-fixing. Under the post-Malik and post-Cronje legal regime, match-fixing comes with a life ban from the game.

By focusing on the bonus point question and determining that his team's chances of making the final would be enhanced, if not guaranteed, by permitting the other side, South Africa, to win, Fleming was alleged to have been a party to 'contriving or attempting to contrive the result of any match'.[22] If indeed there was an order to lose the game, we must be very close to the point at which what is going on is in violation of both the spirit and the *Laws* of the game. If sides are trying to lose, can they be said to be playing cricket in good faith? Does the phrase 'playing cricket in good faith' contain a redundancy? In other words, in the absence of good faith, is one still playing 'cricket'? Yet, the result was allowed to stand, Stephen Fleming was not disciplined, let alone banned for life as provided under the *Code of Conduct*. Everyone agreed to disagree but everyone agreed that what happened was 'not cricket', but of course, it was still cricket. The bonus point system which rewarded larger margins of victory was thought to be at fault since it was open to manipulation and distortion. The exploitation of the rules in a ruthless fashion, even when that involves not trying to win, or to score runs when batting, is still, after the World Cup and New Zealand/South Africa cases, playing the game of cricket. The only question here, and this must always be the case, seems to be one of where the line between playing and not playing the game of cricket is to be drawn. The answer appears to be up for grabs. If not trying to win, or even trying to lose can be part of playing the game, just what is 'cricket'?

If we can now return to our understanding and interpretation of Hansie Cronje's offer of US$250,000 to his teammates to lose in India, we might simply see what happened as a series of democratic conversations about what it meant to them to play (or not) the game. Anything might go. For example, the game's administrators and sponsors are subject to ongoing criticism about heavy playing schedules and particularly about the frequency of often 'meaningless' One-Day Internationals. In fact, this is part of the actual context in which the South Africans might have come to discuss the offer relayed by Cronje. If the players decided that a particular game was in fact for them meaningless, then one might, however tentatively at this point, argue that 'not' playing the game by accepting the bribe, was little more than industrial action through self-help by disgruntled workers.

Again, however, this leaves out of the calculation many relevant contingencies which would have to be brought to bear for any complete understanding of what happened, not the least of which would be Cronje's base and basic greed and dishonesty. Imagine for now that the South African team had all decided to take up the bookmaker's offer and throw the game. I assume that they would have had to do so while still giving the appearance of playing the game. Would we spectators and the players on the opposing side, as well as the umpires, have witnessed and participated in a game of cricket? Would we know? Is that important? What if only seven players had agreed, would the other four have been playing a different game? Is this a Platonic problem of shadows in the judicial and adju-dicative cave called 'playing the game' or is it an Aristotelian game which is no longer a game, or is it another game? Just what are we and they playing at here? Is a fixed cricket match still a cricket match? Is good faith simply a way of making rules about making rules in a matrix of contingency spiralling away from us at all times?

During the infamous Bodyline series, the Australian captain, Bill Woodfull, famously said to the English team manager at the end of a bitter day's play:

> Of two teams out there, one is playing cricket, the other is making no effort to play the game of cricket.[23]

What would Hansie Cronje have made of such a conversation? Could he have been a good faith participant in the collective dialogue about the politics of law and cricket? Was he a good cricketer? Was he a cricketer only part of the time? Or was he a cricketer at all?

Bribery and corruption strike at the heart of any good faith adjudicative process. In essence, the game, or some part of it, is fixed, the result pre-determined, an unfair advantage obtained, the very process of judging tainted and changed. Naturally enough though, in a contingent and nonfoundationalist account, all these statements would have to be subjected to political and analytical scrutiny, contextualized and deconstructed. Is a bribed judge, for example, ever still a judge? Does proof of corruption in the judicial process offer *per se* proof that the outcome was 'wrong'? A guilty accused may be convicted as the result of bribery or police corruption. The 'conviction' is tainted in so far as we consider the process essential to the outcome. But this does not mean in a practical sense that the accused did not commit the crime. These questions have of course always troubled our understanding of judicial bribery and police corruption.[24]

They also now trouble our understanding of cricket and of adjudication within the game and about the game. Several international umpires have reported having been approached by bookmakers to supply information which might have led to match-fixing.[25] More serious accusations have been levied against Pakistani umpire Javed Akhtar. Some have alleged that his seven LBW decisions against South Africa in a Test against England in 1998 may have been the result not of a calculated application of the intricacies of Law 36 to the merits of each delivery, but instead have been 'bought' by bookmakers.[26] The allegations against one umpire are serious and troubling enough, but when combined with doubts about the integrity of past and future results and performances, they give rise to funda-mental questions about what we mean when we speak or write about 'cricket' and even 'law'. Doubts about every match in which Cronje captained South Africa are now part of the interpretive context.[27] Every dropped catch or soft dismissal, once put down to inattentiveness, laziness in stroke play, tiredness, mental lapse etc., are now placed in the match-fixing context. Every questionable LBW decision is fraught with even more doubt than usual.

Some have proposed that we might purge cricket of this taint by eliminating those convicted of match-fixing, like Salim Malik or Hansie Cronje, from the record books. Of course, the suggestion was quickly dismissed first on epistemological and taxonomical grounds i.e. there really are no records kept by an official body. *Wisden*, the sacred text of cricket, is a private undertaking. The 'Bible' of the game is not an 'official' text. Any expunging of Malik, Cronje or Mohammed Azharuddin from *Wisden* would not have been an official sanction or officially sanctioned. The move to remove them was also dismissed because of the forensic impossibility inherent in any such project. If Hansie Cronje is eliminated because he is a cheat, does that mean that every bowler who dismissed him, or every fielder who took a catch from his batting or every batter who scored runs from his bowling, must also lose that part of their own history?[28] When Cronje was killed in a plane crash in South Africa in June 2002, similar debate and controversy surrounded the appropriate place and function of history and memory in our understanding of 'cricket'. Should/would he be mourned as one of South Africa's great players and captains or as an unrepentant cheat and a disgrace who brought shame to his country and himself?[29]

This encapsulates the interpretive, legal and ethical dilemma imposed on us by the bribery and match-fixing scandals. Doubt is magnified to such an extent that we no longer appear to know with any practical certainty where the boundary between good and bad faith is to be found. We struggle for moral, ethical, legal and historical certainty when all we can find is complexity and plasticity. 'It's not cricket' may now come to refer not to some vague, unarticulated but nevertheless understandable ideal of the spirit of the game, but to a more basic epistemological and jurisprudential dilemma. If we cannot know whether any or all of the players or umpires are actually playing cricket, even if they appear to be engaged in that activity, how are we to know or decide anything? If the police manufacture evidence and perjure themselves, how can we believe in the criminal justice system? Yet, in the end, the game of law, just like the game of cricket, goes on. I agree with Mike Marqusee when he writes about the cure for cricket corruption: 'Only in the democratic domain, where cricket and its meanings are shared and shaped by multitudes, can there arise a force strong enough to override the manipulations of the elite.'[30]

I agree with Allan Hutchinson again that: '(Good faith) is more an issue of moral integrity than of analytical accuracy...'.[31]

In the end, cricket can only save itself if it is a democratic exercise in lawmaking by all participants – players, umpires, administrators and fans. The same can be said about law more generally. Just because Hansie Cronje did not play the game does not mean, nor could it ever mean, that the game is not being or cannot be played. That is for us to decide. Just because some police lie, that does not mean that law does not exist, or even that innocent parties have been convicted. That is for us to decide on the basis of other, democratically derived criteria. What follows is my attempt to indicate some of the areas in which we have constructed, and should continue to construct cricket and law, and the *Laws of Cricket*, through interpretive disagreement, compromise, growth and uncertainty. More significantly, I hope, what follows goes some way to demonstrate that the strength, for better or worse, of both cricket and law, can be said to be centred in the very interpretive ambiguity which is inherent in each.

2 The legal theory of cricket

Much of what passes for legal scholarship these days continues to be, quite simply, boring. More important, however, than its distinct lack of aesthetic appeal, is its continuing irrelevance. Not only are esoteric debates about the niceties of the rules of frustration in contract, or about the technical meaning of some obscure wording in an even more obscure legal instrument, irrelevant because they are of interest only to a small minority of lawyers and judges, who constitute an even smaller minority of the populace, but they are irrelevant at a more fundamental level. People, I believe, learn more about law through the mediating effects of popular culture than they ever will through the dull and long ponderings of judges or legal academics on the arcana of taxation or contract law.

There is a strong and growing tradition of exploring the links between law and popular culture in American legal scholarship, to which British legal academics and others are slowly awakening. This is due not so much to any innate superiority of things American but rather because American legal academics have learned a basic truth about the real world. As Stewart Macaulay puts it:

> There is an official law, but there are complementary, overlapping, and con-
> flicting private legal systems as well. School, TV and film, and spectator
> sports offer versions of law that differ from that found in law schools. They
> also offer alternative resources from which people fashion their own under-
> standings of what is necessary, acceptable and just.[1]

The lesson we can learn by expanding the parameter of 'legal' scholarship is a simple one. Law and popular culture come together in a dialogic operation. We learn about law through popular culture and, if we look hard enough, we learn about popular culture through law. More importantly, however, and more funda-mentally, we learn and transmit pieces of knowledge through all our social prac-tices. These practices, from sport to law, are really stories we tell ourselves about ourselves. They offer a complex narrative mythology through which our mutual understandings and misunderstandings are mediated. These messages from our daily lives are not, as many legal scholars and judges would have us believe, divided into strictly distinct and segregated epistemological or phenomenological categories. In reality we freely translate and transmute understandings from one 'part' of our lives to other 'parts' of our existence, both individual and collective, on an ongoing basis. These parts of our lives are not, as some jurisprudential traditionalists would have it, divided into an immutable hierarchy which privileges law and devalues other aspects of our existence.

When Stanley Fish wants to emphasize his views on the futility of legal or literary 'theory', for example, he offers not an analysis of Nietzsche, Gadamer or Derrida, but a description of a conversation between a baseball pitcher and his manager.[2] The point Fish misses, or perhaps more accurately, glosses over, is the complexity of the practices he describes, that is playing baseball and talking about baseball. He appears to assume that each takes place in an environment of mutual understanding between and among the members of the interpretive community. The point I want to emphasize in this book is that even between members of the same interpretive community, the level of mutuality is sometimes overestimated. This does not necessarily mean that we lack a shared understanding of the story we tell when we play or write about cricket, but rather that part of our shared understanding is our knowledge of our *lack* of understanding as well as our comprehension that we can and do live with complexity and contradiction.

If Americans can appeal to the imagery and shared values of their culture through the common experience of 'the national pastime', many in England and other parts of the former Empire, can draw information and inspiration from the 'greatest of games' – cricket.[3] In cricket, we find all that baseball can offer legal academics and more. Cricket does not have 'rules', it has 'laws'; umpires are vested with jurisdiction only upon 'appeal' – the list of analogies and parallels between the sport and the legal system is long. More than the obvious, however, comes from cricket, for it is a game full of blatant and co-existing contradictions – the public and the private,[4] the individual and the team,[5] the spirit of the game and a strict application of the laws.[6] This book is an attempt to make this part of legal scholarship less boring and more relevant. It seeks to tell a story about ourselves and our culture and about the ways in which we go about the construction and deconstruction of social meanings through our experiences of the apparently distinct social texts we call law and cricket. In the words of Steve Redhead, it is time to take law and popular culture seriously and there is nothing more serious than cricket.[7]

A brief set of examples will illustrate the applicability of such analyses to the world of playing cricket, talking about cricket and law teachers writing about cricket. The world of grammar and understanding in various sporting sub-communities is both highly specialized and subtle. Thus, we all 'know' what 'a ball pitched just short of a good length' means, just as lawyers 'know' what 'the damage was clearly foreseeable' means. Yet our knowledge of the meaning of these phrases is highly contextualized. In other words, some phrases mean one thing when defined 'literally', yet mean something else when they occur in some other context. We are able, when discussing or analyzing a cricket contest, to realize that the phrase 'just short of a good length' can depend on the nature of the pitch, the speed and bounce of a particular bowler, where the batter takes guard etc. Because we 'belong' to that context or interpretive community, we can distinguish between and among such cases and imbue phrases with the 'correct' meaning.

It is not unusual, for example, especially when the England team are playing, that they are criticized for failing to win. This failure can be variously attributed to (1) gutless, stupid, conservative captaincy, (2) a general lack of team fighting spirit, often compared unfavourably to the ruthless Australian ethos, (3) the players' lack of skill at critical points in the match and (4) the fact that they no longer 'know how to win'.

The factor 'knowing how to win' is one which all participants in the hermeneutic community which 'understands' or 'knows' cricket, comprehend, just as we all know about a ball pitching just short of a good length. Similarly 'to know how to win' is not, for example, to be taken literally. We do not believe that Michael Vaughan does not understand the *Laws of Cricket* which would require him to score more runs than the other side and dismiss them twice. Nor do we believe that 'knowing how to win' is simply shorthand for (1), (2) or (3), although it may include parts of each of these. We 'know' that you have to 'know how to win', that some captains (for example Bill Lawry of Australia) 'do not know how to win', that others, e.g. Steve Waugh, almost innately 'know how to win'. We also know, for example, that you may indeed have to lose 'to know how to win', although that is not necessarily the case where England are concerned.

We can imbue the phrase with even more subtlety, if we choose. Several years ago, Allan Border's Australian team performed very poorly. Border was criticized for his captaincy – he did not know how to win. Through the process of losing, however, he built the early nucleus of a team which was passed on to Mark Taylor and then to Steve Waugh, and Australia lead the Test match table in the world rankings. Steve Waugh and Ricky Ponting, like most Australians if English commentators are to be believed, knows how to win, how to put the boot on the throat of the opposition to press home the advantage. What was a sign of weakness of character – playing in Border's team with its early losing form, has become, in retrospect, a character building exercise – he 'learned how to win' by losing.

It would even appear that one can 'know how to lose'. When David Gower as England captain lost the Ashes to Australia, he was criticized in a brutal fashion for his team's failure and his lack of leadership. Graham Gooch, on the other hand, later returned from a losing Ashes tour to Australia with his captaincy intact and even enhanced. Similarly, the present England team returns from series defeat after series defeat but with its reputation relatively intact. At the same time, Mark Taylor and then Steve Waugh lead some of the best Test sides in modern history to Ashes wins, triumphs over the West Indies etc., only to have their very place in the side called into question. Even 'knowing how to win' may not be enough. The factors which underlie all of these analyses are incredibly complex and will be addressed, in part at least, in the following sections of this work. What is important to bear in mind is the apparently simplistic message that a phrase like 'to know how to win' encapsulates and embodies a whole complex web of meaning, yet we understand such a phrase because we belong to the correct interpretive community.[8]

Critics of the approach to legal scholarship which I adopt in this book operate from their own epistemological starting point, that 'law' is separate and distinct from all else in society. For them, law is, however imperfect in practice, a science. As a process, law, and especially adjudication, is meant to uncover a strict meaning, a truth. All acts of judging consist simply of the performance of a certain, clear autonomous and established methodology which guarantees the uncovering of a true, 'legal' solution to a given problem.

Such a world-view is, in my experience, and as any cricketer will tell you, blatantly false and counter-experiential. We live in a world where every aspect of our lives is connected in a vast web of shared history and culture. The lived experience of law shows historical shifts in meaning as the 'truth' of a given legal text (for example a Constitution, the *Laws of Cricket*) is adapted to suit changing conditions. It is in the ever-shifting yet apparently established nature of the meaning of legal texts that we can discover the first connection between law, cricket and the meaning of life.

The act of interpretation is not, as the traditionalists would have it, an isolated, scientific inquiry into the one 'real' or 'true' meaning about what is a 'declaration' versus what is a 'forfeiture'. Rather, it is, a process of interaction wherein the reader or interpreter engages the text in an act of 'play' (*spiel*).[9] As Allan Hutchinson argues, it is indeed all in the game. 'Law' is 'play'. From the other end of the problem, moreover, 'play' is law, for 'play' is more than mere 'fun and games', more than mere exercise.

> It is a *significant* function – that is to say, there is some sense to it. In play there is something 'at play' which transcends the immediate needs of life and imparts meaning to the action. All play means something.[10]

Just as 'law' is 'play', 'play' is 'law', for both revolve around a *signifying, meaningful* activity, bound by rules, yet 'free' both inside and outside those rules. As every case is decided on its facts, on its own merits within the flexibility of the doctrine of *stare decisis*, each cricket match is different from every other ever played, although guided and bound by the same *Laws*. Each question of a cross-examination is separate and distinct from every other question, bound as to its relevance and admissibility by all existing rules of evidence. At the same time, each question of a 'good' cross-examination is connected with all other questions not only of that witness but of all previous witnesses and of those to follow. In a similar fashion, every ball of an over is independent, judged on the merits of line and length and the success or failure of the batter. Again, at the same time, we all know that each ball is intimately connected with the other five of the over. Consecutive outswingers determine the conditions for the effectiveness of a subsequent inswinger. Four overs of constant line and length determine the success of a bouncer or a yorker. Five leg breaks determine, in addition to the skill of the sixth delivery itself, whether the wrong 'un, googly or topspinner will have the desired effect. Each ball, like each question put to the witness, has a life of its own and its 'truth' depends on its individual merit. At the same time, 'merit' and 'truth' are connected in a very fundamental way to all that precedes or follows an 'individual' moment, question or ball.

Each question is part of a cross-examination, each cross-examination is part of a case, each case part of an attempt to win, to demonstrate the merit and truth of one party's vision. Each ball is part of an over, each over part of an innings, each innings part of a match, an attempt to demonstrate the merit and truth of one side's 'cricket'.

Thus, each and every part of a trial, a law school course, or a cricket match, is at once bound *and* free, independent *and* connected. Between the apparently dichotomous opposites, a complex narrative occurs. The story of law, legal education and cricket depends for its content and meaning on our decisions about what to remember, underline, exclude or elevate in our reading of the particular text and all other social texts of which it is a part.

In so far as cricket is concerned, under one traditional alternative analysis, we must be aware that cricket has become commodified, that it is a tool of the mass media meant to expose consumer goods for our delight, that its ideological function is to perpetuate ideals of competitiveness and the dominant division of labour. More specifically, the popularity and canonization of the likes of Don Bradman as a batter was, in this view of the world, intimately connected to the broader acceptance in Australian society of the values of capitalism. In the Bradman era, batting and the accumulation of large totals was seen to reflect the associated values of capitalism.

While there can be no doubt that we must situate any activity (sport, cricket or law) in its current social and historical context in order to properly understand its nature and function, these critiques and analyses of sport and of cricket in particular, fail to conceive of the key ideas of context or history in a contextual or historical fashion. As E.P. Thompson puts it, in such discussions, 'the conceptual structure hangs above and dominates social being'.[11] In other words, these analyses fail to recognize the 'whole' truth about cricket and falsely conflate partial facts to a status of totality. They picture capitalist society as a complete hegemonic unity, in which *all* meaning is attributed in a uni-dimensional way. Thus, Don Bradman becomes nothing more than a symbol of capitalist drives to accumulation. All else, his talent, artistry and the collective attachment which all who know cricket feel when his name is mentioned, is but a mask for the brutal reality of 'the system'.

Yet to define and describe cricket and the accumulation of runs as prototypically capitalist is to tell only half the story, for capitalism, even in its Victorian zenith, was not a cultural monolith. Nor is it today.[12] Cricket, as the epitome of capitalism, has always carried within it apparently unresolved and irresolvable contradictions. Even in the paradigmatic W.G. Grace we find the conflict of cricket as 'a violent battle played like a genteel, ritualized garden party' as well as the conflict between 'a new profession' and a game 'practised as if it was a pastime'.[13]

What makes cricket so fascinating as a cultural phenomenon and so similar to law as a social practice, is not its monolithic and one-dimensional connection to the mode of production, but rather the fact that is at once inside *and* outside the mode of production, that it affirms and denies capitalist values, that it is anarchic and governed by *Laws*; that is a team sport dominated by a fascination with individual performances; that it is a bourgeois game dominated in many ways by a proletarian practice; that it is governed by *Laws* which are often supplanted in practice by higher ethical conventional norms; that it is the epitome of British imperialism and colonialism and has in many instances been a driving force for colonial national freedom struggles in places like India and the West Indies. It operates, as does law, at many levels, through multiplicitous contradictions and somehow, inspite of this, it continues to thrive. Indeed it might be argued that cricket, like law, is a system of normativity which thrives and grows because of the contradictions which create it.

Cricket is the 'romantic paradox' wherein N.R. Perera of Sri Lanka can be more proud of his presidency of the Board of Control for Cricket in that country than he was of his function within the Marxist revolutionary movement. It is the fundamental contradiction of the introductory chapter of C.L.R. James' *Beyond a Boundary*, where we meet Matthew Bondman, an entirely unacceptable and disreputable citizen who shone and found social recognition as a batter;[14] it is the contradiction between C.L.R. James, advocate of West Indian independence, Trotskyite Victorian out of his time, and C.L.R. James, the greatest cricket writer of all time; it is the contradiction of reserved, staid, upper-class cricket and Ian Botham as 'the first rock'n' roll cricketer'.[15] (Just as 'law' is a means of social emancipation from a 'legal' regime of slavery, and 'rights' are the means of modern racial emancipation and, at the same time, the means which, in some analyses, keeps them from real freedom.) It is to these fundamental contradictions of our experiences of law and cricket that I now turn.

3   Lord Denning, cricket, law and the meaning of life

In the most well-known case of cricket and the law, *Miller v. Jackson*,[1] Lord Denning waxes eloquent on the importance of cricket in the meaning of life.

> In summertime village cricket is the delight of everyone. Nearly every village has its own cricket field where the young men play and the old men watch. In the village of Lintz in County Durham, they have their own ground, where they have played these last 70 years. They tend it well. The cricket area is well rolled and mown. The outfield is kept short. It has a good club house for the players and seats for the onlookers. They belong to a league, competing with the neighbouring villages. On other evenings after work they practise while the light lasts. Yet now after these 70 years a judge of the High Court has ordered that they must not play there any more. He has issued an injunction to stop them. He has done it at the instance of a newcomer who is no lover of cricket. This newcomer has built, or has had built for him, a house on the edge of the cricket ground which four years ago was a field where cattle grazed. The animals did not mind the cricket.
>
> . . .
>
> And the judge, much against his will, has felt that he must order the cricket club to be stopped: with the consequence, I suppose, that the Lintz Cricket Club will disappear. The cricket ground will be turned to some other use. I expect for more houses or a factory. The young men will turn to other things instead of cricket. The whole village will be much poorer. And all this because of a newcomer who has bought a house there next to the cricket ground.[2]

For Lord Denning, the issue is clear, the consequences dangerous.

> There is a contest here between the interest of the public at large; and the interest of a private individual. The *public* interest lies in protecting the environment by preserving our playing fields in the face of mounting development, and by enabling our youth to enjoy all the benefits of outdoor games, such as cricket and football. The private interest lies in securing the privacy of his home and garden without intrusion or interference by any-one.[3]

Lord Denning, in the text of his judgment in *Miller v. Jackson*, offers us a legal reading of a *social* text, cricket. He urges up, calls upon, invokes images and meanings which are meant to confirm or instil in us, the readers, a vision or interpretation of the text which leaves us with an unmistakable, incontrovertible *meaning*. The dominant imagery which Denning invokes, is, of course, the power and majesty of village cricket. Village cricket is, for Denning, and for the readers who get the message, as we must, quintessentially English.[4] It is more than the sum total of its parts, for cricket is, after all, only a game. But for the reader of the Denning text who is pulled along, the image and meaning of village cricket is much more. It instills, as does Denning's rhetorical flourish, a sense of nostalgia and wonder at the purity and joy of it all. As Mary Mitford put it, 150 years before the tragedy of the Lintz cricket ground: 'Who would think that a little bit of leather, and two pieces of wood, had such a delightful and delighting power!'[5]

Each image employed by Denning is meant for us to consume and interpret in one way, and one way only. For Denning, there is *Truth* and Truth is the essence of cricket. For him, 'village cricket is the delight of everyone'. Cricket is a norm, a universally accepted social practice. It is a way of being-in-the-world which has meaning for us all. As the 'rule of law' is a generally recognized social norm, embodying values which are 'good', so too is 'village cricket'. As the legal system is divided among judges, solicitors, barristers, clerks, secretaries, clients, witnesses, police, so is cricket a universal divided into particular elements or sub-groups, each of which is essential to the constitution of the whole.

'The young men play and old men watch.' There is, for Denning, no hierarchy or division. The players, the young men, are in no way superior to 'the old men' who watch. It is a social endeavour, a social text, democracy embodied at the local level. Without one, the other would be incomplete and 'cricket' would not exist. 'Cricket' is watched *and* played, together, at the same time, one activity complementing the other and together constituting the complete text, 'cricket'. Unfortunately, we must remain ignorant of the fate of the other half of the local population. The 'women', young or old, it would seem, have nothing to do with cricket. They neither watch nor play. Universality in the construction of the good life in democracy is in reality far less than universal.

Like law, cricket for Denning, has dignity, stability and age. The cricket ground is a place 'where they have played these last 70 years'. Like other English social institutions, it must be carefully guarded by all who participate, it must be 'tended', 'well rolled and mown'. It is as English as the country garden, the same techniques apply, the same functions are served.[6] The physical facilities, like the game itself, are for all – 'a good club house for the players and seats for the onlookers'. Perhaps the women have a place inside the club house, preparing the meals for the players.

It is a temporal pastime, fixtures taking place on weekends, practice in the evenings, all away from the normal grind of employment or work. Cricket involves everyone for the joy of the game, not for remuneration. It is a social activity distanced by time and space from the means of production. It is healthy and competitive, for 'they belong to a league'. But they compete 'with the neighbouring villages'. 'Neighbouring' villages indicates not only physical proximity but a psychological closeness, participation in a shared cultural practice with mutual values and neighbourliness and of England – the apparent contradiction of 'friendly competition' which finds its resolution in local cricket.

Into this neighbourhood, this world of shared values and interpretations, enters 'the newcomer', the ideal and evil *Other*, threatening the peace and harmony, the very existence of the community. The newcomer is foreign, *Other*, dangerous. Cricket is tradition, he is *NEW*; the villagers *belong* to the established practices of their cricket, he *comes*, inserts himself, *violates* their peace, threatens their very existence. If he has his way 'the Lintz Cricket Club will disappear'. With the destruction of the village cricket club, as with the destruction of the rule of law, will come all manner of social disruption, the fabric of the community will be torn asunder. 'Houses' or 'a factory' will replace the cricket ground. These materialistic 'things' will replace a sense, a practice and a reality of community. The public space of shared, democratic communal values will disappear to be replaced by the private domain of the dwelling house or of private capital and profit accumulation.

'The young men will turn to other things instead of cricket.' One can only imagine – theft, drunkenness, pillage and plunder. Or worse yet, maybe even football. For if cricket is good and true, all else, which is what they will be left with, is evil and false. 'The whole village will be much the poorer', for, like democracy and the rule of law, cricket hangs by a delicate thread – truth can be destroyed, if we are not careful, 'because of a newcomer who has just bought a house there next to the cricket ground'.

The new, the foreign, the materialistic, all these nefarious elements threaten truth. They threaten the community. They are foreign and tainted with unnaturalness. The outsider threatens cricket. After all, cricket has been played, watched, enjoyed for 70 years. The pitch rolled, the outfield mown, the friendly competition held. Now all this and much more is threatened by an unnatural force. After all, the cattle 'did not mind the cricket', for cricket and nature co-exist, at least in the absence of foot and mouth epidemics. At some deep and fundamental level, like the rule of law, cricket is as *natural*, as English, as inherently and unquestionably good, as the grazing cattle.

Indeed, cricket is so natural, it is *green*; it embodies and enshrines the natural environment so rapidly disappearing and under threat in the countryside, itself in danger of disappearing. The public interest, synonymous with the interest of cricket 'lies in protecting the environment, preserving our playing fields in the face of mounting development. . . .' Its implements, leather and willow, are natural. Its values, fair play, gentlemanly conduct, 'the spirit of the game', are not only natural, they are public values, constitutive of the social text of what it means to be English. In the final analysis, what the newcomer has done 'just isn't cricket'.

This newcomer, this *Other*, threatens us because he *is* Other. He is not part of the community which recognizes and values the social text invoked by Denning.

If he were, he could not possibly contemplate destroying the village cricket ground. He is *Other* and, as such, he is the antithesis of the sense of unity and unitary meaning to which Denning appeals. At the same time, of course, it is only because of this Other that such an appeal can be so strong. The community defines itself not only by those who understand the social text of village cricket but, perhaps even more strongly, by reference to those who do *not* understand. The French and Germans may play football, but they are incapable of ever grasping the subtleties and genius of either the common law or cricket. We define ourselves equally by what we are and what we are not. It is by reference to the non-participant that we feel we belong as much as it is by reference to our fellow members of the community. Our community is defined, must be defined, by those we exclude, those who do not understand us. Indeed, the power of Denning's textualization of cricket exists because the text/practice of cricket he calls upon is threatened by a competing text. Without the Other, there can be no Self.[7]

Yet even the ideal embodiment of the rule of cricket as a social and legal text which in turn embodies all that is English, cannot escape the rule of law. In the 2000 village cricket championship, Werrington lost on the last ball to Usk, missing out on a chance to play in the final at Lord's, the home of cricket. This, if the story went no further, would be a tale of tragedy and triumph, of the battle between bat and ball, of a close encounter in friendly competition. It would, in other words, epitomize the idealized vision of cricket as social text so dear to Lord Denning.

But the story does not end there. While travelling on what would have been a despondent journey home, a Werrington player noticed a road sign which read: 'Welcome to the historic town of Usk.' Usk, population 2,187, winner of the village cricket match, was not, in law and in fact, a village after all. It was a town. Although it fit many of the criteria of the competition, it had a royal charter, a mayor and a town council. The competition's organizers disqualified Usk and the disqualification was upheld by the High Court: 'As in cricket, the umpire's decision is final.'[8]

The Usk vice-captain commented after the judgement:

> Usk is known as a town only for marketing reasons to attract tourists, and the other side did not complain before the match. They only complained after we beat them with the final ball of the game.[9]

Village cricket here fulfils neither of the criteria, it does not involve a 'village' and it is not 'cricket'. Both sides played in the same game; the confrontation between bat and ball gave a result. Yet, on one view of the game of cricket and the law, the real competition took place sometime later between solicitors. One side complained that the game itself was not 'cricket' since one team was unlawfully competing. *Ex ante*, there was no game. The other side claimed that the only competition which counts takes place on the field of play and that any *ex post facto* determination was itself not cricket. It might or might not be cricket but it is law. In this instance the mirror image of cricket is cricket and it is law. This is the fundamental contradiction of cricket and the deconstruction of Lord Denning's epistemological and sociological edifice of cricket and the law. As with Hansie Cronje, the basic questions again are whether there was a game of cricket being played and how can we know?

4 Dante, cricket, law and the meaning of life

If Lord Denning's invocation of the heavenly nature of cricket in English society represents one side of a social text, Simon Barnes' description of Dante's ideal of cricket hell, represents the other side of the coin.[1]

> Here are all the cricketers the world will long despise:
> The chuckers and the sledgers, all the men who cheat,
> Batsmen who refuse to walk, fielders who tell lies,
> Bowlers who make false appeals, those who, just to beat,
> Their foe, will bend or break the custom and the law.[2]

In cricket hell, we find those who would denounce all that Lord Denning holds dear. We find what Simon Rae has recently described as the 'history of skullduggery, sharp practice and downright cheating in the noble game'.[3] They are the cricketers who cheat by making an illegal delivery (chucking) or by distracting their opponents through taunts and jeers (sledgers). They are the cricketers who would deny the truth by refusing to leave the batting crease when they know they have snicked the ball and been caught (refuse to walk). They are the cricketers who deny the truth by claiming to have taken a catch which touched the ground (fielders who tell lies). They are cricketers who attempt to trick or intimidate an umpire into an incorrect decision in their favour (bowlers and fielders who make false appeals). They are cricketers who have rejected the ethos of the game, who have denounced the communal nature of 'friendly competition' and who have adopted the values of winning at all costs ('those who just to beat their foe, will bend or break the custom and the law').

These cricketers have been condemned to hell for the ultimate sin of committing acts which 'just aren't cricket'. Like a crooked judge or a bent copper, they must be treated even more harshly than their 'civilian' counterparts because they have betrayed a fundamental trust which 'we' who know the *truth* of law and of cricket have placed in them. Worse than the 'newcomer' of *Miller v. Jackson*, they have betrayed their own; they are traitors who pretend loyalty to cricket and truth while serving Mammon and falsehood. Like Hansie Cronje, more than the Other, more than any outsider, these are in reality the enemy within. In appearance they share our hermeneutic and ethical understandings of 'cricket' yet they voluntarily place themselves outside the community, for they know the truth and yet they deny it. They are not the unsaved barbarians, they are those who have fallen from grace. They are not unbelievers, they are heretics and apostates. They know better yet they are disloyal.

But, in fact and in law, as the rest of this book will argue and demonstrate, the loyalty we demand here is a loyalty which none can give. Those we condemn to hell must obey 'the custom and the law', yet the custom and the law are often contradictory. Indeed, their proper ordering is mysterious. Remember here Don Oslear and his umpiring fellows and Christopher Martin-Jenkins and his journalistic cronies on the Cronje/Hussain deal. Remember the definitions of 'declaration' and 'forfeiture'. Must we obey the letter of the law or its spirit? Do we give obedience to law or justice, to legalism or equity? Which must predominate? Does the hierarchy of cricket place the *Laws* first or does it subordinate formalism to a higher level of ethical practice? Just who gets sent to cricket's jurisprudential hell?

For Denning, the loyalty we owe is to cricket, to the spirit, to Englishness, a *public* duty. Yet the private duty which he so easily dismisses is 'the privacy of his home and garden without intrusion or interference by anyone'. What could be more an epitome of Englishness (and gender bias) than the maxim that 'everyman's home is his castle'? To obey Denning's vision of *truth*, we must first deny or ignore the fundamental contradiction of the public and the private.[4]

To condemn to hell those who disobey 'the custom and law' we must condemn all cricketers, for there is more often than not a fundamental contradiction between the two norms. To condemn the 'batsmen who refuse to walk', we must deny to the umpire the sole jurisdiction to decide on dismissals upon appeal, thereby for some undermining the entire judicial process. To condemn 'bowlers who make false appeals', we deny the right of access to justice and adjudication and ignore the complexities of the *Laws* of cricket, not to mention engaging in a process of mind reading which must inform any or most such assertions of bad faith. Can 'we' know if the bowler heard a nick or saw a deviation as the ball passed the edge of the bat? Can we always know this, or only sometimes. If so, when?

Most importantly, however, is that to condemn those who breach custom or law is to falsify the 'essence' of both custom and law by conferring on them a naturalistic basis. Theories of civil disobedience, for example, teach that it may sometimes be not only permissible but morally compulsory to breach customs or laws. Sociological studies of our experience of sport as a cultural phenomenon also demonstrate that in some instances violating the rules may be the 'right' thing to do. Even rules are sometimes not rules.

There are some who would argue that no violation of the rules should be encouraged or permitted, just as there are jurists who argue that there is neither a right nor a duty to engage in acts of civil disobedience. An example of such formalism can be found in international soccer for example, where FIFA instructs referees to issue a red card (expel) to any player committing a 'professional foul'. A professional foul is often a deliberately illegal tackle on an opposing player who will be, if the foul is not committed, in a position to score. It is, therefore, in such circumstances, a rational, risk-reducing decision to break the rules by changing a virtually certain goal into a somewhat more risky penalty shot or free kick or the less likely possibility that the referee will miss the penalty altogether. For proponents of strict adherence to the rules and laws of the game, the FIFA action is warranted because rules must be enforced in order to ensure that the result is achieved between two teams playing by the rules. If one team is allowed to breach the rules or laws of the games and emerges triumphant, the very integrity of the sport as lawful contest is open to challenge. Unfortunately, such theories depend upon practical implementation. Complaints about the standard of refereeing at all levels of the game indicate that the theory has not been successfully put into practice. A similar interdiction policy applies to professional fouls in rugby union where the referee is empowered to award a penalty try in those circumstances where a foul clearly prevented the team from scoring. Yet as the first Test in the 2002 Tri Nations series between Australia and New Zealand demonstrated, observers, participants and officials will differ over just when a try was 'certain' enough to justify the award of a penalty try instead of a simple penalty.

On the other hand, our experience of sport indicates that rule-violating behaviour like the 'professional foul' in football, rugby or basketball, is directly and intentionally integrated into the existential norms of participants and others who interpret the particular sport/text. For example, ice hockey violence in Canada and the United States, demonstrates that while fist-fights are illegal, they are accepted by all participants as an important and integral part of the game. Indeed, to refuse to fight, that is to refuse to break the rules, will lead to ostracism and shaming by peer and other reference groups (for example parents and fans).

Moreover, some rule-violating behaviour may be functional as a deterrent to other more serious rule-breaking. Again, the example of ice hockey violence indicates that there is a clear distinction between legitimate (although illegal) fighting (fist-fights) and illegitimate (and still illegal) violence (using the stick as a weapon). Not only is a player who uses his stick as a weapon ostracized and stigmatized as a 'cheap shot artist', but using a stick can cause serious, career-ending injury, and might even incur civil and criminal liability on the perpetrator. Participants in the sport, and spectators and fans, see fist-fighting as legitimate not only because it functions to physically intimidate opponents (a skill or attribute which is honoured and legitimated when it occurs within the rules), thereby making it easier to win in a 'collision' sport, but it is also legitimate because it prevents the occurrence of more violent and dangerous instances of illegality by providing a relatively harmless outlet for aggression. Just as in the world of criminal law and criminological theory, in sport not all illegal acts can be simply lumped into a single category. More specificity and detail are required than simply and simplistically labelling an act 'illegal', if we are truly to understand the act and its place in a complex whole.

Not only do law and custom in sport and in the 'real' world often diverge and contradict each other, but it is often 'customary' to break the law. Indeed, it is not unknown in cricket or other sports that some players are celebrated and others are rendered 'notorious' for pushing and exceeding the boundaries of the *Laws* and of the spirit of the game. Australians are regarded by many other countries as the 'best' sledgers in world cricket. For some, these activities violate the *Laws* of cricket, the spirit of the game and are sharp practice at its worst. For others, the Australian talent for sledging is simply one of many examples of why the team is the best in the world. For them, 'sledging' is not sledging; it is part of an attempt to achieve the 'mental disintegration' of the opposition. The contradictory forces which define the cricket experience and which make it such a fascinating social text are intimately connected to this tension between law and custom and the oft-denied contradiction between law and order. To illustrate the complexities of the legal and social construction of cricket, I shall examine in some detail the nature and function of some of the *Laws* and customs of cricket. By thinking of cricket as another legal system, one can then begin to conceive of Law as a more complex and contradictory social text than traditional legal scholarship would have us believe.

5 Laws, not rules or cricket as adjudication

As fans of the game, particularly those of a traditionalist bent, are wont to point out, cricket is governed not by mere 'rules' but by 'Laws'.[1] For them, and for others, this is a distinction which tells us much about the character of cricket. It indicates the formal, gentlemanly Victorian nature of the game. It also confirms the claims of its supporters that it is, for this and any number of other reasons, the best of all sports. Finally, it indicates, linguistically and grammatically at least, an affinity between the interests of jurists and those of cricket lovers.

Again, to begin this attempt to understand or reveal the complexities of the cricket text, we must place the subject in its historical and social context. At one level, codification in all sports came about as a result of general trends within Victorian capitalist culture. As Midwinter points out, cricket fits into a 'preoccupation with money and book-keeping',[2] and scorekeeping practices reflected this. Besides being related to and reflective of ideals of rationality, efficiency and ordering, however, cricket codification served a more direct mercantile purpose. Gambling on cricket was rife and the stakes often very high.[3] In order to ensure a more rational and fairer betting process and to avoid the market dislocations and distortions of cheating, it was vital that everyone play by and adhere to the same rules. The codification of the *Laws of Cricket* was necessary both to eliminate the evils of free-rein in gambling and to permit orderly competition as cricket matches became more easily arranged over greater distances with the introduction of national postal and rail links.[4] It is then perhaps both ironic and just that gambling should now be at the centre of a set of controversies which raise questions about the very existence of cricket as a practice governed by *Laws* and good faith.

Once the *Laws* came into existence and the game spread and grew in its appeal, a new character entered the social text of cricket. That character is, of course, the umpire. Like the jurist, the cricket umpire is the sole judge and interpreter of the *Laws*. He is the source for decisions concerning scoring, violations or infringement of the *Laws*, and most importantly, of dismissals.

Like their judicial counterpart, the umpire's power commands, and at the same time depends upon, the respect which is given to the position and authority. Unable to summon the police or to invoke the power of contempt, the cricket umpire's effectiveness depends upon the acceptance of authority by players and fans. He is the central and hub figure in the social contract of cricket. Failure to accept rulings during a match without question would lead to a collapse of the rule of law within the cricketing community.

Like a judge, the umpire is vested not only with the interpretation and application of the *Laws*, but is also the sole judge of fair play.[5] Thus he exercises both common law and equitable jurisdiction. The leading guide to officiating in cricket offers the following description of an umpire's attributes.

> An umpire above all must be a person of integrity. When under pressure it is by no means easy to keep calm and to remain completely neutral and unbiased. It is essential to do so. An umpire needs to cope not only with the clinical application of the Laws but with the attitudes of the players, which nowadays are much more aggressive than in the past. He must be firm in control of the game, without being pedantic or officious. He must not let his absolute impartiality be affected by the behaviour of the players, or by the state of the game. He will therefore need a judicial mind which enjoys quickly weighing up evidence. He will need an even temper and good humour to respond wisely to the often hasty and excited actions of the players. He will need confidence in himself to remain calm, fearlessly continuing to control the game according to the Laws. Above all – he will need common sense – a rare quality – to deal with both the unexpected event and the awkward player.[6]

The umpire must decide each case on its merits. He must never engage in the process of 'levelling out' – an attempt to be fair by 'balancing' a known mistake by deliberately making another. From the umpire's perspective such an attempt to achieve 'rough justice' would be counter-productive in the long run for it would lead to players losing confidence in the certainty and validity of each decision as well as in the integrity of the umpire. It must be noted, however, that the other participants in the construction of meaning in cricket, the players, will themselves sometimes operate under a system of 'levelling out'. Thus, for example, a player might well justify a failure to walk on the grounds that he is simply either making up for a past mistake by an umpire in (incorrectly) giving him out or that he is taking precautionary measures against an inevitable future error by the umpire.[7] The *truth* and perfection of cricket as described by Denning here begin to show the cracks and wear and tear of the reality of the judicial process.

Nowhere is the communal and universal bliss of cricket more clearly put aside than in discussions of the very technical and highly legalistic nature of the umpire's jurisdiction. With the obvious exceptions of determining fair and unfair play (Laws 3(7) and 42(2)), and determining the fitness of the ground, the weather or the light,[8] the umpire's principle jurisdiction (with regard to dismissals) is by way of appeal. Under the *Laws*

> Neither umpire shall give a Batsman out, even though he may be out under the Laws, unless appealed to by the fielding side. This shall not debar

a batsman who is out under any of the Laws from leaving his wicket without an appeal having been made.[9]

The new 2000 *Laws* formally enshrine in legislative text that which had previously been only a part of informal, yet lawful practice i.e. a batter leaving the wicket when he thought, or it was clear, he was out. A batter who has been clean bowled, will, in most cases for example, head back to the dressing room. The bowling side will celebrate. In the absence of an appeal to the umpire, a strict interpretation of the *Laws* might have meant that the batter had not in fact or in law, been dismissed, even though everyone knew that he was in fact, beyond any doubt, out.

The *Laws* also limit the form of a valid appeal:

An appeal 'How's That?' shall cover all ways of being out.[10]

As a 'puzzled foreign sportsman' once queried in a letter to the *Times* on 14 July 1932,

...I could not find out why the umpire could not give a decision without being appealed to. In other games one considers it unfair to ask the umpire for a decision. Will you kindly explain to me why it is so for cricket.[11]

In the puzzlement of the foreign sportsman and the apparent rigidity of Law 27, we find the beginning stages of the crumbling of Denning's cricket edifice. Rather than a bucolic, ecologically sound embodiment of all the spirit that is England, we find a game that is rule-bound and formalistic. The umpire has no jurisdiction without an appeal and that appeal must be made within the time limit or else it is statute-barred.[12] In a similar formalistic fashion, while 'How's That?' covers all grounds of dismissal and will be considered as such, an appeal (admittedly rare) of 'How's that for LBW?' will not be answered in the affirmative in those circumstances where, while the batter is not out LBW, because the ball first struck his bat, he has been caught close to the wicket. Under the *Laws*, as interpreted historically by most umpires, the bowler or fielder has limited his appeal and, as a consequence, the umpire's jurisdiction.

Not only must there have been an appeal and the appeal properly formulated, it must be addressed to the umpire with 'jurisdiction'. An appeal to the umpire at the striker's end for LBW would be an appeal 'addressed to the wrong court'. The new 2000 *Laws* attempt to deal with this previous legal formalism through legislative change. Thus, the general jurisdictional provision of Law 27(1) now refers specifically to 'Neither umpire' whereas the 1980 version spoke of 'the umpires'. More importantly, the new wording of Law 27(5) **Answering appeals** now indicates more clearly that

A decision Not out by one umpire shall not prevent the other umpire from giving a decision provided that each is considering only matters within his jurisdiction.

It is also obvious from the text of the *Law* that 'an appeal is an appeal is an appeal' and that umpires must treat each appeal equally, no matter how vociferously or meekly made. For lawyers, as well, it is as obvious that a firmly argued case presented by a senior silk is no more meritorious *per se* than a stumblingly argued position put forward by a junior solicitor. At the same time, it is nonetheless true that the bucolic calm of Denning's world of cricket was frequently violated by vociferous or consistent appealing, perfectly 'legal' and within the bounds of Law 27, yet each appeal meant, in its own way, to intimidate, pressure or coerce the umpire into a favourable decision. Umpires, of course, dismiss any suggestion that such tactics would or could influence them in their judicial duty. They insist, in effect, that 'an appeal *is* an appeal *is* an appeal'.

Indeed, some argue that an umpire must take all the circumstances surrounding the appeal into consideration if he is to make a correct decision. In his description of a New Zealand Tour of Pakistan, Sohaib Alvi, criticized Umpire Badar precisely for failing to take 'extraneous' factors into account.

> Were it not for an ill-judged decision by umpire Badar, the two (Bradburn and Patel) may well have taken New Zealand to victory. First slip had put up a muted appeal, and second slip was not hopeful either. The most significant indicator was that Yousuf had calmed down upon throwing up the ball, and was revitalised only upon seeing the raised finger. It must be said that the umpire should have read between the lines during the few seconds he took to pass sentence.[13]

On this view, umpires must take into account the 'nature' of the appeal because they should 'know' that some circumstantial evidence can serve as a strong indicator of truth. This position is based upon the argument or belief in the umpire's ability to possess and utilize a practical wisdom gained by experience and indeed necessarily part of the existential knowledge and fact of simply 'being an umpire'. Judicial interpretation in playing the game requires a level of practical wisdom, *phroenesis*, which must always go beyond a mere technical knowledge and application of the *Laws*.

In fact however, umpires have always disclaimed any idea of undue influence. While such appeals were within the *Laws*, that is 'legal' in a formal sense, many saw vigorous and persistent appeals as contrary to the spirit of the game, to its customs and practices. While Barnes (or Dante) would banish all transgressors to Hell, strict formalists could argue that there are *no* transgressors because all appeals, no matter how frequent or apparently frivolous, were legal. Others would perhaps choose to send off the transgressors for failing to comply not with the Law but with an even higher norm, the spirit of the game.

Thus Richie Benaud, one of Australia's greatest Test captains and now a respected commentator, criticized the frequent appeals in the 1990 Melbourne Test between Pakistan and Australia. For him the trend to frequent appeals was not to be welcomed: 'I have never seen so much appealing in a Test and it's difficult to recall when I have seen so much frivolous appealing. Players might stop it with the right incentive.'[14]

Benaud did not wish to condemn the transgressors to Hell or even to Purgatory. He would have preferred simply that the captain, in that case, Allan Border, intercede to instil in his team respect not only for the letter of the *Law* but especially for the spirit of the game. The solution to the problem was, for Benaud, an ethical one, arrived at by the members of the community (the players) without recourse to the outside (the *Laws* and the umpires). While the community relies on an inherently hierarchical structure, the captain retains his position largely through his praxis and the respect this instills in the players. Benaud's appeal against appeals was grounded in the democratically based community ethical structure and rejected, at least implicitly, the importance of the external law-based normativity to the practice of cricket.

Writing on the same Test, English commentator Henry Blofeld bemoaned 'this constant appealing' which he argued 'pressures the umpires into making bad decisions', 'rattles umpires', and 'is making the game a sordid spectacle'![15] Blofeld saw the problem at two levels, the formal/legalistic and the ethical. Constant appealing, Blofeld argued, resulted in bad or incorrect decisions, that is decisions not based on the strict application of the law to the facts. In other words, the decisions are 'bad' because they are 'illegal' in that they do not conform with the law. At the second level, conduct like persistent appealing violates the spirit of the game and transforms it from 'game' or 'sport' into 'sordid spectacle'. Decisions, therefore, are 'bad' because they take place in an atmosphere tainted by a disrespect for the 'spirit of the game' and for its underlying and accepted ethical norms. For Blofeld, cricket as Law and cricket as ethical contest occur at one and the same time.

Thus, following Benaud and Blofeld on the same set of facts, we could argue that the Melbourne Test was (a) good cricket because all appeals are acceptable if they conform to the formal requirements of Law 27, (b) bad cricket because frequent appealing leads to an illegal application of Law 27, or (c) bad cricket because no matter how 'formally' correct the appeals may have been, they violated the ethical understanding shared by all who participate that one appeals only in those circumstances where one believes the batter to be out.

Yet another (what I would call a neo-positivist) reading of the frequency of appeals in the Melbourne Test was available. Under this interpretation, offered by Peter Roebuck, the frequent appealing was both consistent with the *Law* and in keeping with broader ideals of the spirit of the game.[16] For Roebuck, Australian Terry Alderman bowled in a style characterized by consistent line and length, 'from stump to stump'. Because of the way he bowled, argued Roebuck, Alderman could and should appeal frequently when the ball struck the pad, because, statistically speaking, there was a good chance that the batter was indeed out LBW. For Roebuck, Alderman (and his teammates) were justified in appealing frequently not only by a strict reading of the text of the *Law*, but also because he and they could and should have a genuine belief that the batter was out. On the same set of 'facts', under the same legal text, and under similar shared understandings about the unwritten ethical norms, at least four (sometimes mutually exclusive and inconsistent) readings of the game of cricket, the nature of the *Law* and the judicial function, were, in the example of frequent appeals in this Melbourne Test, possible. Of course, these apparently inconsistent analyses are not always as inconsistent as they may, at first blush, appear. Among Roebuck, Benaud and Blofeld, for example, a real source of disagreement may simply be 'the facts'. Implicit in the Blofeld/Benaud analysis is the rejection of the validity of the appeals based on their view of the facts i.e. the appeals are frivolous and annoying because the ball would not have hit the stumps. For Roebuck, this was clearly not the case given Alderman's bowling style. It was only possible to become involved in the 'higher' ethical and legal debate surrounding the issue of frequent appeals where one took a particular view of the facts. This does not mean that only one view should be accepted as the 'correct' one, nor does it mean that, given the numerous alternatives, cricket simply lapses into pure relativism. It simply means that we must choose from among the options if we are to give 'meaning' (or meanings) to the text we call cricket, in circumstances such as these. Thus it is also easy to imagine that 'everyone' would agree to condemn a series of appeals as excessive in circumstances where, for example, a spinner was pitching every delivery outside the batter's leg stump and then striking him on the pads. This can 'never' under the *Laws* be out (even if experience teaches us another lesson). A side which appealed each and every time the batter was hit on the pads would quite clearly be engaging in behaviour which was at one and the same time illegal and contrary to the spirit of the game.[17]

A similar situation, involving discussions about the 'appropriateness' or 'legality' of appeals has historically arisen not out of concern over the question of frequency, but out of inquietude over the 'nature' of the appeal itself. While asking the question 'How's that?' covers all types of dismissals, the text of the *Law* has been silent as to the 'manner' in which the question is asked. There is a clear factual difference between a *sotto voce* appeal by a slip fielder and one unanimous shout by the bowler, keeper and all slips. Similarly there is a difference between a quiet appeal and the stated invocation of a pleaful fast bowler, knees bent, eyes aglow, both arms raised to the heavens. In some circumstances, it was argued that the 'nature' of the appeal, especially combined with a surrounding context of frequent appeals, could and did serve to intimidate the umpire into making a 'wrong' decision. Again, while umpires would argue that they are never intimidated, there is at the very least an impression that they are – justice is not seen to be done.

An historical example of the difficulties, debate and passions which arose in such circumstances can be found in the fourth Test between England and the West Indies in Bridgetown, Barbados in April 1990. England batter Bailey was given out (caught behind) by umpire Lloyd Barker after West Indian captain Viv Richards raced down the pitch, arms moving in the air, 'asking the question'. Richards, described his 'little jig' as being 'very ceremonial', adding that he 'was hoping to celebrate getting the batsman out'.[18] Umpire Barker denied that he had been intimidated '. . . to suggest there was any bullying is wrong'.[19]

The British cricket media disagreed. Simon Barnes of the *Times* characterized Richards' behaviour as 'over the top'.[20] Mike Selvey in the *Guardian Weekly* wrote of 'his demented and intimidating charge'.[21] Christopher Martin-Jenkins, broadcasting for the BBC offered the following:

> It wasn't the mistake that was so sad. It was the fact that Lloyd Barker was pressurised into changing his initial decision. If that's gamesmanship or professionalism, I'm not quite sure what cheating is.[22]

Umpire Barker issued defamation writs against Martin-Jenkins and the BBC.

Here, the text of the peaceful game of village cricket in Lintz seems far, far away and long ago. Defamation, professionalism, gamesmanship, intimidation and cheating are not part and parcel of evening practice in County Durham nor do they appear to have much in common with the calm and judicial function of the umpire vested in his jurisdiction through an appeal of 'How's that?'. The umpire says he was not intimidated, although he did later recognize he may actually have been mistaken in giving the batter out. The media, including some members of the West Indian press corps, felt that Richards' behaviour was undignified and probably unwarranted. The umpire's delay in giving the decision, his original hesitation, followed by his affirmative reaction to Richards, might well be interpreted to indicate unseemliness or even to prove an apprehension that justice was not done, but was he in fact intimidated? Do we believe him, a man of enough integrity and ability to justify being chosen as a Test umpire or do we discard his proclamation of innocence and draw a possible, and only a possible, conclusion from the circumstantial evidence? Was Viv Richards' behaviour really unseemly or illegal? Did he violate the spirit of cricket or the letter of the *Law*? Did such an appeal constitute 'unfair play' under the existing provisions of Laws 42(2) and 3(7) or is it simply a case of a violation of the spirit of the game? Section 42(3) of the *Laws* would have indicated that such behaviour was not, by implication at least, 'unfair play' since the only remedy was intervention

> by calling and signalling 'dead ball' in the case of unfair play, but (the umpires) should not otherwise interfere with the progress of the game except as required to do so by the Laws.[23]

In this case, signalling 'dead ball' was in no way a remedy against Richards' actions and this alone would indicate that such an 'intimidatory' appeal, if indeed it was, was not, technically speaking, 'unfair play'.

Common rules of statutory interpretation would also likely lead to the conclusion that Richards' actions could not have been characterized as 'unfair play'. The version of Law 42 which dealt primarily with this issue contained prohibitions on the several types of behaviour which constituted 'unfair play'. Lifting the seam of the ball (42(4)), changing the condition of the ball (42(5)), incommoding the striker (42(6)), obstructing a batsman in running (42(7)), bowling fast short pitched balls (bouncers) to intimidate (42(8)), bowling fast high full pitches (beamers) (42(9)), time wasting (42(10)), damaging the pitch (42(11)) and a batsman unfairly stealing a run (42(12)) were the actions legislated against. It would appear that under no interpretation could an 'intimidatory' appeal constitute unfair play because it was in no way in the same 'category' as the types of behaviour enumerated in Law 42, *ejusdem generis.*

It may have been that under Law 42(13), Richards was guilty of 'generally behaving in a manner which might bring the game into disrepute'. There are, however, some problems even with this approach. First, if his actions did fall under these provisions, there was no immediate remedy available to the aggrieved batter. The remedial steps of Law 42(13), required notifying the captain of the player's infringement, but in this case Richards was the captain. The next step was for the umpire to notify the team executive and relevant governing body. Such provisions indicated that the nature of the remedy and the offence was administrative or ethical rather than formally 'legal', in the sense of covering events as they occurred on the field of play under the *Laws.* They also indicated that the offence, if there is one, is a 'public' one, involving an affront to the game itself rather than a 'private' one allowing redress to the 'injured' batter, or his side.

A more fundamental problem, however, existed. It is only if the umpire felt that Richards was attempting to intimidate him that he could, after all, invoke these provisions. If Richards' actions did not constitute 'unfair play', they were permissible within the *Laws.* Thus it was highly unlikely that he could have been reported for bringing the game into disrepute by acting 'legally', unless one is willing to admit that a higher ethical norm imposes a duty which transcends strict obedience and conformity to the text of the *Laws.* If they were intimidating, then the umpire would be admitting that he was in fact pressured, or felt under pressure to comply, into acquiescence and would himself have been guilty of misconduct. *Ubi jus, ibi remedium?*

At the same time, it must be emphasized that the Viv Richards' affair was hardly unique. The question of the frequency or vociferous nature of appeals has a long history in cricket. Nor can the Richards case be fully understood unless it is placed in a much broader context. To see the issue here as limited simply to the question of the appropriate 'manner and form' of appeals is to reduce the complexity of a real *praxis* (cricket) to a reified world-view (Law). The complex nature of West Indian cricket and society in relation to British racism and imperialism was and is a clear sub-text informing the whole event and context of any England–West Indies Test.

Yet, even to expand the hermeneutic circle to encompass racism and imperialism would not necessarily lead to a full understanding of the Richards' appeal in particular or of the problem in general. One would, for example, have to bring to bear to any interpretation the entire history of the issue in cricket and in doing so, we would quickly understand the impossibility of 'understanding' as the purists would have it. In early Tests, the English accused the Australians of refusing to accept the (English) umpire's decisions. The Australians reciprocated in part by pointing to the English practice of frequent appealing. Thus

> The English have the irritating habit of appealing in chorus at every possible opportunity, presumably with the motive of discommoding the batsman. The sooner this undesirable habit is corrected the better.[24]

We learn not only that the text of frequent appeals was confused with overlayers of nationalism but that the question goes not only to the function of the umpire and his relationship with the fielding side, but that it may also be invoked as a strategy to harass the batter, thereby by-passing the umpire and referring to another interpretive relationship, that of the batter and the fielding side. Each action, every interpretation, takes place within a life-world of complex relations between and among individuals, sub-communities and broader communities, each of which adds to the richness of the hermeneutic mix we call cricket.

Rather than competing, the communities come together as fielders, umpires and batters and are affected by and attribute meaning(s) to frequent appeals. And before Australians think they are saved, it must be noted that whatever may have been the truth of historical allegations that frequent appealing was a distinctly English phenomenon, the Antipodes cannot claim immunity. Arthur Mailey, describing Australian bowler Bill O'Reilly, says

> He roared at umpires and scowled at batsmen. There was no sign of veneer or camouflage when he appealed, nor were there any apologies or beg pardons when the umpire indicated that the batsmen's legs were yards out of line with the stumps.[25]

Nor finally can it be said that frequent appeals are necessarily, as they might appear to be in the Richards or O'Reilly cases, brutish intimidation. Like all textual and interpretive strategies, they themselves are open to interpretation, modification and strategic alteration. One bowler, like Australian Ian Johnson, might issue two or three stifled *sotto voce* appeals, followed by apologies to the umpire for his mistake. In this context, a confident appeal could well convince the umpire *per se* of its correctness.[26] Like the umpire confronted with a batter with a reputation as one who normally walks staying in the crease after an appeal, the umpire in this case of the strategic use of infrequent or frequent appeals is placed in a position of granting the appeal not 'on the facts' of the instant case, but on his presumed practical knowledge of the 'context' which he then imposes to create both a decision and, retroactively, a 'new' set of facts.

Without attempting then to definitely answer any of the questions raised by the Richards' affair, it seems clear that there was uncertainty as to the exact limits and nature of the umpires' judicial function in such circumstances. Questions of players' and umpires' integrity, both real and perceived, were raised, as were questions about the applicability or efficiency of the *Laws*. Indeed, at a basic level, it still remains impossible to define Richards' behaviour as Law-violating or ethics-violating. If the practical distinction in such circumstances is so nebulous, what are we to make of the apparent, self-proclaimed clarity of the distinction between the categories themselves?

However, we now also know that the debate has moved on to a different legal and ethical level. Troubled by the frequency of appeals, and other examples of what cricket administrators began to characterize as 'bad behaviour' on and off the field, legislators, in the form of the International Cricket Council and the MCC, have combined efforts to deal with these questions by changing the legal environment and the technical rules governing behaviour. The Viv Richards' case, were it to happen today, would occur in a changed legal and ethical world. The *Laws of Cricket*, as well as the *ICC Code of Conduct* now offer us apparent textual, legal solutions to what were, just a few years ago, troubling ethical dilemmas to be solved by collective and democratic rule-making. Richie Benaud's plea to the art of captaincy and to the ability of participants to settle and determine the contents of the rules of conduct has been replaced with 'law'. I now turn to a brief introductory discussion of one aspect of the brave new world of cricket and the law.

6 Law, codes and the spirit of the game

Former Australian wicket keeper Rodney Marsh has been appointed to head the newly created England Cricket Academy. In addition to the delicious irony of the colonial teaching the former imperial masters the basics of their own game, it is interesting to note the attitude expressed by Marsh concerning the correct conduct of cricketers on the field, particularly on the question of appealing. Marsh, speaking of his days as head of the Australian Cricket Academy, said

> At the Academy we spend a lot of time talking about the players' attitude to umpires. The basic rule I lay down is 'Don't appeal if you don't think it's out; make it a good one if you do'. It is the players' interest to earn the respect of the umpires. They'll appreciate that behaviour. If you appeal all the time the umpire is more likely to turn down the one that is out through frustration and human nature.[1]

Here, Marsh is expressing an attitude impregnated with pragmatism and utilitarian calculation. He is not asserting that at some basic level of principle the spirit of the game requires and demands good faith appeals. Instead he puts the idea that umpires are only human and that they are in fact both more likely to grant the appeal of a player with a reputation as a 'cautious' appellant and less likely to grant even a meritorious appeal to someone with the opposite reputation. However, neither Marsh's appeal about appeals nor other calls for senior players to set the right example for the good of the game, managed to stifle the growing trend to constant appealing pragmatic.[2] Instead, strict law enforcement measures have been invoked in order to ensure the spirit of the game by threatening the full power of the law if the players do not sort themselves out. Like a gang of juvenile delinquents, players of the greatest of games are now faced with the carrot of compliance and the stick of punishment.

Unlike its previous legislative embodiments, the 2000 *Code* of the *Laws of Cricket* carries with it a *Preamble* dedicated to 'the spirit of the game'. For centuries this idea and ideal of cricket was to be found in the shared and common understandings of those who played and participated in the game. Now, it has been reduced to written text. Some will see this as an exemplary achievement, like all codification projects, as the reduction of centuries of practical achievement to a few simple principles, available to all and now public, textual, in nature. Others will bemoan the state of political and legal reality which has brought us to the stage that we must diminish the democratic, constantly evolving, creative exercise of determining the state of the spirit of the game through *praxis*.

Be that as it may, we are now faced with a new legal text, not just in the substantive changes to the *Laws* in the 2000 *Code*, but in the terms of the *Preamble*. Here, I wish simply to outline some of the key points of the newly codified 'spirit of the game', and to summarize some of the more troubling jurisprudential aspects of the codification process for our understanding of cricket and the law.

The leading interpretive text summarizes the situation as follows:

> The Preamble – The Spirit of Cricket is a direct result of the growing concern about the deterioration in player behaviour on the field of play. Laws 1.4 and 42.1 place the responsibility of ensuring that play is conducted within the spirit of the game – as set out in the Preamble – firmly on the two captains. Should the umpires have any concern that the spirit of the game is not being observed, they should immediately and jointly speak to the captain of the side responsible for the contravention and require him to take the appropriate action.[3]

At first blush, then the provisions of the new *Preamble* appear to offer little new in the way of jurisdictional innovation. The provisions of Law 42(1) of the 1980 *Code* also made it clear that responsibility for '. . . ensuring that play is conducted within the spirit of the game as well as within the Laws fell on the captains'.

What appears to be new in the *Preamble* is first the very existence of the text itself and the clearer enumeration not just of the substantive content of 'the spirit of the game' but also of the procedural mechanisms to be invoked in case of a breach. Thus, Article 2 imposes a clear duty on the captain, which may have been simply implied under the previous set of *Laws*, after the intervention of the umpires 'to take action where required'. Moreover, it is made explicit that the process of setting and reinforcing the parameter of 'the spirit of the game' lies with all participants on the field of play.

> Captains and umpires together set the tone for the conduct of a cricket match. Every player is expected to make an important contribution to this.[4]

Citizens of the republic of cricket not only have rights as enunciated in the *Laws*, now for the first time, they have explicit duties to the game and to their fellow citizens. Indeed, Article 4 clearly enunciates this new legalized ideal of the cricketer as citizen and participant in the law-making, or at least law enforcement process.

The Spirit of the Game involves RESPECT for:
Your opponents
Your own captain and team

The role of the umpires
The game's traditional values.

The legal semiotics of the *Preamble* are fascinating and informative. The 'spirit of the game' is now the 'Spirit of the Game', removed from the lower levels of discursive practice to the majesty of upper case. And not just any upper case. But upper case **bold**. The republican duty imposed on the citizen participant is itself rendered not just in bold type, but is entirely in upper case. Like Aretha Franklin, cricket now demands **RESPECT**. In case there was any doubt about the nature and extent of the duty of respect owed, and those towards whom the ethical relationship must be recognized, the list is at once complete and open-ended; opponents, captain and teammates, the judicial function and the traditional values of the game itself. Thus, the new *Laws* directly impose on all citizen/participants an obligation to respect the rule of law (the umpires etc.) and the democratic values enshrined in the *Laws* and spirit of the game. 'The game's traditional values' are to be respected and one assumes from the rest of the *Preamble*, obeyed upon pain of penalty.

Of course, it might be argued that at some level at least, the enumeration here is self-contradictory and incoherent. Respect for one's own team and captain seem almost by definition to be part of playing a team sport like cricket. Respect for opponents is always and already part of the spirit of competition inherent in the practice of cricket, as is, with notable exceptions and controversies perhaps, respect for the role of the umpire. Finally, of course, one might be forgiven for having thought that respect for the traditional values of the game was, is and will be the very essence of our understanding of the idea of 'the spirit of the game'. In other words, the attempt to embody in legislative language the idea and limitations of the spirit of the game might well be a simple exercise in redundancy. Indeed, one might go further and assert that the idea of respect for the 'game's traditional values' is either rendered meaningless, or else is given an entirely new meaning, by the very existence of the *Preamble*. In either case, this would result in the text becoming a self-defeating legislative nullity.

If one were to adopt this analysis, one would simply assert that chief among 'the game's traditional values' has always been the idea that the spirit of the game has been created, modified and embodied in the constant shifting and evolutionary nature of the legal practice of the game by its participants. Any attempt to legislate this practical law-making exercise immediately undermines its very nature. The traditional values of the game cannot be reduced to a written text because they are ever changing, and they are ever changing in part at least, because they are not embodied in a legislative text.

The essential jurisprudential, democratic and republican dilemma posed by the existence of the text of the *Preamble* becomes clear when it is read in the context of the substantive provisions of the *Laws* themselves. Of course, in the normal course of an interpretive practice this would raise many interesting and intriguing questions about the relationship between a 'preamble' and the *Laws* themselves. Is the former a part of the Code? Is it to be used merely as an interpretive tool? Or is it merely precatory in nature? These are all questions with which lawyers will be familiar from dealing with statutory instruments of all kinds. Further issues which arise concern the choice of linguistic renderings of essential concepts. Are 'the traditions of the game', 'the sprit of the game' and 'fair play' different or synonymous? Are they synonymous all the time or only partially? Fortunately for us, the codifiers of the 2000 *Laws of Cricket* appear to have removed many, but not all, of these tricky issues of legislative intent and interpretive technique.

Let me briefly remind the reader of the operative general textual provisions which must be considered here. First, we find the preamble to the *Preamble* itself.[5]

> Cricket is a game that owes much of its unique appeal to the fact that it should be played not only within its Laws but within the Spirit of the Game. Any action which is seen to abuse this spirit causes injury to the game itself. The major responsibility for ensuring the spirit of the game rests with the captains.

Article 1 imposes the responsibility indicated in the preamble to the *Preamble* on the captains.

> The captains are responsible at all times for ensuring that play is conducted within the Spirit of the Game as well as within the Laws.

The next part of Article 1 deals with **Player's Conduct** and reads

> In the event of a player failing to comply with instructions by an umpire, or criticising by word or action the decisions of an umpire, or showing dissent, or generally behaving in a manner which might bring the game into disrepute, the umpire concerned shall in the first place report the matter to the other umpire and to the player's captain, and instruct the latter to take action.

Article 2 provides that

> According to the Laws the umpires are the sole judges of fair and unfair play. The umpires may intervene at any time and it is the responsibility of the captain to take action where required.

Article 3 authorizes the umpires to intervene *inter alia* in cases of

> Any other action that they consider to be unfair.

Article 5 then provides a partial list of actions which are against the spirit of the game, including

To indulge in cheating or any sharp practice, for instance:

(a)   to appeal knowing that the batsman is not out

(b)   advance towards an umpire in an aggressive manner when appealing.

We must then also consider the provisions of Law 42(1) and (2) which read respectively

1.   Fair and unfair play – responsibility of captains

The responsibility lies with the captains for ensuring that play is conducted within the spirit and traditions of the game, as described in The Preamble – The Spirit of Cricket, as well as within the Laws.

2.   Fair and unfair play – responsibility of umpires

The umpires shall be the sole judges of fair and unfair play. If either umpire considers an action, not covered by the Laws, to be unfair, he shall intervene without appeal, and if the ball is in play, shall call and signal Dead ball and implement the procedure as set out in 18 below.

Finally, the text of Law 42(18) may come into play. It reads in part:

Players' conduct

If there is any breach of the Spirit of the Game by a player failing to comply with the instructions of an umpire, or criticising his decisions by word or action, or showing dissent, or generally behaving in a manner which might bring the game into disrepute, the umpire concerned shall immediately report the matter to the other umpire.

The umpires together shall

(i)   inform the player's captain of the occurrence, instructing the latter to take action.

(ii)   warn him of the gravity of the offence, and tell him that it will be reported to higher authority.

As I have already mentioned, the structure and content of the *Preamble* and the *Laws of Cricket*, for the lawyer trained in manipulating texts, raise several serious and interconnected issues, However, it is important to note here that my concerns are not so much with the technical questions or even the answers to these issues which a legal interpretive exercise might give. Instead, here, as throughout the book, I am trying to outline ways in which the very notions of law and cricket which are seemingly at stake are in fact subject to and informed by underlying epistemological, ideological and ethical positions which each reader and participant brings to these debates. For those who adopt the position that the new *Laws*, including the *Preamble*, were sadly necessary to prevent a further deterioration in the game itself, the reading which they will give to the interactions of the various texts here will be informed by the understanding of the concerns and ideas underlying the expression of legislative purpose. For others, who see either the provisions of the 2000 *Code* as unnecessary or as an unwanted encroachment by a hierarchy on a democratic base of those who play and construct the game through the practice of playing cricket etc., the meanings of the new texts will carry other interpretive possibilities. My goal here is simply to point out some of the difficult issues raised by the texts and their possible interpretations.

The first point which should be made is that the potential interpretive difficulties posed by the existence of a *Preamble* and then a substantive text of the *Laws* are to some extent, although perhaps not entirely, removed by the *Laws* themselves. Thus, as we have just seen, Law 42(1) specifically refers, in so far as the captain's duties are concerned, to the spirit and traditions of the game 'as described in The Preamble'. The legislature itself here incorporates the text of the *Preamble* and gives it legislative force as fully incorporated in the *Laws*.

Of course, one might argue, as matter of the strict reading of the text that this provision is in fact limited to the duty and role of the captains and does not *ipso facto* necessarily incorporate the *Preamble* into the rest of the *Laws*, or even into the rest of Law 42. However, the list of 'offences' listed under the powers of the remedial intervention of umpires (42(18)) would seem to indicate that there has been, by strong implication at the very least, incorporation of the *Preamble* into the *Laws*.

Again, to be somewhat obstreperous or at least taking the text at its word, one can also note that Law 42(2) gives the umpires authority over 'an action, not covered by the Laws'. If it is truly the case that the *Preamble* has been fully incorporated into the text of the substantive provisions of the *Laws*, the exact meaning of these words is rendered problematic. If the spirit and traditions of the game, and all that that entails, form part of the *Laws* by incorporation, it is difficult, if not impossible, to imagine any action 'not covered by the Laws'. Such an action would, on this reading, have to be one which is contained neither in the spirit of the game nor in the substantive provisions of the 2000 *Code* but which is nonetheless a violation of our understanding of 'fair play'. This provision must then be read either as an indication of the less than complete incorporation of the spirit of the game into the *Laws*, or as granting an extraordinarily wide power of intervention to the umpire, above and beyond both law and equity.

Similarly, the provisions of Law 42(1) refer specifically to the captains' duties with regards to the spirit, traditions and Laws of the game, under the heading **Fair and unfair play**. At the same time, Law 42(2) dealing with **Fair and unfair play – responsibility of umpires** contains no such specific reference to the spirit or traditions of the game.[6] The text speaks only of 'fair and unfair play' as well as the aforementioned reference to an action 'not covered by the Laws'. Is the reference to fair and unfair play in Law 42(1), found only in the title, incorporated as a substantive provision into the text of that paragraph? If so, does that mean that a similar reference to 'fair and unfair play' in Law 42(2) then by implication incorporate the references to the game's spirit and traditions from Law 42(2)?[7] Again if this is in fact and in law the case, then we are left once more to ponder the meaning, if any, of some action which is 'not covered by the Laws'.

Further interpretive difficulties also arise here. There is imposed upon the captain a clear and apparently unequivocal duty to ensure compliance with both the traditions and spirit of the game on the one hand, and the *Laws of Cricket* on the other. It seems clear then, from what we 'know' of cricket, that the reference to the *Laws* here has two distinct purposes. First, the issue of incorporation, express or by implication, is problematic and/or irrelevant here. The captain has a clearly defined duty to both, 'as well as' is the language employed by the legislature here. If they were identical through incorporation or otherwise, such a phrase would be redundant, and a basic rule of interpretation is that the author/legislator intends to give meaning to all words in the text.

Secondly, we proceed on the idea that there is still, within the context of the *Laws* themselves, a difference in form and content between the spirit, and ethics of cricket on the one hand, and the literal, technical meaning of the legislative set of *Laws* on the other. There must then be some form of ordering, unless we believe that there can never be a conflict between the *Laws* and the spirit of the game. If there is no conflict then the captain will have no real difficulty in ensuring compliance with both norms. If on the other hand, there is a conflict between the *Laws* and the spirit of the game, then it will be impossible literally and in practice to ensure compliance with the captains' duties as embodiment of the Law, the *Laws* and the spirit of the game. Indeed, much of the rest of this book is dedicated to the idea that one of the things which makes cricket such a great game and such a fertile field of study for lawyers, is that it often poses precisely the apparently stark distinction between strict, formal, literal or positivistic rule-compliance and the obligations imposed by a higher ethical duty. Thus, the provisions of Law 42(1) do little if anything to answer the basic jurisprudential questions of cricket and the law – (a) do we obey the law?; or (b) do we obey the spirit of the game; or finally (c) in acting according to (a), do we violate our duties under (b)?

Finally, a further set of jurisprudential and practical questions is posed by the provisions of the new *Laws of Cricket* and the incorporation of a text which seeks to articulate in part at least the content of the spirit of the game. Umpires must ensure fair play, including preventing players 'behaving in a manner which might bring the game into disrepute' (Article 1 and Law 42(18)). We know again from Article 4 of the *Preamble* that the spirit of the game, in upper case letters, includes respect for 'the game's traditional values'. We also know from Article 5 that one violates the spirit of the game by indulging 'in cheating or any sharp practice' 'for instance' etc. We also know again, that the umpire may intervene under Law 42(2) in relation 'to an action not covered by the Laws'.

Here, briefly are the matters of concern. Law 42(1) requires that the captain ensure compliance with the spirit of the game 'as described in The Preamble'. This presents no, or fewer, difficulties when we are dealing with conduct which is clearly defined and proscribed. Indeed, at first blush one might think that this means simply that the *Preamble* completely codifies the content of the spirit of the game. However, a simple reiteration of the legislative language of the text in question reveals that the captain must ensure compliance with actions which violate nothing more clearly defined than 'the traditional values of the game', or behaviour which 'brings the game into disrepute', or even 'cheating or sharp practice' which is, by the use of the phrase 'for instance' almost certainly not limited to the listed acts, but is much broader in the content or understanding of prohibited actions.

Quite clearly, if and when such vague phrases impose a penalty on a team or individual, there must be serious concerns about issues of natural justice.[8] More importantly, for present purposes, there must also be concerns about the utility and importance in practice of the *Preamble* and many of the new provisions in the 2000 version of the *Laws of Cricket*. The texts themselves leave little doubt that much of the substantive content of the spirit of the game and of sanctions for the breach of that substantive content is and must remain unarticulated. If one takes the position briefly outlined above that cricket rule-making and practice is and always has been deeply informed by an incremental, democratic praxis, this does not, or at least it should not, give rise to basic concern about the nature of the game and the nature of the *Laws* and Laws of the game of cricket. Certainly, one is not prevented in such circumstances from asserting that a particular set of facts reveals a substantive and clear breach of the spirit of the game and should be subject to sanction.

On the other hand, if one adopts the view which seems to underlie the reform process behind the 2000 version of the *Laws* and the *Preamble* in particular, then one is faced with fundamental dilemmas and questions. New provisions incorporated into Law 42, which I shall discuss in more detail in other parts of the book, give new powers of sanctions to the umpires. Bowlers can be ordered out of the attack and penalty runs can now be awarded to the aggrieved side. This quite naturally fits into the world-view and legislative intent informing the new *Laws* i.e. that behaviour was getting out of hand, moral suasion was no longer effective and harsher penalties and sanctions had to be made available to umpires to prevent the game from further degradation.

Yet even if all if this is accepted as true, many of the interpretive and practical dilemmas which have always troubled cricket remain without a clear resolution. Let me briefly return to the idea of the proper relationship between the spirit of the game and the content of the *Laws* (and again ignoring the incorporation issues). The *Preamble* bans 'sharp practice', and activities which 'bring the game into disrepute' which are, according to the text, potentially unlimited concepts. Anyone with even a cursory knowledge of the history of cricket knows that the game is full of, and may even be defined by, 'sharp practice'. We also know that in many cases, some of which I shall study in more detail below, controversies which might be said to have brought the game into disrepute have arisen because a player or a team stands on their rights to a strict application of the *Laws*. Often, this can be seen to be an action in violation of some understanding of the spirit and traditions of the game. This conflict between the spirit and the *Laws* can then be seen to bring the game into disrepute, although for others it is by definition impossible to bring a game into disrepute by demanding that it be played according its own *Laws*. All that need be said for the moment is that despite the best efforts of the MCC and the committee which drafted the new *Laws of Cricket*, the dilemmas which forced them into the belief that the game was in some way being brought into disrepute by player behaviour will not necessarily go away under the new version of the legislation. Cricketers will not be deterred from engaging actively in the hermeneutic practice of constructing and changing the ways in which the game is played. Cricket will still be cricket, indeed it might be argued that cricket will only be cricket as long as it is not completely embodied in the dead, objective scientific and epistemological certainty of a perfect legal text.

By way of conclusion, which is in fact merely another way of further opening and engaging in discussion about cricket and law and cricket as law, let me turn finally to Viv Richards' charging appeal. It is now clear that advancing '...towards an umpire in an aggressive manner when appealing' is considered as sharp practice or cheating in violation of the provisions of Article 5 of the *Preamble* and would in all likelihood, assuming that 'advancing in an aggressive manner' can be understood, applied and interpreted in practice, lead to the invocation of Law 42(18). In fact and in law, the idea that any appeal of 'How's that?', no matter how delivered, is a valid appeal has been modified by the *Laws*. Some appeals are now considered to be cheating or sharp practice.

But even in law, the matter does not end there. If an appeal in this manner is 'cheating or sharp practice' in violation of the spirit of the game, we must still go back to the provisions of the *Laws* to determine what the practical, adjudicative consequences of the new provisions will be. Law 42(18) simply empowers the umpire to inform his colleague, inform the player concerned of his transgression, and inform the captain.[9] No further sanction is envisaged by these provisions. The umpire under Law 42(2) 'shall intervene' and 'shall', if necessary, signal dead ball. Thus, it might be possible to argue that the appeal, if it does constitute 'unfair play', is null and void. Again of course, this would require an interpretive decision that all breaches of the spirit of the game are by definition 'unfair play'. On the other hand, the *Preamble*, which specifically defines aggressive appealing as a breach of the appropriate standards, does not define the action as 'unfair play' but merely as a violation of the spirit of the game. In addition, the same *Preamble* even when dealing with the 'behaviour' which 'might bring the game into disrepute' (Article 1), establishes and possibly limits the umpire's actions to informing his colleague and instructing the captain to intervene. It seems that if one studies the remedial and substantive sections of the new *Code* together, there must at some level still be a distinction, in both fact and law, between and among, 'unfair play', violating the spirit or traditions of the game and 'sharp practice'.

If this is so, we must again turn to complex questions of legislative intent, the meaning of the language of the texts in questions, and the difficult tasks of reading the disparate texts together to make some practical sense of what might happen here. One might argue that Law 42(18) could be read in a highly legalistic manner to render the appeal null and void. But another possibility remains. The mischief in question here is the 'manner' of the appeal. This is not a case of a vexatious appeal made with the belief or 'knowledge' (required by Article 5) that the batter is not out. Thus the batter let us assume, has nicked the ball to a fielder. He is 'out' in some real sense. Is it appropriate or proportionate in terms of legislative intent, deterrence or punishment theory, to deprive the bowler and his side of a wicket because of the 'over enthusiasm' of one fielder? One might of course, convincingly argue here that the whole side should suffer since the problem of aggressive appeals brings the game of cricket into disrepute, it evidences a lack of respect for the game, for one's teammates and captain and for the judicial function and rule of law as embodied by the umpire. In making these arguments, however, one is no longer asserting the objective clarity and certainty of the provisions of the *Laws of Cricket*. Instead one is arguing about what cricket is, what the role of players, umpires, the *Laws* and the spirit of the game are and should be.

Similarly, one might argue that the punishment should fit the crime and that the sanction should target the offender to ensure as much specific deterrence as possible in the circumstances. Imposing the sanctions of censure by the umpires and captain, plus post-match disciplinary measures, hits the offender and offers a measured and proportionate response. By adopting the interpretation of imposing upon the umpire an obligation to call and signal dead ball and render the appeal null and void, one not only punishes those who have not offended, but one also deprives them of their right to appeal. All appeals are valid if rendered in the appropriate form (Law 27(4)). In addition, a temporal element could also be found to be relevant in these circumstances. The 'dismissal' occurred at the point the catch from the edge was taken. The offence necessarily on these facts occurred after the catch was taken. To call dead ball and render any and all appeals useless is to impose a sanction in a retroactive fashion, something generally abhorred by our understanding of the rule of law. It is the behaviour of the fielder after the dismissal which is the valid and appropriate target for censure and sanction here. Again, it goes almost without saying that this particular set of arguments is again grounded not in objective textual analysis but in a set of (unarticulated) beliefs about law, cricket, the spirit of the game and the role and nature of adjudication.

Other interpretive difficulties are not avoided by the now (relatively) clear textual provisions of the 2000 version of the *Laws of Cricket*. Richie Benaud in his commentary on Australia's Channel 9 is continually vexed by a 'new' kind of appellate procedure. Here, the bowler who believes he has caught the edge and the ball has carried and been held by the keeper or a fielder, simply raises his hands to the sky, makes an appeal and continues to run down the edge of the pitch to be met by his celebrating teammates. He never looks in the direction of the umpire to see if the batter has been given out, or only does so after celebrations have begun. For Benaud this type of behaviour indicates at some basic level a disregard for the umpire, his adjudicative function and the actual substance of his decisions. It might even be argued that there is some evidence of an attempt in such circumstances to 'intimidate' or 'trick' the umpire into giving a positive response to the appeal by appearing so certain of the result that it is not even necessary to look for the upraised finger.

Again, one might agree or disagree with Benaud's position, for any number of reasons. However, it seems clear that there is an arguable position being put forward that this type of action could easily be seen to fit within the 'definition' of bringing the game into disrepute. If this is so, then of course, exactly the same interpretive issues which arise concerning the consequences of an overly aggressive appeal again come to the fore. What is equally evident is that the contextual complexity and genius of cricket and cricketers again comes to the fore to defeat any attempt to codify the game and its *Laws*. 'Aggressive appeals' by charging the umpire are replaced by what one might call passive appeals by ignoring the umpire. Each or both or neither might arguably be contrary to the spirit of the game. Legislative intervention may or may not be an answer but it can never be *the* answer. Cricket is and has always been understood as complexity and uncertainty within law and *Laws*. It is this complexity, this uncertainty within law and adjudication, which make cricket the game that fascinates and annoys.

Finally, by way of introduction to issues to which I shall return later, it might be added that a further possibility remains. Nothing in either position or any variant thereof about the nature of appeals and the spirit of the game or the sanctions to be attached to a violation of the traditions of cricket in these circumstances would prevent the batter caught in such cases from voluntarily surrendering his wicket.

Thus under Law 27(1) and (2) a batter 'who is out under any of the Laws' may leave his wicket without any appeal having been made and that batter is considered to be 'dismissed'. Again one might argue that a batter might be prevented from doing so if the combined result of the provisions of Law 23 relating to when a ball is dead would mean that he has therefore not been 'dismissed' under the *Laws* at the time he leaves his wicket. A leading commentary on the *Laws* exposes the apparently uncomplicated position that under the new *Code* there is a clear distinction between a batter who is 'out' and a batter who is 'dismissed'.

> Being out means that the conditions of the appropriate Law apply. Being dismissed means that an umpire has given him out, or he has given himself out by walking from his wicket.[10]

This positivist distinction between the fulfilling of objective conditions (out) and judicial intervention (dismissed), does not however answer the question as to when the objective 'conditions of the appropriate Law apply'. This will always be a matter of some interpretive intervention and often debate. Indeed, the issue under discussion here is but one example. If the ball is 'dead' the batter who edges a catch to a fielder or who is struck on the pads cannot be either 'out' or 'dismissed', since the ball is not in play.

Law 23 is clear in listing when a ball is dead and what many of the consequences of a call and signal of dead ball are. However, it does not clearly establish the basic jurisprudential point which is central for any determination under the circumstances under discussion, i.e. is the ball 'dead' *per se* or is the ball 'dead' only when the umpire says it is? In addition, in the case I am discussing now, when does the ball become dead? If it is dead either *per se* when the spirit of game is violated by an aggressive or passive appeal (if unfair play and the violation of the spirit of the game are the same) or if it is dead after the signal and call by the umpire, the events and facts which constitute the dismissal all precede both or either of those points i.e. a lawful delivery, striking the bat and being fairly caught by a member of the fielding side.

Again, only if we give a retrospective effect to the call of dead ball and a positivistic reading to the dismissals and appeals i.e. the batter is out when given out and only then, could such an interpretation be invoked to prevent the batter from walking. The actual provisions of the new *Laws* clearly belie the last point since it is clear that a batter may be dismissed not just on appeal but when '...he is out under any of the Laws and leaves his wicket...'[11]

Here then, we can offer a reading not just of the technical aspects of the *Laws* or of the incorporation of the spirit of the game within the *Laws*, however vaguely articulated, but we can begin to address the complexities of the umpires' jurisdiction and the effects which players can have on that jurisdiction. First, however, we need to turn to another legislative development which again attempts to codify parts of the spirit of the game and to sanction the violation of those traditions of the game. Here we come to the new judicial official who determines at another level, fair and unfair play, the ICC Match Referee.

7 More law and the spirit of the game

There has been and continues to be, among the highest echelons of the cricket world, a widely held belief that players' behaviour has been and is approaching and crossing over the line of the unacceptable. It no longer appears to be possible to simply refer to the traditions of the game, or to invoke the captain's duty to ensure compliance with the *Laws* and spirit of the game. The idea that the umpire is the sole judge of fair and unfair play, enshrined in legislative text and combined with the ethical convention that an umpire's decision is final and beyond question no longer are enough to ensure compliance by participants in the game of cricket with the rules and *Laws* of the game. Mere anarchy seems ever closer.

For example, in July 1998, the leading umpires in the world met in London and roundly condemned the players for bringing the game into disrepute and undermining the very basis of the rule of law in the game i.e. adherence to the idea and ideal of the judicial function of the umpire. Alan Lee of the *Times* put it succinctly: 'With unprecedented candour, the umpires denounced many modern Test match players as cheats.'[1]

This meeting of the umpires and the nature and results of their discussions highlight the tension which has, I believe, always been present in the game and which raises the very basic jurisprudential question under study here. Not only is there now, as there has always been, a tension between the letter of the *Laws* and the spirit of the game, a conflict between rule formalism and appeals to a higher ethical normative practice, but there is growing evidence of a deeper set of troubles. Participants in the process of playing the game, that is of establishing the actual content of the *Laws* in practice and of the higher normative rules of the spirit of the game, seem to be involved in a sort of conspiracy to pervert the course of justice. In other words, the same basic question posed by the Hansie Cronje affair resurface here in a different but related context. If the players decide as a matter of their daily practice of the game to subvert the *Laws* and some traditional understandings of the spirit of the game, then we must ask whether this is or is not 'cricket' and exactly what do we mean by this.

If we believe, as we must, that the game involves at some level the capacity for unformulated yet substantive behavioural norms and rules of conduct, then we must endeavour to formulate an understanding of the parameter of that democratic impulse. We have always understood, I believe, that there is

more to cricket than the strict letter of the *Laws*, just as we have always understood that the letter of the *Laws* must be adhered to. We know that the spirit of
the game exists, we know that there is behaviour which brings the game into
disrepute. We even know sometimes that such behaviour may be said to exist in
an instance of strict rule formalism. We know, ultimately, that those involved in
playing the game are in fact and in law, participating in a process of rule formation
and rule interpretation. Again, as with Hansie Cronje, the question at the
borders of cricket and 'not cricket' is precisely where we draw the line. For
example, Alan Lee's report of the umpires' meeting in 1998 relates the following
story from West Indian umpire Steve Bucknor.

> Bucknor, who is also uneasy about the undermining effect on umpires of the
> giant video screens at Test grounds, told of a wicketkeeper in the West
> Indies who was recently told he would lose his place in his island's first-class
> team if he did not join his close fielders in every contrived appeal. 'He knew
> it was wrong but, to stay in the side, he went along with it. I only hope his
> conscience gets the better of him. It's my duty to do as much as I can to
> prevent cricketers beating the system but I am deeply saddened by some of
> things I see now.'[2]

I turn to some of the issues posed by the existence of television replay technology later in the book. There are two important and interconnected questions
raised by the example given by Bucknor for present purposes. Again, the fact
that a team 'conspires' to issue contrived appeals in order to obtain a particular
verdict, in other words an adjudication by the umpire that a batter is 'out' when
he is not, is from many perspectives and for many of those who love the game
and cherish its ideals, extremely troublesome. But again, the problem here, above
and beyond the degradation in many people's understanding of what the spirit of
the game actually means in practice, is dwarfed by the more basic problem of the
very epistemological challenge to the existence of 'cricket' which might be seen
to be posed by such 'conspiracies'.

Are these players playing cricket? Do they stop playing cricket when they
appeal, 'knowing' the batter is not out? Is the umpire properly vested with jurisdiction when he answers an appeal which is, in fact and in law, without foundation? How would we know? Is the batter 'out' because the umpire says he is and
that result is entered by the scorers in the official results at the end of play? Has
justice been perverted or merely law? Are they the same? Again, the questions
here are many and complex, and when given further nuance and shade, may
become more clear or more ambiguous. Imagine for a moment a batter who is
clearly 'out' because he has edged a catch to the keeper. Everyone heard the nick
and saw the deviation. Television replays and the technology of the 'snickometer'
confirm this. But the umpire is unsure. The bat passed close to the pad at the
same time as the ball went by the edge. The crowd noise is loud, the deviation
was barely discernible from the natural swing of the bowler. The decision is 'not
out'. The next appeal by the fielding side takes place in circumstances which are

similar except that, for the sake of the example, we assume that the fielding side knows the ball did not hit the bat.

At this level then, the appeal is without merit. It is motivated in large part by feelings of injustice and revenge. The umpire gives the decision in favour of the fielding side. Is the batter 'out'? He is 'dismissed' if and when the umpire upholds the appeal. Has justice been served, even if law has not? Clearly arguments will circulate here within the interpretive community about rule formalism, balancing out and the karma of the game, about conspiracy and about justice versus the individual merits of every adjudicative act. Some will see justice and the best interests of cricket while others will see conspiracy, injustice and a violation of the spirit of the game. Epistemological certainty might be replaced by democratic dispute and disagreement. Very little can be certain, even whether we are indeed talking about the same thing.

Once we get over the epistemological and deontological hurdles we will always encounter in such debates about law-making and judicial interpretation, we can then begin to confront the next level of debate about the appropriate and best measures to be invoked to deal with the 'problem' as we have agreed to define it. Are the issues raised by this and other questions about the current state of the game and about the rule of law and increasing criminality and lawlessness better dealt with through more law or through more democratic, or some would argue, republican rule-making activities?[3]

Umpire Bucknor speaks in favour of a combined effort. He sees his role as umpire to encompass a duty to maintain the 'system'; to keep the players from 'beating' it. At the same time, he makes it clear that a major focus in ensuring the survival of the game, both at the level of the *Laws* and the spirit of the sport, must be in the individual conscience of the wicketkeeper. He urges an ethical solution from individual cricketers who will in some way see the light and realize the error of their ways. This would be in keeping with at least one type of understanding of the participatory rule-making, rule-creation and democratic building of the essential jurisprudential character of the game. Players, as the *Preamble* to the 2000 *Code* of the *Laws of Cricket* makes explicit, have a duty to the game and their teammates and to ensure the ongoing relevance of the spirit of the game.

But this of course faces an immediate and practical hurdle in the circumstances outlined by umpire Bucknor. The wicketkeeper in question was pressured into illegality by his fellow players and/or by the selectors who decide who is picked for inclusion in the side. If they breach their duty to the spirit of the game and to their teammate by 'coercing' his compliance and participation in a conspiracy against the *Laws* and ethical norms of the game, what is he to do? The threat is that in the case of non-participation, he will be excluded from the side. In such a case, he would, by upholding the spirit of the game and the *Laws of Cricket*, be excluded from playing the game. In such a case then, the question of epistemology and deontology once again rears its potentially ugly head. If he is excluded, the rest of the team by definition is in fact and in law doing something which is 'not cricket'. What game are they playing? How do we know and what do we do about it?

The answer for many is clear. We need more law and we need still more adjudication. We need the Match Referee system.

The ICC Code of Conduct

It is not my intention here to offer a full and complete description or analysis of the Match Referee system and of the disciplinary jurisprudence as it has evolved in the world of international cricket. Instead I wish to highlight the general structure and content of the system and the ways in which it fits into the basic issues which I have been discussing. Is more law, in other words, the answer to a perceived or real failure in law?

The *ICC Code of Conduct* applies to Players and Team Officials and has effect in relation to both on and off the field activities.[4] Procedural mechanisms and a structure of penalties are created. In essence, the *Code of Conduct* creates a supplementary set of rules to the *Laws of Cricket* and at the same time, adds a jurisdiction which adjudicates as a supplement to the on field decision-making of the umpires. In other words, the legislative authorities in world cricket believed that the breakdown in law and order demanded the imposition of more law and more order. Part CC of the *Code* creates offences and sets out the appropriate penalties to be imposed by the new judicial official, the Match Referee. The offences which are of relevance here relate both to conduct which could be said to be contrary to the *Laws of Cricket*, including the *Preamble* and to other regulatory provisions imposed by the ICC. Thus Level 1 offences are:

1.1 Breach of the Logo Policy save for breaches relating to a commercial logo or players' bat logo
1.2 Abuse of cricket equipment or clothing, ground equipment or fixtures and fittings
1.3 Showing dissent at an umpire's decision by action or verbal abuse
1.4 Using language that is obscene, offensive or insulting and/or the making of an obscene gesture
1.5 Excessive appealing
1.6 Pointing or gesturing towards the pavilion in an aggressive manner by a bowler or other member of the fielding side upon the dismissal of a batsman.

Quite clearly most of these provisions are intended to further criminalize precisely the types of behaviour which many believe are indicative of the break-down in cricket's version of law and order, and to fill the disciplinary gap left by the umpire's lack of punitive powers. Dissent, sledging, and excessive appealing all clearly show either a disrespect for the umpire's judicial function and office or violate not just the provisions of the *Laws* relating to interfering with the batter, but also conflict with a dominant understanding of the spirit of the game.[5] They are also all the types of activity identified by those who argue that cricket anarchy has arrived or is just around the jurisprudential corner.

Level 2 offences involve either recidivism in relation to Level 1 crimes and misdemeanours or more 'serious' examples of those actions, e.g., 'serious' dissent instead of 'dissent'; 'deliberate and malicious distraction' of the batter. 'Charging or advancing towards the umpire in an aggressive manner when appealing' as opposed to 'excessive' appealing. In addition, public criticism or comment on a match when the comment or criticism are deemed inappropriate, as well as 'inappropriate or deliberate physical contact between players in the course of play' are also criminalized. Again, the clear legislative intent here is to ensure compliance with various elements of the 'spirit of the game' already codified in the *Preamble* and partly in the substantive provisions of the *Laws* and to introduce an additional element of control over acts equivalent to *ex facie* contempt.

Level 3 offences continue the recidivism aspect of the *Code* and introduce the new offence of racial and other insult or vilification, again acts which many would say have been essential elements of certain types of 'sledging'. 'Intimidation' of the umpire or referee also constitutes an offence here and a threat of assault or actual assault become Level 4 offences.

The structure and content of the *Code of Conduct* again clearly demonstrate that the ICC has chosen to adopt a strict law and order approach to the problem identified as the breakdown in law and order. Of course, many of the same interpretive problems will remain. What is the difference between 'dissent' and 'serious dissent'? What is the line of demarcation between 'excessive appealing' and 'charging and advancing' towards the umpire when appealing? Quite clearly, more law will in fact result in more law. Debate will continue to rage around the substantive content of offences. People will differ over not just the gravity of an offence but over the consistency of judicial decision-making by Match Referees.[6] *Wisden* will continue to carry a new rubric 'Crime and Punishment – ICC Code of Conduct – Breaches and Penalties' as a new jurisprudence of cricketing offences is created and defined. No doubt the abilities of the players and others to challenge and stretch the boundaries of the *Laws*, the *Preamble* and the *Code of Conduct* and the spirit of the game will continue.

Before he was exposed as a crook and a cheat, Hansie Cronje, captaining South Africa against India, appeared on the field sporting an earpiece, enabling him to receive instructions and information from the dressing room. Nothing in the *Code* or *Laws* specifically prohibited this. Only some idea that such an act would be 'conduct unbecoming' or 'unfair play' or would 'bring the game into disrepute' could prevent it. Again all the questions and dilemmas about what we even mean when we say 'cricket' or 'not cricket', came to the fore. Is cricket, as some claim, great because it is somehow 'natural', willow, leather, dirt and grass, Lord Denning's pastoral dream? Is it great because it adopts technological advances and adapts to change? Is there some essential difference between someone, another player, coach or manager, listening to or watching television and radio commentary and passing along the insights of expert commentators at a drinks or luncheon interval and the more immediate passing on of similar information via a radio set and earpiece? Is this 'sharp practice' or innovation? Is it cricket or not? Cronje removed the earpiece after the intervention of the match officials and it has not reappeared in international cricket. Is this because of more law, of the threat of sanctions or because after mature discussion and reflection based upon the ideals of the spirit of the game, it was decided by deliberative democracy that this was simply 'not cricket'? Can we know and if so how?[7]

We can know two things. First, more law may, and often does result in ongoing calls for still more law, as gaps are identified or as the original system fails for whatever reason. Secondly, cricketers, umpires, Match Referees and fans will nonetheless continue to dispute, contest and argue over the actual content of the new law and in doing so they will, at some level at least, ensure that democracy continues to play an important role in the rule of law in cricket.

The Code, Conduct and the Rule of Law

Ever since the ICC's introduction of the *Code of Conduct*, the actual content of the *Code* and its structure have undergone substantive modification and clarification. Despite this ongoing process of legislative review and change, law and order continues for many to be on the verge of collapse in the world of international cricket. Abusive Australian crowds led Sri Lankan officials and commentators to call for an increase in the powers of the Match Referee to control fan behaviour.[8] In 2001, Lord MacLaurin of the England and Wales Cricket Board decried and bemoaned not just bad on field behaviour but judicial laxity by Match Referees. For him, 'The administrators have to be tough and if they start removing players when they transgress they will soon come into line. We have to be tough because the game is moving on.'[9]

Here we find not just a tough 'law and order' policy, informed by the criminological insights of punitive practice and zero tolerance ideas, but a clear indication that the players are the primary culprits, aided and abetted by reluctant judicial officials, who are themselves former players. Only the administrators are willing to take a tough stance to save the game. Indeed, progress depends on the past. Some idealized, yet substantively unarticulated notion of the glories of cricket, of its halcyon days, of the spirit of the game would appear to be at work. 'The game is moving on' and at some level it can only do so if we go back to the past. Bring back the cane and the players will soon realize the error of their ways. They might think they are playing cricket but Lord MacLaurin knows better. If not the cane, then let us learn from the experience in other jurisdictions. Like football, let us consider introducing the yellow and red card system for transgressors.[10] This is for many emblematic of the sad state of affairs in cricket jurisprudence today. Not only has respect for the tradition of the game seemingly disappeared, but the only way to save the game is to introduce the legal system from the sport of the working class. All is nearly lost. Only law and more law will save us from anarchy.

The new system of Levels 1–4 for grading offences was introduced specifically to save the game from itself or more precisely from the players and slack officials. Malcolm Speed, the Chief Executive Officer of the ICC explained in the following terms:

We want international cricket to be tough and competitive but we also want to improve its image with the public. Umpires have agreed to support this drive by clamping down on language and behaviour that falls below reasonable standards.[11]

He added

I am not asking for suspensions willy-nilly but that, for serious breaches that warrant suspension, this is the punishment imposed. I want respect for officials, respect for opponents and respect for the spirit of the game.[12]

Speed underlined his position in a letter to Match Referees. Therein he stated:

I have been very pleased that a number of captains have spoken publicly of their intention to ensure that their teams play not only within the Laws but also within the Spirit of the Game. There have, however, been a number of incidents in matches over the past 12 months that have fallen below an acceptable standard. I have no interest in dredging up past incidents, and I point no finger of blame, but it is time to ensure that, moving forward, all of us charged with protecting the reputation of our great game meet the high standards expected.

I would also add that I am concerned that some match officials have not always responded adequately to some of these incidents. As a result, there have been occasions when inappropriate behaviour has gone unpunished and other occasions when penalties have been inadequate to deal fully with the offence committed.[13]

Speed's interventions and the attitude of the ICC towards 'bad behaviour' have been generally well-received and applauded.[14] Yet, as I point out throughout the rest of this book, such behaviour, to a greater or lesser extent, has always been part of international cricket, and indeed of cricket at all levels, from the beginnings of the game to the present day. The argument is not settled as to whether we should stamp out bad behaviour on the field of play, nor whether we should and do support the ideals embodied in our understandings of the traditions and spirit of the game. These are 'motherhood' questions – no one supports unacceptable behaviour, that is why it is unacceptable. The debate is now, as it has always been, over what fits inside and what falls outside the spirit and *Laws* of the game. The debate, with or without the Match Referee and the *Code of Conduct* is now, has always been and will always be, about what is and is not 'cricket'.

Indeed, even a brief and cursory review of some parts of the rule of law and the rules of law since the creation of the new judicial officer, the ICC Match Referee, indicates the ongoing, complex and often contradictory nature of law-making and adjudication which again makes cricket jurisprudence so important for our understanding of the basic principles of law and democracy.

Cricket is not rugby. It is not a contact sport, although this does not mean that physicality, courage and masculine violence are not essential elements of playing the game. But unlike rugby, for example, physical contact between the players is not part of the definitional parameter of lawfully engaging in the sport of cricket. Section 2.5 of the *Code of Conduct* and our general understandings of the spirit of the game make it clear that

> Inappropriate and deliberate physical contact between players in the course of play . . . is contrary to accepted modes of behaviour – it is not cricket.

However, this provision quite clearly does not involve the criminalization of all physical contact. Only contact which is both 'inappropriate and deliberate' falls under the scope of the prohibition. We all know, for example, that it is sometimes unavoidable that a runner trying to make his ground will run into a bowler completing his follow through. Even if such contact might be construed to be 'deliberate' i.e. by both players refusing to deviate from their respective trajectory, it will not in the normal course of events be 'inappropriate'. The bowler is entitled both to continue his natural follow through and to stand his ground. Practice and the history of democratic rule-making impose some obligation on the runner to take whatever evasive action may be necessary. Thus, the question for adjudication by the Match Referee will always be whether the two conditions have been met. The contact must have been both 'deliberate' and 'inappropriate'. It may well be, as a matter of statutory interpretation here, that the inclusion of the criterion 'deliberate' is redundant. Arguably, practice and the spirit of the game indicate that 'inappropriate' contact will be almost by definition 'deliberate', while deliberation cannot be a truly sufficient condition. The history of the law of unlawful collisions under the *Code of Conduct* highlights the interpretive framework and difficulties inherent in attempting to reduce the complexity of 'playing the game' to a limiting set of textual provisions.

Thus, for example, in a 1995 Test between New Zealand and Sri Lanka, Kiwi captain (and lawyer) Ken Rutherford and his Sri Lankan counterpart Arjuna Ranatunga were involved in a verbal exchange.

> The incident which led to (Match Referee Barry) Jarman's involvement came when Ranatunga ran into seam bowler Kerry Walmsley's elbow while attempting a single.
>
> Walmsley, who was reprimanded by Jarman on Saturday for swearing, stood his ground in mid-pitch as Ranatunga bumped into him. The two captains then appeared to exchange angry words.[15]

The physical contact here is undoubted, the verbal exchange which resulted therefrom would appear contrary, at first blush, to the spirit of the game. This is especially the case when the players involved are the captains, who as we have seen, have always been charged by the *Laws* themselves, with ensuring respect for the spirit of the game. At this level, Jarman would have been adjudicating on whether the contact between Ranatunga and Walmsley was deliberate and inappropriate.[16] But, as in all cases, other factors, not apparent at first sight might then enter the calculations involved in a full and complete, and therefore just, adjudicative process. *Inter alia*, one might argue that it would be relevant to consider the past conduct, if not the reputation, of the players involved. Ranatunga, for example, is well known outside his native Sri Lanka and by some in his homeland as being a particularly prickly character. Walmsley already had one 'conviction' in the match. Other questions might also be seen to be relevant to put the collision and its aftermath in its full context. Sri Lankan spinner Muralitharan had been, and is still, accused by some of having a suspect action, of being a chucker and therefore a cheat.[17] In the context of the game in which Ranatunga collided with Walmsley, New Zealand team official John Reid '... tastelessly claimed (during the match) Muralitharan's action was suspect'.[18]

Finally, while the pitch at Napier where the Test was played is normally considered to be hard and true, Sri Lanka arrived to find not only that they faced a 'green top', but a New Zealand bowling attack specifically selected for such a pitch. Included in the side was Walmsley, a 22-year-old seam bowler 'who had only three first-class games behind him'.[19] In other words, they could easily have believed that they 'had been had' by a conspiracy to create conditions favourable to the home side. This is, of course, not unknown in cricket, but it might nonetheless be considered to be 'sharp practice' by some, especially the Sri Lankans under Arjuna Ranatunga. It would not be inconceivable either that the hard feeling evidenced in the incident in question or a judge determining the case, could each be influenced by these factors. One might even assert that the New Zealanders would (or should) be hard pressed to object to Ranatunga's actions since they did not come to the adjudication in question with clean hands. In the end, '... in a statement after a brief disciplinary hearing, Jarman said "common sense prevailed with the charge being withdrawn"'.[20]

Is this a early example of the judicial laxity bemoaned by Malcolm Speed and others? Or on the other hand is it an indication that cricket like all law-making and adjudicative practices, is complex and complicated? Are those involved in judicial decision-making to take instruction or policy direction from the Prime Minister, or Home Secretary or Chief Executive, pushing their own law and order agendas for a variety of reasons or will we permit unrestrained, or less restrained, adjudication to occur? Is common sense, a post-match handshake by the captains a sign of the collapse of law and order and the rule of law, or an example of good judging and good judgment, of the best embodiment of equity and the spirit of the game?

Whatever the position one adopts on the practical, ethical and jurisprudential/jurisdictional issues here, there is little doubt that collisions will continue to occur and Match Referees will be called upon to adjudicate as they were when Darren Gough collided with Roshan Mahanama of Sri Lanka in Jan. 1999,[21] or when two years later Gough came into contact with another Sri Lankan, Indika de Saram;[22] or again when Mohammad Akram of Pakistan ran into Shane Warne;[23] or when Damian Fleming and Chaminda Vass collided[24] or indeed when Australian leg spinner Stuart MacGill crashed into Ramnaresh Sarwan of the West Indies and apologized for the unintended collision.[25]

A final example will demonstrate the complex interconnections between legal prohibitions and various understandings about the spirit of the game. During a One-Day International between Australia and New Zealand, Steve Waugh sustained an injury as the result of contact between him and Kiwi bowler Dion Nash. Attempting a second run Waugh collided with the bowler after Nash appeared to step backward into his path. Then

> Match referee Hanumant Singh referred the matter to Waugh, who refused to accuse his rival of tripping him although yesterday he suggested journalists should satisfy themselves by examining the video.
>
> Hanumant noted that Nash stepped back 'without an apparent reason' and, while the bowler maintained his innocence, he received a caution and was warned to stay out of the way of batsmen in the future. 'To say with any certainty that this was an intentional act would be difficult,' Hanumant said.[26]

Here then we have a case which falls outside the strict letter of the law because in the opinion of the referee it is impossible to determine with certainty whether Nash stepped back deliberately into Waugh's path. The burden of proof and benefit of the doubt must lead to an uncertain finding of intention which must benefit the accused. At the same time, there are strong doubts and suspicions about the bowler's act. There was no 'apparent reason' for him to step back as he did. Waugh simply referred to the video replay evidence which he believed spoke for itself. The Match Referee, while giving the benefit of the doubt to the bowler, nonetheless felt that he had been at the very least careless or reckless and issued a warning. Thus, the formal justice system worked here, the burden of proof and benefit of the doubt were invoked, and justice was served.

Still, there is another set of informal justice or legal mechanisms at work here alongside the strict procedures and rules of the *Code of Conduct*. The Match Referee himself referred to the judgement of the apparently aggrieved party, Waugh, who refused to accuse the alleged perpetrator of acting with criminal intent. It seems clear, however, that at some level Waugh and even Hanumant believed that something was amiss. Again, Waugh asked reporters to simply look at the video evidence. In effect, what appears to be happening here is the invocation of the public/private distinction in combination with some unspoken idea of collective justice outside the formal legal machinery of the game. 'What happens on the field stays on the field' has long been an essential part of the ethos of the game. In fact, the Match Referee and *Code of Conduct* system has called into question this very idea of a public/private distinction in disciplinary matters. Historically, matters were settled between the players themselves or else in private and closed hearings before club or local authorities. Fans, at some level, were excluded from the judicial or at least the juridical system as matters were settled 'in private'. Now, with the Match Referee system and the publicity given to decisions, justice can be seen to be done, although it must be noted that such publicity is a recent occurrence and has come about only after sustained criticism of the ICC.[27]

Nonetheless what the Waugh/Nash case indicates is that there must still be some remaining idea of informal, democratic creation and application of rules of conduct between players. Waugh was unwilling to accuse the bowler openly, but at some level we must all know or suspect that he might well believe that what the bowler did was deliberate. Perhaps they exchanged words on the field, or after the match, or perhaps the next time Nash decided to stand in the way of an oncoming Australian player, a collision might not go in his favour. Similarly, the next time Dion Nash came to the crease with a bat in his hand, it is not inconceivable that Australian bowlers might send a few quick deliveries at his head and body. Anyone who knows about cricket and self-regulation, including any future Match Referee, would be well aware of what was going on in such a case, but, as in the instant example, would be hard pressed to 'prove' deliberation. This 'payback' could be seen to be just and fair according to the best traditions of the game, in which the players set and determine the extent of rule-violating behaviour which will be tolerated and inflict punishment on any transgressor according to tribal tradition. Someone else, faced with the same facts, might well characterize such retribution as lawless hooliganism, a violation of the *Laws* as well as the spirit of the game. Both would be right.

The introduction of the *Code of Conduct* and the Match Referee system has simply created a new type of disciplinary jurisprudence which carries with it its own set of rules, limits and complexities. If we return briefly here to the Viv Richards/umpire Barker case we find yet another example of the ways in which the law of cricket creates more and more law of cricket.

The vexed question of excessive or over-exuberant appeals is neither a new one nor is it one which has gone away since the introduction of the *Code of Conduct* and Match Referee system. Australia were warned for excessive appealing by Match Referee Clive Lloyd during an Ashes Test at Trent Bridge in 1993.[28] The next year the Adelaide Test between South Africa and Australia was marked by over-exuberant and excessive appealing from the visiting side.[29] In the West Indies, England were booed off the field by fans after numerous bat-pad appeals when the batter was, for the fans, the umpires and the Windies batters, obviously not out. A spokesperson for the ICC at the time commented 'Such appeals put unnecessary pressure on the umpires and the captains have been asked to control it.'[30]

They appear not to have listened. Controversy again emerged in 1999 when both South Africa and England were accused of issuing 'dubious appeals';[31] and in 2000 when Arshad Kahn was fined for excessive appealing by the Match Referee in a game against Sri Lanka.[32] When England toured Sri Lanka in the winter of 2001, the issue of excessive appealing again came to the fore.

Tour matches were marked by appeals for everything. Before the first Test, Hanumant Singh, the Match Referee, issued a statement. It said:

> I want it to be an appeal, not a demand. I want to stop people jumping and dancing up and down in front of the umpire and trying to intimidate him.

Sometimes I accept it's genuine excitement, but more often it's an orchestrated attempt to cheat.[33]

The *Code of Conduct* refers to the Level 1 offence of 'excessive appealing'. Even
the Match Referee himself indicates that the mental element of the offence, if
indeed there is one, is sometimes difficult to discern. In order to be 'excessive',
must an appeal carry with it an intention to 'cheat' or 'intimidate'? Is it a strict
liability or *mens rea* offence? What remains unclear on the legislative language
and therefore subject to alternative and competing interpretations by advocates
and judges/umpires/Match Referees, is the actual substantive definition of the
offence in a particular context. Arguably, a single appeal for a dismissal, based on
the circumstances could be, in and of itself, 'excessive', if one assumes that the
noun 'appealing' is singular and does not *per se* refer to a process or series of
events. Thus, assuming a single appeal can constitute 'excessive appealing', then
the Match Referee will have to consider various factual and circumstantial
elements if he is to find the offence proved. There might be something in the
nature and character of the appeal and accompanying behaviour which would
render it 'excessive', again assuming that such behaviour falls short of the Level
2 offence of 'charging or advancing' appeals. Perhaps it is the tone of voice, or
the 'jumping and dancing up and down' which will bring the sanctioning power
down upon the transgressor. Perhaps it will only be if the Match Referee is able
to determine that the dancing and jumping was not simple exuberance but the
indication of bad faith that the offence will be found to have been committed.
Again, it may be that it is the very circumstances of the appeal which establishes
the offence of 'excessive appealing'. Thus, when everyone 'knows' that there is
no good faith basis on the available facts for an appeal, then the appeal will be
ipso facto 'excessive'.

   Again, it might also be the case that a series of appeals will be found to constitute
a single offence of 'excessive appealing'. A Match Referee might adopt the attitude
that some benefit of the doubt either concerning the behaviour (dancing as exuberance), or the good faith basis of one or several appeals, should go to the fielding side
and only after a pattern emerges will he find that 'excessive appealing' has occurred.[34]
In other words and yet again, more law does not indicate more certainty.

   Indeed, the Sri Lanka versus England series was marked by what Simon Rae
describes as having '... provided a masterclass in unacceptable practices'.[35]

   In the first Test, four Sri Lankans were fined by the Match Referee for excessive
appealing. Nonetheless, Kumar Sangakkara, a law student, insisted that the side
would continue to appeal in the second Test. For him then issues and duties of
the various parties in law and in practice were clear.

We should be calling it as we see it and the match referee is there to make
sure we don't overstep the mark.
   When we are in the middle we appeal when we think someone is out and
we don't notice if we are going too far – it's the commentators and the
people who are watching who notice it more.

If eight balls hit the pad you might as well go up for all eight and some-times when you are in the middle you don't know how things look.[36]

The Sri Lankan wicketkeeper then went on to explain that when Muralitharan is bowling in local conditions, he extracts spin and bounce, the ball is moving around and things are both exciting and confusing. Here we see a complex set of arguments and assertions about the nature and practice of appealing and of the epistemology and jurisprudence of 'excessive appealing'.

Simply put, everything is context and context is everything. The pitch and ball act differently in Sri Lanka than they might at Trent Bridge or the WACA. This means that the batter will be hit on the pads, or near or on the bat as he tries to cover the spin. It is difficult if not impossible to know, let us say for a wicketkeeper, if the ball was spinning enough to miss the stumps, or if the batter played a genuine shot at the delivery.[37] In some ways, it is the duty, obligation and right of the keeper in these circumstances to 'ask the question', to appeal. After all, very few, if any, batters will conceivably surrender their wicket in the absence of an appeal and concede that they have been dismissed LBW.[38] The umpire is vested with jurisdiction to decide on dismissals by way of appeal.[39] The form and timing of an appeal are clearly established in the provisions of the *Laws of Cricket*.[40] Why, as many Australian television commentators are wont to ask, should a player or team 'die not knowing'?

The division of responsibility and the legal philosophies are clear for propo-nents here. The umpires must decide if a batter is or is not out. They can only decide when there is an appeal. The game, the result of which depends on taking wickets, i.e. on gaining lawful dismissals, cannot, in fact or law, be played unless players appeal. This is essentially Sangakkara's position. It is the player's job to appeal, it is the umpire's job to adjudicate and it is the Match Referee's job to decide if the appealing was 'excessive'.

The problem arises here because we know that Sangakkara's argument is based on a simple and simplified notion of the legal practice which ignores the very complexity he in fact invokes to justify his continued advocacy for dismissals. There is a problem not of 'appealing' but of 'excessive' appealing. A simple assertion that cricket is complex, that Sri Lankan conditions are difficult, that Murali is an exceptional bowler at home, and that there is a clear legal right to appeal and established mechanisms for the process, can in reality be seen to be an assertion that there is either no such thing as 'excessive' appealing and the *Laws*, *Preamble* and *Code of Conduct* are redundant and of no effect, or as a more limited, but equally problematic assertion that the provisions cannot in practice be applied in the Sri Lankan circumstances.

At both levels, this is what Allan Hutchinson so perceptively describes as antifoundationalism.[41] The rules and circumstances are seen to be so indetermin-ate that 'anything goes'. What this position ignores is the 'fact' that complexity is not a bar to adjudication or law more generally, but is simply the condition in which it occurs.[42] In other words, just because it is complicated, nuanced and subject to epistemological and deontological uncertainty and debate, cricket still exists. And if cricket exists, if the *Laws*, *Preamble* and *Code of Conduct* have meaning because they are interpreted and applied in the context of what we know to be cricket, then so too is there something called 'excessive appealing'.

Speaking of excessive appealing in the game today, Sir Garfield Sobers declared that 'It makes me sick. These things really disgust me.'[43]

But less than three months after Sobers' intervention, India were cautioned for over-appealing in Zimbabwe.[44] The ICC again issued warnings about cracking down on cricket lawlessness. Players appeal. Cricket, like life and like law, goes on. One final set of comparative legal practices highlight not just the complexities and contradictions of the law of appellate practice in cricket but also the possibly changing normative universe in which the Laws and spirit of the game operate.

One could assert that the ideal of players' honesty and integrity in relation to the *Laws* and to the spirit of the game has been part of the spirit of the game itself. Thus, while players might aggressively appeal, asserting in good faith, the positivistic and formalistic idea that it is for them to appeal and for the umpires to decide and that is the way the process of adjudication in cricket has always operated, an underlying ideal of good faith always informed and informs this process. In other words, it would be considered by most members of the interpretive community to be a violation of the spirit of the game for a player in bad faith to appeal when he knows the batter is not out. A player who falsely claims a catch, knowing he has merely trapped the ball after it has hit the ground, is a cheat. A player who appeals not knowing whether he has trapped or lawfully caught the ball is simply relying on his right to appeal and calling upon the umpire to exercise his jurisdiction.

Of course, in the second case there will be some debate and some will assert that the player who does not know if the catch has been taken should therefore not appeal. This is the glorious uncertainty of cricket and the reason we love the game and its legal and ethical debates. Finally, there will be the morally upright player who immediately indicates that the catch was not taken and the appeal should be withdrawn.[45] Here, as for the 'cheat', there is no uncertainty.

The historical case and record of Ian Healy highlights the uncertain certainty and the certain uncertainty which informs the jurisprudential debates here. In one game in the early 1990s against the West Indies, Brian Lara was given out stumped from the bowling of Australian off spinner Greg Matthews. Replays seemed to indicate that Healy had in fact dislodged the stumps with his gloves without the ball. Healy did not appeal, simply indicating that he did not know what had happened. He reported that he believed the ball had hit the stumps and dislodged the bails. Healy was scorned by the Windies for the rest of the series and told to leave their dressing room under apparent threat of physical harm. He had, despite not having appealed, been branded a 'cheat'. When the West Indies returned to Australia for their next tour, another incident arose in which Shane Warne appeared to have bowled Carl Hooper: 'Healy barely appealed for the decision because he considered it so routine. But the fact that the umpires consulted was interpreted by Healy as a sign that his word meant next to nothing.'[46]

Several elements about appeals, jurisdiction, credibility and the spirit of the game come to the fore here. Healy did not loudly invoke the umpires' jurisdiction to adjudicate on appeal since, in his experience and that of virtually all cricketers and umpires, when the stumps fly or the bails are dislodged and the batter is bowled, everybody 'knows' he is out. In this case however, such collective and institutional knowledge was subject to a counter-context of Healy being known as a 'cheat' by the team against which he was playing. He was also known by all those who had seen the replay of the previous incident as one whose 'word' might be subject to some doubt.

Finally, it is also 'known' that it is sometimes difficult when a spinner is bowling and the keeper is standing up to the stumps, to be certain that the ball hit the stumps first or whether it came back off the body, gloves or pads of the keeper. When Shane Warne is spinning the ball out of the rough, on a bouncy and turning wicket at the SCG as he was here, knowing exactly what happened is difficult. Did the umpires consult because of Healy's record and reputation or did they consult because on the other facts, it was difficult for the umpire at the bowler's end, whose view of the ball might have been blocked, as it neared the stumps by the batter? Healy certainly feels that the former interpretive context was predominant in the umpires' minds, although the second explanation might be equally plausible. We probably can never know. What we do and can know is that the content of the ethical obligation imposed upon a fielder to appeal or not to appeal or to withdraw an appeal is uncertain, as is the process of adjudication on the appeal.[47] Do umpires consider each appeal on its merits as they are bound to by their judicial office? Do they consider past practice or reputation in deciding? Is there a conflict between these two positions? What do we mean by the merits of an appeal?

The problem did not go away. Later in the same series,

> Brian Lara fell in controversial circumstances to a catch which the West Indians claimed did not carry to the wicketkeeper. The Australians argued otherwise and countless TV replays could not provide conclusive proof one way or the other.[48]

Lara later confronted the Australian dressing room. No doubt previous encounters between the two, and between Healy and Lara's teammates, on disputed questions of law and fact played a major part in the confrontation. The legal issues were and are clear cut. The ethical issues remain somewhat more problematic. Phillip Derriman outlined the situation in the following terms:

> A well-known former Test umpire was at the SCG to see the Brian Lara catch on Tuesday and later studied slow-motion replays of it. He had no doubt Ian Healy took a legitimate catch, he said yesterday. If he had had to rule on it as a third umpire, he would have flashed the red light.
>
> This question of whether the catch was fair is really still the central issue of the Healy-Lara affair, even if the public's attention has since shifted to the controversy over Lara's stormy reaction.

...

If the catch was unfair, Lara was entitled to feel aggrieved, for Healy must have known the ball hit the ground first. If the catch was fair, as several informed observers have judged it to be, Healy could claim to be the injured party – a victim of his past.[49]

Once again, context in adjudication, law and the spirit of the game is everything. Lara and his teammates, based on the context of their past experience with Healy's claims of 'fair' dismissals, appeared to refuse to take him at his word. Moreover, they appeared to believe that his word is that of a 'liar' and a 'cheat'. For them he is simply a cricketer who claims catches knowing they have not been fairly and lawfully taken. He is condemned to cricketing hell. Derriman, while not necessarily accepting the accusation on the evidence of this case, does recognize that reputation, however unfair or undeserved, or however fair and deserved, can and does play a central role in such disputes. He goes one step further, when he unproblematically asserts that the keeper, if this were the case 'must have known' the ball was trapped or caught after it hit the ground. This is, of course, for many, the *sine qua non*, the condition precedent, for asserting an unethical appeal. If the player does not know, again many would argue that he can and indeed must then 'ask the question' and invoke the lawful jurisdiction of the umpire. Many others would argue that in such cases of doubt, a higher ethical duty to the spirit of the game requires the player to refuse to make an appeal.

For example, when Shane Warne appeared to take a catch at slip to dismiss Pakistan batter Saeed Anwar in a Test at the Gabba in Brisbane, he immediately indicated to the umpire that he was uncertain whether he had in fact caught the ball on the full. The third umpire gave the benefit of the doubt to the Pakistani. Anwar said at the end of the day's play

> 'That was good from Shane Warne, and I think this is what the sport needs', he said. 'I think it's a really good gesture and I thank Shane Warne for it. He did the right thing.'[50]

Warne did 'the right thing', which here is invoked as synonymous with the spirit of the game. Yet several factors intervene to complicate and contextualize the actual content of the ethical norms here. First, Warne did not not appeal. He simply appealed and indicated that he was not sure if the ball had been taken cleanly. This then shifted the decision-making burden and jurisdictional power to the on field umpire who, based on the facts, or doubts as to the facts, sent the case to the third umpire for determination. Warne did not affirm that the batter was not out because he was uncertain. Instead he relayed his uncertainty to the umpire. It may well have been the case, if one were to invoke other practical norms which some would argue should be considered as essential elements in the historical deontological code or spirit of the game, that if he had confirmed his certainty that the ball had carried, in the absence of a third umpire, the on field adjudicator would have given the batter out. Similarly, in the good old days, which if the traditions of the game continue to inform and define the content of the ethical code, if the slip fielder confirmed that he had taken the catch, the batter would have left and surrendered his wicket without requiring a decision from the umpire. It seems clear today that while one might argue that many of these ideas should inform cricket law and practice, they do not in fact receive universal or perhaps even majority support. Times have changed, laws have changed, or perhaps not.

Perhaps Warne acted as he did because he had, not long before, in Australia's successful World Cup campaign, claimed a catch which replays demonstrated had not carried. Does this matter? Certainly, the idea that someone comes to law and equity with some doubt over their veracity will have an effect on their status as a law-abiding citizen and participant in the democratic construction of the living rules of cricket's understanding of lawful and ethical conduct. At the same time, the uncertainty may be based in good faith and in good faith which arises out of past errors. Warne was doubtful of the facts because his certainty had been proved erroneous in the past. Whatever the case may be here, it is clear that for Warne and for Anwar, the 'right thing' was not to withdraw the appeal. Instead it was to pass the decisional onus onto the person vested with that role, the umpire, while at the same time providing the umpire with additional information on which to base his decision or to give up his jurisdiction in this case to the third umpire.

It is only, as Derriman implies, when a player 'knows' the catch has not been taken that an almost universal norm of ethical (and legal) practice can be invoked. In other words, the ethical issue is resolved only when a factual determination can be made that the player 'knew' the ball had not carried. In cases of doubt about this state of factual reality, members of the hermeneutic community differ as to the actual content of the ethical norm to be applied, as subsequent events demonstrated. In the second Test at Lord's in the same season, Healy was again involved in a case of a disputed catch. This time he withdrew his appeal for the dismissal against Graham Thorpe because he did not know if the ball had carried. He was applauded for his sportsmanship and umpire David Shepherd indicated his approval. 'It was probably the first time an umpire has clapped a player for sportsmanship during a Test.'[51]

Here Healy did the right thing, which was not the same as the right thing which Shane Warne had done. He was in doubt about the legality of his 'catch'. He informed the umpire. Healy complied with the ethical norm and by doing so he preserved and maintained the spirit of the game and indeed the *Laws of Cricket*, by preventing a possible erroneous decision by the umpire which would have resulted in a 'miscarriage of justice' for Thorpe. Moreover, it might be argued that this is a more important example of ethically correct behaviour because of Healy's 'record'. His action indicates that he has been rehabilitated in part perhaps as a result of his having been subject to the sanctions of shaming and exclusion by his fellow cricketers. In some ways he has achieved a state of forgiveness and grace. He is a reformed sinner returning from purgatory to the fold of law and justice.

8 The man in white is always right: umpires, judges and the rule of law

Former Australian captain and current Channel 9 commentator, Ian Chappell, offers an excellent historical example of the interpretive ambiguity and complexity surrounding ideas and practices of respect for the umpire's decision in cricket. During a One-Day game against the West Indies at VFL park (during the days of World Series Cricket) Collis King appeared to 'edge' a catch behind to Rodney Marsh from the bowling of Max Walker. Fielding at deep gully, Chappell had a good view of the batter and was certain that King had indeed snicked the ball. Umpire Col Hoy at the non-striker's end gave King not out, and did not check with the umpire at square leg. Chappell, as captain, went to ask umpire Hoy the reason for his decision. For him, if the umpire had refused the appeal because he thought the ball had not struck the bat, that would have been the end of the matter, even if Chappell believed the batter had given an edge. This was, for Chappell, a matter of judgement for the umpire alone and was not open to any dispute. On the other hand, Chappell felt that if the umpire had refused the appeal because he thought the catch had not been made, he was, as captain, perfectly entitled to request that the square leg umpire be consulted.

While Chappell characterizes this as a matter of law, it would perhaps be more correct to say that this is a case where the umpire should seek more assistance on the facts from his colleague who is better placed to determine if indeed the ball carried to the keeper.

The applicable legal provision in such a case under the operative code was Law 27(4) which read

> An umpire may consult with the other Umpire on a point of fact which the latter may have been in a better position to see and shall then give his decision. If, after consultation, there is still doubt remaining the decision shall be in favour of the Batsman.

Several points of law and jurisprudence are important here. First, the consultation was purely voluntary. The *Law's* use of 'may' clearly and unambiguously indicated that the umpire making the decision need not refer to his colleague unless he wished to do so. Secondly, the doubt must be as to an issue of fact and not on a question of law. Thirdly, ambiguity must always favour the batter, that is the respondent and not the appellant who at some level might be said here to bear the burden of persuasion. Finally, the *Law* indicates quite clearly that the consultation between the umpires must occur before the decision had been made. The language used is that the umpire may consult in such cases 'and shall then give his decision'. Arguably in the case described by Chappell the umpire could not have lawfully consulted with his colleague since he had in fact given the 'not out' decision before Chappell's intervention.

But the legal interpretive dilemma or controversy did not necessarily end there. Law 27(6) read

> The Umpire's decision is final. He may alter his decision, provided that such alteration is made promptly.

Here we find two levels of difficulty in the process of cricket adjudication. First, there is the apparent conflict between the two provisions of the *Law*. A decision was at once 'final' and at the same time it could be altered. In practice of course, this might simply have been found to deal with those cases in which an umpire has misspoken. But the language of the provision would also be broad enough to include cases where the umpire recalculated some or several factors which would indicate that a different decision should have been made. Whatever the solution to this apparent ambiguity in the legislative language, other wording of the same provision posed even more fundamental difficulties in the instance outlined by Chappell. The alteration had to be made 'promptly'. Assuming that we can get over the hurdle of interpretation and jurisdiction raised by the requirement that the consultation between umpires must (or should) precede the rendering of a decision, the question here would be whether a change in a decision under these circumstances could be considered to have been made 'promptly'. Here, a decision had been given, the batter is 'not out'. The captain spoke with the umpire, who then engaged in a conversation and consultation with his colleague. It would seem, at some level of common sense at least, that such facts make it difficult to assert that the alteration was made promptly and thus was in conformity with the *Laws* which determine the jurisdiction of the umpires and the procedures to be followed.

It would also still, of course, be possible to characterize the umpire's error here as an error of law. Because he was deciding while operating under a misapprehension as to the 'real' facts, he was committing an error which goes to his jurisdiction and was therefore an error of law. Upon inquiry, umpire Hoy replied that he did not think the ball had carried. He acceded to Chappell's request, asked his colleague at square leg and upon being informed that the ball had indeed been fairly caught by keeper Marsh, changed his decision and gave King out. Despite strong protest from the West Indies, the batter was forced back to the pavilion.

Chappell reported that the West Indian management called him a cheat, but he is adamant that his request to umpire Hoy was both legal and ethical. It might appear that Chappell has some grounds for believing that he was correct since all he did was ask the umpire to proceed according to the provisions of the *Laws* to determine more fully what the 'facts' really were. He was not disputing a fact clearly within the sole jurisdiction of the umpire at the non-striker's end and made it clear that he would never do so. Indeed, had the umpire at square leg indicated that the catch had not been made, Chappell, despite his belief to the contrary, would not have disputed the batter's right to stay at the crease. He simply availed himself of his rights and asked for a full hearing of the facts. At the same time, however, it seems clear that an equally strong argument could be made that even if one were to consider that the umpire's original decision were factually erroneous, the actual legislative language rendered Chappell's request and the umpire's change of heart doubly illegal. The captain was, on this view, not entitled to request a consultation and the umpire, having rendered his decision, was in fact and in law *functus officio*. He was out of time and therefore out of jurisdiction to seek assistance from his colleague. Moreover, he was debarred from changing a decision after such a period of time, unless we are willing to concede that the unfolding of events as described still allowed the reversal to be considered to have been made 'promptly'.

The provisions of the 2000 *Laws of Cricket*, which modify the language of jurisdiction and appeal somewhat do not alter the problem significantly. Thus, Law 27(5) reads

> The umpire at the bowler's end shall answer all appeals except those arising out of any of Laws 35 (Hit wicket), 39 (stumped) or 38 (Run out) when this occurs at the striker's wicket. A decision Not out by one umpire shall not prevent the umpire from giving a decision, provided that each is considering only matters within his jurisdiction. When a batsman has been given Not out, either umpire may, within his jurisdiction, answer a further appeal. . . .

Law 27(6) which deals with consultation reiterates the previous legislative position that consultation is to be on points of fact and is to occur before the decision has been made by the umpire with appropriate jurisdiction. Finally, Law 27(9) states

> An umpire may alter his decision provided that such alteration is made promptly. This apart, an umpire's decision, once made, is final.

We can see clearly here that the language of the new *Laws of Cricket* does not modify or change the problem posed by Chappell's case, nor does it change the judicial error committed by the umpire. The requirement for promptness continues to exist. Consultation must still occur before the decision is rendered and can only take place on a question of fact. The new provisions simply make it clearer, by making it explicit, what decisions fall to the umpire at the striker's and non-striker's or bowler's end.

While it may appear at first blush that any steps by an umpire under Law 27(9) to alter his decision might be said to lead to confusion and a loss of respect for his judgement, this may not be the practical result of such an action. Umpires themselves declare that such alterations, while requiring strength of character, actually serve to increase respect for their decisions because

> There may be embarrassment but there is no disgrace in admitting it and changing the decision as allowed in this section. In the long term he will be more respected for doing so than for obstinately sticking to something he knows to be wrong.[1]

In practice, however, there is some doubt about the judgement which should or will be passed on an umpire who reverses himself. For example, in the fourth Test between England and Australia in 1958–59 at the Adelaide Oval, a batter was using a runner. The umpire, when the ball was hit, moved to his normal position and when the ball was returned and the bails removed for a possible run out, not seeing the runner, he signalled 'out'. He then realized that the runner was behind him and 'that he could not give a run out against a runner he had not seen. He reversed his decision, a courageous thing in a Test.'[2]

In some instances, umpires have reversed themselves not because they did not see the play as in the Adelaide Test case, but simply because they have changed their mind and decided they were wrong.[3] While such actions are generally applauded as courageous and correct because they are seen to conform with notions of formal justice and legality, a more problematic scenario arises, especially in the days of televised instant and slow-motion replays, when the umpire is seen to be wrong by other members of the cricket interpretive community, for example by giving out a batter who was not 'on the facts', out.

This happened during a Test match between Sri Lanka and Pakistan in Colombo. David Shepherd reversed himself in interesting circumstances. Ijaz Ahmed played at a delivery from Muttiah Muralitharan and found himself stranded at the bowler's end as his partner Salim Malik took a step then turned his back to return to his crease. The stumps were broken at the striker's end and Shepherd, standing at the non-striker's end asked his fellow adjudicator at square leg, which batter was out. Umpire K.T. Francis indicated that Ijaz was out and the Pakistani returned to the pavilion. The next batter Inzamam came on and was about to take strike when Shepherd was told on the walkie talkie that Salim should have been given out since he had not grounded his bat. Shepherd called Ijaz back to the crease. Match Referee John Reid was quoted as saying that 'Justice has been done and that is what is important, not how long it took.'[4]

This is one jurisprudential position of course. Yet the actual letter of the law, which must at some level also be said to inform our understanding of 'justice' as well as law, clearly still indicates that the decision must only be altered 'promptly'. There is no clear and unambiguous definition of what 'promptly' means, yet it does seem arguable at least that once a batter has left the field of play and the new player has taken strike, any common sense notion of the temporality of cricket would lead us to the understanding that a decision to recall the departed player is no longer 'prompt'. In this case, after being informed of the 'error' Shepherd consulted with Sri Lankan captain Arjuna Ranatunga.

Again, we know that the *Law* allows the captain to withdraw the appeal but only before the dismissed batter 'has left the playing area'. This is clearly not the case here. Justice then may have been done but only at the expense of the real meaning of the legal text.

The positivist position is, of course, that if the umpire says the batter is out and does not reverse his decision, then the batter is indeed out, or 'dismissed' if one accepts this as an operative and important distinction. On the other hand, formalist or ethically based critiques could be made in such a case. The batter is not 'out' unless his dismissal occurs in accordance with the *Laws*. In such a situation, however, the *Laws* are clear as to the time limit within which an umpire may change his decision. Therefore, a formalist could be forced to admit that while the original decision was erroneous or even illegal, the *Laws* would themselves prohibit a reversal, in effect rendering 'legal' an 'illegal' decision, if such a reversal, as we have seen, did not occur 'promptly'.

Such an instance occurred in the second Test at Lords between the West Indies and England in 1984 when Viv Richards was given out by umpire Barry Meyer. The instant replay indicated that Meyer was wrong and the umpire later 'apologised to Richards and admitted that he had possibly made a mistake, but had realized it too late to recall him'.[5]

On one view, Meyer's action complied with both a formalist and an ethical view of the Law and the umpire's function. Formally, he could not reverse his decision because he did not 'realize' his mistake until it was too late. Morally, he did the right thing by recognizing his error and offering his apology. Of course, at the utilitarian level of winning and losing, an apology is of little consolation to the 'incorrectly' and 'illegally' dismissed batter. At the 'higher' level of the long-term interests of the game, however, Meyer's apology indicates both that the umpire does indeed possess individual integrity and that the spirit of the game is such that he would not, or could not, simply revert to a positivistic position of standing by his decision and thereby refusing to admit even the possibility of an umpire making a mistake. At the same time, others would argue that the judiciary must never be seen publicly to have erred. Like Lord Denning, they might argue that the 'system' is better served if the innocent are hanged or given out than if judges or umpires are seen to be human and fallible.

In the 2001 Test series against Australia, New Zealand complained about the adjudicative competence of Zimbabwe umpire Ian Robinson who had made clear mistakes in turning down several New Zealand appeals. He was booed off the pitch. After watching replays of the calls in question he admitted his mistakes and apologized, arguing only that he was human and like everyone else prone to error.[6] Two weeks later Robinson was also involved in a controversy about his competence in a Test match in India against England.[7] Similarly Daryl Harper of Australia admitted that he had made a mistake in turning down a New Zealand appeal against Justin Langer in the first Test of the same series in which Robinson made his mistakes. Harper was criticized for the admission on the grounds that the integrity of the decision-making process could be brought into disrepute if umpires admitted their mistakes.[8]

Unlike the ideal of Denning's cricketing Heaven in *Miller v. Jackson*, or Dante's cricketer's Hell, the ethical debate is not as clear or as one-sided as it may appear. Brodribb also expresses the dilemma:

> It was brave and commendable action by Meyer to say that he might have been wrong, though some may say that he ought to have kept silent, and upheld the idea of an umpire's infallibility.[9]

It is impossible to resolve here the age-old debate about whether the interests of justice are better served by uncritical devotion and respect for the ideal of judicial infallibility or by open, public critical debate. Suffice it to say that even in a law-based system of being-in-the-world like cricket, hard ethical existential choices and freedom remain, as they do for the justice system when faced with the cases of the Guildford Four or the Birmingham Six, or any number of other cases subject to review and overturned when the conviction has been found to have been 'dangerous'.

In Chappell's case, for example, the question was whether a clean catch had been taken. The umpire at the bowler's end is vested with jurisdiction and must make the decision in response to the appeal. Here, on what I believe is the best and most consistent interpretation of the provisions of the *Laws*, a judicial error was made. In the end of course, the records of the game will still indicate that Collis King was dismissed, caught Marsh, bowled Walker. The question and presence of televised replays, and the innovation of the third umpire, the television replay judge, has both lessened the likelihood of judicial errors and increased the controversies surrounding umpires and their essential roles as adjudicators.

While, as the *Laws* themselves make clear, the umpire's decision is final, this is not, in either fact or law, the final word about the law. The *Laws of Cricket* also provide that

> The captain of the fielding side may withdraw an appeal only with the consent of the umpire within whose jurisdiction the appeal falls and before the outgoing batsman has left the field of play, If such consent is given the umpire concerned shall, if applicable, revoke his decision and recall the batsman.[10]

Some may see such an intervention as a direct affront to the umpire's authority and as causing serious embarrassment to the umpire who has made his decision. From a strictly formalist perspective, it must be underlined, however, that the captain may only withdraw the appeal 'with the consent' of the umpire. Therefore final jurisdiction remains with the umpire. It may be argued, then, that no embarrassment is caused to the umpire both because he retains final jurisdiction over the dismissal and also because a request to withdraw the appeal does not necessarily indicate disagreement with the umpire's decision as a matter of law. Instead it may well indicate a captain's desire to abide not by the law but by a more 'sporting' view of the ethics of the situation. In such cases, the captain does not necessarily seek to dispute the formal correctness of the umpire's decision but rather to inform the umpire that he wishes to proceed under a different set of 'ethical' norms. In this event, the captain merely indicates his desire to change the interpretive canon from one binding text (the *Laws*) to another binding text (the spirit of the game). Of course, under the 2000 *Code*, the captain's duty to ensure compliance with the spirit of the game is further strengthened and reinforced in the textual provisions which have already been discussed. No matter which canonical text is invoked or applied, all participants in the community, it would appear, *know* what the standards are and how they are to be put into practice. Such assertions must always be contextualized and modified on the basis of the actual interpretive law-making practices of playing the game of cricket.

In order to reach any understanding or decision on the matter, we must consider the conflict, disagreement and hermeneutic fluidity surrounding the actual content of the norms of the traditions and spirit of the game, which form the basis of cricket jurisprudence. Moreover, and perhaps more fundamentally, there is the extent and meaning of the provisions of Law 27(8) which need to be studied and explicated. The language of the provision itself makes it quite clear that there is no legal obligation on the captain of the fielding side to withdraw an appeal which has been made by his side, he 'may' do so. At the same time, he is under a more obvious and mandatory obligation to ensure compliance with the spirit of the game; he *is responsible* (*Preamble*, Art. 1 and Law 42(1)) for the spirit of the game. Therefore, if he is responsible in some obligatory sense, one might legitimately inquire why he is under no similar compulsion to withdraw an appeal if the circumstances, which at some level we are all supposed to know, require such an act on his part. If withdrawing an 'unjust' or 'unsporting' appeal is part of the obligations incumbent upon the guardians of the game, why should they not be expected to always act in such a way through the imposition of a specific legal instruction to do so?

The reason, or at least one of the reasons that this legal situation obtains, is that there is still some understanding that the nature and content of norms which embody the spirit of the game are both unknown and unknowable. At the same time, we also 'know' that this may be their very strength as rules of normative import. In other words, despite recent changes to the *Laws* which I have already discussed, there is some recognition that there can in fact be no complete codification of the spirit of the game. By its very nature, such an ethical, deontological code must remain uncodified, subject to interpretation, application and modification as part of the democratic rule-making practices of playing the game. At the same time, this code, and the debate which surrounds its actual content throughout the history of cricket to the present day and for the foreseeable future, must be not just uncodified, but again almost by definition, purely voluntary. If it is to remain meaningful, in any sense consistent with the history and very self-definition of the game, it must not be 'reduced' to writing or compulsion. The spirit of the game can only truly be present and valuable as a juridical set of norms and practices so long as adherence thereto is voluntary and consensual.

It must be a socially constructed ethical normative understanding, accepted, interpreted, applied and modified by the rule-makers themselves. Otherwise, what we would have is in fact and in law the full incorporation of law and equity in which the latter has lost its separate existence as normatively binding. If that were to be the case, for many, cricket would no longer be cricket, and the idea of 'not cricket' would come to mean simply anything reduced to a violation of a written legal prescription.

At the same time, however it is clear that there will always be some connection between the positive content of the *Laws of Cricket* and the spirit of the game. Indeed, it may well be the case that the spirit of the game will, in circumstances relating to the withdrawal of an appeal, be directly related to maintaining and ensuring the strict application of the *Laws* themselves.

Thus, there are cases where a captain's request is based on a belief that an umpire's decision is *wrong* in Law.

> In the Golden Jubilee Test at Bombay in 1979–80 R.W. Taylor, of England, was given out caught at the wicket off Kapil Dev, but the Indian Captain, Viswanath, fielding at slip was as certain as Taylor was that there had been no contact with the ball, and he asked the Umpire to change his decision, which he did.[11]

Such an instance might, *prima facie*, be seen as a direct questioning of the umpire's authority or integrity. This formalist challenge is nonetheless more apparent than real. In such circumstances, the request is based not on the proposition that the umpire has committed an error in relation to 'the Law' in a strict sense but rather that his decision was based on a misapprehension of the 'facts', in other words whether the batter did touch the ball with his bat. In such a case, the captain, fielding at slip, is simply offering, through his request, additional eyewitness testimony to counter his own team's appeal and to give the judiciary the benefit of 'all' the 'facts' so that a correct, i.e. fully informed, decision can be made. The Law and the *Laws* are each best served by such actions.

In addition to this formalistic justification, it may well be that the captain, given all the circumstances, is urging the umpire to invoke a higher order normative system and interpretive canon – the spirit of the game. Here, there is some doubt about the facts and therefore about the formal correctness of the decision. After all, this was the Golden Jubilee Test, a special occasion perhaps imbued almost by definition with the ethically superior norms of the spirit of the game. Finally, this was a request by the home captain in these circumstances. Hospitality as ethics informs the entire set of circumstances. The umpire, granting the request in this context, was simply paying homage both to a formalistic application of the *Laws* which grant him the power to accede to such a request (Law 27(8)) and to the spirit of the otherwise apparently oxymoronic 'friendly competition'. Here, rather than facing a surface and apparent conflict between *Laws* and norms or between principle and policy, there is for cricket a deeper concordance between the two regimes where the conflict is dissolved.

While it is generally true that in such cases, the captain is suggesting that an error of 'fact' has been committed, it is sometimes the case that an umpire has erred in law and the appeal should be withdrawn to avoid an injustice and a violation of the spirit of the game. Thus, in the second Test of the 1991 Australian tour of the West Indies at the Bourda ground in Georgetown, Dean Jones was apparently dismissed. As he left the crease to walk back to the pavilion, it became apparent that the umpire had signalled 'no ball'. With Jones still out of his crease, Carl Hooper of the West Indies removed a stump.[12] Jones was given out 'run out' by the square leg umpire. On these 'facts', the umpire clearly and unequivocally erred in giving Jones out pursuant to Hooper's appeal.

While a batter may be run out from a no-ball (Law 24(15)), Law 27(7) governing appeals also indicated that,

> An umpire shall intervene if satisfied that a batsman, not having been given out, has left his wicket under a misapprehension that he is out. The umpire intervening shall call and signal Dead ball to prevent any further action by the fielding side and shall recall the batsman.

Law 27(5), of the 1980 *Code*, which was in effect at the time, similarly provided

> The Umpires shall intervene if satisfied that a Batsman, not having been given out, has left his wicket under a misapprehension that he has been dismissed.

In this case, Jones left his crease without having been given out. The umpire with jurisdiction at the bowler's end had signalled no-ball. He was clearly not attempting a run, but was leaving his crease 'under a misapprehension'. He was, as everyone on the field of the play, in the stands at the ground and watching on television knew, heading back to the dressing room. He was doing so because he was under the misapprehension that he was 'out'. Here, the umpire should have intervened and called Jones back. He was under a legal obligation to do so. The *Law* employs the word 'shall', when he did not do so, he committed an error of Law by refusing or failing to exercise his jurisdiction. This error was compounded by the other umpire giving Jones out on an appeal which had no basis in fact or law. Because the umpires failed to act and then acted improperly, it could be argued that Viv Richards then had a duty to the spirit of the game and to the letter of the Law, to withdraw his side's appeal. His failure or refusal to do so simply compounded the ethical and legal errors in this case. Again, however, we must always remember that Richards was not under an obligation legally imposed and sanctioned in case of a breach. He had a moral duty to act, but not a legal one.

The Jones' dismissal offers a *sui generis*, yet somehow hermeneutically perfect, example of the law-bound nature of cricket. Unlike most of the other cases already seen, or those discussed in the pages which follow, this instance is one of blatant and outright illegality. The umpires here were both without jurisdiction to give Jones out, the West Indies side was without legal (and even factual) justification in appealing, the two captains failed in their ethical and legal duties to the game and to their teams, all because, it would appear, no one knew the *Laws*. Indeed, it may well be that Richards acted appropriately, or at least ethically, in so far as it might be claimed that he did not know what the *Laws of Cricket* said about situations such as these. If we assume that a breach of the spirit of the game can only be said to occur in circumstances where the player is aware of the norms in question, then it might be the case that Richards did nothing 'wrong' or more precisely, nothing knowingly wrong. If his duty to the spirit of the game carries with it some notion of a mental element to the breach of the relevant norms, then that duty could only exist if and when he knows that the umpires have committed an error at law. If he is unaware of that state of fact and law, he cannot be said, under this analysis, to have breached his duty to the spirit of the game by refusing to recall Jones.

Of course, one might equally argue that even if Richards erroneously believed that the umpires had made no actual mistake of law, that a batter could be given out run out if he leaves his wicket mistakenly believing that he is out, not knowing that 'no ball' has been called, such a strict adherence to the absolute letter of what he thinks is the law is itself a violation of the spirit of the game. In addition, it might also be asserted that part of a captain's obligation to ensure fair play and to maintain the spirit and traditions of the game, is to actually know what the *Laws of Cricket* say. In other words, ignorance of the *Laws*, by the captain of a Test side, is no excuse. Thus, Richards' breach of the spirit of the game at some level predates the Jones' dismissal and was only actualized when that breach resulted in the unjust and unlawful dismissal of another player.

The analyses which could be offered here would be endless. Yet while this is indeed a unique case because it involves a clear 'error of law' by both umpires and by all the players on the field of play (assuming good faith), the debate which followed raises the same types of issues as other examples not based on an error of law and absence of jurisdiction. Then Australian coach, Bob Simpson, complained that Australians would never act in such a way, only to be immediately contradicted by captain Allan Border's statement. Not one of the eminent television commentators, including three former Australian captains, was apparently aware of the actual provisions of the *Laws* in this case, although Richie Benaud subsequently explained that he himself referred to Tom Smith's book to discover that the umpires had erred.[13] The umpires, breaking judicial precedent, attempted to justify their illegal decision after the fact, yet, revealed only 'little more than an embarrassing exercise in self-justification' according to Brindle. Finally, historical reference to the 'good old days' school of interpretation, reinforcing a key point about the content of a captain's obligations, could point to the fact that Sir Donald Bradman studied for and passed the umpire's examination when he played cricket and would no doubt have been aware of the *Laws* governing such a case, unlike Richards or Border. And all of this would be true, and all of this would be cricket.

Nonetheless, a captain's decision to withdraw an appeal against an opponent is most commonly seen as laudatory and as giving evidence of the strength and dominance of higher order ethical considerations ('the spirit of the game'). Indeed, a failure to withdraw an overly formalistic appeal can result in strong condemnation of the captain's moral fibre. But, like all truths in cricket, this truth is not a universal one. During the 1990–91 then Sheffield Shield competition, in a match between Victoria and South Australia, South Australian batter Paul Nobes was using a runner. After a mix-up, Nobes left his crease and started to run. He was run-out short of his ground but Victorian captain Simon O'Donnell withdrew the appeal. Nobes, on 19 at the time, stayed at the crease for 70 further minutes and added 39 runs to his total. The game ended in a draw, when, had Nobes' wicket fallen, Victoria might have had a chance of victory. Although some writers characterized O'Donnell's action as 'a gracious sporting gesture' and a 'marvellous sporting gesture',[14] they were also quick to point out that because of the close race in the competition, O'Donnell's decision, which for them had a direct causal connection to Nobes' additional time and runs and therefore to Victoria's inability to win the match outright, could have cost Victoria a place in the Sheffield Shield Final. As it turned out, Victoria defeated Queensland in the next game, New South Wales did not gain first innings points against Tasmania, and Victoria hosted the Shield Final in 1991. What this case illustrates again, however, is the existence of equally strong counter-narratives in cricket's ethical and legal discourse, in this case utilitarianism *versus* ethical purity. Doing the right thing might nonetheless be condemned as doing the wrong thing.

Both Phil Wilkins and Malcolm Conn, well-respected Australian cricket journalists, while applauding O'Donnell's adherence to the spirit of the game, also appear to have urged an utilitarian hermeneutic i.e. the spirit of the game may have 'cost' Victoria a chance at winning. Just like the bowler who 'shows the ball' instead of *Mankading* a straying batter,[15] O'Donnell's gentlemanly gesture starkly contrasts ethics and results. The commentators on the ABC Radio Network took the analysis a step further and offered a legal formalist rebuke to O'Donnell. Both Keith Stackpole and Peter Roebuck opined that O'Donnell should not have withdrawn the appeal. For Stackpole, 'rules are rules', Nobes made a mistake in leaving his crease, and should pay the price. According to Roebuck, no 'blame' could be attached to the fielder's appeal and therefore O'Donnell was mistaken in asking the umpire to countermand and rescind his decision.

What is important to note here is not whether O'Donnell was correct or whether the Stackpole/Roebuck position was or is today, preferable, but rather the multiplicitous positions which can be proposed and understood by the members of cricket's interpretive community (or communities) as putting forward equally valid truth claims.[16] In addition to O'Donnell's 'ethical' discourse, we can know and understand his decision by reference to models of utilitarianism, legal formalism and even competing ethical discursive practices. For as Stackpole's and Roebuck's arguments revealed, legal formalism is underpinned with moral positioning. For Stackpole, 'rules are rules', and besides the Nobes' case is not like *Mankading* where there might be some moral argument against a formalist application of the Laws. Likewise, Roebuck based his appeal to formalism, in part at least, on the ground that the fielding side here was not to 'blame'. Whatever position we finally support, we nonetheless recognize, because we are part of the interpretive community and *must* therefore recognize, that each claim can pretend to a truth-status.[17]

One final case, which echoes with the jurisprudence created by the 'mistaken' appeals lodged by Ian Healy and with the broader issues under consideration here, brings the evolving and still uncertain nature of the content of the ethical and legal obligations incumbent upon cricketers under the game's current and future regulatory regime. In July 2001 West Indies keeper Ridley Jacobs was suspended for three One-Day Internationals by Match Referee Denis Lindsay during the tour of Zimbabwe. Jacobs was suspended after having been found guilty of breaching the *Code of Conduct* provisions relating to 'bringing the game of cricket into disrepute' and other rules prohibiting 'cheating or sharp practice'. In a One-Day game against India in Harare, replays indicated that a claimed stumping of Indian batter Sehwag actually occurred while Jacobs held the ball in his left hand while breaking the wicket with his right. Law 28(1)(iii) clearly provides that a wicket is put down only when *inter alia* the bail is dislodged or the stump removed by

> ...a fielder, with his hand or arm, providing that the ball is held in the hand or hands so used, or in the hand of the arm so used.

Law 39 declares that a batter is out stumped again only when

> ...his wicket is put down by the wicket-keeper.

In other words, Sehwag is not 'out' because the conditions for his dismissal under the applicable *Laws* have not been met. The appeal had no basis in fact or law. But what is important for the jurisprudential issues under consideration here is that Jacobs did not in fact appeal for the stumping. His transgression, the 'cheating', the 'sharp practice' which brought the game into disrepute was to say nothing and to not take advantage of the opportunities to bring the batter back.

There are several intriguing and interacting aspects of cricket law and practice which are important and worthy of brief examination here. First, we must again refer to the provisions of the *Laws of Cricket* which deal specifically with the withdrawal of an appeal. Law 27(8) specifically refers to the 'captain of the fielding side' with the consent of the umpire being vested with the appropriate jurisdiction to 'recall the batsman'. Thus, strictly speaking, if one reads the plain language of Law 27(8) and gives it its clear meaning, the only person who could have, or should have if this provision is found to incorporate some ethical obligation, recalled the batter is the 'captain', although again he cannot strictly speaking do so. Only the umpire can and may recall the departing batter. At some level then the Match Referee has imposed upon a member of the fielding side a lawful as well as a moral obligation to act in a way which is literally illegal and not permitted under the applicable provisions of the *Laws of Cricket*.

Again, as we have seen, the *Preamble* deals with the spirit of the game and is in fact incorporated into the actual text of the *Laws*. This incorporation of the spirit of the game into the *Laws* poses particular problems of statutory interpretation and legal practice in the Ridley Jacobs' case, a set of problems exacerbated by the possible further difficulties posed by the interactions between and among the *Preamble*, the *Laws* and the *Code of Conduct*.

As we have seen, Article 1 of the *Preamble* clearly places responsibility for ensuring respect for the *Laws* and for the spirit of the game on the shoulders of the captain. It further states that if and when an umpire determines that a player is acting to 'bring the game into disrepute' '. . . the umpire concerned shall in the first place report the matter to the other umpire and to the player's captain, and instruct the latter to take action'.

Article 4 asserts that the spirit of the game involves respect for both your opponents and the game's traditional values. Article 5 defines cheating and sharp practice, against the spirit of the game, to include appealing knowing that the batter is not out. Finally, Article 7 declares that the umpires and captains are responsible for setting the 'tone for the conduct of a cricket match' and that

Every player is expected to make an important contribution to this.

It is, on the facts of the Jacobs' case and on one reading of these various provisions, possible to assert that Jacobs was either in fact under no obligation to the spirit of the game or that he did not in fact violate any of the proscriptions set out in the *Laws* and *Preamble*. The captain is responsible for the spirit of the game and the umpire must inform the captain of any breach of the practices and norms which might bring the game into disrepute. Under Article 2 the umpires are responsible for fair play and may intervene with the captain to ensure that incidents of unfair play are dealt with. This did not as far as we know happen here. While it is against the spirit of the game to appeal falsely, there is no specific provision imposing a duty to revoke an appeal. If there is such a duty the *Laws* clearly impose it on the captain as we have seen. Players are responsible for the 'tone' of a match, but there is no specific indication that this is by definition synonymous with the spirit of the game. And while Article 4 does say that the spirit of the game includes respect for the game and for the opponents, all remedial provisions invoke the direct responsibility of the umpire and the captains, but not the individual players. There must be some doubt here as to the actual content of the obligation imposed upon Jacobs to 'withdraw' an appeal. Further there must even be doubt as to whether it is in keeping with the rules governing the game and the principles of natural justice to impose on him an obligation to act when there is enough textual ambiguity to allow one to argue that the only person who is responsible for such a breach is and should be the captain.

Unlike the *Preamble*, the *ICC Code of Conduct* does in fact and in law apply to each player. Jacobs clearly assumes responsibilities thereunder when he steps on the field of play. The question must still remain however as to the exact nature of his offence. We know that he was found guilty of provision C2:

Players and/or Team Officials shall at no time engage in conduct unbecoming to their status which could bring them or the game of cricket into disrepute.[18]

Paragraph 5.1 of the *Code of Conduct* provides that

Where the facts of or the gravity or seriousness of the alleged incident are not adequately or clearly covered by any of the above offences, the person laying the charge may allege one of the following offences

(A)   breach of Rule C1 – unfair play; or
(B)   breach of Rule C2 – conduct that brings the game into disrepute.

It is not my purpose here to review the law relating to natural justice, procedural fairness and disciplinary bodies. However a simple reading of the text, combined with the fact that the ICC is well aware of the idea that such proceedings must be conducted in accordance with the rules of natural justice, must raise concerns.[19] Section 5.1 in the language which creates the offence under which Jacobs was convicted, does so in circumstances where the gravity or seriousness of the offence are not adequately or clearly covered and again simply reiterates C1 and C2 which are themselves 'unfair play' and 'conduct that brings the game into disrepute'. These provisions seem to create offences which are, in many circumstances, so vague and unknowable as to be unfair and disreputable themselves.

In addition Jacobs was found to have breached the 'cheating or sharp practices' provisions of the *Preamble*. Here we find a judicial determination of the existence of a positive duty to withdraw an appeal under the *Code of Conduct* and the *Preamble* even when, as I have argued, such an action would be a literal impossibility under the *Laws of Cricket*. Referee Lindsay has concluded that the list of offences under Article 5 is merely indicative and not exhaustive. He has created, or discovered, and imposed a positive obligation on all cricketers to withdraw an ill-founded appeal. He has also found that failing to do so brings the game of cricket into disrepute. One must nonetheless ask exactly what the substantive content of such an obligation now is. Does it apply only when the player 'knows' that the appeal is baseless or without an actual legal or factual foundation? Does it apply more broadly when a player 'should' know, or finally does it apply when video evidence for example simply reveals the absence of a proper basis for an appeal regardless of the state of mind of the player? Who bears the burden of proof and what sort of proof will satisfy that burden?

Let us go back to the case of Ian Healy and the disputed catch of Brian Lara or any number of other incidents when there is for some doubt as to whether the ball carried. Usually, in such cases, for others there is no doubt that the ball bounced before it was taken and for still others, no doubt at all that the catch was fair and the batter is out. Is there now an obligation at law and in ethics not to appeal, or to withdraw an appeal by others? What happens to the text of Law 27(8) which clearly gives the captain and only the captain the right to seek permission to withdraw an appeal? Clearly one might for example argue that in the case of factual doubt by a fielder, an ethical and now a legal obligation, since the *Preamble* as interpreted has been incorporated into the *Laws*, not to appeal or to withdraw exists. If there is doubt and controversy, surely the game of cricket is brought into disrepute by such unseemly and controversial legal shenanigans? Of course, one result of an actual obligation such as this being put into regular and consistent practice would be that umpires and appeals would be unnecessary since all claims for dismissals would be good faith and based in legal and factual certainty; this is absurd. We need judges and umpires because there is doubt and uncertainty, and doubt, conflict and uncertainty can be and are founded in good faith disputes about facts and law. If we reduce the application of the obligation not to appeal to cases of 'actual knowledge' we may well limit the number of cases in which it might be found to apply, but we will certainly never eliminate the controversy surrounding Ian Healy and Brian Lara at the SCG. Nor indeed can we at some level be absolutely certain that in the heat of the moment, in a hard fought game, with the speed and dexterity required to effectuate a stumping before the batter grounds his bat or makes back his ground, that the keeper is actually aware that he had the ball in the wrong hand at the time the bail came off.

9 Umpires, decisions and the rule of law

It is clear, however, that whether one sees such situations as inherently conflictual or inherently synthetical, the fundamental issue which remains unresolved is a precise and clear definition of the umpire's position and authority, and of any concomitant duty to the spirit of the game which might also arise. In other words, the real question is how, or indeed whether, given the factual and interpretive ambiguities which surrounded the umpire's adjudicative function at both the formalistic and ethical level, his decisions can receive authority and respect. Is the man in white always right?

Like a liberal democracy, cricket depends for its stability and success on the acceptance of its norms and procedures by those who are subject to them. There is, of course, evidence in our experience of the game that one should, as Ian Botham says, *never argue with an umpire*. Such an admonition is informed by, and confirmed at, many levels of the existential practice of cricket. As we have already seen at the formalistic level of the *Laws*, the *Preamble* and the *Code of Conduct*, any show of dissent is a violation of the normative structures of cricket.

At the practical level, respect for the umpire's decisions is required for several reasons. For the social compact involved in playing any sport, acceptance of the rules and norms of conduct and behaviour is both implicit and necessary. In other words, in order to 'play the game', by definition both sides must agree that they are playing 'the same game'. At another utilitarian level, respect for the finality of the umpire's decision is required if the game is to proceed to a conclusion. Finally, at the ethical and mythological levels, respect for the umpire's decision is required by the gentlemanly and sportsmanlike common traditions and practices of cricket. For example, when fast bowler Ernie McCormick of the Australian team which visited England in 1938 was consistently no-balled by the English umpires, he not only accepted their authority and decision without demur but he offered his apologies to the umpires. To act otherwise, to question or doubt the umpires, would simply not be cricket.

A common current argument or point of contention, however, is that the 'character of cricket' and of cricketers, now legislatively embodied in the various legal texts which govern the game, has changed in the post-war era. These nostalgic invocations of the good old days of the rule of law in cricket, of a universally accepted and respected spirit of the game, have strong ideological appeal. It is hardly surprising that former Prime Minister John Major or Australian leader John Howard are both fans of the game. Unfortunately the ideological appeal of cricket as law and order and the political consequences for some leaders of this set of understandings of the game and of the law, are counterfactual. They are myth, not reality and almost certainly at the most important levels, not law. The entire history of cricket and international Test cricket in particular, is permeated with dramatic instances of total and public disrespect for the integrity of umpires' decisions and for the rule of law in cricket. Writing in the Badminton Library book on cricket in 1882, A.G. Steel described umpires as receiving 'certainly no thanks, and too frequently something which is not altogether unlike abuse'.[1] At the zenith of Victorian culture, umpires, so it would seem, were subject to disrespect and abuse. This, however, did not prevent Steel from describing respect for the umpire's decision as 'The chief principle that tends to harmonise the game...'[2] While these two descriptions of the state of respect for the umpire might appear contradictory, Steel does go on to solve our dilemma when he writes

> First-class amateur cricketers should remember that it is impossible for them to pay too much deference to the decisions of Umpires, as it is from them that the standard or tone of morality in the game is taken.[3]

The general tone of disrespect for the umpire's decision, for the Victorian idealists and their present day acolytes, comes not from the true morality or character of cricket but from the invasion of foreign, lower-class elements. The true morality of cricket which demands complete and utter respect for authority is the morality of the Victorian upper-class. A fine statement and no doubt reflective of one view of Victorian morality which to this day informs one view of the ethical nature of cricket. On the other hand, there is a competing and contradictory view of the nature of ethical values in Victorian England and in Victorian cricket, among cricketers of all classes.

This other view does not reject the ethical merit of accepting an umpire's decision without question. Nor does it suggest that cricket did not, or does not, in fact, reflect these values. It merely puts forward the argument that the ethical or normative context of the game of cricket is a highly complex web of competing structures and values. The events of the earliest Tests between England and Australia as well as current controversies indicate that the interconnections between the Law, ethical norms and cricketing practices are more complex than any simple and simplistic reference to either the mode of production or gentlemanly conduct in Victorian England and far-flung colonies, can solve.

In what is now considered the first Test, in Melbourne in 1877, the ideological norms of sportsmanship, ethical behaviour and respect for the umpire's decision were clearly the practice. Australian captain Dave Gregory was run out and 'walked' before the umpire's decision. The umpires 'gave three decisions in Australia's favour and one in England's favour. Each time the batsman walked without argument when the decision was given.'[4]

During the 1878–79 tour of Australia by Lord Harris' team, however, a different ethos evidenced itself.[5] Billy Murdoch, the Australian batter was given out (run out) by umpire Coulthard, an umpire appointed by the English team. Gregory, the New South Wales captain, protested and refused to play unless Coulthard was withdrawn. The English captain, Lord Harris, rejected the ultimatum, an 'angry mob' of spectators invaded the field, Lord Harris was struck by an enraged fan and the mounted police tried to restore order.

These events could be said to reinforce Steel's view, if one were to see them as a result of the angry behaviour of a bunch of ill-bred colonials. But the context of the SCG 'riot' is more complex than that. First, it must be noted, as already mentioned, that gambling was an important part of Victorian era cricket, both in Australia and in England, and there is some evidence that the crowd were incited by bookmakers anxious over the effect of Murdoch's dismissal on their coffers. Secondly, it must be noted that many of the Australian players, including Gregory, had previously toured England and were convinced that English umpires were in the pay of wealthy amateur cricketers and 'knew which side their bread was buttered on'. For the Australians then, when an English umpire gave an Australian player out, it was, from experience, a case of justice not being done or not appearing to be done. In either case, the fact that umpires were appointed by the opposing sides might well indicate, in light of the historical and even current debates both over neutral umpires, and more frequently over the capacities of all umpires, that Victorian upper-class cricket may well have been 'not cricket'.

Other incidents of disagreement with, or disrespect for, an umpire's decision indicate that the problem has never been limited to the lower classes or to Larrikin Colonials. In a match between Hampshire and Notts in 1922, J.A. Newman lost his temper and kicked down the stumps. His captain asked him to leave the field.[6] A. Ward of Derbyshire refused to bowl after disagreeing with an umpire's decision in a 1973 match with Yorkshire. He too was sent from the field.[7] While both Newman and Ward apologized subsequently and recognized the error of their ways, and while both were immediately disciplined by their captains, their behaviour does indicate a clear transgression of the norms of quiet acquiescence, which if the nostalgics are to be believed, were universally respected.

Similar instances have occurred on a somewhat regular basis in international cricket. In New Zealand, West Indian pace bowler Michael Holding displayed his displeasure with a decision by kicking the stumps from the ground.[8] Again in New Zealand, after being frequently no-balled by umpire Goodall, Colin Croft, 'deliberately barged into umpire Goodall and also knocked the bails off. On the third day, the West Indies refused to come out unless Goodall was removed: after some delay the game continued, but the West Indies threatened to go back home that evening'.[9]

In 1987–88, the English bowler, Graham Dilley, was fined £250 by his own side 'when appeals for a catch were rejected during the first Test match against New Zealand in Christchurch'[10] and he displayed his displeasure. On two separate occasions, English batter Chris Broad demonstrated his own lack of self-control. During the Bicentennial Test in Sydney, after spending seven hours at the crease and scoring 139, he 'petulantly smashed the stumps with his bat after playing on to Waugh. His action was the mark of a man who finds it difficult to accept dismissal, whatever his score at the time'.[11]

For being a poor loser and bringing the game into disrepute, he was promptly fined £500 by his own team management. In Pakistan, after being given out caught at the wicket, he refused to leave the crease, staying for almost a minute and departing only after his partner, Graham Gooch, persuaded him to do so. He was issued, much to the disappointment of Pakistani officials and English writers, only a 'stern reprimand'.[12]

Other brief examples from more recent times demonstrate that even the creation of the new Match Referee system, with the explicit provisions of the *Code of Conduct* outlawing dissent, and the imposition of heavier sanctions, have done little to deter or eliminate dissent.[13] If dissent indeed attacks the very integrity of the judicial system upon which cricket is built, by challenging the authority of the judiciary and the rule of law, one might wonder whether the game of cricket is still being played. At the same time it might also be usefully be noted that of the eighteen 'convictions' recorded under the *Code of Conduct* in the season 1999–2000, only one was in fact for showing dissent. It may now be the case that like much law and order rhetoric, 'the sky is falling' proponents of the decline of cricket behaviour may be overstating their empirical case. Or, it might be that the decline in dissent is attributable to increased vigilance and sanctions. The debate will go on as to which is cricket's chicken and which is the egg.

Following a One-Day game against Australia in 1997, Pakistani player Aamir Sohail was reported by the umpires to the Match Referee for dissent. He stood his ground after having been caught and given out, apparently on the basis that the ball which he struck was above shoulder height, prohibited under One-Day Playing Conditions, and should have been called a no-ball. After finally leaving his crease, he pointed at the umpires who were standing together and spoke to them. He was found to have had a previous conviction for a similar offence, having been fined for tossing his bat when given out in a Test match in Hobart in 1995. He became only the second player to be suspended when Raman Subba Row inflicted a one-match ban.[14]

One can see this as the simple application of a more severe penalty on a repeat offender who has breached an important if not fundamental norm of cricket's rule of law. However, one might also bring other elements to bear which might complicate both our understanding of the application of the law and of the justice issues involved. Sohail's previous conviction for a dissent-based offence also came at the hands of Subba Row. This could mean that the judge had a better and more complete knowledge of the accused's record and comportment. Or, it might be argued, that there is some level at which one might apprehend a possibility of bias or prejudgement here. Is the Match Referee making a decision purely on the merits at the stage of deciding whether the offence has been committed and then invoking the defendant's past acts at the sentencing stage, or is he perhaps (or could it be perceived by an observer) more likely to believe that Sohail committed the offence because he has a past history? I am not suggesting that Subba Row violated the rules of natural justice here or that Sohail was not in fact guilty of the offence in question. Instead I am again pointing out that we can only answer these questions, and we can only take a position on the more basic legal and jurisprudential questions of breakdown of law and order in cricket, if we are willing to admit and examine these complicating factors.

Let us examine Sohail's first offence, the bat throwing incident at Bellerive Oval. At first blush, this appears to yet another example of petulant and generally unacceptable behaviour by a cricketer unhappy with his dismissal. But, as one account indicates, this might be subject again to nuance and deconstruction. Thus, Sohail was dismissed after chipping a simple catch, from a medium pace delivery, to the fielder at mid-wicket. Therefore, his subsequent petulance in throwing his bat, was not an act of 'dissent' strictly speaking, but one of disappointment and disgust at the ease with which he, as a top order batter, surrendered his wicket in a Test match. This does not, of course, necessarily go to the acceptability of his actions, but it does perhaps, in some circumstances, mean that he was not a recidivist when he later disputed his dismissal. For example, under the current provisions of the *Code of Conduct*, it is a Level 1 offence to show dissent (1.3) or abuse cricket equipment (1.2). Under this legal regime, any offence like that which Sohail committed at Hobart would almost certainly fall under the latter (1.2) count.

It is a Level 2 offence to either repeat 'any Level 1 offence' in a specified time period (2.1) or to 'show serious dissent' (2.2). Assuming again that this was the nature of Sohail's action over the no-ball issue, he may or may not have committed a Level 2 offence depending upon whether one considers that he has shown 'dissent' (Level 1, 1.3) or 'serious dissent'. What is clearly open to disputation and legal argument is whether the Hobart offence and the Sydney offence were 'unrelated' as a matter of law. Arguably, one was a case of equipment abuse and the second more clearly an instance of dissent. Of course, it will also have to be borne in mind that Section 5.2 permits the Referee to take into account 'the prior record of the person accused'; again, however, this must apply only to the penalty phase.

Finally, as far as the judicial history of Aamir Sohail is concerned we might turn to the following:

> Sohail rehearsed the shot with such vehemence as he strode off that he dropped the bat, an incident he paid for heavily when referee Raman Subba Row fined him half his match fee and added a two-match suspended sentence.[15]

Arguably, if we were to accept the description here as literally true, then it becomes possible to create an argument that Sohail was in fact and in law 'wrongly convicted'. If he was merely practising the shot on which he was dismissed and the bat, as might be inferred, left his hand accidentally, it could be argued that he did not in fact 'abuse' his cricket equipment. If we believe that

(1) the bat did not just slip and he acted deliberately or (2) he was negligent in not maintaining a proper grip on the bat or (3) his vigorous or vehement practice was negligent or (4) 'abuse' of equipment is a strict or absolute liability offence, or one requiring intent or negligence, then he was rightly convicted. What is evident is that it is not until we address and decide each of these questions that we can even begin to discuss either Sohail's guilt or the basic issue of whether his case or cases offer further proof of the declining standards in relation to behaviour and dissent.

For example, a most vigorous and interesting public debate about the issue of 'the man in white is always right', occurred during a first-class, four-day match between the touring Pakistani team and Victoria in Melbourne in Jan. 1990. In that match, umpire Robin Bailhache, a veteran of 27 Test matches, ordered Pakistani spin-bowler, Mushtaq Ahmed, out of the bowling attack after warning him for running on the pitch.

Law 42(11) stated:

11. *Players Damaging the Pitch*
The Umpires shall intervene and prevent Players from causing damage to the pitch which may assist the Bowlers of either side. See Note (c).

(a) In the event of any member of the fielding side damaging the pitch the Umpire shall follow the procedure of caution, final warning and reporting as set out in 10(a) above.

(b) In the event of a Bowler contravening this Law by running down the pitch after delivering the ball, the Umpire at the Bowler's end shall first caution the Bowler. If this caution is ineffective the Umpire shall adopt the procedures, other than the calling of 'no-ball', of final warning, action against the Bowler and reporting.

(c) In the event of a Batsman damaging the pitch the Umpire at the Bowler's end shall follow the procedures of caution, final warning and reporting as set out in 10(c) above.

Law 42(10)(c) provided for the following system of warnings:

(i) In the first instance he shall caution the Captain of the Fielding side and inform the other Umpire of what has occurred.

(ii) If this caution is ineffective, he shall repeat the above procedure and indicate to the Captain that this is a final warning.

...

Finally, note (c) of Law 42 defined the 'danger area' as follows:

(c) Danger Area
The danger area on the pitch, which must be protected from damage by a Bowler, shall be regarded by the Umpires as the area contained by an

imaginary line 4 ft/1.22 m. from the popping crease, and parallel to it, and within two imaginary and parallel lines drawn down the pitch from points on that line 1 ft/30.48 cm. on either side of the middle stump.[16]

After Bailhache ordered Mushtaq out of the attack, Pakistan team manager Intikhab Alam ordered his team off the field

> Only intense negotiations between Intikhab, Umpires Bailhache and Bill Sheehan, Victorian Cricket Association executive director Ken Jacobs and State coach Ian Redpath saved the game following a 33-minute delay.[17]

The debate which followed the Pakistani walk-off and the issues which are raised by the case point to the fundamental contradictions which pervade not only cricket but, by clear analogy, apply to debates within 'law' about formalism, positivism, ethics, justice, adjudication, interpretation, bias and racism. I will now briefly examine some of them, in an attempt to highlight the complex stories we create for ourselves from and about our social texts, especially those of cricket and law.

From the point of view of a formalistic application of the *Laws*, it would seem to have been quite clear that pursuant to Law 21(3),

(a)   A match shall be lost by a side which, during the match,

  (i)   refuses to play[18]

Under a literal reading it was apparent that when a team leaves the field as did the Pakistanis this *would*, *should* and *does* constitute a 'refusal' to play. This is the view taken by Peter Roebuck who claimed that the Pakistani walk-off 'perpetuated an outrage'. For him there is no doubt that 'By leaving the field Pakistan had conceded the match and so stumps should have been drawn, reports filed, and the game awarded to Victoria.'[19]

If anything is certain in the uncertainty of Law and of Cricket, it is that it is not always clear what the 'correct' legal or ethical decision or outcome should be. On the surface and plain meaning of the text, Roebuck was apparently correct and Law 21(3)(a)(i) was not subject to much contrary interpretation. Yet there are other factors, legal, ethical and practical which make the context of umpire Bailhache's decision and the subsequent Pakistani action more complex than they appear at first sight and which indicate the false security of appeals to plain language and literalist interpretation of what must always be complex social texts and meanings.

First, as a matter of fact and of Law, Law 21(3)(a)(i) only became relevant because the Pakistanis walked off and they only left the field because Bailhache invoked the provisions of Law 42(11) against Mushtaq for running on the pitch. What if the umpire was 'wrong', not in fact but *in law* in applying Law 42(11)? Only an absolute or crude positivist could then claim that some form of

Pakistani protest was not warranted. And it is exactly the Pakistani's position that the umpire acted, in effect, without jurisdiction, ultra vires, illegally.

Under Law 42(11), the umpire who saw a bowler running on the wicket had to follow the procedure set out under paragraph 10(a) of that Law. In other words, he had to give a first caution and then a second and final caution before proceeding to order the bowler out of the attack. According to the Pakistani team manager Intikhab, umpire Bailhache failed to inform the Pakistani captain of the second warning. Under this version of the facts then, the umpire acted improperly and without jurisdiction in ordering Mushtaq out of the attack because the second warning, a condition precedent to such action, had not been given. The walk-off could then be seen to be an attempt to ensure not only that the spirit of the game was upheld, but that the letter of the Law was adhered to as well.

Umpire Bailhache maintained throughout that he

> ... went through all the correct procedures leading up to the event and they just decided they couldn't play under that interpretation and walked off the ground.
> ...
> I did what I thought was right.[20]

It can be said, Bailhache's contention notwithstanding, that the official reason given for permitting play to resume and to not invoke the letter of Law 21(3) was that the officials involved in the subsequent negotiations appear to have accepted the Pakistani contention that they 'believed' only one warning had been given.[21] While this turn of events might be interpreted as merely conforming with the Law which permits an umpire to reverse his decision, that interpretation again would be clearly disingenuous given the Law's formal requirement that the reversal be 'made promptly', not after 33 minutes of negotiation have taken place. Moreover, umpire Bailhache insists that he *did* give two warnings so that only an apparently stretched reading of the Law would allow the element of Pakistani 'belief' to count as one of the elements of the procedure of warnings under Law 42. It is perhaps better and more correct to see the outcome of the negotiations with the Pakistani team as fitting into the category of 'the best interests of the game'.

There are, however, other factors which must be taken into account before anyone can be in a position to even attempt to properly analyze or classify these events. Yet another factual circumstance was invoked by Intikhab to 'justify' his action. According to this new element, Mushtaq was wearing rubber-soled shoes rather than spikes. For the Pakistani this could only mean that he did not *in fact*, damage the pitch. Not surprisingly, Peter Roebuck dismissed this part of the Pakistani position as 'utter balderdash'. Roebuck's attitude to this claim is, of course, a familiar one in legal debates. From his formalist position, the law is the law is the law. Mushtaq ran on the pitch in the danger area as defined, he was properly warned and the full and formal weight of the *Laws* should have been brought down upon him and, following their walk-off, upon the whole of the Pakistani team. No 'fact' other than the umpire's decision is of importance or interest.

Intikhab, on the other hand, proposed that the formalist/literalist approach to the interpretation of the *Laws* should have been replaced by a more liberal, purposive one. For him, the purpose of Law 42(11) was, as the heading itself suggested, to prevent players from damaging the pitch. It is not even that damaging the pitch *per se* is a moral or social evil which must be stamped out. Rather, to take the argument one step further, that which must be prevented, in the words of the Law itself, is a Player 'causing damage to the pitch which may assist the Bowlers of either side'. A pitch damaged in an area which would change the ball's trajectory would give an unfair advantage to the bowler. Intikhab's interpretive position is straightforward, the purpose of Law 42 was to prevent damage which would give an undue advantage to the bowler. Therefore, both the wording and purpose of the legislation indicate that the intent of the Law was not to prevent *all* running on the wicket but rather running which *damages* the danger area. Unlike spiked shoes, rubber-soled shoes do not cause physical damage to the wicket. Therefore umpire Bailhache was incorrect and exceeded his jurisdiction when he issued a warning under Law 42(11), because Law 42(11) applied only in cases of actual *damage* to the pitch.

Besides these various interpretive factors, other elements of the match seen as a whole also serve to make the issues surrounding the walk-off more complex and more heavily contextualized than Roebuck's formalism would allow. First, we have the peculiar nature of the offence and its relationship with the parties involved. Only seven first-class bowlers (including Mushtaq in this match) had ever been warned off, in Australia, for running on the wicket. The Law was one, then, which was rarely applied and this might indicate that it should have been interpreted restrictively if there was any question of it being invoked in circumstances of desuetude.

Despite its rarity, the Law and umpire Bailhache were familiar friends, for it is he who had expelled the last four offenders.[22] Two views of the importance of and interpretation to be given to this fact come readily to mind. First, we have the position of the formalist Roebuck: 'Apparently, too, Bailhache is a stickler for rules, but players know this as children know their teachers and surely can accommodate him.'[23]

Another view, equally appropriate to cricket or to any judiciary, is that the umpire was considered by the players to be a bastard, and that his rigid adherence to the *Laws* was attributable in their view not so much to ideals of truth or duty, but to a petty tyranny. Just as there are difficult judges, there are difficult umpires and they should not be allowed to cloak otherwise unacceptable and unjust behaviour in the mystique and power of their position. Formal mechanisms relating to the removal or judges or umpires for misbehaviour or inappropriate actions, are often lengthy, complicated and subject to great controversy since they raise in stark terms the ideals of an independent judiciary. It may well be that adherence to some understanding of the higher interests of the traditions of the game needs to be invoked and deployed in a democratic fashion by the participants in the process. It might also be useful to ask, since we have undergone a period of legislative change since the Pakistanis left the field, what impact the new text of the *Laws of Cricket* might have here.

Law 42(11) is headed 'Damaging the Pitch – Area to be Protected'. Paragraph (a) now states that

> It is incumbent on all players to avoid unnecessary damage to the pitch. It is unfair for any player to cause deliberate damage to the pitch.

Paragraph (b) defines the area to be protected and Law 42(12) deals with the case at hand of a bowler running on to the pitch in the danger area. It provides in paragraph (a)

> If the bowler, after delivering the ball, runs on the protected area as defined . . . the umpire shall at the first instance, and when the ball is dead,
>
> (i) caution the bowler.

The new provisions also still provide for a system of second warning and on a third violation, for the bowler to be taken out of the attack.[24] Are we now any better off in dealing with umpire Bailhache's actions? The *Laws* no longer make a specific reference to damage which will advantage a bowler. The text now simply refers to the act of deliberately damaging the pitch as 'unfair'. The question which will have to be decided under the new *Laws* is that of the relationship between the provisions of Law 42(11) (a) and 42(12). It is unlawful under the former to 'cause deliberate damage to the pitch'. Under the latter, a breach appears to have been committed if and when a bowler 'runs on the protected area'. Again, we face a familiar set of questions. Is it in reality and under a correct interpretation of the *Laws* an offence to run on the danger area or is it still necessary to add an element of 'causing deliberate damage'? In other words, one interpretive strategy would argue that the offence in 42(1) is one of strict or absolute liability. It requires only that a bowler run on the area regardless of either actual damage or 'deliberation'. This is the view offered by one leading text for umpires. Thus

> It must be realized that the offence here is not damaging the pitch, though this may be a consequence; the offence is running on the protected area in the follow through.[25]

The other position would assert the necessary connection between the two sections and would urge a broad and purposive hermeneutic technique and practice. The second text involves no change from the 1980 *Code*. The purpose of these provisions is clearly expressed and known to practitioners. Its goal is to prevent deliberate damage to the pitch, and regardless of the change in the legislative language, this is meant to prevent disadvantaging a batter and giving an advantage to a bowler as the surface deteriorates 'unnaturally'. Thus, a bowler must run on the proscribed area and intend to and perhaps even actually, inflict damage. I will not further belabour the point. Suffice it to say that the interpretive possibilities of cricket in these circumstances remain open.

At the same time, a judgement can be made on the issue of the legality and/or appropriateness of the Pakistani response to the Bailhache decision only by considering further factors which together constitute the entire context of the match. For example, we might also consider the fact that Intikhab, the team manager, had, as a player, been warned off in a match between Pakistan and Queensland some 17 years previously.[26] Nor was this the only run-in between Bailhache and the Pakistani bowlers. After the walk-off and subsequent return, heated words were exchanged between the Pakistanis and the umpire when he warned and no-balled Aaqib Javed for intimidatory bowling. During one occurrence, Aaqib bowled three bouncers at Victorian captain Simon O'Donnell, was warned by the umpire and promptly reacted by bowling a fourth.[27] It would be possible to see such action as nothing more, as does Roebuck, than childish behaviour, if one's view is informed by an unadulterated and narrow formalism. The bouncers, the warning, the reaction, the no-balling all took place in the context of all the factors I have mentioned in discussing this match and in the context of one more key factor which has not yet been discussed, bias, or more politely, perceptions of bias, with an undercurrent of nationalism and racism. Given persistent Pakistani complaints about the quality and prejudice of umpires on their various tours, it is impossible not to interpret these events as being at least partially influenced by these factors, either 'in reality' or as a perception which shapes the Pakistani view of many questionable umpiring decisions, particularly in Australia.

Additional credibility is given to the Pakistani position by two factors. The first is that, as has been seen, disputes with umpires have a long and storied history and many of them have occurred between visiting teams and 'home' umpires. At the level of the perception of some participants, nationalistic bias has been a consistent element in Test match and international umpiring. The second reason which makes it more difficult to dismiss or criticize in absolutist terms the actions of the Pakistani team, is the fact that what is considered by almost everyone in the game as the most (in)famous event of disrespect for the *Laws of Cricket* and the sanctity of an umpire's conduct and decision occurred in Pakistan. It involved, not the Pakistan team, but the team which is, in the mythology of 'the man in white is always right', meant to embody respect for the higher ethics of the game. Of course, I am speaking about the infamous finger-pointing row between then English captain Mike Gatting and Pakistani umpire Shakoor Rana.[28]

During the Faisalabad Test, England were bowling. Near the end of the day's play, Gatting moved David Capel from his position at deep square leg to one closer to the wicket in order to prevent a single. As Eddie Hemmings commenced his bowling run-up, Gatting signalled to Capel that he was now in a correct position. Umpire Shakoor stopped play to inform the Pakistani batter Salim Malik of Capel's new position. He reproached Gatting for unfairly moving Capel behind Salim's back. Gatting demurred. The language was basic, and Gatting is part of cricket immortality for the pictures of this finger-wagging confrontation.

Shakoor refused to return to the field the next day unless Gatting apologized, Gatting refused, the third day's play was lost to negotiation; after further discussions on the next (rest) day could not produce a compromise, the Test and County Cricket Board (TCCB), English cricket's governing body at the time, instructed Gatting to apologize, which he reluctantly did. The English side decided to continue to play under protest and issued a public statement declaring:

> What is beyond dispute is that the umpire was the first to use abusive language to the England Captain. This was clearly heard by England players close to the incident. Mike Gatting was ready to apologise two days ago for his response, provided the umpire would do the same.
>
> . . .
>
> The incident was sad for cricket but the solution forced upon us is even sadder.[29]

For the formalist or even the cricket moralist, the fact that Gatting is to be thoroughly condemned for breaking the written and unwritten rules of cricket law and etiquette is beyond dispute. With the benefit of hindsight, such moralizing is easier for many of us to accept, given that Gatting later lost the captaincy allegedly for cavorting with a 'barmaid' in his hotel room on his birthday and led a rebel English tour to *apartheid* South Africa. But neither facile moralizing nor retroactive justification based on subsequent moral failures offer much succour in dealing with the issues of the contradictions and complexities of cricket law and practice raised by this and similar events. Again, the many factors which should enter into the moral/legal calculus are confusing, as are the various interpretive perspectives which are open on the hermeneutic circle. In addition to the obvious national hermeneutic perspectives, English, Pakistani, or more 'neutral' Australian, it would also be possible to view these events from the standpoint of other interpretive sub-communities e.g. umpires who have been 'abused' by players, players who have been 'abused' by umpires. Each, like varying accounts of 'events' in civil or criminal trials, is founded in a validity claim, the 'objectivity' of which its proponents would all loudly proclaim.

There is, again, dispute over the 'facts'. Gatting claims that he did warn Salim about the fielding change, Shakoor's contention is that Gatting heaped abuse at him. There is, of course, a strong moral argument that Gatting, no matter the provocation, should never have replied as he did, and the English players' public statement would indicate that Gatting himself would agree. On the other hand, there is an equally strong argument that Shakoor's behaviour was inappropriate. Even if Gatting did heap abuse on him, the normal and judicially correct thing to do would be to maintain his personal dignity and to ensure respect for his position, in other words, to simply ignore Gatting's provocation. If, on the other hand, Shakoor did indeed curse and hurl abuse at Gatting, then his entire behaviour was unjudicial and deserving of the strongest censure, perhaps even by Gatting.

Yet, even this slightly more contextualized critique does not approach the deep and true texture of events which reached a head at Faisalabad. From the 1961–62 tour of Pakistan by Ted Dexter's England side, English players had always suspected and complained about the bias and incompetence of Pakistani umpires and the Pakistanis had as vociferously expressed their lack of confidence in English umpires. On the 1982 Pakistani tour of England, umpire David Constant had given a decision crucial to the English victory. Imran Khan, the captain of Pakistan, publicly criticized Constant and attributed Pakistan's defeat to his errors. In their 1987 tour to England, Pakistan requested that Constant not umpire but the TCCB refused their request and again Constant was involved in more contentious decisions. Hajeeb Ahsan, the Pakistani tour manager, branded Constant 'a disgraceful person'.[30]

With this history, the Gatting team came to Pakistan. Chris Broad as already mentioned refused to leave the crease after being given out by umpire Shakeel Khan, against whom England had previously launched a protest/request similar to that made by Pakistan in reference to Constant. Broad was issued only with a stern reprimand and Peter Lush, England tour manager, publicly criticized the umpiring and called for neutral umpires.

With this history, the English went to Faisalabad for a match to be umpired by Shakoor of whom Martin Johnson comments:

> ...The umpire's reputation for upsetting visiting teams, notably when the New Zealand captain, J.V. Coney led his team off the field in protest during the Karachi Test in 1984–85, was already known to (the English).[31]

With this history, the English went into the second day. There was 'one unsavoury incident, following Shakoor's rejection of a bat-pad appeal from Bill Athey'[32] when, as they say, the jurisprudential shit hit the legal fan. As the brief discussion indicates we are no longer faced with a hypothetical or formalistic world in which the umpire's integrity is never questioned or never questionable. Instead, we are in the world of real cricket where attacks on the integrity and reliability of umpires have a long, somewhat sordid, institutional history. We are not in the world of the morally pure *versus* the ethically corrupt. We are in our world of each and every side questioning the integrity of the other's umpires and in some cases, of their own umpires.[33] We are in a world where even the inevitable move to neutral umpires in Test Cricket has not necessarily reduced dissent or the degree to which judicial competence is challenged. We are in a world where the complexity of even what would appear to be a simple text like cricket is such that the Shakoor–Gatting confrontation will add another layer upon which all debate, discussion and interpretation of the idea of respect of the umpire will be built.

If the finger-waving confrontation of Mike Gatting with umpire Rana marked the low-water mark for cricket at the time, there can be little doubt that for many in England and Australia in particular, the 'antics' of Arjuna Ranatunga as captain of Sri Lanka helped sink the game to new depths. For them, Ranatunga embodied and exemplified the disintegration of the rule of law in the game and therefore he posed a threat to very concept and normative understandings of 'cricket'.

Of course, it is not possible to properly situate the various aspects of the Arjuna case and controversies without some attempt to grasp the subtleties and historical context of Sri Lankan cricket. While it is beyond the scope of this work to offer any such detailed examination, we must nonetheless attempt to bring to our interpretation of the facts and law of the examples which follow here some idea of the history of English colonialism in Ceylon, the role of the English public school model in forming not just a governing elite but a cricketing elite. We must remember the tensions and conflicts between city and country dwellers. Battles and struggles between Sinhalese and Tamil, and between Christian and Buddhist Sinhalese must inform all our readings of the Ranatunga text. Conflicts between various board members in cricket's governing body and between the board and the government are never far from the surface of Sri Lankan cricket.[34] Litigation over broadcasting and sponsorship rights also present commercial, legal and ethical considerations which must be understood here.[35] We must also bring to our reading of what follows an understanding of the ongoing tensions between 'white' and 'black' cricket, the role of the metropole and the settler dominions and the conflict with the subcontinent in world cricket.[36]

Relations between Sri Lanka and Australia in the world of cricket have never been easy. The Sri Lankans were at the time of the first run ins with Ranatunga the most recent members of the Test-playing community and were considered to be the easy beats of the game. When they came to Australia in 1995–96, they were met with less than first-class training facilities and a shortened Test series. Australians at some level clearly believed that it was part of their duty to the game, cricket's 'white man's burden', to play the Sri Lankans but for them it really was not something they wanted to do. Into this context came the Sri Lankans, captained by Arjuna Ranatunga. Trent Bouts, writing in *Wisden*, reported on the animosity between the teams. Australian misbehaviour, intimidation and racist sledging were to some extent to be expected, '... the street-smart Ranatunga was no angel either'.[37]

The tour was marked and marred by controversy. The visitors were 'illegally' accused of ball-tampering.[38] Their star spinner, Muttiah Muralitharan, the only Tamil in the team, was called for 'throwing' and accused of being a cheat.[39] The Sri Lankans retaliated with charges of bias and racism. Relations did not improve. Following an increase in the intensity of the civil war between Tamils and Sinhalese, the Australians controversially refused to play their match in the 1996 World Cup scheduled to take place in Sri Lanka.[40] That Australia never even considered cancelling an Ashes tour to England at the height of IRA bombing campaigns might indicate that there is and was something more than fear of physical safety at work here.[41] The construction of 'Third World' violence as epistemologically distinct from terrorism in the Mother Country is one which continues to operate. Australia lost to Sri Lanka in the final game and the easy beats of world cricket became world champions in the One-Day game.

Two years later, in late 1998, and early 1999, Sri Lanka returned to tour Australia. Controversy again surrounded the visit. Sri Lanka, still smarting from the no-balling of Murali for throwing, demanded that umpire Darrell Hair be removed from the panel of umpires to stand in the series. The ACB and the ICC hemmed and hawed, and dithered while the tension rose. On the one hand, everyone wanted to avoid a repeat of the unfriendly atmosphere which had informed the last tour as a result of the legal controversies over ball-tampering and chucking. At the same time, many bristled at the idea that one team could dictate who adjudicated in Test matches. This threatened the understanding of the rule of law and ethical normative standard of the spirit of the game. Umpires are unbiased and competent. If the home board and/or the ICC named an umpire as eligible to stand, then no team could accuse that umpire of unjudicial behaviour or attitudes informed by bias without challenging the ideal of judicial neutrality and objectivity in adjudication. In the end, Darrell Hair 'did the right thing' and decided to stand aside for the good of the game.

For some, this was a sad day for cricket and the law. Political pressure and extra-judicial factors had resulted in the humiliating removal, albeit 'voluntarily', of an umpire for reasons which had nothing to do with his competence or abilities. For others, chiefly Sri Lankan supporters, this was the triumph of the rule of law and justice in cricket. Justice must not only be done but must be seen to be done. If one side has good faith reasons to fear that adjudication will not be fair, then this apprehended bias must be acknowledged and the process of judging and applying the law be seen to be fair by the removal of even the potential for bias. Finally, still others might agree that the rule of law has indeed been respected and upheld, not by the pernicious motivations of the Sri Lankans, or by the pusillanimous behaviour of officialdom in Melbourne or London, but by Darrell Hair. His decision to withdraw indicates that when faced with a crisis not of his making and not informed by law, he nonetheless decided that the rule of law and the traditions of cricket, the spirit of the game, compelled him to make the sacrifice, both monetary and psychological, to step aside. He assumed a personal injustice 'for the good of the game'.[42] Each and every one of these readings is or could be correct. None will impose itself objectively on the basis of the 'facts' or the 'law' of the case.

With Hair gone, one might have expected that the series of games in Australia would unfold without any extraordinary developments. Of course, that expectation again would have to be grounded in a belief that the only objection the Sri Lankans had was to Hair, that they then intended to comply with the best traditions of the game. Similarly, it would depend on the idea that the other teams involved, Australia in the Tests and One-Day series and England in the One-Dayers, had no other history or problems in their relationships with the

Sri Lankans. Nothing could be farther from the truth and this is, yet again, why cricket and the law are such fascinating topics of study.

Ranatunga, rightly or wrongly, had a reputation as a niggler. He had personal traits and tactical skills which managed to get under the skins of his opponents. One could argue that this was just the way he was, or that it was calculated to give his team an advantage and demonstrated his skills as a captain. One could argue that his ability to niggle opponents was also informed by his experiences as a 'colonial' cricketer and by the biases of others when faced with such opponents. When an Ian Botham or Ian Chappell resorted to such tactics, Australians and English fans delighted in the skills and *nous* of their captains. When Ranatunga or now Sourav Ganguly of India behave in a similar manner, they are low-life cheating scum who besmirch the traditions of the game. Again, neither the law not the facts will determine the correct interpretive approach here.

What is beyond doubt is that tensions were high and the players did not like each other. Ranatunga used the *Laws* to engage in a 'favourite' tactic to call for a runner while batting. Australia's acting captain Shane Warne objected but Ranatunga persisted in his claim that the injury was not a pre-existing one, but one which had occurred in the game. Thus, 'A Runner shall be allowed for a Batsman who during the match is incapacitated by illness or injury.'[43]

Australian commentators and players were not impressed.

> On the field the Sri Lankans under Ranatunga play a giggly sort of game which gets under their opponents' skins. The captain leads the way, especially with his regular stunt of calling for a runner while batting.
> . . .
> What can the umpires do? They cannot query the honesty of the man every time; they cannot have his injury examined in the middle of an innings. He has them over the barrel.
>
> Yet in this instance the injury cleared up in two days, and Ranatunga showed no signs of it on Saturday. Warne and many others could be forgiven for doubting the genuineness of that injury.
>
> What's worse, Ranatunga gloats about this by walking singles whenever he can, this is his way of thumbing his nose at his opponents. 'No, I'm not fit, but what are you going to do about it?'[44]

The conclusions are obvious, for any red-blooded Australian reader at least, Ranatunga is a liar and a cheat. He abuses his opponents and the umpires by invoking his 'right' to a runner when he knows that he is breaching the *Laws* and the spirit of the game in doing so. He uses blackmail and extortion on the cricket pitch. He is not playing cricket because everyone 'knows' that he needs the runner not because of an injury sustained while playing the game but because, as Australians were known to say at the time, 'he had a few too many curries' and was not in proper shape. Here his offence to the game, and its *Laws*, is compounded and exacerbated in Australian eyes, because he breaches unwritten laws and codes and ethical norms and basic understandings about what it means to play cricket. This is not in reference to using a runner, or invoking the *Laws* in a bad faith manner. There is something more fundamental at stake here. He is undermining and 'thumbing his nose' at the cult of virility. He is unfit and he is unfit and proud of it. This is not the sunburned hardened Australian male, being hit by bouncers, sledging, and giving his all for his country. This is a fat, effeminate foreigner, walking, yes walking his singles!!!. No scurrying between wickets in an attempt to hurry the throw and steal another run in a masculine Australian fashion. He walks and he smiles as he does it. He is un-Australian and this is his greatest sin. Sharp practice, relying on the literal wording of the *Laws of Cricket*, even 'cheating', these are all parts of Australian cricket, as long as they are conducted in a manly fashion. Subcontinental cricketers like Ranatunga break the code of the code. They are wristy and girly. They are not real men. That is their crime.

Ranatunga compounded his innate criminality as a Sri Lankan cricketer in Australia when he took his team off the field and remonstrated with the umpires when Emerson no-balled Muralitharan. The game was delayed for 14 minutes while Ranatunga consulted with team management, and sought the intervention of the Match Referee. Reaction was immediate and unanimous, at least in Australia and England. Alec Stewart called the game the least enjoyable he had ever played in. Ranatunga was attacked by Malcolm Conn for his 'disgraceful behaviour': 'The failure by a captain to accept an umpire's decision, no matter how much he may disagree with it, is a threat to cricket's fabric.'[45]

This is the central and most important point about all of the controversy which surrounded this case. Ranatunga was reported and summoned before the Match Referee. He showed up accompanied by two lawyers who threatened a legal challenge to the *Code of Conduct* system in which the Referee was both prosecutor and judge.[46] Here the problems are clear. Cricket depends on the authority of the umpire. Umpires are neutral embodiments of judicial impartiality and the objective application of the *Laws* of the game. Ranatunga directly challenged that idea and ideal and then exacerbated the problem by challenging the new legal system put in place to ensure respect for the old legal system. Here, too much law is barely enough. Not only did Ranatunga challenge the traditional understandings of what it means to play cricket on the field, he challenged the legality of the system of discipline to which he and his Board had agreed.[47]

Putting aside the important administrative law questions which will always arise in sports discipline matters, the central issue here must be what has happened to the rule of law and the spirit of the game. Mike Gatting pointed his finger in Rana's face and was forced to apologize. He recognized, at least publicly and officially, that dissent and disrespect for judicial office, were inconsistent with the spirit of the game. Ranatunga effectively escaped punishment when he had publicly remonstrated with the umpires, stopped play for 14 minutes and showed up at the disciplinary hearing with two lawyers in tow.

Of course, there is some counter-narrative available here. The Sri Lankans were convinced that umpire Emerson was acting in bad faith when he no-balled Murali. He was not judging in an objective manner and according to the *Laws* and traditions of the game. He was not acting in a judicial manner. The question here then goes back to the idea of good faith and adjudication.

For Malcolm Conn and others, the idea of respect for the umpire's jurisdiction and decision-making power and integrity goes to the very 'fabric of the game'. One must respect the umpire's decision 'no matter how much' one disagrees with it. Clearly the idea of respect for the judicial function of the umpire and respect for decisions once rendered does go to the heart of the game. Yet it is also evident that this general statement of law and ethics has never been, legally or ethically, literally part of the fabric of the game. Bad decisions may be in effect overridden by a player indicating for example that the ball was not fairly caught, or by a captain recalling a batter. Players, even in the days of video replays and *Code of Conduct* violations, continue to shake their heads and wait at the wicket when given out 'incorrectly'. Bowlers still grab their caps or sweaters from the umpire at the end of an over in which they have had a 'good' appeal rejected.

There is of course a degree of difference and distinction between each of these instances and what Ranatunga did. Bowlers who grab their garments may be fined for their behaviour and they do not take their team off the field. Similarly, a player may disagree with an umpire's decision to turn down an LBW appeal, believing that the ball would have hit the stumps. But this does not, even when accompanied by some disrespectful behaviour which might result in punishment from the Match Referee, constitute an attack on the fabric of the game. In other circumstances, the umpire may have been wrong on the facts, for example, in giving out a batter LBW, because everyone else knows that the ball pitched outside leg stump. Such a decision is wrong in fact and in law, the umpire had in reality no jurisdiction to render the judgement he did, but no player will order his side not to take any further part in the game following such a decision.

For Ranatunga and his supporters, there was arguably in fact and in law a qualitative and essential difference here. The umpire only appeared to be acting as an umpire, in fact he is not 'judging', he is cheating. If the umpire is no longer acting as an umpire, then the argument goes, one is not attacking the fabric of the game by refusing to comply with his decisions because they are in fact and in law, not really decisions. The real attack on the fabric of the game comes from the umpire who is no longer an umpire. The defence of the spirit and *Laws* of the game comes through 'disrespecting' the umpire who is not one, by upholding the ideal of neutral adjudication and good faith. One is compelled to respect bad and incompetent judges because the higher interests of the game, its traditions and spirit all require such conduct. Other mechanisms may be available to deal with the problem. But one is not compelled by the spirit or essential fabric of the game to respect the (non) decisions of the (non) umpire. One's ethical obligation on the contrary is to resist.

Thus, perhaps Ranatunga's decision to bring legal counsel to the Referee's hearing was informed by a desire to point out the essential illegality of the hearing, not because of some poorly drafted potential violation of the maxim *nemo judex in sua causa*, but because one cannot be charged with bringing the game into disrepute for upholding the basic principle of good faith in adjudication.

One cannot bring the game of cricket into disrepute if the game of cricket is no longer being played by the umpire.

Such jurisprudential investigations would perhaps sit more comfortably if two criteria were met. First, we would need some kind of legal and discursive consensus on the idea of 'bad' umpiring, which must be respected and 'bad faith' umpiring which would need to be rejected. No such consensus is likely to arise. This brings me to the second jurisprudential condition precedent. It would be perhaps easier to talk about consensus and bad faith concerning respect for the judicial integrity and the rule of law if the plaintiff/hero were not Arjuna Ranatunga.

Even supporters of Sri Lanka, including players, were not unanimously enamoured of Ranatunga. He was and is a controversial figure and not universally admired or respected as a captain.[48] The idea here is that the plaintiff/defendant who pretends to be upholding the best traditions of the game, of seeking justice against arbitrary tyranny disguised as law, must come with clean hands. He must not be someone who uses and abuses the letter of the *Laws* for his own advantage. He must be the ideal cricketer in order to uphold the ideals of cricket. He cannot be Arjuna Ranatunga. More tellingly, he cannot in all likelihood, be anyone who has ever played the game.

Once again, we find ourselves facing the fundamental epistemological, deontological and jurisprudential questions which go to the heart of adjudication and cricket. If *Laws* are to be applied, and players are to obey the injunctions of the adjudicators, there must be, at some level, a combination of coercion and consent. Participants in the game contract to accept the rules and norms of the contest. If they did not share this good faith understanding of what it meant to play cricket, the very basis of 'cricket' would cease to exist. We have already seen the complexities and subtleties which must be confronted if we wish to concretize the meaning of this 'agreement' of what is and is not cricket. Nonetheless, at some point, that agreement must be found. At the same time, since the game itself imposes obligations and rules, there must be a form of sanction or coercion for breach. A batter is out if he is caught, a no-ball penalizes a bowler for over-stepping etc. Again, what is a fair catch, or whether the bowler did overstep are sometimes easily accepted and sometimes deeply contested questions of fact and law. Players may in the park, the backyard or on a Test match field, accept the consequences of breaching the *Laws* and coerce themselves. Or they may be coerced by a process of adjudication. The umpire hears appeals, investigates, observes and adjudicates. The players accept that decision, and moreover, for the broader spirit of the game, or the utilitarian benefit of all concerned, they accept even bad or wrong decisions. Yet it seems clear to anyone who has played or watched the game of cricket, that the ideal of the 'man in white is always right', has always been subjected to stresses, strains and outright breaches. Mike Gatting's finger, Arjuna Ranatunga's walk off etc., embody an alternate reality in which the umpire's adjudication is directly challenged.

A batter, when an appeal for caught behind is made, might rub his arm or shoulder, indicating again to the umpire, the 'fact' that the ball did not hit the bat and he should be given not out. Some consider this sharp practice, some consider it outright and unambiguous cheating. Others would say that it is simply a way of ensuring that the process of adjudication takes place with a full and complete set of facts. There has been, is and will be debate about the proper jurisprudential characterization to be given to such incidents. But what if we move forward in time? An appeal has been made, the batter rubs his arm, the umpire decides and the decision is that the batter is out. He stays at his crease. He continues to rub his shoulder. Here, we have, for most members of the interpretative community, an act of dissent. This is not an attempt to help the process of adjudication, this is an act of defiance, of disputation. It is, for many, the epitome of 'not cricket'. The umpire had decided. The batter must leave without further ado. Of course, we know that this is an ideal, never realized in consistent practice. Arm rubbing, delay, or open remonstration with the umpire, or smashing the stumps out of the ground, can be and are considered to be unlawful 'dissent'. For some, there is a gradation here, from acceptable to unacceptable dissent. For others, there is only a gradation among different forms of unacceptable dissent. For years, the 'man in white is always right' competed in practice and in law, with this ethical debate and confusion, or for others, with this practice of open defiance which threatened the very existence of the game. Finally, after what must be seen to be some sort of consensus that such actions were bringing the game into disrepute and challenging the very existence of lawful authority in adjudication, the ICC stepped in and introduced its *Code of Conduct* provisions which deal specifically with 'dissent'.

The *Code of Conduct* can be seen primarily in two lights. First, it might be read as the codification of pre-existing consensual norms of ethical behaviour. Secondly, it might be seen as an attempt by the hierarchical authorities of the game's administration to stamp out player misbehaviour which had reached, for whatever reasons, unacceptable levels. Whatever legislative intention and political history one wishes to ascribe to the *Code of Conduct*, it seems to establish clearly one basic jurisprudential position. Unwritten norms of ethical behaviour and respect for the rule of law in adjudication had not had a sufficient deterrent or regulatory impact. Law and order had to some extent broken down. A formal mechanism which not only specified as much as possible the limits of acceptable behaviour, and imposed, through the introduction of the Match Referee as a new level of adjudicative authority, a new set of formal penalties beyond self-regulation, was deemed necessary. The breakdown in law and order required more law to impose more order.[49]

I need not enter into a complete and encyclopedic review here of all of the cases of 'dissent' under the *Code of Conduct* since its inception in the 1990s. It is however important to note a couple of preliminary legal facts before turning to a brief enumeration and discussion of the jurisprudence of dissent. First, it appears that dissent continues to be the single most important category of offence under the *Code of Conduct*. Again, there are subtle and often important taxonomical issues which will need to inform future discussion and analysis of this emerging area of law in cricket, but I shall simply stick here to broadly accepted ideas of what constitutes 'dissent'. For example, a batter who is given out LBW in doubtful circumstances or who is out caught to a ball he believes has not carried and smashes the stumps with his bat as he leaves the crease, will in all likelihood be considered to have his action fall within the accepted idea of dissent. On the other hand, a batter who smashes the stumps after being bowled, such as Grant Flower in Trinidad in March 2000, is acting out of disgust or frustration.[50] He has committed an offence under the *Code of Conduct*, but not of 'dissent'. Similarly, when Nasser Hussain broke the glass door of the dressing room fridge after being given out LBW, he might have been dissenting or frustrated, but was convicted under the provisions dealing with bringing the game into disrepute.[51]

Secondly, it does not appear from the statistical and narrative evidence that more law has in fact resulted definitively in more order. Of course, since dissent was not a specific offence and there was never a really efficient, adequate or public forum for adjudicating on this question, before the *Code of Conduct*, we have no real basis for comparison. The number of cases of dissent before the *Code of Conduct* is and will be unknown. What we do and can know is again that cases of dissent appear to be the most numerous single type of violation of the *Code of Conduct* provisions and that dissent persists. The number of cases may have gone up or down, but the typology remains unchanged. Dissent is still manifested by players. The deterrent effect must at some point in time be subjected to careful analysis.

For my purposes here, however, I shall content myself with a brief review of dissent cases as reported by the ICC. The *Code* deals with dissent in several provisions. A player commits a Level 1 offence for

Showing dissent at an umpire's decision by action or verbal abuse.[52]

A Level 2 breach is

Showing serious dissent at an umpire's decision by action or verbal abuse.[53]

Repeated misdeeds are elevated to Level 3 and 4 offences.[54]

Violations of the dissent prohibitions in the *Code of Conduct* were prominent from the earliest days of the introduction of the new regime. Batters objected to decisions giving them out, bowlers did not appreciate appeals being turned down. Verbal objections, grabbing the sweater from the umpire at the end of an unsuccessful over and similar actions featured in the first year of Match Referee adjudication. Aqib Javed became the first player to be suspended for misconduct after his second conviction for dissent in 1992. In that same year, Rashid Latif, Peter Kirsten, Manoj Prabhakar, Allan Border and Merv Hughes were all found guilty of dissent-based offences.[55] Nine out of the ten convictions in that first year were 'dissent'-based if one adds to the list Pakistani captain Javed Miandad who was reprimanded for failing to control Aqib Javed. One other important trend began, in retrospect, to emerge from the beginning of the new legal regime. The country of origin of offenders also indicates the widespread nature of dissent, and again at some level, brings into question the existence or extent of an ethical standard of accepting the umpire's decision without question. Since the introduction of the *Code of Conduct* limitations on dissent, offenders have come across the spectrum of international cricket. Pakistan and India lead the pack, but Australia, South Africa, Zimbabwe and New Zealand are not far behind. Sri Lanka are as prone to dissent as the Mother Country, and the West Indies, of the established Test nations, are the least likely to object to the umpire's decision.[56] In 1993, all five of the offenders against the *Code of Conduct*, Desmond Haynes, Allan Border, Merv Hughes, Vinod Kambli and Andrew Jones, were found guilty of dissent.[57]

The next year, showing dissent continued to feature prominently in the list of breaches. Peter Kirsten was fined twice in the same match against Australia in Adelaide, first for dissenting when a teammate was given out LBW, and again when he fell to the same fate. Michael Atherton was fined when he objected to an LBW decision. An Indian wicketkeeper, and a South African and Australian bowler were each punished for dissent for objecting to decisions denying an appeal for a catch. Guy Whittal of Zimbabwe on the other hand was fined for objecting to a decision giving him out caught and Brian Lara for the same reaction to a successful stumping. Finally, the litigious Arjuna Ranatunga was fined by Match Referee Peter Burge for showing dissent by indicating that the ball came off his pad when given out caught behind.[58] Clearly from the earliest days of the new legal system of prohibition, players continued to breach the legal and ethical norms requiring them to respect the umpire's decision and they did so in a variety of ways. As fielders and batters, as victims and unsuccessful appellants, for catches and LBW, the opportunities to accept the umpire's decision and get on with the game were avoided and replaced, by senior players for the most part, by open resistance to the idea that the umpire is either right or his decision, whether right or wrong, must be accepted.

In 1995, Wasim Akram showed his dissent by snatching his hat from the umpire after an unsuccessful appeal. South African wicketkeeper David Richardson, a solicitor, hit a stump out of the ground after being run out.[59] The next year, Danny Morrison, New Zealand bowler, and also a solicitor, was fined for sinking to his knees and hitting the wicket after an LBW appeal was rejected, and David Johnson of South Africa stood his ground rubbing his shoulder after being given out caught behind.[60] In 1997, Aamir Sohail of Pakistan and Mohammed Azharuddin of India were found guilty of lingering at the crease after being given out. South African spinner Pat Symcox was convicted the same year of objecting to the umpire's refusal of a bat-pad appeal.[61] Graham Thorpe of England was reprimanded for standing his ground for seven seconds after having been given out and Adam Parore and Stephen Fleming of New Zealand were punished for dissenting over a rejected appeal for caught behind.[62]

The next year Shahid Afridi also lingered at the crease and in 2000 Arshad Khan of Pakistan did the same.[63] In 2001, England batter Graeme Hick questioned an umpire's decision in the first Test at Galle, while in the second Test at Kandy, Sanath Jayasuriya of the home team showed 'dissent by gesticulating while walking back to the pavilion'.[64] Glenn McGrath became the first offender of 2002 when he too remained at the crease after being given out in a One-Day International against New Zealand. He compounded his crime by gesturing and verbally abusing the umpire and was suspended for the next match.[65]

Again, this summary highlighting of only some of the dissent cases indicates the ongoing problem for the game and its system of law. Dissent, if not rife, continues to manifest itself on a regular basis. Charges are laid, trials are held, convictions entered, sentences imposed, and the crime wave continues. Is there an ethical code of respect for judicial authority? Has there ever been one? Is it different now? One of the key ideas which informs respect for the umpire or judge's opinion and findings must again be the fundamental notion of good faith. Part of this broader concept is based on the twin ideas of competence and neutrality. In cricket history, these questions have constituted the twin axes for jurisprudential and legal controversy. Are umpires unbiased adjudicators and are they capable arbiters of truth, law and justice on the field of play? I turn now to these questions.

10 The man in white is always right (but he is not always neutral)

It should be clear that no matter how cogently worded the *Laws of Cricket* may be and no matter how many years of practice have built up for us to call upon in cases of doubt or uncertainty, at a basic level, an umpire is bound by the nature of the game to make mistakes. Just as a judge may mistakenly believe in the credibility of a clever liar, thereby reaching an 'incorrect decision', an umpire dealing with the blur of a fast bowler and listening for a nick of the bat, or lifting his eyes quickly from the bowler's front foot to follow the flight and pitch of the ball to determine if the batter is out LBW, can easily be mistaken. As noted and respected former umpire Dickie Bird puts it:

> We are dealing with inches and fractions of seconds and are bound to fall into error at some time or another. What it is important to realise, however, is that umpires all over the world are honest men doing their best in difficult circumstances, without fear or favour.[1]

For these reasons, Bird historically opposed the creation of an international panel from which neutral umpires would be selected to stand in Tests. Proponents of the neutral umpire panel did not dispute Bird's contention that umpires are human and fallible, nor did they argue that members of such a panel would never err. They did argue, however, that not all umpires are equal and that only the best should serve in Tests, the pinnacle of cricket. Finally, they argued that there was enough historical and continuing evidence of at least an appearance of bias by 'home' umpires and that the apprehensions which follow would be best eliminated for the continuing good and credibility of cricket. While situations such as those described by Nandy where Indian umpires in a match against England '. . . not only jumped in joy when they gave English players out, but also broke into tears when they had to decide against Indian players'[2] were not common, it was felt there was a need for the introduction of neutral umpires.

Concerns, as we have seen, from New Zealand and England cricketers, about the neutrality and impartiality of Pakistani umpires were not based purely in colonialist and racist mythologies. In the early 1980s, two Pakistani umpires Khalid Aziz and Shoaib Mir, resigned because they refused to continue to follow directions on how to make decisions and what decisions to make.[3]

Early Australian teams visiting England criticized English umpires as biased. This was dismissed as the snivelling of the Colonials and as nothing more than a result which their own behaviour served to bring about.[4] Australians made similar complaints in domestic cricket where, again, umpires were identified with their respective teams.[5] By the 1880s, however, the domestic scene had changed and Australians concentrated for the most part on the merits of play rather than the merits of the umpiring.

Internationally, however, complaints about hometown bias continued. West Indian players complained about New Zealand umpires,[6] Indian players complained about Sri Lankans,[7] and as we have seen, England, Pakistan and Australia complained about each other's umpires. The case for neutral umpires became clearer and appeals for the system louder. Finally, John Hampshire and John Holder of England stood in the Pakistan–India Test series of 1989 and the Pakistani Board of Control for Cricket announced that Pakistan would not tour abroad unless Test series were supervised by umpires from neutral countries.[8]

After much debate the ICC introduced a series of measures under which a number of umpires would be nominated by their Boards to stand in international matches. All Tests would then be presided over by one 'domestic' umpire and one 'international' umpire who would not come from the visiting country. Here, at the official level of discourse about adjudication, the signifier 'neutral' was for the most part scrupulously avoided. This was made necessary because of the general unwillingness to face up publicly to the fact that two different, sometimes separate and sometimes interconnected issues were at play here. The first criticism of umpires at the time was one grounded in 'incompetence'. In other words, many umpires standing in Tests were just not 'good' umpires because they lacked the technical skills to adjudicate correctly. Injustices and illegalities occurred because umpires did not meet the basic standard of competence required as a *sine qua non* of judicial activity.[9] The rule of law was under threat because the norm of behaviour which required respect and unquestioning acceptance of umpires' decisions was becoming more difficult to enforce in such circumstances. If the umpires lacked even the most basic skills, the game of cricket could not in effect take place because there was no 'certainty' that adjudication would occur within basic minimal standards.

Of course, we shall still need to interrogate exactly what it is we mean by 'competence'. Is it the same as perfection? Certainly some advocates of the continued and expanded use of technology in adjudication, seem, by implication at least to adopt this position. Others argue that ideas of judicial competence include the notion of error, in other words because adjudication is a human interpretive activity, some level of error is to be expected. Of course, there will be built into this idea an understanding of minimum ability. Umpires, like judges, are not expected to be perfect, but they are expected to perform at a minimum level of ability which will include a collective understanding of 'easy' and 'hard' cases. Errors in hard cases will be acceptable while mistakes in what 'everybody' knows is an easy case will be an indication of incompetence. While it might be a simple and unproblematic proposition to assert the commonly accepted norm in such general terms, it is a much more difficult task to decide what is competence in more specific instances. As we shall see throughout the book, much of the debate about law-making and law application in cricket seems to occur around those cases in which some argue that there is in fact no doubt and everyone on the opposing side agrees in theory but not in substance. For the former, batter *x* was clearly out, for the latter, the same batter was clearly not out. A recent empirical study of umpiring 'competence' highlights many of the problems under review.

In the 2001/02 season, involving Tests between New Zealand and South Africa, and a triangular One-Day series with the same sides, the ACB subjected every appeal to *ex post facto* video review in order to determine the error rate of umpiring decisions. Putting aside here the important epistemological and methodological issues of how 'error' was determined under such a system, the ACB found that of 363 appeals, the umpires were 'right' 345 times. This produces a score of 95 per cent or an error rate of 5/100.[10] The problem, as the ACB recognized, is that because this is the first study of its kind, there is no point of comparison. Do these figures place these umpires at the top or the bottom of their profession? Is an error rate of 5 per cent high, low or average? Is it acceptable? In other words, we know that umpires in these international matches got it right much more often than they committed an error. At the same time, we know that batters were given out when they should not have been. Bowlers were given wickets when they should not have, and batters were allowed to bat when they should have been on their way to the pavilion. Conversely, bowlers were denied wickets they should have received and batters were out when they should have been allowed to continue. Is this fair? Is it law? Is it cricket? Again, all we can say with any certainty here is that adjudication, even by the most competent umpires available, will be subject to error. The fact itself will not lead us to the truth about law or about cricket. How we classify and construct this 'fact' of and about the 'acceptable' level of error, and what we mean by 'error', will determine our definition of competence in adjudication.

The second type of critique of the then current umpiring system was based on ideas of 'bias' and 'bad faith'. In other words, when umpires were not incompetent, they were biased in favour of the home team or against the visitors. Here again, a minimum standard for all adjudication is under threat. Bad faith in the end means that umpires are acting in a non-judicial fashion, deciding not on the merits and applying the appropriate rules to the best of their ability but according to prejudice and bias. Once more, in those circumstances injustice was the natural consequence. Cricket was not cricket in such conditions.

Even the creation of the panel of umpires to stand in Test matches accompanied by an arrangement as to funding left unanswered difficulties, not the least of which was the perception for some of the existing disparity between Test-playing countries.

While the move to neutral, or to be more technically accurate 'international', Test umpires was inevitable, it did very little to clarify or eliminate the ambiguities which limit and determine the process of cricket adjudication. While the element of national bias was meant to disappear (or take on a different guise as Nandy postulates), this was clearly not the case. In effect, only one half of the problem was even addressed under this system. A home umpire was still to stand and adjudicate in every Test match. His decisions would be just as final as those of the visiting neutral umpire. They would also be as prone to allegations of bias, incompetence and racism as they had always been. Sri Lanka, for example, was involved in a well-publicized international controversy when it objected to the selection of Australian Darrell Hair as an umpire in any match in which they played, on the ground that he was biased against them. This alleged bias first manifested itself when Hair stood as the 'home' umpire in games in Australia, but the Sri Lankans objected to him acting as the 'neutral' umpire in games played elsewhere. Thus the idea of a 'neutral' umpire did not eliminate the old attacks on either competence or bias grounds. It simply replaced the context in which such debates occurred.

During the Australian tour of India in 1998, the visitors and the accompanying media complained bitterly about the standard of umpiring and about the decisions which went against them. These complaints were aimed at both the Indian umpires and the 'neutral' umpire. In the Test at Chennai/Madras, the Australians complained bitterly about several decisions.

> Ironically three of the decisions were given by English umpire George Sharp. Two were absolutely dreadful. This should help establish a view that, by and large, umpires around the world are not cheats, just bad umpires.[11]

On the other hand, when India toured Australia the next year, the series was beset by allegations and accusations that the home umpires were biased against the visitors and that the bias was informed by racism.[12] Allegations of incompetence and bias were also levelled at the neutral umpire. The Pakistanis made similar assertions about Australian umpiring.[13] The umpires objected and protested to the ACB, which disciplined and stood down the leading Australian umpire Darrell Hair, not for bias or incompetence, but for speaking out publicly about complaints of incompetence and racism levelled against him.[14]

In 2000, Sri Lanka complained about a perceived lack of competence and neutrality by Pakistani umpire Riazuddin.[15] Zimbabwe also complained about Riazuddin's competence.[16] England expressed concerns about the technical abilities of Pakistani umpire Javed Akhtar.[17] Indians have complained about the adjudication skills and ability of New Zealander Steve Dunne, standing in India as the 'neutral' umpire.[18] The 2001 series between England and Sri Lanka in Sri Lanka was marred and marked by dissent, excessive appeals and general disgust at the incompetence of several decisions.[19] Simon Rae wrote of the series: 'The umpiring was undeniably poor. Of the 40 wickets that fell in the first two Tests, the *Independent* reckoned that 22 were the result of bad decisions.'[20]

Finally, in April 2002, the ICC caught on to the fact that the 'neutral' umpire system was not working precisely because it still left itself open to ongoing and irrebuttable attack on the joint grounds of bias and incompetence. Instead, it introduced a new system of elite umpires. Here, in Test matches, both the umpires who would be chosen to adjudicate will be selected from the elite panel. The One-Day selections will, for the time being, be made up of one elite panel member and one international member, i.e. the most competent local umpires, in theory at least. Members of the panels were selected in part on the basis of past performance and after consultation with all the captains of Test-playing nations. The ICC clearly wishes to be seen to be ensuring that adjudication will now take place in an atmosphere imbued with confidence and competence.

> Umpiring is one of the toughest tasks in international sport and this panel represents the best decision makers in the game. Their skills will help improve the overall standard of umpiring at the international level and set an example for the next generation of top class umpires to follow.[21]

Nonetheless, debates and controversies about issues of 'competence' continue to circulate. During the Indian tour of the West Indies in early 2002, the elite system of umpiring was used. Daryl Harper of Australia and Ashoka de Silva of Sri Lanka stood in the matches. One local commentator summarized the situation as follows:

> The game of cricket is filled with bad umpiring decisions, they are part of the game, and over time the players have come to accept them on the reasoning that umpires, being human, can and will make mistakes and that in a career they balance themselves out.[22]

Yet the mistakes allegedly made by Harper and de Silva meant that their '…skill…deserves to be questioned'.[23] Again there is nothing surprising here, no new jurisprudential or practical issues are raised. What is of interest is that the idea of competence and skill in adjudication will not go away. That under the new elite system the questions and debates remain the same is the most important legal insight here.[24]

11 Technology, adjudication and law

As debate continued and continues around issues of umpiring competence, a further complicating factor has entered the jurisprudential arena. Here we confront the intersection of technology and law, and of the ideology of adjudication. For those who seek certainty and an 'objective' truth as the goal of every act of interpretation, the idea of using 'technology' if not to judge, then to assist the judiciary in their task of finding the truth, has a strong, if not overwhelmingly persuasive appeal. The idea here is that in many cases, television replays have for several years given viewers at home and fans in the stadium an almost instant basis for judging the facts, and then assessing the 'correctness' of the umpire's decisions for themselves. Why should not umpires themselves have access to the same technology? This would result in 'better' decisions and decision-making. Correct decisions could be reached because umpires could see what really happened. They would have more time to adjudicate than they have in being forced to determine with the naked eye an appeal for a run out or a stumping for example. Thus, the right decision would be more likely. Moreover, if correct decisions were made more often as a result of referring to technological assistance, then the whole process of decision-making would gain more respect.[1]

Here human frailty would be replaced by the reproduction of truth by television camera. The facts would be established once and for all and from that would follow the simple and mechanical application of the appropriate legal rule. There is, of course, some obvious truth to the matter. Recourse to replays for run out decisions or stumpings would allow for a more careful examination of events and facts than adjudication by the naked eye permits. This would and should then lead to more accurate decision-making and thence to greater respect for the judicial function. Certainty and accuracy will negative and displace debates about the problem of umpiring competence since technology is by definition competent.

Here, however, several objections can be and were raised. First, by introducing technology, the game's authorities would be at some level offering up further admissions that there was in fact a certain level of incompetence which had led the game into disrespect. This admission erases the difference between competence and perfection. Instead it asserts that there is a truth and that any falling short of that measure is not a simple good faith mistake and acceptable human error, but failure and incompetence.

This idea of truth, of objectivity brings into question both the understanding of adjudication in cricket and of the nature of the game.[2] For some, there must be some direct relationship between objective perfection and truth in adjudication, For others, there can be neither truth nor perfection. In the cricket context this comes down to the idea of what it means to play the game. Is cricket a human undertaking, played under rules of human construction and interpreted by humans, or is it an objective mechanical operation? Of course, there are variations to these positions, some important, some of only hypothetical and theoretical importance. The real question here is about the nature and practice of rule-application in the game. Is cricket a human game subject to objective laws or one in which adjudication by umpires is an essential element? In other words, could we have a game of cricket under the *Laws* with two teams of 11 players and machine, or computer-generated adjudication? Do we need umpires for there to be 'cricket' or do we simply need adjudication of some type?

If umpires are not necessary, their presence is the consequence not of the taxonomy of the idea 'cricket', but of the imperfection of computer technology. With Hawkeye,[3] television and computer-generated projections, some kind of technology similar to the Cyclops used in tennis for service line calls,[4] there is no need for human umpires and adjudication could be a simple matter of applying facts to law in a database.

If umpires are necessary, then the introduction of technology can be seen to assist in their function but not to replace them. The question will then always be one of striking a balance between the use of available technology and the foundational idea that umpires are essential to the law-making activity we call 'cricket'.[5] Some will argue for more technology, some will assert that we need less. The debate will always be informed by some understanding of what we mean by adjudication and what the goals of the process are. Are we after 'truth', or a process that allows us contingent access to something we will call 'truth' until we learn more or have 'better' access to a still contingent understanding?

What do we mean by law and how does it fit with our understandings of the search for truth? What about justice? Can it exist without 'truth', or without 'law'? In this area, there is still a fundamental conflict in debates about the use of televised replays. There are those who believe that there is a truth which is reproduced in televisual images. For them, technology allows umpires to apply the law to the 'facts', as objective reality, law and justice become one. Others will believe that television images are themselves texts to be interpreted and given meaning through a contextualization of that text 'TV replay' with other texts, for example the *Laws of Cricket*.

Neither text can or does represent reality or objectivity in the sense understood by proponents of the first position. Instead, by reading and applying the various texts in context, TV replay, the applicable law, the game at hand, the history of the *Laws* and the game etc., we create the world of law and cricket which is made up of these interpretive objects, texts, which we read and apply.

The answers which we give to any or all of these questions will be determined by what we believe 'cricket' to be and will in turn determine our understandings of 'cricket'. What is certain is that certainty is elusive. In Feb. 2000, respected English umpire David Shepherd encouraged and applauded the use of television technology in adjudication and called for more of it.[6] Later Shepherd and West Indian umpire Eddie Nichols were publicly shamed and humiliated after replays of several dismissals they had given during a Test between England and Pakistan were shown to have come from balls delivered by bowlers overstepping the front line of the crease. Shepherd later revealed he almost gave up his umpiring career as a result.[7]

In 'fact', if not in law, the batters were not out since the delivery which 'dismissed' them was a no-ball. Spectators were treated to constant replays of the bowler overstepping, the umpire failing to detect or signal the transgression and then to the umpire raising his finger to confirm the dismissal.[8] This simply replicated the performance of South African television in the 1997 series between Australia and the home side.

Is this the failure of law-making, of law application or part of the human activity which makes cricket such an enjoyable game and important jurisprudential activity? Some would argue that technology exists to determine if the bowler oversteps and should be used. To fail to do so allows injustice to prosper. Batters are given out to no-balls, the rule of law in cricket teeters on the brink of anarchy. On the other hand, this would mean that every delivery would need to be scrutinized by a video umpire as a possible no-ball. The delay would be considerable in a game which is often criticized for being too slow as it is. What about the injustice on the batter in such circumstances? Say he hits the ball and attempts a single and is caught short of his ground. He can be run out from a no-ball.[9] The penalty for a no-ball is one run.[10] Had he known that the ball was a no-ball he might not have chosen to try for a single. The lack of immediate decision-making in this case would result in him being out in circumstances which could be seen to be unjust and illegal. Where he relies solely on the jurisdiction of the umpire at the non-striker's end, his dismissal might still be in the eye of some both unlawful and unjust, but they will take on a different character and typology. Introducing technology would not by definition remove injustice or ensure more legality, it would merely change the type of disputes about illegality and injustice which might arise.

Indeed, there are cogent arguments, or ridiculous ones depending both on one's perspective and broader jurisprudential ideological position, that the insistence on examples of judicial error in the no-ball case miss the point about the law and the nature and role of adjudication itself. Thus Peter Roebuck asserts,

> Cricket hasn't changed much. Some umpires are pedants and others are broadminded. Some call 'no balls' with the enthusiasm of zealous traffic wardens and are reluctant to decide anything else. Others only bother if a bowler takes too much too often. This latter school of thought attracts most of the better men and many of the better umpires, including Venkat. None of the local commentators has ever worn a white coat in serious company.[11]

Again, Roebuck's comments will be applauded or rejected depending on how one views the nature and scope of adjudication and what philosophical position one finds most comfortable. A legal formalist will condemn any umpiring which disregards the letter of the law, while others will concur with the observation that adjudication is practical wisdom, *phroenesis*, not formalism. Whatever one thinks, technology itself will not provide the answer.

What I wish to do in what follows is to offer a brief summary of the legal regime which now regulates the use of technology, more precisely televised replays, in adjudication. Then I shall examine a few examples of the ways in which the new legal regime has in fact been put into practice in order to evaluate the main jurisprudential issues raised by that system of adjudication.

The Law

Over the past few years, the ICC has introduced a series of *Rules and Regulations* governing the use of televised replays in international matches. The *Laws of Cricket* remain unchanged and refer only to the two umpires who stand at the non-striker's end and at square leg. The ICC *Rules and Regulations* have created another level of judicial authority for the interpretation and application of the *Laws*, the third umpire, or television replay official. The *Rules and Regulations* now permit the third umpire to adjudicate by the now familiar system of red and green lights in cases of appeals for dismissals by way of run out, stumped, caught and hit wicket. He may also decide on issues concerning boundary decisions (did the fielder touch the boundary and the ball at the same time? etc.) and to determine which batter is out when they have both run to the same end.[12]

The issues arising from this last part of the third umpire's jurisdiction are illustrated in the following case. During a One-Day series between India and Australia, Mark Waugh and Darren Lehmann were batting. As is often the case with Waugh, there was a mix up and both Australians ended up at the same end. The bails were removed and Lehmann walked off. Indian captain Sourav Ganguly remonstrated with the umpires and asked for a replay to determine which of the two batters should have been given out. Somewhat bizarrely, given Ganguly's disciplinary record and the clear wording of the *Rules* which forbid any player from asking for a referral to the third umpire, he was not disciplined for his actions.[13] Waugh went on to score 133 not out and Australia won the game. The problem was exacerbated by revelations that there was in fact no camera angle available which would have shown which of the batters should have been given out.[14]

Again, decisions or non-decisions are interpretive practices, subject to debate, argument and disagreement. At some level, the creation of a new jurisdiction to allow better decision-making and more certainty has created nothing other than more uncertainty and dispute over questions of law and fact. In the Mark Waugh case, there was no available technology which would have allowed interpretive access to the 'correct' answer. For some this is evidence of the failures of technologically based umpiring and supports a return to pure adjudication by on-field umpires. For others, this is strong evidence that error is caused by the lack of appropriate technology and offers support for more adjudication by properly equipped third umpires.

The text of the *Regulation* offers several interesting and important insights into the restructuring of the judicial process in cricket and the limits set on jurisdictional questions. It is clear from the subordinate legislation that the creation of the new jurisdiction of the replay official, third umpire, or television umpire, as he is variously called, is dependent upon the on-field umpire. Thus paragraph, 2.1(c) sets out the first limitations on the appellate jurisdiction of the replay official.

> The on-field umpire has the discretion whether to call for a TV replay or not and should take a common-sense approach.

Thus, if the umpire on the field feels that he can decide without referring to the replay, he can and should do so. At the same time, if there is some doubt, if he was not in a good position, or if he was unsighted for example, or events occurred too quickly, then he should and will seek assistance. All of this would be part of a 'common sense' approach. At this level, the creation of the new adjudicative position is clearly supplementary and subjected to the jurisdiction and discretion of the traditional umpires. The third umpire has no independent authority and can act only when called upon to do so by the umpires on the field.

At the same time our experience of this form of adjudication also indicates that the idea of an easily determined 'common sense' about when the umpire 'should' (but not 'must') refer to his colleague 'in the booth', is not as straightforward as one might believe after a simple reading of the text. Thus, we know that whether the umpire refers to the third official or not, fans watching at home, or at the game, will be treated to incessant replays of any controversial decision. Thus, there will be unofficial and public review of his decision whatever he does. In such a case, it could be part of a common sense approach for the umpire to refer every decision to the third umpire, thus relieving himself in some way of the 'responsibility' for any controversial decision. In fact, it is common practice for the umpire on the field to act in just this way. Some see this as an excellent development, allowing again under this view for more certainty in adjudication. Others argue that there are practical and jurisprudential issues of some consequence raised by this type of judicial behaviour. First, as already seen, it slows down the game. Although the third umpire is instructed to take 30 seconds to decide, this is only a guideline. Since he is entitled to take as many views of the play as are required to reach a decision, the guide is often ignored.[15] In addition, he finds himself in the same position as the on-field umpire in so far as public review is concerned. Fans in the stands and at home are seeing what he sees. Any 'incorrect' decision will be subject to instant judgement by telespectators. Indeed, some administrators have taken steps to limit the number of replays that can be seen at the game because constant views of umpiring 'mistakes' was felt to be bringing the game into disrepute.[16]

The second problem is that some see the recourse to video replay as an abdication of judicial responsibility by on-field officials. They are, so the argument goes, umpires. It is their job to decide and that is what they do; if they make a mistake, so be it. A decision by those empowered to decide is more important at some level than the correctness of that decision. A hesitant, unconfident umpire is a bad umpire. Referring to the video official is an indication that the umpire has little confidence in his own abilities. Given the limitations on the jurisdiction of TV officials to some types of dismissal, this lack of confidence, and the public recognition of the lack of confidence as evidenced in constant referrals to the third umpire, will have an adverse impact on the umpire's ability to decide, to adjudicate in those cases where he cannot have access to replays. In such cases, a mistaken determination will be made all the more problematic because of the perceived lack of confidence. An umpire with the courage of his convictions, so the argument goes, will take a different view of 'common sense' and only refer those decisions about which there is or can be real doubt. An umpire who refers a run out decision to the video official when the batter is a metre short of his ground is a bad umpire, lacking in common sense and judicial courage, and will be seen as such, both by players and by fans.

Finally another aspect of the jurisdictional position of the third umpire needs to be underlined here. The *Rules* make it clear that only the umpire may seek the assistance of the video umpire. Players may not make a direct appeal or even ask the umpire to refer the case to the video officials. Such actions on the field of play constitute 'dissent' and are subject to disciplinary action by the Match Referee.[17] In 1995, Ajay Jadeja of India and Mushtaq Ahmed of Pakistan were fined 10 per cent of their match fee for such an action.[18] The next year Hansie Cronje of South Africa was fined 50 per cent of his match fee for the same offence.[19] In 1997, Aamir Sohail was found guilty of the same offence in aggravated circumstances and was suspended for one match.[20] Once more, this clearly establishes the idea that the umpires remain masters of their own jurisdiction to decide on appeals. The third umpire has a limited jurisdiction, both in terms of the types of questions on which he may adjudicate but also in terms of when and under what circumstances he may be called upon to decide.

This does not mean that umpires are not prone to pressure and to context and that recourse to the third umpire may on some occasions be blatantly illegal and at the instigation of the players. Just such a situation obtained in the fifth Test between England and South Africa at Newlands, Cape Town in 1996. Graham Thorpe was originally given not out by umpire Dave Orchard after a run out appeal. Replays clearly showed that he was short of his ground. The crowd protested as did the South Africans. After consultation with fellow umpire Steve Randell, and at the urging of the South Africans, Orchard called for the video replay and Thorpe was given out.

Here the questions and issues are of major jurisprudential importance. Thorpe, on the 'facts', was out. In law, however, he was given not out. This is, at some level, an injustice or at the very least an incorrect umpiring decision. Had Orchard asked for help instead of deciding for himself, Thorpe would have been given out. Fact and law would have coincided and justice would have been seen to have been done. Instead, while the ultimate result was 'correct', i.e. no one argues that Thorpe had made his ground, the process by which it was reached may be seen to have been 'just' or 'unjust'. The conclusion one reaches on this point will be determined by one's ideas of adjudication, jurisdiction, democracy, technology and the rule of law. The South African players' decision to unlawfully appeal to the umpire to seek the assistance of the replay official was instigated in part by the crowd reaction to the replay screen. Here democracy, input by many members of the hermeneutic community of cricket observers, had a direct impact on the more discreet communities or sub-communities of players and officials. This is, then, either democracy in action or mob rule.

Similarly, the South African demand for a replay and adjudication on the replay was either an attempt to seek justice, to 'right a wrong', or else a cynical manipulation of the system and a blatant disregard for the rule of law. The umpire's decision to refer the decision to a replay was 'just' or the completely unlawful result of intimidation. Alan Lee puts his position as follows:

> The most significant of all the ramifications, however, is that this was an instance of a dismissal – and a crucial one – being imposed on an unwilling umpire by the ever more manipulative hand of television. Without TV replays, or even with no substantial crowd, Thorpe would not have been given out. This would have been an injustice, of course, but it would have been a decision taken by an umpire, in whom such power has always been invested, rather than one brought about by influences outside the running of the game.
>
> . . .
>
> My own objections to the system have been eased by the many occasions on which borderline decisions have been referred, and thus ruled upon correctly. But it works only if the technology is used consistently and if, when it is not, players accept the ruling.
>
>   The episode yesterday was a case of the umpire's decision not being final, and for reasons that cricket must not regard with complacency.[21]

At this level then, the introduction of technology in the form of television and video replays for decision-making purposes must always be established as an interpretive tool, an aid to adjudication and not as a way of allowing technology to decide. In the end, even when the third umpire is called upon and is vested with jurisdiction, he decides. An umpire still assesses the 'facts' and applies the *Law*. This is and must remain for many the most important point here. Adjudication still involves interpretation. Texts and images are interpreted in the booth just as they are on the field of play.

For example, it is important to underline here that there will be, until technology is perfected and until adjudicators become aware before they arise of potential problems, serious concerns about even the basic capacities of the technological innovation to provide factually 'accurate' views of what has happened on the field.[22] In the early days of adjudication on run outs for example, it became clear that when a batter was using a runner, a practical factual problem arose. When the injured batter is facing, the runner stands well wide of the playing surface. This has sometimes posed problems in ordinary adjudication since the runner will be out of view of the umpire. In replay situations, it became clear that adjudication was in some cases impossible because the TV official could not tell with any accuracy if the runner's bat had been grounded behind the line before the bails were removed. The crease line simply did not extend far enough to be able to tell where the bat and the line were in relation to each other. Of course, the solution is and was obvious. The line was extended. A low-tech solution to a high-tech legal problem.

Still, in the absence of further technological innovation, adjudication for stumpings and run outs still remains fraught with a similar problem. How can the umpire tell when the bat is grounded? Given the three dimensional reality represented in televisual two dimensionality, whether the bat is actually touching the ground or the grass is sometime impossible to tell.[23] Similar concerns arise and continue to cause debate in instances of fielders claiming catches close to the ground. In such cases the umpire must give the benefit of the doubt to the batter. Similarly, the angle of the camera or the fact, again, that a fielder is blocking the view of the stumps or the crease may mean that the third umpire simply cannot be sure when or if the batter grounded his bat or the bail was dislodged by the keeper.[24] In the fifth Test of the 1999 Ashes series at the SCG, Michael Slater was given not out for just such a reason.

> ...It transpired that the cameras on which [third umpire Simon] Taufel relied were not perpendicular to the crease, and that the bowler Such, had inadvertently obscured the precise instant of the stumps' disintegration.[25]

Slater, on 35 at the time, went on to score 123 and Australia won by 98 runs. Of course, we can never know what might have happened had Peter Such not been in the way or the cameras better placed. What we do know is that in all televised replay decisions, there must still be interpretation and adjudication. In other words, the 'facts' of televisual reality cannot replicate, duplicate or signify the facts in reality. In the 2002 Nat West One-Day series between England, India and Sri Lanka, dark coloured stumps and bails were used. On more than one occasion, the third umpire was unable to 'fully' adjudicate on run out appeals because the television monitors and replays could not, particularly with the blue uniforms of the England and Sri Lankan players at the stumps, accurately allow the viewer to determine the exact moment when the bails were dislodged. The technological solution would of course simply have been to use white bails, allowing the contrast to assist in adjudication. Adjudication is interpretation and in the absence of a clear text to be interpreted, the umpire can only decide not to decide.

The idea that certainty now reigns in cricket adjudication, or at least part of cricket adjudication is based in the epistemological error that insists that television is truth.[26] Even a brief review of some examples of decided cases under the new regime will amply demonstrate that television will not change in any fundamental way the freedom and constraint of adjudication involved in playing the game of cricket. At the same time, it is important to bear in mind that there will always exist, as long as adjudication in the booth is in the hands of a human umpire, no matter how expert, 'errors' can and will occur.[27] These errors will be due to carelessness, inattention, stupidity, malice, bias etc. In other words, this form of adjudication will inevitably be subject to criticism grounded in issues of bias and incompetence, just as all adjudication which has preceded it has been.[28]

In the earliest days of the technology, the problem was that the reality presented by television replays was simply inadequate to allow proper adjudication. Camera angles, the position of fielders and batters etc. often obscured the view of the wicket to such an extent that the third umpire could simply not decide.[29] Sometimes, as in the Port-of-Spain Test between England and the Windies, the TV replay umpire did not have access to all the angles of replay available to television viewers at home. In that game, he gave Adam Hollioake out run out. The replays to which he had access did not show that the wicketkeeper had dislodged the bail with his glove before he caught the ball.[30] In another case, South African wicketkeeper Dave Richardson was given out despite everyone agreeing that he beaten the attempt to run him out. The third umpire shared this view. Unfortunately for Richardson, the umpire revealed: 'I pressed the right button, but the wrong light came on.'[31]

Today the on-field umpires can communicate by means of walkie talkie with the third umpire and vice versa in such cases, but the fact remains that Richardson is and was given out, not by an umpire or by an umpiring error, but by technology.

But the problem of error in interpretation remains a key part of third umpire adjudication. Here, of course, the problem is not technological fallibility but human interpretative practice. In addition, of course, one must also see the use of the third umpire not just as a legal question. We must also interrogate ethical issues to see if they have been affected in any way by the introduction of the television replay official. Let us take the example of catches which are 'claimed' here. We know that traditional understandings of cricketing jurisprudence and normativity impose an obligation on any player who 'knows' that he did not take a catch cleanly not to appeal or to withdraw an appeal made by a teammate. Not to do so is 'cheating', 'sharp practice' and 'not cricket'. Indeed, it might be argued that the introduction of televised replays, slow motion video, freeze frames and the development of technology which allows the image of the ball to be 'blown up' at the moment of the catch, might have a positive impact by exposing cheats to the public and to their fellow players, the umpires and Match Referees. Conversely, there is the vexed question of 'walking' and whether a batter will or should remain at the wicket pending adjudication by the third umpire.[32]

For the fielder (and for the batter in some cases) the question which remains is what should be done in those cases in which there is some doubt, in which the player believes he has taken the catch but is unsure. Should he appeal or in the absence of certainty is there some moral obligation not to invoke the jurisdiction of the umpire? Now it might be argued that one can more easily and ethically refer the matter for adjudication. If there is any doubt, the *Rules* now impose two further stages of judicial decision-making. Paragraph 2.3, which deals with catches, imposes the obligation not found in the *Law* dealing with catches (Law 32) but contained in the general provisions of Laws 3(13) and 27(6) for the umpire to consult with his colleague in cases of doubt.[33] If that process does not decide the appeal, recourse can be had to the third umpire. Thus, a fielder in some doubt can appeal, certain that if the *Law* is followed to its full extent, three umpires will be involved in determining if the catch has been made. This might well be seen as removing any existing ethical obligation not to appeal and to confirm the idea again that umpires are there to decide and any determination as to whether the ball carried or was taken cleanly should be left to them.[34]

As one might imagine, the matter does not end there. Again there must be a point at which adjudication occurs. The umpire may be certain that the catch was or was not taken and will decide accordingly, assuming again that he is not 'cowed' into referring the case to the third umpire for fear of public criticism. The second umpire may be certain and convince his colleague to decide. Finally, if the case is referred to the third umpire, he must decide. He must interpret the images. Whatever he decides, like all other instances of doubt and debate, this will be open to approval or criticism.

Thus in an Ashes Test match in 1998, the England team lodged an official letter of protest as the result of a decision by the replay official. They argued in fact and in law, that he was wrong. Mark Taylor appealed for a low catch of Mike Atherton taken from the bowling of spinner Stuart MacGill. The English manager Graham Gooch put their case as follows: 'The TV umpire [Paul Angley] made a decision in a very short space of time. Mark Taylor has nothing to apologise for. He asked a legitimate question about the catch and tomorrow we'll get on with the game'.[35]

The issues here are of course familiar. The *Rules* now state that a decision should be made in 30 seconds. The English side claimed that the umpire decided too quickly. Replays on Channel 9's television coverage, according to columnist Phil Wilkins, left '... only grave reservations as to whether Taylor had swept the ball up on the half-volley'.[36]

The umpires consulted, the third umpire viewed the replay until satisfied that the catch had been taken and Atherton was given out. Channel 9 commentators were left in some doubt but Wilkins' own reaction was that Taylor had taken '... a brilliant reflex catch, as clean as a whistle, whatever waling emerges from Fleet Street'.[37]

The ethical position seems clearly established. The English have no complaints about Taylor's right to appeal or the appropriateness of his actions. The debate is over the law, the facts and the interpretive process. Was the catch taken? Could one tell at all? Could one tell so quickly? Was this another case of whingeing Pom syndrome? Again the answer one gives to any, some, or all of these questions will not be determined by objective reality but by a complex set of starting points, ideological and political positions and by what one believes one saw on the television. There is nothing different in this interpretive process. It is, as Allan Hutchinson would say, all in the game. Again, of course, it is important to underline the ethical terrain on which these debates also took place. Taylor believed he had taken the catch, Atherton stood his ground. He felt no obligation to accept the word of the Australian captain and walk; he waited for the three umpires to decide. Even then, the decision was not acceptable to the English. Walking, gentlemanly conduct, a player's word is his bond, the umpire's decision is sacred – all of these ethical norms of real 'cricket' seem to have been replaced by technological adjudication.

Two separate adjudicative instances, each of which took place in Australia and each of which involved the 'third umpire', offer final evidence that technology will never to able to provide the certainty its proponents seem to seek. Technology will never reduce uncertainty in adjudication because television replays do not judge, umpires do. Replays are an interpretive tool, they are not interpretation. The provisions of Law 35 of the 1980 *Code*, 'Hit Wicket', and their interpretation in each of two cases, offer convincing evidence of the glorious uncertainty of cricket and the law.

The *Law* in its relevant provisions stated:

The Striker shall be out Hit Wicket if, while the ball is in play:–

(a)   His wicket is broken with any part of his person, dress, or equipment as a result of any action taken by him in preparing to receive or in receiving a delivery, or in setting off for his first run, immediately after playing, or playing at, the ball.

The *Note* to the *Law* added:

A Batsman is not out this Law should his wicket be broken in any of the ways referred to in 1(a) above if:–

(i)   It occurs while he is in the act of running, other than in setting off for his first run immediately after playing at the ball. . . .

For the purposes of the two cases under examination here, the key point is that the wicket must be broken either while the batter is preparing to receive or is receiving the delivery or upon setting off for his first run 'immediately' after 'playing or playing at' the ball. There is a temporal limitation placed on the applicability of the *Law*. If the wicket is broken at some other time, the batter is not out 'Hit Wicket'.[38] The first case occurred during a tour match between Victoria and the visiting West Indies team in 1996. Brian Lara was hit on the gloves by a rising delivery from Victorian bowler David Saker. The ball flew over the gully area and Lara stood watching the ball fall safely, before setting off on a run after being called through by his partner. They ran two, after which the Victorians noticed that one of the bails at Lara's end was on the ground. They appealed and the square leg umpire referred the case to the third umpire, who had jurisdiction over Hit Wicket decisions. After reviewing the evidence, the official gave Lara out. The West Indians were not content. The twelfth man was sent on to the field to query the umpires who claimed that the matter was out of their hands once the replay official had ruled. They were *functus officio*, in administrative law terms without jurisdiction. The Windies' management raised the issue again during the tea break but were told that nothing could be done.[39] Here the point of dispute was not whether Lara had dislodged the bail. The issue was whether he had done so 'in setting off for his first run, immediately after playing' as required by the *Law*. The Windies claimed that it was clearly established by the evidence that Lara hesitated at the wicket, looking for and at the ball, before setting off on a run. If this were the case, he had not started on his first run 'immediately'. As a matter of law, on the facts, he could not be given out 'Hit Wicket'. There was no factual basis for his dismissal and the third umpire as a result committed an error of law. If the Windies' interpretation of the facts is correct, and it appears to be, then they are almost certainly correct, unless 'immediately' is given another interpretation.

This would permit the passage of a short period of time, assuming that the passage of time was still, for example, part of the whole process of playing and starting off on the first run. Under this interpretation, the phrases 'immediately after playing' and 'setting off for his first run immediately after playing at the ball', could arguably be said to evidence a legislative intent to penalize a batter who puts down his wicket in the period of playing his shot and attempting a first run. This period would be interpreted as 'immediate', depending on the circumstances. In other words, there are two possibilities here. First, that the umpire made an error of law in deciding that Lara hit the wicket 'immediately' after playing the ball and the batter was erroneously and without any foundation in law, given out. Secondly, that the umpire's interpretation of 'immediately' can be and is justified and that Lara is out. Each can be justified on the facts and on legally sound arguments about the interpretation of the provisions of the *Law*. In cases such as this, a television replay adds evidence, allows the umpire a chance to review what has happened. It does not interpret and give legal and practical effect or meaning to the word 'immediately'. We do that as we watch the replay and listen to debates about the meaning of the *Law*. The Windies' management does that, the umpire does too. Television may rule our lives but it does not rule the *Laws*.

This becomes even more evident in the second case of Hit Wicket jurisprudence. During a Test between Australia and South Africa at the Adelaide Oval, Mark Waugh was proving to be an obstacle to a South African victory. He had been batting all day and frustrating the visitors in their quest. Waugh was hit on the elbow by a rising delivery. He, '...took three steps backwards and then appeared to nonchalantly flick the bails off the stumps with his bat'.[40]

The South Africans appealed, the third umpire watched the television replay and Waugh was given not out. The South Africans protested, expert television commentators disagreed about the legality of the umpire's verdict. Waugh later revealed that he had lost feeling temporarily in his elbow and that the bat had hit the stumps as the result of an uncontrollable involuntary action. His defence was the cricket equivalent of reflex action or automatism in law.[41]

Yet his defence was irrelevant. The entire decision depended on the meaning given to the words, 'in receiving a delivery'. Waugh did not set off on a run, so the interpretive context is somewhat different here than the one under which the case of *Saker v. Lara* was decided. Was Waugh still 'receiving the ball' when his bat hit his wicket? Clearly the South Africans asserted that the umpire should take a similarly holistic interpretive position to that adopted in *Lara's* case. They would see the entire process of being struck and stepping back after having been hit as one circumstance of 'receiving a delivery'. For the umpire however, Waugh at some point prior to hitting his stumps, had stopped 'receiving' and even though the ball was not yet dead, some other legal situation obtained. Since he was no longer receiving the ball and he was not setting off on a run, none of the conditions precedent to a dismissal for 'Hit Wicket' was fulfilled and Waugh was not out.

The interpretive situation can be described as follows:

> Umpires may have some difficulty in deciding when the striker has finished receiving a delivery. Both the follow through of the bat after hitting the ball and movement to ensure that his bat does not make contact with the ball must be included as part of receiving it.[42]

Waugh's actions clearly do not fall within the type described here, although the list is not exhaustive. Nonetheless the replay official clearly decided that the *Law* could only apply while the batter was receiving the ball and that he was, when his bat hit the stumps, no longer in that position.

Again, the players disagreed among themselves. South Africans appealed and dissented; Waugh maintained his innocence. The third umpire gave him not out and Mark Waugh saved his country from defeat by ending the day unbeaten on 115 not out, after having been dropped by South Africa when he was on 1, 96, 107 and 108. The presence of technology here played no role in interpretation except in providing some evidence once again upon which the correct judicial determination could be made. The crucial element was the umpire's interpretation of what he saw in light of the text of the legal provision. In the end, no matter how many replays we watch, Mark Waugh was not out at the end of the day because of an umpire's determination of the practical, contextual meaning of 'receiving a delivery'. *Phroenesis* versus technology. Adjudication wins every time. Otherwise, it just would not be cricket.

12 Leg before wicket, causation and the rule of law

Easily the most controversial of all the *Laws* in its practical application is the leg before wicket (LBW) rule. Law 36, modified, changed and applied in every game of cricket. According to former Test umpire Don Oslear 'This law causes more doubt, disagreement, debate and discussion than all of the other 41 put together.'[1]

Yet another authoritative text on the *Laws* and adjudication in cricket argues that an umpire's skill and reputation can be determined by the ability with which this *Law* is applied: 'LBW might be termed a high profile Law. The esteem, or otherwise, in which an umpire is held will depend very much on his ability, consistency and fairness in judging appeals for LBW.'[2]

Sunil Gavaskar, commenting on the umpiring in a One-Day game during the 2002 winter tour by England to India claimed quite simply that the visitors were 'robbed' as the result of a poor LBW decision: 'Leg-before wicket decisions are never the easiest to give nor are they unanimously accepted by the fielding side or the batting side, but the speed at which they were given made them look worse.'[3]

Clearly, arguments about bias and competence in adjudication inform almost every discussion about LBW decisions. The problems of drafting and applying the *Law* have resulted in almost constant claims that cricket is in crisis.[4] At the very least, LBW decisions by umpires are questioned, attacked, queried and accepted with a begrudging reluctance which seems grounded more in cricket fatalism than in any notion that the umpire's decision was in any jurisprudential way, correct.[5]

The first recorded LBW dismissal came in 1798, before that date LBW dismissals were a form of 'bowled'.[6] When 'padding-up' to the ball became a more popular technique for batters, the LBW *Law*, already controversial, had to be changed. The *Law* had already been amended nine times, between 1774 and 1831. Discussions, debates and changes took place between 1888 and 1901 and again in 1937, a change took place as a result of Bodyline,[7] so that today we have a law which reads:

Law 36   LEG BEFORE WICKET
1.   Out LBW
The Striker is out LBW in the circumstances set out below:
(a) The bowler delivers a ball not being a No ball
and (b) the ball, if it is not intercepted full pitch, pitches in line between wicket and wicket or on the off side of the striker's wicket

and (c) the ball not having previously touched his bat, the striker intercepts
the ball, either full pitch or after pitching, with any part of his person
and (d) the point of impact, even if above the level of the bails, either (i) is
between wicket and wicket

or (ii) is either between wicket and wicket or outside the line of the off
stump, if the striker has made no genuine attempt to play the ball with his
bat
and (e) but for the interception, the ball would have hit the wicket.

While there are what might be called some strictly formalistic issues which arise
from the interpretive practice surrounding Law 36, the primary difficulty which
informs the on-going debate concerning LBW appeals and decisions is one
clearly relating to the law/fact *nexus*.[8] The controversy surrounding LBW decisions is directly analogous to the debate over contentious causation problems in
the law of torts.[9] Even if we are able to put aside the question of LBW dismissals
for intentionally padding up, and its dependence on a determination on whether
the batter was playing a 'genuine' stroke and assume that the ball has not
pitched outside the leg stump, a basic jurisprudential dilemma remains. The
umpire is still faced with answering a speculative 'but for' question – 'But for' the
intervention of the 'pads' would the ball have continued on to strike the wicket?
Given the complexity of the issues involved, it is little wonder, for example, that
the *Laws* prefer, in the case of a ball which then goes on to the stumps, to consider
the batter 'bowled'. In such a case, as in all matters of judicial decision-making,
'certainty' is to be preferred to what must, in the end, be speculation about
events which did not occur.[10]

In addition to answering the final 'but for' question, the umpire must also
determine a vast array of condition-precedent issues – did the ball pitch from
wicket to wicket? Did it pitch on the off-side? If it is a full toss or yorker, would it
have pitched wicket to wicket? Is the point of impact in line with the wicket?
Did the ball strike the bat or the pad first?

In addition to answering these 'factual' and sometimes speculative questions
which directly relate to the applicability of Law 36, the umpire at the non-striker's
end must also immediately before turning his mind to them, examine the position
of the bowler's front and back feet to determine whether the delivery is a legal
one or a no-ball.[11] He might also, and at the same time, turn his attention to
determining whether the bowler is delivering a fair ball or 'chucking'.[12] In the
end, after all these considerations, the umpire's decision rests on speculation, no
matter how certain he might be. His only basis for decision is a *would have*.

It is little wonder then that LBW continues to create much heated debate and
controversy. Anyone standing in the position of the umpire at the non-striker's
end (as we appear to be when watching the match on television) can offer an
opinion as to whether the ball would have struck the wicket and television and
radio commentators do not hesitate to enter into prolonged discussion about the
umpire's decision in any given case.[13] Some appear to operate from the legal
perspective that umpires are today more prone to 'give' an LBW and an equally

strong perception that they are very often mistaken. There is a clear belief not only that the judicial process is not an objective scientific application of facts to law but that it is acceptable and necessary to openly and strongly criticize the umpire.

Yet while managers and journalists are free to question the validity of LBW decisions, players do not necessarily enjoy such freedom. Not all members of the various sub-interpretive communities which create and tell a story of cricket enjoy the same interpretive freedom. Since the introduction of the *ICC Code of Conduct*, of course, dissent by batters and bowlers in relation to LBW appeals and decisions, have been dealt with and punished by the Match Referee.

Added to the 'legal', 'factual' and 'speculative' issues of the LBW *Law* are the problems associated with the general questions of competence and of the national bias of umpires. If in many cases there is a practical, operative interpretive assumption by those involved that umpiring decisions may be based not solely on scientific objectivity but also on national favouritism, this problem of bias (real or apprehended) in judicial decision-making in cricket is exacerbated by the very speculative nature of the LBW *Law* itself. If there is bias, or if bias is feared or perceived, it is most likely to reveal or manifest itself in a decision-making situation, where, by definition, there must be elements of doubt and speculation or where institutional interpretive restraints may apply less strictly. In other words, the interpretation given by the umpire to the text of a factual situation involving Law 36 is immediately open to doubt because there is no ethos of shared meaning binding the interpretive community.[14] If an interpretation relies for its authority on the interpretive community's shared understanding of the interpretation's truth, or at least its truth claim, and if that community's under-standing of truth is expressed ideologically in terms of 'science' or 'objectivity', then any interpretation which can be discovered to assert nothing more than 'opinion' is bound to be not only less authoritative but, almost ironically, more free and unbounded.[15] It is, in fact, an interpretation more open to interpretation than one bounded by a collective understanding.[16] This is clearly the situation, or at least the perceived situation, of the LBW *Law*. Because of the interpretive and factual freedom involved, appeals to formalism are destined to founder on the rocky ground of practical impossibility or complexity. Indeed, it may well be that simple positivism can make its strongest case here where no appeal to science or objectivity will be acceptable to various members of the interpretive community.

Although it is seemingly impossible to determine whether 'in fact' each LBW decision is 'correct', or conversely, whether the individual decision was infected with bias, there is some evidence based on statistical compilation and analysis to indicate that, as in all other aspects of cricket practice, the answers are them-selves ambiguous and open to many highly contextualized interpretations. Science, in other words, proves the unscientific nature of science and of life.

In a 1981 study of all previous Test LBW decisions, John Sumner and Michael Mobley came up with statistics interesting enough not to stop debate but to rekindle it.[17] Their results showed that allegations or suspicions of bias may in some cases find a statistically relevant basis while, in other cases, the facts do not speak for themselves. For example, the only countries where a statistically significant percentage of home-nation bias was detectable were India, Pakistan and South Africa, with Indian umpires being the most likely to give out visiting batters LBW. In the West Indies, by contrast, West Indian umpires are more likely to give out their 'own' batters than any other country's umpires, and in New Zealand, visiting players were less likely to be given out LBW than anywhere else. Dismissals for LBW ranged from 32 per cent of all fallen wickets in the West Indies to 27 per cent in Australia.

While one reading of these results would permit us to assume that there is definitive home-team bias in some cases and not in others, such a conclusion cannot be justified in any *one* case. Even if one assumes, for example, that Indian umpires tend to harshly treat visiting batters in a statistical sense, this can in no way determine whether an individual dismissal of an Australian batter at Delhi was biased, partially biased (doubt resolved against the visitor's interest) or based totally and solely on the fact the ball would have hit the stumps. We simply cannot develop any epistemological basis on which to analyse a phenomenological occurrence, or in some cases, a non-occurrence, that is a refusal to adjudge the batter LBW. Similarly, the reluctance of New Zealand umpires, statistically, to give out visiting players LBW has no bearing on the fact that a particular decision may be right or wrong. At the same time, moreover, such statistically based analyses or inferences in relation to certainty may simply miss the point. Any particular umpire, making one decision on an LBW appeal, may well have, in his own mind, dismissed any uncertainty as to the facts of the delivery. Therefore, while the decision may have been from our 'outside' view of the facts, wrong, inside the judicial mind, he may well have been acting 'objectively' and in good faith with no consideration as to statistical tendencies of umpires and without any 'subjective' doubt as to the correctness of his decision.

Likewise, the reluctance of Australian umpires to give any batters out LBW, as well as the fact that there is no statistically valid difference between LBW dismissals of Australian or visiting batters, on one view, indicates that there is no evidence of bias. At the same time, however, the fact that statistically reluctant Australian umpires dismissed six Pakistanis LBW in one innings in a particular match, might indicate or allow us to infer a counter-statistical presumption of nationalistic bias. What is clear is that nothing in the debate over the LBW *Law* in theory or in practice is clear. What makes the debate so vociferous and ongoing is that no one – umpires, players or spectators – can find solace in rule formalism, nor can the debate simply shift to the purely ethical level. Unlike debates surrounding the practical application of other *Laws*, no clear-cut area of narrative discourse (*Laws versus* the spirit of the game) is possible. Every debate on LBW is obviously and publicly 'just' a matter of interpretation. While we may all belong to the same interpretive community, there remains no agreement as to the final and correct community interpretation nor indeed is there agreement as to the text (facts) we are supposed to agree to interpret.

In addition, just as the debate over the practical application of the LBW *Law* is situated in the shifting sands of disagreement over issues of 'fact', national bias or plain incompetence, further complexities can be added to more deeply contextualize the issues. As Sumner and Mobley pointed out, other 'non-legal' factors must be considered even when considering the validity of the statistics.[18] Are Australian batters more prone to LBW decisions in England because of their unfamiliarity with the nature of English wickets? Would such unfamiliarity cause hesitancy or back-foot stroke-play which might result in the ball striking the pad with the player in his crease? Are Australian umpires reluctant to give LBW dismissals because the bouncy pitch found most commonly in Australian conditions makes it less certain the ball would have struck the stumps? If so, does this mean that where they do allow LBW appeals they are more certain and therefore that Australian LBW decisions are more factually accurate? Does the same argument apply in reverse to English players in Australia? Can the tendency of West Indians to be dismissed at home be explained by some cultural idea-type of flair and natural, exuberant stroke play of West Indian master blasters? Is the New Zealand umpires' reluctance to give out visitors attributable to a native Kiwi politeness?

Of course, we must also be open to the interpretive possibility of umpiring which is simply bad or wrong. Simon Rae writes of the 2000/01 Sri Lankan tour by England.

> The bowler was the Sri Lankan captain Sanath Jayasuriya, who was bowling left-arm orthodox spinners from over the wicket on or outside the leg stump. A ball pitching a good nine inches outside the leg stump turned and hit (Alec) Stewart on the leg. Up went Jayasuriya, backed up by the irrepressible wicket-keeper Sangakkara, and to the amazement of everyone watching, up went the umpire's finger. Stewart publicly described it as the worst decision he had ever experienced in first-class cricket.[19]

We would need to enter many other circumstances into the interpretive matrix in order to offer a full reading of the legal text, over-appealing, tension and bitterness between the teams etc. But to focus on the 'facts' and the law of the case, a ball pitching outside leg stump can never legally justify an LBW decision. Here the umpire made a 'bad' decision. He was wrong. Yet we will not know if he was wrong because he was evil or incompetent; whether he had a moment of inattention or was badgered into the decision by insistent pleas from the Sri Lankan bowlers and fielders; whether he did not like Stewart and wreaked his revenge on him or made a mistake; whether Sri Lankan umpires are bad or simply more prone to give LBW decisions than others.

Simply posing these questions would indicate that neither rule formalism nor appeals to some universal ethic or spirit of the game can provide answers to the most hotly contested and on-going debate in 'legal' cricket. When we add to the confusion by pointing out that many Australians, with the advent of Shane Warne as a main strike bowler, now argue that the LBW *Law*, by denying *de jure* an appeal for dismissal on any delivery which pitches outside leg stump has deprived and devalued the game by favouring off-spin bowling, to the detriment of leg spin. A leg spinner may strike the batter on the pads, right in front of the stumps with a ball going on to hit the wicket, but especially if he is coming around the wicket, he will never get the batter out LBW because the ball will invariably pitch outside leg stump. Not only is the bowler disadvantaged, but the spectator is treated to the boring spectacle of the batter simply padding the ball away with impunity. The LBW *Law* was introduced and remains to force batters to play with the bat, to engage in the defining battle between bat and ball. Given that the leg side prohibition has much to do with preventing a vicious 'Bodyline' style attack of a fast bowler spearing in deliveries at the body of a right handed striker, the legislative purpose of the *Law* is not served and the game suffers as a result of maintaining the letter of the *Law* in such circumstances, which violate the spirit of the confrontation between bat and ball. Here, then, the nature, function, application and validity of Law 36 are all sent into a maelstrom of uncertainty.[20] The LBW *Law* is of so much concern quite simply because it is most apparently uncertain. The 1937 *Law*, like Bodyline itself, was a clear manifestation of cricket's early entry into the contingent interpretive world of 'post-modernism'.

Here, as in other cases we have already seen, proponents of legal change seek certainty in technological innovation. For several years, there have been claims that we have the technology which will enable us to remove the uncertainty from LBW decisions and therefore to prevent a constant state of jurisprudential crisis in the game. Umpires were being criticized for dismissing batters incorrectly, and for not giving out batters who should have been. Too many appeals were given; umpire Javed Akhtar gave eight batters out LBW in a test between England and South Africa and was condemned for bad decision-making. Other umpires were reluctant to give any batter out LBW and were attacked as gutless.[21] In order to restore law and order and respect for the process of judicial decision-making, as in many instances, appeals were made for technological help.

South African and New Zealand scientists made claims in the 1990s for the most foolproof technological system, a contest which might have tended to indicate that certainty was still far from our grasp.[22] In the 2001 season in England, Channel 4 and Sky, followed by other broadcasters, introduced 'Hawkeye', technology borrowed and adapted from military use to produce a virtual track of the ball after it hits the pad to 'determine' where it would have gone. Some argue that the technology is so good that it must be introduced not as a way in which television commentators and viewers can second guess or approve of the umpire's decision but as the adjudicator for LBW appeals. Of course, all of the familiar arguments are raised here. Referring LBW appeals to the third umpire would inevitably slow things down in a game which can be more than slow enough already. Conversely, as Mike Selvey argues, introducing such a system may well speed things up too much. More batters might be dismissed LBW, leading to games ending more quickly.[23] On the other hand, Dickie Bird's recent conversion to support for the technology is in fact informed by his interpretation that it proves that he was more often right than wrong. He was an umpire who was believed to be 'hard' on LBWs, deciding to give the benefit of the doubt to the batter. He claimed that 'Hawkeye' shows that more often than is commonly accepted the ball would have passed over the stumps, thus justifying his judicial reticence.[24]

For some, uncertainty is good and exciting and part of the indeterminacy which makes cricket such an enjoyable social practice and legal text. Technology is not perfect. Even 'Hawkeye' has to work on probabilities and mathematical projections since the ball never goes on to hit the wicket in such cases. It is still, even with 'Hawkeye'-type technologies, difficult to determine if part of the ball pitched in line with the leg stump. In the absence of technology to assist the technology, determinations would still be speculative and interpretive. Technology would serve to provide an aura of certainty in a process still by definition deeply informed by interpretation and therefore by uncertainty and contingency. For example, as Ian Botham pointed out during the Sky Sports coverage of the first Test of the 2002 series between Sri Lanka and England at Lord's, a certain degree of scepticism was still required about 'Hawkeye'-type technology. Cricketers and umpires, he argued, know that there is a hill, or slope at Lord's. The ball tends to follow that hill, and will, depending on the circumstances, miss the stumps even when it appears that it would be travelling straight on. For Botham, technology cannot know this. It is only as good as the information it receives and if it 'thinks' that the wicket at Lord's is a flat plane, it will be wrong. This is the uncertainty of cricket which is, or should be, the certain knowledge of players and umpires. Of course, an obvious reply to this would be to point out that any such information about the grade of the slope etc. at a particular ground can easily be measured by modern surveying techniques and factored into the computer program which drives the technology. The problem is not that something is knowable only to cricketers and umpires, but that that particular knowledge has not been rendered into the zeros and ones which drive 'Hawkeye'.

All of these problems, concerns and debates resurfaced in July 2002 when the ICC decided to trial the introduction of television replay adjudication for LBW decisions. On-field umpires will be permitted to refer to the third umpire LBW decisions, but only in limited circumstances. The question of whether the ball would have hit the stumps is still left in the hands of the umpire at the non-striker's end. He may refer the question of whether the ball pitched outside leg or whether it struck the inside edge of the bat before hitting the pads. One assumes therefore that the issue of the trajectory of the ball will constitute a condition precedent to any referral to the replay umpire. In other words, the umpire will be satisfied that the ball would have gone on to hit the stumps but will have some doubt as to where the ball pitched or if the batter struck the ball.[25] In the ICC Champions Trophy match between the West Indies and South Africa, Rudi Koertzen became the first replay official called upon to adjudicate on an LBW appeal.[26]

ICC cricket manager, solicitor and former South African keeper Dave Richardson articulated the by now familiar reason for the trial: 'Leg before wicket is one of the areas where umpires are making mistakes, time and time again.'[27]

Technology is thus introduced into the adjudicative process in this part of cricket and the law as a result of the incompetence critique. In other words, umpires are not capable of meeting minimum standards for deciding LBW cases. Of course, the referral of the decision to the third umpire does not in and of itself solve this problem. First, the incompetent umpire must at some level be aware of his incompetence and make the decision to refer the case, unless of course we reach the point where all decisions are sent to the television replay official. Secondly, the television replay official must be in a position to decide, for example, where the ball pitched. Given our own experience of watching televised replays during matches, it is not difficult to imagine that this will, because it is in and of itself yet another act of interpretation by a judicial official, result in error. Finally of course, if incompetence in LBW cases is such a problem, one must ask why the law reform practice here does not refer the question of whether the ball would have hit the stumps to a third umpire as well. Surely it is possible to argue that technology is in fact better suited to 'adjudicate' on this question that it is on the bat-pad issue for example since no human intervention by way of interpretation of video images is required?

Players and former umpires have objected to the move. They argue that the new system will slow down the game; that it will lead to a further lack of competence of umpires who will no longer have to make difficult decisions and learn from their mistakes in the *phroenesis* of judging appeals; that umpires will become simple ball counters etc.[28] In the end, of course, the position one takes on the future of LBW adjudication will be informed by the ideological and political standpoint from which one reaches their jurisprudential position. Are incompetence and judicial error part of the human uncertainty which make cricket cricket, or are they aspects of the game to be stamped out in order to ensure that the contest between bat and ball is unimpeded by adjudicative mistake? Do we want law or perfect justice? How can we know?

13 Mankad, Javed, Hilditch, Sarfraz and the rule of law

Law 38(1) of the 1980 *Code* described when a batter is 'run out' as follows:

LAW 38   RUN OUT
1.   Out Run Out
Either Batsman shall be out Run Out if in running or at any time while the ball is in play – except in the circumstances described in Law 39. (Stumped) – he is out of his ground and his wicket is put down by the opposite side. If, however, a Batsman in running makes good his ground he shall not be out Run Out, if he subsequently leaves his ground, in order to avoid injury, and the wicket is put down.

Law 29 defined a batter 'out of his ground'.

LAW 29   BATSMAN OUT OF HIS GROUND
1.   When out of his Ground
A Batsman shall be considered to be out of his ground unless some part of his bat in his hand or of his person is grounded behind the line of the popping crease.

Law 24(5) regulated and foresaw the possibility of a bowler trying to run-out the non-striker before his delivery.

5.   Bowler Attempting to Run Out Non-Striker Before Delivery
If the Bowler, before delivering the ball, attempts to run out the non-Striker, any runs which result shall be allowed and shall be scored as no balls. Such an attempt shall not count as a ball in the over. The Umpire shall not call 'no ball'. See Law 42.12. (Batsman Unfairly Stealing a Run).

The situation where a Bowler runs out a non-striker who has strayed from his ground before a delivery ('backing up') is known in Australia as *Mankading*. The practice of *Mankading* is named after Indian bowler M.H. 'Vinoo' Mankad, the first player to achieve such a dismissal in a Test match when he ran out the wandering W.A. Brown at the SCG in the 1947–48 series between the two countries. While *Mankading* is a statistically rare occurrence in cricket in general, and even rarer in Test cricket, it is the clearest and starkest example of the conflict between legal formalism in cricket and an ideal of the game based on higher or more important 'ethical' norms.[1]

The *Laws* clearly foresaw and permitted such a form of dismissal. Many believe that recent amendments to the legal structure will make such incidents less likely in the future, but they do remain legally and ethically possible in playing the game of cricket and the law.[2]

In the judicial world of the freedom and constraint of cricket adjudication, formalism clearly dominates as the unique value.[3] The umpire has no choice and *must* give the batter 'out'. But rule formalism is not problematic in any situation unless there is a counter-norm to which one can appeal. What makes the issue of *Mankading* so interesting, of course, is that there *is* just such a counternorm. There is an ethical practice in cricket that the bowler who sees a non-striker backing up, should, before removing the bails to run him out, 'show the ball', i.e. hold the ball over the stumps to indicate that the bowler is aware of the batter's transgression and to issue a warning that the next time he backs-up, he will be run out. The bowler must, to act both ethically and legally, put the non-striker 'on notice' of his default or breach.

This ethical practice complies with standards of fair play and sportsmanship and stands in sharp distinction to the practice of the bowler 'standing on his rights' to effectuate an immediate dismissal. Moreover, a dismissal which follows showing the ball is *both* legally *and* morally acceptable. The batter has been warned and therefore chooses to act at his own risk in knowledge of the *Law* and of all the facts. In the ethical world view of cricket, a batter who chooses to back-up after such a warning *deserves* to be run out because, in backing-up, he is attempting to gain an unfair advantage by shortening the length between his position and his target – the crease at the other end – to score a run and he has received a fair warning of the penalty he will pay for his transgression. Indeed, the non-striker's decision to back-up may be based on a more sophisticated cost–benefit analysis than a simple desire to gain a speedy run. It may well be that the player at the non-striker's end is an acknowledged batter, while the player on strike is a tail-ender. In such circumstances, it is vitally important for the recognized batter to take as much of the strike as possible. His backing-up, therefore, has an even deeper utilitarian importance in this case. Once shown the ball, he can only back-up with the full knowledge that he risks being run-out and leaving a non-batter at the crease. All the costs are known and must be internalized.

'Showing the ball' does occur in fact and is applauded as being in conformity with the spirit of the game. In a Reliance Cup Match in Lahore against Pakistan, Courtney Walsh, the West Indian fast bowler, sacrificed a victory for his team, when, in the last over of a close match, Salim Jaffer backed-up.

> Walsh refused the easy temptation to run out his opponent in one of those larger-than-life demonstrations of sportsmanship which will be extolled wherever the game is played. He deservedly won an International Fair Play Award.[4]

In the 1996 World Cup, Walsh again 'showed the ball'. He

> . . . declined to run out Stuart Law when the latter was backing up too far at the non-striker's end. Instead he stopped his run up, gave Law a warning glare, the eyes steady and pinprick-focused, and returned to his mark.[5]

In a One-Day game between India and Pakistan in Australia in 2000, the Indians upheld what many believe is the binding ethical norm.

> With one ball left at the Gabba and the scores tied on 195, paceman Venkatesh Prasad skidded to a halt in delivery stride, hand and ball hovering over the stumps, threatening Pakistan's Waqar Younis lest the tailender should seek a flying start to steal the winning run.[6]

Pakistan ran a bye off the last ball to win by 2 wickets.

In these instances we see the different ways in which the bowler may 'show the ball', from a glare to a literal compliance with the ethical practice. We also see more importantly that at some level a practice continues to inform the actions of some bowlers whereby they forfeit or delay their chances to win by applying the letter of the law. For them, in finals, in the World Cup, in a match between 'traditional enemies', the spirit of the game emerges triumphant.

There is, however, some confusion over the exact meaning of *Mankading*, a confusion stemming from the basic contradiction between rule formalism and ethical practice. For some, *Mankading* means the sharp practice of running out the batter under the *Laws* without supplying the 'conventional' warning. For others, *Mankading* describes a running out of the non-striker by a bowler who has complied with both his moral and legal obligations. In the first sense of the word, *Mankading* is a term of moral disapproval while in the second form, it is more purely descriptive. In fact, when Mankad himself ran out Brown, he *did* comply with his ethical obligation to warn the batter.[7] Historically and factually then, *Mankading* should refer only to the ethically correct practice of a bowler running out a straying batter.

Whatever the technically correct or the folk-meaning of *Mankading* may be, it is quite obvious that it is a classic example of the distinction between law and ethics in cricket, a distinction which arises in analogous situations as well. For example, thinking play has ceased, but without a call of 'dead ball' or 'over' from the umpire (Laws 3, 23 and 22) a batter may leave his crease to repair or 'pat down' the pitch. Technically and formally he is out of his ground and can be run out.

Thus, in a Test match with Australia, the great Victorian and 'greatest cricketer ever', W.G. Grace relied on the letter of the Law when S.P. Jones left the crease to pat the wicket.[8] Grace instructed the keeper to remove the bails and appealed for a dismissal to umpire Bob Thoms. After verifying what Grace wanted, the umpire said: 'It is not cricket, but I must give the batsman out.'[9]

A similar situation occurred in a NSW–Victoria match in 1934 when Jack Fingleton was given out in like circumstances. In that case, however, ethics prevailed and Bill Woodfull, the opposing captain, asked the umpire to withdraw his decision. Woodfull's act was applauded in the press.

> It is the spirit of cricket that has made the game what it is today and those who sacrifice advantages to do the sporting thing, particularly in big cricket, do the game a great service.[10]

The issue involved in *Mankading* then appears, on the surface, to be a simple conflict between the wording and plain meaning of the *Laws* on the one hand, and accepted ethical practice on the other. Even a cursory glance, however, reveals that there is no such thing, in this context, as a simple issue. When Alan Hurst ran out Sikander Bakht in Perth, he was, depending on one's view (a) simply legally correct without any moral connotation being attached to his actions, (b) or his was both legally and morally correct or (c) he was legally correct and immoral. For the pure positivist, he was legally correct because he acted in accordance with the law. Morality is, in such situations, legally irrelevant. From another perspective, he was legally correct and morally upright in his behaviour because obedience to the legal norm is *per se* moral. Finally, he was legally correct in a formalist sense, but immoral because he violated the standards of an ethical practice which he implicitly accepted by agreeing to participate in cricket. Membership in that community of cricket players is determined not merely by adherence to the letter of the Law but by the acknowledgement that one is bound by the traditions and unwritten norms of the community. Depending upon one's definition of the relationship, if any, between cricket, law and the meaning of life, Alan Hurst was a law-abiding citizen, a good citizen or an outsider and bad guy.

Former Australian captain, Ian Chappell, adopts the batter's point of view, and adds a new layer of legal and ethical complexity. Chappell has no sympathy for any player 'stupid enough to be out of his ground' before the bowler delivers the ball. For him, the question of 'showing the ball' is of no practical or moral import. Young cricketers are taught from their earliest days in the game to back-up with the bat grounded behind the crease while watching the ball leave the bowler's hand. This practice has the practical advantage of allowing the non-striker to perhaps learn something about the bowler's technique which he might use when he advances to the striker's end. It also has the advantage of being a technique, which, if observed, will mean that the batter can never be *Mankaded*. From this perspective, the moral and ethical dilemmas facing the bowler over the question of whether to 'show the ball' become irrelevant. The situation should never arise if the batter is playing 'good' cricket. If it does, he is playing 'bad' cricket and has no one to blame but himself. If one wishes to assert, however, that there is some moral obligation in such circumstances, Chappell is especially adamant that the moral obligation, if there is one, is on the non-striker who must pay the price for his decision. For Chappell the situation is analogous to that of batter moving down the pitch to a spinner. No one would expect that the player should receive a warning that he will be stumped if he persists. In each case, the batter is seeking a physical advantage over the bowler, to change the flight of the ball or to steal a short single. As such, he must expect to suffer the consequences if he miscalculates. If he then decides to act, he must accept the consequences of those actions and not seek to avoid moral responsibility by imposing some obligation on another.

The point of view one adopts on this issue is determined by a number of factors as adherents of one ideal judge those who belong to a different group according to these different factors as interpretive possibility is piled upon interpretive possibility. For Brodribb, for example, *Mankading* (without warning) is an act which can only 'smack of sharp practice'.[11] In addition to his apparent anti-formalism, Brodribb's opinion is informed by a clear nationalistic bias for he hastened to point out that, as far as *Mankading* was concerned 'only 8 have occurred in English cricket, and only three of these since 1894'.[12] Not only is a *Mankading* bowler an 'outsider' because of his unethical conduct but he is an outsider from Denningesque 'true' cricket because he is a foreigner, a 'newcomer' who, unlike the cows, does not like cricket. Indeed, one feels, how could he really like or understand cricket since he is after all, not an Englishman?

Ian Chappell offered the following as a study of the moral, ethical and legal choices facing bowlers when a batter backs-up too far. In the 1968/69 series against the West Indies at the fourth Test in Adelaide, Australian Ian Redpath backed-up well out of his crease. Charlie Griffith of the West Indies *Mankaded* Redpath. This run out changed the match from one where Australia looked comfortable in chasing the West Indies total for victory to one where the team was left with only one wicket standing and were forced to settle for a draw.

At the fifth Test in Sydney, Redpath again backed up well out of his crease. This time the West Indian bowler Wes Hall stopped next to the stumps, showed the ball, shook his head and said to Redpath, 'Man, you must be some kind of fucking idiot.'

In these two cases, the bowlers Griffith and Hall chose different courses of action. The former stood on his rights, acted according to the letter of the *Law* and punished Redpath for bad cricket. The latter chose a more personal form of rebuke. Yet, as Chappell points out, Wes Hall could not be classified as any less a hard-nosed competitor than Griffith. He simply acted in a different way, and one as consistent with our understanding of cricket as Griffith's decision to *Mankad* Redpath. Here, the moral and ethical choice is an individual one and not one which a cricketer like Chappell would condemn one way or the other.

John Woodcock shared in Ian Botham's and Phil Edmonds' condemnation of Ewan Chatfield for *Mankading* Derek Randall. The Englishmen invoked the custom of showing the ball, and claimed that Chatfield violated that unwritten ethical norm.[13] Others would choose to adopt a different moral hermeneutic point of reference. For example, it should be pointed out that when Randall came in to bat, the previous partnership of Rose and Boycott had made only 25 in almost one and a half hours so that part of Randall's function was to speed up the scoring rate. Thus, his backing-up can be seen, again, as an attempt to gain an (unfair) advantage both for himself and his team. To *Mankad* him, in such circumstances, is both appropriate and morally justified. This was certainly the attitude adopted by the local press, who stood loyally by invoking both legal formalism ('What the blazes are rules for, if they're not to be observed?') and obedience, in one form or another, to the moral imperative of 'showing the ball'. Thus, New Zealand press reports indicated that Richard Hadlee, Chatfield's teammate, 'had warned several English batsmen for backing up too quickly earlier in the match'.[14] On either view, legal formalism or moral imperative, the relevant reaction to the incident can be, and were, seen in an entirely different interpretive light.

At the same time, neither Chappell as a batter, nor Hall, Botham, Edmonds or Griffith as bowlers, have an interpretive monopoly on such events. Griffith's *Mankading* of Stackpole received extensive press coverage and others did not hesitate to offer their views on the moral propriety of Griffith's action. West Indian captain Gary Sobers apparently offered his apologies to Bill Lawry of Australia after the day's play, indicating perhaps his disapproval but it must be noted that Sobers' apparent moral condemnation of Griffith did not extend so far as to cause him to ask the umpire to withdraw the appeal.[15] Sobers apparently viewed the action as immoral but did not wish to impose a *legal* sanction on his player or his team by invoking ethical practices to supersede legalities. Nor perhaps did he wish to publicly *shame* his player by asking the umpire for permission to withdraw the appeal.

The crowd, on the other hand, had no truck with legal niceties and 'reacted angrily, hooting Griffith as he ran up to bowl his next two balls, and when the team left the field at the tea adjournment'.[16] Bill O'Reilly, speaking perhaps as a former bowler, adopted a position which urged a deep union between law and morality. Writing of Griffith's 'tremendous effort' throughout the innings he added:

> He raised local ire by running Ian Redpath out as he backed up, too enthusi-astically, when Australia was claiming short runs galore. Griffith was fully entitled to the action he took. He would have been foolish not to have bore it.[17]

Not only does the bowler in such situations have a legal entitlement and a moral duty, but he is, for O'Reilly, virtually under an existential sense of obligation to himself and other bowlers to *Mankad* a straying batter. He must interfere with the non-striker's wanderings for to do otherwise he would be a 'fool', not a bowler. For O'Reilly, Griffith was under a moral and a legal obligation not just to himself, but to his fellow members of the fraternity of bowlers, to *Mankad* Redpath. His duty to himself, to his fellow bowlers, to his team and to the *Laws* all coincide in this moment of praxis.[18]

The moral and legal situation of Griffith's place in the historical jurisprudence of cricket and law is further complicated by a careful review of other facts. It might, for example, also be noted that Griffith had, metaphorically at least, 'shown the ball' to the Australians for, as Phil Wilkins pointed out, Griffith had, while fielding, spoken to several Australian batters and warned them that were backing-up too far and too early and were in danger of being run out. Even if one were to assert that a bowler has a moral duty to 'show the ball' before *Mankading* a player, it would be possible to argue that a certain interpretive ambiguity surrounds even such an apparently clear moral imperative. A bowler might 'show the ball' with a head or eye movement for 'showing the ball' is not to be interpreted literally. Rather, it is a metaphor for a proper warning, for a required notice of default to the non-striker. In addition, it might be argued that the moral duty to warn does not exist in ontologically or temporally rigid confines. In other words, there is nothing in the hermeneutic shared understanding of 'showing the ball' which requires a bowler *qua* bowler to warn the batter immediately prior to *Mankading* him. Rather, the notice requirement is a broader and more temporally flexible standard. It is what lawyers would understand as an equitable notice rather than a legal one which is required. Thus, on the facts, Griffith did warn Redpath when as a fielder he warned Australian players of the danger. His moral obligation is a public one, to the spirit of the game and to the Australian side, not to each Aussie batter trying to steal a short single. In this case, even when he 'failed' to 'warn' Redpath, Griffith did, in fact and in 'law', act in accordance with both the legal and the ethical standards surrounding the practice of *Mankading*. Because of the moral complexity involved in such cases, however, and because of the multiplicity of interpreters, not all other participants share this perspective. Cricket officials and sportswriters in the West Indies, for example, condemned not Griffith, but his captain Sobers for apologizing to Lawry.[19] Bill Lawry simultaneously criticized the morality of Griffith's action and offered his view on Australia's ethical superiority: 'It is one of the laws of cricket, but I would be disappointed if one of our players did it in the Sydney Test.'[20]

Interestingly, Lawry apparently did not indicate whether he, as captain, would withdraw an appeal in such an incident. Of course, he would not be faced with this dilemma given the Australians' higher moral standards.

Of course, as we have already seen, the Sydney Test was marked by Wes Hall's warning to Redpath. It was also marked by Griffith adding yet more texture to the issue of *Mankading*. Bill O'Reilly again offered an intriguing account:

> Stopping one delivery to trap Redpath out of his crease, he nonchalantly gave the batter an extension of time, even though he had been warned previously by Hall.
>
> I prefer to think that Griffith's action there stemmed more from a feeling of pity, than from him having been cowed by a lot of uninformed criticism over his Adelaide coup.[21]

O'Reilly, quite naturally, cannot betray his previously stated belief that Griffith had acted correctly on all accounts in Adelaide. What he does admit here is the possibility that in certain contexts with the result assured, a new factor, human pity, may enter into a bowler's moral calculus when dealing with a straying batter. Griffith's actions, simply and yet with great complexity point out again that any number of moral interpretations and practices can exist, even within the same person. We will still recognize him as a 'bowler' who plays 'cricket' although we cannot offer any single reading of what either of these texts mean. *Mankading* is and can be alternatively legal and ethical, legal and unethical, cricket and not cricket, yet it is and must be part of the game which even those who condemn it must recognize as such.

Bill Lawrie's reaction to Griffith's *Mankad* of Redpath was based, in part, at least, on a publicly declared nationalist bias. Conversely, nationalist biases and stereotypes, may be used to reinforce the ethically superior status of someone who, like Courtney Walsh, 'shows the ball'. Not only did Walsh counter 'a winning is everything' ethos with his action, but he demonstrated himself as able to rise above such considerations and to actively participate in more than an adherence to an abstract ideal of the spirit of cricket. His actions occurred in a match against Pakistan, some members of which are considered by their opponents to be 'notorious' louts. A former manager of Pakistan has stated his belief that cheating is 'absolutely necessary' in professional cricket today.[22] 'We' all know that Pakistani bowlers tamper with the ball.[23] Salim Malik has been banned for life because of his involvement in match-fixing and bribery scandals. Walsh could perhaps have been forgiven even by some moralists had he *Mankaded* the batter in his match against Pakistan. After all, there are limits to the notions of fair play and 'turning the other cheek'. That Walsh chose to take the ethical high road against an 'unworthy' opponent for some only enhances his moral stature.

Given even the ethical ambiguity to which an analysis of Walsh's behaviour might be open, it is hardly surprising that any categorization of Hurst's action against Sikander cannot take place with any degree of accuracy, or interpretive certainty, unless it is further contextualized. In this case, a further *Law* must be examined as must the facts of the Sarfraz–Hilditch affair.

Law 33, as in effect at the time, provided:

1. Out Handled the Ball

Either Batsman on appeal shall be out Handled the Ball if he wilfully touches the ball while in play with the hand not holding the bat unless he does so with the consent of the opposite side

and, of course, until the ball is called 'Dead', it is 'in play'. As a result of the interpretive ambiguity surrounding the idea of 'consent' of the fielding side which could range from a verbal request to a silent compliance by action, there were and still are conflicting formal and ethical norms in cricket concerning the correct 'practice' to be followed by a batter. One set of standards urged a batter to *never* handle the ball. Under this 'practice' he would incur no danger of running afoul of a less than liberal umpire's interpretation of the presence or absence of 'consent' by the fielding side. At the same time, he would not breach any rule of etiquette which frowned upon a batter touching the ball at any time. He would also conform with a utilitarian practice which called for no cooperation with the fielding side who should be made to do all the work. In addition, he would eliminate one chance for sharp practice by the fielding team.

On the other hand, there is an ethical view of cooperation, gentlemanliness and good conduct which would urge a batter, when play is effectively and 'in practice' over, to politely assist by returning a ball laying at his feet rather than compelling the wicketkeeper, or bowler, or fielder to come to the crease to retrieve the ball. A concomitant of this ethical practice is that the fielding team, the beneficiaries of a good faith and sportsmanlike gesture of assistance, would not rely on a literal, legalistic interpretation of Law 33 and appeal for a dismissal of the batter.

This ethical norm was apparently absent from the Test series between Pakistan and Australia in 1978–79.[24] At the first Test in Melbourne, Javed Miandad ran out Rodney Hogg of Australia who was inspecting the pitch. In retaliation, at Perth, Hurst *Mankaded* Sikander and later in the same match, Sarfraz successfully appealed for 'handled the ball' against Hilditch, the non-striker, who 'picked up the ball and helpfully tossed it back to Sarfraz'.[25]

In each case, then, the ethical and legal debate occurred and was situated within a much broader and richer context than a simple 'Hurst *Mankaded* Sikander' or 'Sarfraz dismissed Hilditch "handled the ball"' would indicate. Even without considering the rich preceding history of cricket and conflict between the two sides, the events of 1979 offer a rich hermeneutic backdrop for us to consider when we seek to explore the interpretive framework of the various communities who tell the story of cricket.

When Javed ran out Hogg, he violated an ethical norm but complied with the letter of the *Law*, as had the 'great' W.G. Grace. At the same time, however, Pakistani captain, Mushtaq Mohammed, attempted to withdraw the appeal, but the batter had already abandoned his position. This attempt to invoke the ethical norm, by withdrawing the appeal, was rejected by an accurate and formalist application of the *Laws*, which, as we have seen, impose a clear temporal limit on the ability of an umpire to accede to any such request. Throughout these events, legal formalism, a strict adherence to the literal text of the operative legal norms, not surprisingly, was the stance adopted by the umpires.

When Hurst *Mankaded* Sikander, he acted, or so we can assume, in retaliation against Javed. The actual *Mankading* was formally justified and if one believes in the synonymous relationship between legality and morality, it was ethically justified as well. On the other hand, Hurst operated outside one understanding of the ethical convention by failing to 'show the ball' and deserved, from the cricket moralist, condemnation. Again, however, a situationalist morality could see Hurst's formal and rigid adherence to the rules as justifiable retribution, a moral 'tit for tat' against Javed's unethical, but legally permissible, run out of Hogg. The Pakistanis did not deserve moral considerations because they behaved immorally. On the other hand, this position is weakened somewhat by two factors. First, it conflates individual and collective culpability. Why should the Pakistani team in general or Sikander in particular, be denied moral status because of the actions of Javed? Secondly, the Pakistani team through the agency of their captain, Mushtaq, had, in fact, attempted to act morally by seeking to withdraw the appeal. To condemn them as an immoral team is therefore 'factually' incorrect and morally inconsistent in individualized utilitarian terms. At the same time, and conversely, it must not be forgotten that Sikander was to some extent morally culpable, if we accept the position defended by Ian Chappell for example, for backing-up.

Finally, we could, under the same circumstances, condemn Hurst on the grounds that it is never morally correct to engage in acts of retribution. His act or omission in breaking the convention by failing to show the ball was *per se* immoral and cannot be justified by an appeal to morally or utilitarian-based retribution arguments. Indeed, one might assert, *a fortiori*, that ethically and morally behaviour has real meaning and importance only when it occurs in a context of competing unethical activity. In a morally unproblematic universe or interpretive community, ethical activity has little moral and pedagogic meaning because it is the norm. Ethical behaviour in the face of an unethical opponent gives true existential and propaedeutic import to such acts.

Similar analyses are available in relation to Sarfraz's appeal against Hilditch. It was technically correct and on one view of the law/morality *nexus* morally justified. On another view, it was violative of a convention and immoral. It was, or was not, justifiable on the basis of *retribution*. At the same time, the ethical norms governing Hilditch's conduct are perhaps somewhat unclear. On one view of the ethical and practical imperatives surrounding the 'handled the ball' *Law*, a batter should *never* have touched the ball. If one accepts that such a view carries with it or is informed by 'moral' as well as utilitarian concerns, then Hilditch himself must carry some degree of blameworthiness which, depending on one's overall moral framework, will or will not relieve or diminish Sarfraz's own moral culpability. Again, and *a contrario*, this analysis ignores the moral weight and suasion of an analogy with the conventional requirement that the bowler 'show the ball' before *Mankading* the batter. In such a case, the batter who is out of his crease and backing-up is also morally culpable for gaining an advantage in his run. Yet, in these circumstances, the moral purpose and weight of the convention is nonetheless to force the *bowler* to act first and to conform to the moral duty imposed on him. The runner becomes morally culpable only when he ignores the warning. The same situation obtains, by analogy at least, in the Sarfraz–Hilditch *scenario*, so that on this analysis, the morally culpable actor is Sarfraz.

Bill O'Reilly, in his account of these incidents, did not mince words or hesitate to pass moral judgement. He described the Hilditch dismissal as 'the ugliest act of reprisal I have ever seen' and distanced himself from such practices by stating: 'I am glad that no such melancholy performance hangs heavily on my cricket conscience, nor could it on any man I played with or against in my cricket career, first, second or Nth class.'[26]

Here O'Reilly is invoking a standard position in ethical and legal discourse. It is a call to harken back to the good old days, the golden age, when men were men, and no one, from park cricket to Test match, would act in such a way as to violate the spirit of the game. I have already demonstrated, and more examples will follow, that this is simply a counter-factual position. The good old days were not all that good and 'immorality' has always been part of the game. But O'Reilly himself demonstrated the fallacy of his position. First, by acknowledging that Sarfraz was acting in retaliation, he opened the door to a more deeply contextualized interpretation than his simple moral imperative would at first blush appear to allow. Secondly, and more importantly, he himself recognized the existence of competing legal, moral and factual texts in his description of Hurst's *Mankading* of Sikander. On legal formalism he allowed that: 'Nothing in the rule book says that the bowler should deliver a warning. . . .'

He then asserted a competing extra-legal counter-text, 'But sportsmanship and accepted rules of behaviour insist that there is a moral side which the bowler must observe.'

Then, we come to the real 'factual' stumbling blocks: 'Hurst, himself, is the only man who knows for certain whether he gave Sikander the office. He might have done it either with a gesture or just a threatening look.'

'Showing the ball', as interpreted and practiced in the real-live text of cricket again does not necessarily take on a literal meaning. Rather, 'showing the ball' is a metaphor for *any* warning to the batter that he is engaging in morally reprehensible behaviour. Because this warning can be in the form of 'a gesture' or 'a threatening look', it may not be perceived by the other members of the interpretive sub-communities – the umpires, the players and the crowd. The communication can, in such circumstances, be a private one but if given, it complies with the code of public morality. Our external moral condemnation must be tempered here because we cannot know if the code has been broken or adhered to.

Finally, there is another 'fact' which contributes to the moral and ethical complexity surrounding the formal legal correctness of *Mankading*. Sikander 'was wholly involved in his job of trying to keep his partnership with Iqbal alive by running short singles'. He was acting in a strict utilitarian fashion, serving his team's purpose. On these 'facts', Hurst was acting in a morally correct manner by preventing Sikander's sharp practice. Moreover, he was acting legally and he served a strict utilitarian function by stopping the opposition's quick accumulation of runs. In this interpretive context, 'near cheating' appears instead to be part of a morally acceptable context of playing cricket in accordance with the *Laws* and spirit of the game.

Rippon condemns each incident as 'petty behaviour' of 'infant school' cricketers,[27] while Brodribb defines the Hilditch dismissal as 'shameful'.[28] Yet we know, in fact that such incidents occur. We are also aware of the degree of outrage they spark. Finally, we know that 'sporting' gestures like Courtney Walsh's are greeted with much acclaim and granted awards. All of these things which we know about the law and ethics of such situations within the hermeneutic community of cricket indicate that normative compliance with the higher standard of 'true' cricket is not necessarily or universally accepted or acceptable. Lord Denning's 'newcomer' and other violators of the canon are not always perceived, nor do they perceive themselves, as *Other*. Sarfraz, Hurst, Hilditch, Chatfield, Botham, Javed et al., were all cricketers and would consider themselves to be cricketers yet they operate in the same interpretive world under different interpretive canons and precepts. Each was playing cricket, yet each chose to play under a different set of interpretive rules. Some actions are dismissed by others as 'not cricket' yet are perceived by the actors themselves precisely as being 'cricket'. Both the ontological and epistemological status of the 'text' appears to be in some dispute, yet the game of cricket remains recognizable as such to the various members of the interpretive community. Indeed, at the end of the series in which Sarfraz, Hurst et al. made their contributions to cricket jurisprudence, Asif Iqbal, Pakistani vice-captain condemned both teams' behaviour. He said: 'I think it was disgusting. I don't want to be associated with any team that reverts to those tactics. It was a shameful performance from both teams.'

Yet, while even some of the players themselves might feel a certain shame, they nevertheless recognized both the strict legality of each of these actions, and the fact that some see such legality as fulfilling a moral function as well. We are all still talking about the same thing even when we have fundamental jurisprudential conflicts and debates over the content and meaning of the ethical normativity of 'it's not cricket'. Here there is not just a conflict between the *Laws of Cricket* and the spirit of the game. Instead there is conflict between and among participants in the hermeneutic community about the form, content and existence of the ethical standard.

Moral opprobrium and abuse are heaped on offenders against the moral code by observers, commentators and other players, if and when they can agree on the content of the moral obligation. Even some umpires, bound as they are to an institutional practice of complete formalism, find ways to invoke formalistic principles as a sign of moral disapproval. Ted Jones offered the following anecdote.

> Some years ago whilst umpiring a match I was slightly upset when a bowler removed the bails at the end of his run up with the non-striker out of his ground and appealed 'How's that?' Under the laws of cricket I had no option but to give the batsman out. Normally a bowler will 'show' the ball to the non-striker thereby warning him to stay within his ground during subsequent bowling actions. Having thus dismissed a prolific run getter the bowler then had the temerity to appeal for 'Timed Out' as the incoming batsman was a little tardy in appearing. Not one of my favourite bowlers I hasten to add; my colleague and I dismissed the timed out appeal![29]

Jones, the rule- and role-constrained adjudicator can appear to apply the *Law* while in reality he is imposing a competing moral text. What is more, Jones can do so while experiencing no apparent existential bad faith or self-doubt. In this case it might be possible to infer that the incoming batter may well have been out of time and should have been given out 'timed out'. If such is the case then, Jones has acted in an illegal, bad faith and unjudicial manner. He has flouted the law in order to achieve what he perceives and understands to be a 'just' result. Yet, this clearly violates his own rule formalism. Despite this, he still understands himself to be a cricket umpire.

Even in the debate between formalism and moralism, as the complexities of the *Mankad* and related debate demonstrate, the weapons of one discourse may be turned in a radical interpretive turn against themselves or, in what may amount to the same thing, in favour of their apparent opponent. Appearance and reality take on a postmodern tinge even in the certain world of legal formalism.

Finally, it should be noted that the law reform process has imposed a new interpretive and substantive framework on the form of dismissal 'Handled the Ball'. The new text of Law 33(2) (ii) now provides that a batter will not be out handled the ball if

> . . . he uses his hand or hands to return the ball to any member of the fielding side without the consent of that side.

Thus, legislative intervention following the series of controversial incidents which brought the game into disrepute in the eyes of many, appears to have recognized that the practice of appealing for a dismissal in these circumstances was perceived to be 'legal' but unethical. The *Law* now seems to have eliminated the possibility of such behaviour by making the act of returning the ball to the fielding side, even without permission, a lawful act. But, of course, that is not the case. The *Laws* have simply moved the illegal nature of the act from the 'handled the ball' category to the 'obstructing the field' category. Thus, Law 37(4), now provides

> Either batsman is out under this Law if, without the consent of the fielding side and while the ball is in play, he uses his bat or person to return the ball to any member of that side.

Legislative rationalization and reorganization now simply mean that the old separate offences of hitting the ball twice and handling the ball are now covered under the single offence of Law 37(4). 'Sharp practice' is still permissible. The only thing which has changed is the entry recording the dismissal in the scorebook. The same interpretive, normative and ethical dilemmas remain. For example, when Michael Vaughan was dismissed in a match against India for handling the ball, he appeared, in the words of one commentator, 'very hurt' at his dismissal. He claimed that he was just returning the ball to the fielding side. But on another view

> He should have first seen the replay of his dismissal. He had no idea where the ball was and when he discovered that it was spinning precariously close to his stumps, he brought his hand on it to stop it. That's out both within the letter of the laws of cricket and its spirit.[30]

Here at some level the debate is the familiar one. There is for some an issue of morality and legal formalism to be sorted out. For Kureishi there is neither. The interpretation on the facts is that the batter used his hand to stop the ball from hitting the stumps. That is, in effect, exactly the type of circumstance the *Law* is meant to prevent, and he deserved to be dismissed. There is no ethical issue here because he is not, as he might have claimed, simply and innocuously returning the ball after the danger has passed but before the ball is dead. In those circumstances the formalist and positivist reading of the *Laws* might conflict with the some ethical norm. However, the amendments to the *Laws* seem to eliminate even this idea. Had the ball not been in danger of hitting the stumps (Law 33), Vaughan would still have been dismissed under Law 37(4). He had, at the level of legal positivism, even less of an argument than he would have had before the legislative changes. Mark Nicholas made a similar point when he wrote

> Later, he said he was merely handing the ball to the close fielder and, though he knew the relevant law, he felt it unsporting of the Indians to appeal. Having seen the replay a few times, it does not look as if that was the case. Were it so, the victim would have a point, though here again the law is clear in explaining that the batsman should seek permission to hand the ball to a fielder, otherwise he can be given out for obstructing the field. Either way, Vaughan made a cock of it, and has learned a nasty lesson.[31]

Nicholas' comments seem to indicate belief in the continued existence of an ethical norm under which the Indian appeal would be legal but still 'unsporting'. It might equally be asserted as a matter of interpretation and legislative history, that the legislature has specifically reduced, if not eliminated, the parameter or possibility of any assertion of an extant moral norm in such cases. By reconfirming that returning the ball to a fielder without permission is illegal and by placing the action in the substantive offence of 'obstructing the field', the lawmakers have in fact reiterated that such actions are unacceptable. They could have, had the argument about the spirit of the game forbidding such sharp practice as an appeal in such circumstances been part of the ideals and legal universe of the game of cricket, made it clear in the *Laws*. They did not do this. Instead, they carefully amended the *Laws* not just in relation to the substantive modes of dismissal of 'handled the ball' and 'obstructing the field', but they added the *Preamble* to the 2000 *Code*. As we have already seen the incorporation of the ideals of fair play and the sprit and traditions of the game was central to the new legislative text. That they left the substantive norm that a batter can be dismissed for returning a live ball to a fielder as part of the *Laws of Cricket*, indicates that there is no norm, ethical or legal, which would, could or should prevent an appeal in such circumstances.

One might also add that there is no indication that the ICC Match Referee saw anything about Vaughan's dismissal which would contravene the prohibitions against sharp practice or which would bring the game into disrepute. This does not necessarily mean that there is no ethical norm about such appeals in certain circumstances. It might indicate that Vaughan had violated the *Law* in this case in such a way that no ethical question could have been raised about the appeal.

It might also indicate that the ethical standard does not rise to the level of making such appeals 'sharp practice' etc. If this is the case, the existence of the *Preamble*, and the *ICC Code of Conduct*, still leave unanswered a central jurisprudential question for cricket and the law. Is it possible to conceive of any circumstance in which reliance on the strict application of the formal text of the *Laws of Cricket* could or should result in a violation of the 'spirit of the game'?

On the 'handled the ball'/'obstructing the field' question, it appears that Ian Chappell is vindicated in law and in morality. Do not touch the ball and you are safe. Stupidity will be punished.

14 It's not cricket: underarm bowling, legality and the meaning of life

No other case in recent cricket memory has so epitomized the conflict between law and morality than the infamous underarm incident at Melbourne in Feb. 1981. In a One-Day match with New Zealand, with the visitors needing six from the last ball for a tie, Australian captain Greg Chappell ordered the bowler, his brother Trevor, to deliver a 'mullygrubber', that is an underarm delivery rolled along the ground. Trevor complied and 'A stunned New Zealand batsman blocked it.'[1]

Australia won and the battle was on. On television, former Australian captain Richie Benaud called the Chappells' action 'the most gutless thing I have ever seen on a cricket field'.[2]

Kiwi Prime Minister (Sir) Robert Muldoon called the underarm delivery an 'act of cowardice' and stated he now understood the reason Australia's One-Day uniform is 'yellow'. The ACB condemned and censured Chappell for not meeting the duty of an Australian captain to uphold the spirit of the game. Australian Prime Minister Malcolm Fraser bemoaned the loss of the good and decent tradition of cricket. The incident became part of Australian and New Zealand popular cultural history and is compared in terms of jurisprudential and cultural importance with Bodyline.[3]

The underarm incident continues to serve as an almost universal signifier in Australian–New Zealand sporting contacts. Some of the metaphors and social translations are humorous, others filled with a more serious sense of national outrage at the triumph of legal formalism over cricket's (and society's) higher values. The manager of the New Zealand blind cricket team complained that Australia had an advantage in such competitions because all bowling was underarm. During a One-Day match played at Hobart, the Kiwi PM's Christmas Party focused on the television coverage of the game.[4] As Australia approached the New Zealand total and required two runs off the last ball to win

> ...underarm bowling jokes swept the room. New Zealanders have not forgotten Trevor Chappell's final, unplayable ball on his brother Greg's orders, that ended a 1981 Melbourne one-day final so sourly, denying New Zealand a chancy six off the last ball.[5]

While these references are clearly accompanied with good humour, and the text of the underarm bowling incident takes on a different meaning with the passage of time, another adoption of the referent offered a chance to combine a seemingly 'neutral' legal formalism with a strong personal and social desire for revenge. During a trans-Tasman Test in netball, the Australian team was late coming on to the floor after the half-time break, and the New Zealand team restarted the game without their opponents. In other words a contest between two teams was actually briefly occurring with only one team present. For the Kiwis it was clear what sporting interpretive context informed their reaction to Australian tardiness. The incident had evened the score for cricket's infamous underarm delivery.

Reaction at the time of the Chappell brothers' incident was, as might be expected, heated. Television and radio stations were inundated with telephone calls, some seeking the number of the Kiwi's Melbourne Hotel in order to apologize, others calling for Greg [but interestingly not Trevor] Chappell's scalp.[6] New Zealanders were equally vociferous in their complaints. A local judge said 'I hope there are no Australians coming up before me this morning.'[7] New Zealand feeling remained heated one year later when Chappell led the Australians to Auckland.[8] Editorial writers bemoaned not only Chappell's poor sportsmanship, but branded him a traitor to his country. His action, it was said, was 'an act that will sour anyone who ever held sportsmanship dear. It was contrary to the Australian spirit.'[9]

The incident itself was cast in the broader context of Australia–New Zealand relations. Like Australian Prime Minister John Howard's frequent invocation of cricket metaphors to explain and clarify political questions, Chappell's mullygrubber was itself placed in the broader socio-political context of Australia's condescending attitude towards its trans-Tasman neighbour. Instead of limiting itself to the cricket pitch – it's just a game – the underarm delivery, precisely *because* it took place on the cricket pitch, took on a broader interpretive political function. As the editorial writer for the *Sydney Morning Herald* put it the next day:

> New Zealanders will however, undoubtedly use the 'underarm' incident for years to come as a metaphor for the way Australians continue to show lack of consideration to a trans-Tasman relative and friend. This is a disregard that transcends everything that has happened this cricket season – all the controversial LBW decisions, the undue protection by umpires of Australian tail-end batsmen and the non-granting of legitimate catches.

The editorial writers and politicians were not the only ones to see a broader social and political hermeneutic at work. For the cricket fans, Chappell's decision symbolized and embodied other broader issues from capitalism: 'Maybe Manning Clarke is right when he says that Mammon has taken over in this fair country of ours', to class: 'Cricket, the game loved by many kinds of people from judges to housewives, actors to building workers, appears to have died. In its place is cricket, a sport for boozing ockers and yobbos...', to literary criticism: 'Test cricket is drama. Limited over cricket is farce. Mr Chappell introduced into the farce a further dash of comedy', to religion: 'Sadly, we have seen our national sporting reputation sold for the proverbial 30 pieces of silver', to the counternarrative of formalism: 'Greg Chappell's action but places him on a sparsely populated pedestal of "thinking" captains who have brains as well as just co-ordination.'

Finally, at least two readers saw parallels with another significant and signifying social, political and legal text, the 1975 Constitutional Crisis in Australia when the lawfully elected Whitlam government was dismissed by the Governor-General's use of the reserve power and replaced by Malcolm Fraser's Liberals: 'Mr Fraser approached the zenith in hypocrisy with his denunciation of Chappell's methods. Surely the Prime Minister used the rules of the game to his own advantage in 1975' and 'Has there been a more sensational event in Australia since Sir John Kerr sacked Mr Whitlam?'[10]

Other members of cricket's interpretive community also jumped into the hermeneutic circle. Former Australian bowler, noted journalist and iconoclast, Bill O'Reilly, joined in on the side of morality. His feelings of private and public outrage were clearly stated:

> As a patriotic Australian, influenced by all the tough spots through which my Test career took one, I felt humiliated. It was an injury to all the great players who have played over the past 100 years.[11]

O'Reilly here seeks to utilize and invoke a classic interpretive and legal strategy. His appeal, yet again, is to the past, to the historically constituted community of players, its morality and its internal rule of law. By making this appeal in these circumstances he is clearly seeking to exclude Chappell (and his team) from the community of Australian cricketers ('I implore the selectors to brush this team aside', id), to banish them from the group of those who may impose an authentic meaning on what is for O'Reilly, an exclusive, elite and private text. Like those who seek to cherish and preserve the sacred traditions of the Bench and the Bar, to confirm them as guardians of the Ark, O'Reilly wishes under the guise of a universal and public moral code to impose a limited and private morality. This does not necessarily mean that the content of this morality is one which is not shared by other interpretive sub-communities in cricket. It does mean, however, that we must always guard against those who seek to legitimate private moral codes by imbuing them, by mere assertion, with a broader public status, especially given O'Reilly's position on *Mankading* and his reputation as an aggressive, if not intimidatory, appellant. This does not mean that it is not possible to construct an ethically and legally consistent position which adopts these interpretations of various moral and legal questions. It does mean however, that each element of that position needs to be clearly articulated and interrogated without any elevation to Truth status simply because O'Reilly played for Australia.

Finally, authoritative representatives of another interpretive sub-community, umpires, jumped into the fray. Don Oslear, the English Test umpire condemned Greg Chappell for violating the spirit of the game. Asked how he could have reacted had been standing in the match, he replied: 'I might have said, "Come on Greg, It's been a tremendous game. Let's bowl it up".'[12]

Here we have a rather surprising addition to the interpretive canon. Rather than relying on the traditional ideals of rule formalism and judicial neutrality and invoking standards of passivity, Oslear takes the position that umpires must play an active role in upholding the spirit of the game. That entity must dominate and take precedence over the letter of the *Law*. Perhaps Oslear, looking at events from a distance, is speaking from principle, perhaps he is simply being disingenuous, but whatever the case, it is interesting to note that nothing he says indicates that he could or would have intervened beyond mere imprecation. Had he been present, had Chappell rejected his imprecations and bowled underarm, whatever his own moral view, he *could* not, as an umpire, have acted any differently than did the two umpires who were actually present. At that actual practically real point of obedience to the letter of the law, personal morality must be set aside. Unless, again, Oslear is willing to argue that the umpire's jurisdiction of 'fair and unfair' play, for example, could be extended to allow him to assert an injunctive power to prohibit an act which is legally permissible and permitted but ethically suspect. This idea, that the spirit of the game is superior to strict adherence to the formal content of the *Laws of Cricket*, whatever its moral, deontological status, has never, in such circumstances, had an actual legal consequence or effect.

The issues surrounding the underarm incident are myriad. At the surface level, the conflict is a straightforward one of rule formalism confronting an unwritten ethical norm, for, needless to say, at the time, Chappell's underarm delivery was perfectly 'legal'. At the same time, however, something deeper and more contextually important arises from even a cursory analysis of the 'case'.

First, like all events to which we attribute significance and which we imbue with meaning, the underarm bowling affair occurs in a particular context. For example, the Chappell incident takes on importance only because of a conflict, yet again, between the *Law* and convention. But there is in the debate around this case, as in all cases where it is convenient or necessary, a tendency to forget history and grant one's position the status of a universal and transcendent epistemological basis. The 'it is legal' argument from this position appears much less problematic than the conventional 'it's not cricket' argument. As a matter of historical fact, for example, until 1864, it was illegal to bowl *overarm* and any bowler attempting to do so was no-balled. It was not until 1878 that Australia became the first team to use a specialist overarm attack.[13] Appeals to the *absolute* ontological immorality of Chappell's decision lose their argument with the history of the game and its *Laws*.

Secondly, again perhaps mostly as an historical curiosity, is the phrase 'it's not cricket' which embodies the argument of the proponents of anti-formalist ethical versions of the game in general and of those who condemn the Chappells in particular. The phrase was apparently originally coined by Rev. James Pycroft to express his displeasure at and disapproval of *overarm bowling*. In a neat historical, contextual flip, 'it isn't cricket' has left its original place in the interpretive community to stand as moral armament for those on the opposite end of its historical positioning. Truth and falsehood shift as time and community practices and texts shift.

Historical counter-facts to one side however, it is obvious that the underarm bowling incident raises many questions. First, as in other instances we have seen, it was *legal*, and for the sake of brevity, *immoral*. Unlike other types of 'sharp practice', however, there was something special enough about this affair that the *Laws* of One-Day Cricket were changed so that it could not be repeated. Why was outrage so great and the weight of ethical norms so powerful that the formalist trend was turned on its head and traditional practice enshrined in the rules?

A first and most plausible reason for the reaction and outrage also finds, in a bizarre way, its sources in the historical or perhaps mythological, origins of the game. Overarm, roundarm bowling was, according to cricket legend, first developed by a woman. As Frindall explains:

> The first woman technically to assist the development of cricket was Christina Willes, later Mrs Hodges. It is generally accepted that she originated round-arm bowling *c* 1807 when she practised with her brother John in the barn of their home at Tonford, near Canterbury. Her full skirt of the period made the legitimate bowling style of the times impossible. John, who was to become a squire and sports patron, found round-arm bowling difficult to play, adopted it himself, was the first to be no-balled for employing it in a major match... and had the satisfaction of seeing the style made legal six years later in 1828.[14]

While it was originated by a woman, overarm bowling, especially fast bowling, is now clearly associated with virility and manliness, which are essential elements (*infra*) of the moral and social nature of cricket. The contest between bat and ball which characterizes and defines the game is embodied for many in the confrontation between a batter and a bowler capable of delivering the ball at high speed. Fast bowlers are the big, virile men of the team and the ability to stand up to a 'barrage' or 'attack' of bouncers from these big men is a sign of the courage and virility of batters. What happened in the underarm bowling incident was that Greg Chappell, in the words of one writer 'failed the virility test',[15] or as Richie Benaud put it, he was 'gutless'. As Australian captain in an international match, he represented all Australians (read Australian men) as weak, wimpish, hiding behind the rules, rather than facing destiny 'like a man', a fact exacerbated by traditional Australian attitudes of superiority towards New Zealanders, especially in cricket. The decision to change the rule was a decision in favour of masculinity. No longer could an Australian hide behind the skirts of the Law, he would have to put his manhood on the line.

Connected with the virility explanation is the fact that Chappell might have achieved the same result in a masculine and virile way, and in a way which would both conform with the *Laws* and the spirit of the game. As McVicar pointed out: 'If the same result could have been effected by Lillee rocketing down a bouncer, everyone would have preened.'[16]

Even Harold Larwood, the fast bowler who followed Douglas Jardine's orders to such devastating effect in the Bodyline series (*infra*), condemned Chappell's actions: 'It was a bloody stupid thing to do and I hope it will never happen again.' When asked if he would have acted like Trevor Chappell, following his captain's order to bowl underarm, he replied: 'No, definitely not. No one in my time would have done anything like that.'[17]

It is immediately difficult to characterize Larwood's response as anything but disingenuous or at best evasive. Jardine never hesitated to stand on the letter of the *Law* to achieve victory and it is impossible to believe that he would by definition have seen anything 'immoral' about underarm bowling if it would achieve the desired result. This was the very nature of Bodyline and the legal and moral conflict which arose as a result. Jardine insisted that his tactics were perfectly legal and the Australians claimed that what England were doing, 'just wasn't cricket'. Nor is it possible to imagine the working-class bowler Larwood disobeying an order from his captain, Mr Jardine. Again, there is ample proof that legal formalism and sharp practice have a continuous presence in the practice of cricket so that Larwood's invocation of the 'good old days' can hardly be persuasive.

Yet beneath this text which seemingly refutes Larwood's position, there lies an equally, if not more, persuasive argument to strongly support his view that he would not have been faced with such a situation (or even if faced with such an order he might have refused). The text which supports Larwood is one which arises frequently in discussions of the underarm incident, that is once more the cult of virility.

One reason Chappell is condemned for the mullygrubber incident is that his action is seen as unmanly, as violating a strong social imperative, and an even stronger cricket imperative, that a man should be a man and not hide behind the letter of the *Law* and use a weak, feminine underarm delivery. Larwood, Jardine and Bodyline cannot be placed in the same interpretive matrix. While standing on the letter of the *Law*, Bodyline does so from the other side of the hermeneutic circle. In its very essence, Bodyline is manly, virile, masculine. It is about fast bowlers bowling fast. It is about assault and attack, it is war on the oval. If it stands on the letter of the Law, it stands against a weaker, more feminine 'gentle'-manly spirit of the game. Bodyline points out and underlines the androgynous (*infra*) nature of cricket – both the *Laws* and the spirit – because it demonstrates when contrasted with the underarm incident, that one can stand by the Law and still be a man, or one can stand by the *Law* and be regarded as a wimp. Larwood, then, is right when he says that no one, not even Jardine, would have ordered him to bowl underarm because such an action, while legal would have violated the spirit of Bodyline, which *was* legal but more especially and more essentially it was masculine.

Another possible explanation, not at all inconsistent with the virility thesis, is that the public outrage over Chappell's actions arose as a result of a deep disquiet about the newly evident and growing commercialization of cricket. Chappell's action was seen as a public manifestation of all that was wrong with this phenomenon. For supporters of the Denningesque tradition, Chappell's decision demonstrated the nefarious impact of the Other, with its own, contraindicated code of 'professionalism', 'gamesmanship' and 'win at all costs'. For supporters of the 'new' cricket, Chappell's order and his brother's compliance (as a good wage-slave?) constituted perhaps an embarrassing display of the Emperor's new clothes.

But neither explanation is completely satisfactory, nor is it total or holistic. To explain away the underarm delivery as the result of commercialization overlooks and ignores a strong connection between the interests of capitalism and the interests of patriarchy. Commonly, weak, wimpish behaviour is unacceptable under both. It is also to ignore the historical (*infra*) connections between commercial interests and cricket. If there has always been such a connection, commercialization cannot have been the only reason or explanation for the underarm bowling incident, for such actions would have been common and acceptable. Again, any attempt to explain anything about cricket by an appeal to a one-dimensional master referent must always fall victim to the inevitable and inherent complexities both of the practice of the game and the practice of talking about the game.

At the same time, the virility thesis is not, and cannot be, universally acceptable or applicable, even in these apparently clear circumstances. After the game, Geoff Howarth, the New Zealand captain 'wondered whether he would have had the guts to do what Chappell did'.

Is it gutless to hide behind the *Law* or does it take guts to use the letter of the *Law*, knowing that in 'standing up for your rights', you will be roundly condemned for doing so? For example, when Javed Miandad of Pakistan hit a six off the last ball in the final of the Australasian Cup of 1986 against India, at least one journalist from that country chided the team for not being 'professional enough' to have bowled the ball so short it would have rolled to the batter.[18] In the domain of legal and ethical discourse, judgements about the moral infirmity of Greg Chappell appear to rest in the shifting and uncertain sands of ethical indeterminacy, part of a situation in which even the construction of the dominant trope of masculinity in a phallogocentric world (see *infra*) is more and more uncertain. If capitalism, law and cricket all demanded that Chappell act like a man, how can each be blamed for his failure to do so?

It is easy, in the underarm incident as in all other aspects of cricket, Law and life, to tell other stories from other perspectives. While the dominant and lasting canon relates to the immorality of Greg Chappell's order to his brother, other sub-texts, albeit slightly tongue in cheek, permit us either to place blame on Chappell from another perspective, or, in a unique twist, to put the moral culpability purely on Brian McKechnie, the New Zealand batter who faced the final and fateful delivery from Trevor.

In the first instance, Chappell can be faulted not from the point of view of some moral condemnation of his insistence on legal formalism or by assaulting his 'manhood', but more particularly on 'the facts'. On this view, Chappell must be criticized because he made a bad utilitarian calculation. McKechnie could not have hit even a regular delivery for six.[19] Chappell's decision to bowl underarm was therefore *wrong* on the facts because a 'normal' cricket delivery would have had the same result. He then could have avoided all the moral outcry which followed his action and achieved exactly the same result. This is confirmed not only by Larwood's analysis but *ex post facto* by Trevor Chappell. As his brother Ian relates the story, some years after the incident Trevor was invited to New Zealand to compete in a double-wicket competition. 'Someone with a sense of humour' partnered him with McKechnie. Upon his return home, Trevor was heard to complain that not only had McKechnie not hit a six, he had not been able to manage a single boundary during the entire competition. Greg Chappell could have, and should have avoided all the controversy surrounding the under-arm incident if only he had known.

At the same, it is possible to tell a story about what a skilled batter could have done even against an underarm delivery. In this narrative matrix, the moral culpability falls not on either of the Chappells but on McKechnie for failing to be a good batter. Ian Chappell tells a story of the great Australian batter Doug Walters' reaction to the incident. Walters simply expressed his disgust at McKechnie's inability to hit the mullygrubber for six. As his teammates shook their heads in disbelief, Walters offered to prove his theory. At net practice at the SCG, someone rolled an underarm delivery at Walters. Walters moved down the wicket, kicked the ball into the air with his front foot and hit the ball onto Driver Avenue. While his teammates pointed out his theoretical vulnerability to an LBW appeal, Walters nonetheless 'proved' once again that in cricket any number of stories, from any number of perspectives, can be told, each as 'valid' as every other. Legal formalism and ethical debate can never be simply or crudely deployed or asserted as complete explanations.

15 The chucker as outlaw – legality, morality and exclusion in cricket

'Chucking' and 'throwing' are the terms used by cricketers to refer to bowling actions which violate the terms of Law 24(2) and (3). In most instances, it is simply short-hand for calling the offender a cheat.[1] The issues which surround the chucking debate in cricket again find their sources in the history of the game. Like most other debates we have seen, they raise issues of law – the meaning of Law 24(2) and (3), its correct interpretation and its application in specific situations – and issues of ethics – is chucking immoral as well as illegal? Why is it treated more harshly in the ethical practices of cricket than breaches of other *Laws*?

Like the bizarre mirror image of the underarm bowling incident, the issue of chucking has its origins in the dramatic paradigm shift which took place in cricket with the development and legalization of round-arm, overarm bowling. Not only were there obvious interpretive difficulties in deciding whether the bowler was illegally straightening his arm, but the earlier *Laws* gave sole jurisdiction for the issue to the bowler's end umpire. As we have already seen, it would be and is extremely difficult for that umpire to check the position of the bowler's feet, his arm motion and follow the flight and pitch of the ball for a possible LBW decision, all in an instantaneous flurry of action. While the *Law* was been amended so that 'either Umpire' may now no-ball a bowler for throwing, many interpretive difficulties surrounding the issue not just of chucking generally but of the proper jurisdiction of the umpire, as we shall see, remain.

The history of the game shows clearly that umpires have not always acted in a forthright way in upholding the letter and spirit of the *Law* when the vexed question of 'illegal deliveries' arises. History also shows that when umpires do act to enforce the *Law*, that can be the beginning rather than the end of controversy. Debates about the definition and sanction for chucking raged for the 20-year period between 1882 and 1902. When Australian umpire Jim Phillips took a public stand by enforcing the *Law* and no-balling bowlers, the controversy came to a head and, for a time at least, chucking was stamped out.[2]

It is interesting and telling to note, however, that while it was an umpire's adherence to the *Laws* and his institutional duty to 'courageously stamp out unfair play', which served as the catalyst to the anti-chucking movement, the apparently true and effective sanctioning of the alleged breaches of the *Law* came about through the means of an internal form of alternative dispute resolution and self-regulation. Thus, after Phillips took the initiative, 'a meeting of the English County captains in late 1901 agreed not to bowl 14 players they all agreed were throwers, the problem was temporarily solved'.[3]

This 'fact' is highly illustrative. First, it is clear that at this time in cricket's history at least, various participants in the process/text of 'cricket' were actively involved in formulating and inventing the meanings and interpretations which were given to it. In other words, the County captains were an acknowledged interpretive community whose attributions of 'meaning' carried great weight and authority. The *Laws* and the spirit of cricket were imbued with significance by the daily 'practices' of interpreters other than umpires. The legislative text of the *Law* was authenticated and its practical application altered by a community functioning as a source of folk or informal law.

At the same time, of course, it must be remembered that the County Cricket structure in England was determined and informed by the distinction between amateurs and professionals – the Gentlemen and the Players, reinforced itself by the absurdities of separate dressing rooms, entrance gates and the semiotic practice of identifying status by whether one's initials preceded or followed one's surname.

The interpretive community of the County captains, then, was one of upper-class amateurs and not *per se* representative of the ethos of other members of a broader 'cricket' community. Moreover, it is not amiss to point out that fast bowlers, who would be among those subject to suspicion of chucking, were at that time (and continued to be) the proletarians of cricket, both by their class origins outside cricket and by their function as the workhorses (or infantry?) of the attack. The English County captains' meeting, whatever the 'technical' accuracy of its assessment of the 14 players banned as throwers, clearly operated by imposing *prima facie* an upper-class amateur interpretation on the practices (and livelihood) of many of the working-class members of their teams. An interpretive 'community' is not necessarily a broad-based, democratic interpretive community, nor is an 'accepted' interpretation one which is accepted because it was arrived at through a conscious, open, free and democratic hermeneutic practice.

Once again, however, even apparently *certain* and defined categories like class and amateurism, as well as an apparent universal interpretive community like the County captains, tend to fray at the interpretive seams. Two captains, MacLaren of Lancashire and England and Prince Ranjitsinjhi of Sussex, demurred and continued to bowl the alleged chuckers in their teams.[4] The universality of the interpretive community foundered not only on county loyalty and a potential utilitarianism (the bowlers concerned took wickets) but also because it was perceived then, as it would later be in Australia, that some of the agreement that everyone 'knew' who threw was based not in 'fact' or shared knowledge but on the 'fact' that they were effective bowlers. In Lancashire, where Crossland and Meld were accused of chucking, the allegations were met with the counter-allegation that: 'We never had the slightest doubt the Crossland's pace had quite as much to do with the outcry against him as his alleged unfairness.'[5]

Furthermore, simple class analysis about the proletarian nature of bowlers is countered, in one instance at least, by the facts. One of the bowlers to be no-balled for throwing was C.B. Fry, the very epitome of the English gentleman amateur. Fry was singled out for the most vociferous attacks for throwing, ironically perhaps because he was an amateur and a gentleman.[6] While professionals might be expected because of their origins to show a certain disregard for the *Laws*, it was incumbent upon the gentlemen to uphold both the letter of the *Law* and the spirit of the game. Here, Fry had fallen from grace for he had betrayed his station. He should have known better, indeed he *must* have known better. He has forsaken his fellows. By chucking, he had renounced membership in the community of gentlemen and by definition, although not in practice, in the community of cricket.

Notwithstanding these additional complexities, interesting insights into the general and specific operations of the *Laws* and spirit of cricket emerge from the 1901 meeting of the County captains. The players 'banned were 14 players they all agreed were throwers'. At one level, this is a classic example of the experiential nature of our understanding about truth and law. If we operate within a system of rules (law or cricket) our knowledge about their practice comes not so much from a scientific and rational study or understanding, but from our lived experience of them. We know a tort or a crime or a contract when we see one because we have seen torts and crimes and contracts before. We have a lived, experiential base for our 'knowledge' of them. For us, law is existential and sometimes ontological, not epistemological. Similarly, we 'know', or rather the County captains know, what throwing is, not because of an intimate knowledge of the *arcana* of Law 24, but because to possess that knowledge of Law 24 is what it actually means to be a County cricket captain.[7] As part of their shared experience of 'cricket', 'they all agreed' the players in question were throwers. Cricket Law and the spirit of the game are not technical skills, rather the technical skills (*techné*) are part of the practical wisdom (*phroenesis*) of what it means 'to play cricket'.

Perhaps the most important interpretive 'fact' to come out of this 1901 meeting is that the captains did 'all agree' that the players in question were throwers. As we have seen, the controversy had raged for 20 years and nothing was done until an Australian umpire, Phillips, took action and began to enforce the *Law* by no-balling offending bowlers. During this time, people involved in cricket 'knew' as they could not fail to 'know' by the very nature of their involvement and participation in the game, yet they did nothing.

Nor did the inaction suddenly disappear after 1901. Just as the problem of suspect actions did not disappear, neither did the strange reaction of umpires, players and administrators to their 'knowledge' of ongoing breaches of the law.

Thus, when Frank Chester, the most famous umpire in the world in the 1950s, said of Cuan McCarthy, the South African bowler, 'I'm convinced this man throws, Sir Pelham', Warner thought it wasn't quite the form to no-ball him: 'These people are our guests.' Chester was restrained, therefore, from intervening though he spent the afternoon ostentatiously gazing into the middle distance whenever McCarthy was bowling.[8]

Some of this reluctance to act can perhaps be explained, by reference to Sir Pelham Warner's code of gentlemanly conduct. It was just not the done thing to condemn one's fellows or one's guests, even if they were cheats. But the explanation is unsatisfactory and incomplete. At various times, there have been large public outcries against chucking. Chuckers are ostracized and treated as the pariahs of the game, they are cheats. Moreover, once again, reliance on Warner's gentlemanly code brings one into direct conflict with the *Law formalism* which epitomizes so much of cricket. The law is the law and there is a *Law* dealing with 'unfair deliveries'.

A study of history of the Ian Meckiff case illustrates better than most just how blatant and unresolvable are the legal and moral debates which surround chucking.[9] When the controversy around Meckiff's action arose, there was a strange juxtaposition between the vociferous nature of the attacks in the English press and by English players on the Australian fast bowler and his success against England: '... after his 6 for 38 set up an Australian win in the second Test at Melbourne, the full wrath of Fleet Street descended on him.'[10]

He had already taken 8 wickets in the first Test. After much debate and controversy, Meckiff was no-balled by Australian umpire Colin Egar in the Brisbane Test against South Africa in Nov. 1963 and never played for Australia again. Whether Meckiff's action was illegal is still a matter for debate, as is the question of whether his action was any different from that of many other fast bowlers. What is more fascinating than these 'factual' debates is the morality play which surrounded, and continues to surround, Ian Meckiff's bowling action and more recent cases of bowlers accused of being chuckers.

It is clear from the circumstances, for example, that Meckiff's action became more problematic for the English as his success in taking wickets from them increased. Again, several 'meanings' can be attached to this. One could, for example, argue that English protests were grounded on nothing more than basic utilitarianism. They would be better off if Meckiff could be made to go away. Complaints about the 'legality' of his action, therefore, were a subterfuge and the *Law* was used, as it often is in 'real' life, simply as a means to an end.

On the other hand, we could see the English invocation of 'rights talk' in the same moral light as one view of *Mankading*.[11] The bowler who uses an illegal action is attempting, through his breach of the *Laws*, to gain an unfair advantage over his opponents. One could take an absolutist moral and legal stand and say he should be no-balled, the *Laws* invoked against him each time, an ethical and legal zero tolerance policy against chucking and chuckers. Or one might decide to take a moral and legal stand which tries to achieve a compromise between Pelham Warner's gentlemanly turning of a blind eye (and the other cheek) on the one hand and standing on the strict enforcement of one's rights on the other. Just as the batter who in backing-up tries to gain an unfair advantage should first be 'shown the ball', a bowler with a suspect action should perhaps first be queried or, as seemed to be the case, ignored as long as he does not obtain a *real* advantage – 'no harm, no foul' – or, as in rugby or soccer, it may be best 'to play the advantage', i.e. not interfere unless a breach of the rule has an actual adverse impact on the victim. In circumstances where the thrower is not taking wickets, his action, like prostitution or marijuana use, is a 'victimless crime'. From this perspective, what appears to be cynical utilitarianism may be seen to involve a slightly more complex moral calculus.

Whatever the motivation behind the English press reaction and Colin Egar's decision to no-ball Meckiff, it is clear from the aftermath of such events that something very special is involved in cricketers' debates about chucking. Following these incidents, Meckiff was 'harassed at his office and on the golf course by people who called him a cheat'.[12] In addition

> His children were called 'chucker' by neighbourhood kids, and his relatives were repeatedly confronted by friends who asked 'Does Ian really throw?' Some of his closest friends addressed him sourly as 'Chucker'. When he bowled a few spinners to school boys, one of them called 'No ball!' If he landed in a bunker at golf, other players suggested he 'chuck it out'. The strain of these jibes caused his health to crack and he had to undergo medical care.[13]

What is it about chucking that would create such an atmosphere? What code of honour did Ian Meckiff violate which called for such a drastic imposition and expression of moral opprobrium? It might be argued that chucking is cheating because it is a direct violation of the *Law*. But other *Laws* are violated all the time in cricket, yet no bowler is ostracized for a no-ball call after overstepping the crease. Some would perhaps suggest that chucking is not only a technical violation of *Law* but is a real, illegal attempt to gain an advantage. Again, so are many other violations, yet, the best type of example of trying to gain an advantage over a batter, 'sledging', is not only a violation of *Law* but it is something of a proud Australian tradition. The reaction against chucking is perhaps so vehement and condemnation so fierce because it occurs in the confrontation between the bowler and the opposing striker, the most telling one-on-one in the game, and a test of both players' character and manhood. Does the bowler somehow fail this test of character by backing down in the confrontation, by making an illegal delivery to gain an unfair advantage? This explanation somehow feels close to the truth for it brings together elements of law, ethics and the cult of virility, all so important to the 'character of cricket'. But on examination, it too falls into incompleteness.

Greg Chappell fell down in the virility sweepstakes, on one view of the underarm bowling incident, yet he was not driven out of the game or attacked as vehemently or for as long as was Meckiff. Chappell is still considered a great Australian cricketer and captain. Nor can reference to the simple fact that Chappell's unmanliness was 'legal' while Meckiff's was not, suffice to explain their different fates.

As far as the 'context' of Meckiff's cheating, in the violent confrontation between bat and ball, in the gladiatorial clash of foes, this explanation too fails, for as we shall see, the prohibition against 'fast, short-pitched' bowling, which also has regulated the terms of engagement between demon-bowler and batter, was and is still violated on a regular basis. Bowlers who use intimidatory tactics against batters, who aim to and do, strike the batter on the body, are not driven from the game, harassed and banished, they are the folk heroes of Bay 13 at the MCG. Like Meckiff they deliver illegal balls at the batter in order to gain an advantage, often in violation of the *Laws* and the spirit of the game, but their fate is not ostracism, it is canonization and adulation.

Still other moral and legal issues are raised and left unresolved by the context of the chucking controversy. The familiar issue of intimidating umpires (*supra*) again arises here. Not only did Bill Dowling, chair of the ACB at the time of the 1960 Meckiff controversy, condemn press attacks as attempts to intimidate umpires, but he and Sir Donald Bradman pointed out that such reports were contrary both to cricket's concept of fair play and of the basic presumptions of the Golden Thread of the common law, and the presumption of innocence. Meckiff, roundly condemned by one and all as a thrower, had not yet appeared in England, yet he was found guilty of a heinous cricket offence in the press.[14]

Not only must we bear in mind the effect of such public opinion on the ethical and legal context of interpretations of *the Laws of Cricket*, but we must also remember that Dowling's and Bradman's remarks indicate that the matter of Meckiff's chucking was not one on which there was universal consensus. Meckiff had been accepted and chosen by his captain and his country's selectors and had not yet been no-balled for throwing by any of the umpires who had watched him before the complaints were heard over the sound of falling English wickets. This could mean that the ACB and Australian cricketers were cheats or it could, more probably, mean they did not think or 'know' that Meckiff threw.

As the meeting in 1901 of the English County captains on the chucking controversy of that era demonstrates, this very idea of the practical wisdom and knowledge of the actors in the game of cricket is highly problematic. In addition, as we know from our experience of the criminal justice system, and of the theory and practice of propaganda, it is quite possible to create 'facts' simply through a concerted effort to change public perception. 'Crime' reaches epidemic proportions, not from empirical truth, but simply because crime stories feature on the evening news. A similar process of chipping away at accepted legal principles and interpretations through changing social circumstances, including public perception and opinion, is the very process of the evolution of the common law method and system.

When Colin Egar no-balled Ian Meckiff in Brisbane, this does not mean that Meckiff actually threw or that he always had been, as the English claimed, a chucker. Nor does it mean that Egar was acting in bad faith when he declared Meckiff a chucker by no-balling him.[15] What it does mean is that the 'fact' of Meckiff's chucking is an interpretive construct, made up of and connected with a complex *matrix* of physical phenomena, public perceptions, ethical and legal dilemmas and a host of other factors.

These factors are combined with the problematic nature of the interpretive community (or communities) of cricket and its (or their) 'knowledge' of chucking. Pollard refers to the actual definition of throwing as '... the game's most complex problem, still unresolved', and states that John Arlott, one of the game's great observers and traditionalists, 'said the job of explaining a throw for the law book was one for the barristers, not cricket writers'.[16] It is obvious, then, than any claim of 'knowledge' as to what 'chucking' means is filtered through many complex and confusing factors, to which still others, like racism and nationalism, must be added, if the historical context which informs the chain of being of cricket (and of chucking) is to be understood.

In Australia, Aboriginal fast bowlers Albert 'Alec' Henry, Eddie Gilbert and Jack Marsh have all been at the centre of the throwing controversies of their eras.[17] In a country where no Aboriginal has ever played Test cricket, it would not be disingenuous to propagate the idea that decisions to no-ball all three were, in part at least, informed by an inherent Australian racism, or at least an Australian racism which is part of that country's cricket tradition.[18] Marsh even went so far as to have a doctor put his arm in a splint which made it physically impossible for him to throw. He played until the luncheon interval in the contraption and his 'natural' bowling action and effectiveness in attack were in no way hampered. The umpire as in Gregory's case left in humiliation and Marsh was not again accused of chucking.[19]

In addition to utilitarianism, formalism, moralism, racism and class-bias, the interpretive content of 'chucking' may also be informed by nationalism. Charlie Griffith, the West Indian fast bowler, was harassed and driven out of the game as a thrower and among the main proponents of this view of his action were the Australians and the English.[20] On the other hand, the West Indians defended their own bowler, as had the Australians during Meckiff's ordeal and to this day Sir Garfield Sobers, former captain of the West Indies team, claims that Griffith did not throw and that he was 'crucified'.[21]

None of what I have said means that the umpires who no-balled Marsh or the Australians who attacked Griffith's actions were blinded by nationalist bias or utilitarian desires to rid themselves of a fearsome opponent. I simply assert that what the chucking issue, in all its complexity demonstrates, is that cricket, like Law, is a social text which we imbue with meanings which are sometimes fixed or apparently universal and sometimes fluid and subject to 'local' specificities. Our 'knowledge' of cricket, its *Laws* and ethics, its ethos and praxis, is an ever-changing text on which we inscribe and from which we erase meanings of which even we are sometimes unaware. In spite of this, or perhaps because of it, tit-for-tat allegations of chucking arise from time to time.[22]

Yet, as at least one commentator has had the apparent good sense to point out, the problem with chucking should not be allegations of chucking or national defence of one's own bowlers. The problem with chucking is chucking itself.

My own view on efforts by captains and cricket boards to defend the suspect actions of their bowlers has always been that it is just not cricket. It is an extremely disappointing scenario that allows an Arjuna Ranatunga or a PCB to make an international issue of what should remain a strictly cricketing problem of a technical nature, and subsequently takes away the powers of umpires on the field to rule on unfair bowling actions. Just as sadly, numerous cricket commentators of immense knowledge and experience have supported such essentially political moves, forsaking the time-honoured values of cricket.[23]

Yet if one thing is clear about chucking, it is that the time-honoured traditions of the game, and the technical application of the *Laws* on the field by the umpires, have never been, and probably can never be, anything but 'political'. The recent legal and ethical controversies surrounding Sri Lankan spinner Muttiah Muralitharan and Pakistani quick bowler Shoaib Akhtar amply demonstrate this.

16 Murali, Shoaib and the jurisprudence of chucking

As cricket moved into the 1990s and then into the twenty-first century, we can find striking evidence of the repetition of by now familiar themes. Allegations and insinuations about the legality of some bowlers' actions emerged. Questions about the appropriate interpretation of the *Laws* dealing with illegal deliveries were raised. Umpires who 'called' bowlers for throwing were vilified as racists and cheats, or lauded for their courage in upholding the letter of the law and the true spirit of the game. The battle between bat and ball was saved from cheating bowlers or endangered by overzealous adjudication. Doubts seemed to emerge as wickets fell, indicating again for some that throwing has more to do with success than a desire to stamp out cheating. Bowlers resorted to the modern equivalent of 'bowling in splints' as expert medical advice and biomechanical analyses were trotted out to prove that the bowler's arm was congenitally deformed and that what might have looked like throwing was in fact nothing more than an optical illusion. In other words, in this area of the law and *Laws* of cricket there was and is little new under the jurisprudential sun.

The first important case in cricket's renewed battle about and around throwing came to the fore in 1995 when doubts began to emerge about the action of Sri Lankan spinner Muttiah Muralitharan. Then coach of New Zealand, John Reid, voiced in public the idea that Murali might well be a chucker: 'I don't want to crucify the guy but I want to convey the feelings of my team...We do have doubts about his action and believe an investigation is needed.'[1]

The conflicts and controversial legal and moral implications of chucking are immediately evidenced by Reid's intervention. First, we note the serious moral censure which has historically been carried in accusations of throwing. The New Zealand coach described the possible effect of the accusations in Biblical terms – 'crucify'. Secondly, we can see, at least by implication, the competing counter-narrative. The New Zealanders are 'concerned' here because doubts about a bowler's action go again to the very core of the game, of what it means to play cricket. The contest between bat and ball, between bowler and batter, is tarnished and lacking in good faith if it is unfair, and it is unfair if the bowler is not engaging in the confrontation in a lawful manner.

Finally, the New Zealanders concern could have been construed and understood as having been influenced by the fact that they were on a long run of failure in

Test matches. Murali had taken 5 wickets for 64 runs in the first Test. We have already seen that the series was marred by physical contact between players and that New Zealand stood accused of its own sharp practices by preparing a green pitch and loading its side with seam bowlers.[2] The idea that doubts about the spinner's action came from some objective respect for and love of the *Laws* and spirit of the game might be belied by other factors which operated at the time.

When the Sri Lankan side arrived in Australia after their visit to New Zealand, doubts and rumours continued to circulate about the legality of Murali's action. Following a tour match in Queensland the Australian umpires standing in the game apparently reported their concerns about the legality of some of his deliveries. The Match Referee Graham Dowling, himself a former captain of New Zealand, met with Sri Lankan team officials prior to the first Test in Perth and raised concerns about throwing. Team manager, and another former captain, Duleep Mendis dismissed the rumours about his bowler's action, 'He has played all over the world before different umpires and there was no problem, so I don't think at this stage we should discuss it.'[3]

Mendis here raises several questions and issues of both procedural and substantive import for our understanding of the jurisprudence of throwing and the case of Muttiah Muralitharan. First, he asserts that Murali had played before and never been called by an umpire. Of course, as we have already seen in this and other contexts, this can in fact and in law be proof of nothing more than the assertion itself. Because he had not been called for throwing, we cannot simply assume that this means that he has not, does not or will not throw. There may be some assumptions about the legality of his action based on judicial inaction, but these assumptions are not proof and they can not, at a basic level of legality, determine a future judgement about his deliveries. In chucking, as in all matters of law and legality, each case must be decided on its merits. As far as throwing is concerned, this means that each and every delivery, in theory at least, must be judged for conformity with the *Law* relating to unfair deliveries.

In addition, it might also be the case that as a matter of 'law', Mendis is over-stating his case. We now know, *ex post facto*, that officials on and off the field, umpires, Match Referees and those at the ICC offices in London, had held suspicions about Murali's action for some time: 'ICC divulged that umpires, via match referees, had expressed doubts about his legitimacy for more than two years.'[4]

Australian umpire Darrell Hair, to whom we shall return shortly, later admitted that he had intended to call Murali for throwing at a tournament in Sharjah in Oct. but that '... he was dissuaded by the International Cricket Council representative'.[5]

Here we encounter a set of legal practices which first of all call into question the soundness of Mendis' statement and secondly which indicate the existence of a legal counter-narrative to strict ideas of an ethos of legal formalism in cricket adjudication. In other words, umpires had in fact expressed concerns about the legality of Murali's bowling action and a statement that he had not been called by any umpires previously, while factually correct, does not convey the whole legal story of events up to this time. A simple assertion, or implication, that because he had not been called for throwing, Murali's action had been 'approved' as legal is on the facts and in law not correct. At the same time, there is evidence here that a new legal system had informally been established which had little, if anything, to do with the *Laws of Cricket*. Instead of calling a bowler for throwing when entitled (and obliged) to do so under the *Laws*, umpires reported their concerns to the ICC Match Referee who then passed on the information to the game's headquarters in London.

We must confront a basic contradiction between strict adherence to the letter of the law and an attitude of informal or alternative justice systems. Instead of invoking the law as written, and thereby, as we have seen, bringing down on the bowler all of the moral stigma attached to having been branded a chucker and therefore a cheat, umpires quietly report the offender to the authorities who then, we must assume, are supposed to take some kind of remedial action. In cases such as this, for example, the home board could be informed, and the bowler could receive tuition to correct the faults in his delivery action, failing which he could be dropped from the side.[6] The *Law* and the law would be served here if the bowler learned to deliver legal balls to the batter or if he failed to learn this, he would no longer participate in the game and cheating would not occur. Such diversion programmes are increasingly part of juvenile justice programmes for example. Instead of humiliation and ostracism as a result of the labelling process which necessarily comes with the historic practice and understanding of the public legal spectacle of being branded a cheat for violating this *Law* in particular, the bowler is reintegrated into the game, or at least is given a chance to do so. All of this can be and has been supported in terms of both individualized and collective justice – the bowler is 'saved', and the interests of the *Laws* and spirit of the game are preserved in the long run.

Of course, there is one major difference between what must or should have been the ideas informing the ICC practice in 1994 and 1995 around Murali and others, and diversion or reintegrative justice reforms. In the latter, the victim must be involved and an essential part of the reintegration of the perpetrator is the idea of confrontation with the victim of the offence and making them whole in some way. In the informal reporting world of what we can assume was happening in world cricket, the immediate victims, the batters here, are never confronted by the wrongdoer nor are they made whole. If a wicket falls to a delivery the umpire suspects might have been illegal, and the informal system is in place, there is nothing from the victim's perspective but injustice. They should have received the benefit of a no-ball. Instead their wicket has fallen and goes in the record books to the credit of the bowler. The *Law* on fair deliveries is not respected and the batter is the victim of a never-remedied injustice. From this perspective, the failure to adhere to the rule of law and the application of the normative structures of the *Laws of Cricket*, which are supposed to regulate the confrontation between bat and ball, results in a fundamental illegality and a basic injustice.

Finally, it is also important to underline as a matter of law and jurisprudence, that even if we assume that the bowler in question has undergone remedial treatment and training, that can never be a guarantee of the future legality of every delivery he will bowl in his career. A pardon and reintegration into the game can only ever cover past conduct. It cannot result in an irrebuttable presumption that every delivery will be legal. That would not only be factually absurd, but it would remove from the jurisdiction of the judicial authority who has always been assumed to be in the best position to render decisions on such matters, the umpire, the ability to intervene to stop actual illegal conduct. This is the point at which recent and ongoing debates on chucking appear to founder into jurisprudential and legal nonsense. No bowler, as a matter of law and practice, can ever truly be said not to throw until an umpire on the field of play adjudicates on a particular delivery. There might be factual generalizations based on empirical evidence, i.e. a bowler has never had his delivery questioned and therefore we can practically affirm that he is not a chucker. But this can never be a legal principle. In the end, as we shall see in some more detail later, the umpire must always be in a position to make the decisions under the *Laws* in the course of the game. If this is not the case, then it is obvious that the nature of the game will change and wickets will fall 'illegally' to no-balls but with no remedial redress available to the batter who has been harmed.

On the surface of the Murali case as it unfolded, the legal system seemed to operate under its traditional jurisdictional and normative schemes. Officials refused to comment publicly about confidential Match Referee reports and instead left enforcement of the anti-throwing provisions in the hands of the umpires on the field.[7] Murali played in the first Test at the WACA in Perth before umpires Peter Parker of Australia and Khizar Hayat of Pakistan. Although there were other legal issues of some import arising out of this game, Murali's action went unchallenged on the field.[8] The same did not obtain at the second five-day game between the sides, the Boxing Day Test at the MCG. Umpire Darrell Hair, an Australian, who we now know had previously reported his doubts about Murali's action, called Murali seven times in three overs. Instead of following the practice invoked by Richie Benaud when Ian Meckiff was no-balled and removing his bowler from the attack, Sri Lankan captain Arjuna Ranatunga, put the bowler on from the other end. Umpire Steve Dunne of New Zealand did not call Murali. We do now know, however, that Hair stood ready to call Murali again from the other end had the Sri Lankans persisted in bowling the spinner.

An international uproar followed, proving once again the gravity of 'chucking' for the very definition of the game, and from the content of the uproar, also demonstrating the apparently immutable content of jurisprudential debates in cricket. The first reactions, from respected Australian cricket writer Phil Wilkins, indicate the inherent problems and misunderstandings of both law and fact which surround chucking and cheating in cricket law.

First of all, Wilkins reproduced the philosophically unsound and legally incorrect idea that Murali was somehow safe because he had passed previous muster: 'Despite the widespread reservations, Muralidharan entered the Melbourne Test innocuously, having been "cleared" in the Perth Test by umpires Khizar Hayat, of Pakistan, and Peter Parker, of Australia.'[9]

Again, I need not belabour the point here. Whether he had been cleared or not is unknown, given what we know about the informal justice system which was at some level operating in international cricket at the time concerning illegal deliveries. Moreover, as I have already argued, being 'cleared' does not mean, at law, the same thing as being 'clear' for the future. Being found 'not guilty' at one trial can never mean that an accused will never be convicted of another offence in the future, and no one would make such an absurd claim about criminal law. This is something we all seem to know about law but conveniently forget when we are talking about cricket and the law. Yet the misconception continues to inform not just cricket debate but legal, quasi-judicial practice. For example, in May 2002, Adam Gilchrist made some comments in an informal setting during which he stated that he believed that Murali did 'throw'. He was immediately subjected to an Australian Cricket Board (ACB) disciplinary proceeding for violating the prohibition on making detrimental public comments.[10] Rule 10 of the ACB Code of Behaviour states in part: 'Players and officials must not make any public or media comment which is detrimental to the interests of the game...'.

There are several interesting points here which no doubt will be litigated in the future. Is the circumstance of an informal set of comments at a 'private' gathering at which some journalists may be present sufficient to constitute 'public or media comment' in violation of the Code? On the ABC Television programme *The Fat*, broadcast on 27 May 2002, Gilchrist made clear that he was not aware of the presence of journalists and considered his comments to be only brief and impromptu remarks in response to a friendly inquiry at a luncheon. At the same time of course this raises a familiar issue of 'free speech' and sporting association bans, for example on comments relating to refereeing decisions. But more importantly for the issue here is the ACB's official reason justifying the proceedings against Gilchrist. CEO James Sutherland stated:

> Muttiah Muralitharan's action has been cleared by the International Cricket Council (ICC) after an exhaustive review. The ICC has a rigid and comprehensive process in place to continually assess the legality of bowling actions and the ACB supports this process.[11]

Again, even the ICC bowling review procedures permit the umpires in any match to apply the provisions of the *Laws* of cricket relating to unfair deliveries. The fact that a bowler has been cleared does not mean that he does not throw, or that he will not throw in the future. Here the question appears to be exactly what in Gilchrist's comments are 'detrimental to the interests of the game'. Is it that he questioned the legality of a bowler's action? Is it that he by implication challenged the validity of the ICC decision or the ICC process? Is it that by implication he associated the ACB with this alleged imputed attack on the ICC? Is it detrimental to the game to question the ICC throwing committee? Is this the administrative equivalent of 'dissent' over an umpire's decision? What is being protected here – Murali's reputation, the ICC, the ACB and which if any of those when attacked is detrimental to the game of cricket? Gilchrist's comments and his interview on the ABC indicate that he was not casting aspersions on Murali's character. He rang the Sri Lankan in London to explain and apologize for any misunderstanding. His comments were aimed at administrators and coaches who allow bowlers with suspect actions to continue uncorrected. Surely one could see these comments as being in the best interest of the game. Instead, the ACB appears to be adopting an innovative jurisprudential idea combining contempt of court and *stare decisis*, deciding that a player may not address any issue which has been 'dealt' with by the judicial apparatus. Of course, the issue has not been 'dealt with' in any definitive way unless and until we accept the idea that the ICC's committee on throwing has the power to 'clear' a bowler to cheat forever once a decision has been made about the legality of his action.

Gilchrist was found guilty of the offence and given a reprimand by the ACB.[12] Apparently the substantive character of the offence which to some extent still remains unarticulated is that his comments were detrimental to the character and interests of the game, 'particularly in the context of the ACB's relationship with other countries'.[13] Still, the essential element of the offence for which Gilchrist was convicted appears to remain obscure. Which relationship(s) are under threat here? Australian/Sri Lankan relations have hardly been harmonious historically. Is the question here the relationship with all other members of the ICC and/or those with representatives on the throwing committee? Surely this would mean that no cricketer can ever make any comment on any issue relating to international cricket. Again, a major legal problem for cricket adjudication may be looming here. There are complex issues of the extent and nature of the contractual relationship which ties Gilchrist to the ACB. There are serious concerns about the content and applicability of the rules of natural justice in such a context. Gilchrist's livelihood was, in theory at least, on the line in such a hearing. How can such a serious matter be fairly adjudicated when the substantive nature of the offence charged is still not clearly and explicitly outlined? 'Detrimental to the interests of the game' is arguably so vague as to be without any meaning. How can comments that another player is in effect being allowed to cheat with impunity be detrimental to the interests of the game? If true, what is detrimental to the interests of the game is the fact that such activity in violation of the *Laws of Cricket* is being allowed to continue unchecked. Indeed, the idea of the relations with, in this instance, the BCCSL, being harmed is arguably risible. If they, as the history of their actions in several cases, including their defence of Murali, which involved an orchestrated walk off under Ranatunga's captaincy, act in such a way as to allow 'chuckers' to be part of their Test sides, how can Gilchrist's comments be detrimental to the game?

In the 2002 series between England and Sri Lanka, Ruchira Perera was reported for illegal deliveries. The Sri Lankan authorities in that case simply relied on the technical wording of the regulations relating to Stage 1 breaches under the new ICC system dealing with illegal deliveries, which require a review of the bowler's action by the home Board, and 'threatened' to include him in their team for the next match.[14] In the end, Perera was not selected. Instead Muralitharan came back from injury and appeared in the second Test at Edgbaston. Perera did play in the subsequent tour match against an MCC eleven, after receiving tuition from the Sri Lankan bowling adviser, Daryl Foster. The change in his action for some '. . . was evident but his bouncer still invites suspicions . . .'[15]

Perera was not chosen for the third and final Test at Old Trafford. Not surprisingly perhaps, Sri Lankan politician and former captain, Arjuna Ranatunga, criticized Perera's omission by the selectors. He opined that he would not have hesitated to pick the fast bowler if only to have a psychological impact on his opponents and thereby to help his team to victory.[16]

The idea that Gilchrist's statements could have been detrimental to the game of cricket in these circumstances is extremely problematic. Chucking is on the agenda of public discourse about cricket, yet the Australian vice-captain and number one batter in the world cannot comment about suspect actions. When he did so, he was reprimanded for bringing the game of cricket into disrepute.

When the decision to convict and punish Gilchrist was reported, the criticism of the ACB continued: 'The ACB has worn flak all week for jumping on Gilchrist for answering his questions honestly, and with a view common among a majority of players around the world.'[17]

In addition to expressing concerns about the chilling effect of the ACB's actions and the future reluctance of players to make any honest comments about the game, this reaction raises another more obvious question. If it is true that the majority of the world's cricketers think that Murali is a chucker, what on earth is going on at the ICC Committee level, or among international elite umpires? Do players misunderstand the *Law* on unfair deliveries? Does anyone know what throwing is?

England batter Mark Butcher made an adverse comment about the legality of Ruchira Perera's action in a newspaper column after the first Test against Sri Lanka in 2002. After the ACB action against Gilchrist, Butcher expressed fears that he too would be prosecuted. He did issue an apology, was finally fined £1,000 plus £500 costs.[18] There is of course an important difference here. Perera was reported after that match for 'throwing'. At the time of Butcher's comments he had yet to be reviewed and 'passed' by his Board under the Stage 1 provisions of the ICC regulations. Therefore, Butcher was not 'in contempt' of the ICC. He might still be considered to be 'guilty' if it is argued that he made a comment on a case which is 'before the courts' and therefore somehow interfered with the prosecution of an action.[19] Once again, however, 'chucking' appears to throw common sense and intelligent analysis out of the window in favour of moral panic.

To return to the specifics of Phil Wilkins' commentary on the original no-balling of Murali, we can see all of these contradictions and indications that common sense and dispassionate discourse about the 'law' are replaced by something else. Wilkins makes an even more telling point on the contradictions, misunderstandings and disagreements which continue to surround the law and ethics of chucking in the world of cricket. For him and many others, 'The curious feature of the seven occasions Hair called Muralidharan was that it was done from behind the bowler – not from square leg.'[20]

On previous occasions where bowlers had been called for throwing, it had been common for the decision to come from the square leg umpire. Indeed, when Ian Meckiff was called by Col Egar this was the case. The crowd at the time implored Richie Benaud to adopt the policy which Arjuna would use in 1995, i.e. to put the bowler on at the other end, to give the other umpire a chance to judge his delivery from square leg and not from the bowler's end.[21] There are of course practical reasons, based in the way the game is played and judged, which inform this idea that the square leg umpire should decide in chucking cases. His view, facing the bowler, albeit at an angle, better allows him to detect any change in the position of the arm just before, or as the ball is delivered. Secondly, there is the idea, again based on practical experience, that the umpire at the non-striker's end has other things on his mind and within his jurisdiction. He must keep an eye on the bowler's front foot to ensure that it is behind the line of the crease. He must also be aware of whether the back foot of the bowler is cutting the crease. Finally, he must ensure that his eyes move from the feet or foot of the bowler as the ball is released in order to be certain where the ball pitches in case of a possible LBW appeal. He cannot, according to this view, do all of these things, fulfil his legally imposed jurisdictional responsibilities in other words, and at the same time, determine whether the delivery action of the bowler's arm is legal.

Of course, as always, there are strong counter-arguments and narratives about the question in general and the case in particular. There is nothing objectively determined about the perspective of the square leg umpire, who is, as noted, always looking at an angle and at an angle which increases as the bowler falls away with the delivery. Nor is there anything in the physical world which would lead us to conclude that a straightening arm or elbow cannot be detected from behind. Moreover, on the facts of the actual case, we know that Hair actually stood well back from the normal umpiring position close to the stumps, in order to get a better viewing angle. Here, Hair stood up to watch the bowler's feet for the front foot no-ball violation and then stood back because of his concerns about the arm during the delivery. Of course, one might wish to make an argument that Hair was committing the same type of error about facts and the *Laws* as supporters of Murali have made. In other words, just because the bowler's front foot was lawfully placed on previous deliveries, this cannot mean that for future deliveries one can be certain that he would not overstep. One might assume that his delivery stride would be consistent but one cannot be assured of this as an absolute certainty based on the past. Indeed, we know from the application of the front foot no-ball law itself, that bowlers only infringe occasionally. In fact and in law, what we arrive at here is a position on the proper use of judicial discretion and the idea of police 'prioritizing' between and among serious and less serious crimes. Quite obviously here Hair was willing to forego the enforcement of the front foot no-ball *Law* and focus on the more serious chucking issue. And again, we must run the risk that in doing so he will miss a violation of the front foot *Law*, find no illegality in the delivery action, and a wicket will fall. Once more, the batter here would be the victim of a miscarriage of justice and law in the name of a judicially determined greater good. Since we know that Hair only called Murali in approximately 38 per cent of the deliveries on which he adjudicated, i.e. 7/18, there is at some level a significant chance that he may have missed a front foot no-ball.

In any event, no one really cared about this hypothetical possibility. They focused on the idea that the non-striker's end umpire should not make a decision on the chucking question.[22] Not only do these objections ignore the facts not just of the case but the laws of physics and geometry as experienced on the cricket field, but they also ignore the actual wording of the *Laws of Cricket* as they then read. Law 24(2) of the 1980 *Code* clearly and unequivocally stated that:

> If **either Umpire** is not entirely satisfied with the absolute fairness of a delivery in this respect he shall call and signal 'no ball' instantly upon delivery. (emphasis added)

There can be no doubt here that Hair had lawful jurisdiction to no-ball Murali if and when the substantive conditions of the breach of the *Law* were satisfied. It was clearly contemplated by the legislators that either umpire could be in a position to make the determination of an illegal delivery. If the practice of the square leg umpire making the call had some absolute basis in physical reality or such a strong place in the informing ethos of the game, then surely the *Laws* would have reflected those realities and norms. That the provisions of the *Laws* gave the power to Hair is a strong indication in such circumstances that an umpire at the non-striker's end can and should, indeed must (**shall** is the operative word in the legal text itself), make such a call.

Of course, all of this is further complicated by the fact that Arjuna changed the end from which Murali bowled instead of taking him off altogether. This meant that Hair stood then at square leg and Dunne at the bowler's end. Neither umpire called Murali then. The positions of the two umpires here arguably work together to buttress the arguments of those who would criticize Hair's earlier decisions. First, Umpire Dunne did not no-ball the bowler, either from the square leg position, or from behind the stumps. For critics this appears to support the idea that Hair was mistaken, on a frolic of his own, or up to no good and acting in a non-judicial manner. Once again, in fact and in law, this 'proves' no such thing. Dunne may not have called the bowler for a number of reasons. First, he may well have been satisfied with the legality of the Sri Lankan's action. On the other hand, he may have possessed doubts but acted on the understanding that he would report his suspicions to the Match Referee after the end of play, as had been the umpiring practice for some time. He may also have felt that since Hair had made the point publicly and officially about Murali, there was no need for further legal action. He may have wished to spare the young bowler further humiliation. He may have feared retribution and reaction. We do not and cannot know. Any or all of these factors, or any combination of them, may have been operating.

Secondly, the fact that Hair did not no-ball the bowler when he switched ends does not prove that the action was legal. Hair may have felt that the angle and view from square leg were not such that he could exercise his jurisdiction. Indeed, the critics may find their answer in subsequent revelations. We now know that Hair informed the Sri Lankan authorities at the tea interval that if Murali continued to bowl, he would call him for throwing from his position at square leg.[23] Perhaps he did not call him before the break because of some mistaken belief that his umpiring partner would back him up and no-ball Murali from the non-striker's end. Indeed, Hair himself says that he had previous discussions with Dunne at the Sharjah tournament during which the Kiwi umpire apparently made clear his doubts about the spinner's action.[24] Perhaps he thought that there was, as Richie Benaud had indicated years earlier in the Meckiff case, some kind of legal and ethical practice that a captain would withdraw his bowler in such circumstances and was giving Ranatunga a chance not just to comply with the norm, but also by doing so, to reduce the humiliation of the bowler. The captain, after all, bears a responsibility to the *Laws* and to the spirit of the game. There may have been in Hair's mind the idea that he would give Ranatunga the chance to do the right thing. Once it became apparent that the Sri Lankan captain would not comply with this understanding of his ethical and legal obligations, then Hair decided to invoke once again the letter of the *Law* and the norms of legal formalism. Indeed, Hair himself confirms many of these hypotheses. He says that he did not feel that the action could be best seen from square leg. He expresses anger and disappointment that Ranatunga did not withdraw the bowler.[25] Finally, he insists that after seeing Murali bowl again in Australia, he remained convinced that his bowling action was 'diabolical'.[26]

Critics of Hair were unrelenting in their attacks. In addition to the issue of umpiring solidarity and debate over which umpiring position best entitled the umpire to make a no-ball decision, there was the vital question of why Hair decided to act when and where he did, at the MCG in front of over 50,000 fans and millions of viewers tuned into the Australian national ritual of the Boxing Day Test.[27] Peter Roebuck epitomizes the approaches of the critics.

His front-page story was unequivocal in its moral and legal outrage and condemnation. The no-balling of Muralitharan by Hair at the MCG constituted a 'humiliation' and 'almost an execution'.[28] All of this, or a large part of it at least, could be put down to the public forum in which it occurred:

> And it was not done quietly, in some hallowed corner of cricket officialdom, with the senior men of the International Cricket Council studying film and gravely reaching their verdict.
>
> It was done, instead, in front of a crowd of 55,239 on the first day of a match scheduled to last five. It was done when he was playing for his country. It was done in a foreign land. It happened in his 54th first-class match, and his 23rd Test.[29]

After a lengthy review he concluded:

> Events left an unpleasant taste in the mouth. This must not happen
> again. I don't think he throws. But I do believe that such matters must be
> resolved after long and careful consideration, and in private.[30]

Roebuck's intervention is at once extraordinary and typical. His invocation of
the fact that Murali had played in many Tests and first-class matches is by now
familiar and as useless from the point of evidence or analysis as it always is.
His assertion, by implication, that there was something unfriendly to visitors
(or perhaps something more ominous) is equally problematic and typical.
Murali was under suspicion and not just by Australians or by Darrell Hair.
Most problematically, there is the idea of secrecy and privacy in adjudication
invoked here.

One of the most troubling and disconcerting elements which has surrounded
many aspects of cricket's confrontations with law and legality, has always been
the idea of secrecy. Transgressors were punished for bad 'public' i.e. on field,
behaviour, in private and behind closed doors, if and when they were punished
at all. This was clearly to the detriment of the game and its public image.
Particularly in the age of world-wide television audiences and large screen replays at
the game itself, the idea that decisions about incidents of illegality can take
place away from public view is, to say the least, unrealistic. Now, here, Roebuck
wants to convene a secret tribunal. Presumably, if after a review of the evidence,
Murali is banished and disappears from the game, Roebuck would have us
believe that he and we should then 'accept the umpire's decision' even if we, like
he, don't believe that Murali is a cheat or a thrower. Of course, one might first
ask why we should accept, authorize and approve of a decision reached in secret, on
secret evidence? What does that tell us about the understanding we should have
of the rule of law, democracy and the ethical ideal embodied in our construction
of what is and is not 'cricket'?

And what does it tell us about respect for the rule of law as embodied in the *Laws*
of the game of cricket? Hair did what he was entitled to do, what he thought was
the right thing, and finally what he was obliged to do under the provisions of the
Laws in force at the time. And he did it in public. Roebuck argues that it would
be somehow fairer, more just, better, more morally acceptable, to arrive at a
similar conclusion behind closed doors.

He compounds his factual, legal and jurisprudential errors when he adds that

> So far as can be told, Muralitharan's action has been condemned by one
> man. Either that or the rest are too meek to take the first step. Far better for
> those appointed to decide such matters to come together so that the young
> man can be passed or condemned once and for all.[31]

Again, doubts had been circulating about Murali for some time. New Zealand
coach John Reid had publicly raised the issue months before Sri Lanka came to

Australia. Reid's remarks and other indications about Murali were reported in Roebuck's own newspaper. He had in fact been 'condemned' by more than one man. Perhaps others were 'meek' or gutless in not taking action sooner. Perhaps the informal justice mechanisms on the other hand were imperfect. In neither case can Hair on these facts alone be condemned for interpreting and applying the *Laws*. Finally, Roebuck repeats the fallacy of adjudication which surrounds these debates about cricket, chucking and the law. Murali cannot be cleared, or passed (nor can in reality he be condemned) once and for all. It is not an offence against the *Laws of Cricket* to 'be a chucker'. It is a breach 'to chuck'. The crime of chucking is on the wording of the *Laws of Cricket* simply one of several ways in which a delivery can be unfair and therefore unlawful. It is true that it may well be an offence against some unarticulated norm of the spirit of the game to 'be a chucker', but this is not technically a matter of law or adjudication. At a practical level, it would apparently be difficult to include a player who 'is a chucker' in the side. He might be called at any time, slowing down the game, giving away free runs, removing a bowler from effective participation in the attack and adversely effecting the fielding side's ability to limit runs and take wickets.

At the same time, however, it is commonly accepted within cricket practice and discourse, that there is in fact, in law and even ethically speaking a difference between someone who throws occasionally and someone who is a chucker.[32] In many cases, doubt and suspicion surrounds a quick bowler's action when he bowls a bouncer, or a spinner's 'quicker' ball. These may be illegal deliveries if and when they occur but that does not, in the minds of most observers today, make a bowler a chucker. It makes him someone who occasionally infringes the *Laws* on fair deliveries. Gideon Haigh argues that the principle of avoiding moral conclusions based on infringements of the *Law* should be almost universally applied in cases of those suspected of throwing. For him,

> The point here is that nobody is cheating. If Muralitharan's action is infringing the laws of cricket, it is not because he has premeditated the gaining of an unfair advantage over his opposition. Those who have been unfortunate enough to arouse the ire of umpires for 'throwing' in the past have almost without exception, been innocent of connivance.[33]

For Haigh, there is no evidence of intent to break the *Laws* or disrupt and corrupt the contest between bat and ball. 'Throwing' here for him should carry no moral stigma. This might be subjected to further contextualization. There may well be some difference in fact, law and morality between someone who has infringed the *Law* against throwing and someone who has a basic or fundamental physical and mechanical problem with their ordinary, standard, 'natural' delivery technique. This person is a 'chucker', that is someone who in the very act of bowling appears to violate the *Laws* of the game as they define and regulate fair deliveries. If that person were allowed to continue unchecked, then the defining confrontation between bat and ball would be compromised. Thus, not only is Roebuck's idea that a bowler can be cleared or passed once and for all problematic, but it fails to distinguish properly between someone who throws and someone who is a thrower. Even in the latter case, it is not beyond the realm of possibility, experience or law, to imagine that biomechanical review, expert advice, radical or minor changes in technique and positioning, can in fact transform someone from being a chucker to someone who complies with the *Laws* of the game.[34] This can, of course, only be confirmed in light of experience and public adjudication on each and every ball delivered in a match. That is and can only be the job of an umpire.

In fact and in law, repeatedly, these conceptual, taxonomical and jurisprudential errors are repeated. The Murali controversy was no exception. Then West Indian captain Richie Richardson offered his view that because Murali had not been called previously that would prove that he did not throw.[35] Former Australian off-spinner Bruce Yardley opined that Murali's action was an optical illusion and caused by a defect in his arm. His coach confirmed the permanently bent arm theory.[36]

Biomechanical experts and medical professionals were brought in to confirm the diagnosis which would 'prove' that it was medically impossible for Murali to chuck.[37] Yardley's comments also bear examination on another point central to the law and jurisprudence of cricket and chucking. He stated: 'I don't believe any of us has got the right to dictate a young player's career like that. When there's so much uncertainty, how can one man play God like that?'[38]

Again, a player's career is not in jeopardy unless we ignore the distinction between a chucker and someone who throws occasionally on the one hand, and fail to apply it properly to the facts of the case at hand on the other. More importantly, and this is a theme which emerges as informing comments like those of Yardley and Roebuck and others, there are two levels of jurisprudential and legal critique operating here.

First, the *Laws of Cricket* themselves give the umpires these 'god-like powers'. In the case of throwing, the general and inherent power of the judiciary is exacerbated and increased by the practical and legal difficulties which have both informed the development of the *Law* and the interpretation of the text. It is, as almost everyone will attest, extremely difficult, if not impossible, to accurately define a 'throw' in the confines of the legislative language of the *Laws of Cricket*. At the same time, there is some level of consensus among participants in the hermeneutic practices of playing and adjudicating cricket that one can know a throw when one sees one or at least one can recognize a lawful ball when one sees that. There is also a consensus that 'throwing' does give an unfair advantage in fact and in *Law* if not stopped to the bowler.[39] He can deliver the ball more quickly or impart more or different spin if he throws rather than bowls the ball. In addition to, or because of, these difficulties and the consensus surrounding the unfair nature of throwing, the *Laws* at the time of Murali's encounter with Judge Hair gave a wide discretion to the umpire. Indeed, the wording again imposed a duty to act and a burden on the umpire which is significantly different from the process of adjudication in other matters. Again, Law 24(2) read

If either umpire is not entirely satisfied with the absolute fairness of a delivery . . . he shall call and signal 'no ball' instantly upon delivery.

Moreover, as we have already seen in the discussion of the history of pre-Murali throwing cases, the operative *Note* defined a throw *inter alia* as a delivery which 'in the opinion of either Umpire' involves the straightening of the arm. Thus the adjudication process for throwing, if not conferring god-like powers on the umpires, did give them extremely broad jurisdiction to act when in their 'opinion' they were not 'entirely satisfied' about the 'absolute fairness' of the delivery. Here, the benefit of doubt and opinion went to uphold the *Law* and to, to whatever extent, 'punish' the bowler.

We find the two real levels of objection to Hair's decision. The combination of wide discretion and the consequences of the umpire's call of no-ball. Shame, exclusion, outlaw status and the punishment of chuckers had always been severe and without recourse. If one believes, as do both Yardley and Roebuck and no doubt the Sri Lankan officials, that Murali's action was legal, then one's outrage at the decision will be compounded. Not only is the discretion vague and wide-ranging, but the consequences are as severe as they can be for a cricketer who becomes not a cricketer but a cheat. These concerns are then made even worse if all of this involves an 'innocent' party. Of course, Murali is or was not innocent in a formalist or positivist sense, since he was, according to the judge and the law, guilty. He is and was innocent because some believe that he does not throw.

The rhetoric and legal and factual assertions which surround the Darrell Hair no-balling of Murali in Melbourne again all seem to circulate around one basic ethical and moral position which has always appeared to inform debates about chuckers and chucking. That position is that which dictates that the contest between bat and ball must be constructed and understood as being the central element of the spectacle and legal event known as cricket. A chucker is someone who disrupts the centrality of that event and seeks to subvert the basic collective understanding of the game. 'It's not cricket' precisely because, according to our common legal and ethical understandings of the game, chucking is 'not cricket'. It is something else – baseball perhaps where pitchers throw, but not cricket, whose rituals, morals and collective legal understandings depend on the fair contest of natural skills, which must of course, occur in the entirely constructed and artificial definition and practice of 'bowling'. What is vital is the understanding shared by all participants in the game, players, umpires and fans alike, that the definitions of the legal limits of the battle between bat and ball must in these circumstances be shared and imposed on all.

Thus, writers could speak of Murali as he 'confronts the humiliation of being exiled into a group of only nine Test cricketers accused of throwing',[40] or of being 'branded as a thrower',[41] or as 'an unassuming young man who has been crucified'.[42] Here we find the informing ethical narrative of chucking jurisprudence. There is in the minds of all those concerned, whether they think Murali innocent or not, some underlying understanding of the seriousness of the offence of throwing, of being 'branded'. The scarlet letter 'C' for chucker is stamped on the body of the excluded former member of the community of cricket. Chucking is again literally and figuratively, 'not cricket'.

But the story did not and does not end there. Sri Lanka insisted on Murali's innocence, despite revelations of longstanding doubts about the legitimacy of his action and Hair's no-balling of the bowler. His team announced their decision to include him in the side for the next match, a One-Day game against the West Indies at Hobart.[43] Despite the scrutiny of two Australian umpires, Terry Prue and Steve Davis, Murali bowled his full compliment of ten overs, returning 2/46, without being 'called' during the match. For many of Hair's critics this seemed to vindicate their position that he was in error in calling Murali at Melbourne. His action had been watched carefully by two qualified Australian umpires who were obviously aware of the controversy and questions of fact and law weighing on them in Tasmania. That they did not no-ball Murali was then invoked as 'an unequivocal endorsement' of Murali's action.[44]

The legal issues then moved to Brisbane where Murali was no-balled again. This time, Australian umpire Ross Emerson, standing in his first International One-Day match no-balled the Sri Lankan seven times in three overs, replicating the findings of Darrell Hair. Moreover, the other umpire, standing at square leg, Tony McQuillan, also no-balled Murali on one occasion but since Emerson had also delivered that verdict, his call was to no effect at law although it did confirm that both umpires were not satisfied with Murali's action.[45] Not surprisingly, uproar ensued. In addition to the by now familiar allegations of incompetence, bias, unfairness etc., one further factual and legal issue emerged. Once he had been no-balled for throwing his regular delivery, Murali, following suggestions from acting captain Aravinda de Silva, switched to wrist spin. He was again no-balled. For many commentators and observers this offered proof positive that umpire Emerson was engaged in an entirely unobjective and unjudicial vendetta. For them, because of the nature of a leg spin delivery, it is virtually impossible to 'throw' when bowling that sort of ball. Emerson's call when Murali was bowling leg spin was proof for them that the decision was not, because it could not be, a good faith determination by the adjudicator.[46] The umpires were escorted from the field by police at the end of play.[47] The Sri Lankans expressed not just their disappointment but their shock and outrage especially at the no-balling of the leg spin deliveries. They threatened to bring legal action over what they saw as a conspiracy and a plot to impugn the integrity of Sri Lankan cricket and cricketers, even when there was no longer even the pretence of a factual basis for the decision-making.[48] Of course, it almost goes without saying, the debate and controversy did not end there.

Murali underwent tests by medical and other experts and was 'passed'. He was named in the Sri Lankan World Cup team and Darrell Hair, because of Sri Lankan objections, did not stand in any of their matches. Sri Lanka won the World Cup, exacting sweet revenge by beating Australia in the final.[49] The ICC revised the legal system dealing with illegal deliveries and a panel system was instituted to review any bowler accused or suspected of throwing. When that panel intervened and banned Shoaib Akhtar of Pakistan, it was abolished by the ICC on the grounds that its jurisdiction and powers would be subject to serious legal objections for breaching the principles of natural justice. Another system, under which international cricket now operates, was created. In the new and current system, a series of remedial and review steps are taken following the reporting of a bowler before the ultimate sanction of banning can be imposed. This is the jurisdictional jurisprudence and law reform activity created by the Muralitharan affair and its aftermath.[50]

Murali and the Jurisprudence of Chucking Redux

Two years later, Murali returned to New Zealand and controversy about his action resurfaced. Bruce Yardley, former Australian spinner and himself one of the few cricketers to have been called for throwing, again leaped to his protégé's defence, but this did not quell rising concerns about his unorthodox style.[51] The next year, Yardley again defended Murali from throwing accusations.[52] Later that same year, during a tour of England in which wickets fell to the unorthodox spinner,[53] doubts again were raised, this time by England coach David Lloyd who 'made his opinions known' to the proper authorities. David Hopps summarizes the legal and ethical issues of the 1998 tour as follows:

> Muttiah Muralitharan continues to charm every dispassionate observer, but England will forever murmur privately that he is a chucker. Properly cleared of throwing by the International Cricket Council after extensive medical and video evidence, the Sri Lankan spinner has long been found innocent, but still must endure insinuations that he is guilty.[54]

Here, the jurisprudential confusion results not just from the speculations of the passionate and sometimes ill-informed or biased observer, but from the structures of legality itself. Under the new system of the panel on throwing instituted by the ICC, the legal regulatory system of cricket has at some level institutionalized confusion and conflict. The provisions of Law 24(2) are left on the books. On field adjudication by the umpires however is 'replaced' by a system of reporting, study and adjudication. But the basic problem of chucking and the law remains unchanged and perhaps is made worse. Here we have a quasi-legal regulatory system the result of which appears to be that in this case, for example, Murali is 'cleared' – he 'has long been found innocent'. But the confusion and fundamental error about the nature of law, adjudication and cricket remains as previously argued. An expert panel which views video tape and medical evidence about a bowler's action can really and in the final analysis reach two related conclusions about the bowler if it finds him 'innocent'. It can, by seeing and studying his delivery action, in a statistically valid sample, reach the finding that he is (a) not a chucker, i.e., that he does not normally or usually throw the ball and (b) that he did not chuck any of the balls they saw. What they cannot do as a matter of logic or law, as long as the throwing provisions remain in the statute books, is to say that he will not ever throw in the future. This is precisely the judicial function of the umpire, to determine on the merits of each delivery according to the law. Not only is any contrary assertion illogical, but it would violate fundamental ideas we all have about law, fairness and most importantly about what is or is not cricket. If we conclude that Murali has been cleared, declared innocent in the sense in which Hopps and others appear to use these terms, the logical conclusion would be the spinner has been in fact and in law, given a licence to cheat. This is why we can only ever know if Murali or any other bowler is a chucker, or more accurately if he has thrown a particular delivery if we maintain the factual and legal interpretive functions of the umpire. This does not mean that the *Laws* are perfect and could not benefit from a change, which as we shall see has in fact taken place. Nor does it mean that the ICC panel system is without merit. Captains can meet and discuss bowlers' actions, ICC expert panels can offer their opinion and advice and remedial steps can be undertaken. All of these measures are in keeping with traditional practices and are consistent with maintaining not just our understandings of the ethics of cricket, but also of the distinction between someone who might throw and someone who might be a chucker.

It simply means that we must decide, at some point, about the fairness of the contest between bat and ball, and that decision is, I would argue, best left to the adjudication of the umpires on the merits of each and every delivery.

Some chose to characterize Lloyd's remarks as 'churlish, nastily-sour' and he was finally reprimanded by the English authorities.[55] But it is important not to suffer from conceptual and taxonomical confusion. One might well debate whether comments about an opponent's action should be voiced in public, and how such comments should be regulated by local boards or under *ICC Code of Conduct* provisions. Mark Butcher and Adam Gilchrist would no doubt have views on these issues. But that does not go to the heart of the issue here. Is Murali a chucker? Does he throw? When? Is he a cheat? If so, why? If not, why not? David Lloyd was not the first person to question the legality of his action. He was no-balled by three different umpires, and reported to the ICC before that. Given the factual, legal and jurisprudential complexities which surround the questions, a determination by the ICC panel does not definitively answer these questions. David Lloyd wanted the ICC to reopen the case.[56] Again, rumour and speculation do not constitute proof, but they do raise again and again the most intriguing aspect of all these cases. Why is being a chucker so bad?

At the end of 1998, after Lloyd again raised the question about Murali, the Sri Lankans returned to Australia. After some furious negotiations, Hair was not named (or 'voluntarily' withdrew) to officiate in any of their matches. The issues raised here involve questions not just of the personal integrity of the umpire accused of bias, but also issues of the integrity of the rule of law and the notion of abiding by the umpire's decision. They are not new and I address them in the context of another recent case in the chapter which follows.

The return of the main controversy was not long in coming. Speculation surrounded his action and the decision-making process of the umpires who would stand in the series. Match Referee Peter Van der Merwe reported that he would forward complaints about Murali's action to the ICC.[57] Finally, Murali was no-balled for throwing during a One-Day game against England at the Adelaide Oval. Umpire Emerson, who had already no-balled Murali at the Gabba in 1996, again called the spinner. Ranatunga argued with the umpires and took his team off the field for 15 minutes. As was the case with the Pakistanis and umpire Bailhache in the tour match which we have already seen, one might ask why the umpires did not declare that the Sri Lankans had forfeited the match? One might also ask once again important questions about what is understood in such circumstances about respect for judicial authority and the rule of law. And finally, is Murali a chucker?

The traditional defences and debates quickly came to the surface. The congenital deformity issue was again in the public forum.[58] Australian fans continued the collective practice of shouting 'no-ball' in unison on every Murali delivery. The Sri Lankans were outraged by this behaviour.[59] Peter Roebuck bemoaned the fact that Murali had been '…cat-called with unpardonable rudeness'.[60] Yet at some level the Australian crowds, behind the larrikin humour and probably a dose of good old fashioned Australian racism, were reflecting doubt as to the factual and legal situation. Murali had been no-balled. The Sri Lankan side and management continued to support the perfect and constant validity of Murali's action despite years of doubts from other quarters. They refused to consider remedial work because for them there was no doubt about any of his deliveries.[61] Then Australian coach Bob Simpson even put into doubt whether in fact Murali had been 'cleared' by the ICC. Instead, Simpson declared that the ICC had merely allowed Murali to continue pending conclusive evidence. Of course, the legal and ethical issues which I have already discussed are only compounded by Simpson's intervention.[62]

Again, if Murali were a chucker, as opposed to someone who might throw, the 'unpardonable rudeness' of the Australian crowd could be seen and understood as the heaping of moral disapproval on a confirmed and unrepentant cheat. Again, almost all of the positions which are adopted in debates and controversies surrounding chucking are themselves grounded in a combination of pre-determined legal and ethical standpoints. The position one takes on whether someone is or is not a chucker, and the ethical sanction one believes should be associated with chucking, will always then determine where one is situated in all jurisprudential discussions. Is chucking a serious moral offence or one warranting understanding and compassion? Is the accused a chucker or someone who throws? Are we dealing with inadvertent rule-breaking or outright cheating?

When umpire Emerson no-balled Murali again, the juxtaposed legal arguments were starkly raised. For many, Emerson was a rogue, a maverick, biased or more interested in surrounding himself with controversy and glory than in an objective determination of the facts in a judicial and therefore good faith manner. For others, he was a courageous umpire, standing up against enormous pressure from the media, the ACB, the Sri Lankans etc., and applying the *Law* despite the majority desire to see legality (and justice?) ignored for purposes of expediency.[63] The ACB used the revelation that Emerson was on stress-related leave from his government job at the time he no-balled Murali to relieve him of further umpiring duties and later to remove him from the elite panel of umpires.[64] In a strange but not unexpected twist, it was not the bowler in this case who is shamed and excluded from the community of cricket, but the outlaw judge, the umpire. Emerson according to this version of the story was mentally unfit to act in a judicial manner and capacity. His decision about Murali's action was probably informed not by an unbiased evaluation of the facts but by an unbalanced mind. The Law can be saved by his removal and exclusion.

Of course, this does not, nor can it, answer the most important questions. Is Murali a chucker? The fact that Emerson was on stress leave from his other job does not in and of itself prove that he was mentally incapable of acting as an umpire. No one at the time noticed anything erratic or unjudicial about his behaviour except that he no-balled Murali for throwing. This naturally can only be characterized as erratic or unjudicial if we reach the conclusion that Murali is not a chucker or that he never throws. Again, this is a conclusion based on an assumption rather than a decision grounded in an independent adjudicative process of judging each and every delivery on its merits. Even if we accept that Emerson was stressed and under pressure, that cannot as an absolute certainty eliminate the possibility that he was in fact and in law correct in no-balling the spinner. He may have been 'crazy' and Murali may have thrown, the two are not logically mutually exclusive.

What is clear beyond any doubt is that at some level the controversy surrounding Emerson and Murali, like that surrounding Hair and Murali earlier, had a chilling effect on adjudication and on umpires' ability or willingness to act and enforce the *Laws of Cricket*. The earlier accepted ethical norms of the game, epitomized by Richie Benaud removing the suspect Ian Meckiff from the attack, and Meckiff's immediate retirement, at least had the benefit of certainty and of legal and judicial continuity. There was a fundamental shared understanding within the interpretive community of cricket that if Col Egar called Meckiff, Meckiff was a chucker, and it was Meckiff who had to go. In the case of Muttiah Muralitharan, the opposite hermeneutic seems to have been at work. The umpire is suspect, the umpire is breaching the norms by branding a bowler a cheat. Hair did not stand in games because the Sri Lankans protested; Emerson was removed and shamed out of the game; Murali continued to bowl, as he does today.

I am not suggesting that the old system of ethical judgement which resulted in the total and complete ostracism of the bowler in question, which ignored the important distinction between a chucker and a delivery which is thrown, is to be preferred. Instead I seek to point out that somehow the ethical paradigm has been for many dramatically reversed in a relatively short period of time. In addition, the reversal of the ethical paradigm has a direct impact on what we understand of the judicial function and the rule of law. Here, the idea is that the umpire is not in the best position to decide, expert panels must adjudicate with all the problems associated with this new position on adjudication and law.

It is little wonder, then, that when Murali signed to play county cricket in the summer of 1999, the umpire's Association decided in effect to abandon their on field adjudicative function and not call Murali for any suspect delivery. Instead, umpires were instructed to report their concerns in writing to officials.

> The hysterical reaction which followed umpire Ross Emerson's decision to call Muralitharan for throwing, which resulted in an on-field row between the official and Sri Lankan captain Arjuna Ranatunga, is a situation that England's cricket rulers are anxious to avoid.[65]

Again proponents of Murali and of a change in the jurisprudence of chucking or at least of the jurisdiction of chucking, would be pleased with this course of action. Decisions would not be made on the field but by experts behind closed doors; the bowler would be spared further shame and humiliation. On the other hand, of course, one might be led to believe that disrespect for judicial office, bullying and contempt had triumphed over the rule of law in cricket. Umpires are told here not to apply one of the *Laws* of the game as it is written. They are told that if a batter is out to a questionable delivery, they should put their concerns in writing. The question of justice in cases of individual confrontations between bat and ball is trumped by what some might see to be a concern for broader justice issues and still others define as pragmatism, politics and blackmail. What does this tell us about good faith and adjudication?

An umpire who believes that Murali (or any other bowler) is a thrower, or that he has thrown a particular delivery, or more precisely, an umpire who is not assured of the absolute fairness of a particular ball, must, according to his superiors here, not apply the *Law*. If the batter plays a shot and is caught, or is trapped in front of his stumps and hit on the pads, the umpire must not signal no-ball, but for the 'good of the game', the batter must be given out. Here we have not rule formalism, in which an umpire is forced to give a batter out because the letter of the *Law* indicates that he must. Instead, we have anti-rule formalism, an intriguing jurisprudential development, in which the umpire must give the batter out despite what the *Law* says. The best interests of the game are to be protected and upheld by ignoring rather than by applying the *Laws of Cricket*. I have already given examples of the ways in which rule formalism can be said to violate the ethical norms of the spirit of the game and of the conflicts between law and ethics which arise in the course of constructing what is and what is not cricket. Here we have a mirror image of this in which the spirit of the game is made synonymous with the administrators' decisions about the 'best interests of the game' and umpires are told not to apply the law because of this higher concern.

What would we make of an umpire in the following situation? Murali bowls a delivery which the umpire believes to violate the provisions of Law 24(2) as then in effect. The ball pitches correctly and hits the batter on the pads. If the delivery were a fair one the umpire is certain that the batter would be out LBW. What is he to do? If he gives the batter out, he is refusing to apply the prohibitions on throwing, he is ignoring one *Law* and applying another, Law 36. He is following orders not to apply one *Law*. If on the other hand, he knows that he cannot at some level enforce Law 24(2) and call Murali for throwing because he has been ordered not to, can he lawfully and ethically refuse to give the batter out LBW, not because he has not been struck on the pads, in line with the stumps by a delivery that would go on to hit the stumps but for the intervention of the striker's pads, but instead because he does not wish to impose an injustice on the batter? He could justify his decision, entirely in bad faith, by informing the appellants if he wished to do so, that the ball was bouncing or spinning too much to allow him to be certain. Justice would be served (to the batter at least) in such a case by judicial bad faith. What of justice to Murali or to the game? Does not a simple application of the *Law* against throwing serve everyone – bowler, batter, cricket? Is an umpire who complies with an order not to apply the *Law* still acting as an umpire? Are we still watching a cricket match if the umpires are not applying the *Laws of Cricket*?

As with Ian Meckiff, the case of Muttiah Muralitharan raises more questions and doubts that it answers or settles. Murali continues to bowl for Sri Lanka, to devastating effect, especially on the friendly wickets of his homeland. Some say that he is the greatest spinner in history, some say he is the greatest bowler in history. Others declare that if he stays healthy he will end his career as the taker of most wickets by a significant margin over the next best bowler.[66] In Feb. 2002, former Indian spinner Bishen Bedi was quoted as saying

> If Murali doesn't chuck, then show me how to bowl.
> . . .
> It's just too bad, honestly. . . . Some people are blind . . . Will a blind man be allowed to fly an aircraft? So should a bowler be allowed to chuck just because he has deformed arm?[67]

The next month, comments attributed to Michael Holding and Bob Woolmer again raised doubts about Murali's action.[68] Is he a chucker? Will he be the greatest wicket-taker of all time and a cheat at the same time? Will we ever know? And what about Shoaib?

Shoaib Akhtar and Adjudication in Cricket

The prohibitions against throwing in the *Laws of Cricket* do not discriminate. Spinners can chuck and fast bowlers can throw. The 'greatest spinner in the game', Murali, can be called for chucking and the pretender to the crown of the world's fastest bowler, Shoaib Akhtar of Pakistan, can be surrounded by throwing accusations and suspicions. In May 1999, several media commentators in Sri Lanka and India made adverse judgements about the legality of Shoaib's action.[69] Here at least the Australians had no role to play although that would change. When Pakistan arrived in Australia for their tour in Nov. 1999, controversy about chucking was not long in coming. During a tour match against Western Australia at the WACA, Shoaib was videotaped at the behest of the umpires standing in the match. The umpires were Terry Prue and Ross Emerson.[70] Removed from the international panel by the ACB, following the no-balling of

Murali, Emerson had continued to be an umpire in good standing in Western Australia. His banishment from the game was at this time only relative. Yet his status as rogue umpire was only confirmed by the legal imbroglio created by the videotaping procedure.

The tape was forwarded to the ACB which refused to take any action.[71] Instead of expressing their concerns over Shoaib's action, as required, in their official match report, the umpires directed their complaints and the videotape to the ACB. At the most basic level of established procedures, their videotaping and failure to report to the Match Referee, were highly irregular, if not illegal. The ACB took the position that since the video had come into their possession in such an irregular fashion, and since they therefore had received no official statement of concern over Shoaib, they would and could do nothing. They had not been, in administrative terms, vested with jurisdiction. Nonetheless, unofficial discourse about the chucking allegations circulated. Phil Wilkins somewhat misleadingly wrote that 'His slinging action has never previously been questioned.'[72]

We know of course that controversy over Shoaib's action had emerged in media comments on the subcontinent several months earlier. Unless Wilkins is referring here only to 'official' concerns, his statement ignores these prior comments. Moreover, the concerns of umpires Emerson and Prue are not in fact or in law 'official' because of the fundamental procedural flaws affecting them.

Former Australian batter Dean Jones and former South African Test player Barry Richards both blasted Emerson. Their complaint is again familiar and pitched at two interconnected levels. First, for them Akhtar is not a chucker. Secondly, any allegation of chucking is a serious one, perhaps the most devastating one which can be levelled against a bowler. 'If a bowler is called a "chucker", which is what Emerson has implied in the case of Shoaib, then it amounts to nothing less than saying that the bowler is a cheat.'[73]

Once again, the position one takes on the factual question and the jurisprudential and ethical stance one adopts about the taxonomy of chucking appear to be intimately linked. If one believes that a bowler has a legitimate action, then obviously any allegation of cheating will be a serious attack on the moral integrity of an honest cricketer. If, on the other hand, one believes that a bowler is in fact a chucker, then he is a 'cheat' and should be removed from the game. Any potential distinction between someone who is a chucker and someone who might throw an occasional delivery disappears as legal and ethical positions are staked out.

Later in the same tour, however, things would become 'official' and the new regulatory mechanisms of the ICC throwing panel would come into play. At the third Test in Perth, an official report, signed by the two umpires, Darrell Hair and Peter Willey, and by the ICC Match Referee, John Reid, was sent back to England with Willey. Shoaib, however tentatively, had been officially branded a chucker by an Australian, an English umpire and former Test cricketer, Willey and a former captain of New Zealand, Reid.[74] Of course, as we have already seen, both Reid and Hair had some level of involvement in the earlier controversies about Muralitharan as chucker. Others rejected any idea that Shoaib's action was illegal. Former Australian pace pair Dennis Lillee and Jeff Thomson expressed their outrage at the idea that Shoaib was anything but a legitimate fast bowler.[75] Some in Pakistan saw a conspiracy against them, particularly given the facts that Hair was once again involved and this was the first time, after having been under the jurisdiction of numerous international umpires and Match Referees, that Shoaib had been reported.[76]

What is perhaps most intriguing about the Shoaib case, since all these other comments and allegations are merely repetitions of previous chucking scandals, is the fact that it became known very early on in the series of events that the officials' concerns centered only on Shoaib's action when he bowled his 'express' delivery or bouncer. They apparently noted in their report to the ICC that Shoaib had suffered a shoulder injury and that this had caused him to alter his action, leading to him throwing some deliveries.[77] In other words, from the very beginning the issue of fact, law and ethics could be argued to have been clearly delimited. On this view, Shoaib was not being accused of 'being a chucker'. Instead he was charged with the lesser offence of occasionally throwing a ball. He was not being labelled, despite some protestations to the contrary, an inveterate cheat, but someone who sometimes breaches the law. The breach of the law was not caused by an intention to cheat and gain an unfair advantage in the defining confrontation between bat and ball, but was the result of physical misfortune. Remedial action was possible and with it reintegration into the world community of cricket.

At the same time it is also important to note that the video evidence against Akhtar, which was compiled and submitted to the ICC, showed between 50 and 60 deliveries from the Hobart and Perth Tests which were considered to be problematic.[78] In other words, almost ten full overs of deliveries were illegal. The question here then is one of line drawing and taxonomical definition. When does one cross the line from 'occasional' throwing to throwing as an essential or core part of one's being? One over, two per match? If one is a fast bowler of Shoaib's pace, and if one throws nearly every really quick delivery or bouncer, can one still be a 'bowler' without chucking?

After lengthy study, the ICC determined that Shoaib had fundamental difficulties with this type of delivery and banned him under the then new regulations on throwing.[79] Not unexpectedly, the Pakistanis protested, appealed and used the ICC's own legal and factual norms against them. They mounted a series of legal and factual defences of their quick bowler. They argued that the ban was wrong because Akhtar was not a chucker. Moreover, the ban, they claimed would prevent Shoaib from playing in the One-Day series against Australia. Because the bowling of bouncers is banned in One-Day Cricket and any bouncer is automatically called a no-ball, it was factually and legally absurd to ban the bowler. His problem was with bouncers. He could not bowl bouncers in One-Day Cricket. Therefore he would not chuck, therefore he should not be banned for chucking.[80]

While attractive for its logic and apparent consistency, the Pakistani argument suffers from several possible counter-arguments. The ICC ban is not meant to prevent a bowler from 'bowling' certain types of deliveries which he does not in fact 'bowl'. Instead it is meant to eliminate the possibility of infringement by keeping him off the field of play. Remedial action is imposed in order to ensure that this goal is met. Moreover and more conclusively, it is also the case that concerns were apparently raised not just over his bouncer, but over his 'effort' ball. It is perfectly possible for someone like Shoaib in this case to put the extra effort to extract additional pace (not bounce) into a delivery that is an 'effort' ball, but not a bouncer. The banning of bouncers from the One-Day game could therefore be no guarantee that Shoaib would not resort to the type of delivery which was thought by Willey, Reid and Hair to be problematic.

Finally, we know that it is not every 'bouncer' which is banned from One-Day Cricket. Certain types of deliveries for example are limited by a *numerus clausus* but not banned while others are banned outright. Still others, while pitched 'short' or 'shorter' than usual, will be perfectly legal. The Pakistani assertion that bouncers are banned in One-Day Cricket so Shoaib should not be banned needs to be, as most claims about cricket and the law, interrogated and examined very closely before being accepted.

Then Chair of the ICC, Jagmohan Dalmiya, not for the last time, decided to ignore the ruling of the lawfully constituted adjudicator and overturned the ban on Shoaib. Dalmiya's reversal, for which there was apparently no textual jurisdictional basis, was grounded in a combination of the argument, uncontested, that bouncers are banned in One-Day games and a fear that the throwing review mechanism established by the ICC was legally flawed and open to challenge in the courts.[81] Many criticized the ICC for inconsistency and for failing to back up its expert panel. Others hailed the decision permitting Shoaib to play as embodying justice for a wrongly accused bowler.[82]

Five months later, while on tour in the West Indies, Shoaib was stood down from a match after the ICC requested that he not play pending further review of his suspect action.[83] Controversy and conflict were avoided when Akhtar suffered an injury which resulted in him being sent home without playing. He did return to the side which toured New Zealand where he was reported following a One-Day game by Kiwi umpires Steve Dunne, who stood at the other end when Darrell Hair no-balled Muralitharan, and Doug Cowie.[84]

Shoaib went home and then travelled to Australia for remedial work on his action with Dennis Lillee and biomechanical study at the University of Western Australia.[85] According to the medical experts, Shoaib, like almost all alleged throwers in the past few years, appears to be a freak of nature. A congenital problem creates an optical illusion that he throws when in fact he does not. Umpires, expert panels, Match Referees and many others continue to suffer from these delusions. Doubts again surfaced about his action during a Pakistani visit to the Sharjah tournament where South African referee Denis Lindsay and the umpires reviewed video footage of his action, '...many observers who watched him bowling in the first two matches of the ongoing triangular tournament believed that all was not well (sic) Shoaib's action'.[86]

He was officially reported by Lindsay, and umpires Rudi Koertzen and George Sharp.[87] Because this was the second time he had been mentioned in official reports, he entered Stage 2 of the ICC process. Under this system, a first report or on field no-ball call, invokes Stage 1, in which the Home Board of the player is advised and remedial action, if required, taken; the Home Board reports back to the ICC with its assessment. A second report in a 12-month period, as was the case here, results in the ICC appointing a bowling adviser of its own to assist and evaluate the bowler. If a third report is issued in the period, the Bowling Review Group meets and holds a formal hearing. After deliberation, a simple majority vote that the player has chucked in violation of Law 24(2) means that the player is banned for a period of 12 months.[88] It is interesting to note here that while a system of reporting, review, tuition and expert panels is involved, the very first sentence of the Terms of Reference states

> Nothing in the following shall override an Umpire's responsibility to apply Law 24.

At Stages 1 and 2, it is also clearly set out that while the bowler may continue to bowl, he is still subject to the *Laws* and may be called for throwing. Again the issues and questions of law are complex but many have already been discussed. What is striking here is the way in which the reporting system has actually worked. There continues to be a fundamental difficulty which we must confront. If the umpire has a duty to enforce Law 24, and if the duty remains unchanged, how can an umpire then be said to be acting consistently and in conformity with his duty to the *Laws* if he participates in the reporting process without calling the bowler on the field? If he has concerns and doubts, then the provisions of the 1980 *Code* version of Law 24(2) which we have seen in detail must clearly be met. The umpire cannot be 'entirely satisfied with the absolute fairness' of a delivery if he brings his concerns to the attention of the Match Referee at the end of the day's play, and if that is the case, he must call no-ball. The plain language of the Terms of Reference clearly confirms that nothing therein relieves him of that obligation.

The changes to the *Laws* in the 2000 *Code*, do not, I believe, change much here. Law 24(2) now reads:

> For a delivery to be fair in respect of the arm the ball must not be thrown. See 3 below. Although it is the primary responsibility of the striker's end umpire to ensure the fairness of a delivery in this respect, there is nothing in this Law to debar the bowler's end umpire from calling and signaling No ball if he considers that the ball has been thrown.
>
> (a)   If, in the opinion of either umpire, the ball has been thrown, he shall
>
> > (i)   call and signal no ball.
> > (ii)   caution the bowler, when the ball is dead. This caution shall apply throughout the innings.
> > (iii) inform the other umpire, the batsmen at the wicket, the captain of the fielding side and, as soon as practicable, the captain of the batting side of what has occurred.

(b)   If either umpire considers that after such caution a further delivery by the same bowler in that innings is thrown, the umpire concerned shall repeat the procedure set out in (a) above, indicating to the bowler that this is a final warning. This warning shall apply throughout the innings.

(c)   If either umpire considers that a further delivery by the same bowler in that innings is thrown,

> (i)   the umpire concerned shall call and signal No ball. When the ball is dead he shall inform the other umpire, the batsmen at the wicket and, as soon as practicable, the captain of the batting side of what has occurred.
>
> (ii)   the umpire at the bowler's end shall direct the captain of the fielding side to take the bowler off forthwith. The over shall be completed by another bowler, who shall neither have bowled the previous over nor be allowed to bowl the next over. The bowler thus taken off shall not bowl again in that innings.
>
> (iii) the umpires together shall report the occurrence as soon as possible to the Executive of the fielding side and any Governing Body responsible for the match, who shall take such action as is considered appropriate against the captain and bowler concerned.

3.   Definition of fair delivery – the arm

A ball is fairly delivered in respect of the arm if, once the bowler's arm has reached the level of the shoulder in the delivery swing, the elbow joint is not straightened partially or completely from that point until the ball has left the hand. This definition shall not debar a bowler from flexing or rotating the wrist in the delivery swing.

There are several points of legal interpretive interest for discussion. First, it is now clear that the jurisdiction to call a thrower rests with both umpires and either is entitled to adjudicate. Secondly, the spectacle of a bowler being no-balled seven times in three overs will never repeat itself. The umpires now have a legal authority to order the captain to remove a bowler on the third no-ball for throwing in an innings. This is an excellent practical example of the idea that the breakdown in cricket law and order (and ethics) has had to have been met with the response of more law. If the Richie Benaud ethos of removing Ian Meckiff as soon as he was no-balled for throwing is no longer accepted or implemented by captains, the umpire will sooner rather than later impose the removal of the offender. In addition, it is important to note that the provisions now also provide, at least by implication, a further reinforcement of some ethical duty on the captain in such circumstances. The authority to whom the umpires report 'shall' take appropriate action, not just with regard to the offender himself, the bowler, but the captain as well. Perhaps, the captain is to be punished because he should have been aware of doubts over his bowler's action and done something about it, although a captain is not always a selector and this will necessarily further complicate the analysis. If a captain cannot determine who is in his side, then it would be unfair to argue that the *Law* should be read to punish him for something over which he has no control. It would be a brave captain indeed who would jeopardize his own position and the chances of his team by, for example, refusing to give the ball to a bowler he believes to be a thrower but who has been selected to play in the match.

Perhaps it is better and more appropriate in the practical context of playing the game of cricket, to read this provision as seeking to impose a duty on the captain to act before the full force of the *Law* is imposed on the field of play by the umpires. Thus, once a bowler is called for throwing, it might be argued that the *Law* reaffirms previous practice and imposes indirectly by implication a duty to immediately remove the bowler from the attack. Indeed, it can clearly be argued that the captain's duty to ensure that the spirit of the game is respected imposes this duty already. A *fortiori*, the new provisions impose on him a legal as well as a moral duty when his bowler has been no-balled for throwing.

Whatever the result or the correct reading of this part of the *Law* may be, it still seems clear that the *Law*, for all its attempts at more clarity, its emphasis on the idea of 'throwing' etc., leaves the judgement about violations and breaches of its substantive norms to the 'opinion' of the umpire. Therefore, at this level, the dilemma and contradiction of what we are to make of the on field umpire who refuses to call a player for throwing but still reports the bowler after the game, while arguably attenuated by the rewording of the *Law*, must continue to trouble us.

In Shoaib's case, the problems do and did not end there. As required by their own regulations, the ICC named Michael Holding as official advisor in the case.[89] The Pakistanis persisted in their claims that Shoaib was not a chucker and that the apparent anomaly in his action could be explained by the hyper-mobility of his joints.[90] In a letter to the ICC two days later the PCB in effect protested against Holding's nomination and pleaded that Shoaib was a special case. In essence their argument was that because the biomechanical report from the University of Western Australia had already examined and explained Shoaib's action in terms of medical 'impossibility', there was no need for Holding's appointment. Since the purpose of the adviser under the regulations is to offer counsel about possible corrective modifications to a bowler's action, he could not serve this function here. There was nothing unsound about Akhtar's delivery. The *Law* could not apply because the facts established with absolute certainty that the law could not apply.[91] The Australian scientists reviewed tapes of Shoaib's action and confirmed their earlier findings. The PCB passed the scientific report to the ICC.[92]

Shoaib continues to bowl often to devastating effect. During the Pakistani series against the West Indies in Feb. 2002, several commentators on the television coverage commented on Shoaib's action. Michael Holding was among them.

> Holding, now a respected international television commentator, noted during Shoaib's spell on Monday that there was 'a definite kink' in his elbow after it passed shoulder height and before straightening on delivery.[93]

During the shortened New Zealand tour of Pakistan in 2002, Shoaib sent New Zealand stumps flying with a ferocious display of fast bowling in the first Test at

Lahore. He took 6/11 in the first innings. Bryan Waddle commentating on Radio Sport for New Zealand openly questioned the legitimacy of Akhtar's action.[94] Is Shoaib a chucker? Where are the umpires? What is the law?

Brett Lee, Shoaib and Chucking Jurisprudence

It is not just Australian umpires who have been embroiled in recent chucking controversies. At least one Australian international cricketer, fast bowler Brett Lee, has been named as a chucker. Lee, who vies with Shoaib Akhtar for the title of the world's fastest bowler, has come under judicial and quasi-judicial scrutiny for his action in the recent past. Again, the accusations and defences raised have a familiar ring to them. Lee's devastating pace might make one believe, if one were prone to conspiracy theories in relation to chucking, that it is his potential as a strike bowler rather than any actual defect in his action that is at the root of some of the accusations against him. Similarly, one can find echoes of biomechanical explanations from past cases in the Australian defence of their bowler, with revelations that a broken arm in his youth has resulted in an apparently bent arm action.[95]

Rumours and unofficial complaints about Lee's action began to circulate in late 1999, at the time of an India/Australia series. Reports at the time indicated that Indian coach, Kapil Dev and consultant Bob Simpson, both experienced international cricketers and members of the ICC panel of experts on throwing questions, raised doubts about the legality of Lee's action, although Dev denied the reports.[96] The apparent whispering campaign was all the more significant since its timing coincided with reports and inquiries surrounding Shoaib; chucking by fast bowlers was on the legal and ethical agenda of international cricket.[97]

Although at this time no official report had been filed by any umpire or Match Referee, Australian authorities consulted the same biomechanical experts who would report on Shoaib and enlisted the support of fast bowling legend and Lee mentor Dennis Lillee. Australians also sought to derail ICC judicial intervention by pointing out that

> In Lee's favour is the fact that Hair umpired him in the India-NSW game in early December and no report on him was submitted to the Australian Cricket Board despite rumours that the Indian tour management had expressed concerns about the legitimacy of his action.[98]

The legal argument involved is easily discerned. Darrell Hair is the kind of umpire who will not tolerate chucking. His record in the Murali case clearly establishes his judicial history and integrity on the question of violations of Law 24(2). Since he did not call or report Lee in the match in question, he, a stickler for imposing proper bowling actions, passed Lee. The fast bowler had the judicial seal of approval. Of course, two counter-narratives are once more readily available. Each would and will be persuasive again depending on one's jurisprudential stance on the question of chucking and adjudication. The first interpretation would argue that Hair is in fact not a tough judge with a reputation for strictly enforcing the prohibitions on chucking. Rather, for supporters of this view, he came to the Murali case with a pre-existing prejudice, informed on the grounds of ethnic bias, or some other prejudgement. That he passed Lee in this instance would simply confirm the belief that he is not an unmitigated opponent of chucking, but an opponent of what he claims is Sri Lankan malfeasance. Finding an Australian bowler not guilty of throwing allegations would hardly be surprising for a holder of this position.

Secondly, if one were to adopt a more formal and legalistic reading of events in the Sydney match, one would simply argue yet again that there is no larger significance to the fact that Lee was not called or reported beyond that fact itself. In other words, just because Lee was not called at the SCG, we cannot assume that he will not be called in the future. He may simply have passed muster in the way he bowled in that particular match, which is no proof, although it might be some indication that he is not, nor will he ever be, guilty of throwing.

Indeed, that is exactly what came to pass. During a three-match series in New Zealand, two different umpires, both Indian, reported their suspicions about Lee's action to the ICC. Umpire Venkataraghavan reported Lee in the first Test and Umpire Jayaprakash reported him in the third Test.[99] Many of the by now well-known questions and issues of law and fact which have surrounded throwing cases again emerged from the Lee accusations. Australian officialdom was outraged by the delay between the umpires' reporting of Lee and public notification from the ICC. The New Zealand tour took place in March–April but the ACB was not informed until late June. Again, as in the earlier cases of Murali and Shoaib, serious and interesting questions about ICC procedures and our understanding of ideas of natural justice, speedy trials and the public nature of hearings when faced with serious allegations all arise again here.[100]

Still other important issues also arise. The two umpires who reported Lee in New Zealand were Indians. The original 'whispering campaign' against Lee originated among the Indian cricket hierarchy. Were the umpires subject to undue influence? Were they biased by virtue of their national origin? Lee was reported in the first and third Tests, in which the Indians stood. In the second Test, where the 'neutral' or international umpire was Riazuddin of Pakistan, Lee took 3/49 from 17 overs and was not subject to a negative finding. Nor did, as far as we know, the New Zealand umpires in any of the Tests find any difficulty with Lee's action. Bobby Bowden in the first Test, Dave Quested in the second and Steve Dunne in the third, all appear to have let Lee's action go.

We could read these facts to indicate that the Indian umpires were biased and had another agenda in reporting Lee. Or we could take note of the fact that, if Australians believe that Darrell Hair has a particular reputation in relation to throwing and we must draw some inferences and conclusions from that, umpire Venkat is and has been considered one of the top umpires in the world. He is a former Indian Test player and spin bowler. As a former bowler and top rated international umpire, one might simply argue that he is extremely well placed to judge suspicious actions. In addition, we might well applaud the umpires for exercising their 'discretion' and for confining their concerns to a written report instead of no-balling Lee on the field. Conversely, we might slam them for failing to uphold their sworn duty to the *Laws of Cricket* for allowing unfair deliveries to be bowled.

Similarly, we can draw either positive or negative inferences from the 'inaction' of the other officials. Perhaps they found no problem with Lee's delivery. Perhaps they were not well placed to judge when Lee was bowling. Perhaps they had seen what had happened to Darrell Hair and Emerson when they had no-balled Murali and were more interested in self-preservation. We simply cannot know. The interpretation we choose to apply to the facts and law of the Lee case will again be informed by any number of legal and factual prejudices we bring to our own interpretation of these interpretations. That is again what makes cricket as a legal practice so intriguing and so potentially democratic.

Michael Holding, a member of the ICC panel and someone who knows more than a little about bowling very fast, summarizes many of the concerns and issues which have been encountered throughout this study of the jurisprudence of throwing. He writes:

> Bans are difficult to justify in any case, unless a bowler chucks every ball. If certain deliveries have been identified as a problem – and for the sake of argument let's imagine a player who bowls leg-breaks but throws his variation off-break – then how can you ban someone outright? Whether we are talking about fast or slow bowlers, the best thing is for the player and his national board to work together on adjusting his approach.
>
> Cricket has always had its chuckers, and I don't believe it has ever been a major problem for the game. Sure, if a bowler throws a high proportion of his deliveries, something needs to be done. But what we don't need is a witch-hunt with anybody who looks slightly suspect being accused.[101]

Holding allows us to return once more to what should be a fundamental distinction between a chucker and someone who throws occasionally. One needs to be ostracized, the other helped back into the community. Yet, because we seem incapable of identifying the difference in practice, there is an ongoing concern about 'accusations', 'witch hunts' and 'crucifixions'. Again, the label 'chucker' or 'thrower' carries a moral sanction which is, at some level, incapable of moral or legal subtlety. Lee, like Shoaib, was suspected of throwing only his 'effort ball'. He was not therefore necessarily 'accused' of being a chucker but possibly only of chucking from time to time depending on the frequency of his fastest deliveries and/or bouncers. The legal and ethical consequences of the distinction in this case, as in most of the others under review here, nonetheless seem to be, despite Holding's analysis, incapable of articulation in most discussions and interventions on the topic.

Lee was 'cleared of any suspicion' in Aug. 2000, and while battling injury, continues to bowl for Australia.[102] This idea that he has been 'cleared of any suspicion' is not a categorical legal or factual truth. He may or may not throw in the future if he ever did or did not in the past. If he is not a chucker, that is a bowler who almost never 'bowls', that does not, nor can it ever mean that he has been 'cleared' for the future. That is not law and it can never be cricket, at least not as long as Law 24(2) remains on the books and umpires are charged with enforcing and applying that *Law* in each and every game of cricket, as each and every ball is delivered and played. The text of cricket and the law has the glorious uncertainty of requiring it to be played in order for there to be law and for there to be cricket. And it is a game and legal practice determined one ball at a time.

Other Recent Cases of Chucking and the Law

While the cases of Murali, Shoaib and Lee are the best known of the most recent decisions relating to the laws against chucking, the world of cricket throws up other examples of breaches of the prohibition against unfair deliveries, each of which in their own way raises intriguing legal and ethical questions.

Courtney Walsh played 122 Tests for the West Indies. He took 483 wickets at an average of 24.25 and took 5 wickets in an innings 21 times. He was one of the greatest fast bowlers in the history of the game. He also was suspected of being a chucker. Although he was never no-balled for throwing or reported by an umpire or a Match Referee, rumours about the legality of his action circulated. In fact, the allegation more precisely was not that he was a chucker, but that his bouncer action involved a bent arm. He was, it was alleged, a bowler who threw the occasional delivery. In 1995, Australian journalists and commentators published reports, some of which named Walsh, that there was a chucker in the West Indian attack. Photos of Walsh's delivery action were published and commentators seemed certain that the illegality of the action was 'blatant'.[103] In Jan. 2000, Ian Chappell named Walsh as someone who had a 'chink' in his action, without branding him a chucker.[104] Pakistan retaliated to accusations against Shoaib by requesting a video of Walsh from the ICC.[105] Walsh retired as the leading wicket-taker in history. He was never warned, no-balled, or subjected to an official inquiry, yet some still insisted that he threw his bouncer. At this point, it is not important or even necessary to determine whether Walsh did or did not throw. What is interesting here is that his 'case' never became a case. Despite clear allegations from some quarters that he threw his bouncer, Walsh left the game not like Ian Meckiff, branded a cheat and hounded for years, but as a true star and hero of the sport.

Others have been branded chuckers after having been reported and then have returned to the game after changing their action or having been subjected, like Brett Lee and Shoaib' to further biomechanical or coaching scrutiny. In England, Mark Wagh was called for throwing and underwent rehabilitative work and returned to the game.[106] English bowler James Kirtley was reported by an International Match Referee and despite claims of support and arguments about the misleading persuasive power of optical illusions from his homeland, he was called upon to change his bowling action.[107] Kirtley was named in the England squad for the ICC Champions Trophy in Sept. 2002. Yet even then he was plagued by notions that remedial work had not been completely successful and familiar themes reemerged. Thus,

> In a global competition such as the Champions Trophy his action is sure to come under scrutiny once more. During his time in Zimbabwe he was reported as having an unsatisfactory action, with hyper-extension of his elbow cited as the cause.
>
> This in itself is legal so long as no attempt is made to straighten the arm from there. After work with the bowling coach Bob Cottam last winter to try to iron out the kink, he was deemed clean by the England and Wales Cricket Board. But an offending bowler is only as clean as his last delivery, and there is a suspicion that when he is searching for the 'effort' ball he reverts to type.[108]

In Australian domestic cricket, in cases involving umpires Hair, McQuillan and Emerson, several bowlers were called, reported or suspected of throwing. At some level, one might argue that these cases offer some evidence that the involvement of these umpires in the no-balling of Murali was perfectly consistent with their decision-making practices in Australian domestic cricket. Accusations of ethnic or other bias might then be countered by demonstrating that they no-balled Australians as well as Sri Lankans. Thus Greg Rowell was reported by McQuillan in an interstate match and withdrew from further play to work on his action.[109] Ian Hewitt of Victoria came under scrutiny and concern from Darrell Hair,[110] Ross Emerson called Queensland spinner Geoff Foley for throwing in an interstate match in Hobart in 1998.[111]

Henry Olonga of Zimbabwe was no-balled by home umpire Ian Robinson in 1995. He underwent remedial training with Dennis Lillee and returned to bowl for his country.[112] Grant Flower of Zimbabwe was no-balled and removed from the attack under the new provisions of the *Laws of Cricket* by Darrell Hair. The local panel reviewed his action and found no problem with his delivery; he was returned to the side.[113] In a Test against India in Delhi later in the same year, Umpires Venkat and John Hampshire of England experienced difficulties with Flower's action and spoke to his captain, who removed him temporarily from the attack. Match Referee Barry Jarman reported 'After seeing Grant Flower bowl yesterday, both umpires and myself were not entirely happy with the legality of all of his deliveries'[114] then added: 'We understand that Grant Flower was no-balled by umpire Darrell Hair but was cleared . . . but there is no such thing as cleared.'[115]

This is the point which I have been making throughout this discussion. A bowler, as Mike Selvey puts it, 'is only as clean as his last delivery'. Still, one might ask again why the umpires here did not no-ball Flower. Perhaps there is now some clear distinction between the old language of the *Law* and the new provisions which require that the umpire be of the 'opinion' that 'the ball has been thrown'. Under the 1980 *Code*, the level of doubt was arguably lower, requiring only that an umpire be 'not entirely satisfied with the absolute fairness' of the delivery.

One could argue, based on the idea that such an interpretation is consistent with the legislative decision to change the operative language, that the umpires had doubts which fell short of leading them to the opinion that the ball was thrown. Under the *Law* they could not no-ball the bowler but could, under the operative provisions of the regulatory system dealing with throwing, review his action after the end of play. One might assert that this is a misreading of their duty under the *Laws* or that it is indeed consistent with the new text which has operated a change to the substantive offence with which they are called upon to deal. What seems clear from this and many of the other instances we have seen is that there is still a competing and conflicting idea and understanding of the legal system of adjudication to be followed and invoked in such cases. One involves instant adjudication as the game is played, the other deliberation at the end of the day's play.

Other cases highlight and underline many of these same issues and concerns. In Pakistani cricket, Shahid Afridi has come under suspicion for several years, but has been cleared by the PCB after being reported by Barry Jarman.[116] Pakistani fast bowler Shabbir Ahmed was reported and banned, but eventually cleared to return after modifying his action.[117] Pakistani spinner, Shoaib Malik was reported by the umpires following a match in Sharjah in 2001.[118] The PCB panel detected a problem with Malik's 'other one' and ordered him to undergo remedial work.[119]

In Sri Lanka, Murali was not the only bowler to fall afoul of throwing allegations. Jayantha Silva and Ruwan Kalpage were reported for throwing.[120] Off spinner Kumara Dharmasena has come under constant scrutiny and has only returned to the game after a two-year period in which he was effectively excluded as a 'chucker'.[121] In 2001, fast bowler Suresh Perera was reported for throwing.[122] For the first Test at Lord's in May 2002, when Murali was unable to bowl due to a shoulder injury as already briefly mentioned, Ruchira Perera was named in the side by the Sri Lankan management. During the Sky TV coverage of the match, both Ian Botham and David Lloyd spoke of Perera's bowling action as having a 'kink' and a 'problem'. Both lauded the Sri Lankan decision to 'support' their bowler and at the same time urged remedial action. At some level this commentary evidences the way in which the ICC reporting system for throwing now operates. Yet it must be for some nonetheless disconcerting that commentators would laud an administration's support for a bowler who may well be 'cheating' and would ignore the fundamental unfairness for a batter who is compelled to face such a bowler without having the *Law* and the umpire there to protect him from what the same commentators believe to be unfair deliveries. The concern in legal and ethical discourse surrounding chucking now appears to focus almost exclusively on the question of the accused and the effect the charges and label will have on him. There is virtually no discussion of the 'rights of the victim' here, the batter who faces unfair and therefore unlawful deliveries. The confrontation between bat and ball which is the defining essence of cricket is corrupted yet the contest is allowed to continue.

The Match Referee, Gundappa Viswanath, and the two umpires, Daryl Harper and Srinivas Venkataraghavan, reported Perera at the conclusion of the Test.

Immediately thereafter the Sri Lankan management officials acknowledged that they had received notification of the report and that they intended to comply with the applicable ICC regulations. They further pointed out, however, that those regulations permitted them to name Perera in the side for the next match.

> The same umpires are officiating in Birmingham and, having assessed the footage, may decide there is evidence enough. To play Perera would be a risk and, though in accordance with the regulations, would raise ethical questions.[123]

This potential imbroglio surrounding Perera embodies and epitomizes both the strengths and weaknesses of the current legal regime regulating chucking and chuckers. Gone are the days of instant and permanent exile and shaming which Ian Meckiff and others suffered. 'Chuckers' are now examined, corrected if necessary, and allowed to return to the game when their action has been cleared. At the same time however, the new system also removes at some level the ethical norm whereby 'chuckers' were seen to be engaged in some basic unfairness and should be removed from the attack. Here, the Sri Lankans are perfectly correct in putting forward the position that under Stage 1 of the procedures, once a bowler has been properly reported, the only thing the administrators are required to do is review and assess the action within six weeks. Section 5 specifically provides

> Throughout this period the player will be permitted to continue playing. At any time through this period the player is subject to being called on the field or reported by the umpire/referee.[124]

The normative context is clear. The player may play and the *Laws* and regulations will continue to apply. The Board may select the player, although in doing so they run the risk that the player may be called for throwing or reported again. If he is reported or called, then the provisions of Stage 2 come into effect, but again the player may continue to bowl.[125] The 'real' risk only arises if the bowler is called by the umpires during the match and the suspension provisions of Law 24(2) come into effect. At the same time, during either Stage 1 or 2, there might exist some ethical normative sanction which would operate to brand a bowler who continues to bowl in such circumstances as a chucker, and the Board and captain who persist in bowling him as violators of some idea of the 'spirit of the game'. Of course, the existence of such an ethical standard seems doubtful given the specific provision of the regulations which permits the bowler to continue playing. Again, the relationship between the written code of the *Laws* and the unwritten norms of the spirit of the game is uncertain at several levels. Is there a conflict? Is there an existing unwritten norm? What is its content? Can we imagine, within the realm of cricket jurisprudence, a captain being sanctioned by a Match Referee for violating his duty to uphold the spirit of the game for bowling a player twice reported for throwing? Can we imagine, in other words, a system of legal sanction which would punish a cricketer for abiding by the strict limits of the *Law* because to do so would violate the spirit of the game?

One further issue emerges. What about some idea of 'fairness' or of the spirit of the game in so far as opposing batters are concerned? If there is an ethical norm which should cause administrators to think twice before naming a bowler who has been reported in a side to play in a Test, at some level that norm must, or at least should, relate not just to ideas of shaming and exclusion or fairness for the bowler, but should also aim to ensure fairness for the batter in the confrontation between leather and willow. Of course, one might argue that such fairness is assured by the continuing operation of the *Laws of Cricket*, if the bowler throws, the umpires, can, should and must no-ball him. Yet we know that in this case, as in many others, that the umpires did not no-ball Perera. Of course, it is possible to argue that they did so because their doubts about his action fell short of the standard imposed by the new wording of the *Laws*. They may have had doubts which did not rise to the stage of allowing them to form the opinion that a delivery was thrown as now required. Indeed, these doubts may have reached this level after review of the videos which gave rise to the decision to report the bowler. But that cannot have a direct effect on the process of adjudication on a particular delivery in a future match. Just as video evidence cannot 'clear' a bowler neither can it 'convict' him for the future. At the same time, they may have been reluctant to call the bowler because they feared retribution, humiliation or abuse. They may not have called no-ball because they believed that the private remedy of reporting is, for whatever combination of reasons, to be preferred to a public declaration of illegality.

The issues of fairness, law and adjudication all arise here because there is a potential conflict, in practice, between the reporting procedures, and the actual normative provisions of the *Laws of Cricket*. It is not beyond the realm of possibility to believe that given (1) the moral sanction which has traditionally been attached to a bowler called for throwing, (2) the existence of an alternative reporting mechanism, and (3) the uproar and controversy surrounding the integrity of umpires in recent throwing cases, that some umpires may believe that it is the best interests of the bowler, the game and their reputation to invoke the reporting mechanism rather than the immediate and public sanction of the *Law*. Yet again, this places the batter and the batter's side at a distinct disadvantage. He and they must face a bowler who, assuming that the umpires are of this opinion, 'throws' and is allowed to get away with it. If we assume for the sake of argument that this was the case with Perera, this is the legal and ethical situation of unfairness which obtains.[126] In the first innings, Perera took 3 wickets for 48 runs and in the second, he had a return of 2/90. Several possibilities arise. He threw any or all of his wicket-taking deliveries; the batters are out to an illegal delivery and suffer a direct and immediate injustice. This might effect not just the outcome of the game, but it might also have a direct impact on a particular player's income, career and reputation. A batter who is on the edge of the team, lucky to have been selected, given one more chance to prove himself, might well in such a case find his representative career at an end because he was dismissed for a low score or to a bad shot. If Perera had been no-balled, the batter would have had a chance to go on to make a score and cement his place in the side. Similarly, the wicket might fall at an important juncture in the game, with well-known flow on effects. We cannot know, but we can know that if a bowler is allowed to throw, this possibility of direct and serious personal and collective injustice will always exist.

Even if Perera did not throw any or all of his wicket-taking deliveries, the unjust possible consequences of not applying the *Laws* persist. Under the *Laws*, on the third illegal delivery, the bowler is removed from the attack. This might mean that some or all of the batters dismissed by Perera would not have had to face him at all in the game and therefore another entire set of possibilities might have arisen. With the removal of a strike bowler, the attack is weakened, the other bowlers and part-timers have to take up the slack and replace the overs he would have bowled. Again, any number of consequences might have unfolded as a result. More or fewer wickets might fall, they might fall at different times, more or fewer runs might have been scored etc. What we can and do know with absolute certainty is that none of these possibilities will arise unless and until the umpires apply the *Law* on the field of play. Allowing a chucker to bowl simply increases the possibility of possible injustice.

Other chucking cases have also been on cricket's jurisprudential and law and order agenda. In India, off-spinner Rajesh Chauhan was suspected, cleared and suspected again.[127] More interestingly, spinner Harbhajan Singh was also charged with being a chucker in 1998.[128] In what many Indian and Australian fans call the greatest Test series in history, the Indian team brought Steve Waugh's side's amazing consecutive winning streak to an exciting end in March 2001. The most devastating Indian bowler, the man probably most responsible for controlling and eliminating the threat of Australian batting was Harbhajan Singh.[129] In the short space of three years he had gone from pariah, being a 'chucker', to being a national hero.[130] Indeed, the delivery which made Harbhajan such a deadly force was his 'other one' or 'Doosra', the very ball which he allegedly threw before Fred Titmus 'straightened' the kink in his action. Harbhajan's return to the Indian cricket side may be seen to evidence both the idea of redemption and reintegration through hard work and to the necessity of grounding the ethical discourse about chucking in contextualization and subtlety. Gone are, or should be, the days, of Ian Meckiff's exile and shame, replaced by our ability to understand and define 'chucking' and 'chuckers' with more accuracy and fairness.

It may also be seen as evidence of how cheaters still manage to sneak into the game, to challenge and undermine the authority and authenticity of the basic confrontation between bat and ball. Lest this be seen as a typical example and embodiment of the phenomenon of a supporter of the losing side accusing the best bowler in the opposition of being a chucker simply because of his and their success, let me cite two relatively neutral expert authorities for the proposition that the legality of Harbhajan's action is not beyond doubt. No less an authority on bowling than Fred Trueman wrote that: 'The actions of Harbhajan Singh and Sarandeep Singh are, in my judgment, highly questionable and should be looked at closely.'[131]

Trueman finds support not from whingeing Australians but from one of Harbhajan's fellow Indians, former Test spinner Bishen Bedi Singh. He wrote that Harbhajan's floater or arm ball was not bowled in the traditional and legal manner, using the shoulder but illegally using a bent and straightening elbow.[132] Again, of course, Bedi is in effect arguing that Harbajhan is not a 'chucker' in his natural style or his normal delivery. It is the exceptional ball, the arm ball, which is of course a potentially devastating and wicket-taking delivery for any spinner, which is illegal. Thus, the problem here is that the bowler breaks the *Law* and delivers an unfair ball from time to time. In the circumstances of a batter confronting a spinner, trying to read the ball out of the hand, in the air or off the pitch, the legal, practical and ethical difficulty is that the definitional battle between leather and willow is unfair, the bowler is cheating and the batter suffers a fundamental disadvantage. Deception is part and parcel of every bowler's, but especially every spinner's, arsenal. Deception is not *per se* not cricket, it is at the heart of this part of the game. To see the stumps sent flying by a ball which has completely deceived a batter is one of the joyful moments of any cricket contest; it is deception and it is cricket because it is lawful deception. To see a batter beaten in similar circumstances by an illegal delivery is not cricket, it tarnishes the essential elements of the game. A bowler who gets extra pace or spin, who deceives his opponent by breaking the *Laws* of the game, is not playing cricket. He is doing and playing something; or she is.

To return to the mythological origins of overarm bowling and the ethical injunction embodied in 'it's not cricket', the world of women's cricket has also been rocked by throwing allegations. At the 2000 World Cup in New Zealand, bowlers from the host country, India and the Netherlands were all reported for having suspect actions.[133] Law, like ethical injunctions and the game of cricket, can be full of delicious irony.

17 Bouncers: terror and the rule of law in cricket

The late, great West Indies pace bowler Malcolm Marshall put his views as follows:

> I am a fast bowler and I have a job to do. There is a law dealing with intimidatory bowling and the umpires are there to judge. If they believe I am exceeding the limit, they must step in. Once you keep winning, you will always hear about fast bowling. A bouncer is part of a fast bowler's armoury. If you pitch up and you are driven all the time, people won't think much of you.[1]

Marshall gave voice to many of the legal and ethical issues which arose from a consideration of Law 42(8) of the 1980 *Code*. The provisions of the current *Laws* dealing with 'bouncers' are found in Law 42(6) and (7). What Marshall expressed first was a view of the law which is both formalist and moral. For him, there was a moral imperative incumbent upon him as a 'fast bowler'. At the same time, he is quite clearly a formalist in his attitude to the division of interpretive labour which must occur on the cricket field. The determination of breaches of the *Laws* and responsibility for policing and enforcing the *Laws* clearly lie with the umpires. Marshall simply bowled as he bowled, including bouncers, and if he violated the law it was up to the umpire to step in.[2]

Marshall also recognized another type of practical interpretive strategy at work here as it is in other areas of cricket (and law). Like 'chucking', 'deliberate bowling of fast short pitched balls', becomes especially problematic when success accompanies their (apparent) use. It is quite clear to followers of the game that much of the debate which raged about bouncers arose as a direct result of Clive Lloyd's successful introduction of an all pace attack in the West Indies' Test side. Bouncers are bad when the other side uses them and worse when the other side uses them successfully.

Marshall indicated in an unembarrassed way that the virility cult and martial imagery also have a great deal to do with interpretive views about bouncers. For him, bouncers were part of his 'armoury', they were a weapon to be used in the battle which was also simply part of his job. At the same time, his own self-worth both in terms of his 'internal' view of himself and the value and respect he received from others, and which they give to him, all form part of the *matrix* of meanings which can be attached to the bowling of bouncers. If he did not use the bouncer, he would be 'driven all the time, people won't think much of you'. He will not be playing cricket or playing cricket well if he does not use the bouncer as a weapon in the confrontation between bat and ball. At this level, utilitarian functions also enter into, and interact with, other elements of the calculus. If a bowler *is* driven all the time because he does not use bouncers and simply pitches up, he will be ineffective and inefficient as well as a poor practitioner of his craft. His craft will suffer, as will his moral and market worth if he does not break or at least tempt the limits of the law. It may well be that part of the cult hero status we accord to fast bowlers is due to their very outlaw nature. Unlike Denning's 'newcomer' who violates the spirit of the game and is condemned as Other, and unlike Ian Meckiff who 'breaks' the law and is ostracized, a fast bowler who challenges the authority of the law and the authority of the opposing batter is treated as a hero precisely because of his flirtation with illegality. He is not Other, one we despise and fear, rather he is the very embodiment of 'character', of a fine exponent of the defining characteristics of the game, the confrontation between bat and ball.[3]

Before examining the complex moral nature of Law 42(8) as it was practiced, and of the current texts of Law 42(6) and (7), it is also useful and important to note the many interpretive 'legal' problems raised by the bouncer issue. A simple reading of the text of the *Law* itself flags many of the difficulties which face the umpire who must, in the real life situation of a fast bowler in full flight, interpret and apply the 'letter of the Law'.

At the outset, the reader can see that not all fast short-pitched balls were or are 'unfair' or illegal. Thus an illegal bouncer is not part of an absolute liability offence, unlike a throw or a front-foot no-ball. It is, on the contrary, a question of fact and law, and a highly nuanced one at that. Under the *Law* of the 1980 *Code*, the umpire was required to engage in an interpretive process aimed at determining whether the bouncer constituted 'an attempt to intimidate the Striker'. As all criminal lawyers will note, as in 'attempt', the actual success of the intimidation was *per se* irrelevant but it could be considered under a different rubric (for example relative skill of the striker). The new provision changes the legal test. Thus:

> Bowling of fast short pitched balls is dangerous and unfair if the umpire at the bowler's end considers that by their repetition and taking into account their length, height and direction they are likely to inflict physical injury on the striker, irrespective of the protective equipment he may be wearing.

The constitutive elements of the offence have undergone a substantive change. 'Intimidation' or an 'attempt' to intimidate have now been replaced by the concept of 'injury', or more precisely the likelihood of injury.

A number of factors, or tests, must still be applied by the umpire to each ball which might be an 'intentional' bouncer under the old *Law*. Thus, the length, height and direction are all to be considered. And each must be considered not in the abstract but according to the actual context of the particular case. For example, the idea of a ball which is 'short'-pitched will depend on a variety of circumstances. A short-pitched ball at one ground may well be not 'short' or not so short at another. The condition of the wicket as the days of play in a Test pass will also need to be taken into account. Once there is a *prima facie* case based on these factors, the umpire must enter into the most difficult stage of his adjudication. Was there *intent* or was the ball 'likely to inflict physical injury on the striker?' To the lawyer, this is as recognizable and complex and confusing as debate over the mental element of crime. The first part of the test appeared to require the determination of the actual subjective state of mind of the bowler.[4] Intention appears to imply a kind of subjective or even moral guilt by the bowler. As the well-regarded former Test umpire Dickie Bird said:

> Judging intention is a tricky business even in the ordered atmosphere of a court-room and can be infinitely more difficult with tense young men trying to project a ball quickly enough to get it through the defense of some obdurate batsman.[5]

Of course, as lawyers know from examples as different as a murder trial and the interpretation of a contract, it is perfectly plausible to engage in an inquiry into 'subjective' intention by examining, as the law itself provides, all the relevant 'objective' circumstances.

While 'intended to' implied a subjective element, 'likely to inflict physical injury' seems to impose a more general, objective absolute liability standard based on concepts of probability and causation. Practice would indicate, however, that the 'or' in Law 42(8) was interpreted in practice as conjunctive and not disjunctive, and therefore that the likelihood of causing physical injury was a factor which went to the umpire's judgement of intention. Yet, as former England captain and commentator Tony Greig likes to point out, even this question of likely physical injury is increasingly problematic in an era where a batter wears not only heavy leg-guards and gloves, but a batting helmet with face guard, a chest protector and an arm guard. In 'fact', this technology makes 'injury' less likely than ever, although we all know from bruising encounters with cricket balls both that the concept of 'injury' needed to be subjected to careful analysis and that injuries, however defined, still occur. The new text deals with this complexity by eliminating it from the umpire's consideration. A key factor which must be added and considered with all else in the umpire's split second adjudication was and is 'the relative skill of the Striker'. That this factor is one which must (*shall* also be taken into consideration) be part of the calculus, indicates clearly that legal 'formalism' plays only a small part in judicial decision-making under the bouncer provisions of Law 42. The 'relative skill of the Striker' requirement underlines not only the highly contextualized nature of an umpire's task, but also gives a strong indication of a 'legislative intention' that a purposive approach should be adopted.

The 'relative skill of the Striker' demonstrates that to fully understand and apply the bouncer *Law*, the umpire must have an intimate knowledge of the complete 'text' of cricket. Generally speaking, the bowling of three consecutive bouncers to any top order player in any Test side could be perfectly justified as a fair and legal tactic against a world-class batter. On the other hand, a single head-high bouncer to a tail-ender could well have been a clear attempt to intimidate or be likely to injure. Again, however, even these factors are highly individualized and contextualized. As Dickie Bird put it:

> These days there are very few mugs with the bat and the vast majority of cricketers fancy their chances of chipping in with the odd runs so it is basically a matter of keeping a sense of proportion and dealing with each individual case on its merits.[6]

Not only must the umpire display a good deal of practical wisdom and knowledge about the game, the bowler and the batter, but he must be aware that even as far as individuals are concerned, a change in context can and does require a different interpretation of the same legal text. A batting bunny can become, with practice and application, a reasonable batter. The umpire must show the ability to adjust his interpretation as the actual circumstances of the batter change. A tail-ender at the beginning of his innings may be subjected to one interpretation of the *Law*, but as the same batter also displays 'tenacity and courage' to bat into the 70s, he will probably find the umpire's interpretation of his 'relative ability' to be relatively changed.

A good practical example of interpretive realities of adjudication in the area of short-pitched bowling under the 1980 *Code* provisions can be found in the first Test between the West Indies and Australia in March 1991 at Sabina Park. Australian fast bowler Craig McDermott was warned by umpire Steve Bucknor for bowling too many bouncers (four in two overs) at Gus Logie. Many factors must have influenced umpire Bucknor's decision, but the most important no doubt was the fact that Logie had been injured earlier in the match when a ball struck his helmet and squeaked through the grille. Thus, while Logie was a batter of some ability, his 'relative' ability needed to be taken into account and that relative ability was, in the umpire's view, affected by Logie's experience of helmet 'failure'. No doubt this factor was given further weight by the 'fact' that both David Boon and Mark Taylor of Australia had suffered injuries in similar fashion in the same game and McDermott himself had been hurt by a ball passing through the protective grille in the preceding warm-up match against Jamaica.

At the same time, of course, the Australian side could offer a perfectly acceptable and valid explanation of the bouncer strategy for Logie which arguably would not involve a violation of Law 42. Logie had returned to bat after his injury and was at the crease with the members of the West Indian tail. McDermott was bouncing Logie at the end of each over to keep him away from the strike so that his bowling partner could try to dismiss the tail-ender.[7] This idea of keeping a player at one end by bowling in such a way as to prevent them from scoring is a well-accepted and current practice in the game and a recognized part of the game's tactics. Once more, what this 'case' illustrates is not whether umpire Bucknor was right or wrong in warning McDermott under Law 42 but that, despite claims to the contrary by cricket commentators, lawyers or judges, there is almost never a 'case' where what one has to do is 'simply apply the facts to the legal principle' in order to be assured of a correct and objectively true result.

Thus, in discussing the famous fast-bowling incident when Ewan Chatfield of New Zealand was struck on the head by a bouncer from John Lever of England, Henry Blofeld made it clear that Chatfield 'on the facts' could have expected a bouncer because he was no longer, on that day, a tail-ender. Moreover, Lever's action indicated an attempt not to 'intimidate' but to use the bouncer to obtain a dismissal.

> It is difficult to say whether Chatfield, who has recovered very quickly although he may have a hairline fracture of the skull, or Lever was the unluckiest. Lever had in no way infringed the laws surrounding the over-use of short balls. Chatfield had batted intelligently for 75 minutes, and was by then entitled to be treated as a batsman. Lever's intention was to have him caught off the glove and he had moved his gully three yards closer only two balls before for this very purpose. No one that I have met in Auckland today has held Lever in any way to blame for what happened.
>
> Congdon, the New Zealand captain, and Bruce Hosking, their team manager, were both most emphatic about this, and Lever's own reactions to what he had done, and the distressed state in which he has been, show a man who has never borne physical malice against a batsman in his life.[8]

There is even room, in the interpretive context of bouncers, as there is in some civil and criminal trials for *ex post facto* proof of intention.

The interpretive and practical difficulties surrounding the enforcement of the *Law* on bouncers are best seen, not so much in incidents of refusal or reluctance by umpires to enforce the prohibition, but by examining a particularly controversial incident where the *Law* was enforced.

In the third Test in the 1980–81 series against New Zealand at the MCG, umpire Robin Bailhache, whose contributions to cricket jurisprudence we have already encountered, called no-ball after Australian tail-ender Jim Higgs was caught behind of the bowling of Lance Cairns.[9]

On the face of it, there should be nothing controversial about such a decision. The call of no-ball is the appropriate and legal measure to be taken by an umpire when he determines that there has been a violation of the fast short-pitched delivery provisions of Law 42. On the face of it, umpire Bailhache was simply doing what the *Laws of Cricket* told him to do. But, as should be obvious, what appears on the face of things to be a simple 'case', in both law and cricket, can often turn out to be much more complicated and deeply textured upon closer examination. Such is the case here. A look at the 'facts' and 'the law' will reveal the difficulties surrounding the practical implementation of the prohibition against intimidatory bowling. As we know, Law 42(8) prohibited fast, short-pitched balls intended to intimidate or to cause injury to, the batter. In this instance, the ball was not fast and could hardly, even taking into account Higgs' skill, or lack thereof, with the bat, be seen to have been meant to intimidate.

Lance Cairns was no more than a medium pace bowler, and like Greg Chappell, his bouncers were meant to surprise the batter, not to hurt. On this view of the facts alone umpire Bailhache was clearly 'wrong in law' in invoking Law 42. The delivery simply was not 'fast'. Moreover, this was the first bouncer Higgs had received although he had already spent 28 minutes at the crease for only one run. Although the strict letter of the *Law* did not prevent an umpire from calling no-ball on the first bouncer a striker received, there is nonetheless an interpretive practice in cricket which would strongly militate against such a decision. Because intimidatory bowling must necessarily take place in a broader context, and because of the complex nature of the factors which had to be considered under Law 42(8), it was highly unlikely that a single delivery, especially from a medium pacer like Cairns, could be said to have met the legal criteria of an offending bouncer. Again, a more likely 'interpretation' of the Cairns delivery was that it was meant not to intimidate Higgs, but to catch him by surprise and to take his wicket, as it did. Indeed, descriptions of Higgs' reaction to the delivery point to and confirm surprise, rather than intimidation as the key 'mental' element of the alleged offence. Bill O'Reilly described Higgs having '. . . got himself out in a flurry of arms, knees and bumps-a-daisy as he tried to get out of the way', and Mungo MacCallum wrote that he faced Cairns' 'totally innocuous, very short, quite slow bouncer'. . . By a series of physical contortions, Higgs somehow managed to get himself caught behind.

Adding to the controversial and arguably legally incorrect nature of Bailhache's decision was his obvious failure to place additional contextual factors into his interpretation/application of Law 42(8). At the time, Doug Walters was on 77 and at the other end with Higgs. Australia had just lost 3 wickets for none and were depending on Higgs to hold up his end while the recognized batter Walters added to his team's score. After the no-ball call, instead of being all out for 279, Australia went on to 321 and Walters to his century. This does not mean that umpire Bailhache reached his decision because of home team bias, nor does it mean that in applying the *Law*, an umpire should consider the impact of his decision on either team. To remain true to the 'judicial' nature of his position, he must decide simply by applying the facts to the *Law*. But it does not violate his judicial impartiality, rather it is part of that judicial impartiality and skill in adjudication, to insist that an umpire take into account *all* the factors which make up the context in which he must render his decision, before he makes his judgement. In the context of this Test, with these players, it was perfectly conceivable that New Zealand would choose to focus its attack on Higgs, the batting bunny, in order to get the final Australian wicket. Therefore, umpire Bailhache was again, wrong, on the facts, in this context, when he decided that the Cairns' delivery was meant to intimidate Higgs, for the entire focus of the New Zealand attack must have been on getting his wicket as quickly as possible. Even putting an interpretation more favourable to umpire Bailhache on the facts and assuming that 'intimidation' was an element of the delivery does not make his no-ball call legally correct. Even if a Cairns' bouncer could be said to have intimidated Higgs, only the purest and most obtuse legal formalist could support the umpire's decision here. The intimidation of batters by bowlers has always been a part of the text/ game of cricket and was a part of the game when Law 42(8) was passed. It was clearly not part of the legislator's intent to eliminate all 'intimidation' from the confrontation between bat and ball. Some intimidation is even today essential to the game if the bowlers are to prevent batters from gaining hegemony, as they have in the One-Day arena. Umpire Bailhache was wrong in law in this case because he clearly misinterpreted the legislative intent behind Law 42(8). If Cairns did intend to intimidate Higgs, such intimidation was clearly not prohibited by the *Law*.

Finally, umpire Bailhache's decision was tainted by yet another element of possible illegality. Pictures of the incident show that the umpire's call of no-ball came well after the ball had struck Higgs bat and the wicketkeeper had made the catch. While no one would suggest that umpires should not show calm, cool and dispassionate deliberation in making their decisions, it would seem from these facts that a strong argument about the appearance or apprehension of judicial bias could be made. If umpire Bailhache was clearly of the opinion that even one bouncer from Cairns to a player like Higgs was intimidatory and illegal, he should have called no-ball as soon as he saw Cairns pitch the ball short. His failure to do so and his slowness in making the call until the catch was taken, in light of all the other surrounding circumstances, could lead one to infer that the decision was tainted by bias and resulted only because Higgs was caught. As any administrative lawyer will know, this does not mean that Bailhache was biased but rather that someone reviewing the decision and all the circumstances surrounding the decision could draw a reasonable inference or apprehension of such bias. For all these reasons, Bailhache clearly erred in law in his decision.

What the preceding case indicates and the interpretive purpose it serves, is not that Bailhache was right or wrong. Rather, it demonstrates that, in cricket as in law, the more one situates a seemingly clear text in its real and concrete circumstances, and the more one understands about the various sub-texts of these circumstances themselves, the more easily one sees that there is nothing easy about attributing meaning to such texts. Indeed, it is possible that such cases can give rise not only to detailed *ex post facto* speculation but to occasional prescient, although somewhat confused, prognostication. Writing of the Higgs–Cairns– Bailhache incident a little more than a month before the infamous Mullygrubber incident, Mungo MacCallum opined prophetically 'It is widely rumoured that future touring sides will be required to bowl under-arm to bad Australian batsmen.'

It should also be remembered that another contextualization may allow our practical knowledge of the game to permit the bowling of bouncers at bowlers who are batting in a situation, which but for the additional factor, would have constituted illegal and for some, unethical activity. The factor which adds to the context is retribution as moral imperative. If a team resorts to the use of fast, short-pitched bowling, it can expect, as an 'accepted' practice, that the other side will retaliate, and, depending on the circumstances, that they will retaliate either under criteria of collective guilt (bouncers at strikers not individually responsible), or under criteria of individual liability (bouncers at the bowlers who come in to bat). In any case, it is an accepted interpretive practice that this will occur and, from the perspective of the players as an interpretive community, the umpire is not expected to intervene. While there may be factual disagreements as to whether retribution is called for or as to whether retribution has exceeded the original offence, it is generally accepted that 'We bowl short at them, they bowl short at us – it's as simple as that.'[10]

Finally, to state the obvious, the 'relative ability' of a batter depends not so much on his actual position in the batting order (e.g. a tail-ender), but on the reasons for his being where he is on the day. If things go normally, a tail-ender will bat in his usual place. If, however, a night-watchman is required, he may 'come in' at number three or four. The umpire must know this (as he undoubtedly will) and treat the batter as an individual, not as an actual or real number three or four as we would otherwise understand.

Given the technical legalistic and interpretative difficulties of this part of Law 42, it is little wonder that the issue of intimidatory bowling has always been, and continues to be, one which gives rise to heated debate. Although umpires like Dickie Bird expressed a willingness to apply the *Law* when necessary, they also admitted that there was a great deal of inconsistency among their colleagues.[11] Indeed for Bird, the jurisprudential and jurisdictional issues are clear. It is not a question of further and ongoing legislative intervention. Instead all that is needed is judicial integrity.

> Intimidatory bowling has always been a contentious issue, and I guess it always will be, but it is no good to keep changing the law. It is almost impossible to legislate properly for it. I make no apologies for repeating that it should be down to the strength and discretion of the umpire.[12]

As with LBW appeals and chucking, complex fact situations and interpretive difficulties lead naturally to dispute and disagreement.

For example, during the Melbourne Test against Pakistan in 1990, Australian quick Merv Hughes bowled six bouncers in nine deliveries at Pakistani tail-ender Tauseef Ahmed. Tauseef was struck on the elbow, the forearm and had his groin protector (box) shattered during the Test. The umpires took no action. Intikhab, the Pakistani manager, bemoaned the umpires' failure to intervene and Richie Benaud thought that the situation was extraordinary.[13] It is important to underline that neither Intikhab nor Benaud objected to the use of bouncers *per se*. Rather, in the context, they believed that the number of short deliveries to a tail-ender constituted intimidation. For Intikhab, the problem was simply one of the umpires failing to act to stop a blatant breach of the *Laws*.

> 'I'm not saying they should not bowl bouncers,' . . .
> 'Why not? [It's like] asking a spinner not to turn the ball.'

'The umpires have been given enough power to handle the game. It is up to them to control it.'[14]

For Benaud the problem was not only one of illegality, but also of an affront to the aesthetic and tactical beauty of the game: 'Apart from anything else, it bastardises cricket because, surely, the bouncer should be used as the shock weapon, not the basic delivery.'[15]

Then Australian captain Allan Border offered a more prosaic and positivistic analysis, pointing to the fact that Pakistani bowling star Wasim Akram had delivered five successive bouncers to Hughes without the intervention of the umpires. Who cares about bad or incorrect umpiring as long as they are consistently bad for both sides?

It is little wonder, then, that such universal and ongoing controversy had led to a call for law reform. Some saw the outlawing of bouncers as the simplest and most effective weapon, while others argued that further criminalization was not necessary and 'not cricket'.[16] For members of this camp, the problem was not with the *Law*, or even with the umpires, but, as in the case of chucking, in the common and apparently accurate perception that cricket administrators and governing bodies did not support umpires who vigorously enforced the *Laws*.[17] Law and order problems are not due to the laws on the books or the cops on the beat, but to the gutless elected officials and bureaucrats who let politics triumph over principle. As Dickie Bird explained,

> As Clive Lloyd once said, 'When Dickie has applied the law we have accepted it. If he is strong and steps in, that is fine by us. We might not agree with him, but it is his decision. He is consistent in its application, and we respect him for it.'[18]

Again, judicial competence and integrity are essential for all participants to understand what it means to play the game of cricket and the law. When this system of adjudication breaks down, the law and the game come under threat.

Besides these technical difficulties and failures of official adjudication, one again cannot fully understand the issues involved in the practice of cricket as it related to Law 42(8) without a further 'contextualization' of events and ideas. For example, students, admirers and former brilliant practitioners of the game like India's Nari Contractor (who was almost killed by a Charlie Griffith bouncer in 1962) and former Australian captain Ian Chappell pointed out that there is a practical, tradition-based, self-regulatory, technical solution to the issue, a solution which can be seen as either a substitute or a supplement for stricter law enforcement.[19] For them, a solution was to teach young cricketers to hook. A hook shot, if successful, proves the adage that the best defence is attack. Rather than the batter being intimidated by the bouncer, a successful hook to the boundary of a high delivery will intimidate the bowler and deter him from any further such use of the bouncer.

To a cricket narrative of bowlers' intimidation of batter and the question of legal formalism is added a counter-narrative of a practice of players dealing with their own problems, a counter-narrative of self-help, of the playing community operating and offering solutions without interference from the outsider. To this narrative and counter-narrative, with their own subtle contexts, sub-texts and inter-connection, with other parts of a great cricket story, must be added consideration of other factors.[20] As great West Indian fast bowlers Malcolm Marshall and Michael Holding pointed out, much debate about the 'illegal' use of intimidating bowling could be attributed to the tremendous historical success of the West Indies' all pace attack.[21] Other countries, most notably Australia, who used fearsome pace attacks to such effect that in the 1975–76 series against that team, Lillee and Thomson, a pair of Australian fast bowlers who became cult heroes as a result of their unending pace barrage, allegedly caused Viv Richards to suffer a breakdown and be put under psychiatric care, began to raise objections to West Indian tactics.[22] Lillee and Thomson were rarely no-balled for bowling bouncers and Richards, as West Indian captain, went on to command the world's best (and most vicious) attack.

Besides national bias and changing perspectives depending on one's own bouncer capabilities, other technical, ethical and social interpretive frameworks can be overlaid with ones already mentioned. Differing wickets and batting 'experiences' can cause one to attach different meanings to the idea of 'intimidation'. A batter brought up on hard, dry bouncing wickets in Australia, South Africa or the West Indies has an entirely different experience of bouncers and is able to develop a more successful technical armoury against them than is a player raised on English wickets or brought up against the spin attacks of Indian or Pakistani teams.[23] With technical equipment like helmets and pads now available, a new dilemma arises. Are players less fearful, thereby reducing the possibility of 'intimidation' or are bowlers more likely to aim an attack at the body knowing their victim will be at least partly protected? And what of the effect of such equipment on the tradition-based response to bouncers posed by Contractor and Chappell? Are players today not more likely, as Sir Garfield Sobers contends, to simply duck at the arrival of a bouncer knowing they are well-protected if they misjudge the ball?

The virility cult also raises its head again. Bouncers, fast bowlers, ducking batters, these are, for some, part of what makes cricket an exciting spectator sport. Australians, for some reason or bizarre national trait, manifest this desire for violent cricket most publicly. Not only must the foe be beaten in the score, but he must be conquered physically as well. Total victory can be achieved only through the physical and mental disintegration of the opponent. Bouncers are good because they are manly. More bouncers are better because they are more virile, more masculine. Appeals like Richie Benaud's for the aesthetics of cricket compete with the Sam Peckinpah aesthetic of blood and violence. Each exists in cricket and imposes its meaning on the practice of the game. Added to the cult of virility in Australian cricket is a layer of nationalism, especially where English teams are concerned. Jeff Thomson best summarizes the situation: 'I couldn't wait to have a crack at 'em [the English team]. I thought: "Stuff that stiff upper lip brat. Let's see how stiff it is when it's split".'[24]

If we add to all these factors from interpretive difficulties to the virility cult, the final factor that bouncers, violence and action have strong commercial audience appeal, and we must recognize that commercial interests have always informed some visions of the cricket text, one can only conclude, yet again, that Law 42 on short-pitched fast bowling is not as simple as it seems.

Finally into the debate about bouncers and to counter-cries for stricter law enforcement practices come the ethic and practice of the fast bowler–batter confrontation. This meeting is more than one informed by the virility cult, or nationalistic fervour or commercial self-interest. While it is all of these things, it is also the moment at which these players seek to impose their own meaning on the story of their lives – it is an instant of existential authenticity and self-definition. Players define themselves by their ability to withstand a barrage of bouncers, or conversely by their capacity to intimidate batters.

Here, the ethical practice of self-definition comes into stark and immediate conflict with the letter of the *Law*. This interpretive praxis demands and requires precisely that which was forbidden by the *Law* – intimidation and injury. Fast bowlers define themselves in terms of intimidation: 'I try to hit a batsman in the rib cage when I bowl a purposeful bouncer, and I want it to hurt so much that the batsman doesn't want to face me any more.'[25] and batters in turn look down upon their fellows who fail the test.[26]

A classic example of the existential self-examination in such cases is described by Michael Manley in his discussion of the 1989 Test series between the West Indies and Pakistan and the confrontation between Gilchrist the bowler and Hanif the batter.

> ...those sixteen hours exposed him to nearly forty overs from Gilchrist, then arguably the fastest bowler in the world and certainly the most hostile. For hour after hour, Hanif dealt with balls in excess of 90 miles per hour, rearing past a head fractionally withdrawn at the last moment. Who can tell what tiny increments of fear were lodging in the back of his mind, as lodge they must in the back of the mind of every batsman who has to face really hostile bowling. Apprehension forms like stalagmite in a cave, imperceptible to the eye within short periods. But in the wider span of time there is suddenly the evidence of a process and of a measurable result accumulating drop by drop.[27]

Here we see the classic challenge of gladiatorial combat and the ideal of existential self-definition. Each player attempts to impose his own meaning on the text of his life by imposing himself on the text of the Other and on the broader context of cricket. The letter of the *Law* is stretched and violated if the higher goal of playing the game demands it. And finally, time itself takes on new meaning as the 'moment' of self-definition occurs over a period of hours and perhaps days and weeks. Yet injury and intimidation nonetheless occur in the presence of a legal text forbidding 'intimidation' and 'injury'. Law-violating behaviour can, in such contexts, define what 'is cricket', just as in other circumstances, something can be 'not cricket' if it breaks the letter of the *Law*. Conversely, standing on one's rights and insisting on a strict application of the very letter of the *Law* can, in other circumstances, embody the very definition of precisely what is considered to be 'not cricket'.

Of course, the current version of the *Law* has brought important modifications to the practice of fast bowling and to questions surrounding bouncers. It will always be important to bear in mind that these legislative changes, like the debates surrounding the interpretation of the old *Law*, will inevitably effect the fundamental confrontation between bat and ball. They level the playing field, they give an advantage to the batter, they fail to stop bowlers' dominance, depending on one's starting point in the process and practice of legal interpretation.

In addition to the removal of the 'intimidation' factor, the new provisions also specify in the text of the *Law* itself that height, direction and frequency are to be taken into account. It is also important to underline that the *Law* specifically instructs that 'their frequency' is to be considered. It appears that from the use of the plural pronoun 'their' and the plural noun 'balls', as well as from the plain meaning of 'frequency', that a single bouncer cannot as a matter of *Law* constitute a dangerous and unfair delivery.

It can however still constitute an 'unfair' delivery under the provisions of Law 42(6) (ii) which provides that any ball which pitches and passes or would have passed over head height of the striker, is 'unfair' even though by definition it does not threaten physical injury. Furthermore, the same provision allows such a delivery to count as one of the 'series' or as an element of 'frequency'. Thus the *Law* distinguishes between a fast short-pitched delivery which is both dangerous and unfair and one which is simply unfair. Here, while there is a specific legislative connection permitted between two types of delivery, there appears to be some qualitative distinction in the purpose of the prohibition. In one the aim is to prevent opportunities for injury to the batter and in the other the goal appears more directly to concern the ideal of the battle between bat and ball. Like a wide, a bouncer that passes over head height can be virtually impossible to play. Of course, we would need to return here to familiar arguments about the hook shot as essential to the confrontation between bat and ball.

Finally the new *Law* now allows the umpire after a warning procedure to remove a bowler who violates the prohibitions against fast short-pitched deliveries which are unfair and dangerous, or which are simply 'unfair', from the attack for the remainder of the innings (Law 42(7)). As with other legal and ethical controversies which had 'plagued' cricket, it has been decided to modify law in an effort to modify behaviour. Given, however, the fact that the current provisions of the *Law* still require not just the existence of a state of 'facts' – short-pitched balls, and then an interpretive matrix involving a 'consideration' of the 'likelihood' of injury, with a series of other relevant factors set out by the legislature to assist but not to determine the adjudication process, it is unlikely that bouncers will disappear as a result of the law reform efforts here. Instead, again, it is regulatory reform which has had the biggest impact on the way the game is played and defined.

Thus, in Test matches, the ICC simply replaced Law 42(6) with Playing Conditions which limit the number of bouncers per over to two. They define a bouncer, or fast short-pitched ball, as one which passes or would have passed above shoulder height but not above the head. The sanction of removal remains.[28] Other short-pitched deliveries are subject to regulation as unfair and dangerous in the event they are likely to cause injury.

Again, the *Laws* in and of themselves were believed not to work. When law does not work, in cricket as in politics, more law is the answer. And the legislature levels the field or disadvantages bowler or batter by removing a weapon or an unfair advantage. The *Law* is clear, the meaning is up for grabs. The idea of bowlers pitching the ball so that it will surprise the batter and strike him on the body is not reduced or eliminated by the new *Law* or by the Playing Conditions. The determination of the validity and legality of the tactics of the bowler will still be left, as long as the ball is kept below the shoulders, to the common sense, pragmatic, contextual interpretive skill of the umpire. As importantly, the practice of the law and interpretation will also be informed by the evolving legal and ethical practices of the way the game is actually played.

In the 2001 series against South Africa, Brett Lee was heavily criticized in the Australian media for his concerted attack in the first Test against Makhaya Ntini and Nantie Hayward. Both are bowlers and neither is renowned for his skill with the bat. Lee delivered four consecutive 'bouncers' to the two batters. The two deliveries to Ntini hit him on the helmet and one of the deliveries followed Hayward as he bailed out to leg. Steve Waugh supported his bowler against media critics and delivered a clear exposition of the current understanding of accepted practice among the players' interpretive community.

> 'It's Test match cricket. When Brett goes in, he's going to cop it,' said Waugh of Lee, who was struck on the hand by a short ball from Hayward in the first innings.
>
> These days you're earning big money, you've got a responsibility to learn how to bat. It's not like it was 20 years ago when it was not professional and there was sort of a bowler's code.
>
> Our bowlers work very hard on their batting, and we expect other tailenders to do likewise. There's no favours out there in the middle of a Test match, and I think the way Brett bowled – it's Test match cricket.[29]

Malcolm Marshall would be proud, at least at one level. Test match cricket is a manly pursuit. A fast bowler is a man and part of the team. It is his job to help win by bowling fast. Yet Waugh and Lee have gone one step further. Not only is Test cricket a manly pursuit, it is now a professional activity. This means that the stakes are higher, cricket is a career. In addition, the stakes at play also impose a new obligation on all players; they must meet new standards and targets. This is the age of global capital and of performance indicators. Cricket cannot escape management expertise and review. There are no tailenders; there are only Test cricketers. The old rule, that a bowler did not bounce another bowler is replaced by a new standard, a professional standard. Shaun Pollock, South African captain, himself a bowler, and the son and nephew of South African Test cricketers, supported Waugh's interpretation.

> It's part and parcel of the game, I guess. You've got to try and intimidate players and try to get them out...In my dad's day there was a bowlers' union, but that's long gone, and if you stay within the rules, then there's no complaint.[30]

The comments by Pollock and Waugh indicate and underline the mutability of codes of conduct, ethical behaviour and the spirit of the game. These norms change over time and sometimes the pace of change is rapid. In March 1994, Courtney Walsh was criticized by members of the English press and former English captain Graham Gooch for his barrage of short-pitched deliveries aimed at England bowler Devon Malcolm. Malcolm was then described as one of the worst number 11 batters in world cricket, 'Walsh's bowling was a disgrace. Given the nature of the combatants, it was the worst most observers could remember.'[31]

At the time, many participants in the interpretive practice of cricket believed that the ethical standards of the game imposed an obligation not to bowl as aggressively as Walsh did at an incompetent batter like tail-ender Malcolm. Seven years later, even the 'victim's' captain recognized that the norm no longer applied. Instead all that is left is the letter of the *Laws of Cricket* and Test match Playing Conditions.

The *Laws* are there to regulate conduct and umpires are there to interpret and apply the law. Lee was not 'officially' warned or taken off as a result of his attack on the South African bowlers. The umpire simply had a quiet word after his delivery to Hayward.

The real debate here appears to centre around the function of bowling bouncers in a particular context. For former Australian batter, Dean Jones, there was no illegality or immorality involved in Lee's bowling at tail-enders, even if he did so to soften them up. The morality and legal purpose of the practice, established by the West Indies, and adopted by other nations who saw the successes which followed the practice, was to allow the wicket to be taken. The idea was to make the tail-ender back away so he could be bowled or forced to play a shot guaranteed to offer an easy catch.[32]

Noted legal ethicist Glenn McGrath explained the players' code again in terms of masculinity and belonging.

> If Hayward made an effort to stand behind the ball, one he wouldn't get hurt as much and, two, we'd respect him a lot more and there'd be nothing said.
>
> . . .
>
> Intimidation is part of a bowler's armoury.[33]

For journalist Richard Hinds, however, 'Lee's fourth and final bumper to Hayward crossed the line that distinguishes the legitimate working-over of a batsman from assault and battery.'[34]

Everyone at some level recognizes and applies the changed standards of legal and ethical practice. The old 'rule' that it was not on to bounce bowlers has disappeared and the ethical, practical and legal context has changed as a result of democratic experience. The debate now is merely one which occurs at the margins. Where is the line crossed? 'Working-over' the batter is permissible, although arguably strictly forbidden by the letter of the *Law*. Too much working-over is illegitimate. Working-over for the sake of working-over is not permissible. Punishing to take a wicket is not only permissible but required under the code of ethical conduct of the players themselves. Fast bowlers bowl fast, batters get out of the way, or they hit the ball to the boundary, or they get hit. Umpires know this, fans know this, players know this.

Indeed, the reaction in relation to the Lee versus Hayward confrontation can be compared instructively with the actions of Indian spinner Anil Kumble in the Antigua Test against the West Indies in May 2002. Kumble was struck on the head by a bouncer from Mervyn Dillon. His jaw was broken. He was ruled out of the rest of the series and told to return to India for reconstructive surgery. Nonetheless he bowled again in the match, coming back with his head and jaw swathed in bandages. He took the prize wicket of Brian Lara.

Here was a man and a man's man. A bowler who was struck by a bouncer and came back from his sickbed to engage in the struggle between bat and ball with one of world's finest player's wicket at stake. For Australians, this brought back memories of Rick McCosker whose jaw was broken in the Centenary Test by Bob Willis. He returned to bat with his face bandaged and is to this day considered a 'role model', the physical embodiment of Australian manliness on the cricket pitch.[35] He was no Nantie Hayward, backing away to leg. He was a real cricketer. And everyone knows that, just as everyone knows that Dillon's bouncer to a spin bowler facing him was also a manly act and part of the game.

The letter of the *Law* is clear, yet it will not be applied as written because to do so would render the game being played 'not cricket'. In other words, as Allan Hutchinson again says, it is all in the game. Or as Dickie Bird might put it, it is down to the umpires to interpret and enforce the *Laws* and to players to play the game. If and when the two practices coincide or diverge we encounter the jurisprudential complexities of just what we mean by what is and what is not 'cricket', and what is and is not 'law'.

18 Ball-tampering and the rule of law

In cricket, in recent years, no issue better captures the idea of good and evil, right and wrong, law and order *versus* criminality, than the vexed problem of allegations of 'ball-tampering'. The idea that the fielding/bowling side deliberately interferes with the ball, most commonly either by lifting the seam or defacing one side, goes to the heart of the 'contest between bat and ball'. The confrontation between batter and bowler encapsulates 'cricket' as contest – the batter trying to score runs, the bowler attempting to capture wickets, the two vital elements in calculating winning and losing. The idea of 'fair play', of 'cricket' necessarily includes the idea that the confrontation must be one of skill and 'natural' talent, of 'bat against ball', of willow and leather. Allegations of ball-tampering therefore go to the very heart of what it means to play cricket and conversely what it means to 'cheat'.

When the MCC modified the *Laws of Cricket* to redefine and clarify the nature and content of the offence, Don Oslear proclaimed 'With these dramatic changes, we are now getting closer to the punishment fitting the crime and that is no bad thing.'[1] Oslear is no stranger to ball-tampering issues. He explains his concerns not just over the incidence of ball-tampering but with the history of official inaction in dealing harshly and consistently in order to weed out this activity which he obviously considers to be cheating of the worst kind.[2] Indeed Oslear has claimed that he was driven from the game as a result of his support for Allan Lamb's allegations of ball-tampering against Pakistani cricketers.[3] Whatever one makes of Oslear's allegations of high-level cover-up over the issue, it is clear, as I shall briefly review in the following sections, that the issue of ball-tampering raises fundamental questions and issues of law and morality in the world of cricket. Again, to tamper with the ball in order to gain an unlawful advantage is possibly the worst offence one can imagine since it, like throwing, goes to the heart of the contest between bat and ball.

It is therefore appropriate that the *Laws of Cricket* historically dealt with the issue under the provisions relating to **Unfair Play, Law 42**.[4]

Law 42(4) of the 1980 *Code* read as follows:

Lifting the Seam
A player shall not lift the seam of the ball for any reason. Should this be done, the umpires shall change the ball for one of similar condition to that in use prior to the contravention.

Law 42(5) further stated:

Changing the condition of the Ball
Any member of the fielding side may polish the ball provided that such polishing wastes no time and that no artificial substance is used. No-one shall rub the ball on the ground or use any artificial substance or take any other action to alter the condition of the ball.

In the event of a contravention of this Law, the Umpires, after consultation, shall change the ball for one of similar condition to that in use prior to the contravention. This Law does not prevent a member of the fielding side from drying a wet ball, or removing mud from the ball.

Note (a) instructed the umpires to make frequent and irregular inspections of the ball while note (b) allowed the ball to be dried on a towel or with sawdust.

The provisions of the new anti-tampering section of the *Laws* can again be found under the fair and unfair play rules of Law 42(3). The new language of the *Law* attempts to clarify first with greater precision what a player may or may not do with the ball and second establishes a fundamental change in the remedial powers of the umpires in dealing with this aspect of unfair play. Bowlers may now be ordered out of the attack and penalty runs awarded to the batting side in cases of unlawful interference with the ball.

3. The match ball – changing its condition

(a) Any fielder may

   (i) polish the ball provided that no artificial substance is used and that such polishing wastes no time.
   (ii) remove mud from the ball under the supervision of the umpire.
   (iii) dry a wet ball on a towel.

(b) It is unfair for anyone to rub the ball on the ground for any reason, interfere with any of the seams or the surface of the ball, use any implement, or take any other action whatsoever which is likely to alter the condition of the ball, except as permitted in (a) above.

(c) The umpires shall make frequent and irregular inspections of the ball.

(d) In the event of any fielder changing the condition of the ball unfairly, as set out in (b) above, the umpires after consultation shall

(i)   change the ball forthwith. It shall be for the umpires to decide on the replacement ball, which shall, in their opinion, have had wear comparable with that which the previous ball had received immediately prior to the contravention.

(ii)   inform the batsmen that the ball has been changed.

(iii) award 5 penalty runs to the batting side. See 17 below.

(iv)   inform the captain of the fielding side that the reason for the action was the unfair interference with the ball.

(v)   inform the captain of the batting side as soon as practicable of what has occurred.

(vi)   report the occurrence as soon as possible to the Executive of the fielding side and any Governing Body responsible for the match, who shall take such action as is considered appropriate against the captain and team concerned.

(e) If there is any further instance of unfairly changing the condition of the ball in that innings, the umpires after consultation shall

(i)   repeat the procedure in (d)(i), (ii) and (iii) above.

(ii)   inform the captain of the fielding side of the reason for the action taken and direct him to take off forthwith the bowler who delivered the immediately preceding ball. The bowler thus taken off shall not be allowed to bowl again in that innings.

(iii) inform the captain of the batting side as soon as practicable of what has occurred.

(iv)   report this further occurrence as soon as possible to the Executive of the fielding side and any Governing Body responsible for the match, who shall take such action as is considered appropriate against the captain and team concerned.

Finally, it should also be noted that the ICC Test Match Playing Conditions and One-Day International Playing Conditions each stipulate that

> The umpires shall retain possession of the match ball(s) throughout the duration of the match when play is not actually taking place. During play umpires shall periodically and irregularly inspect the condition of the ball and shall retain possession of it at the fall of a wicket, a drinks interval, at the end of each over, or any other disruption in play.[5]

The *Laws* therefore clearly establish in both the former and current texts that which can be done with/to the ball and those actions which are illegal. They seek to strike a balance between allowing the bowler's side to maintain the ball (polishing and drying) in a condition which allows him to perform his assigned task of dismissing the batter and permitting the batter to face a ball which has only been subjected to the effects of natural wear and tear. In other words, the *Laws* function to ensure the classic 'confrontation between bat and ball'.

The problem, of course, is that, like much else in life, law and cricket, the only thing that remains certain is the reign of uncertainty. 'Common wisdom', custom, all that we know about cricket, can and does change. Change is not always accepted since it upsets a strong desire for certainty and the 'old ways'. The reluctance to accept change is a common characteristic between cricket and the legal system. Indeed, change in cricket is often accompanied not just by reluctance and unwillingness, but by a steadfast refusal to believe that the change in question is possible except by deceit, trickery and 'cheating'. Thus it was and is with allegations of 'ball-tampering'. Now we arrive at the first jurisprudential development in relation to the text of the 1980 provisions of Law 42(4) and (5), the vexed question of 'reverse swing'.

Traditionally, the ability of right arm bowlers to swing the ball, more precisely, to swing the ball into the right-handed batters, was associated with opening bowlers in combination with the meteorological forces of nature, the shiny new ball, a bit of moisture in the air and some cloud cover early in the morning.[6] As the ball became worn, it would swing less and more in the expected 'natural' fashion, i.e. away from the bat. Thus, more predictability from the batter's perspective was brought into the game as the ball became older. This was confirmed in the player's mind by watching the bowler's grip on the ball at the point of release. An outswinger grip, the placement of the seam and that of the polished side of the ball, all allowed the batter facing to 'know' with certainty that if the ball moved in the air, it would move away. While his ability to take advantage of this 'knowledge' still depended on a number of factors such as his skill with the bat, the field placings, where the ball pitched and whether it moved off the pitch, the striker still enjoyed a relative advantage over the old ball bowler because of his certainty in relation to the issue of swing.

Then along came the Pakistanis, particularly Imran Khan and his protégés, Waqar Younis and Wasim Akram. This trio, along with Aqib Javed and others, could somehow make the old ball swing in the air into the batter. The effect was dramatic and traumatic. A ball that should have swung away suddenly came at very high speeds at the batter, crashing into middle stump or painfully smashing into the toes. Not only did the 'reverse swing' deliveries take wickets but they also served to sow doubt in the striker's mind, turning the tide in the bowler's favour in the 'confrontation' between 'bat and ball'.[7] Of course, this sudden change to what 'we' thought we knew about cricket balls and how they behaved quickly brought about what appears to have become the standard response to such epistemological upheavals and paradigm shifts – accusations of cheating. And the cries continued as Wasim and Waqar became the best pace bowling duo in the world and as England crashed to even more Test defeats.

Soon the physicists were on the case. While their objective studies seemed to demonstrate conclusively that 'reverse swing' was both explicable in scientific terms and achievable without cheating this did little to stop the murmurings in the cricket world that the Pakistanis were up to no good.[8] The issue for this part of the cricketing world at least had little or nothing to do with physics and everything to do with 'cricket' and 'truth'. The discourse here was not to be scientific but legal and ethical.

The intersection between cricket and the law reached its most logical point in Nov. 1993, when former Pakistani bowler and legal expert Sarfraz Nawaz brought a defamation suit against England batter Allan Lamb. Lamb, in his role as journalist, had written an article in the *Daily Mirror* in which he asserted that when they were teammates at Northamptonshire, Sarfraz had shown him how to get 'reverse' swing by defacing the ball. In other words, Lamb claimed that Sarfraz was a 'cheat'. It is important to note that Lamb's Article was the culmination of much speculation in the English media about the Pakistani's ability to achieve the phenomenon of 'reverse swing' without breaching the *Laws of Cricket*.[9] After several days of hearings which saw the introduction of video evidence apparently showing Pakistani 'ball-tampering', the suit was dropped.[10] Ball-tampering as part of cricket and law remained unresolved.

This was not however the only case of litigation involving Pakistani and English cricketers and the vexed question of ball-tampering allegations. This time, the plaintiffs were English, the defendant Pakistani, but the context and circumstances relatively unchanged. Ian Botham and Allan Lamb sued Imran Khan after Khan wrote an article accusing the pair essentially of being low-class, uncouth English racists concerning their previous allegations against Pakistani players.[11] During the course of proceedings Imran claimed that Keith Miller of Australia was a ball-tamperer since he had clearly indicated that he lifted the seam of the ball. Also during the trial, Imran withdrew allegations of ball-tampering against Botham when he admitted that he accepted Botham's assertion, verified by David Gower, that he had merely been squeezing the ball back into shape during the incident in question, 'But Imran said he believed Botham had still been technically guilty of ball-tampering.'[12]

Here we come to one of the intriguing issues not just of the jurisprudence of ball-tampering *per se* but of cricket legality generally. Imran is in fact withdrawing the allegation that Botham was a 'cheat' while maintaining his assertion that he was still guilty of a technical breach of the prohibitions dealing with changing the condition of the ball. We arrive once again at a basic issue of liability both civil and criminal, the mental element associated with the guilty conduct and more fundamentally to a potential conflict between the technical content of the legal provisions of the game's governing juridical text and the ethically informed norms of existential and deontological practice within the interpretive community.

In other words, a technical violation of the *Laws* may be an offence but unless it is accompanied by some intention aimed at circumventing either the legislative purpose of the text, or the generally informing ideal of a confrontation between bat and ball, it is not 'cheating'. This latter offence must be seen not just in the context and limits of legal formality, but within a broader understanding of the way in which the rules of appropriate conduct are understood by the players of the game and those called upon to adjudicate.

In 2002, for example, Bob Austen of the Association of Cricket Umpires and Scorers discussed the common practice of loading up one side of the ball with sweat and saliva in order to assist in obtaining reverse swing. Such acts are not just common and accepted by the players, but because of the accepted belief that they are also legal, they are conducted in public. Yet for Austen, these actions potentially breach the wording of Law 42(3). The problem here is not just one between players' understandings of accepted and acceptable practice on the one hand and some umpires' technical legal reading of the legal text. Instead, it is also a problem grounded in the poor and ambiguous drafting of the terms of the *Law* itself. Thus, paragraph (a) (i) permits 'polishing' *inter alia* 'provided that no artificial substance is used'. By strong implication, the use of natural substances such as sweat and saliva would be permitted here. However, the use of these substances is permissible only in the process of 'polishing' the ball. Arguably, loading up one side of the ball in order to create an imbalance in the weight distribution of the ball to allow it to swing is not within either the accepted common sense meaning or legislative intent behind 'polishing'. In such a case, the provisions of sub-paragraph (b) prohibiting any action likely to alter the condition of the ball would come into play.

In other words, Austen is correct unless and until the understanding of 'polishing' is interpreted, as it seems to be by players of the game and indeed by most umpires who witness the actions and do not intervene, to include this practice. In such a case, the activities of bowlers and others in relation to bodily fluids and the ball are perfectly lawful.[13]

Of course, there are here, in the Khan and Botham case, as there always are, interpretive grounds for disagreement. One could easily argue that the ball-tampering provisions of the *Laws* are themselves found within the legislative and broader interpretive framework of the rules relating to 'fair and unfair play'. Any violation of the prohibition in place here is therefore a *per se* breach of the spirit of the game, which at the very least must be informed by and grounded within the ideals of fair play. Indeed, the text of the *Law* itself makes clear exactly what can and cannot be done to the ball. There is no provision which would have allowed the players themselves to employ self-help mechanisms to beat the ball back into shape. However, at the same time, it might well be pointed out that the text of then Law 42(4) and (5) did allow some ambiguity even in so far as Imran's assertion that Botham's actions constituted a technical breach of the prohibition against ball-tampering.

For example, Law 42(4) specifically and only forbade lifting the seam. Squeezing the ball back into shape does not, generally speaking, constitute lifting the seam. Law 42(5) also prohibited very specific acts relating to 'polishing', 'rubbing', or 'drying the ball'. Only the heading of the section speaks more generally of 'Changing the Condition of the Ball'. Obviously an available argument about the proper legislative interpretation relating to this provision would assert that the *Law* was penal in nature and should have been interpreted restrictively. Moreover, the title of a provision should not, as a matter of well-accepted interpretive practice, impose a prohibition not covered by the actual language of the substantive text itself. Thus, while pounding and squeezing the ball back into shape may be in common parlance 'changing the condition of the ball', such acts were not specifically included in the limited definition and description of what constituted changing the condition of the ball pursuant to the legislative text.[14] Arguably, as a matter of law, Imran's distinction between 'cheating' and a technical violation of the anti-tampering provisions might itself have been subjected to this type of legal argument. Finally, however, another textual provision might have been seen to buttress Imran's position on the 'illegality' of Botham's actions.

Law 5(5) provided that

> In the event of a ball during play being lost, or, in the opinion of the Umpires, becoming unfit for play, the Umpires shall allow it to be replaced...

Here it seems clear that the umpires, who are the sole judges of fair and unfair play generally, are also vested with the sole jurisdiction to decide if the ball has become unusable. In the circumstances under review here, it would appear that the actions of Botham deprived the umpires of the power to exercise their discretionary jurisdiction. Therefore, what Botham did was a violation of the *Laws* either if we are willing to give a broad and liberal interpretation to the anti-tampering provisions or if we see his actions as an affront to the unique jurisdiction of the umpires in relation to changing the ball. Anyone who watches or plays the game will be familiar with the common practice, particularly in the latter stages of a One-Day game of the batter asking the umpires to look at the ball and to change it because they are having difficulty seeing the dirtied surface of the white leather covering or because it has become knocked out of shape. It seems obvious that dissatisfaction with the shape or state of the ball is to be dealt with by the umpire. Squeezing or pounding the ball back into shape in such circumstances is 'illegal', if not unethical. Once more, what the Imran, Botham and Lamb case indicates is not the clarity of the *Laws of Cricket* or the universality of normative understandings about the spirit of the game, but instead the uncertainty of all interpretive practices within the jurisprudence of cricket.

For those who thought the truth about 'reverse swing' and Pakistani 'cheating' would or could be determined as a matter of law, the decision to withdraw and cease the proceedings in the Sarfraz case seemed to have deprived them of an answer in their search for truth. The Imran case offered a second opportunity, in slightly different legal circumstances, to address many of the same issues. Even the final majority verdict in favour of the defendant, raised as many questions as it answered, in the arcane and technical world of defamation law. But the questions about ball-tampering, cheating, reverse swing etc. seemed to persist.

It may well be argued that the evidence adduced at the trial was more than sufficient to demonstrate the validity of 'cheating' claims and assertions that Pakistani success can only be attributed to malfeasance. Conversely it may be asserted that the evidence showed no such thing and that the issue here is not as clear cut as Allan Lamb and his supporters might want us to believe.

The debate here raises several factual, legal and ethical questions. The first question, one of mixed fact and law, is 'Are balls tampered with?' The second question, which rests on a certain positive answer to the first is, 'Who tampers with the balls?' A third question, which may be related or unrelated to the answers to either or both of the first two questions, is, 'Does tampering affect the way the ball swings?' A fourth query might ask, again either with or without relation with any of the preceding, 'Is it possible to achieve "reverse swing" without cheating?' Or one might put it this way, 'Is all "reverse swing" achieved by cheating' in other words by tampering with the ball in violation of the *Laws of Cricket*?

It seems clear to me that each of these questions is important if one wishes to approach a full 'understanding' of the issues surrounding the legal and ethical debate which sought to impose a synonymous relationship between 'reverse swing' and 'ball-tampering'. It is equally clear that one can answer affirmatively or in the negative to most of these queries without automatically leaping to the conclusion that all bowlers who achieve reverse swing were or are 'cheats'. It also seems clear that, as a matter of jurisprudential logic consistent with the common law system and its apparently inherent respect for and reliance upon the principles of the 'rule of law', it would be inconsistent, unfair and a form of intellectual cheating, to assume that even if we could be satisfied that balls are tampered with in order to achieve reverse swing, all Pakistani bowlers are cheats or an individual Pakistani bowler in a particular circumstance did in fact cheat. Without proof in each case, we would be installing a system of collective guilt and responsibility which is inconsistent with the legal system in general and with the *Laws of Cricket* in particular. At the very least, those who saw in the *Sarfraz v. Lamb* case, and in the subsequent proceedings against Imran Khan, the opportunity to justify their position on the issue of ball-tampering were operating on a system of beliefs about law and justice which was and is inconsistent and unjust.

This position is further exacerbated by the nature of the evidence adduced at the Sarfraz hearing and apparently allowed by the Court under rules of admissibility. Even if it is proven beyond all doubt and to the satisfaction of everyone that the ball was tampered with in those instances where video evidence was put before the courts, Sarfraz Nawaz had long before retired from cricket. If the libellous statement was that Sarfraz had shown Lamb how to cheat after a County match 12 years previously, it is difficult to imagine how an incident in a One-Day International or a Test in 1992 could 'prove' the factual basis of Lamb's assertion unless the finder of fact was willing to draw the problematic conclusion that because one former Pakistani bowler knew how to tamper with the ball 12 years ago and Pakistani bowlers now know how to tamper with the ball, he, and he alone, necessarily must have showed them how to do it. A less forceful argument, but one based on the same erroneous jurisprudential assumptions, would be that events 12 years after the alleged incident clearly and cogently demonstrate that the incident did in fact occur. This is ridiculous on its face yet it seems to have been key to the jurisprudential position adopted by Lamb's supporters. It also seems to be the position of those who persist in the conjunctive claims that 'reverse swing' is the result of cheating, that the Pakistanis are the ones who get the ball to swing the other way, therefore the Pakistanis are cheats.

What, then, are the legal and jurisprudential lessons which might, at this stage of the inquiry at least, be gleaned from the Sarfraz/Imran/Lamb/Botham affairs? First, it is now possible to answer the question as to whether ball-tampering did/does occur. A year or so after the Sarfraz/Lamb case, Pakistani cricket authorities suspended indefinitely fast bowler Asadullah Butt after he was caught tampering with a ball during a domestic first class fixture.[15] Imran Khan confessed to his biographer that he had on several occasions lifted the seam and defaced one side of the ball.[16]

According to Ivo Tennant's account of Imran's bowling practice,

> If Law 42 on short-pitched bowling was flouted by Imran, so was the spirit of the game. Although in other respects a fair sportsman, he tampered with the ball on occasion, scratching the side and lifting the seam and once, playing for Sussex against Hampshire in 1981, asking the 12th man to bring on a bottle cap. The upshot was that the ball began to move around as not before in the match. Sussex won and the umpires were none the wiser.[17]

Khan's 'admission' caused a furore and he was finally forced to resign from the ICC's cricket committee. Many saw Khan's confession as proof positive for the more general assertion that the Pakistanis were cheats or at the very least that many of their more recent successes could be attributed to ball-tampering.[18] In an interesting twist, which adds yet another dimension to the legal debate here, Khan argued not only that ball-tampering had always gone on and therefore was an accepted part of the ethos of the game, but that this was a fact which was recognized by the better-educated elements associated with the game. All the fuss about the *Laws* and about clamping down on cheating came, according to Imran at least, from the lower classes. Implicitly at least, they should simply mind their betters, for they obviously suffer from a dramatic case of false consciousness when it comes to the ideology of the rule of law.[19] This, in effect, was the type of statement which caused Botham and Lamb to take offence and take action.

Whatever the class content of the ball-tampering issue may be, Khan's confession of transgression and the reaction to it indicated yet again that there is more at play here than a simple discussion of the 'facts' or even of the 'law' might, at first blush, lead us to believe. As I have already mentioned above, a fundamental factual and jurisprudential fallacy, the fallacy of 'collective guilt', is apparently at work here. The fact that Imran has admitted to 'cheating' does not logically or as matter of law, in any way lead to the conclusion that any other Pakistani bowler, from Sarfraz to Wasim and Waqar, has, in fact or in law, 'cheated' unless one admits that it is acceptable to draw from such notoriously unreliable 'propensity' or 'similar fact' evidence the conclusion that if one Pakistani admits to cheating, they are all guilty of cheating. While such a conclusion is not uncommon and is perfectly consistent with the idea that 'Pakistan are the least popular of the Test playing countries',[20] it also does much to reveal a more basic fact about 'cricket'. Underneath the surface of claims which invoke nothing more than a morally righteous support for 'right' over 'wrong', for 'fair play' over 'cheating', for the rule of law over law-breaking, we can often find evidence of a much more traditional and common discourse of racial, ethnic, religious prejudice and hatred. In other words, regardless of the merits of the case in any particular instance, 'rule of law' discourse in cricket, particularly in the case of allegations of 'Pakistani ball-tampering' is almost always and inevitably informed by the discourses and historical practices of colonialism, religion, ethnicity and race. What attention to this heritage as underlying and informing many claims and protests about the *Laws* in such instances reveals is not the 'truth' or 'falsity' of the 'factual' issue about 'ball-tampering', but rather how easily legal discourse can assume a guise of value neutrality while at the same time being potentially informed by a fundamentally racist set of preconceived notions and practices.

The way in which this rule of law discourse serves to buttress racism as an acceptable hidden discourse becomes clearer when we move away from the epistemological category of 'Pakistani ball-tampering' to a related but separate epistemological category of 'other ball-tampering'. As Imran Khan asserts and others agree, ball-tampering has a long history in the game.[21] The sun cream which many Australian bowlers wear to prevent skin cancer has long been suspected of finding its way mysteriously onto the cricket ball, for example. Indeed, Australian, English and New Zealand bowlers have all admitted in the recent past to having 'doctored' the ball in ways which were contrary to both the 'spirit of the game' and to the *Laws of Cricket*.[22] In 1996, Victorian captain and former Australian cricketer, Dean Jones, alleged that New South Wales tampered with the ball in an interstate game.[23] I am not suggesting that the conclusion to be drawn from these admissions of 'wide-spread' 'cheating' by fast bowlers is to admit defeat, throw in the towel and scrap the provisions of the *Laws* dealing with ball-tampering. Nor would I even assert that the preferred course of action is that 'we' simply should therefore admit that 'cheating' happens and we should not express such great surprise when ball-tampering occurs. What I am suggesting, however, is that we take note of the fact that it is clear to anyone who studies this issue in even the most cursory fashion that we are in fact faced in each case with 'similar fact situations', i.e. 'ball-tampering', and with the clear applicability of the same legal text, the *Laws of Cricket*. One can equally assume from the nature of the rhetoric which one encounters in this field, that we are also faced with a universal set of ethical norms neatly and concisely found in the phrase 'the spirit of the game'. Yet the 'legal' and ethical discourse (perhaps silence would be more accurate here) which surrounds these other revelations about 'ball-tampering' clearly indicate that they fall within a separate and distinct legal category. In other words, even the most vociferous critics of confessed tamperers, Lawson and Pringle, have been willing to tolerate these confessions of illegality in a way which they were apparently unwilling to countenance in relation to Pakistani cricketers. Derek Pringle and Geoff Lawson have not been 'shamed' or 'shunned' or condemned or excluded from the community of cricket. Not only did the transgressors escape virtually unpunished by the forces of law or of equity, but whatever guilt they may carry and that appears to be minimal, is clearly attributed and attributable to them personally.

The discourse of 'collective guilt' which so clearly and insistently underlies most mainstream interventions about 'Pakistani ball-tampering' has disappeared from discussions of 'cheating' by Anglo-Saxon cricketers from the Mother Country and the settler dominions. No one has asserted, nor would they dare assert, that because Derek Pringle has confessed to doctoring the ball, all English fast bowlers are cheats or more outrageously, that English cricket is corrupt.[24] Yet, the applicable legal text and the equitable principles which appear to apply to all cases of illegally obtained 'reverse swing' remain 'unchanged'. I wish simply to underline here the now trite point that law is not ever 'just' law, it is always, for all its claims to neutrality, something else as well. Nor would it appear, is 'justice' ever 'just'. At least not if you are a Pakistani fast bowler who takes a lot of English and Australian wickets.

Thus, the answers to the first two questions raised earlier about 'ball-tampering', i.e. does tampering occur and if so, who does it, are to be 'yes' and 'quite a few people'. However, it appears that the questions themselves may be overly simplistic if not actually misleading. Quite clearly the legal and jurisprudential debates which surround the issue of 'ball-tampering' are themselves only accessible if one is willing to examine the discourses which appear to underlie claims to neutrality and justice. What is clear is that these discourses about law and justice in this context must themselves be more deeply contextualized. At the same time it is important to remember and to underline the fact that the discourses and the contexts which inform them are of course historically contingent and mutable. In fact and in law, as I have argued throughout this book, all discourses are mutable and contextual. In relation to 'ball-tampering', it appears that the mutability nonetheless, as far as legal and ethical discourse are concerned, takes place in a context in which two separate epistemological categories have been established and which operate as primary referents. Thus, as a matter of cricket and as a matter of law, there appear to have been both 'ball-tampering' and 'Pakistani ball-tampering'. While these constructs continue to operate as ideological limiting factors on much of the discussion about illegality and 'ball-tampering', it is also the case that the 'factual' and historical evolution of other texts and practices can operate to have some impact on the actual content and context of the dominant epistemological categories themselves.

Indeed, at a 'practical' level, even the current legal and ethical discourses about one part of the 'ball-tampering' meta-narrative offer clear evidence of the mutability of that discourse itself.

In 1993, for example, it was widely accepted that 'reverse swing' of the old ball was an effect available only to the Pakistanis and which was widely believed to be available to them only by defacing the ball. By 1995, that part of the discourse which asserted that only the Pakistanis could get the old ball to swing in to the right-handed batter was no longer part of Australian cricket talk.[25] In the intervening period, New South Wales quick Glenn McGrath had entered the Australian side, toured, and become the major strike bowler in Australia's Worrell Trophy victory in the Caribbean and most importantly, had developed the ability to move the old ball in the air into the batter. Shortly thereafter, the three-Test series between Pakistan and Australia saw the television commentators on Channel 9 and the ABC Radio broadcasters consistently comment on the ability of all three bowlers, Wasim, Waqar and McGrath to get 'reverse swing'. They also offered scientific explanations of the phenomenon to viewers and listeners. It seemed, by the laws of physics and the jurisprudence of reverse swing, that if an Australian could do it, cheating no longer entered into the equation and there was no need to invoke the legal text. Since then, of course, the interpretive circumstances and context have been completely altered at least at this level of discourse. All cricket commentary in Australia and in England, and elsewhere, now includes specific references to the ability of some bowlers to 'swing the old ball'. We are shown on replays how to polish one side of the ball and even how to load it with sweat in order to properly alter its aerodynamic properties to allow for reverse swing. English and Australian bowlers might even be chosen in a side and brought into the attack at certain times because of their ability to extract reverse swing. The taking-up of the new ball is often delayed in order to allow these bowlers to continue to challenge the batter. In other words, for many, the old idea that reverse swing was evidence of cheating in the basic confrontation between bat and ball has now become a legitimate and exciting aspect of that essential battle within cricket.

This is not, however, the end of discourses about law and ethics in relation to the questions of 'reverse swing' and 'ball-tampering'. For it still appears that basic assertions and understandings of the *Laws* and ethics of cricket jurisprudence are in this context informed by a meta-narrative which claims that 'the Pakistanis are cheats'.

Michael Atherton's Ball: England's Glorious Tradition of the Rule of Law

Nowhere is the process of creating separate epistemological categories to cover seemingly identical events more clear in the history of cricket's legal and ethical 'crises' than in the case of then England captain Michael Atherton's infamous brush with the law. Here we can witness and learn from what is possibly the finest example of common law reasoning to emerge from cricket jurisprudence. As all lawyers trained in the common law tradition know, the genius of the system resides in its ability to advance by a process of incremental change through a style of legal reasoning and argument which 'distinguishes' seemingly similar factual and legal circumstances from precedent. Herein lies the fascination for the law and jurisprudence of cricket in Atherton's case for, on the surface, in this instance in the television coverage, we quite clearly have a case of 'ball-tampering', albeit not by a Pakistani. However, as any decent trial lawyer will tell you, eyewitness testimony is notoriously unreliable and, as O.J. Simpson and any number of professional footballers will tell you, the 'law' is never as clear as it might at first blush appear.

The 'facts' of the Atherton case are by now well-known. During the television broadcast of the Lord's Test against South Africa, the camera caught, and replayed again and again, Atherton appearing to put his hand into his pocket, removing his hand and rubbing the ball, which he then returned to the bowler. Atherton's activities were characterized by Peter Burge, the ICC Match Referee, as an 'unfamiliar action'. Burge investigated the incident and after being informed by the umpires, England's Dickie Bird and Australian Steve Randall, that they could find no evidence that the ball had in fact been 'tampered' with, he questioned Atherton.[26]

Although Atherton was effectively cleared of 'ball-tampering' because there was no physical evidence that the condition of the ball had been altered, the case did not stop there. During his 'explanation' to the Match Referee, Atherton was asked if he had resin in his pocket, to which he apparently answered truthfully that he did not. The 'facts' of the case become somewhat murkier at this point. On one version, Atherton simply kept quiet at this moment and did not go on to tell the Match Referee that he had dirt in his pocket. On another version, he answered untruthfully that he did not have any dirt in his pocket. Thus, Atherton either committed some type of 'sin' of omission by keeping silent or else he committed the more 'serious' sin of commission, in other words, he lied. While opinion apparently remains divided on the facts, it now appears that he did in fact reply in the negative when Referee Burge put the 'dirt question' to him.[27]

According to Atherton's own version of events, he was asked three questions: first, if he had an explanation for his actions; secondly if he had resin in his pocket and thirdly if he had any other artificial substance in his pocket. He replied to the first query that he was drying his hands and with a simple 'no' to the other two.[28]

The next day Atherton explained to the public that he had kept dirt in his pocket in order to keep his fingers and palms dry from sweat in order 'to keep the ball as dry as possible on one side to help our bowlers to get reverse swing'.[29] Two interesting, if somewhat subsidiary, facts emerge from Atherton's explanation. The first is the idea that English bowlers were then thought to be able to achieve 'reverse swing', apparently without cheating. The second is that Atherton could have saved himself and the adjudicators who had to deal with his case a lot of trouble if only he had realized that he could have achieved the goal of helping the bowlers get 'reverse swing' by actually keeping his hands sweaty. By loading up one side of the ball with perspiration, exactly the same imbalance which promotes 'reverse swing' in the first place can be obtained. He could have achieved his stated aim by perfectly 'legal' means without having to resort to his 'unfamiliar action'.

Be that as it may, the fallout from the case was immediate. Atherton was fined by the England management and rebuked in the Match Referee's Report for misleading the Referee 'by not giving a full and frank disclosure when given the opportunity to do so'.[30] Burge however refused to impose a further penalty, stating that the 'fine and the resultant publicity and public scrutiny of the England captain is a sufficient penalty in the circumstances...'.[31]

The public scrutiny which followed was indeed harsh and calls for Atherton's sacking were numerous and vociferous.[32] But Atherton continued to captain England. Many of my Australian friends claimed with absolute certainty and with no small measure of delight that Michael Atherton was a 'cheat' and a 'liar'. Obviously, the decision of the Match Referee to censure Atherton and the TCCB's decision to levy the fine indicate that Atherton was, at the very least, guilty of something. This raises the first level of inquiry for those of us concerned with cricket and the 'rule of law', an investigation into the law of this case.

The most obvious area of investigation is that first pursued and then rejected as unfounded by Peter Burge, a violation of then Law 42(5) – **Changing the Condition of the Ball**. The text merits reproduction here:

> Any member of the fielding side may polish the ball provided that such polishing wastes no time and that no artificial substance is used. No-one shall rub the ball on the ground or use any artificial substance or take any other action to alter the condition of the ball.
> ...
> The Law does not prevent a member of the fielding side from drying a wet ball, or removing mud from the ball.

Note (b) provided that:

> A wet ball may be dried on a towel or with sawdust.

Clearly, a successful 'legal' solution to the Atherton case on the issue of 'ball-tampering' again requires a careful reading of the statutory text. However, before that reading can be carried out and the law applied, the 'facts' in issue must be established. There are no doubt those who believe, on the evidence of their eyes, that Mike Atherton's actions as revealed on the television screen were not consistent with his claim that he was drying his hands with dirt from his pocket. For them, he was clearly rubbing something on or into the ball, that something being a substance which came for his pockets. On this sceptical reading of the facts the legal solution becomes 'clear' since Atherton thereunder was seen to use an 'artificial substance to alter the condition of the ball'. Even under this hypothesis, however, a certain textual/factual ambiguity remains, in what to make of the 'fact' accepted by the judicial officers concerned, the umpires and the Match Referee, that no change occurred to the condition of the ball. In other words, did the *Law* require that the artificial substance actually alter the condition of the ball or was it sufficient that the act be done with the 'intent' of altering the ball? In terms familiar to criminal lawyers, did Law 42(5) deal only with the substantive, principal offence or did it also include 'attempts'?

Jonathan Agnew was clearly of the view that the ancillary offence of attempting to alter the condition of the ball was included within the terms of the *Law*. He wrote:

> The point is that Atherton was attempting in my opinion to change the condition of the ball in contravention of Law 42.5. It is no less a crime because he didn't succeed in altering its state.[33]

It would appear at first glance that as a matter of 'law' Agnew may be correct. There is nothing to indicate that the general principle of law that attempts to commit the substantive offence are to be included is not a part of the *Laws of Cricket* generally or of Law 42(5) in particular. Surely the clear legislative purpose of protecting the batter and assuring a fair contest between bat and ball cannot be seen to depend on the skill of the law-breaker in achieving the aim of altering the condition of the ball. The *Law* itself speaks of actions 'to alter the condition of the ball' not of actions which in fact alter the condition of the ball, thereby giving credence and support to the position adopted by Agnew. However, as all good lawyers will tell you, nothing is as simple as it appears to be, especially not the 'plain language' of a statutory instrument. While the language of the *Law* might well have been read to indicate that 'attempts' were covered by legislative intent, it might well have been argued that, on the other hand, that part of the legal text which specifically empowered the umpires to intervene and take action in the case of 'ball-tampering' stated:

> In the event of a contravention of this Law, the umpires, after consultation, shall change the ball for one of similar condition to that in use prior to the contravention.

A 'plain reading' of this part of Law 42(5) would indicate that perhaps Agnew leaped to an incorrect conclusion in arguing that 'attempts' were contemplated under the provisions of the *Law*. This section of the statute clearly drew a direct connection between the concept of 'contravention', i.e. 'tampering' or 'altering', and a ball that had, in fact, been altered. In this case, the umpires must intervene and replace the ball with one of similar condition. In other words, it is clearly arguable that a contravention has occurred only when the ball had actually been changed in some way. Of course, the interpretative difficulties do not stop there. One could also assert that a 'contravention' is not necessarily limited to the case of actual alteration but that only in the case of that type of contravention did the umpires have the duty to change the ball. Under such a reading, attempts would still have been 'covered' by the *Law*. In addition, even if one accepts the argument that because of the wording of the second paragraph of Law 42(5), attempts to alter the condition of the ball were not covered by those provisions, it would have been open to assert that such attempts would nonetheless constitute a breach of the equitable concept of 'fair play' of which the umpires are the sole judges (Laws 3(7) and 42(2) of the 1980 *Code*).

Such an argument would have to establish the nature of the concept itself and also would have to establish that the general legal and equitable concept of 'fair play' existed above and beyond or at least as a supplement to the provisions of the *Laws of Cricket*. While it would be quite easy to establish the 'fact' that attempting to alter the condition of the ball is a violation of the 'spirit of the game' and/or of fair play, it might be more difficult to argue as a matter of legal textual interpretation that the general power of the umpires to determine 'fair and unfair play' under Law 3 superseded or supplemented the clearly enumerated circumstances of Law 42 which carried the general heading **Unfair Play**.

The question to be asked, in other words, once again, as a matter of statutory interpretation, is whether the text of Law 42 exhausted (and exhausts) the types or instances of 'fair and unfair play' over which the umpires have sole jurisdiction or whether on the other hand, the general jurisdiction over 'fair play' could have been extended to cover instances which are excluded from the application of Law 42. In such a case, the umpires and/or the Match Referee could have concluded that Atherton violated the duties imposed on the captain in relation to the ideals of the game. In such circumstances, there would have been no need to invoke the 'remedial' requirements of changing the ball, either in fact or as a matter of interpretation, tying the umpires' jurisdiction to those cases where the remedy was required.

Instead, Atherton's legal status could be determined by reference to another provision and to the remedies available under the *ICC Code of Conduct*. This discussion does not offer an answer to the many questions posed by the arguments of Jonathan Agnew and his supporters who see in Atherton's actions a clear violation of a particular provision of the *Laws of Cricket* or to the issue raised by appeals to a general, but still statutory, concept of the 'spirit of the game'. My goal is simply to point out that there are, in fact and in law, no simple solutions.

This point becomes even clearer and even more effective in undermining the substantive certainty of those who claim legal and factual certainty in the debates over the jurisprudence of cricket when one examines the Atherton case from the other available 'factual' perspective. If one operates from an interpretive position which accepts that he had only dirt in his pocket, and that he used the dirt to dry his hands and, based on the video evidence, the ball as well, the issues do not suddenly become any less complex. As a primary matter, it is clear that all that has just been written on the matter of attempt may apply *a fortiori* if we accept that there was neither a defacing of the ball or any 'intention' to tamper with it. But, of course, the matter does not end here. Even assuming that one could get past these difficulties, it remains clear that several other difficulties of statutory interpretation and equity remain both for Atherton's supporters and his detractors. If Atherton is found to have 'polished' the ball and not simply to have dried his hands, the question which still must be addressed under the operative provisions of then Law 42(5) is whether 'dirt' was an artificial substance under the *Law*.

On a literal reading, or at least on one literal reading, 'dirt' is perhaps the most 'natural' of substances. However, as any good postmodernist would tell you, the very concepts of 'natural' and 'artificial' are the most problematic and least literal of all concepts.[34] Moreover, the *Law* further prohibited the rubbing of the ball on the ground, indicating that in some circumstance at least, 'dirt' is not kosher. Of course, it is possible to argue first that the provisions relating to polishing the ball and artificial substances are distinct as a matter of drafting from the provisions prohibiting the rubbing of the ball on the ground. Secondly, the second sentence of this paragraph mentions both 'the ground' and 'artificial substance', indicating as a matter of construction that 'the ground', which may or may not include 'dirt', is not an artificial substance. Thirdly, it can be asserted that the purpose of the prohibition against rubbing the ball in the dirt is to prevent the process of abrasion, not to serve as a blanket ban on 'dirt'. Of course, this argument could then be used by Atherton's opponents to argue that 'dirt', depending on its nature and consistency, might well be abrasive, in which case it should be included *mutatis mutandis* either under the prohibition on artificial substances or on rubbing the ball on the ground or under the final catch-all phrase '*or take any other action to alter the condition of the ball*' which quite clearly can be read to include taking an action with a 'natural' substance which might alter the condition of the ball.

In addition to these interpretive dilemmas, Atherton's assertion that he was using the 'dirt' to dry his hands, given the fact that some of the 'dirt' clearly made its way onto the ball, raises issues in relation to the provisions of Law 42 (5) permitting the drying of the ball. Again, a plain reading of the *Law* might show that while the fielding side is permitted to dry the ball, they are only permitted to do so under Note (b) by using a towel or sawdust. Indeed, Atherton himself has claimed that he was in fact drying the ball. He writes: 'I was not altering the condition of the ball, however; I was trying to *maintain* its dry and rough condition.'[35]

Again, it would be necessary to examine the legislative language and intent behind these provisions. If the ball becomes wet, at some level of fact, drying it is not 'maintaining' its condition. To dry the ball here is to 'alter' its condition from that of a wet ball to that of a dry ball. Clearly the legislature indicates that some form of drying is permitted but by seeming to limit the types of activity which fall under the idea of legal drying, by implication at least, one might argue that the *Laws* contain support for the notion of unlawful drying.

This again raises several interpretative difficulties. Is this list imitative? Are towels and sawdust the only drying instruments permitted? If the answer to this is affirmative, that would mean that a member of the fielding side contravenes the *Law* when he dries the ball for example on the tail of his shirt. Is a shirt-tail to be assimilated to a towel as a matter of statutory interpretation? If so, is 'dirt' sawdust for the same purpose? If the list is to be read strictly, then putting dirt on the ball in an attempt to keep it dry is clearly a violation of the provisions of Law 42(5). It is little wonder then that the Atherton case lead to some strong calls for the redrafting of the provisions of the *Laws of Cricket* dealing with ball-tampering.[36] But this is not the end of the Michael Atherton case. Whatever position one adopts in relation to the interpretation of the intricacies of Law 42(5), whether one thinks Atherton transgressed or not, there remains one more important issue. What of Atherton's conduct before the Match Referee?

As I mentioned already, it appears that many now believe that Peter Burge did in fact ask Atherton if he had anything in his pocket and that Atherton replied in the negative. According to Atherton's account, he was asked only about 'artificial' substances. In the immediate aftermath of the case, Burge had been subjected to some criticism and his legal skills were called into question, for apparently 'failing to ask the question'.[37] Perhaps the criticism was based on the fact that the ICC Match Referee more closely resembles a French *juge d'instruction* with his concomitant judicial and investigative powers and function than he resembles a common law judge. Be that as it may, on the best reading of the 'facts' for Atherton, he committed a sin of omission by failing to tell the complete truth to the Referee. On the more likely reading of the state of the facts, Atherton lied to the Referee.

As noted above it was this 'lie' which caused the greatest concern to Burge 'because of the effect on the image of cricket'.[38] And it is the lie which makes Mike Atherton's case all the more fascinating from the perspective of cricket's claims to ethical status as the embodiment of the 'rule of law'. Here again, it is at the intersection of fact, law and ethics that the contingent nature of such claims becomes evident. Under the 1980 *Code*, Law 42(1) provided:

'The captains are responsible at all times for ensuring that play is conducted within the spirit of the game as well as within the Laws.'

It is clearly a matter of some debate whether Mike Atherton breached his duty as captain both to the spirit and *Laws of Cricket* when he put his hand in his pocket at Lord's. It seems to be beyond debate that he breached his duty to the spirit of the game if and when he 'lied' to Peter Burge. A strict reading of the case might cause a literalist to argue that the captain's duty under Law 42(1) is limited to the conduct of 'play' and that it cannot be read to extend to any time beyond the day's play. Surely this is an example of literalism gone mad. In any event, Atherton was also bound by his contract with the TCCB to uphold the spirit of the game and was fined for his failure to do so. In addition, he was at the very least bound as a player by the *ICC Code of Conduct* prohibition against bringing the game into disrepute.[39] On whatever legal or ethical text/discourse one wishes to base oneself, Atherton was clearly in breach of fundamental norms of conduct when he lied, by omission or commission, to Peter Burge. Moreover, Atherton was the captain of England, a position which carries with it in the echoes of the colonial past which are still alive in the discourse of the game, a special duty to the mythological spirit of the game. He stated that 'I was to learn that the England cricket captain was expected to act with greater moral probity than the highest officers in the land...'[40]

It is also the case that the Test match in question occurred at Lord's, the home of cricket, a geographic/semiotic signifier which still carries with it many of the same messages in relation to the spirit of the game as does the England captaincy. Finally, the Test was against South Africa upon that country's return to world cricket after years of apartheid isolation. Atherton's actions had for many the unfortunate effect of granting some kind of moral high ground to the still lily-white South Africans. Some like Peter Roebuck claimed that Atherton's transgression in the grand scheme of things was a minor one.[41] But Roebuck's assertion goes to the issue of the importance of the breach of the substantive provisions of the *Laws* relating to the question of 'ball-tampering' and not, it would seem to the broader ethical issue.[42]

Even under the current version of the *Laws of Cricket*, there might well still be some question about the nature and degree of Atherton's culpability. Again, the heading of the relevant provision still refers to 'The match ball – changing the condition' and prohibits polishing with an 'artificial substance'. Atherton did not actually 'change the condition' of the ball unless we interpret the prohibition as including drying a wet ball. Of course, it is not stretching the language or intent of the provisions to assert and argue that a wet ball is not the same as a dry ball and that a change from one state to another is a change in its condition. Sawdust has been removed from the *Law* and now only a towel may be used. But even here, the strict language of the *Law* is not meant to be read literally or strictly. Thus it is suggested that

> Drying on sawdust is no longer permitted. It is permitted to dry the ball only on a towel, though umpires may reasonably extend this to the players' clothes – trousers, shirt, sweater and so on.[43]

Furthermore, the new wording of Law 42(3) (b) refers specifically to an action which 'is likely to alter the condition of the ball'. While the possible 'intent' element of the previous text may now be seen to have been removed and replaced with a strict liability basis for breach, it is still necessary to find that the action in question would be likely to change the ball's condition. Again, this 'fact' is a condition which is an essential element of the offence. Atherton could well have been found guilty under these new provisions provided it is determined that changing the condition of the ball includes going from wet to dry. Whatever Atherton's liability under the former or present *Laws* relating to ball-tampering, it seems beyond question that he committed a major breach of legal and ethical norms when he committed cricket's equivalent of perjury. Yet, as I noted above, despite an initial outcry in parts of the media and the cricketing fraternity, Atherton's case was dealt with by shaming, public exposure and a small set of fines. He retained his captaincy. The case of Michael Atherton with its legal, interpretative difficulties may well be more accurately classified as a case of 'perjury' or 'perversion of the course of justice' or 'wasting police time' rather than as a case of 'ball-tampering'. Nonetheless it remains true that it originally started off as what appeared to be a clear-cut case of 'ball-tampering' and remains classified as such by many observers of the game.

Whatever jurisprudential taxonomy one decides to apply in this case, however, it is clear that it was treated by all concerned, almost from the outset, as something different from a 'Pakistani ball-tampering case'. It serves as a classic example of the way in which the apparently neutral discourses and practices surrounding the legal and ethical issues in question actually serve to establish a dual system of legal rules and ultimately of 'justice'. This epistemological and juridical duality is confirmed by subsequent events. During the 1995 Test at the Wanderers Ground in Johannesburg, Atherton batted for almost 15 hours and scored 185 not out to save England from what appeared to be certain defeat. The press reaction underscored the continuing presence of colonial discourse in cricket and the game's links with the faded glories of days gone by. Atherton was treated as hero of the great colonial struggles of yore. Martin Johnson wrote as follows:

> Before this tour is out, Jack Russell is planning to take his paints and easel out to the old colonial garrison at Rorke's Drift, but as far as he and Michael Atherton are now concerned, they have already been there and picked up their Vcs. This was behind-the-sandbag heroism on an epic scale.[44]

Mike Selvey, writing in the *Guardian Weekly* from which one might naively have expected better wrote:

> The medals for valour awarded in the aftermath of the defence of the mission station at Rorke's Drift are testament to the fact that resistance and heroism in the face of overwhelming odds are not unknown in these parts. The Victoria Cross is not awarded for cricket, of course, but something should be struck immediately and pinned to the chest of Mike Atherton.[45]

Perhaps Selvey can be forgiven his exuberance given Atherton's and the *Guardian's* Manchester origins, but the image of a much younger Michael Caine holding off the rampaging Boer quicks in the movie version of 'The Mike Atherton Story', does little for one's faith in either the state of cricket journalism or the long-term ethical memory of English cricket. Michael Atherton was a convicted deceiver, a man who breached his duty to the game and to his country. Then, he became a national hero, saving his country from defeat and disgrace. This may well speak volumes for the rehabilitative nature and success of English cricket's judiciary and management. If so, perhaps they should be placed in charge of HM Prisons and probationary matters. On the other hand it may speak volumes for the double standard applied in these cases. Is it possible to imagine the case of a Pakistani Test cricketer who is suspected of 'ball-tampering', is seen by millions on TV putting his hand in his pockets, rubbing the same hand on the ball, claiming that he was only drying his hand on some dirt and lying to the ICC Referee about the whole thing and for whose virtues as a cricketer would be extolled by the English press a couple of years later? I think not. Yet Mike Atherton was a national hero. But my friends in Sydney were convinced he was a 'cheat'. This is no doubt attributable to the fact that as Australians they have a different set of historical experiences, such as Bodyline, which allowed them and me to read the context of Mike Atherton's case in a much different interpretive context. For them, I suspect, the same rule applies to England captains as to all Pakistani cricketers, assume they are all 'cheats' of some kind or another and you won't be far wrong.

More Balls: Judicial and Legislative Rule-Making and Ball-Tampering

Since the debate surrounding 'ball-tampering' consistently invokes the legal and ethical norms surrounding the game of cricket, it is appropriate at this point to examine another example of 'legal' discourse relating to 'ball-tampering'. During the course of the abortive Sarfraz/Lamb case, the defendant called Umpire Don Oslear to the stand. Umpire Oslear testified that the Pakistanis had apparently tampered with the ball during a One-Day International at Lord's where Oslear was third umpire. He also testified that during the Headingley Test of the same series, the ball appeared to have been interfered with.[46]

Oslear's testimony and subsequent statements raise several important issues about the functions of law-making and law enforcement in cricket. Why, for example, had no umpire spoken out prior to the Sarfraz case? Several possible explanations present themselves. Umpires may have been, as Oslear apparently asserts, cowed into silence by the game's governing legislative and administrative bodies, the MCC, the TCCB or the ICC.[47] The matter may have been dealt with internally and under a rule of silence attributable to the seriousness of the allegations and cricket's historical tendency to deal with issues of serious law-breaking and transgression behind closed doors. Or, finally, whatever damage Oslear claims occurred to the balls in question, there may have been no or insufficient evidence of tampering. Under such circumstances, it would have been unwise and unfair, not to say possibly defamatory, for any umpire to have spoken publicly. Of course, any good lawyer would also have to question the motives which might have inspired Oslear to come forward. On the one hand, he could be seen as a white knight, going public in his whistleblower role to reveal misconduct at the highest levels. On the other hand, he could be seen as an embittered ex-employee, a man who had received notice that his career was ending, the author of a forthcoming book on umpiring, the sales of which would not be hurt by public controversy.[48] The TCCB responded to Oslear's claims of victimization by characterizing them as 'unfounded and disingenuous' and by pointing out that his compulsory retirement had been notified to him well before his testimony in the Sarfraz/Lamb case.[49] Of course, it is not unusual for whistleblowers to be branded as miscreants in an effort to discredit their evidence. Whatever the 'facts' surrounding Oslear's decision to go public with his revelations, the revelations themselves raise some vital issues about the jurisprudence of the rule of law in cricket, again particularly when 'Pakistani ball-tampering' is the underlying epistemological juridical framework.[50]

Oslear's claims include not just allegations of Pakistani ball-tampering, but of judicial incompetence, jurisdictional error and cover-up. Serious allegations indeed since they call into question the ability of the umpires and the ICC Match Referees and the game's administrators. According to Oslear and others, Umpires John Hampshire and Ken Palmer noticed a change in the ball's condition and at lunch, brought it to the attention of the Referee, former West Indian wicketkeeper Deryck Murray. Murray ordered the ball to be changed. It is alleged that the Pakistani manager Intikhab Alam and captain Javed Miandad tried to have the decision to change the ball rescinded. The TCCB refused to comment on the issue on the grounds that umpires' reports are confidential. Oslear charged that Murray changed an original statement about 'ball-tampering' under Pakistani pressure.[51]

Again, Oslear's allegations raise some vitally important issues for the jurisprudence of cricket. The continuing reluctance of the game's governing bodies, the TCCB as it then was, the ICC and the ACB in Australia, to realize that issues of 'public' interest and controversy must see the light of day and not be couched in terms of secrecy and confidentiality or else they risk alienating the media and the cricket-loving public, is a subject of continuing amazement in this day of freedom of information and the omnipresence of the TV cameras.[52] Whatever interests are protected by such confidentiality are not only clearly outweighed by the general public's right to know but also by the damage which is caused to individual and collective reputations, not to mention the reputation of the game and its administrators, when 'facts' are kept hidden and can only be the subject of mis-information, rumour, innuendo and the process of selective leaking. Justice quite clearly must be seen to be done, an adage which continues to escape cricket's administrative and judicial rulers who continue to rely on outdated notions of confidentiality and respect for the umpires, or in this case, the Referee's decision, grounded, it seems in some more fundamentally misplaced notion that only they know what is right and good for the game. Such elitist notions surely have no place in the construction of a democratic and public discourse of 'justice' and the 'rule of law' which informs the idea/l of 'cricket'.

Of equal importance here, in the case as outlined by Umpire Oslear, is the failure of the first level of judicial intervention, the umpires, to act in accordance with the fundamental principles of 'natural justice' and of the 'rule of law'. It seems clear that in this case, the umpires believed that something was amiss with the ball. It is equally clear that they allowed the ball to be used until the lunch break and only then, at the behest of the Match Referee, did they remove the ball from play. This course of action was clearly wrong in both law and equity. First, the text of the applicable *Law* is clear and unambiguous. Law 42, Note (a) clearly imposed a duty on the umpires to inspect the condition of the ball:

> 'Umpires **shall** make frequent and irregular inspections of the condition of the ball.' (emphasis added)

Under both paragraph (4) (**lifting the seam**) and (5) (**changing the condition of the ball**), the umpires were also clearly instructed to intervene in the case of contravention:

'...the umpires **shall** change the ball...(4) and

'...the umpires, after consultation, **shall** change the ball...(5). (emphasis added)

Because the umpires in this case failed to change the ball, only two conclusions are possible. Either there was no tampering in their opinion and so no change was required (or in the case of a violation of paragraph (5), one of them did not agree that tampering occurred and unanimity was deemed to be required under a reading of 'consultation', see below) or else they quite clearly failed in their duty to apply the *Laws of Cricket* and abdicated their responsibility as judicial rule-makers in favour of intervention by an appellate or superior supervisory jurisdiction, the ICC Match Referee. In administrative law terms they failed to exercise their jurisdiction and this failure (assuming that there either was tampering or the ball was in such a deteriorated condition that the subsequent decision to replace it was justified) is bad enough on its face. In addition to their specific duty under Law 42, Law 3(7) clearly vested the umpires with a general and residual jurisdiction which they failed to exercise:

'The umpires shall be the sole judges of fair and unfair play.'

Additionally, Law 5(5), dealing specifically with the ball also clearly instructed the umpires to act by removing the ball from play in certain circumstances:

In the event of a ball during play being lost or, in the opinion of the umpires, becoming unfit for play, the umpires shall allow it to be replaced by one that in their opinion has had a similar amount of wear. If a ball is to be replaced, the umpires shall inform the batsman.

If judges refuse to judge, the 'rule of law' quite quickly loses any substantive or even procedural basis upon which it might claim legitimacy. This has been and continues to be a major jurisprudential dilemma in cricket adjudication since the introduction of the Match Referee and the third umpire. There is a perception, supported by instances such as this, that umpires on the field of play are reluctant to adjudicate, instead they tend to abdicate their authority to 'higher' or other officials. But the difficulties and injustices in this case do not stop here. By failing to confiscate and remove the ball from play the minute they suspected tampering had occurred as they are required to do under the *Laws*, the umpires perpetrated a further set of injustices on the players of both the England and the Pakistani sides. As mentioned already, the purpose of the provisions of Law 42(4) and (5) was clearly to ensure a fair contest between bat and ball, the essence of 'cricket'. If the bowler can tamper with the ball, he will be able to gain an unfair advantage over the batter in their confrontation. By allowing a ball which they knew or believed to be (if this hypothesis is correct) damaged through illegal actions by the fielding side, to be used after such tampering was detected, in fact and in law, the umpires imposed upon the England batters a disadvantage.[53] Not only did the umpires, by refusing to exercise their jurisdiction, betray an abstract duty to the notion of the 'rule of law' but they betrayed their real, concrete duty to the batting side to ensure 'fair play'.

But the injustice does not stop here. In addition to the practical and legal disadvantage imposed on the side batting, the umpires here deprived the Pakistani side in general and the bowlers in particular, of a key element in their right to self-defence. If the umpires are in agreement that the ball appears to have been tampered with, they were under a duty to immediately withdraw the ball from play because of the clear language of the *Laws of Cricket* and of their duty to 'protect' the batting side. They were also obliged at law to confiscate the ball in order to allow it to be presented in evidence to a superior appellate or supervisory jurisdiction, the Match Referee. This would have permitted the 'accused' to be presented with the evidence against him/them and therefore with the opportunity to argue his/their defence. By allowing a ball to continue to be used, the umpires permitted clear and potentially effective 'tampering' with the evidence to occur. In these circumstances, the Pakistanis were deprived of any real opportunity to defend themselves against allegations that they illegally damaged the ball. Moreover, in the circumstances, the Match Referee could not rely on the physical, forensic evidence itself since it had to all intents and purposes been destroyed. The verdict can only be considered in such circumstances to be unsafe and unreliable.[54] Perhaps that is why Deryck Murray chose not to elaborate on the umpires' 'allegations'.

In a bizarre twist, then, the 'Pakistani ball-tampering' case offers interesting lessons to those who claim for cricket some status as a discourse which embodies those fundamental legal and ethical norms summarized in the phrase 'the rule of law'. In essence, cricket was not able to give real life and meaning to these norms in relation to this case. The failure was attributable to several causes, chief among which were, I believe, the inherent racism which undergirds the seemingly neutral 'legal' rhetoric applied in combination with the fundamental failure of the system to follow its own rules and procedures. This does not mean that the umpires or Match Referee were influenced by personal racial or other prejudice against the Pakistani team. Instead, it is the way in which media reports construct the actions and failures of the officials which reflects and constructs the idea of 'Pakistani ball-tampering' as epistemologically different which is evidence of a particular prejudice. In this case, both the 'rule of law' and the principles of 'natural justice' were honoured more in the breach than in the observance. But this does not mean that there are no other lessons beyond the substantively empty nature of legal discourse to be drawn from the fall-out of the Sarfraz/Lamb case. We now know, for example, that 'ball-tampering' does occur and that 'everybody' does it. We know that 'ball-tampering' is illegal and immoral and that umpires and Referees have the power and jurisdiction to deal with it, although in this case they failed miserably in their job.

Indeed, we also know that the issue of 'ball-tampering' has remained on the legal agenda of cricket. So much so that recent legislative interventions by the

ICC have attempted to assist the umpires in exercising their general jurisdiction under the *Laws of Cricket* by giving them further and better particulars. The *ICC Code of Conduct* has now legislatively expanded upon the umpires' duty to inspect the ball under Law 42(4) (5). The Match Referee is instructed to ask the umpires to 'inspect the ball on a regular basis...to look for signs of ball doctoring'.[55] In addition to their re-emphasized adjudicatory role, the ICC has also vested in the umpires, in relation to the problem of 'ball-tampering', a community policing, crime control function. *Test Match Playing Condition* 8 now instructs the umpires to maintain a process of inspection and guardianship over the ball.

Despite all of the 'legal' knowledge which is open to anyone who wishes to read in the 'jurisprudence' of reverse swing and 'ball-tampering', from Sarfraz/ Lamb/Khan/Botham/Atherton, to the *Laws* and *Playing Conditions*, one fact remains virtually unchallenged. 'We' still know that, whatever clever, O.J.-style legal arguments which might be mounted to accuse the accusers or shift the focus to the umpires and their various LAPD-style procedural and forensic failures and mis-handling of evidence, the Pakistanis are cheats.

Australian Balls: Pakistan and Sri Lanka 1995

If one were to attempt to encapsulate the basic premises of the idea of the 'rule of law' in the common law tradition, a good starting point would be the doctrine and practice of precedent. Courts, as judicial decision-makers, are bound by previous decisions on the same matter. This gives primacy to the values of predictability and consistency. Like cases will be treated alike, subjected to the same rules and outcomes. On the flip side of the respect of the values of predictability and consistency, is the substantive ideal that 'wrong' decisions will be overturned in the interests of justice. Thus, the common law maintains a balance between consistency and predictability on the one hand, and the ability to adapt to changing circumstances in the interests of justice and efficiency on the other. In lay terms, the common law possesses the capacity to change by 'learning from its mistakes'. This ability has evolved over time and through experience. It is as much a matter of lived practice as it is a matter of principle, much like the child who learns not to touch a hot stove both from its parents' repeated warnings and from the pain caused when it ignores the warnings and experiences truth for itself.

One would think, then, that cricket's law-makers and decision-makers would have learned from the mistakes of the past. With its long institutional and collective memory combined with a highly developed rule-making tradition and practice, cricket, perhaps more than any other sporting activity could be said to embody the 'genius of the common law'. Cricket's 'ball-tampering' episodes have been fraught with legal and jurisprudential difficulties, leading to a sustained critique of the legal system, in both its legislative and judicial branches. These criticisms have led not only to a greater awareness of the legal and factual stumbling blocks but to clear legislative intervention to aid the judicial rule-makers, the umpires, in their tasks. In other words, cricket has had its hand burned and has clearly learned its lesson on the stove of 'ball-tampering', or not.

Events surrounding 'ball-tampering' scandals in Australia in the 1995–96 cricket season revealed quite clearly that theory and practice in rule-making and adjudication were still quite far apart. Moreover, it would seem that the epistemological duplicity which has informed judicial and ethical debate on the 'ball-tampering' issue continued to flourish. Once again there is the legal and jurisprudential category of 'Pakistani ball-tampering' and a separate category of 'ball-tampering'. However, recent Australian cases also revealed the substantive 'legal' and 'factual' vacuity of these taxonomic differences.

During its first real tour match against Western Australia at the WACA in Perth, Pakistan was once again subjected to 'ball-tampering' allegations. The headlines left not much doubt:

Pakistan 'ball-tampering' probe
Unseamly-Pakistanis fend off calls of ball-tampering – again
We're no cheats[56]

As a result of the umpires' 'suspicions', the ACB took control of a ball used in the match. The ball allegedly showed 'signs of excessive scarring inconsistent with customary wear and tear'.[57] More particularly, 'the cross seam on the rough side of the ball in Western Australia's first innings appeared to have been lifted'.[58] Suspicion was apparently raised when acting captain Amir Sohail on occasion refused or failed to return the ball to the umpires as required under the playing conditions.[59]

As is usual in cases of 'Pakistani ball-tampering', the nature of the evidence invoked in support of the prosecution's case was of a type not normally admissible in other standard legal instances. Apparently the exceptions to the hearsay evidence rule now include in their number a 'Pakistanis are cheats' heading. Thus, Australian journalist Trent Bouts could include the following two hearsay-packed paragraphs in his 'report':

> Although several WA players were unaware of any problems with the ball, another said last night he heard the umpires say more than once: 'they're playing with the ball'.
> It is understood the ACB has been told television operators covering the game have pictures which provide intriguing viewing some in close-up.

The ACB did little to counter the weight of this hearsay-infected journalistic coverage of the 'allegations' when it chose to invoke the traditional administrative response of 'confidentiality' and refused further comment. Unfortunately for the Australian administrators, events soon overtook the ACB and it was forced to act, but in a most unexpected manner.

From the earliest reports, Pakistani officials denied that tampering had taken place, arguing that they had in fact asked the umpires to change the ball because it was deteriorating faster than expected on the WACA pitch. The Pakistani team pointed out that the umpires' Match Report did not carry any mention of the alleged 'ball-tampering', nor had the umpires or the ACB raised the matter with tour manager Intikhab Alam.[60] In other words, none of the available legal or administrative means for informing the accused of the 'charges' against them had been invoked. As it turns out, the Pakistanis were correct. The umpires' Report said nothing about the 'ball-tampering' concerns. Instead, the umpires had written of their worries in a separate letter to the ACB. Herein lies one of several legal and jurisdictional errors tainting this case. Umpires Terry Prue and Ross Emerson were stood down for a match by the ACB for failing to do their duty by including the 'ball-tampering' allegations in the official Match Report to the Board. Because the allegations were not part of the Match Report, the ACB adopted the legally correct position that it was without jurisdiction in the matter and refused to take any further action.[61]

Here again is a case of 'Pakistani ball-tampering' reduced to the level of Keystone Kops law enforcement and O.J.-type forensic screw-ups. The umpires failed to exercise their jurisdiction properly by putting their concerns or allegations of 'ball-tampering' in the proper form, thereby depriving the ACB of the authority to investigate. For many, this is yet another example of procedural concerns clouding the 'real' issue of substantive guilt. Thus, for Trent Bouts, who had already muddied the jurisprudential waters with his hearsay-tainted reporting, the investigation: '... floundered on a technicality because the umpires involved failed to comply with reporting procedures'.[62]

Of course, this 'technicality' also included what some might consider, in cases other than those of 'Pakistani ball-tampering', the important legal norm of the right of the accused to have proper notice of the charges. Since the allegations were not included in the umpires' Report, the Pakistanis had no official notice of the 'charges' against them and had to rely on the not-too-subtle press reports to learn of the allegations. More importantly, as in the previous English case, the umpires had failed in an even more fundamental way to exercise their jurisdiction by refusing to change the ball that they suspected had been tampered with. Indeed, according to their letter to the ACB and the subsequent press reports, in their opinion, the ball did in fact show signs of physical change. As I have already argued, this is not just a failure to exercise the authority vested in them under the *Laws of Cricket*, but it also potentially imposes an unfair disadvantage on the Western Australian players in the 'confrontation between bat and ball' and denies the accused Pakistani team the right to confront the evidence against them.

This last concern becomes even more crucial when placed in the broader context of facts which became known subsequently. Throughout the summer, for example, all teams playing Tests in Australia (Australia, Pakistan and Sri Lanka) consistently complained about the quality and endurance of the Kookaburra balls used in Test and First Class matches. In addition, the WACA pitch had been invaded over the winter months by an attack of algae which wreaked havoc on the ground and which may have resulted in the wicket being more 'roughed up' than usual. In other words, it would have been open to the Pakistanis, if charged with 'ball-tampering' in relation to the match against WA, to raise a factual/legal defence based on the poor quality of the balls in use and on the 'unnatural' natural conditions which obtained at Perth at the time of the alleged offence. Such a defence, either of 'manufacturing defect' or 'abnormal' wear and tear, became impossible because of the failure of the umpires to do their jobs properly and to act in accordance with the 'rule of law'. Of course, for writers like Trent Bouts, this would all simply remain in the category of 'a technicality' since, after all, this is case of 'Pakistani ball-tampering'. In fact, it was matter of some chagrin that 'Although Australian umpires continued to watch the Pakistanis like hawks, he was never caught red-handed.'[63] Damned clever buggers, those Pakis!!!

Indeed, the strength and resilience of the epistemological categorization which surrounds the taxonomy of 'ball-tampering' *versus* 'Pakistani ball-tampering' became even clearer with subsequent events in the antipodean summer of 1995, again at the WACA ground. This time the case occurred during the first Test between Sri Lanka and Australia. During the 17th over of Australia's first innings, the umpires stopped play and remonstrated on the field of play with Sri Lankan captain Arjuna Ranatunga. After the close of the day's play, the ICC Match Referee, former New Zealand test cricketer Graham Dowling, issued a formal report/press release announcing that the ball had been interfered with by 'a member or members' of the Sri Lankan team.[64] Subsequent reports indicated that this case was distinguishable from the previous 'Pakistani ball-tampering' incident since the damage to the ball was a case of lifting the main seam as opposed to the Pakistani attack on the cross-seam. This Sri Lankan form of ball-tampering was an action apparently meant to assist spinner Muralitharan who was bowling at the time.[65]

On the surface, the treatment of the allegations of Sri Lankan and Pakistani ball-tampering appear to be identical. Here we have two sets of dark-skinned cricketers, each with bizarre, un-Australian religious beliefs and 'wristy' stroke play, accused of 'ball-tampering', of cheating. Each was condemned in similar terms in headlines. The importance of the Sri Lankan case was underlined when it was pointed out in media accounts that, with the exception of the Mike Atherton affair, this was the only time a Test side had been found guilty of the offence of 'ball-tampering'.[66] In fact, of course, on a strict reading of the 'judgement' in the Atherton case, he had not been convicted of 'ball-tampering' but of misleading the Match Referee and of carrying unauthorized 'dirt' in his trouser pocket. Under this distinguishing reading of the Atherton case, the Sri Lankans became the first side ever convicted of such an offence in the Test arena. Putting aside this technical 'legal' quibble, the sentiment in the press immediately following Dowling's decision finding the Sri Lankans guilty was clear. Not only was much made of their guilt and transgression, but Dowling's 'sentence', a finding of guilt, followed by a stern warning against any future transgression, was criticized for its leniency.[67] The press wanted a harsher punishment.

But sentiment and 'facts', in the world of 'legal' analysis of the Sri Lankan ball-tampering case quickly turned. The following day, Australian television's Channel 9 commentators revealed that their careful examination of the coverage of the 17th over revealed nothing untoward to them.[68] And further reporting revealed yet another instance of 'jurisdictional' error by the umpires. Yet again they had failed to exercise their power and duties under the *Laws* and *Playing Conditions* to change the ball once 'evidence' of tampering appeared. Once more, issues of fairness to the batting side arose as do the same issues of natural justice and the right of the accused to confront the evidence. Even Phil Wilkins expressed surprise that the umpires had not removed the ball from play, although he indicated that the ball could have been removed at lunch.[69] The fact that this would not have allowed the Sri Lankans to be confronted with the evidence against them, that is 'a ball damaged in the 17th over' but with one after 28 overs did not seem to bother Wilkins. It did, however, bother Ian Chappell, who pointed out that the ball had in fact spent a certain amount of time in the stands after a couple of Michael Slater hits for six, as well as crashing into the boundary during Muralitharan's spell. The idea that the ball's condition was unchanged from over 17 to over 28 was unthinkable.

This time the press jumped to the defence of the Sri Lankans, pointing out that they were unfairly prohibited from commenting on the allegations against them by the *ICC Code of Conduct* while the allegations had been given a great deal of publicity.[70] The irony that they themselves had been among the first to announce the Sri Lankans' guilt appeared lost on the Australian media. Subsequent columns also pointed out that in addition to this breach of the rules of natural justice, the umpires failed to change the ball, thereby denying the Sri Lankans the opportunity to confront and challenge the evidence against them; that the balls used in Australia had posed wear problems for all sides; that the Perth wicket was unusually rough due to the winter algae attack; that the ball in use on the third day also showed unusual signs of wear but no allegation was made against the bowling side; that the Match Referee's report was written before the Sri Lankans were given a chance to speak in their defence and finally that it was in fact umpire Khizar Hayat of Pakistan who insisted that there had been tampering, while Australian umpire Peter Parker apparently did not concur.[71]

Each of these issues raises interesting and important legal and jurisprudential questions. Many of the concerns about the umpires' failures in relation to the changing of the ball have already been discussed at some length. What continues to be surprising is the failure of the umpires, the ACB and the ICC to learn to keep their hands off the juridical stove. The case of 'Sri Lankan ball-tampering' does, however, raise some questions of law and practice which are of original impression. The first of these is the effect and impact of the so-called 'gag rule' on the perception of justice being done as well as on the actual possibility of justice being done. The *ICC Code of Conduct* at the time dealt with the issue of public comment by players and management both directly and indirectly, as does the current version of the *Code*. Paragraph 2 contained a general prohibition on engaging in conduct 'unbecoming to an International Player or Team Official which could bring them or the game into disrepute'. The current *Code* prohibits 'conduct unbecoming to their status which could bring them or the game of cricket into disrepute' (C2). Given cricket's history, its general practice of keeping disputes in house and 'confidential' and the ruling norm of never questioning a decision, it is clearly arguable that as a matter of law, this provision could be applied to prevent any discussion of the Match Referee's rulings. But the drafters of the *Code of Conduct* have not left the issue open to such interpretative manoeuvrings. Paragraphs 7 and 8 of the *Code* read as follows:

7. Players and Team Officials shall not disclose or comment upon any alleged breach of the Code or upon any hearing, report or decision arising from such breach.

8. Players or Team Officials shall not make any public pronouncement or media comment which is detrimental either to the game in general; or to a particular tour in which they are involved; or about any tour between other Countries which is taking place; or to relations between the Boards of the competing teams.

The current *Code* makes it a Level 2 offence to engage in

Public criticism of, or inappropriate comment on a match related incident or match official.[72]

Clearly under these provisions, the Sri Lankans were forbidden from commenting upon a decision of Referee Dowling which branded them as 'cheats'. One could read this as manifesting a desire by cricket's ruling bodies to ensure the integrity and dignity of proceedings before the Match Referee and to guarantee that he can exercise his supervisory judicial function free from dissent and public criticism from those subjected to sanctions or hearings. On the other hand, one could read this as yet another in a long list of examples of cricket's attempts to keep its scandals quiet and away from the light of public scrutiny. If only the judge is allowed to comment through the release of press statements and rulings there can be no way open for anyone to make an informed comment. All discussion of legal and ethical issues, the very issues which make cricket 'cricket' are stymied.[73]

Of course, it is arguable that the parties have, by adhering to the ICC and by participating in the rule-making process, clearly given their consent not only to the exercise of jurisdiction by the Match Referee but also to the content of the rules in the *Code of Conduct* which prohibit them from making public comments or statements about disciplinary hearings. Whatever weight and persuasiveness one wishes to afford to this 'consent to silence' argument, the situation becomes somewhat more untenable when one takes into account the allegation that the Referee had written his report in the case of apparent Sri Lankan 'ball-tampering' incident before he had heard their defence. This, if true, is perhaps the most clear-cut and blatant example of a breach of the rules of natural justice it is possible to imagine. To make a decision before hearing both sides of the case is not in keeping with the norms of the 'rule of law' which are so often invoked in cricket's legal discourse. Worse still, the allegations, if true, establish that Referee Dowling acted in breach of the very ICC *Regulations* establishing the nature and function of the ICC Match Referee. Not only had the umpires in this case failed to act according to the *Laws* and *Playing Conditions*, but Referee Dowling had failed to comply with the 'statute' granting him jurisdiction. Article 4 of the ICC *Regulations* defining the role of the Referee is entitled '**Procedure for dealing with disciplinary matters**' and specifies quite clearly in sub-paragraph (b) (**Hearings**) that:

> After a report has been received and proper notification given . . . , the following procedures must be carried out:
>
> (i)   A Hearing should be arranged as soon as possible and practicable, bearing in mind that, unless there are exceptional circumstances, a decision should be made no later than twenty-four hours after an incident . . . .
>
> (ii) The Hearing should be attended by the person who is the subject of the Report, his Captain and Team Manager (if applicable), and the initiator of the Report, none of whom can be denied the right to appear at the hearing . . . .
>
> . . .
>
> (iv) The Referee must hear details of the alleged breach of the Code and other offence and decide on the action to be taken in a manner which accords with the principles of natural justice and which best ensures the fair and prompt determination of the breach or offence. In particular, the Referee must allow the person who is the subject of the Report to give evidence and produce proof, either verbally or in writing.[74]

The action attributed to Referee Dowling is in clear breach of these explicit norms. Moreover, the *Code* and *Regulations* issued by the ICC contained an **Appendix 1**, entitled **Guidelines on the Principles of Natural Justice**.[75] The Appendix clearly outlined in even more detail the type of hearing which was to be afforded to the accused before any finding could be made against him. In this, as in other ball-tampering cases, especially where the evidence has not been preserved, the umpires and particularly the ICC Match Referees fell far short of the standards required by the 'rule of law' and natural justice. Trent Bouts, having changed his jurisprudential tune, wrote:

> The officials got things seriously wrong in the Perth Test. Umpires Khizar Hayat of Pakistan and Peter Parker of Queensland failed to impound the ball when they suspected interference and referee Graham Dowling, the former New Zealand captain, gave the impression that he had made his mind up that the Sri Lankans were guilty even before the post-match hearing began. ICC overturned his verdict.[76]

Another factual and legal complication in relation to events in the 17th over at the WACA is presented by the identity of one of the umpires involved, Pakistani Khizar Hayat. As several of the stories published in the days after the 'ball-tampering' allegations came to light pointed out, Hayat's stay in Australia had not been an unproblematic one. Questions about his, as well as England's Dickie Bird's, ability to continue to adjudicate in Test matches had been raised earlier following a series of controversial decisions. In relation to the WACA incident, it was asserted that he was the one of the two umpires who was convinced that tampering had taken place. Australian Peter Parker apparently did not entirely agree. By itself, this raises an important interpretative question about the meaning of the 'consultation' required under Law 42(5) and still demanded under Law 42(3) of the 2000 *Code*. Does this 'consultation', after which the ball shall be changed, mean that 'agreement' or 'consensus' must be reached, or does it simply impose a procedural rather than a substantive condition? It would appear that an argument based on the statutory text that the requirement is substantive, i.e. that there must be agreement can be asserted since the *Law* states that the 'umpires' in the plural must change the ball in the case of tampering. In these circumstances, it would appear that umpire Parker's 'agreement' may have been somewhat reluctant, bringing into question the validity or complete legality of the umpires' actions in the Perth Test. Any argument on this issue is made all the more problematic by the fact that the umpires acted illegally by failing to act, thereby tainting their subsequent actions in reporting the Sri Lankans itself with a possible 'illegality'.

These arguments are made even more problematic when the other criticisms of umpire Hayat are considered and brought into the equation. Classically there is Peter Roebuck's assertion that 'Khizar Hayat may know a thing or two about cricket balls'. This statement may be read on the one hand as a reflection of the umpire's skill and knowledge of the game. On the other hand, it might as easily be read as yet another insinuation that there is a separate epistemological/ jurisprudential category 'Pakistani ball-tampering' with which the Pakistani umpire Hayat would be familiar. Additionally, there is the entire history of Australian–Pakistani cricket relations combined with the more general debates about the role, value and neutrality of third-country umpires, which were circulating at the time. Finally, the fact is that in this same Test, umpire Hayat made the controversial decision that gave Test debutant Australian batter Ricky Ponting out LBW for 96. It was not beyond the realm of speculation, particularly for Australians, that umpire Hayat's decision somehow represented Pakistani 'revenge' against all the injustices, real or perceived, which inform Pakistani– Australian cricket relations.[77] At the same time it is equally possible that Hayat simply made a mistake or that he was/is incompetent in applying the LBW *Law*.

But, finally, what is important from the point of view of the jurisprudence of cricket and the rule of law is the fact that all of these factors came quickly into the debate over 'Sri Lankan ball-tampering' in a way which they never had in relation to cases of 'Pakistani ball-tampering'. Almost all of the editorial and columnist commentary, with the possible exception of Phil Wilkins, emphasized the denial of natural justice to the Sri Lankans by the precipitous decision-making of the Referee, the umpires' error in neglecting to preserve the evidence by removing the ball from play, the apparent failure to consider the possibilities of manufacturing defects or abnormal wear and tear caused by the 'new' Perth wicket and the injustice in these circumstances of the ICC gag rule. The fact that this is a 'distinguishable case' was perhaps best summarized by Mike Coward (who, in fairness, it should be noted is one of the few writers to point to anti-Pakistani bias as informing debate in those cases) who writes: 'Sri Lanka, universally known for their scrupulous fairness as a cricket team, stand accused of cheating in a test match.'[78]

Coward reflects here the generalized impression that the charges against the Sri Lankans were unfair and probably unfounded. Like all other writers dealing with the case, except perhaps Wilkins, he supports the idea that an injustice, both substantive and procedural, had been done in this case. Much has been written in relation to the Sri Lankans' feelings of hurt and outrage at the charges and in support of their attempts to gain an apology from the ICC for the Referee's decision, again on both procedural and substantive grounds.[79] The Sri Lankans continued their efforts to receive an apology and threatened legal action for damages. Lawyers, forensic experts and former Test umpires in Sri Lanka became involved in the campaign and offered estimates that damages could go as high as US$25 million '(s)ince it is a matter involving not one individual but a whole nation . . . .'.[80] Again, the legal issues involved in getting the ICC to apologize for a decision which was, under the rules 'final'[81] are interesting. There was no apparent formal statutory provision in the ICC Charter or the regulations for any appeal mechanism. While an action in damages or for judicial review for the breaches of the rules of natural justice were both possible, there seemed to be no way in which the Sri Lankans could 'legally' proceed with their complaint or upon which the ICC could respond to it.[82]

The ICC stepped forward to clarify, confirm and further obfuscate some of these issues. It confirmed, in practice if not in theory, its inherent appellate jurisdiction by acting on the Sri Lankan request/demand for an apology by issuing a statement expressing 'its sincere regrets' to the Sri Lankan Board and stating that: '. . . the Sri Lankan team therefore stands exonerated of a breach of Law 42.5.'[83]

However, the statement of the ICC, negotiated with Sri Lankan cricket administrators, stopped short of a complete apology to the Sri Lankans. For some, they were released on a 'technicality' because of the umpires' failure to save the ball and to allow it to be examined and confronted by all parties as evidence. The Sri Lankans, on this view, received the ICC equivalent of a 'pardon' or more precisely, the verdict against them was found to be unsafe and unfair, although the 'fact' of tampering apparently remains on the 'record'.[84] Indeed, the Richards' statement makes it clear that the major criticism is levelled by the ICC at the two umpires who failed to act pursuant to Law 42(5) and remove the ball. The ICC is not critical of Referee Dowling, who according to the statement, reviewed the ball at lunch when the ball was 28 overs old, and who confirmed the umpires' opinion that the condition of the ball had been altered.

Thus, while apologizing to the Sri Lankans, the ICC statement confirms the 'fact' that the umpires and Dowling found, by implication at least, that the ball had been tampered with. The umpires were correctly criticized for their failure to withdraw the ball.[85] The 'ball-tampering' allegation was however allowed to remain as part of the ICC statement on the case. Umpire Parker's declaration that after the inspection of the ball at the end of the 16th over, that is the over before umpire Hayat questioned the condition of the ball, he had found the ball to be uncontaminated by any apparent attempts to alter its condition, also remains as part of the evidence in the case.

In addition, serious legal questions remained in so far as other aspects of the case are concerned. Reports of disagreement between Hayat and Parker once more highlighted concerns expressed above about the nature and content of the 'consultation' requirement of Law 42(5). Umpire Hayat's apparent failure to accede to the requests of both his umpiring partner and of the Referee to change the ball raised serious questions about his knowledge of the *Laws* and of his function as umpire. These issues go directly to his competence as a member of the judiciary and of those who had appointed him to the international umpiring panel.[86] Moreover, grave concerns about the role of the ICC Match Referee and of the ICC's supervision of the function needed to be answered. It would appear that the problem involved was both a practical existential one and one caused by a conflict in the 'legislation' under which the office of Match Referee was created and the nature and extent of its powers delimited.

At the practical level, if one umpire fails to heed the opinion, based on the *Laws*, of his colleague and then continues to act in a way which is not in accordance with the *Laws* after the intervention of the Match Referee, there seems to be little that can be done at that time to address the issue. In essence, umpiring is supposed to be a balance between a cooperative venture between the 'men in white' who are to function largely as a team, helping and supporting each other in the event of difficulties and individual judicial responsibility. When one umpire refuses to comply with this ethical judicial practice, the situation becomes somewhat akin to that of a judge who begins to act in an erratic and legally questionable way. At this moment, the value of cooperation, as well as the fundamental question of whether the individual is now really acting 'like a judge' or 'like an umpire' comes to the fore.[87] In each instance, these questions, informed by a set of ethical and practical norms grounded in an idea of the nature of the judicial function and office, come into stark conflict with a keystone of the ideology and practice of 'the rule of law', the concept of the 'independence of the judiciary'. While most jurisdictions now have developed mechanisms, both informal and formal, for getting rid of the recalcitrant and the incompetent member of the judiciary, these mechanisms, almost by definitional necessity, must remain awkward and time-consuming if the principle of judicial independence is to remain important and respected. This situation, and the dilemma posed by it, is further complicated by the 'statute' defining the role of the ICC Match Referee. Under these provisions, the Referee was empowered to see that:

the full implications of Law 42.1 (the spirit of the game and the role of the captain) are properly understood and upheld[88]

and

to liaise with the appointed Umpires, but not in any way to interfere with their traditional role.[89]

This latter provision was confirmed by another provision:

The Referee must not interfere with the traditional role of Umpires but should urge Umpires to be decisive in upholding the Law.[90]

The current *Code of Conduct* simply states that

The Referee shall, at all times liaise with the Umpires on any matter the Referee considers appropriate provided that the Referee shall not interfere with the role of the Umpires under the Laws of Cricket.[91]

Thus, it appears that while the Referee is the official representative of the ICC and is charge of enforcing the *Code of Conduct*, his relationship to the umpires is limited both by the traditional respect for the ideal of judicial independence and by the language of the statute which gives primacy to the role of the umpires as the guardians of the *Laws* and spirit of the game, particularly in this instance in relation to then Law 42(5) and the general jurisdiction under Law 3(7). In this particular case then, Referee Dowling could do little beyond what he apparently did, i.e. plead that the ball be changed. If umpire Hayat refused or failed to comply, the Referee was bound by his own terms of reference to respect that 'decision' even if, it seems, the 'decision' might not have been, in law or jurisprudential taxonomy, 'a decision' which was legally correct.

However, one more factor needs to be entered into the equation here. Given umpire Hayat's refusal to remove the ball from play after detecting 'tampering' at the end of over 17, and the fact that he did not see the ball until lunch 11 overs later, Referee Dowling, in fairness to the accused and out of respect to the requirements of the rules governing his power, should have realized that any verdict based only on the umpire's word, in the absence of the ball and of video evidence confirming the umpire's 'opinion', would be, by definition, unfair.[92] He should, therefore, have refused to give any further consideration to the charges. For his failure to do so, he should have been censured by the ICC. Instead the ICC ignored this flaw as well as his apparent failure to hold a proper hearing and reaffirmed in its statement the fact that he supported the umpires' contention in relation to 'ball-tampering'. Part of the difficulty is the wording of the ICC *Regulations* which did not grant the Referee a clear jurisdiction in such cases to take his own actions. But a more serious failure appears to be the ICC's reluctance to realize the full logical, legal and jurisprudential consequences of the only uncontested 'fact' in this whole case, that the umpires did not change the ball when they were required to do so under the *Law* and under the law. The inevitable consequence of this legally established fact is that the rules of fundamental fairness and natural justice were ignored, rendering any subsequent 'finding' of 'fact' null and void.

Once more, however, what is most clearly demonstrated here in the public and even in the Sri Lankan reaction to these events is the clear existence of a separate category of 'Pakistani ball-tampering'. Thus, evidence that Australian Kookaburra cricket balls may have been suffering from a manufacturing problem causing them to suffer greater than normal wear and tear, or evidence that the WACA pitch might have been causing damage to cricket balls because of unusual algal growth, or the absence of video evidence of 'tampering', or the failure of the umpires and the Match Referee to observe the rules of natural justice, apparently raise legitimate doubts in 'our' minds about Sri Lankan 'ball-tampering' charges but not about Pakistani 'guilt'.

Indeed, evidence that allegations arose in the Pakistani tour match against Western Australia may even have been invoked as admissible and relevant evidence in pleading the Sri Lankan case for innocence. But the subsequent events involving the Sri Lankans seem to carry little, if any, weight in raising 'post-conviction' queries about the soundness of the 'verdict' in the Pakistani case. The Sri Lankans are, after all, 'universally known for their scrupulous fairness as a cricket team' while we all know, 'the Pakistanis are cheats'.[93] Why they even go so far as accusing umpires of misconduct in relation to the condition of the ball.[94] We all know that the recent history of 'ball-tampering' as an offence has been dealt with the utmost probity, skill and respect for the rules of natural justice and the 'rule of law' by cricket's judicial officers. Those Pakistanis, they will stoop to anything.

Of course, the interpretive complexities surrounding ball-tampering and allegations of cheating and unethical conduct do not end there. We might, for example, ask whether allegations concerning Sri Lankan malpractice would continue today to be met, in Australia or elsewhere, with a counternarrative of Ceylonese gentlemanliness. Controversy and strong evidence of a Sri Lankan reluctance to accept being bound by the normal course of adjudication and rule-making in cricket has emerged as a 'trait' of their game. Chucking controversies continue to dog the team's best bowler and Arjuna Ranatunga left the game with a reputation as an annoying and niggling performer who did not necessarily resile from pushing the limits of acceptable behaviour. In his work on the history of the *Laws* and spirit of the game, Simon Rae writes of Ranatunga in a 1998–99 match in England as follows:

> The match was played in the worst possible spirit, with Ranatunga in regular conflict with the umpires and the England side, making what Christopher Martin-Jenkins described as 'a calculated public exhibition of himself' in his determined attempts to have the game run the way he wanted it. The stump microphone picked up Stewart's opinion that his behaviour was 'appalling

for a country's captain.' Having shown an absolute disregard for the preamble to Law 42 . . . , Ranatunga compounded his defiance by turning up to the post-match disciplinary hearing accompanied by two lawyers.[95]

It would be possible to write an entire volume dedicated alone to the jurisprudential exploits of Arjuna Ranatunga and I shall not belabour the obvious here. Suffice it to say that this text must also be placed in the context of colonial history, Sri Lankan national identity, possible contradictory attitudes by some interpreters to the same acts by different cricketers, not to mention the recent disciplinary record of Sri Lankan cricketers during the England tour to their country. Simply put, yet again, previous declarations about the sporting ethos of Sri Lankan cricketers and cricket would, as always, need to be revisited and reexamined if we are to be faithful interpreters and appliers of legal principles to the game of cricket.

Indeed, a brief examination of ball-tampering in international cricket since the Sri Lankan imbroglio in Perth further strengthens the idea of the glorious uncertainty of cricket and the law.

Balls, Cheats and the Rule of Law

In late 1997, allegations of ball-tampering by a visiting team in Australia again surfaced, this time against the South Africans. Two separate incidents were brought under media review. In the first, Hansie Cronje was shown

> . . . dropping the white ball to the ground during a break in the December 4 match at the SCG, rolling it over with his foot, and pressing the spikes in the front of his shoe into the ball. Cronje denied any intention, saying he was only playing with the ball.[96]

The issues here are by now familiar, particularly Cronje's defence that he did not possess the requisite intent to commit the offence. The *Law* in effect at the time speaks only of 'any other action to alter the condition of the ball'. The first level of inquiry must again be one involving the definition of the offence in the text. Is an 'action to alter the condition' to be read as an 'action *intended* to alter the condition' or as 'an action *likely to* alter the condition'. If the latter interpretation is correct then Hansie Cronje's defence must collapse since it is clear that stomping on the ball, playfully or otherwise, will likely alter the condition. On the other hand, even if one assumes that an 'intentional' element exists, there is a distinction well-known to lawyers between motive and intent. Cronje's motive may have been playful, but he did intend to stand on the ball and therefore, on one available reading at least, committing the offence.

The second case of alleged ball-tampering is also one which offers interesting legal possibilities. In a tour match, Umpire Terry Prue questioned the South African practice of returning the ball from the fielders to the keeper by bouncing the ball into the rough surfaces of the centre square. Cronje replied

I said that's the way we pass the ball from one bloke to another. Sometimes we do it out of fun and sometime we do it to get the ball a little bit rough on the one side.[97]

Cronje asserted that throwing the ball along or into the ground was not the same thing as the prohibited act of rubbing the ball on the ground, and that only the latter was prohibited. He seems to have conveniently forgotten the 'any other action' provision which, along with Cronje's admission of intent to alter the condition of the ball would seem quite conclusively to turn him into both a law-breaker and a cheat (now not an astonishing revelation). Naturally, at the time the South Africans reacted with outrage at any such suggestion either of technical transgression of the *Laws* or of an ethical violation. Indeed, Malcolm Knox referred to Cronje's record in support of the South Africans' plea of innocence.

Cronje's record is unblemished by any suggestion of foul play. As national captain he has twice recalled opposing batsmen to the wicket after they had been given out what the South Africans considered poor decisions.[98]

The South African coach tried to shift the blame onto the apparent accusers, claiming that the attack on Cronje was an attempt at gamesmanship by the Australians before the Test series. Australian journalists at some level appeared to back up either Cronje's claim of innocence or to diminish the gravity of the offence. In some way, they argued, Cronje was being punished for a naive and honest admission.

Cronje stands guilty more of naiveté than deliberate cheating. Scuffing the ball in various ways has been a worldwide practice since the advent of reverse swing in the 1980s. Players are often caught in the shady zone between accepted practices and the letter of the law.

The extent to which this has become a grey area became clear when Cronje made the self-incriminating statement that his players had been throwing the ball on to the wicket at Devonport while returning it to keeper and bowler 'to rough it up on one side'.

Honesty, candour and the wish to be helpful deepened Cronje's trouble. As one South African insider ranted, 'This would never have happened with Kepler Wessels. Kepler would have told the media to—off.'[99]

This is followed by a lengthy of the Cronje family history as persecuted Huguenots in Catholic France to explain the decent and honest character of the South African captain. Several points should be briefly highlighted here. First, it seems clear that for Knox and others, there is a distinction between ball-tampering as a technical violation of the *Law* ('the grey area'), and a case of ball-tampering as cheating. Secondly, there is a clear statement that the practice of technical rule violation has been and continues to be a well-established practice. Thirdly, the very character of Cronje precludes us from defining and treating him as a cheat. He is a gentleman, he recalls batters wrongly given out etc. I do not wish to contest either of the first two points. It is clear from this case and the others that I have discussed in this chapter that there have been and are always contextual subtleties and nuances of circumstance which make blanket assertions about either law-breaking or unethical behaviour, even in the basic confrontation between bat and ball which is the essence of 'cricket', impossible.

What I would like to underline, however, is that the argument about character is itself *per se* problematic. There is no logical or even legal position which would allow us to state with certainty that an individual of a certain character did not commit a particular offence at some specified time and place. We can make arguments about propensity and about the relevance of past patterns or behaviour in relation to penalties, but the law is always extremely reluctant to admit such evidence as probative or determinative of guilt or innocence. Indeed, given what we now know about Cronje's 'character' as a cheat of the worst kind, does this again allow or compel a retrospective analysis of his 'intent' when he placed his foot on the ball, or permit a re-evaluation of the practice by his side in returning the ball? When did he start to cheat? Did he start to cheat by accepting bribes as the result of the same character flaw which led him to admit to scuffing the ball? Is his transgression as ball-tamperer made worse because we now know he was a match-fixer? Finally, of course, there is the possibly still problematic question about the legality of throwing the ball into the wicket area which caused much of the Cronje controversy in the first place. Don Oslear, no friend of ball-tamperers writes

> The attempts by players to cause damage to the surface of the ball, other than by legal means, have become so sophisticated in recent years that a regulation has been brought in that forbids players to deliberately skim the ball over the surface of the ground in returning it to the wicketkeeper. This was always done when the ball was thrown down onto the worn bowling ends of recently used pitches. I had departed the professional game when this regulation was brought in but I feel it must be very hard to prove.[100]

During the 2001 cricket season in Australia, Richie Benaud and his fellow commentators on more than one occasion pointed out instances of such bouncing returns to the keeper and raised the issue of the effect of such practices on the ball. Again, it seems that long-time practice, ethical norms and the actual application and meaning of a relatively plain and clear legal text all raise fundamental and largely unanswered questions for various members of cricket's interpretive and adjudicative communities.

Whatever our answer to these legal and moral questions about cricket jurisprudence it seems clear that the overriding feature of the rule of law in cricket discourse continues to be the creation and ongoing deployment of the taxonomical and deontological category of 'Pakistani ball-tampering'. Thus, in the 1999 World Cup in England, allegations of tampering against the Pakistani quicks once again emerged. Following a match against Australia at Headingley,

Pakistan again stood charged with seeking an unfair and unlawful advantage in the battle between bat and ball. The allegations centred around assertions that Pakistan did something funny with the seam, that the only explanation for their ability with reverse swing was that they cheated. Tony Greig, former England captain and Australian television commentator, said that he was certain that something was amiss

> I asked the camera to home in on because I had been watching the fielding side closely for some time. The ball went to deep long-on and they seemed to be working very hard on the ball as it came back across to the bowler. There is no doubt they gave the seam some work...[101]

Pakistan were subsequently reported by Match Referee John Reid of New Zealand for interfering with the ball in a match against South Africa in the same tournament.[102] Once more the basis of the allegations is the reverse swing achieved by the Pakistani bowlers.

> 'Let's just say those guys certainly swing the ball a long way', an unnamed Australian opponent said. 'They are great bowlers but other sides have great bowlers too. They cannot swing it as prodigiously. When you play as players you can see what they are doing'.[103]

The interpretive context has been modified to some extent. Reverse swing is now part of the game and great bowlers from all sides can make the ball move 'the wrong way'. Now the problem is defined in different terms. There is 'reverse swing' and there is 'Pakistani reverse swing'. One is the result of ability and hard work, the other the consequence of law-breaking and cheating. Finally, in 2000, the law for many caught up with the mythology.

During a Singer Trophy match between Pakistan and South Africa, Waqar Younis became the first player banned by an ICC Match Referee for ball-tampering. Again, John Reid of New Zealand found that, based on video evidence, Younis had scratched the ball and lifted the quarter seam. He was suspended while Azhar Mamood was fined and captain Moin Khan was also disciplined, this time for failing in his duty as captain to ensure compliance with the spirit of the game.[104] Waqar was also fined by Pakistan's Cricket Board for bringing the country's name into disrepute.[105]

Of course, the 'facts' do not even begin to tell the whole interpretive or jurisprudential story. For many the finding by Reid and the imposition of a suspension against Waqar, as well as the disciplining of the two other players, came none too soon. Some of those in this group might also respond with a strong hint of juridical cynicism that the finding that Waqar brought the name of Pakistan cricket into disrepute is somewhat problematic since he was surely not alone in this and the reputation of the country did not have a long way to fall.

At the same time, it must still be pointed out that Australian, English and South African cricketers have been accused with good reason of tampering with the ball. The idea that this is a peculiarly Pakistani phenomenon either in quality or quantity is far from the legal truth. In addition, there must still be some serious legal and ethical inquiries before we accept that the only truths of the Waqar case are that the law finally caught up with the evildoers and that the Pakistani players simply got what they deserved following the due process of law.

Such an inquiry might begin with the judicial history of Match Referee John Reid and Pakistani cricket. Following Reid's actions as Match Referee of a Pakistani tour to Australia in 1999, Pakistan objected to Reid's nomination by the ICC for the 2000 series of games against Sri Lanka in Pakistan. Following much publicity about Reid's appointment, and despite the fact that the ICC *Code of Conduct* specifically prohibits either team from objecting to the naming of an individual,[106] Reid suddenly became unavailable.[107]

When he punished Waqar, he was met with allegations from various Pakistani officials that he was biased against them. He was also accused of having breached the *Code of Conduct* provisions himself by reaching his decision on video evidence and without involving the umpires.[108] The Pakistanis protested to the ICC, Reid took the unusual step of publicly defending himself and asserting that everybody who saw the footage in question knew who 'the guilty party' was.[109] The relevant point is not to offer a definitive reading of the jurisprudence of ball-tampering. Instead, I wish once more to highlight the ways in which debates about substantive legal rules and the ethical content of the spirit of the game, which are so often invoked by cricket and judicial nostalgics, must be understood in all their complexity. When we celebrate cricket as the greatest game of all, or when we debate and invoke the spirit of the game, we are in fact celebrating and invoking the fundamental uncertainties of life and of law. We may well be convinced that Waqar interfered with the seam. We may fervently believe that this is a violation not just of the *Laws of Cricket* but of the best traditions of the game. But if we are to adhere to the basic ideal of good faith which must inform all juridical and ethical practices, we are bound to admit that there is much more to ball-tampering than meets the judicial eye. Indeed, in the examination of the latest ball-tampering controversy to rock and shock world cricket, the nonfoundationalist truth of interpretive freedom becomes even more obvious.

19 The little master, ball-tampering and the rule of law

In late 2001 and early 2002, the cricketing world was rocked by a scandal which, for many, went to the very existence of the game and the rule of law within the sport. The catalyst for the firestorm of debate and disagreement appeared to circulate around allegations concerning Indian batter Sachin Tendulkar. A more complete review and analysis of events, however, raises questions not just about law and order in the world of cricket, but also as to the very legal taxonomies which can and do inform our understandings of the game. In other words, while the debate on the surface and in part of its reality concerned a finding by an ICC Match Referee that Tendulkar had in fact tampered with the seam of a ball, other issues of equal import must be taken into account if we are to begin to understand the legal and other questions raised by the case. At issue here are, in no particular order, the internal politics of power within the ICC, tensions and feelings which still surround the idea that 'white' ICC officials are biased against cricketers of colour, the independence of cricket's judicial authorities, and respect for the integrity of decision-making processes and the rule of law within cricket.

Yet, before we even turn to events in South Africa in the last months of 2001, we must briefly focus on events in Australia earlier in the same year. During a particularly mean-spirited encounter between India and Pakistan in a One-Day match in Adelaide, Pakistan felt themselves to be the victims not just of a 48-run Indian victory, but of illegal and unethical behaviour by their opponents. They complained to the Match Referee, former West Indies player, Cammie Smith, that several players from India had engaged in sledging. The Referee dismissed the charges for lack of evidence. More seriously, and more importantly for events ten months later in South Africa, the Pakistanis accused Indian superstar Sachin Tendulkar of tampering with the ball.[1] Referee Smith called the Pakistani charges 'frivolous' and proceeded no further.[2] One easily finds here many of the familiar discursive and rhetorical legal strategies which have traditionally informed such incidents. There are, for some, suspicions about the clean hands of the accusers when Pakistan complains that others tamper with the ball. There is the possibility that the ICC Match Referee system is open to abuse and that complains of misbehaviour may be more grounded in strategy, politics or revenge than in genuine legal dispute. Indeed, the secrecy and gag rule which surround parts of the process may be seen to exacerbate this particular danger. In this case, Pakistani captain Wasim Akram typically invoked the closed and private nature of disputes and of the quasi-judicial proceedings and would not be drawn into further comment even when the allegations had been made public.[3]

Yet all observers of the game will nonetheless recognize the two primary aspects of Indian reactions to the accusations. The first is the expected defence of the accused based on his sterling character and unblemished reputation. Team manager Kapil Dev issued the following statement about Tendulkar: 'Here is a man who has stayed away from controversy from the time he has played international cricket. He has been playing for more than 10 years.'[4]

Once again the defence of character is raised as an absolute bar to any thought that a particular cricketer might have engaged in law-breaking and/or unethical behaviour. I can only repeat here, without casting any aspersions on Tendulkar, that such a defence is legally and indeed morally unconvincing. Character evidence can only be persuasive, it can never be conclusive. An unblemished history of law-abiding behaviour does not categorically exclude the possibility that on a particular set of facts, in a particular set of circumstances, such an individual may have broken the rules. It may make this less likely, but this is almost never the thrust of such defences in the world of cricket and the law.

Of equal importance is the next part of Kapil's plea of innocence and moral outrage. Not only is the victim of the accusation of irreproachable character, but the same can not be said of the accusers: 'We were shocked. Here is a team like Pakistan accusing the Indian captain of ball tampering. Underline Pakistan.'[5]

The hermeneutic and jurisprudential context being deployed here is clear and beyond doubt. Suspected and convicted in the eyes of the cricketing world as ball-tampering cheats, the Pakistanis now have the unmitigated gall to accuse one of the most respected players in the world of cheating. The moral outrage of the Indians is palpable. Notorious cheats are casting aspersions, after losing the game it might be added, on the character and ethical status of one of the game's gentlemen. Consider the source and no credibility at all can be attributed to the charges.

The outrage is exacerbated since the accusers seem to be harking back to traditional enmity, based on nationalistic and religious stereotypes, the history of colonialism and regional politics between India and Pakistan. On the other hand recent history indicates that Indians are beyond such petty considerations when it comes to upholding the *Laws* and spirit of the game. When Pakistani bowler Shoaib Akhtar was reported for throwing, it was the Indian head of the ICC, Jagmohan Dalmiya, who fought off the racist accusers and reinstated the Pakistani bowler. Now the ungrateful and disreputable Pakistanis are reverting to baser tactics.

Of course, in so far as the actual accusations against Sachin are concerned, a jurisprudential cynic might argue the legal equivalent of the adage 'it takes one to know one'. In other words, who would be better suited to detect unlawful interference with the seam than a Pakistani cricketer? Perhaps an ICC Match Referee.

During the relevant Test match against South Africa in Port Elizabeth, Tendulkar was seen on television video replays '...appearing to run his fingernails along the seam of the ball while bowling on the third day of the second Test...'[6]

The television camera operator in charge of the close-up video reported

> The commentators were talking about how Tendulkar was able to swing the ball both ways and therefore how he was holding the ball. I have the most powerful lens so it is my job to get the tight close-ups to illustrate what the commentators are talking about.
>
> While I was doing that we clearly saw him running his thumbnail around the seam several times, like he had been doing earlier.[7]

Once more the jurisprudence of reverse swing and the ethics of lifting the seam reared their ugly heads in international cricket.

Match Referee Mike Denness had a busy time. In addition to the possible charges against Tendulkar, he had to consider potential aggressive and excessive appealing violations against bowler Harbhajan Singh, wicketkeeper Deep Dasgupta, and fielders Shiv Sunder Das and Virender Sehwag. Captain Sourav Ganguly was also charged for failing in his duty to uphold his obligations under Law 42.[8]

Tendulkar was convicted, fined 75 per cent of his match fee and banned for one Test, suspended. The others were also found guilty. Most significantly, Test debutant Sehwag was banned for the next Test.[9] The reaction was immediate and vociferous; India threatened to cancel its 2002 tour of England.[10] More immediately, the BCCI called for the removal of Denness as Referee for the next Test and appealed against the decision suspending and fining their players.[11] Not surprisingly, the ICC refused both the appeal and the request for Denness' removal.[12]

Once again, the presence of a clear and unambiguous legal text has little impact on the jurisprudential, ethical and political discourse surrounding this case. Paragraph D 1(c) states that '...neither team will have a right of objection to a referee's appointment'.

We know, of course, from the case of previous Pakistani response to the nomination of New Zealander John Reid as Match Referee that such a provision has not acted as a bar either to an objection being lodged, nor to the ICC apparently caving in to political pressure. Yet in this case the ruling body remained firm. Denness remained and his decisions were confirmed.

The stakes of the debate and the issues in conflict are by now familiar. There is, if we limit the discussion to the ball-tampering allegations against Tendulkar, the mixed question of law and fact as to whether Denness was correct to have convicted him. Combined with, and informing the outcome of the first set of questions for many, is the feeling among subcontinental cricketers and officials that imperial adjudicators and the old dominions somehow either conspire or are biased against them, both at the substantive and penalty phases of decision-making. Further, intertwined with these concerns and considerations are ideas about respect for the rule of law and the integrity of decision-making and decision-makers within cricket's world of law and ethics.

Some would assert that the most important value is that we must 'respect the umpire's decision' even when the decision may be 'wrong' on the facts. The integrity of the judicial process and of the game itself are dependent upon this essential norm of behaviour and respect for the process of adjudication. Others would assert that such a normative practice is dependent upon the exercise of judicial functions by those charged with them in both a competent and good faith manner. Democracy in cricket demands that umpires and Match Referees be above suspicion of bias or lack of technical ability. Moreover, we also must return here to the seriousness of the charge of ball-tampering and the impact of Denness' guilty verdict. If one sees ball-tampering as a form of outright cheating, then a conviction on such a charge again is tantamount to a finding that the individual is guilty not only of some technical infringement of a legal norm, but that he has breached a fundamental ethical rule. To be cheat is to be excluded from the world of gentlemen cricketers, it is be 'not cricket'.

In such interpretive circumstances this an attack on the very character and integrity of the individual. When the cricketer is Sachin Tendulkar, the man who may well challenge Don Bradman in terms of cricketing greatness and who embodies many of the hopes and aspirations of his country every time he enters the field of play, the insult is collective. An accusation and finding that Sachin is a cheat is for many a declaration that Indians are cheats, that Indian cricket is in fact and in law 'not cricket'. Here, a simple allegation that Tendulkar lifted or otherwise interfered with the seam is very much more than an allegation that Tendulkar lifted the seam.

Thus, the question was raised in the Indian Parliament and street protests took place throughout the country.

> The emergence of the controversy at the highest level only reflects the prevailing mood in the entire country, known the world over for treating cricket with religious fervour. Protest marches in Kolkata, Mumbai and Bhopal have attracted huge crowds, with placards denouncing the ICC and Denness jostling for space with massive posters of national icon Tendulkar.[13]

On the other hand, many supported the ICC and Denness as they invoked not just the general idea that the rule of law demands respect for the adjudicative function of the umpire but the sad practical history of umpiring incompetence and player misbehaviour. In other words, the Match Referee system was imposed after agreement at the highest levels in the game that umpires were being placed under inordinate and unacceptable pressure and that the players were getting out of hand.[14] These arguments indicate not just a traditional understanding of respect for the umpires' decisions as the base on which the entire structure of legality in cricket must depend, but more fundamentally go to the heart of law and order debates within cricket at at least two levels.

First, there is the idea that many participants in the collective construction of meaning in the game, and by this we must mean the players, are no longer willing to respect traditional understandings of the collective norms informing adjudication and law-abiding behaviour in the game. At this level, I am not concerned with whether this is in fact true. It is sufficient that a certain proportion of the game's hermeneutic community believed it to be true.

As I have already pointed out, what is happening at this level of the debate is a determination by the hierarchy of the game that the lower level participants, i.e. the players, are out of control and that the game can only exist if the law and *Laws* are respected. What is needed is more law, and more order. The *Preamble* of the 2000 *Code* makes it clear that the spirit of the game must be rendered in writing so that the normative content of the ethical aspect of cricket can be made explicit and known. At the same time, the *Laws* must be toughened up and finally, the umpires must be assisted by another level of judicial authority. The response to a breakdown in law and order is more law and more order.

Secondly, this new law and order regime must be imposed and enforced at the level of a centralized administration. The ICC, not the players, or even local boards, must be entrusted with supervisory and final jurisdiction. The locals and the players have failed, the central government must intervene. This tension, not just over the form and content of the rule of law in cricket, but over the appropriate division of governance mechanisms, has a long history in the game. The Tendulkar case simply brought many of the simmering tensions once more to the surface.

Thus, almost all former Indian cricketers who commented on the case pointed out the by now familiar tropes of legal discourse in cricket. For them, double standards are applied to subcontinental cricketers who are punished more harshly than perpetrators from the white nations. Evidence of bias is everywhere. Sachin is a cricketer of unsullied reputation so something else must be going on and that something else must be bias.[15] Australian captain Steve Waugh, on the other hand, criticized the penalty as being too soft. For him, ball-tampering is a serious offence and the penalties meted out in cases of transgression must be harsh.

> I guess it's a smear on your reputation that's pretty severe, but if they're going to do it properly they may as well go the full way and make an issue of it. Unless you get a ban it's not a penalty.
>
> I think it's been going on too long ball tampering. Affecting the state of the ball and it's about time people started paying the penalty.[16]

Indians replied with a series of *tu quoque* responses pointing out that the Australians had better put their own disciplinary house in order before criticizing anyone else.[17] Still, at a very basic level, despite all the contextualization which is both necessary and interesting if we are to understand the furore which surrounded the Tendulkar conviction, the basic question is for many the nature of the offence at law and the ethical norm at play. What is ball-tampering and is it cheating?

Thus, the Pakistanis, who are not necessarily best friends with Indian cricket and who had a few months earlier accused Tendulkar of the very offence, stepped into the fray and sought to invoke the case and the penalty imposed in the Tendulkar case in Waqar's favour. For them, the suspended ban on Sachin indicated that there were inconsistent sentencing practices which adversely effected their player. The ban imposed on Waqar unjustly tarnished him.

> Although the ICC cannot reverse the one-man [sic] ban on Waqar, the least it can do is to remove the stigma against the name of the champion fast bowler who has been a scourge for the batsmen throughout his career.[18]

For the Pakistanis the stigmatizing aspect of ball-tampering appears at this stage to arise not from the fact of conviction but from the penalty imposed. But this view is not shared by other critics of Denness' decision. For them, the problem lies squarely with the conviction itself. More fundamentally, the twin questions of the substantive definition of the offence and of the ethical status of the lawbreaker again come to the forefront of all legal debates around ball-tampering.

Partab Ramchaud makes the argument as he sees it on the facts and evidence available to Denness.

> Cleaning dirt from the ball and tampering with it are two very different things. Television footage – including a couple of close-ups – would seem to indicate that Tendulkar is cleaning the seam of the ball. As is well known, dirt is bound to accumulate on the ball, especially in the damp weather conditions prevalent during the Port Elizabeth Test. It is common practice, then, for fielders and bowlers to remove dirt with the nails.[19]

Tendulkar did not use a bottle cap and engage in flagrant abuse of the condition of the ball as is the case in allegations of Pakistani ball-tampering. He did not on the available evidence lift the seam, he merely cleaned it. He did not contravene the *Law* and he is no cheat, or so the argument goes.

Whether he is or is not a cheat is a question to which I shall turn shortly, but the fact that he is a lawbreaker, if we accept Ramchaud's version of the facts as uncontroverted, is beyond doubt. Let us assume Tendulkar did not breach the prohibition of interfering with the seam. Let us further assume that his actions do not fall under the wording of the general phrase banning any other action likely to interfere with the condition of the ball, which we have already seen. Tendulkar simply removed mud from the seam, dirt accumulated from the wet conditions at the ground. Law 42(3) (a) (ii) clearly states 'Any player may . . . remove mud from the ball under the supervision of the umpire.'

A plain and I believe relatively uncontroversial reading of the text would indicate that anyone removing mud from the ball without the supervision of the umpire is committing a violation of the *Law* and is guilty of ball-tampering. Tendulkar then even on the facts as presented by his own defender here has committed the offence of which he was charged and found guilty. He removed mud from the ball in illegal circumstances and is clearly liable for changing the condition of the ball from one with mud in the seams to one without, or with less mud in the seams. Of course, it would still be open to argue that the nature of the breach involved is merely a technical one, doing something without the umpire's permission which he would no doubt have been allowed to do if he had only asked. Such an interpretive position would be based on the idea that the very nature of the violation of the provisions of Law 42(3) can be by definition more or less serious. Interfering with the seam, or using a Pakistani bottle cap, would be serious violations of both the legal and ethical norms at play. Removing mud without permission is the equivalent of a 5 km per hour or 5 mph breach of a speed limit. A technical offence but one which is minor and does not involve moral turpitude.

The text of the *Law* itself makes no such distinctions. It is placed prominently in the section of the *Laws of Cricket* which deal with 'Fair and Unfair Play'. It lists what players may and may not do to and with the ball. Any change or attempt to change the condition of the ball is treated the same and is defined as unfair play. The contrary view, one which asserts a gradation of tampering must be grounded in some understanding derived from the way the game has been and is played and the *Law* has been interpreted. There must be some evidence that Denness was wrong to interpret Tendulkar's action as law-violating and serious in nature. Perhaps the argument is better formulated not in terms of the act but in terms of the mental element of the offence. Here one would posit that the nature of the act and indeed of the offence is in fact and in law different from other types of acts which would violate other prohibitions in the same statute. Interfering with the seam or rubbing the ball in the ground etc. appear to be acts which require high degrees of deliberation. On the other hand, doing something without the permission or supervision of the umpire which one most likely would have been allowed to do if one had sought and obtained the authority seems to be not a deliberate act of commission but one of oversight, or at the worst, a negligent omission.

Again, many of these arguments are familiar by now and are likely to as persuasive as one wants them to be taking into account many other interpretive contexts and factors. Indeed, one might find persuasive the reading that what Tendulkar did was a mere and minor technical violation of the *Law*. Then one might go on to condemn the picayune interpretation and harshness of the punishment as proof positive of judicial bias. Not only is all of this dependent on the biases one brings to one's own act of legal interpretation in the case of Sachin Tendulkar, but it is also dependent on being able to accept that Ramchaud's interpretive account of what the video shows is in fact accurate. This in turn will be yet another act of interpretive intervention and contextualization in the almost infinite regress of cricket and the law. Finally, of course, the story does not end here.

The Indians continued their protests and refused to comply with the Denness decision. Most crucially they named Sehwag, who had received a ban from the Match Referee, in the side for the next five-day game against the South Africans, in direct defiance of the judicial decision. The ICC threatened to withdraw official Test status from any match in which Sehwag played before serving his ban. The Indians refused to take the field if Denness were appointed as Match Referee.[20] The ICC stood by their judge. The South African government intervened in support of the board despite a possible threat to South Africa's position as host for the World Cup.[21] Proving once again that politics does indeed make for strange bedfellows, Pakistan came out in support of India,[22] Sri Lanka and England backed the ICC.[23] The South Africans and Indians played anyway and South African Denis Lindsay acted as Match Referee in the unofficial clash between the sides.[24] Anarchy was apparently loosed upon the cricket world.

I do not intend to investigate or outline the political negotiations and compromises which followed as England renegotiated the terms of the India tour, the ICC decided to appoint a 'review panel' to investigate issues surrounding the use of Match Referees and then debated with an apparently recalcitrant India over the membership of the panel. Press and media coverage at the time was extensive and the issues are quite well known.

What is important is to underline the taxonomical shift which occurred, almost unnoticed by many, as the controversy surrounding the India/South Africa series evolved. The case went from being the Tendulkar ball-tampering case to become the Sehwag excessive appeal banning case. The stakes for many were understood as traditional assertions about bias and colonialism in cricket. For others, they involved instead a plan by Dalmiya to institute a Bush-like New World Order in cricket by organizing and controlling a breakaway, television-driven 'Asian' dominated cricket competition.[25] Tensions between and among various member states of the ICC, internal divisions in the Indian Board,[26] regional resentments[27] and the profit motive all underlined the politics of the debates which swirled in world cricket at the end of 2001. All of this in the end seems to have little or anything at all to do with the original legal dilemmas which allegedly provoked the outrage in the first place. Few if any references can be found after the first two or three days to Sachin Tendulkar's status as lawbreaker, cheat or gentleman. The precipitating legal excuse for the debate was the ICC's insistence that Denness be supported and that the ban on Sehwag be respected. Ironically, at the beginning of the jurisprudential debate, the ban on Sehwag was not perceived to be particularly harsh or unjust.

Excessive appealing has been the subject of increased surveillance, harsher penalties, greater control, and general condemnation as violating the game's informing ethical rules. Former Indian captain and coach Ajit Wadekar stated at the same time as he condemned the treatment of Sachin, 'I can only say that we should come down hard on excessive appealing.'[28]

A former President of the Board of Cricket Control of India Raj Singh Dungarpur, went even further,

> In the case of excessive appealing, I admit that the Indians are not totally above board. There is a 'Nayan Mongia' culture that has set into the team in the recent past....Look at Virender Sehwag, he has played just two Tests, and he has already been suspended. That is completely atrocious. I like Sourav Ganguly as a captain, but he is poor communicator. What were the

coach and captain doing at this time? They should have spoken to the boys and made sure things never came to such a pass.[29]

The legal question at this level, even within Indian cricket circles, seems unproblematic. Excessive appealing is bad, it is against the spirit of the game and should be stamped out. There is no apparent criticism of Denness or his decisions on this point, yet it was precisely on this point that the Indians based their subsequent refusal to comply with the judicial office and respect the rulings of the Match Referee. It would appear that the entire debate had little to do with the facts and the law in the actual cases at hand and everything to do with other interpretive strategies and political goals. This does not mean that this case is entirely different from many, if not all, other legal controversies in the world of cricket and law. The issues at stake and the various claims about bias, double standards etc. have almost always been a part of disputes about cricket and the law. The issue is that on the surface and even deeper in the series of events it looks as if the Indians, with the connivance of the South Africans, who do not necessarily have great credibility in the eyes of many when it comes to arguing about the high moral standards at the heart of cricket, chose to ignore the rules when it did not suit their other ends.

The Chair of the interim committee of the Sri Lankan Cricket Board, Vijaya Malalasekara, put it this way, 'You don't agree to independent judges and suddenly sack them because you don't like how they rule.'[30]

This is a succinct summary of the basic jurisprudential and ethical principle of the supporters of the ICC in the specific case and for supporters of the rule of law more broadly speaking. In this case, the ICC stood by its ideal of the rule of law and supported Denness' decisions and called upon all concerned to respect his status as a Match Referee. At the same time, it subverted this arguably formalist understanding of legality and legitimacy and agreed to appoint a special commission of former Test players to examine the propriety of Denness' judgement. Dalmiya tried to compel the ICC to name members of his choosing and once again the notion that more law could cure the absence of a shared understanding of cricket legality caused the collapse of the commission.[31]

In the end, the competing visions of cricket as cricket and cricket as politics, or cricket as law, are in fact and in practice different versions of the same idea. Cricket is politics, but it is also and must always be cricket. There must be some confrontation between bat and ball, some application of the *Laws* on the field of play.[32] What is clear from the history of adjudication generally or in cases of alleged ball-tampering in particular is that this has never been an absolute and immutable truth in cricket. Umpires and now Match Referees have always been criticized and condemned, accused of cheating, bias and incompetence by players and administrators alike. Players have asserted their rights to a strict and literal interpretation and application of the *Laws of Cricket* and argued that they have not breached them when convenient. Administrators and commercial interests have attempted to appropriate the game for their own ends, from Kerry Packer and Rupert Murdoch to Mr Dalmiya. At the same time, cricket has always invoked and enforced some ideal notion that it is above and beyond such flaws and frailties. Batters walk, fielders signal that they have not fairly caught the ball, captains recall batters wrongfully dismissed. Cricketers relish the confrontation between bat and ball and use bottle caps to change the condition of the ball. The umpires' decisions must always be accepted, or sometimes not. That is cricket.

20 Delay and over-rates: temporality and the meaning of cricket

In these days of fast food and fast money, it seems on the surface that cricket, especially when it reaches the apogee of Test matches, offers a respite and a return to those days of halcyon cricket invoked by Lord Denning's vision of peaceful and bucolic splendour. After all, a five-day Test does not offer a quick fix but a slow, deliberate build-up. It is more like our other life experiences, before globalized economies, with peaks and valleys, ebbs and flows, missed opportunities and opportunities seized, all coming not in a 60-minute interval, with breaks for commercials but over a more human time-frame. As spectators, we have time to get to know the participants in a Test, they perform in front of our gaze for hours and days, allowing their true character to be revealed. If there is one element of cricket which has remained essential to its character, it is this sense of expanded time. If one aspect of cricket distinguishes it from the modern age of sport between TV adverts, it is this sense of time expanded to real dimensions. Of course, there is the ever-vexing question of the One-Day game. This is a version of cricket created for and determined by, the demands of our modern televisual reality. 'Limited' overs cricket is for the purist and true believer not really cricket by the very fact of its artificially constrained temporal limits. There is 'real' cricket and then there is the pyjama game. Different players, different crowds, different rules, 'not cricket'. It appears the ultimate irony, then, that one of the major controversies in modern Test cricket involved the issue of time wasting.

Again, at one level, the speed of play is regulated by formal *Laws*. Law 16 governs issues of time as they relate to the commencement or termination of overs immediately preceding intervals. Law 16(6) describes the rules governing the number of overs which *must* be bowled in the last hour of play. Law 42(9) and (10) place intentional time wasting in the category of unfair play. The provisions of the 2000 *Code* now clearly establish as a matter of *Law*, that time wasting can occur as the result of actions (or inaction) by both the fielding side and the batters. When time wasting is attributable to the fielding side, the *Law* now provides that after an official warning to the captain, any further violation can result in the awarding of five penalty runs to the other team, if the time wasting occurs before an over has begun (Law 42(9) (b) (i)) or if it occurs while an over is underway, the umpire shall order the removal of the bowler for the rest of that innings (Law 42(9) (b) (ii)). If the time wasting is attributable to the batting side, again following an official warning, the umpire shall award five penalty runs to the opposition. In any case of time wasting, the offence is reportable and subject to administrative penalties imposed by the Match Referee.

Once again, however, the practical application of the *Laws* is much more difficult, complex, nuanced than a formalist reading might indicate. While umpires publicly declare their jurisdiction over delaying tactics and announce their willingness to intervene, the *Law* is rarely invoked on the field of play.[1] Law 42(10) of the 1980 *Code*, the predecessor provision to the current *Law* proved to be almost entirely ineffective. Again, however, the question is whether the text of the statute was unenforceable for some inherent reason or whether the 'problem' was attributable either to a lack of judicial competence or to some collective understanding by some members of the interpretive community that the higher purposes of cricket, such as winning, were better served by ignoring or violating the letter of the *Law*.

For example, when an England tour of the West Indies gave rise to several incidents of apparently deliberate time wasting, the frustration of many was exacerbated by the complete absence of legal control and intervention. Despite an ongoing outcry from the influential cricket press and despite the traditions of a game couched at other times in a strict rule formalism, umpires still refused to intervene. During the Antigua Test, Allan Lamb of England was the guilty party, holding up play by complaining about the noise of transistor radios in the crowd, 'It was no louder than at any previous stage in this cacophony of a ground, but the umpire went along with Lamb's blatant ploy.'[2]

In the third Test in Trinidad, acting West Indian captain Desmond Haynes 'slowed his bowlers to a rate of 12 overs in a two-hour session'. His tactics were described by one writer as having 'nothing to do with cricket and everything to do with cynicism'.[3] In the fourth Test in Barbados, England were the culprit as: 'The over-rate was dropped to the cynical depths of less than 11 per hour...'[4] and 'The final over before lunch, bowled by De Freitas, took almost seven minutes and contained the full range of tricks from retying the bootlace to unnecessary field change.'[5]

It is clear that each side engaged in unfair and illegal practices and they did so with impunity. Why, in the *Law formalism* of cricket was this allowed to occur? Many factors deserve consideration. At the practical level, tying a bootlace, shining the ball, taking a long run-up, are all things a fast bowler does in carrying out his task. As each ball of an over constitutes a mere subtext of the larger texts of that over, that innings, that match, that series, that career etc., it may well be argued that it is difficult in practice to draw a clear line between delay and the ordinary time a bowler needs to properly fulfil his task. Similarly, each field placing is part of larger contexts and a captain may, for example, choose to add a slip or take one away for a silly point or a deep fine leg depending on the delivery which he expects from his knowledge of the bowler, which knowledge includes such factors as the batter's tendencies, the bowler's tendencies (a yorker, a bouncer, or a surprise inswinger after a series of outswingers), the weather, the pitch and so on. Furthermore, a change in field positions may be 'required' by the batter at the crease. A right- and left-hand combination will require a change in field placings after each single. The presence of a top order player in form at the striker's end may well inspire the fielding captain to change his field placings by installing a leg-slip or a deep leg-side fielder because he knows of that batter's proclivities for leg-side play. No one, however, would argue that the captain had engaged in deliberate time-wasting in setting his field against the particular batter. To the contrary, many would simply assert that it is exactly this type of strategic and tactical confrontation that makes for good 'cricket'. At the same time, we 'know' from experience, that there are fielding changes which are good tactics and fielding changes which are simply meant to waste time. A 'good' captain, one who plays the game, will be one who manages to delay when required while appearing to be doing something else.

In addition, time and some form of delay approaching 'unfair play' under the *Law*, but not in direct or blatant violation of the *Law*, can be an important factor in the fast bowler's strategy. A batter may be made to 'wait a little, to sweat a little' while he ponders the next delivery in an expected barrage of bouncers or any delivery on an unpredictable wicket. A batter on 49 or 99 will be subjected to delay by the bowler, the placing of fielders close to the bat, not because such delay and fielding changes are strategically important at this stage of the contest, but because the captain wants to increase the mental pressure tactically. This psychological battle of wits and nerves between bowler and batter is a key part of the rich text of cricket, for players, umpires and spectators. For an umpire to make a decision warning a bowler, or captain for slow play may be perceived as risking an error which could upset the whole rhythm of the game if the delay, in fact, or in the perception of other members of the interpretive community, is a justified and essential part of the larger text. An umpire faced with committing such an error might believe, even mistakenly, that he should not take such a risk because to do so would threaten his status as a member of that community.[6]

At the other end, and as the *Law* now provides and recognizes, it may well be that delay is desired and practised not by the bowler but by one or both members of the batting side. A fielding side, sensing victory, may wish to hurry in order to dismiss the other team before the close of play or the passage of time or impending weather forces a draw or in order to commence its innings on that day. It may wish, after a declaration or having been dismissed, simply to get stuck into the other side which may have spent a long time in the field and not be psychologically or physically in their best batting form. On such occasions, it is in the interests of the batting side to slow things down by readjusting their pads, changing their gloves, swotting flies, patting the pitch, conferring with their partner, or taking overly long to recover from being hit by an innocuous delivery.

As in the case of the bowling side, such occurrences seen in isolation are simply things a batter does as a batter and to determine if his pad is loose or he really is hurt is a difficult and risky business for the umpire-participant in the interpretive community. Again, it is also the case that, for example, a batter struggling to carry his bat through an innings, to reach his century, or to stay in the crease to force a 'well-deserved' draw or a surprising victory, as V.V.S. Laxman did against

Australia in India, are very exciting aspects of the game. Rather than making the game boring and dull, such occasions create and maintain a great deal of attention and keep the spectator on the edge of their seat.[7] Similarly, watching a tail-ender trying to keep out the best bowlers in the opposition in order to ensure a draw or participate in an unexpected win can be among the most interesting and even exciting experiences for the spectator and his teammates in the dressing rooms as well.

No matter how appealing and necessary the case for a deep contextualization of cricket may be, however, it remains equally true that players, umpires and spectators, just as they can tell the difference between boring and exciting occupations of the crease, can and do distinguish between valid use and even wasting of time and unconscionable and illegal delay. It is simply and completely one of the things one 'knows' if one 'knows' cricket. As a leading text for umpires indicates 'The umpire has to judge when these things are being taken too far – again a check that his colleague takes a similar view is advisable.'[8]

The issue will always be complex and always occur in a context of which all are aware. It is a question of judgement, of adjudication and of discretion. Mike Selvey could write of the way in which Allan Lamb 'cynically disregarded the laws' and described time wasting as 'cricket's equivalent of the professional foul', in a Test against the West Indies. But this consensus may be more apparent than real. The professional foul is part of the game. In some circumstances it is an accepted and acceptable part of the game, in others it is punished and outlawed. A cynical disregard for the *Laws* may be clever and skilful captaincy. Such a judgement will be dependent first on how one interprets the *Laws* to be applied in the context in question. Secondly, it will, or may be, dependent on how one might interpret a possibly competing or superior ethical norm of the spirit of the game. Thirdly, it must always call into question the role of the umpire as adjudicator. The possibilities, while not endless, are nonetheless many and no simple declaration of a universally acceptable and accepted norm will or should be allowed to stand alone and unchallenged.

The debate surrounding the problem of time wasting proves, once again, the problem of the simultaneous conjunction and disjunction of rule formalism and ethical informalism in cricket (and in law). Outrage over events in the West Indies series was apparently 'unanimous', yet the entire West Indian side participated in the 'illegality' and the umpires did not intervene. The call from media observers was for, at one and the same time, a strict enforcement of the *Laws and* adherence to the spirit of the game. Of course, two captains of Test-playing nations and all the players on both teams at some level seem to have employed and practised a different set of values. As we have seen, the joining together of these two forces or narratives is often an unsolvable logical and/or practical contradiction. Here, however, the two seem to operate, if not at the same level, in practice at least towards a shared ideological goal. When Mike Selvey referred to time wasting as 'cricket's equivalent of the professional foul', he was invoking an anti-utilitarian law and order stance to make the breaking of the rules inefficient. For Christopher Martin-Jenkins, 'time wasting' as evidenced by both sides made further inroads into the gradual erosion of the old saying 'it's not cricket'.[9] These assertions of collective moral outrage against the violation of the norms and practices of the interpretive community demonstrate for proponents of the anti-time wasting camp, a common purpose between law and morality. What they indicated, as did the mirror image cry of 'Good show old boy' after Courtney Walsh 'showed the ball', was that both the old legal order and the ethical community were under threat, or perceived themselves to be under threat, from a common enemy. That common enemy is the apparently 'new' ethos of professionalism – win at all costs or at least avoid defeat at all costs. Bowl bouncers at opposition bowlers when they are at the crease, delay. It is a blatant and publicly cynical utilitarianism, it is under-arm bowling, physical intimidation and delaying tactics. It directly and openly challenges the ethos not only of the *Laws* but of the entire narrative of true cricket.

It is, in the final analysis, a fundamental contradiction of cricket, law and life that we feel more comfortable about a moral dilemma when it is below the surface, or when our ideological imagining of it is couched in terms of other values we accept and understand. It is Enron and WorldCom, international wheeler-dealers, the little companies from Texas and Tennessee, competing with and beating allcomers in the world of big business on their own terms. Finally, it is the collapse of the empire, blamed on slack legal regulators or watchdogs who turned a blind eye in the wake of success. It is the national bubble burst in public for all to see the Emperor has no clothes.

This existential psychological disquiet as our norms and *Laws* change makes us nervous. Certainty about cricket and law are replaced by context and uncertainty. We are now facing a narrative which some of us claim to barely recognize and is exacerbated in this context by the engine of nationalism. West Indians saw the English as culprits and the English blamed it all on the West Indian pace attack.[10] Subcontinental bowlers throw, Brett Lee is wrongly accused. We find various assertions that Australians would never do it, but Sourav Ganguly can never be above suspicion.

Finally, the law had to step in. We have already seen the modifications to the 2000 *Code* of the *Laws of Cricket*. However, as is often the case in these days of delegated legislation and government by regulation, it is not the formal text of the official legislative version of the law which has the most direct and important impact on the way the game is played, but the 'delegated legislation' of the *ICC Code of Conduct* and the Match Referee system. This has been supplemented by the use of special 'Playing Conditions' for Test matches and finally by the intersection of law and technology. The advent of sophisticated lighting systems and facilities at Test match grounds has meant that gloomy weather no longer need prevent a full day's play (unless one is playing at Trent Bridge in Aug. 2002).

Thus, the *Code of Conduct* now provides that in addition to the requirements established for the last hour of the day's play found in the *Laws*, the Match Referee is empowered to calculate the over rate of each day's play and to impose appropriate monetary sanctions in the case of undue delay, on either the bowling or batting side.[11] The *Code* also makes specific provisions for the Match Referee to allow for certain events which should not be counted against either side, e.g., to treat an injured player. Other events beyond the control of the players are also to be taken into consideration.[12] These circumstances are not limited by specific legislative or regulatory language and therefore require that the Match Referee, like the umpire in enforcing the provisions of the *Laws*, engage in subtle, contextualized adjudication. For example, a game played in damp conditions, where the field has not been completely dried, might mean that the fielding side will have to dry the ball more frequently, or that the bowler will have to call for ground staff to repair the area near the wicket for his run up or delivery stride, or that he will need to remove accumulated dirt from his spikes etc. A Match Referee will need to take these circumstances and these acts into account in determining if there has been deliberate time wasting. He will also be able to ensure, along with the umpires, that such delay will not have its desired effect. The Test Match Playing Conditions contain extensive provisions allowing for additional time to be added to a day's play for a variety of reasons. In addition, they allow, in some circumstances, for the use of lights to permit play to go on.[13] Cleaning the spikes may be a safety measure to ensure the bowler does not injure himself by slipping in the delivery stride or it may be a way of waiting until the rain comes, or of making the batter stew. 'We' will know, or not, depending on the context.

We also face, as we try to interpret this changing text, or as we refuse to interpret the text and call for a return to the old stories, the familiar stories, an even clearer, although perhaps apparently minor, contradiction of cricket. Cricket is a game where one obvious solution to slow play is to turn to more slow bowlers. In cricket, slow is fast and fast is slow. The solution to the problem is to bring more spin bowlers into the attack because as we all know slow bowlers work faster.[14]

This is not the first time we see that cricket is situated in a key *locus* (or minor truism) of post-modernism, the transposition of the temporal realm. Slow is fast, fast is slow. Once again, however, even cricket's post-modernism can deconstruct itself. Complaints were made in 1880 of the slowness of slow bowling.[15] Then, slow was slow and fast was fast, but uncertainty has always been a certain part of playing the game.

The real effect of spin bowling, either in an orthodox delivery or in a googly is not in the physical (the spin, the batter's eyes or the spinner's hand) but in the perception – the combination of the physical and the mental which is 'reality', but which is deception. As Wilfred Rhodes put it: 'If a batsman thinks it's spinning, then it's spinning.'[16]

Thus, when Shane Warne bowled Mike Gatting with 'that ball', everyone understood the look of befuddlement and stunned amazement on Gatting's face. And everyone knew that 'our' understanding of cricket and the possibilities of experience had been fundamentally changed by a spinning ball. The reality of cricket is the collective consciousness-creation of the community who give meaning to the text both through their readings and mis-readings.

One final example embodies the changing and contextualized nature of discussions and debates about the law and ethics of time wasting in cricket. During the final stages of a Test match between the West Indies and South Africa at

Kensington Oval, Bridgetown, Windies tail-enders Dinanath Ramnarine and Mervyn Dillon brought to the fore all the issues we have been looking at. With 20 minutes of play and 3 wickets in hand, the West Indies were hanging on for a draw. Ramnarine and Dillon called for on field treatment and consistently stepped away from the wicket, claiming to be affected by cramp. Of course, any player may take steps to protect himself from the debilitating effects of leg cramps. Conditions and the fact that this was the final afternoon of a five-day match may well have meant that cramp was in fact hampering the players. The on field umpires spoke to Ramnarine, possibly to give him a formal warning under Law 42(9). Match Referee Mike Denness called in the two batters and captain Carl Hooper to investigate why the game was slowed down, but no formal action was taken. In other words, the umpires on the field did not invoke their powers under the terms of Law 42(9) to issue a formal warning, or to award penalty runs. Nor did they use their authority under Law 42(9) or under the general provisions of the *Code of Conduct* to report the players to the Match Referee for 'sharp practice' or bringing the game into disrepute. Finally, the Match Referee, after speaking with the parties, did not himself report, try or convict the batters or their captain under the applicable provisions of the *Laws* and the *Code of Conduct*. No legal action was taken despite the widespread belief and suspicion that the West Indies players may well have been engaged in a deliberate attempt to waste time.

We have already seen that the *Laws* now incorporate not just the formal provisions of the substantive *Laws* of the game, but also through the Preamble, the ethical norms of the spirit of the game. It is undisputed that the spirit of the game and the general normative prohibition against bringing the game into disrepute were all operative here. Given the absence of judicial intervention by the umpires or the Match Referee, we could arguably and justifiably conclude that the tail-enders were in fact suffering. This would mean that whatever delay they caused was not 'unfair' or 'time wasting'.

Even if this were not the case, we might also argue that there may also be some ethical norm which encourages such actions (assuming them to have been tactical rather than real) in such circumstances. In other words, for tail-enders to 'get' cramps with few wickets in hand on the fifth day of a Test, to try to save the game is not 'sharp practice' or 'cheating' or 'unfair' or 'against the spirit of the game'. It is good cricket, clever play, lawful manipulation of the circumstances for a permissible and laudable utilitarian purpose. It is not 'not cricket', it is instead 'good cricket'.

But the story does not end there. Further complexity is added at several points of the story of over rates and delay. The South Africans were using their spinners, as is often the case on a deteriorating wicket on the final day. Therefore, they had already bowled the minimum number of overs required in the final hour of play.[17] The time 'wasted' was as a result time 'lost' but not time 'required' for there in other circumstances to have been a full and complete Test.

At this point one could mount a purposive interpretation of the various legislative and regulatory instruments which deal with over rates and time wasting and assert that the real purpose of the *Laws* here is to ensure a minimum number of overs per day and a minimum number of overs in the last hour. Since this twin goal had been met, the West Indies players were not engaging, even in bad faith, in behaviour which violated the *Laws*. Of course, there are equally available counter-narratives and interpretations which would invoke the spirit of the game, the mischief of time wasting regardless of the number of overs bowled, the clear language of the *Laws* which can be read apart from the minimum over requirement etc. Again what is important is not the resolution of the legal and ethical problem, but a recognition of its existence and complexity.

What is even more intriguing is the fact that several senior West Indian players apparently apologized for Dillon's and Ramnarine's tactics after play had finished. For them, such behaviour was unsportsmanlike, and in violation of the spirit of the game. The batters prevented the game of cricket in its essence from happening by avoiding the confrontation between bat and ball.[18]

Thus while they were not censured or sanctioned by the official forces of law and order present and in power at the match, the players were condemned by their fellows and peers, players in their own side, who felt betrayed by their teammates here. This raises not just important issues and facts for any debate about the conduct and construction of the idea of the spirit of the game as a set of normative standards, it also raises key elements about the complexity of any such claims or standards. Why did the two players engage in such conduct? Did they deliberately breach the rules of the spirit of the game, or did they think that other imperatives – preserving their wickets, saving the game etc. were more important and outweighed the ethical content of the spirit of the game? Did they know that the content of the normative system of the spirit of the game compelled them to face up to the bowlers and engage in the confrontation between bat and ball? Does the fact that 'senior' players were the ones to offer an apology to their opponents operate as an important factor here and if so, how? On the one hand one might see this 'generational' divide as one indicating that the younger players who breached the norms were ignorant of the content of their moral and ethical obligations. If this is the case, this would mean that they might be seen to have acted in a morally incorrect or even reprehensible way, but also that their actions were not malicious but grounded in ignorance. One might also find further moral and ethical failures among the senior players who did not meet their obligations to educate properly and inform younger members of the interpretive community of the content of the moral system in which they were expected to operate. We could then argue that the most serious ethical and moral failure, as well as legal breach, was that attributable to the captain, Carl Hooper, who is legally obliged to ensure that the spirit of the game is upheld and respected by his side.

On the other hand, it might be possible to argue here that the generational divide is not one informed by ignorance on the one hand and knowledge but pedagogical failure on the other. Instead, it might be the case that younger cricketers have a different understanding or view of the spirit of the game. Perhaps, as cricketers having grown up with the professionalization of the sport, they simply believe that the goal and purpose of the game is to win, and that this is the moral, ethical and legal imperative imposed on them when they play for their country.

Finally, it would also be necessary, if we wanted to gain a more complete understanding of the issues at work here, to introduce into our analyses concepts of geography and politics in West Indies cricket. Both Ramnarine and Dillon are from Trinidad. The president of the Trinidad and Tobago Cricket Board condemned their tactics as contrary to the spirit of the game and insisted that had they been playing while 'wearing national colours', the Board would have held an inquiry.[19] In fact, the West Indies did issue a severe reprimand against the two players, deeming their actions as contrary to the best interests of West Indies cricket. There are obviously at work complex historical and geo-political factors, e.g. West Indies cricket as a federal and not a national project; historical internal divides within Trinidad and Tobago cricket between 'black' and 'Indian' cricketers etc. What is clear from the aftermath of the Ramnarine and Dillon case is that what is and is not cricket, in law and in ethics, even after extensive legislative and regulatory reform over the problem of over rates and delay in international cricket, remains at some level hotly contested, disputed hermeneutic territory.

21 Ethical discourse, legal narrative and the meaning of cricket

It is by now apparent that one dominant narrative about cricket believes that there is a higher order to the game, a 'true' meaning of cricket, one which was practised in the days of yore. Here sportsmanship was the gentlemanly code of conduct followed by one and all and the *Laws*, if anything, simply reflected, reinforced and supported the higher and truer game. This is clearly the ideological sub-text which informs Denning's and 'Dante's' imageries of cricket heaven and hell. It is also the narrative to which we refer when we impose an obligation on the bowler to 'show the ball' before *Mankading* the batter who backs up too far. It is the story we tell about how we 'know' what chucking is and perhaps why we condemn and harass Ian Meckiff and finally it is the history to which we refer when we condemn today's players for excessive 'professionalism'.

There is, equally obviously, a competing narrative which is necessarily implied by the first. The basis of this narrative is the practice of standing on one's rights and at the same time stretching or breaking the law to gain an advantage. It is an internally inconsistent, yet practically 'successful', history of legal formalism and professional, utilitarian rule bending and flouting. It is a barrage of bouncers which is blatantly illegal but cheered by the crowd. It is the story of strict legality, law and order, the judge who must obey the law no matter what he believes personally, and at the same time, the ballad of the outlaw as hero.

In fact, each and every one of these stories about cricket is now and always has been a true representation of what we know of cricket. Each age has seen itself as falling into degeneracy by ignoring the ethical norms of its ancestors. Each period has therefore referred to some mythical golden age where the ethical dilemmas and contradictions of modern life either did not exist or were dealt with in black and white terms of right and wrong, of cricket and not cricket. What really makes cricket so fascinating as an area of jurisprudential and ethical study is that all of this is false. There have always been moral and ethical dilemmas in the game. There have always been 'sharp practices' and legal formalism from W.G. Grace to Sarfraz, and in today's world of full-time professional cricketers, umpires and the twin legal authority of instant replays and Match Referees. And there have always been those who see cricket as a sport played according to *Laws* and those who see it as a test of character involving ideals higher than rigid formalism. Each version of cricket is true and false at the same time. Each contains and must contain in order to remain coherent and consistent, its own interacting contradictions and inconsistencies. Out of these contradictions, we fashion our narratives and our 'knowledge' of cricket, law and the meaning of life.

The *Laws of Cricket* themselves enshrine and confirm the existence of another (higher?) narrative order. Law 42, as I have pointed out throughout this book, makes the captains 'responsible at all time for ensuring that play is conducted within the spirit of the game as well as within the Laws'. Cricket in its idealized form, and even as practised, is imbued in many instances with a quasi-religious invocation of a higher spirit which makes all its adherents better human beings. At its best and greatest political potential, it offers us a vision of the synthesis of the dialectical tension between Self and Other found in the fundamental contradiction inherent in law and adjudication.[1] It offers an example of the union of the individual and the team. It is a magical space and time which include, not only the 'best' of conventional social values but 'It offsets these values against the superior aspects of social life to provide a playful but serious critique of everyday life.'[2]

At the same time, of course, it does indeed teach and reinforce traditional ethical values in a non-dialectical non-transcendable way. It teaches, through its combination of formalism and ethics, the dangers of non-conformity, as Ian Meckiff discovered, even when the process of expulsion is itself tainted through the violation of 'due process' or 'fair play' norms. In effect, cricket teaches not a process-oriented (playing the game) ideal but a goal-orientation (expulsion, ostracism) for rule-violators, or at least for some rule-violators, depending on which rules they have broken and when. The inner circle of those who accept the norms are rewarded and encouraged by fair play, while the outsider suffers immediate judgement (no due-process for drug dealers or chuckers).[3]

Even at the basic ethical level, there is debate, uncertainty, ambiguity and contradiction. Some argue from an absolutist position that rule-violative behaviour is never morally acceptable and always places the violator 'outside' the normative paradigm of the sport. As we have seen, however, such a rule and moral absolutism is met by practical counter-narratives constructed by those who participate in the sport, for example the professional foul in soccer, the fist-fight in ice hockey, the occasional off-the-ball niggle in rugby. In these counter-narratives, rule-violative behaviour is often expected or even commanded by the interpretive community who 'know' that legal and moral formalism are only one side of a many-sided coin.[4] Again, the legal structures of many sports mirror this moral relativism. There are, in various football codes, for example, some fouls which are more serious than others and which can result in immediate expulsion. On the other hand, there are cases where a player is permitted a certain number of 'minor' transgressions before these are transformed, by way of a legal presumption, into a major offence. In soccer, two yellow cards equal a red card, but at the same time, a single offence may cause the referee to issue an immediate expulsion order. In basketball, perhaps the best example, a player may commit multiple (five or six) transgressions before being banished.

Sport in general and cricket in particular, teaches its participants many conflicting lessons about law and ethics, but these lessons are no different from the contradictory messages of other parts of popular culture or of law itself. While it may be true that '(s)porting youngsters are as likely to learn to cheat as they are to learn the spirit of fair play',[5] this is not, as the Denning narrative would have us believe, the result of the notorious influence of modernity and progress, of incomers disturbing the utopian rule of law in cricket and society, nor is it the result of a 'new professionalism'; nor, finally, is it the only lesson taught or learned. It is simply one lesson which has always been part of the contradictory ethical and moral nature of cricket and of Law.

The great Doctor Grace was not beyond standing on his rights under the *Laws* to have a batter run out while out of his crease patting down the pitch. Even such an ardent supporter of the spirit of the game and of Dr Grace as Neville Cardus was forced to concede that Grace was nothing more on occasion than a product of his time and that those times did not always produce perfect citizens. Cardus had to admit that all Victorians, W.G. included, had 'a bit of fraud' about them and that, in fact, Grace was 'too clever to cheat'.[6] Ashis Nandy, an advocate both of 'true' cricket and its dialectical usefulness in creating an alternative view of society, quotes C.B. Snow on Grace:

> He was a cheat on and off the cricket field. He exhibited the exact opposite of... virtues: including meanness, trickery, and, perhaps, oddest of all, physical cowardice.[7]

> Grace was not alone, nor was his the only era of sharp practices, ethical laxity and legal formalism as a mask for personal and public immorality.

And one might add, as long as there have been imprecations to follow the spirit of the game there have been those, like Grace, Sarfraz, Hurst, Ranatunga or Chappell who have invoked the code of legal formalism. And equally, we might add, such acts have been met with applause *and* condemnation.

Finally, one might add, as long as there have been laws and law-breakers, there have been heroes and outlaws. As long as there have been ethical norms, there have been saints and sinners, the holy and the heretic, and it is often difficult to distinguish between the two or to know what criteria to use in reaching a judgement about where any individual or act might be placed in the ethical and legal taxonomy. The same Australian cricket crowd that makes folk-heroes of Dennis Lillee, Merv Hughes and Brett Lee and screams for more as their deliveries pitch short and break an arm, will jeer Richie Benaud for successfully appealing against West Indies' batter Joe Solomon whose cap had fallen off and disturbed the wicket.[8] They will pack the streets of Melbourne to participate in a ticker-tape parade to farewell Sir Frank Worrell's team. The crowd will cheer the bouncer barrage and yet applaud the opposing batter as he reaches his century and as he leaves the field upon his dismissal. The players will 'sledge' and bowl bouncers and barge into the opposing player as he takes a single but they will also join in the applause as he reaches his 100 and no one will see a contradiction in any of this. The practice of sledging offers a classic and illustrative example of many of the legal and ethical contradictions which make up the complex textual practice of cricket.

22 You... – sledging and cricket as ethical discourse

'Sledging', the practice of talking to or at a batter or fielder, of howling insults and racist jibes, is an apparently essential part of cricket practice. While Law 42(6)of the 1980 *Code* made it a part of unfair play if 'any Player of the fielding side incommodes the Striker by any noise or action while he is receiving a ball', umpires rarely, if ever, intervened. 'Sledging' also occurred outside the limits of the *Laws*, i.e. it occurred *not* just when the batter was receiving the ball but before and after. While it is almost clearly illegal, sledging is a current and 'accepted' ethical practice in some cricket circles. From weekend games to the international arena, sledging is and has been a 'part of the game', just another aspect of the 'friendly' psychological warfare between the two sides of manly men. Others see it as a totally unacceptable, illegal and immoral behaviour which must be stamped out. With the ever-increasing presence of on-field microphones and cameras, zoom lenses etc., what was historically part of the confrontation between players in the 'private' realm of play, has become part of the publicly accessible information for all spectators. As the game becomes more and more image-conscious, in part due to marketing and commercial pressures and practices, administrators and officials have become more and more aware that many aspects of 'sledging' and associated practices are now detrimental to the 'game' in the larger sense.

Thus, response in this area, as in other formerly unregulated or self-regulated parts of the legal regime of cricket, has been to juridify the game. More law and more order are the order of the day. The 2000 *Code* of *the Laws of Cricket* contains new anti-sledging provisions. Law 42(4), as with many of the amendments to the *Laws* dealing with the various offences of unfair play includes new remedial powers for the umpires. Sledging, if we place our faith in the wording of the legislative text, will not be regulated from now on by the inherent agreements among participants about what the parameter of acceptable behaviour is or should be, but by umpires who may penalize offenders.

It is unfair for any member of the fielding side deliberately to distract the striker while he is preparing to receive or receiving a delivery.

(a) If either umpire considers that any action by a member of the fielding side is such an attempt, at the first instance he shall

(i)   immediately call and signal Dead ball
(ii)   warn the captain of the fielding side that the action is unfair and indicate that this is a first and final warning
(iii)   inform the other umpire and the batsmen of what has occurred.

Neither batsman shall be dismissed from that delivery and the ball shall not count as one of the over.

(b)   If there is any further such deliberate attempt in that innings, by any member of the fielding side, the procedures, other than warning, as set out in (a) above shall apply. Additionally, the umpire at the bowler's end shall

(i)   award 5 penalty runs to the batting side . . . .
(ii)   inform the captain of the fielding side of the reason for this action and, as soon as practicable, inform the captain of the batting side.
(iii)   report the occurrence, together with the other umpire, as soon as possible to the Executive of the fielding side and any Governing Body responsible for the match, who shall take such action as is considered appropriate against the captain and the player and players concerned.[1]

Once again we find a further legislative norm not just juridifying the content of play in the game of cricket, but reinforcing the idea that a captain must bear moral and legal responsibility for fair play by his team.

Of course, this legal provision does not encompass all the incidents and actions which we would enter into the taxonomy 'sledging'. It is temporally limited to the time at which a batter is preparing to receive or is receiving a delivery. It is limited to members of the fielding side.[2] Thus, verbal abuse hurled at a batter before he takes guard for example would not fall under a strict reading of the prohibition, nor would words spoken as he is completing a run, or after he has been dismissed, nor are words or gestures which are addressed from either batter to the bowler or any other member of the fielding side. Yet we know that such confrontations can and do occur as part of the way in which the game is played. Steve Waugh's perhaps apocryphal comment to Herschelle Gibbs after the South African had dropped an easy catch, inquiring how it felt to have cost his team the World Cup, for example, would be a classic example of a 'sledge' not covered by Law 42(4), yet would have all the intended consequences sledging is meant to achieve. In that incident, Gibbs appeared to have taken an easy catch to dismiss Waugh, but dropped the ball in attempting an early and over-hasty celebration of the fall of a key wicket.[3]

Michael Henderson wrote

What a fool Gibbs made of himself. In future he may be more prudent. There is far too much of this indiscriminate hurling of the ball when a catch has been taken, or, in this case, not. It serves little purpose except to remind the batsman, in a showy way, that he is out.[4]

There are two sanctions here. First, the catch is not taken and the batter lives to fight on. Secondly, the internal hermeneutic practices of cricketers are embodied. The throwing of the ball in the air can be seen either and both as a celebration and or as a 'sledge'. The batter is sent on his way, having been shown in no uncertain terms that he is out. Waugh's alleged riposte is exactly that, a reply to the fielder's sledge. It is the tit for tat, the give and take of the essential and formative confrontation between bat and ball which is cricket. It is playing the game and establishing the parameter of acceptable practice through practice.

Yet many such acts, gestures and comments are now apparently covered under the provisions of the *Code of Conduct*. Thus, it is a Level 1 offence for a player caught

> Using language that is obscene, offensive or insulting and/or the making of an obscene gesture[5]

Or

> Pointing or gesturing towards the pavilion in an aggressive manner by a bowler or other member of the fielding side upon the dismissal of a batsman.[6]

Level 2 offences include

> Using language that is obscene, offensive or of a seriously insulting nature to another player, umpire, referee, Team Official or spectator.[7]

Threats or abuse which would fall under general legal norms of racial and other vilification constitute Level 3 offences and more serious examples of similar actions are Level 4 infractions.[8]

Interestingly, even the *ICC Code of Conduct* contains a specific recognition that 'sledging' or repartee on the field are an essential part of the game. Article 2.9 adds

> It is acknowledged that there will be verbal exchanges between players in the course of play. Rather than seeking to eliminate these exchanges entirely, umpires will look to lay charges when this falls below an acceptance (sic) standard. In this instance, language will be interpreted to include gestures.

This provision raises some intriguing questions of statutory interpretation. First, because this 'explanatory memorandum' is included in the text of the prohibition, it must, one could argue, have both a substantive and interpretive function.

Secondly, because it is found in Article 2.9, one must ask whether it is of general or specific application. In other words, is the idea of permitting some verbal exchanges limited only to Level 2 offences or does it apply equally to the prohibited conduct in Levels 1, 3 and 4 as well? Thirdly, does the extension of the definition of language to include the non-verbal semiotics of cricket extend again to the offences created in the other sections of the *Code of Conduct* or does it apply only to Level 2 offences?

Whatever response ICC Match Referees or judges called upon in cases of potential judicial review will give to these questions, the most important aspect of Article 2.9 is the recognition that it accords to the hermeneutic and juridical practices of interpreting the game according to the norms of those who play it. Exchanges will not be prohibited but limited. Those which fall below or outside the 'acceptance' standard will be punished. Here of course, we will confront the basic and ongoing conflict of interpretations which informs almost all of cricket jurisprudence. Who sets and who interprets and applies, in theory and practice, the acceptable and unacceptable?[9] Players clearly in most instances have some notion of the boundary between what can be and what should not be said on the field. This applies not just to cricket but to other sports as well. For example, at the beginning of the 2002 Australian Rules season, the game was rocked by a scandal as Melbourne captain Wayne Carey admitted to an affair with Anthony Stevens' wife. Stevens was Carey's friend and teammate. He was also the vice-captain. Carey resigned. There are several interesting aspects to the Carey case which could be applied to the interpretive context of cricket, especially Australian men's cricket. Carey's offence here was not that he committed adultery and thereby offended some strict Australian morality. Instead, it was that he committed adultery with the wife of a friend and teammate. He broke the rules of 'mateship'.

But what is most directly apposite for discussions here is the fact that other players in the AFL made it crystal clear that any on field references to the affair, i.e. sledging, were strictly off limits. From a sport which has had several well-known public incidents of racial abuse in the recent past, this might seem somewhat contradictory and problematic. And of course it is. But the essential fact remains that the players themselves set and determined as part of the social and legal practice of playing the game exactly what was and was not acceptable sledging.[10]

The same might well obtain in cricket. Similarly, individual umpires might be more or less sensitive to different types of abuse, accepting or condemning behaviour in a manner which might well be inconsistent between and among the community of umpires. A similar situation might well also evolve in the next jurisdictional level of adjudication, between and among Match Referees. Again, some might be more or less tolerant. Consistency in adjudication is a hallmark not just of the rule of law but of our understanding of good umpiring in the practice of cricket adjudication. Commentators and fans, as well as players, are frustrated when an umpire makes what they believe to be a 'bad' or 'wrong' decision, but they are even more upset when an umpire makes inconsistent decisions. If he decides in a consistent manner not to give LBW decisions because he believes the bounce of the pitch makes such adjudication uncertain, bowlers may be unhappy when an apparently good appeal is turned down, but they will be even more concerned if, when their side is batting, the same appeals are given.[11]

At the same time, of course, consistency requires that like be treated alike. Context may change, tempers may flair for a variety of reasons and good umpires and competent Match Referees will be judged according to how sensitive they are to those contextual elements.[12] An Australia/England Ashes match, or a Test between India and Pakistan, or a confrontation between a fast bowler and a top batter might and do all generate tension and conflict. Tension might arise because of a perceived breach of the *Laws* or spirit of the game. A batter who refuses to walk, for example, after a fielder has claimed a catch, if given not out by the umpire or after a replay, might well 'deserve' a send off if and when his wicket falls. Similarly, the historical and geographical dimensions of the game will also require sensitivity and context. While Rudi Koertzen may well be able to detect sledging in Afrikaans from a South African player, umpire Venkat may not. Australians for example are almost universally convinced that Urdu abuse is a constant part of their tours to parts of the subcontinent but most umpires and Match Referees would be hard pressed, in the absence of Berlitz for cricket judges, to detect the difference between ordinary chat between teammates and unacceptable abuse addressed at a batter.

Two examples of the context in which such cases will and should be judged points out the complexity of deciding the level and type of judicial intervention which might be appropriate or required if there is to be a balance between formal and informal mechanisms of rule-making and rule-application in cricket. During the 1999/2000 season in Australia, the visiting Pakistanis were involved in hard fought and sometimes bitter matches with the home side. Events at home, including a military coup and the removal of the PCB by the government and ongoing bribery allegations and investigations did not lighten the mood.[13] At the end of the Test series, the Pakistanis went home and were scheduled to return for the triangular One-Day series in the new year. There was press speculation at the time that they would in fact not come back to Australia because they were intending to protest about Australian sledging in the Test series. Reaction in Australia was as expected one of denial and also one which emphasized the importance of context, 'The Australians had plenty to say, but Waqar Younis, for one, is believed to have given plenty back.'[14]

This is a typical Australian response to sledging allegations and debates. On the one hand 'we' do not sledge and at the same time the other side is just as bad. The most important aspect of the Australian replies to sledging issues however is the insistence that sledging is part of the game as played. Included in this construction of the practice of sledging is the idea that cricketers themselves sort things out on the field or after play and the intervention of the law is unwarranted and unwelcome.[15] This does not mean that Australians in general or cricketers in particular believe that there are no limits to on field behaviour and verbal exchange. It means that a dominant Australian interpretation of sledging relies on democratic, participatory rule-making and enforcement mechanisms. Fortunately or unfortunately, the world cricket community and the ICC appear to have rejected this view. What remains to be seen is the balance which might still be struck by umpires and Match Referees between the necessary interactions of players on the field and unnecessary, and therefore illegal, behaviour.

One case from the 2002 visit to South Africa by Australia offers an early illustration of the potential development of a contextualized jurisprudence of sledging. This followed the 'whitewash' triumph of the all-conquering Australians in the series between the countries in Australia in late 2001. South Africa introduced new blood into their side, including 20-year-old batter Graeme Smith. In May 2002, Smith wrote about the unending barrage of sledging directed at him by the Australians. He claims to have been threatened with physical injury, and told he was 'not f—ing good enough' to be on the field before he had taken strike for the first time. He also wrote that 'All Warne does is call you a c—all day.'[16]

There are several intriguing and informative points about the evolving practice and jurisprudence of sledging. First, Smith is willing to break '... the traditional reluctance of elite players to bring on-field sledging incidents into the public domain.'[17]

This is, as we have already seen, an ongoing debate and dilemma in this and other arenas of cricket and the law. The fragility of the public/private distinction, the willingness or reluctance to bring issues into a broader hermeneutic circle, private and manly dispute resolution, what happens on the field should stay on the field are themes which continue to dominate part of the issue here. At the same time, we have the ongoing confirmation that Australians seem to lead the world of cricket jurisprudence in this particular domain. We also see yet again that the part of sledging discourse, if not its central function, is an attack on the masculinity and therefore on the ability of a player. Smith was told he was not good enough to be part of men's business. The 'c' word is again deployed to mark the object of exclusionary discourse as a 'woman', as a lack, as an absence, as Other in the world of elite cricket. Finally, we look at this comment from Smith: 'And I remember looking at [umpire] Rudi Koertzen and he just shrugged his shoulders as if to say, "I know it's rough kid, but that's the way it is".'[18]

Accordingly, we get some idea at least that for one umpire, the 'acceptance' level includes the use of obscenities and sexist vulgarity. It is a rough world out there and Smith believes that he was told to grow up and accept it. Steve Waugh defended his team against the allegations by stating that there was an ICC *Code of Conduct* and had his players breached it, they would have been reported by the umpires.[19] Ricky Ponting, captain of the One-Day side, and later Glenn McGrath, invoked the public/private distinction and the unwritten code that what happens on the field stays on the field.[20] Smith rejected Ponting's assertion and stated that he believed in a different construction of the public/private distinction and in the idea of membership in cricket's hermeneutic and adjudicative community. On the rule that on-field statements should remain between the players, Smith said:

I'm not aware of any agreement about that. Why should on-field exchanges be kept secret from the public? Cricket is a spectator sport and the paying public have every right to know the details of what is said.[21]

Ponting argued that complaints about sledging from Smith and his teammate Justin Ontong were grounded in 'cultural differences' between what is acceptable in Australian cricket and what South Africans might be willing to tolerate. Michael Bevan makes a simple assertion that Australians play within the rules of the game and if they did not, the system of umpires and Match Referees would have punished them.[22] Smith retorted that the Australians could not take what they dished out and McGrath alleged that Smith was himself an active sledger. At the same time Ponting asserted that while 'friendly banter' and 'gamesmanship' were acceptable, 'personal attacks' were unacceptable and he as captain would not tolerate such incidents. Exactly where 'I'm going to f—ing kill you' fits in this scheme of things is so far undecided.[23] Of course, by writing as he did about his experiences, Smith is indicating that for some members of the interpretive community, the 'acceptance' standard is not the same as for others. For Glenn McGrath, Smith's position in the hermeneutic community is determined by his relative inexperience. Not only did he breach the unwritten rule which Australians insist must inform practice in this area, but his rights as a player in only a 'handful of games' means that either that he has no authority to speak or that what he says must not be accepted.[24] In other words, the interpretive community itself is one in which an authority and authorization based in hierarchy must be recognized and upheld. Smith, as the newcomer, must go through his masculine rites of passage and bear up to abuse like a man. By speaking out about that abuse, he has been refused admission into the group of international cricketers. What is, can and should be, said on the field is here up for grabs subject to ongoing and democratic contestation and determination. Sledging is indeterminate. Indeed, it is possible to imagine that had Smith succeeded in weathering the storm of abuse against him, and gone on to score runs and cement a place in the side, the nature of the sledging would have changed. He would have been seen to have passed the manhood test at some stage and the idea that he was not 'f—ing good enough' would have disappeared. Now that he has gone public and betrayed the private nature of cricket's masculinity totem, one can only wonder what kind of sledging he has exposed himself to in the future. Again, all that we can know is that sledging in form and content is indeterminate and as flexible as the multiplicity of circumstances available to sledgers, and open to interpretation by 'sledgees' and umpires. The practice of adjudication will, indeed must be, as indeterminate and fixed as the practice of the participants in the community permits.

The jurisprudence of sledging, taking into account the contextualization recognized by Article 2.9, will only evolve and be accepted if such interpretive and legal subtleties become part of the practice and process of adjudication. For the most part, reported cases since the introduction of the *Code of Conduct* and Match Referee system seem to involve either obvious heated exchanges between players or 'send offs' directed at departing batters. Such cases seem to pose few problems in so far as the written text regulating sledging and related practices is concerned. Public 'argy bargy' would clearly be seen by most to 'bring the game into disrepute'. Section 1.6 of the *Code of Conduct* clearly forbids 'pointing or gesturing towards the pavilion' upon dismissal. When Shane Warne and Merv Hughes were fined and reprimanded for verbal abuse of South African batters in a Test match at Johannesburg in 1994, for example, no one was particularly surprised or outraged. Phil Wilkins wrote

> Warne's volley of abuse of Andrew Hudson (60) as the opener left the wicket after being bowled around his legs was completely out of order and warranted the strongest disciplinary action.[25]

In 1995, Chris Lewis of England was fined in an Ashes Test after gesturing Craig McDermott of Australia to the pavilion, Brian Strang of Zimbabwe was found guilty of the same offence in a One-Day International against Pakistan, and Pakistanis Nazir and Aqib Javed were found guilty of making offensive gestures following the dismissals of opposing batters.[26] That same year, Kerry Walmsley of New Zealand was reprimanded for audible bad language on the field of play and fellow New Zealander Roger Twose was found to have verbally abused Sanjay Manjrekar of India for claiming a catch after crossing the boundary.[27]

Further, Asanka Gurusinghe of Sri Lanka was reprimanded for comments made to an opposing player during a game against Australia in the following year.[28] Ijaz Ahmed of Pakistan and Adam Huckle and Alastair Campbell of Zimbabwe were penalized in 1997 for abusing outgoing batters.[29] In 1998, Paul Adams of South Africa was caught on video replay by the third umpire giving a send off to a batter. That same year, Ricky Ponting of Australia and Harbhajan Singh engaged in a confrontation after Ponting was dismissed and both were cited. Glenn McGrath was given a suspended fine for verbally abusing Alan Mullaly at the MCG.[30] McGrath was again hauled before the Match Referee in 1999 for spitting in the direction of a West Indian player. The suspended fine was imposed. Shoaib Akhtar was fined for crude and abusive language after dismissing a batter, while Alastair Campbell was again cited for abusing his opponents, as were his teammates Neil Johnson and Murray Goodwin.[31] Guy Whittall and Lance Klusener of Zimbabwe and South Africa and Craig McMillan and Shaun Pollock, of New Zealand and South Africa, were all found guilty following on field confrontations in 2000.[32]

Even this brief recitation of sledging-related incidents since the introduction of the *Code of Conduct* indicates that the phenomenon has been and continues to be part of the game. Even in the presence of specific and general prohibitions, regulating and forbidding the conduct, players continue to sledge. Bowlers send batters on their way, players stand toe to toe on the field. I am not suggesting here that the behaviour is somehow acceptable. What I do believe is clear is that for some members of the hermeneutic community of cricket and the law such actions are accepted as part of the game. There is then, at some level at least a conflict between the written legal text and practice. This might indicate that the law is at odds with the ethical practice of the game, or it might indicate that the practice of the game is in such instances both illegal and unethical. The existence of robbery does not indicate a general acceptance of theft. At the same time of course, even a more detailed and careful analysis of cricket jurisprudence in relation to sledging will not tell the whole story. There will always be the unexplored yet omnipresent reality of sledging at the local levels of the game.[33] There will, or should be, the largely unwritten law under the *Code of Conduct*, of sledging exchanges on the field which are judged by the umpires to be within the realm of 'acceptance'. Umpires like Rudi Koertzen will shrug at players like Smith and tell him to get on with 'playing the game'. There will also be cases where, for whatever reason, the umpires and Match Referee do not in fact intervene but other regulatory bodies, such as the player's board will impose a sanction. In the Sharjah Cup final in Nov. 2001, Shoaib Akhtar sledged Mahela Jayawardena of Sri Lanka. The previous ball had been sent to the boundary by the batter and upon dismissing the Sri Lankan Shoaib was over-enthusiastic. Match Referee Denis Lindsay took no action but the Disciplinary Committee of the PCB investigated their bowler's conduct.[34] Finally, there will be the continuing insistence, both within and outside the *Code of Conduct* and the *Laws of Cricket*, that sledging is and must be, part of the game and subject only, or mostly, to self-regulation.

Those who have historically seen sledging as part of the game, as recognized in part by the *Code of Conduct*, nonetheless recognize that there are ways in which self-regulation can accomplish more effectively the goals of those who wish to impose an external form of regulation on the game. In other words, the players can take care of the sledging problem themselves. As Ian Chappell explains, 'Any batsman who is even slightly interested in putting up a fight for his wicket will back away from the crease if he's being harassed by a close fieldsman.'

For Chappell, then, the confrontation is between the fielders and the batter. It is open to the striker to silence his opponents simply by exerting interpretive control over the game. If he is unready to bat, he backs away, proceedings come to halt and recommence only if and when the sledging ceases or he becomes comfortable with what is happening and can ignore it.

Not only can this form of self-regulation in itself be effective, but it can also serve as a means to involve the judiciary (the umpire) without having to make a formal complaint. The batter who backs away '...will warn (the umpire) that trouble may be brewing. If the fieldsman continues the conversation, he'll draw a swift reprimand.'[35]

In such a case, because the umpire 'knows' that the striker has left the crease for a reason, that interpretive knowledge which comes from the fact of his membership in the 'interpretive community' will cause him to intervene 'informally' so that justice may be done and the game may proceed. All of this occurs without the spectators, commentators, or home listeners and viewers necessarily being aware of what is happening, indicating that, as lawyers already know, one of the key values of 'informal justice' mechanisms is the element of privacy and secrecy.

Australian theory and jurisprudential practice are informative here. Australian Test captain Steve Waugh was highly critical of the introduction of new legal measures to limit and restrict 'sledging'. One of the main arguments presented here was one which disputes the very existence of 'sledging' as an unacceptable violation of the ethical norms and standards of cricket. For Waugh and many Australians, what others call 'sledging' he sees as part of an overall tactic and strategy of 'mental disintegration' aimed at opponents.[36] From aggressive batting, to wicket-taking field placings, and attacking bowling, Australia aims to overwhelm the opposition and to win the psychological battle of cricket.[37] Sledging is merely part of an overall practice of winning cricket. It is nothing more morally unacceptable than 'Vicious sarcasm, witty ripostes, psychological one-upmanship and just plain trouble-stirring...'[38]

To legislate to stamp out these practices would be not just to change the way the normative standards of the game have been determined, created and interpreted by the players in the practical context of playing the game, but it would diminish and perhaps change the very character of the game, by removing 'character' from the game. On this view, the confrontation between the sides is a contest for superiority of physical and mental skill and toughness; it is, as it has always been, about character and manliness.[39]

Again, many who reject the Australian view of sledging and argue for its abolition and for the increased regulation now found in the *Laws* and the *Code of Conduct*, do so at the level of both legality and morality. They urge umpires to enforce the letter of the law and go so far as to advocate the introduction of soccer's system of yellow and red cards to deal with sledgers.[40] At the same time they invoke concepts of gentlemanly behaviour and the spirit of the game. Their moral, ethical and ideological sub-textual point of reference usually revolves around a contrast between the ethical practices of the 'golden age' and today's immoral 'professionalism'. They choose to ignore or forget the fact that in reality W.G.'s elder brother, Dr E.M. Grace, was notorious for chattering in order to distract batters. Although some would argue that today's version of sledging is qualitatively different from such 'sharp practices', it would appear that the difference is more of a quantitative kind and that the quantity is in part at least determined by our technological capacities.[41] This must once more naturally raise the basic question as to whether more law is, or indeed can be, the answer.

Nowadays, Australians are perceived to be the most noted practitioners of sledging.[42] The rise in the practice is generally attributed to Ian Chappell's captaincy. (It is worth noting that this was also a period of international success for Australian cricket. This could mean that sledging nourished success, or it could it mean that opponents raised the issue because they were losing.) A review of the history of adjudication and of the developing jurisprudence of sledging under the *ICC Code of Conduct* appears to confirm the accepted wisdom. It should be noted, however, that any detailed analysis of this case law would need to be based on a subtle and contextualized analysis grounded in a firmly established taxonomy. For example, when Michael Atherton was reprimanded by Match Referee Singh during a controversial Test in Kandy, he was found to have engaged in a verbal exchange with both the Sri Lankan wicketkeeper and then with umpire Rudi Koertzen. Part of his offence could be defined as 'sledging' while part of it would equally be seen to fall within the idea of 'dissent'. When Glenn McGrath was fined for violating the 'foul language' provisions of the *Code of Conduct* at Bangalore in March 2001, he addressed the language at, or employed it in the presence of, the umpire. That is not in these circumstances what would be considered to fall under the definition of sledging. It is not my intention here to establish a complete epistemology of sledging. Instead, I simply wish to underline yet again the unavoidable necessity of context and care in legal analysis of the legal textual practices of cricket. Whatever the subtle points of difference and of parameter-setting, it does, to return to the point here, appear that Australia are, along with Zimbabwe, the worst offenders when it comes to what might be called sledging, in international cricket. The rest of the Test-playing countries fall somewhere below these standards with the West Indies and Bangladesh having the fewest convictions. Although the England touring team to that country in 2001 did officially complain of sledging in a tour match, Sri Lanka have been found guilty of only two sledging-type offences by ICC Match Referees.[43]

Yet, the controversial history of Sri Lankan and Australian confrontations serves to illustrate some of the many legal and ethical issues and contradictions which arose historically in the area of sledging. During the test between Sri Lanka and Australia at the Bellerive Oval in Hobart in Dec. 1989, Sri Lanka batter Rumesh Ratnayake ran into Australian fast bowler Greg Campbell while he was completing a run and Campbell was finishing his follow through. According to the Sri Lankans, Campbell had engaged in sledging and called Rumesh 'a black cunt'. Reactions after the Test, as reported in the media, illustrate the competing narrative and sub-textual interpretations which inform the legal and ethical debate over sledging.[44]

Sri Lankan captain Arjuna Ranatunga explained that he 'understood' the Australian attitude to sledging and racist remarks but that his team came as gentlemen and only got stronger as the other side behaved in an ungentlemanly way. The manager of the visiting team Nisal Seneratne applauded the general 'expressive' approach of the Australians to cricket and urged his team to adopt the same attitude. At the same time, he felt that sledging went too far. For him, it required the adoption of the soccer system of 'carding' players. He explained his views on good aggression *versus* sledging as follows:

> Aggression, even to an argument or a small brawl, could be admitted as an instance of ones blood rushing up.
>
> . . .
>
> But one could not condone any type of word which disturbs not only the player, but also his character.[45]

For Jeff Wells, the so-called 'professionalism' of sledging simply destroyed 'any tenets of decency that the game may once have clung to…'.[46] Australian officials saw things from a different perspective and therefore from a different set of 'facts'.

Australian captain, Allan Border, claimed to have heard no racist slurs and 'pompously'[47] dismissed events on the field as '...nothing different than what you'd expect in a red-blooded test match'.[48]

Here are encapsulated, again, the stark contrasts of the competing texts of cricket which dissolve into shades of grey. On the one hand, a nation of dark-skinned players visiting a nation of white-skinned players, a nation with a distinct and sordid history and current practice of racism. At the same time, we find an aristocratic brown-skinned man wondering why the Sri Lankans are complaining about being called 'black', when, in fact, they are.[49] All the complex issues of the psychology of racism come to the fore in a context which is, after all, just a game.

Those who bring to the game an urge to gentlemanly sportsmanship find themselves face to face with those to whom it is simply another red-blooded affair. This time, however, in a strange reversal of the history of colonialism and imperialism (*infra*), the 'gentlemen' are black.[50] But the gentlemanly code of conduct is only part of, and not inconsistent with, the virility cult of their opponents. Even the representative for the gentlemen does not decry aggression or even physical violence in the heat of the moment as contrary to the spirit of the game. A gentleman '...could not condone any type of word which disturbs not only the player, but also his character'.[51]

The virility cult and the spirit of the game coincide exactly at the juncture of the public and the private. An insult to one's character as a player ('you *slow-bowling cunt*') would apparently be an acceptable part of good healthy aggressive cricket because it would address issues relevant to one's performance and function *qua* player, in other words, one's *public* persona – that part of oneself one exposes as a price of entry into the interpretive community. Conversely, to attack an opponent's character, or fundamental private being ('you *black* cunt'), transgresses the norms of gentlemanly behaviour as it enters the area of the private realm.[52] It is not cricket because it is not relevant to cricket. Each appeal to the apparently universal norm of acceptability in the context of sledging, as in other areas of cricket and the law, is in fact a highly localized discursive practice.

One might wish to add two other interpretive factors into the mix. One is the apparent popularity of the 'c' word when professional male athletes, especially Australians, engage in sledging. This is, according to Graeme Smith of South Africa, an ongoing trait of Australian sledging. The semiotics and gender politics at play here are fascinating and complex, and fit quite clearly into the historical constructions of Australian masculinity and the cult of virility within cricket.

Secondly, one might also want to engage in an extended history of Arjuna Ranatunga, batter, captain and present day Sri Lankan politician if we wish to arrive at a more complete understanding of the ideal of the gentlemanly status of Sri Lankan cricket then and now.

In any event, the call for respect for the spirit of the game is almost always accompanied by a call for further legal regulation of those who offend. The normative discourses of law and the spirit of the game are, here at least, not incommensurable. Statements bemoaning the death of the spirit of the game ignore history and ignore the complex interrelationship between law and ethical behaviour on the one hand (e.g. sledging) and the apparently complete and utter disjunction between the two narratives in other instances (e.g. *Mankading*). Of course, under the *Code of Conduct*, the language allegedly employed by the Australians against their Sri Lankan opponents, if proved, would constitute a serious breach and at the very least would be a Level 3 offence, for which the penalty, 'shall be' a ban of between two to four Tests or four to eight One-Day Internationals.

And yet the aggressive gentlemen are not the only ones capable of invoking a higher moral or legal tone. Turning defence into attack, Australian coach Bob Simpson urges the Sri Lankans to put their proof to the test, '. . . because it is a very serious slur on the character of our players. It is an easy charge to lay.'[53]

Almost instantaneously, the alleged perpetrators occupy the high ground. Fair play *and* the rule of law demand that their reputations be cleared! In a further reversal of the moral order of things, the public/private distinction and the normative practices of the interpretive community are turned in full force against the 'victim'. Ranatunga, like Smith, but not for the first or last time, has violated the unwritten 'code of silence', he is an outcast, a traitor, because he has 'squealed'. Not only does such conduct violate the cult of virility whereby one is supposed to suffer in silence, to *take it like a man*, but the public statement violates the *private* nature of the alleged offence and apparent disagreement.[54] It should be settled by the players themselves according to their own decision-making and narrative structures and not in the press by *outsiders*. In this case, as more recently in the Smith case, the players clearly perceive themselves as the authoritative interpreters and seek to exclude all others from the hermeneutic circle. This is a consistent, and perhaps democratic, normative test invoked in debates about sledging and the law and politics of regulation in cricket.

In 1997, Brian Lara publicly accused the Australian side of engaging in 'all day sledging' against West Indian batter Robert Samuels, during a Test in Perth. The problem here was again situated at two levels. There was some debate and disagreement about the degree and seriousness of the offence. For the Australians whatever happened was part of what it means to play cricket. The more serious point of contention was over Lara's remarks which were public. The idea of player self-regulation as the normative and deontological context in which such issues are debated and determined had been attacked and undermined by Lara doing something which for the Australians just was 'not cricket'. Shane Warne spoke of his disappointment over his former friend's outburst.

> They say things to us. You don't hear us coming out saying they got stuck into a young bloke playing his first couple of games.
>
> It's sport and you play and if you think the odd jibe can help get a guy out or whatever well fine. That's all part and parcel of it. Everyone who's played sport knows it happens.
>
> If you've got a problem with it or you think someone's gone too far you pull them aside after the game over a beer or whatever and say 'mate, you're going a bit far'. You sort it out there.
>
> You don't come out and say what he said. That was disgraceful.[55]

The alleged perpetrators of the substantive offence are once again placing themselves in the position of the victims of an even more grave breach of normative standards. Cricket is a manly game, an encounter of give and take. It is also, at some level, a private battle. What happens on the pitch stays on the pitch. Mateship, the friendly settling of disputes over a post-game beer, these are the ethical *grundnorms* of cricket and sledging. One does not, if one is a man and a cricketer, which are here indistinguishable, whinge and whine in public.

This was not the only time that Brian Lara's idea of the appropriate normative and ethical content of the rules of sledging and his belief in the appropriate legal regulatory mechanism to deal with apparent breaches of the substantive norms would bring him into conflict with Australian legal ideology and practice. When Glenn McGrath was fined for spitting in a Test match against the Windies, Lara as captain complained directly to the Match Referee. The Australians were outraged. For them, Lara had once more taken the formal law into his own hands. Steve Waugh argued

> It was definitely handled the wrong way, there's no doubt about that.... It should have gone through the right channels. If you've got a complaint you make it via your manager to the match referee.[56]

Here one might take Waugh literally and see his objection as purely procedural. At the same time, given the history of relations with Lara, and the context of Australian attitudes about manly confrontation on the field, it might be possible to read Waugh's comments as containing the implicit idea that Lara's complaint should not have gone at all to the Match Referee but should have been settled between the sides. The West Indies' manager was former captain Clive Lloyd. Lloyd could have been seen by Waugh and the Australians coming from 'the old school' world of manly men and friendly post-match drinks as an alternative dispute resolution mechanism. Under this reading, Lara would have complained to Lloyd, Lloyd would have approached the Australian team, McGrath would have said 'sorry mate', and the matter would have been settled in an informal manner.[57]

Once more, of course, it is always possible to tell a different, equally plausible and true story about sledging and its analogues. In this narrative, displays of slanging and verbal disputes on the field may be experienced by 'the victims' not as an effective attack on them, but rather as clear evidence of the perpetrator's weakness. In the final One-Day International between the West Indies and Australia in 1991, for example, several incidents took place where words were exchanged. The Australians took a positive view and felt that such events

> ... are a symptom that the West Indies are feeling uncomfortable under the sort of pressure which enabled Australia to complete a crushing 4–1 defeat on the home side in the one-day series.[58]

In each and every one of these cases, all the stories we tell about sledging in cricket are true and all the facts are real. ICC Match Referees and umpires are now under a legal obligation, imposed by the *Laws of Cricket*, the playing regulations and the *Code of Conduct*, not just to punish and deter such conduct, but to determine the parameter in which such conduct may lawfully occur.

Finally, one can also detect in more recent debates about sledging a change in both tone and content of the idea of appropriate conduct, of settling scores between players and identifying the victim of a particular sledging-related incident. In his autobiography, former Sri Lankan player Roshan Mahanama accused Australian bowler Glenn McGrath of having called Sanath Jayasuriya a 'black monkey' during a One-Day game at the SCG in 1995–96,[59] McGrath issued a heated denial. Jayasuriya apparently confirmed his former teammate's claims.[60] Again we find accusations that Australian sledging of Sri Lankan opponents was racially based. Not only do such activities violate the now clear provisions of the *ICC Code of Conduct*, they probably violate Australian law as well.[61] Moreover, at some level one would like to believe that they are contrary to the spirit of the game, although such an assertion may founder on the available empirical evidence. But whatever the case, the Australian reaction to the claims is instructive of some possible hermeneutic and legal changes to our understandings of sledging and cricket discourse.

The ACB issued a denial of the allegations 'in the strongest possible terms'. The official position is that the incident did not take place but that the ACB is and will remain committed to policies and practices aimed at stamping out racial abuse. Gone are the days of when what is said on the field stays on the field and associated assertions of the 'private' nature of such activities. The ACB is in agreement with socially accepted and government-mandated ideas of intolerance for intolerance. The public/private split has been redefined as has the substantive content of acceptable discourse. And at the same time, cricket practice here has been juridified. The ACB claimed in McGrath's defence that there was no evidence supporting the claim in part because neither the umpires nor the Match Referee had filed an official report verifying the complaint. Here then we find a new characteristic part of cricket as a social, historical and legal practice. If there is no report, no legal text, there is no 'event'. Here the absence of legal 'proof' is equated with the absence of 'reality', surely a problematic development. Moreover, one might add generally yet another reference here to the specific provisions of the current *Code of Conduct* dealing with sledging. Once more

> It is acknowledged that there will be verbal exchanges between players in the course of play. Rather than seeking to eliminate these exchanges entirely, umpires will look to lay charges when this falls below an acceptance standard.[62]

I am not suggesting here that McGrath made the statement alleged. Nor am I suggesting that any umpire today would find that such a statement, were it to be made, would not constitute a clear breach of the *Code*. Instead I want to underline the more general point that there will be things said which will not be reported. The Law, the *Code*, makes specific and explicit provision for this. Any general assertion that because a statement was not reported it was not made, because a fact is not reduced to law, it does not exist, is now legally and empirically incorrect.

Indeed, events and interpretive context become even more problematic and complex when one further investigates what the legal authorities at the time did or did not say and begins to make inquiries into the character of the accused. McGrath has been suspended from international cricket for misbehaviour and has multiple convictions. While none of his previous offences relates to sledging or racial abuse, he is known for his aggression and hot temper and his legal record confirms this. One might therefore, in any legal analysis of the case, at least raise the issue of whether such evidence is relevant or admissible in determining questions of either propensity or credibility. One of the umpires present on the day of the alleged offence was Peter Parker who is not reported to have denied that such statements were made. Instead he stated, as one would expect, that he himself did not witness or overhear such a statement.[63] Finally, the other umpire standing in the match, Steve Randell, was not interviewed. At the time he was in prison in Tasmania serving time for multiple convictions for sexual assault on pupils while he was schoolteacher. Serious issues of credibility may be raised concerning any account Randell might give.

In any event, 'black c—' and 'black monkeys' seem to be off the legal list of acceptable discourse. And Glenn McGrath sought legal advice concerning Mahanama's allegation. Once what is said or alleged to have been said on the field comes off the field it enters the domain of Australian defamation law. The interesting question, already addressed in part by Australian courts in previous litigation, would be whether it is defamatory to accuse an Australian cricketer of being a 'sledger' or whether an accusation of racism is required to bring his name into disrepute. Indeed, it might well be argued that accusing an Australian of being racist, or of racially abusing Sri Lankan cricketers, would not be an assertion which would lower or damage his reputation in the minds of the community.

While the normative hermeneutic context about and around sledging may be evolving as context and social practices, as well as legal norms themselves, are brought to bear, the limits of sledging will continue to be 'determined' by those for whom the spirit of the game is still invoked in each and every instance. And we continue to 'know' exactly what it means; or not.

23 Walking, the judicial function and the meaning of law

There are occasions when, in cricket, even a direct legal decision by an umpire is challenged by a player. The number of convictions recorded under the dissent provisions of the *ICC Code of Conduct* offers an indication of the existence of an ethos under which players are willing to dispute clear indications by the umpire that they were out.

On the other hand, there is in cricket an ethical practice which assumes that a batter who has 'nicked' the ball and who has been caught, should (*and must*) leave the crease and 'walk' back to the pavilion without waiting for an appeal or the umpire's decision.[1] While there are some minor legal questions involved, walking, in reality, poses in stark terms fundamental issues about the very existence of unwritten ethical norms in the text of cricket.

Sir Garfield Sobers writes in his autobiography that he always walked, although he does note that even in his time in the game the practice was far from universal.[2] Yet for him the moral code imposed on players by the spirit of the game compelled him not only to walk but also to condemn those who did not. He recounts a game in which Basil d'Oliveira of England refused to walk when the fielder indicated he had been caught.[3] For the rest of his stay at the crease, d'Oliveira was taunted by Sobers and maligned as a cheat. When he was finally out for 88, no member of the West Indies team applauded his efforts as he made his way back to the pavilion.

The ethical norm and correct sanction were clearly 'known' and invoked in this case. Sledging, which might otherwise have violated the same ethical code, became acceptable and even necessary to sanction d'Oliveira and to shame him as a transgressor.[4] Further sanction involved a kind of 'shunning' in which members of the community refuse to recognize or have intercourse with another member who has violated their norms. Thus, the Windies players refused to acknowledge d'Oliveira's fine spell at the crease, an event which for them was fundamentally tainted and not worthy of recognition because it was, in effect, not cricket.

But the practice of shunning by cricketers for those who fail to heed the moral command to walk is not as universal or unbending as the code of the Amish. As Sobers recounts in concluding his story, d'Oliveira joined the West Indies team for a drink after the match.

I have always believed that any disputes on the field of play should be forgotten when play finishes and that was the case this time. I offered Dolly a drink. Neither of us had any hard feelings.[5]

For both the transgressor and the moral guardian the sin of refusing to walk was a public one, committed on the field of play, against a code governing conduct in that space and for that time. When the public event was over, the sin was expurgated and could not, by definition, be attributed to the private individual.[6]

While for Sobers the code and its means of implementation were clear and he 'knew' what they meant, walking was not as he himself says, a universal ethical norm among cricketers, and others confirm his view. Yorkshire cricketers, for example, are notorious for developing their own esoteric code of conduct which has little to do with any ideal of general cricketing spirit. Sobers himself points out the different views of walking which compete for an interpretive acceptance. Some players will walk after they have made a century, some players will walk sometimes but not all the time, Australians hardly ever walk and Indians and Pakistanis never do.[7] According to others, the great Indian batter Sunil Gavaskar walked early in his career but in his later stages in the game, he opted to stay put and had to accept the moral consequences of his act.[8]

The debate and differences concerning the theory and practice of walking do not necessarily indicate disagreement between upholders of a high moral vision and lower order utilitarians, although this is sometimes the case. What is indicated most clearly is that even for those who would recognize and cherish the existence of a 'spirit of the game', there is no one overarching and binding interpretation of what that phrase 'means'. It also indicates that, besides the absence of a universal 'meaning' or social 'knowledge' of the code (text) by members of the interpretive community (and communities), there is clear-cut, moral and factual debate over each sub-textual element of the larger code. Many proponents of showing the ball before *Mankading* a batter or people who would condemn the Chappells for the underarm incident, would deny that there is *any* moral imperative for a batter to walk. Similarly, those who would impose on obligation to walk for an edge caught behind would never think of asking a batter to walk because he thought or 'knew' that a delivery that struck his pads had him LBW. Each sub-text, even for the self-defined moral purist, is highly contextualized and situated in an atmosphere informed by situational ethics and variegated historical practices.

One of the elements of the context, national traits, has already been signalled. Australians have a reputation for not being walkers. Some might wish to attribute this (if true) to a unique Australian character quirk, or to the desire to win at all costs, to the professionalism and larrikin behaviour which has always characterized Aussie cricket – in short, to an Australian immorality and cultural tendency to make heroes out of outlaws like Ned Kelly. But such explanations miss the key point of the complex and often contradictory nature of any cricket ethos. The case of Richie Benaud is a classic example. Benaud is commonly and widely acknowledged as one of Australia's greatest all-rounders, as one of its greatest captains, and the most articulate and knowledgeable commentator on the game today. It was Benaud who condemned Merv Hughes' bouncer attack on Tauseef and referred in less than flattering terms to the ethical propriety of the Chappell mullygrubber. Richie Benaud has to answer to none for his love of cricket and respect for its history and spirit.

It is the same Richie Benaud, however, who has confessed that during the Test at Lord's in 1954 he nicked a delivery from Fred Trueman and was caught behind before he had scored.[9] He did not walk, was given not out and went on to score 97 runs and to lead Australia to their first victory in England for eight years. Did Benaud cheat? Is he an immoral character who insulted the essence of cricket? Is he an ugly utilitarian who simply wanted to take every advantage for victory's sake?

Benaud would reject these claims and indeed, whether one agrees with the premises which inform his justification for not walking, one is forced to admit they are not totally amoral. For him, his failure to walk is for the most part informed by a legal (and ethical) positivism which was inculcated in him from his earliest cricket training.

> It had always been drummed in to me that as soon as an appeal is made I must look at the umpire and if he says 'out' or 'not out' I must obey that decision instantly and without any display of emotion.[10]

For Benaud, then, to walk would be counter-intuitive. His cricket training taught him to obey the Law without question and that the sole judge of legality was the umpire. This combination of moral training and legal positivism would make it impossible for Benaud to walk. To do so would violate the strict role division between player and umpire upon which many of the ethical norms of cricket depend. In addition to this ethical–legal explanation, however, Benaud offers a more causalistic one. He describes how on one occasion he *did* begin to walk, thinking the ball had struck his bat, only then realizing it had struck his shirt. But it was 'too late' for '. . . there is no going back once you have started to move'.[11]

What Benaud is arguing for here is a sort of 'levelling' from a batter's perspective. To walk is to risk a mistake for which another future mistake, the other way, may never come, leaving things unbalanced, not 'levelled'. On the other hand, to refuse to walk and stay in the crease, when given 'not out', even though one knows one *is* out, is to allow for the fact that there have been or will be other times when one was or will be given out in error. To stay put is to allow 'fate' to level things out. Gavaskar offered the same probabilistic (although mathematically incorrect) explanation for his refusal to walk.[12]

Such an attitude is not as utilitarian or self-justificatory as it may appear when one considers that the decision to walk or not to walk takes place in a highly confused and complex situation in which not even the 'facts' are what they appear to be, and one in which the discovery of the 'facts' is part of the same process of confusion and contextualization. In giving his decision for a caught-behind appeal, an umpire, who must and does employ his local knowledge and practical wisdom in adjudicating, may be influenced by the reputation and actions of the batter who may be known as 'a walker'. If the player stays put, the umpire might consider this as a factor in the final determination as to whether there was an edge. If, on the other hand, the batter is 'known' as one who *never* walks, the umpire might in the alternative ignore this fact and take no notice of his immobility, or he may decide that doubt should be decided against the batter who makes his job harder or who has had mistakes benefit him in the past. In such complex situations where a 'fact' may not be a 'fact', the ethos of walking is less clear than the moralistic defenders of the purity of the game would have us believe.

The situation becomes even more complex when the 'issue' over which there is factual doubt is not whether the batter touched the ball with his bat, but whether the fielder or wicketkeeper made the catch before the ball hit the ground. In many such cases, the umpire simply cannot see. Here, a double ethos is involved. It is incumbent upon the fielder to declare honestly if the ball 'carried'. If the answer is affirmative, the batter must walk without the benefit of a decision from the umpire, who, if technically and actually unsighted, will give the doubt to the batter. Sir Garfield Sobers clearly followed these moral strictures and condemned those who did not.[13] In the Centenary Test of 1977, Australian wicketkeeper Rod Marsh indicated that a ball hit by Derek Randall of England had not in fact carried and Randall was recalled to the crease after having been (incorrectly) given out by Umpire Tom Brocks. All this occurred when he was on 161. Thirteen runs later, Randall paid his own obeisance to the spirit of the game when he walked off after a bat-pad catch.[14]

During one of Australia's many Ashes victories in England in the past few years, the universality of this aspect of the spirit of cricket was again at the centre of debate. Eddie Hemmings, the English bowler and tail-ender, was apparently caught at third slip, off the bowling of Geoff Lawson, by Steve Waugh. Waugh maintained he made the catch, Hemmings stayed put, as umpires Shepherd and Plews 'were not convinced the ball had carried and could not confirm the catch'.[15] There was uproar as the Australians insisted that because Waugh acknowledged making the catch, Hemmings had a moral duty to walk. In these circumstances, to stay at the crease is not only to violate expected moral standards of the interpretive community but to, in effect, contest the veracity and trustworthiness of one's opponents. The outrage was exacerbated in this case because of another of the ethical sub-texts of the less-than universal ethos of walking. For some, one's moral duty to walk and to accept the truthfulness of the opposing fielder apparently increases as one's prowess as a batter decreases. Therefore, while a top-order batter might be morally justified in staying in the crease in such circumstances, a lower order player like spinner Hemmings, who, after all is in the game not to bat but to bowl, can make no such claim.[16]

Finally, yet another factual historical and cultural possible sub-text emerges. Without questioning Steve Waugh's actual integrity, it is plausible to posit that Hemmings may have refused to walk not only because he did not believe in, or choose to participate in, the ethos of walking, or because he adopted a pure positivism and leaves only when the umpire tells him to, but because there is 'evidence' in the culture, as part of the bank of interpretive 'facts' and 'knowledge' about playing cricket with Australians, that they 'claim' catches they have not made.

In the 1987–88 Test season, in a match at the MCG, Australian wicketkeeper Greg Dyer claimed a catch behind off Andrew Jones of New Zealand who was given out. Televised replays clearly showed Dyer had not made the catch. The Dyer incident itself contains many interpretive complexities. Because it took place against New Zealand it was immediately placed in the interpretive matrix of the Chappell mullygrubber as Kiwi newspaper headlines trumpeted: 'Jones dismissal has that underarm odour.'[17]

In light of this further interpretive complexity, to blindly accuse Hemmings in such circumstances of moral turpitude ignores a considered examination of all the confused and confusing 'facts' which make walking in particular, and the very existence of an epistemological universal 'game of cricket', in general, something about which we have not much knowledge at all.

Ian Chappell also adopts the view that a batter should never walk. For him, as for Benaud, there is a strict division of labour between players and umpires. Umpires are there to make decisions on appeals and it is up to them to reach this decision unaided. Thus, Chappell willingly condemns attempts to influence an umpire's decision, by rubbing the elbow or touching the thigh pad as either 'cheating', or as trying to make a fool of the umpire. Chappell also condemns those who might 'walk' after they have made a century but not before. If such a batter has developed a reputation as a 'walker' and he is subsequently 'out' on a duck, the umpire may be influenced by that reputation and refuse the appeal. Not only is the player's attitude inconsistent, but the umpire is clearly misinterpreting the 'facts'. In this case, the batter is not a 'walker', he is a 'walker after he has scored a century'. To reach a decision based on this reputation, or at least to be influenced by it, before the player has reached the landmark score, is to confuse two clearly distinct fact-situations by conflating a specific 'fact' into a universal truth.

At the same time as presenting these principled and 'jurisdictional' reasons for not walking, Chappell also offers a more practical argument against any moral obligation to walk. As he puts it, 'Not all players are honest'. To put your trust in a fielder who claims a catch may be to fall victim and lose your wicket to cheating. A refusal to walk in the absence of the umpire's decision simply avoids this possibility. Chappell illustrates his point with an anecdote which occurred during a Test in South Africa. Chappell drove to Tiger Lance at point but did not see if the ball had carried. Lance appealed, but the umpire did not react. Chappell asked Lance if he had caught the ball and upon receiving an affirmative response, headed back to the pavilion.

After play, South African Eddie Barlow came to the Australian dressing room to apologize and to confirm that Lance had made the 'catch' on the first bounce. When asked to explain his affirmative reply to Chappell's question, Lance is reported to have replied 'He asked me if I caught it. He didn't ask how many times it bounced before I caught it.' Chappell never walked again.

At the same time, it must always be recognized that on some occasions a fielder will sometimes claim a catch in good faith, which subsequent evidence reveals was not the case. At other times, the fielder may simply not know if the ball has carried or if, à la Steve Waugh, he has picked up after it has bounced while the fielder was in the process of falling to the ground. The question that arises here is whether if the fielder expresses doubt that does or should have any influence on the issue of walking or on judicial decision-making. As the various cases which we have already seen involving former Australian wicketkeeper Ian Healy indicate, the issues involved are complex. What can be said yet again is that any and all claims to the existence of an ethical obligation, imposed by the spirit of the game, in such circumstances cannot bear up to even the briefest legal and factual scrutiny.

Finally, the doubt may be in the mind of the umpire. This of course becomes relevant if one adopts the 'Australian' ethos of letting the umpire decide and respecting that position. For example, in a tour match against a Board XI in Barbados, South Africa were outraged when Travis Dowlin appeared to offer a simple caught and bowled to spinner Paul Adams.

> As the South Africans celebrated, the batsman stood his ground, waiting for a decision which never came.
>
> Umpire Vincent Bullen at square-leg appeared to have the best view of the incident but a request by the South Africans for a judgement brought no more than a shrug of the shoulders.[18]

The South Africans had not been impressed during the Trent Bridge Test in 1998 when Mike Atherton refused to walk after having gloved a catch off the bowling of Allan Donald. Atherton was thereafter peppered with short-pitched bowling and only one member of the fielding side applauded his subsequent half-century.[19] Yet even Donald, who spearheaded the attack on Atherton confirmed that Atherton was perfectly within his rights to wait for the umpire to decide. In other words, there may have been a moral imperative in this case, but that did not necessarily outweigh the invocation of legal formalism and the right to adjudication. Nor did the moral imperative outweigh a simple utilitarian calculus which may have been operating as well. A batter like Atherton is there to occupy the crease and score runs. By refusing to walk and waiting for the umpire's decision, Atherton is just doing his job and fulfilling his designated role for his team. Indeed, there is one sanction under Law here and another set of sanctions for the ethical breach. The batter may be verbally abused for refusing to walk, he may be the object of short-pitched bowling and he may be ostracized by the withdrawal of the traditional gentlemanly praise offered to an opposing cricketer who reaches a batting milestone. He is refused the recognition due to a member of the community because his actions have placed him outside that community, albeit temporarily. And English batters are not the only ones who wait for the process of legal adjudication. In a One-Day match against New Zealand in Australia in Jan. 2002, wicketkeeper Mark Boucher of South Africa stood his ground and awaited a decision on an apparent caught and bowled. The umpire believed, mistakenly, that it was a bump ball and Boucher was allowed to remain at the crease. He said, 'The umpire's there to make a decision, and he made a decision that I was in. So there it was.'[20] The law is the law is the law.

Into the complexities of the walking question, enters a complementary narrative order in which a batter, after having reached a milestone or having benefited from an apparently erroneous decision which permits him to stay at the crease, will 'give up his wicket'. In each case, the ethical motivation behind such an action appears to be different. In the first, the player has reached an individual or team milestone and gives up his wicket either as a selfish or an altruistic act. For example, he may be tired, injured or bored and wish to return to the relative comfort of the pavilion, or he may know that the next batter needs to score X runs for a personal record or to reestablish himself after a dry run. In the second, while violating one ethical norm by not walking, the batter may seek to atone for his sin by walking *ex post facto*, by giving up his wicket. In each case again, the 'facts' and what we ' know' about them compete in various interpretations for validity and narrative acceptance. Sometimes, members of the various sub-communities (especially the players) will 'know' that a batter has given up or thrown away his wicket while others (the spectators) can only guess or speculate about the 'facts'.

Finally, there is the related possibility of giving up someone else's wicket. In such a case we can find many ethical and factual meanings, the most interesting of which is a form of moral self-regulation and censure by the players themselves. The infamous case of Geoffrey Boycott offers the best example of these possibilities. While statistically a 'great' batter, Boycott is almost universally remembered as a boring and selfish player who put his own individual achievements ahead of the requirements of his team or his teammates. There is of course a counter-narrative that if a great player acquires runs, his team will benefit thereby creating a symbiotic relationship between the individual and the collective. Phil Edmonds offers the following, perhaps apocryphal story:

> So then Botham went in out of turn to hurry things up. His version of what happened next is that he played out to short extra cover and called for a run that wasn't there. Boyks ran towards him saying: 'What have you done? What have you done?' Botham says that he ran straight past Boycott and shouted: 'I've run you out, you cunt!' I don't know if that's the truth, but it's Both's version.[21]

In this case apparent facts and morality give way to a more subtle, deeper interpretation. What the spectator may see as poor running by Boycott or bad calling by Botham is in reality a deep morality play. The selfish player is deliberately run out by his partner who is imposing a collective sanction on him for ignoring the team's interest. What makes this ethical self-regulation even more effective, of course, is that it is a punishment which would truly have an adverse impact on Boycott. While shunning or ostracism would be ineffective against the iconoclast, forcing his wicket (and his average) to fall would hit Boycott at his most psychologically vulnerable point. Only another member of the interpretive community, like Botham, would both know this and be in a position to put it into practice.

The uniqueness of the internal hermeneutic practice of self-regulation finds some confirmation in an 'outside' account of Botham's run out of Boycott, and at the same time, it is obvious from the same account that even an 'outsider' can have some understanding of what happens 'out in the middle'. Although he could not *know* what Botham said to Boycott as they crossed, John Woodcock of *The Times* can offer *speculation* which is extremely close to the internal truth of the players themselves. He wrote in his account of the day's play:

> Botham, the next man in, called Boycott for what would have been the sharpest of singles into the covers. Loud and clear, Boycott sent Botham back, but on he ran, deaf to the injunction, until he had passed his dumbfounded captain, then making sure that it was Boycott who was out. Put it down, if you like to too much adrenaline. Botham is a young and high-spirited cricketer, and he had some reason this evening for thinking that in the time left he could do more for his side than Boycott, to judge from the way Boycott was batting.[22]

Into the complex and intriguing moral and ethical narratives about walking comes a final factor. The introduction of televised replays in recent years has helped to add more 'information' and more controversy to this issue. Fans and players could now, for example, see whether an edge had been taken. In cases of doubt, the even more recent use of the 'snickometer' allows us to determine with apparently greater assurance and accuracy if the bat has come into contact with the ball. In these cases, we now 'know' whether the batter is out and therefore whether the moral duty to walk has been triggered. But it is in another area of the difficulties and contradictions which surround ethical discourse about walking that televised replays have themselves been the cause of controversy.

As we have already seen, there has always been debate about whether a batter should walk when a fielder has claimed a catch. In this case the question is not whether the ball has struck the bat but whether the ball has carried and been taken cleanly. One version of cricket ethics, one idea and ideal of what is and is not 'cricket', demands that if a fielder claims such a catch the batter should walk. This is grounded in a normative assumption that cricket is a game and sport based on the integrity and honesty of the participants. It is the epitome of Victorian gentlemanly conduct and no Victorian gentleman would lie. Again, there are competing counter-narratives grounded in a variety of ethical and legal norms. Not all cricketers, as Ian Chappell would say, are in fact honest. The umpires, not the players, decide on dismissals. A batter is there to occupy the crease and score runs. Umpires and players might be uncertain about whether the ball has carried and been taken cleanly.

Television replays are, it is believed by some, the answer to the legal, ethical and factual dilemmas posed by such cases. Technology and science can save us from uncertainty. The third umpire, with access to multiple replays, can determine in fact and then in law whether a catch has been taken. During the 2002 Test series between India and England, the ethics and law of walking in combination with the issues of adjudication grounded in technology came to the fore. During the Trent Bridge Test, Alec Stewart appeared to have been caught brilliantly by Virender Sehwag at slip. Stewart stood his ground while the Indians celebrated the fall of a key England wicket. The third umpire, after viewing several angles of the catch on replay, ruled in Stewart's favour. The outcry was immediate.

Commenting on Channel 4's coverage, Mike Atherton bemoaned the fact that in such circumstances, no batter would ever leave the crease voluntarily. This marked the end of walking. This would mean that a cricketer's word would no longer carry any weight with his fellow players, and the spirit of the game would suffer irreparable harm. Delay would further blight the sport as replay after replay is consulted. Inevitably, doubt would benefit the batter and legitimate catches would not be recognized by the process of adjudication. Not only would this cast doubt on the judicial process, but it would cause aspersions against the good character of the fielder claiming the catch.[23]

Of course, each and every one of these points has already and always been made about the ethical situation surrounding walking. Furthermore, the idea of relying on television replays has also been criticized for, *inter alia*, delay and the impact it would have on the ethical self-regulation of play by the participants. What was and is of importance in the Sehwag/Stewart case is what Channel 4's luncheon interval coverage demonstrated. Dermot Reeve was shown holding a cricket ball close to the ground from various camera angles. This experiment demonstrated beyond any reasonable doubt that it was in fact (or 'virtually') impossible to determine, because of the angle and distance of the cameras, when the ball was touching the ground and when it was legally trapped in the fielder's hand. The doubt from which Stewart benefited was doubt created not by the 'facts' but by the technology used to eliminate doubt. Stewart should have walked because he was out. No one will ever, in the utilitarian world of cricket today, walk, because technology will always provide the certainty of uncertainty for catches close to the ground. In fact, Australian cricket has banned the use of replays for adjudication in catching situations precisely for this reason. There, experience showed that appeals for such dismissals were always turned down by the third umpire because replays created sufficient doubt to benefit the batter. Further and more careful review demonstrated that real catches went unrewarded. Adjudication was returned to the on field umpires and unofficial, democratic law-making, including decisions about whether to walk, left to the players.

Of course, this is again more than just a story about the use of technology in adjudication. Feelings between the two sides at Trent Bridge were not necessarily friendly. Earlier, in the One-Day series which preceded the Test matches, Darren Gough had accused the Indians of sharp practice and strict rule formalism in requesting ball changes.[24] Indian captain Sourav Ganguly had been the victim of 'bad' umpiring decisions in the same Test.[25] All of these, and many other factors, would have been at play when Stewart elected to stay at his crease and wait for the umpires to adjudicate. All of these and many other factors will be (or not) of importance in any attempt we make to attribute meaning and content to our understanding of the ethics of walking in cricket.

What each of the 'stories' or narratives about cricket shows is that there is a multifaceted interconnection and overlap between various parts of the game and the knowledge and ideas we have and create about them. These connections and overlaps act so that cricket informs and is informed by both 'internal' and 'external' forces. The social text of our lives acts upon cricket, just as the lessons we learn from cricket through our practice and experience of it, act upon the other aspects of our existence. The phrase 'it's not cricket', for all its ambiguities and fundamental contradictions, is nonetheless one which deeply resonates in our daily lives. We, in turn, reflect our other values back on to the game, as we scream for, or bemoan, yet another bouncer barrage or mercilessly harass Ian Meckiff while applauding the successful intimidation of opponents through racist, sexist and homophobic jibes. It is to this interaction of broader social texts and the story of cricket I now wish to turn.

24 Other stories about cricket, law and the meaning of life

In the spring of 1990 Conservative Party ideologist and ideologue Norman Tebbit created a storm of controversy in Britain when he criticized many 'Asian' immigrants to Britain for their 'disloyalty'. It appeared to Mr Tebbit that recent and not-so-recent arrivals to the hallowed shores of Mother England retained a fundamental allegiance to the land of their 'origins'. What is interesting here is not so much the apparently racist nature of the remarks (for who could expect anything else from the Tories?) but the fact that Tebbit appealed to the so-called 'cricket test' to make his point. According to Tebbit, too many Asians failed a fundamental and basic standard of patriotic loyalty:

> by cheering for the country they had come from rather than the one they now lived in. 'It's an interesting test' he said. 'Are you still harking back to where you came from, or where you are?'[1]

This is, of course, not the first time that cricket and politics, either domestic or international, have mixed. Bodyline (*infra*) and the underarm bowling incident both created public debate on the politics of cricket. Rebel tours to apartheid South Africa continued to make headlines. The reaction from Tebbit's Tory colleagues is, however, fascinating. Many simply distanced themselves from the substantive ideological implications of his remarks. The majority of other right-wingers took a different approach and 'thought he had been "unwise" to make the cricket analogy'.[2] From the context, it seems that Tebbit's comments were 'unwise' for two reasons. First, they were remarks which, even if true, were better left unsaid. Secondly, and more importantly, it simply is 'not cricket' to speak of cricket in political terms. To do so demeans both politics and cricket – it demolishes the public/private distinction and violates principles of fair play and gentlemanly conduct. Of course, this version of cricket has a deep and clear ideological base and reflects only one still important interpretation of cricket. It must however, compete with other interpretations which would argue that while Tebbit's statement is offensive in the extreme, it is not at all inconsistent with cricket as we 'know' it.

This underlying tension in English cricket, between visions of England (or more incorrectly in cricketing terms, Britain) as white and a multiracial England, emerged again in the mid-1990s. An Article appeared in the *Wisden Cricket Monthly*, asserting that English players of West Indian origin did not share the same mentality as their white teammates and that they were 'resentful and separatist'. A firestorm of controversy erupted. England cricketers Devon Malcolm and Phil DeFreitas issued writs for defamation. England captain Michael Atherton resigned from the magazine's board. The editor issued an apology and paid an undisclosed sum of damages.[3]

Yet debates about the loyalty of non-white, non-native born Britons continue to circulate around issues of national identity and citizenship. Following the civil unrest in the summer of 2001, David Blunkett sought to introduce a number of measures, including basic English proficiency tests for citizenship qualification. The idea that systemic racism, policing problems, economic deprivation etc. might have some influence on the alienation felt by members of immigrant populations apparently had no effect on the latest New Labour version of the old Tebbit cricket test.[4]

One of the dominant and consistent legal and moral functions of cricket is to draw and maintain the lines of division between them and us, to describe and exclude the Other. In this, cricket is no different from any other interpretive community or practice, which must, by definition, exclude outsiders.[5] But it is only in examining those who are excluded, and how and why they are excluded, and conversely, how the Other finally gains inclusion, that we can begin to understand the narrative complexity of cricket and of Law.

At one level, the question for many is quite clear and the boundaries as precise as they can be. 'Cricket should not, in my view, be played by foreigners. Where they do play it, they can leave one out.'[6]

This, of course, leaves unanswered the fundamental question as to exactly who these 'foreigners' are. One evident answer, in a patriarchal culture, is that women are 'foreigners' to the discourse and practice of cricket and there can be no doubt that gender has played, and continues to play, a key role in the narrative structures of cricket.

It is quite evident, from some public opinion samples, that cricket is a sport with a strong male bias among its followers. This should come as no surprise considering that the cult of virility is, and always has been, a primary component of a major sub-text of cricket. Its historical and cultural roots in Victorian England indicate that not only should the masculine ideal of patriarchal society inform cricket discourse, but the converse 'ideal of the passive and vulnerable female' should also be reflected in the culture of cricket, as it was in the Victorian ideology of sport in general.[7] Such ideals are carried forth today, not only in the dominant and obvious male bias in the sport but through the subtle ideological messages which surround and inform our impressions of it. At the most obvious level of televised cricket, the image and textual imaginations of cricket is one of athletic young men in action, while the cameras pan the crown for passive, sun-bathing adoring females.

Other ideological messages which tell us clearly that cricket is a male game, meant for men only, are found in stories about the banning of wives from cricket tours so that there are no 'distractions' and the players can keep their minds on what is truly important. Now, of course, some of the narrative structures have changed and cricketers may be more 'sensitive' and caring. Adam Gilchrist left the Australian team in the One-Day series in 2001/02 to return home to Perth to be with his wife and young child. At the same time, press coverage in that country focuses on the Australian 'Second XI, the players' wives and girlfriends'.[8] Television news dedicates time when the English-born wives of Glenn McGrath and Michael Bevan chose Australia Day to become citizens of their husband's homeland. At the same time, other traditional narratives of masculinity and femininity continue to circulate as tales of the beer-drinking prowess of the Australian male,[9] or in stories of how the code of gentlemanly conduct and fair play permits the good fun of the New South Wales players taking Colin Milburn, the English batter who played Sheffield Shield cricket for Western Australia, the night before his innings in an important game, out for a 'drink': 'In an inspired act, NSW players, knowing about Milburn's unquenchable thirst, worked in shifts to keep him in drinking. Next day Milburn was out for 15, and NSW won by 13 runs.'[10]

All in good fun, or the spirit of male bonding, and the spirit of the game and, as a bonus, 'we' won.

The alcohol–cricket relationship is not, however, one which is universally admired or accepted. When Martin Crowe completed his innings of 299 in a world record partnership of 467 with Andrew Jones against Sri Lanka, he 'told a television interviewer he couldn't wait for a DB beer and thrust a bottle in front of the camera'. While the usual arguments were trotted out by both sides in the debate, the most intriguing aspect of this 'case' is that for some, there was a direct interpretive relationship between Crowe's feat at the wicket and his subsequent promotion of the sponsor's product. In other words, on this interpretation, his cricketing achievement was diminished by his *post*-game act. Cricket is not seen as just a game, but the meaning of what happens on the field is directly influenced by the meaning of what happens off the field.[11]

Other messages about the male nature of cricket come from other unlikely sources but the overall effect on the popular imagination is the same. The first 'black' to play for South Africa, Makhaya Ntini, was sentenced for rape and then acquitted. Questions of race, gender, violence, sexuality and the politics of apartheid all had to be considered in order to even begin to understand what the simple facts of the law of sexual assault and Ntini's conviction could mean for cricket. The outsider of South African cricket had become the insider only to be excluded again, for reasons which many supporters would be likely to conclude were simply in the nature of a black man in any event. His conviction brought into the public imagination the reality of sexual violence in South Africa and his subsequent acquittal brought him back into the fold of many endeavours on the cricket pitch.[12] Gender, sexuality, race, and law have all offered contradictory and informative readings of the texts and practices of cricket.

In late 1989, for example, New Zealand and Australian media coverage focused on the trial of a prostitute and her boyfriend charged with the killing of a client in an S & M session gone wrong.[13] The case was hardly too surprising or worthy of much coverage or popular attention until we learn that the victim was Peter Plumley-Walker, one of Auckland's most respected cricket umpires. Speculation of his possible homosexual connections were rife as were reports that 'pornographic' negatives were found in his home. Here was a *real* story, one of the boys who wasn't, or perhaps was too much, a shocking tale which reveals what happens when the public/private distinction is transgressed and the outsider is exposed as being, or perhaps as posing and passing, as one of us. Just as sex scandals involving the judiciary are more important and interesting because they involve guardians and upholders of the moral and legal fibre of the community, so too is this case important because it points at and identifies the traitor in our midst and warns us to be ever vigilant. Plumley-Walker was not bad because he may have been gay or even because he may have enjoyed alternative sexual practices, he was bad because he was a cricket umpire who may have been gay and into S & M. He betrayed the sacred trust of the virility cult which defines for many what is and is not cricket.

Similar issues arose in Australia when Test umpire Steve Randell was charged and convicted on sex assault cases arising out of his tenure as a teacher in various Tasmanian schools.[14] The betrayal of trust which is the crucial signifying element of sexual abuse cases involving teachers is here amplified by Randell's status as Test umpire. He has violated his fiduciary duty not just to the young girls involved but to the game of cricket, his judicial office and the country. He is a 'child molesting ex-umpire'. His status as an outsider must be confirmed by the game and defined and reinforced specifically in relation to his former judicial function.

Likewise, when Geoff Boycott was convicted by a French court for physically assaulting his former lover, his employers dismissed him from his position as expert commentator, yet he was immediately hired by a competitor.[15] The questions which arise here demonstrate the complex nature of the relationships between and among male sexuality, violence, the law and cricket. Does the fact that Boycott is an abuser disqualify him as a expert in the game of cricket? The level of his knowledge of the game is unchanged. Perhaps the problem here is that his reputation as a batterer would damage his credibility. Or perhaps, the fact that the French court did not believe his story of his partner's injuries brands him a liar and therefore unfit to comment on the great game. In the end of course, not everyone shared these views and he was reemployed to offer his views on the game. Perhaps it is simply the case that being an abuser of domestic partners and a liar are completely separate from his qualifications for the job at hand.

This certainly seemed to be the case for Australian and English commentator Peter Roebuck. Roebuck was convicted of common assault for beating three young South African cricketers at his home. He caned them after they failed to live up to his standards in private coaching sessions. The judge said of Roebuck and his actions, 'It does seem so unusual that it must have been done to satisfy some need in you, whatever that may have been.'[16]

Here there are no doubt complex stories about power relations, sexuality and the benefits and costs of a public school education, which would need to be told in order to understand the intersections with cricket, law and the spirit of the game. Yet Roebuck continues to employed as a journalist and comments regularly on the leading issues of the game. His status as a convicted criminal, who assaults young men in his charge, apparently does not disqualify him from being part of the broader cricketing community, yet Steve Randell is a pariah to the game and its moral standards.

In other contexts, the law outside cricket plays a role in determining the nature, extent and content of the game's sphere of self-regulation. Commercial interests and the social value of male bonding have all changed with the times and the pressures of international marketing campaigns. Players' contracts contain good behaviour provisions.[17] As we have already seen the ICC *Code of Conduct* brings new normative constraints into the lives of cricketers, both on and off the field. When Pakistani and then South African cricketers tour the West Indies, for example, sampling, or allegedly sampling the local ganja involves not just partaking of a local medicinal herb, but the commission of a criminal offence, breach of contract and *Code of Conduct* provisions dealing with bringing the game into disrepute. The police, the Board and the 'game' all have an interest in this part of off field behaviour which has been taken from previous understandings of the private domain and made part of the public life of cricketers.[18] Similar concerns arise in Indian, English and Australian cricket, whether one is dealing with 'recreational' drugs or those which might more directly and intentionally effect performance on the field of play.[19] Regulation here involves issue of social norms, the police, the redefinition of the public/private distinction and important issues of workers' and employers' rights to privacy as far as the former are concerned and to regulate behaviour outside the workplace for the latter.

Of course, the extent to which any of these norms will directly effect the rights and obligations of players will always be determined by context and this will be determined itself by many factors. For example, had any of the alleged 'sexual' transgressors been involved in good clean fun with a young woman, they would no doubt have been congratulated and welcomed as one of the boys. Imran Khan continues to enjoy his status as great cricketer, political leader, husband and hunk despite reports that he fathered an illegitimate child.[20] Even Brian Lara, whose girlfriend filed assault charges with police against him, continued and continues to be admired throughout the cricket world.[21] Ted Dexter, when appointed as Chairman of the England Committee, and referring to Mike Gatting's dismissal as captain, clearly set down the ground rules of acceptable behaviour several years ago: 'There will be an extremely strict code. Rule number one: that they are extremely good looking ladies.'[22]

Other practical worldly issues now also invade the isolated and pristine old boy's club of the cricket world as the last bastions of male dominance tumble or dig in against an assault from the outside world. In 1990, Lancashire County Cricket Club finally allowed women to become full members. Ironically and tellingly, Lancashire had in fact, if not always in law, been trumped by modern medical technology and the socially constructed nature of gender divisions

> when it was revealed at the meeting that a member who had joined the club as Mr Keith Hall was in fact Miss Stephanie Lloyd: Mr Hall having become Miss Lloyd after a sex change operation. Thus, there was already a woman member in their midst.[23]

The legal and ethical moral issues of transsexuality inform even the text of the all-male bastion of cricket club membership.[24] At the same time, Middlesex County Cricket Club, the tenants at Lord's, the Mecca of Cricket, to use not an inapt metaphor, refused to allow full membership status to women, creating not only domestic but international difficulties. The Melbourne Cricket Club and Middlesex have an agreement allowing reciprocal privileges to members.[25] Except, of course, that Melbourne has women members who 'will not be allowed into the pavilion',[26] creating possibilities of legal actions under domestic, EC and International Covenants by aggrieved Melburnians. Cricket and anti-discrimination law collided as Britain entered Europe. 'Human rights' threatened the sovereignty of the most sovereign of English sporting and cultural bastions. The struggle for women's rights at the home of cricket continued for several more years until the ways of democracy and modernity triumphed over stasis and 'traditional' values.[27] A year earlier the first woman president of an English county cricket club headed Surrey. She was Betty Surridge, described in reports announcing her revolutionary victory as 'The widow of Surrey legend Stuart Surridge...' The report added that her '...husband captained Surrey through five successive championship wins in the 1950s'.[28] For the wire services this was apparently qualification enough.

Elsewhere women struggled to become members of the leading cricket clubs as well.[29] They also continue to battle for legitimacy, sponsorship recognition or simply the right to play the game.[30] Here of course, the story of gender, or at least of the female gender and cricket replicates the story of gender and society. The text of cricket is the text of the society of which it is a part. Inequality, lack of access to economic benefits, religious and cultural constructions of women which limit the activities and possibilities in which they are entitled to participate, these are stories and struggles which are represented in the microcosm of cricket as social and legal text. Such broader social, cultural and legal practices are not of course limited to 'gender' as narrowly defined. The politics of gender and employment, with implications for questions of class and economic power, as well as the political and social constructions of reproductive rights emerged in a case in 1998 when a female employee of the England and Wales Cricket Board convinced an industrial tribunal that her employers lived in a 'culture of misogyny' and had pressured her to have an abortion and had later sacked her.[31] Nor is gender always the only element in a complex mix of undesirable traits which upholders of the traditions of the game find offensive. Issues of geography, class and race also enter into the mix for those who wish to see no changes to the 'spirit of the game'. In 2001, controversy swirled around the opening of memorial gates for Yorkshire legend Sir Len Hutton. Former Prime Minister John Major, for whom cricket and politics always managed to mix, found himself embroiled in this domestic version of Yorkshire patriotism/parochialism. Major was invited to open the gates in a public ceremony along with Hutton's widow. He was denounced as a 'southerner' who knew nothing of the county. As president of Surrey, moreover, he was the enemy. The controversy did not end there.

The gates themselves showed among other scenes 'Asian' women in saris watching Hutton batting. Again the locals objected. Two versions of the objections can be put forward. The more 'innocent' of the two is a claim that when Hutton played for Yorkshire and for England, Asian women did not attend cricket matches. In other words, any objection to the artist's rendering of the gate has nothing to do with 'race' or 'gender' but with a desire to ensure historical accuracy in honouring a native son. Club officials defended the design as an attempt to reflect the multi-racial reality of Yorkshire and Yorkshire cricket today. In this defence can be read a response to the second interpretation of objections, i.e. that Asians and Asian women have no place in Yorkshire or Yorkshire cricket.[32] This idea is influenced by the reality of Yorkshire cricket.

> Shamefully Tendulkar is still the only Asian to play first XI cricket for the club, despite the existence of flourishing Asian cricket leagues and the near manic support of local fans. The loony musings of a bunch of former players become all the more damaging when they are seen to represent a county famous for its bigotry.[33]

Neither of these readings or any of the possible alternatives is necessarily complete or an accurate representation of the complexities of gender, race, regionalism or any of the other elements of narrative possibility which might be said to inform the gate case. Again, what needs to be underlined here is the reality of complexity and of the connections between and among different elements which make up our understandings of cricket and of the law.

Briefly we will return to the issues of gender and sexuality which in the case of men's or male cricket introduce intriguing and complex legal and ethical elements. In 1994, Australian representative cricketer Denise Annetts brought a discrimination complaint following her dropping from the national team. She asserted that she had been removed from the side because she was a heterosexual in a team dominated by lesbians. Here again the issues of law, politics and ethics are many and complex. At one level Annetts' claim could be seen to have brought comfort to those who believe not just in the inherent masculinity of cricket, but in the concomitant impossibility of something called 'women's cricket'. Only men can play cricket and any woman who does play the game must be 'masculine' or in the vernacular understandings of women's sport in general, only dykes play sport.[34] Of course, there are conflicting and complicating narrative understandings at work here as well since all red-blooded sports fans, who are by definition male, would of course distinguish between Anna Kournikova and butch women cricketers.

At the same time, the types of response to Annetts' allegations were also representative of the multiplicity of discourses which circulate around these issues. Some could deny the reality of a lesbian presence in the game. Some could admit such a presence but reduce or eliminate its relevance by asserting that sexuality is not relevant to what happens on the field, where of course, the defining characteristic must still be the confrontation between bat and ball. This would then lead to the conclusion that Annetts could only have been dropped on criteria relating to her skill and not to her sexual preferences or practices. Finally, there was the technical legal dilemma that the operative anti-discrimination provisions in place at the time did not permit Annetts' claim to be litigated. It was not against the law to discriminate against heterosexuals.[35]

Finally, it must be noted that whatever sexuality may be at play, for men or for women on the cricket pitch the discursive practices are almost invariably those of masculinity and maleness. Thus, one need not assert values grounded in social or biological essentialism to argue that for example when the Australian women's cricket captain issues statements attacking New Zealand cricket as boring and overly defensive and her own national brand as 'adventurous', it is possible to detect strains of Australian masculine bravado and aggression.[36] Similarly, like their male colleagues, Australian women cricketers are known as the worst sledgers in world cricket. They comment on the size of opposing batters' backsides and on their ugliness. Clare Connnor, the England captain, demonstrates the interconnection with other aspects of cricket practice when she recounts that when she 'walked' after giving what she thought had been a catch, she was called 'f—ing stupid' by the Australians for not waiting for the umpire's decision.[37] Sledging epitomizes and embodies ideas of aggression, disrespect, an attack aimed at 'mental disintegration'. Moreover, it is 'not cricket' for many who see it, as I have already argued, as violating the ideals of the spirit of the game. In the Australian attitude, in both the men's and women's games, we find what some would argue is clear evidence that there is some belief that the 'spirit of the game', 'ethical norms' or the idea of cricketers as 'gentlemen' (somewhat ironically in the last instance) are 'female' ideas. They embody weakness. Walking, giving up your wicket before the umpire decides, is cowardly. These female attributes enshrine fluidity and uncertainty, female characteristics etc. The Law is fixed, certain and it regulates the confrontation between bat and ball between men and 'men'. Unwritten rules of ethical behaviour feminize the game by bringing doubt into play and by attempting to assert that there is in fact something more to playing the game than the battle between willow and leather. The idea of something being 'not cricket' is itself not cricket because of this feminizing and extra-legal normative structure which it tries to impose on manly encounters.

Still other aspects of cricket reflect 'male' attitudes and values, and tend to confirm the feminizing and therefore bad, influence of ethical discourse. Besides the sneering *double entendre* of references to 'bowling a maiden over' (nudge,

nudge, wink, wink, say no more), it is clear that the militaristic and violence-oriented discourse which accompanies the sport (like most other sports) reinforces dominant male values. The macho, moustachioed attacks of a Dennis Lillee, a Michael Holding or a Wasim Akram against opposing batters clearly encapsulated and enshrined a male view of the world.

All of these points are so obvious as to be trite. They also tend to oversimplify the psycho-social complexities of the narratives of sex and gender. It could well be argued, for example, that the fascination we have for such stories as the Plumley-Warner affair stems not from our rejection of sadomasochism, but from the fact that all our relationships and the law itself are informed by the interactive phenomena of domination and submission.[38] It can also be argued that bowling, with its discourse of 'delivery' and 'maiden' is a feminine discursive practice while batting carries with it clear phallic, and therefore, phallogocentric discourse. A more interesting view and one which represents a more nuanced analysis of the competing discursive practices and the potential utopian kernel in cricket is put forward by Ashis Nandy in *The Tao of Cricket*

> Cricket allows each of its specializations – bowling, batting or fielding – to be a play of the masculine and feminine where a particular style – masculine or feminine – is enriched by the presence of its opposite and by the transcendence of the socially assigned gender meaning given to it. Thus, the masculinity of batting, to be truly masculine, must not only be informed with some amount of femininity, but also transcend the sexual differences.[39]

Cricket, like all social narratives, contains both a major or dominant cultural textual referent (male culture), and a competing, sometimes dialectical, 'minor literature'[40] which occurs in different time, space and manner, for some type of temporarily ascendant hegemony over the 'meaning' of the story. Nowhere is this more evident than in the 'minor' text of 'women's cricket'.

In its very semiotic structure, 'women's cricket' is reduced to a secondary minor and purely referential (and reverential) role vis-à-vis the main code. Real or true cricket is simply 'cricket', women's cricket is demeaned by the necessary addition of the adjective and by the entire dominant socially constructed discourse which imbues 'women's' with meaning in our culture. At the same time, cricket has been played by women since at least the middle of the fifteenth century, and played at major grounds at that.[41] In addition, the very masculine practice of overarm, roundarm bowling was, in cricket mythology at least, developed by a woman. But this long history does not mean that women's cricket has been able to avoid relegation to 'traditional' secondary status.

The first woman to be recorded in *Wisden*, the cricketing Bible, in the 'Births and Deaths of Cricketers' section, was Martha Grace (née Peacock), mother of the famous Grace brothers.[42] Her contribution to cricket is the only and traditional contribution open to a woman, as a mother who gave birth to and nurtured successful cricketers. Her value was determined solely in relation to her pre-determined role in the patriarchal system of reproduction.

Nor have the issues changed much for today's women who wish to play 'cricket'. At the simple technical level of equipment manufacture, there has been little or no access to specialized women's equipment and many women are forced to adapt junior or small men's equipment to their physical attributes and characteristics. Unlike the top male cricketers, the leading women cricketers, who represent their county, state or country are amateurs who not only receive no remuneration for their cricketing skills (pay equity), but they do not even receive complimentary equipment from the manufacturers who benefit from the public display of their trademarks when the women play.[43]

'Women's cricket' is virtually ignored by the mainstream media or put in as an afterthought when it receives any attention.[44] When it does receive recognition, it comes in the form of male referents, or in titillating discussion about the hegemony of lesbians in the sport. Yet there is some slow emergence that gender equality, or struggles over issues of gender equality have had some impact on cricket discourse and practice. In Australia, although not noticeably in England, for example, a significant proportion of commentary on the game has incorporated ideas and principles of gender-neutral language.

Some would argue that the imperatives of changing cultural *mores* require the 'neutralization' of cricket's lexicon so that, for example, batsman becomes 'batter'. Others would argue that because of the linguistic and cultural literary traditions of cricket, everyone should become a 'batsman'. The first narrative wants to tell, or at least begin, a new story about cricket, creating a new text and a new textual practice. The second view wants women to be treated as true cricketers according to the historically validated practices of the game. Proponents of the former interpretive practice would likely denounce their sisters who adopt the latter view as traitors who simply want to be men and confuse male discourse with universality. Their batsmen sisters would in turn denounce these women for ignoring facts, history and reality by trying to impose a theoretical and a contextual construct on a textual practice steeped in the traditions of the interpretive community. It would appear for the time being that the latter view has won out in England. As Rachel Heyhoe Flint explains:

> Another move firmly to establish women as cricketers was taken at the International Women's Cricket Council in Melbourne in 1985 'that all players should be known as batsmen – not batswomen or batspersons'. One newspaper report on England's Test in Brisbane in January 1985 referred to a player as the 'nightwatchbatsperson', which was enough to drive any sub-editor to small type![45]

The debate over gender-neutral language in law, literature and cricket indicates just how complex the issues are surrounding every single debate over meaning and practice and how interconnected each single debate is with others raging inside and outside that particular interpretive community. Another example of the *matrix* of questions which arise in the interpretive practice of cricket is the issue of violence.

Debates over fast-bowling practices and sledging are two examples of cricket sub-texts where the issue of violence arises. At the same time, violence is quite clearly an issue which in our legal and social culture is a key element in debates about gender. Yet, as it is a mistake to see spouse abuse *solely* in term of gender in criminological debate, so too is it an oversimple explanation to dismiss violence in cricket as nothing more than male violence manifesting itself in the male world of cricket.

It is not possible to discount the importance of the physical and linguistic practice of violence to all that imbues it with meaning, epitomized by the well-known public declarations of cricketers about intimidating opponents. It is equally not possible to ignore the other contexts which inform the context in which the acts of violence occur. To take the most well-known example, the Dennis Lillee–Javed Miandad encounter, it is impossible to simply attribute this set-to with Javed raising his bat to Lillee who kicked Miandad, without considering the individuals involved.[46] Lillee is well known for his temper, his sledging and his 'hatred' of batters. Javed, for all his skills as a batter, was almost universally disliked by Australian cricket's participants who saw him as a whinger and a cheat. Similarly, prior to (and after) the incident, Australia–Pakistan cricket has been highly contentious with allegations of doctored pitches, biased umpiring, whingeing and cheating. This Javed–Lillee set-to therefore involves not only the male culture of *macho mano-a-mano*, but debates about the function of umpires and respect for the rule of law, about cheating and sharp practice, nationalism and racism and even basic human personal dislike. It raises, like all other cricket issues, questions about law, ethics and the meaning of life.

The Javed–Lillee clash become part of the folklore and interpretive traditions of Australian–Pakistan encounters. Each match adds more interpretive texture to every other, and indeed, we may now add a deeper retrospective understanding to the Lillee incident. All other clashes, allegations, incidents between the two countries and with third countries since then also make up the interpretive context. Legal issues are raised and applied as to whether the bowler or the runner has the right of way just as they are raised in every traffic collision. The role and function of the umpires and captains again become relevant, as is the instant tactical and psychological situation. The physical and psychological intimidation of opposing players might enter into any Australian utilitarian calculation. Allegations of bookmaking and bribery, of ball-tampering etc. then add yet other layers to the interpretive matrix. Fears of 'terrorist' attacks and inadequate safety and security measures result in Australia pulling out of its scheduled 2002 tour of Pakistan. Desperate attempts are made to reschedule the matches in 'neutral' venues. The PCB enters yet another financial and political crisis as a result of cancelled tours and so on.[47]

The psycho-social power of the imagery conjured up in the interpreter's mind of the links between present and past must be factors which enter into any interpretation about interpretation not only of this cricket text but of all legal and social appeals to precedent. We have already seen the ways in which verbal and physical confrontations often serve to construct the parameter of exactly what we mean when we speak of 'cricket', and which seem to give to cricket a distinctive and clearly masculine shape. Incidents of verbal or physical violence in cricket also serve to bring more aspects of the game to the fore. The incident which we have already seen involving Viv Richards and his running appeal again serves as a useful example here. After the on field events, and post-game commentary, Richards appeared to make things worse by failing to lead his team onto the field the next day, opting instead to enter the press box and apparently threaten Tim Lawton, a journalist with the *Daily Express*, with physical violence.[48] The English press had a field day, publishing such headlines as 'Richards on the rampage', 'What's wrong with Viv?', 'King Richards rules shrinking Kingdom', and 'Viv's last stand'.[49]

To fully understand and interpret all these events one must consider not only the concerns about intimidatory appeals (*supra*) or the success of the West Indies against England at the time or simply the notion that the press reported 'the facts'. It would also be necessary to consider the function and place of cricket in West Indian colonial and post-colonial society, as well the nature of British tabloid journalism and its ideological and political role in English society and culture. But most of all, one must place the comments and actions of Vivian Richards into the complex and multilayered issues of race and racism in general and the racial politics of the West Indies in particular.

What few in the English media appear to have understood is the importance of race and cricket in the West Indies.[50] From the campaign to have a black man as captain, to Richards' own statements about the superiority of black cricketers, race is and has been at the *crux* of Windies cricket.[51] Not only did Richards' reference to the superiority of black cricket upset the East Indian community, who as people of colour have a long cricketing tradition, but it naturally raised the ire of racist and colonialist elements in the English press who no doubt believe that cricket is, after all, still an English game. For them, all others play cricket only at the sufferance and under the leadership of the MCC and all else that is English, including the gentleman's code under which no one ever threatens a journalist.[52]

Yet even under the gentlemanly code of true cricket, racism has a long and inglorious history. Even the great Ranji, an Indian prince, could not invoke his aristocratic status and appeal to upper-class solidarity to gain entry into the English Test side against Australia in 1896. Instead, he entered the side because at the time the county which hosted the Test selected the home side. The officials at Old Trafford (Lancashire) went against the whole of the England selectors and Ranji repaid their trust with a debut innings of 154 not out.

Even his entry into the side, his aristocratic origins and brilliant and elegant style (he is said to have perfected the leg glance) could not protect him from the contradiction between the liberal Victorian values of reward for meritorious effort and the deep racism of that same Victorian society. An anecdote reported by Nandy highlights the apparently irresolvable nature of the conflict.

> It is said that once when playing a test he hit a mighty six off an Australian bowler. An English spectator proudly clapped and turning to the Australian

sitting next to him said, 'He is a prince, you know. Do you have a prince in your team?' The Australian had to admit, defensively, that Australia did not. The very next ball Ranji was clean bowled. This time the Englishman muttered under his breath, 'bloody nigger'. All his life Ranji had to live out the reality of this apocryphal story. The clapping and the pride was genuine; so was the swearing. Ranji heard the former; he pretended that he had not heard the latter.[53]

Ranji was not the only one who lived with this fundamental contradiction of society's racism and its complex impact on how we interpret the text of cricket. During his inquiry into the Brixton riots in 1981, a social upheaval caused by factors of race, class, unemployment and alienation, Lord Scarman took time out to watch a cricket match between the youth of Brixton and the police. For Scarman, in part at least, cricket offered the perfect example of the cure to these social ills:

> It's all a matter of getting on with each other, doing things together, that's all I can say. It's civilised and it's cheerful, it's fun, and a bit of competition just adds spice to it. It's all so simple. Of course, I went to see grounds available too and it's marvellous to have the use of the Oval, but you can't always get the Oval.[54]

Just as saving the Lintz Cricket Club for Lord Denning would save the youth of County Durham from 'turning to other things', the existential alienation and violence of a young black man's existence in Brixton, or now an Asian youth in Bradford, would on this view of the world vanish if only a few wickets were laid, a few overs bowled and a few boundaries hit.

Issues of race, ethnicity and religion have always informed the practices of cricket. Purists insist, as they always have, that cricket is game, a confrontation between bat and ball. For them, anything which falls outside the limited confines of pure game-playing is irrelevant and detrimental to the spirit of the game. Yet we know that cricket, like law, is never, and has never been, pure, in this sense. As the game meant to embody the purity and values of the colonial power, cricket was always political. It was part of what it meant to be 'English', just as it became part of what it meant to be Indian, Pakistani, Australian etc. As soon as race or ethnicity, mixed in many places with religious affiliation, became part of national identity it was clear that these elements would infect and inform another key component of national identity, i.e. 'cricket'.

Thus, in the West Indies, the struggle for control and autonomy, for decolonization, became embodied in the battle for a black captain of the cricket team. In India and Pakistan, religion became dominant signifiers of national and international political struggle. The selection of Yousef Youhana, a Christian, in the Pakistani side in the 1990s was of significance in a country beset with conflict between secular and religious 'fundamentalist' forces of national identity. In the ICC Champions Trophy match between Pakistan and Sri Lanka, Saeed Anwar turned down an easy single and Youhana was run out. Anwar sports an 'Islamic beard' and was outspoken against US intervention in Afghanistan. The ICC anti-corruption unit immediately studied the incident for fear that something other than cricketing incompetence was at play.[55]

In India, the election of the BJP and the local political power of Shiv Sena, created an 'official' political identity between 'Hindu' and 'India'.[56] When former captain Mohammed Azharuddin was named and shamed in cricket's bribery scandal, what had been the secular triumph of a Muslim as Indian captain became an Indian Dreyfus affair. Azharuddin was a traitor, like all Muslims, he could never truly be 'Indian', his loyalties, to game and to country lay elsewhere.

In Sri Lanka, the position between Tamils and Sinhalese informs cricket selection and administration. In Australia, no Aboriginal has ever been selected to play cricket for his country. In the Mother country, English cricket is beset by debates over the questionable loyalties of 'Asian' fans and players. The psychological make-up of Afro-Caribbean cricketers is brought into question in a leading publication on the sport.[57] Debates about crowd loyalty, national identity and the 'cricket test' for patriotism surface during every tour by a sub-continental side. Race, ethnicity and religion are everywhere.

But nowhere are these issues of more importance for the questions of constructing cricket and national identity than in the 'racial' states of Southern Africa, Zimbabwe and South Africa. There race informs much of politics on a daily basis, or at least politics is constructed in terms of race, perhaps for other purposes. What is important to explore now is how this issue informs the social, political and legal text of cricket.

The political crisis over land ownership in Zimbabwe, constructed in terms of race and loyalty, of national identity is the most obvious example of the way in which the politics of race has direct and indirect impacts on the practices of the game. As the so-called war veterans, Robert Mugabe's political supporters, began their takeovers of white-owned farms as part of a policy of land redistribution, the Zimbabwe cricket team was being thrashed in England. One of the reasons given in the press and by the players was their concern for the safety of their families at home during the political crisis.[58] At one level of course this is evidence of a deeper malaise on the issue of race in Zimbabwe and in Zimbabwean cricket. The cricketers on the national team were almost to a man white. Their concern for the safety of their families was grounded in the history of land ownership, colonialism, the national liberation struggle etc. Of course, the cynical manipulation of the rule of law, historical inequalities and racial tensions by Mugabe and his cronies can easily be said to have influenced the political and social reality of violence and murder in the country. 'Race' and loyalty in Zimbabwean politics easily become a code for party affiliation, cronyism, corruption, murder and the cynical manipulation of public opinion for personal motives.

The cricketers' concerns were real, but the reality was and is complex. For these reasons, several MPs called for the cancellation of the ECB tour of Zimbabwe in autumn 2001.[59] The manipulations, sackings of the judiciary and intimidation which characterized Mugabe's electoral campaign offended many political and cricketing sensibilities. The relevant question is whether the call to cancel the tour was influenced more by fear for the physical safety of the players given the widespread nature of political violence in the country or if it was informed by some notion of condoning an antidemocratic political regime. If the latter explanation obtains, we return to the complex issues of apartheid era boycotts and rebel tours, in a mirror image. Here 'cricket' and 'democracy' are made synonymous. Indeed, even the converse argument accepts this political hermeneutic. Thus, cricket is a valuable tool for spreading and demonstrating the values of fair play and the rule of law which are central to the functioning of any democracy. By touring, the England team would offer a demonstrable alternative to the people and the government of Zimbabwe would see that there is nothing to fear from democracy and much to be gained. Cricket is democracy, the real issue here becomes which solution relating to playing the game is better suited to making the link obvious.

In the more specific cricketing context, the Zimbabwean game offers clear examples of the way in which the intimate connection between national identity and race is played out in the sport. Zimbabwe is predominately black, cricket is predominately, and especially at the elite level, white. There is a state of *de facto* racial discrimination, based in the socio-economic and historical legacies of colonial occupation, UDI and black power. The real question, for many, in both Zimbabwe and South Africa, is whether and how, the game can be made to represent the ideals of a multiracial democracy. In other words, is it possible for blacks and whites in Zimbabwe to play cricket as Zimbabweans or will the heritage of colonial racism simply drive out whites from the sport as they are removed from the political and social structures? In spring 2001, the Zimbabwe Cricket Union, the game's governing body, announced an 'aggressive campaign to eliminate racial discrimination within cricket at all levels'.[60] Two months later, the Union's Task Force announced its findings and recommendations.[61] The key point here, as in South Africa, is the conflict embodied in the mandate of the Task Force between the 'political' goals of the project and the 'cricket' consequences of those goals. The Task Force was to find ways to ensure '... the full, equitable, and sustainable nationwide integration of Zimbabwean cricket in the shortest possible time with the least possible reduction in individual and team performance'.

No one can doubt the laudable ideal of fully integrated cricket in Zimbabwe. Nor can one be certain of the game's survival and growth unless it becomes a mass sport and not one for a 'few white farmers'. The conflict here, as always when one is dealing with political and legal measures to ensure equality and integration, is between 'equality', however constructed, and 'the least possible reduction in individual and team performance', i.e. merit as defined by immediate on-field performance and abilities. Two months later, the apparent split in priorities became real as black and Indian clubs withdrew in protest over white political manipulation to thwart integration and Zimbabwe internationals Andy Flower and Heath Streak became embroiled in race issues.[62] In Nov. of the same year, former captain Alistair Campbell was disciplined for comments he made attacking racial quotas in selection and the process of transformation mandated by administrative authorities.[63] The Board denounced Campbell and asserted that no racial 'quotas' existed in Zimbabwean cricket, simply goals. Here again we see the way in which the semiotics of race and cricket combine in arguments about the legal regime which regulates the game.

Once more we confront the dilemmas at both a legal and ethical level posed and created by historical and persistent racial discrimination. Debates about quotas, qualification, merit, affirmative action, reverse discrimination etc. have circulated and continue, within legal and political discourse, in many countries. In the cricketing context, the question is posed starkly since national identity and race are intertwined with issues of success on the playing field. 'Winning' comes to signify national success and independence, integration counts only when victory is achieved on the field of play.

The problem then is 'merit'. How to name the best side and include members of the racially oppressed group(s)? Opponents of quotas will simply assert that the 'best' team must always be selected and that the idea of individual 'merit' or ability as a cricketer is an objective criterion. It must also be the sole criterion. Of course, we know as lawyers and as cricketers that things are never as simple as that. Selectors exercise judgement which can often indicate prejudice or at least the consideration of a complex understanding of merit. Bowlers are chosen not because they possess the best statistics but because of ground conditions. A quick bowler may be left out because the wicket is expected to take spin; an all-rounder may be left in or out depending on factors effecting the 'balance' of the side; a veteran player may be given 'one more chance' to prove he has not lost form completely; a new player may be 'blooded' as the selectors look to the future. None of these situations is objective in any strictly limited scientific sense, nor is the sole criterion ever really naming the best 11 players in the country. Finding the 'best' players selected on 'merit' is not and has never been the objective science of selection. Choosing the best 11 players in the circumstances is the art of selection.

The question here is whether 'race' is a relevant circumstance. The debate here 'should' be whether a particular player meets the minimum qualifications as a cricketer believed to be capable of playing at the level for which he is chosen. As long as an incompetent is not chosen, or more precisely, as long as say an 'incompetent' black is no more 'incompetent' than a white player, clearly race may and indeed in some circumstances for many 'should' be relevant. Indeed, it is clearly the case for those who know and follow cricket that the idea that many of the white players selected to play for that country are 'competent' is almost risible. Zimbabwe are, especially in the Test arena, not very good.

The century scored by Hamilton Masakadza on debut against the West Indies highlights another issue relating to 'merit'.[64] He became the first 'black' player to score a century for Zimbabwe. Most of the 'black' players who had risen up the hierarchy of cricket in that country had done so as bowlers, and as fast bowlers. Without entering into the merits of the individuals concerned, it is not difficult to assert that this might be due more to the mythologies of racial stereotyping than to objective evaluations of particular skills. According to this myth, blacks are 'natural' athletes best suited to brute force and bowling fast. They do not have the temperament to develop the subtle techniques of a top batter. Once again, the reality of the way the game is played, the idea and ideal of 'merit' and the legal and ethical issues which evolve around these political and social narrative structures are more complex than many would have us believe.

The situation in South Africa, so long the pariah of international cricket for its refusal to consider 'merit' in selection, grounding its selection policies and administrative structures in the ideology of apartheid, further exemplifies these complexities and contradictions. I shall not discuss here the sordid history of cricket under apartheid. Instead, I want to examine briefly events surrounding the 2001/02 confrontations between the South African side and the Australians. More particularly, I want to highlight the issues of racially specific selection controversies which circulated in the Australian summer. Earlier, especially in 1999, the governing authorities of South African cricket had instituted and institutionalized a practice of racially based selection quotas.[65] Of course, the usual arguments about the balance between remedies for problems of historical oppression and questions of 'merit' surrounded these policies and practices.[66] In addition, there has always been concern about the racial taxonomy used in South African cricket. Selection criteria which establish the quotas for team composition at both the provincial and national levels refer to 'non-white' players. This means first, that at some level, there is an implicit and explicit idea that team composition is *a priori* racialized and racially based, i.e. the white race is the pre-existing norm. This raises several important questions. Is 'white' a race? Is it a race in South Africa or as an objective category? What does this mean? Similarly, is 'non-white' a racial category in and of itself or is it more precisely an agglomeration of all groupings other than 'white'? What is the impact and importance of continuing to afford predominance in the battle against racism to the racial category 'white'? What is the impact of using and continuing to deploy racial categories to combat the legal and political evils of racial categorization of the national population under apartheid? On the one hand, the deployment of the taxonomical structures here, of 'white' and 'non-white' can be seen in pragmatic and political terms as a short-term solution imposed by the continuing nature of race-based divisions in South African society. On the other hand, it might be possible to argue, or at least to consider, that such policies in and of themselves simply replicate the inherent evils of apartheid's objective assumption of racial categories as scientific, social and religious reality.

Indeed, the divide between 'white' and 'non-white' in selection criteria also hides the persistence of apartheid-era discourse in South African society and in descriptions of South African cricket. Herschelle Gibbs and Paul Adams are almost always described as 'coloured' or 'Cape coloured' cricketers, while Makhaya Ntini is a 'black' or 'African' cricketer. Shaun Pollock, on the other hand, is always the South African captain or a South African all-rounder or the son and nephew of former 'cricketers' or 'South African' cricketers, Graeme and Peter Pollock. Neither he nor his father and uncle are ever described as white, or in racially specific terms. Again, white remains the non-racial signifier, the norm of cricket. At the same time, apartheid-era distinctions between mixed race 'coloured' and 'black' continue at a very important and significant semiotic level of law and politics in cricket to be deployed as natural and relevant divisions.

These issues came to a head during the Australian summer of 2001/02. Makhaya Ntini was dropped from the side 'on form' to be replaced by Allan Donald. Donald had been known earlier in his career as 'white lightning' or the fastest 'white' bowler in the world of cricket. Here the dominant racial signifier was 'black', simply because of the 'natural' abilities of West Indian bowlers to bowl fast. Again, the deployment of racial taxonomies and signifiers in the world of cricket has been and is deeply problematic and in need of deep contextualization.

In Australia, in 2001/02, Donald had been struggling with injury and there were serious doubts about his fitness. In addition, it was pointed out by several observers that if Ntini were dropped for lack of form, i.e. on merit, then what was Lance Klusener who had been 'through a bad trot with the bat' still doing in the side? The issue here again was whether there is or was something objectively knowable as 'merit' or 'form' or whether the category was conveniently deployed in different ways and contexts depending on the 'race' of the player.

The South African Sports Minister intervened, raising the issue of racially disparate treatment.[67] Selectors for the third Test at Sydney chose to replace Klusener with Jacques Rudolph and spinner Nicky Boje was preferred to fast bowler Nantie Hayward. Boje, a 'coloured' player was the only non-white in the side. His selection could be of course, and may well have been, justified on merit. Sydney is a wicket historically friendly to spinners although that has not been the case more recently. Nonetheless the selection of Boje fits within generally accepted ideas of merit as understood in the particular context of criteria relevant to selection, in this case, the nature of the wicket. He has been a part of South African Test and One-Day teams for several years.

The selectors were overturned by the president of the UCB who ordered that Justin Ontong be selected in the place of Rudolph, in order to ensure compliance with the quota of two non-white players in the team.[68] Ontong is 'coloured', Rudolph is 'white'.

Problems immediately emerged. It appeared that the President intervened without fully consulting the tour selectors. More importantly, the issue of 'merit' came to the fore of discussions. Ontong had only played in one tour match in Australia and had never been selected in a Test team. His game against New South Wales was not the most successful of his career, he made a pair. Rudolph, on the other hand, had made a half century in each of the two tour games in which he had appeared. Nonetheless, supporters of Ontong's selection did make at least one merit-based argument for his selection. South Africa had already lost the Test series. The Sydney Test therefore did not 'count'. This was a perfect opportunity to 'blood' a young cricketer of colour and to expose him to the opportunities of top class competition for the present and the future.

As I have already argued, the idea of blooding a new, younger player is an accepted part of traditional selection practices. Therefore, there is at this level a perfectly acceptable and accepted justification of the Ontong selection, but again only if one classifies him as a 'young' cricketer instead of as a cricketer of colour. Peter Roebuck presented the traditional critique of the South African policy, once again carefully couched in objective terms of 'merit'.

> Ontong himself has been turned into a plaything. The idea of pushing coloured and black players along applies better in youth and first class cricket than it does in the Test arena where tens of thousands watch and history judges.
>
> ...
>
> Sooner or later it was bound to happen, Sooner or later politics and cricket were bound to fall out.
>
> ...
>
> Life is much simpler in this country where everyone agrees that the strongest team must take the field.[69]

Here we find all of the traditional narrative and ethical devices about 'merit', quotas and affirmative and then some. The 'beneficiaries' of such selections suffer emotional, psychological and personal trauma because they and everyone else knows they do not deserve to be there. Their humiliation is both personal and public. History judges, but apparently history must be limited to entries in the scorebook. The history of exclusion, oppression and murder which inform apartheid are of no concern here. They are of no relevance because there is a difference, at the epistemological and deontological levels, as well as in law, between cricket and politics. Cricket here is the game, the confrontation between bat and ball, not race. A careful review of Roebuck's concern for Muttiah Muralitharan and allegations of chucking might reveal the relevance of racial categories in some cases and not in others. More importantly, of course, here Roebuck praises Australian cricket and Australian democracy by implication as being institutional circumstances where selection is purely based on merit.

Under this view of the world of Australian cricketing democracy, no Aboriginal cricketer has ever played wearing the baggy green cap because no Aboriginal cricketer has ever been good enough. No cricketer has ever been chosen for Australia on a basis other than merit. Of course, one might wish to interrogate Roebuck's assertion and language more clearly here. He claims that in Australia, 'everyone agrees that the strongest team must take the field'. This can easily be read and interpreted as imposing some criterion beyond individual merit as relevant for selection. What is important is the 'strongest team'. This may not necessarily ever or always be synonymous with selection on individual merit. A left hander may be chosen to play and to open the batting in order to make the team stronger. A left and right handed opening pair upsets the line of the bowlers and requires the fielders to change position more regularly. An all-rounder again may be selected because he is a stronger bowler than batter, or vice versa, depending on team balance. This may make a better team but it may also mean that a 'better' player is left out. Again, one might argue that all of these considerations are still related to the defining question of the confrontation between bat and ball while 'race' is irrelevant to this *grundnorm*. That of course is true if two conditions obtain. First, that the player selected on the basis of 'race' is incompetent in the battle of bat and ball and secondly, if one defines cricket purely and simply in those limited terms. Surely we all know by now as we always have, that playing the game has never been only about the 'playing the game in the literal sense'. Roebuck's analysis, like all narratives about cricket, tells us as much about the game by what is omitted or dismissed as irrelevant as that which is considered and presented as essential.

Again, the question here is never really about the merits of a particular player or of the criteria informing his selection. Instead, the issues are moral, ethical, political, historical and legal. Debates about affirmative action and effective legal remedies to deal with the legacies of historically entrenched racism and its consequences are full of these issues. Can legal remedies and regulatory mechanisms which are themselves grounded in 'race' be truly effective in eliminating historically created and ongoing discrimination based on race? Is the problem the reality of discrimination or more fundamentally the evil of the taxonomy itself? Race is of course real but it is a lived and contextual reality. Can a legally reconstructed reality which keeps the taxonomy of racial difference in place ever eliminate that taxonomy? These are basic and essential questions which challenge us all in our daily lives and practices and which must inform 'anti-racist' legal tactics and strategies. What is certain here as elsewhere is that race and even racism are 'not cricket' while at the same time being perfectly central to our understanding of the game. Race is cricket, just as cricket has always been, in part, about race.

In July 2002, the South African United Cricket Board decided that the best way of solving the delicate problems of racially based selection, poor international performances and the upcoming World Cup at home was to drop the controversial 'quota' system and replace it with one based entirely on merit.[70] Indeed, the system was justified as a self-fulfilling prophecy. There are now, it would appear, enough cricketers of colour of both provincial and national quality that all selections can proceed on merit and a racially mixed and representative side will almost inevitably result in any event. Guidelines have replaced strictly enforceable lawful injunctions. Imposed legal norms have been replaced by a form of self-regulation and market-based mechanisms. Provincial B teams are encouraged to select at least 50 per cent non-white players, of whom at least one should be a black African, in order to ensure an ongoing supply of cricketers of colour for higher level sides. Cricket is racial, but race is not quite cricket.

Before feelings of smug superiority set in, it is important to note that the text of Australian cricket is not immune from the interpretive weight of this society's racist and ethnic biases. Tim Zoehrer and Michael Dimattina operated at the fringes of Test selection, and Michael Kasprowicz and Simon Katich have played for Australia. Yet, Len Pascoe (né Durtanovich) was the first person of non-Anglo-Celtic origin to play regularly for his country and that did not occur until the mid-1970's.

No Aboriginal has ever played test cricket for Australia, and only a few (Eddie Gilbert, Queensland, Alex Henry, Queensland, Ian King, Queensland and Jack Marsh, New South Wales) have ever played first-class cricket in that country, despite the fact that one, Marsh, was clearly one of the best players of his time.[71] Gilbert, was a proficient enough bowler to bowl Don Bradman for a duck.[72]

Nor can it be said that Aboriginal Australians have not contributed to the story of international cricket. The first 'Australian' team to tour England was, in fact, an all-Aboriginal side which went there in 1868.[73] From the beginnings of Australian cricket, Aborigines have played the game yet their involvement has only rarely reached the top levels of the sport or public consciousness about the nature and content of cricket in Australia.[74] While the blatant racism of Australian culture and such popular imagery as the iconic 'White Australian Policy' could be trotted out as short-hand explanations, they are little more than inadequate statements of the obvious. The racial character of cricket in Australia must be seen in light of more complex and deeper explanations of sport and indeed of society in Australia.

It is, for example, possible to argue that the virtual exclusion of Aboriginals from the text of cricket history is due to a combination of several factors. Some see the exclusion of Aboriginal cricketers as a necessary consequence of the Australian (white) definition of the role of cricket. As fear of the possible effects of the 'convict stain' on Australia's capabilities grew, it was exacerbated by a feeling that the climate of the country could affect the European stock as 'it had evidently done to the despised and decaying people'.[75] Climate, geography and the political and social history of the origins of white Australians informed and increased their racism and made it vital that they obtain prowess at cricket, for through the means of playing and excelling at this most English of games they could eliminate their own psycho-social fear and self-loathing, just as they could by replicating other traditions and institutions inherited from the Mother Country – such as monarchy, a divided legal profession, allowing for the creation of an elite, white and a male Bar. At the same time, Aboriginal society was being wiped out as Australians of European heritage saw the games between themselves and Aboriginal people not as the interaction of two cultures but as part of a more competitive and destructive relationship. Again cricket, culture, social psychology, even climate inform and make much more subtle and complex what appears at first blush as simple 'racism'. This does not mean that *simple* racism does not exist in Australian society or in Australian cricket. It does mean that any examination of 'race' and 'cricket' must attempt to get beyond the simple and the simplistic to uncover the complexities of both parts of the equation.

Another element, already indicated by obvious reference to many of the events and texts already described, without which 'cricket' means nothing, is the complex relationship between imperialism and nationalism in the history and current practice of the game. Clearly, cricket is an originally English game and those countries which play it at the international Test level – England, Australia, the West Indies, India, New Zealand, Pakistan, South Africa, Sri Lanka, Zimbabwe and Bangladesh – are either the Mother Country itself or former colonies into which the game was introduced by the forces of colonialism and imperialism. The greatest irony of cricket is that it has been turned in almost every former colony from a weapon and tool of anglicization to a linchpin in struggles for national identity and anti-imperialism. The core elements of rule of law discourse which are so deeply embedded in cricket as a practice became basic normative references for opponents of the imperial master and the hypocrisies and contradictions of colonial rule. The role of cricket in the former English colonies demonstrates most clearly its contradictory character and its dialectical potential as a text which can and does provide a utopian vision for the future of the interpretive community. Cricket is both an imperial Victorian game and the 'national' game of India, Sri Lanka, Pakistan, the West Indies, Bangladesh and Australia. 'Each of the interpretations is true and each has the capacity to serve as the basis of a myth. The interpreter has to choose.'[76] At this level, at least, cricket, far outstrips law as an important national social artefact. While there is a trend in each country to develop a 'national' legal system, reliance on English precedent is still a dominating factor in many cricket-playing jurisdictions. Cricket, on the other hand, offers a strong national counter-narrative.

Cricket, as Norman Tebbit, John Howard, John Major and just about anyone one might run into at the bar at Lord's would attest, is and has always been a game which has served as a metaphor for loyalty and for a set of particular understandings about patriotism. Indeed, cricketers were so loyal that they stopped playing first-class cricket in England out of patriotic duty during World War I.[77] Cricket was later a unifying and humanizing element in German POW camps during World War II. The New Zealand cricket museum contains copies of reports of 'Tests' played by English, Australian and Kiwi prisoners. Cricket has always been deployed, however contradictorily, as a tool and symbol of humanity, so much so that the connections between Victorian England and the colonies were best epitomized by reference to the universal trope of cricket.

> The peculiar feature of the Jubilee has been the way in which it has drawn attention to the bonds between England and its dependencies: and the batsman of the day who is acknowledged to be the most consummate in style and all-round power (though he may not be at the head of the averages) is an Indian prince [Ranji].[78]

No cricket text, however, no political, legal, historical, social text, is as clear and unambiguous as the proponents of literalism and plain language, or computer-generated legal argument, or televised replays and third umpires, would have us believe. Each 'national culture' (and every other sub-culture making up that totality) has written its own story of self-identity. As we know, every case of self-identity involves a stage of differentiation from the Other with whom one must also in part identify to know ourselves as Other than Other.[79] Each cricketing nation owes its identity (as does each legal culture in these nations) to a conflicted mixture of independence from, and dependence on, the Mother Country.

In India, for example, cricket has gone through and continues to live with, deep and basic contradictions, yet it survives as a sport of unique national status.[80] From its origins as a princely pastime under the Raj, it has become a catalyst for Indian national sporting identity. From the days of princely patronage and sponsorship, it is now intimately linked at the domestic level with state bureaucracy and commercial private enterprise support. From its former elitist nature under imperialism, it passed through a stage of ethnic and religiously based sectarian organization to a phase of accommodation with the complex cultural and social make-up of Indian society. The rise of Hindu nationalism, the bribery scandal involving cricketers and bookmakers, many of whom were Muslim Indians, and conflict with Pakistan have more recently placed ideas of Indian identity and cricket in a still more complex social, political and legal frame.

Historically, cricket served as a motor-force for Indian self-definition and nationalism despite the inherent contradictions of the game's organization. Ranji, despite his apoliticism at home and *supra*-Englishness abroad, was made into an nationalist hero because he had beaten the colonizers at their own game. This phenomenon is one of the two key factors of the relationship between cricket and nationalism in the British colonies. To beat the Mother Country at its own game demonstrated starkly and publicly that the ideology of superiority/ inferiority which was central to British imperialism was manifestly untrue. In other words, by taking on and interpreting the text of Englishness and imbuing that text with a new and better (Indian – West Indian – Australian) narrative, the colonies demonstrated their ability to exist on a basis of equality. The best English gentlemen were no longer necessarily English nor gentlemen and the experiential basis, the textually embodied validity of national identity could be readily confirmed by a glance at the cricket scoreboard.

The other motor-force operating in this hermeneutic and dialectical reversal of cricket as the social text of imperialism was the fact that in the practice of the game itself, the self-contradictory charade of Victorian upright moralism was exposed. As Nandy says: '[Victorian Cricket] allowed Indians to assess their colonial rulers by western values reflected in the official philosophy of cricket, and to find the rulers wanting.'[81]

Not only at the physical and technical level of successful competition were the contradictions of cricket and colonialism exposed, but at the level of lived ideology cricket could not survive its own open textuality. The dominant ideological code of merit and sportsmanship was exposed to the interpretive light of the real experiences of racism, sharp practices and legal formalism. To succeed at cricket against the colonizer demonstrated not only the falsehood of the myth of inequality but the lie of the English gentleman and the experiential basis of textual validity could again be readily confirmed by a glance at a cricket scoreboard.

Rather than abandoning the game because it was a lie, however, the former colonies have acknowledged the open-textured state of cricket's being-in-the-world to imbue it with a new, native truth. Cricket has been to a greater or lesser extent, localized and democratized. This reversal of cricket's dominant mythico-legal system is not, however, clear and interpretively closed either. The idea/ideology of the 'spirit of the game' and of 'cricket as character' continue to play a strong and continuing formal ethical function in the new 'national crickets', an ethical function which is itself constantly challenged and changed by other local and international circumstances and events. Cricket remains, in its post-colonial stage, a contradictory and ambivalent game.

It is this ambivalence which has prompted many like freedom fighter and political thinker Ram Manoher Lohia (1910–1947), to denounce cricket as a colonial relic and yet eagerly go to watch test matches. [footnote omitted][82]

And it is this same ambivalence which allows Ashis Nandy to argue that 'true' cricket is Indian or at least, that it coincides with Eastern religions' views of fate and character, that the spirit of the game is Indian and that it is being destroyed as India becomes part of the global economy and culture.

The Indians can hope to win the way traditional cricket allows them to win, by being Indians, or they can try to win the way modern cricket encourages them to win, by mortgaging their future to a unilinear theory of history. It is also the argument of the book that such mortgaging and the vision of certain victory over the white man which goes with it, may turn out to be a prescription for a civilizational defeat if pushed to its logical conclusion. But then, I am also aware that seeing a victory as a camouflaged defeat, for reasons which have to do with the means employed to win, requires a cultural self-confidence which is increasingly available only at the peripheries of Indian society.[83]

Of course, we must also be aware of other concerns and issues in Indian and then in 'sub-continental' cricket. The 'Hinduization' of the game, as a result of broader political developments is but one example. Conflicts over Kashmir determine when, where and if matches will be played between India and Pakistan. The rise of Sri Lanka as a One-Day and to a lesser extent Test side has rebalanced and challenged issues of national identity, rivalry and Indian military intervention in the Tamil issue. Bangladesh has now entered the Test arena and questions of wealth disparity, television rights and the legacy of secession from Pakistan will continue to inform understandings of 'cricket' in that context.

Familiar, and at the same time different, considerations and contradictions acted and act upon cricket as national identity in the West Indies. The long struggle to allow a black man the symbolic post of captain coincides with the long struggle to overturn colonial rule for independence.[84] At the same time, local factors and contradictions have always continued to operate. Selectors must consider practical and traditional representational balance among constituent members of the federation in each Test side, just as we must all consider historical and cultural differences between and among the members of the West Indies Federation when discussing the complexities of racism. Thus, Sir Frank Worrell was able to further his cricket career by moving from the strict confines of Barbados to the relatively freer climate of Jamaica and Viv Richards' comments about the inherent superiority of Afro-Caribbean cricketers inflame the passions of 'East Indian' Trinidadians. Various cricket clubs and allegiances thereto in the West Indies functioned under a complex system of racial and class distinction which might strike the 'outsider' as absurd but which, to the insider members of that community was a factual complexity with which they dealt and into which they poured existential meaning(s) on a daily basis.[85]

West Indian cricket also carried with it the shape and tone of outside racial interpretations and stereotypes. A West Indian batter has 'style' and 'natural flair', while the dogged English side must spend hours in the nets. But this is in fact nothing more than the old 'scientific' racist idea of black athletes' 'natural' ability. At the same time, however, part of this identification has been transformed by the interpretive practices of the colonized group itself. Self-identification with physical prowess is one which has been internalized by the West Indians themselves – Viv Richards is the 'Master Blaster' and the all-out pace attack is symbolic of a forceful collective self-identity. Historically, however, such a collective social self-identity could and did inflict heavy personal costs upon individual cricketers who carried the entire weight of history and cultural identity on their shoulders. C.L.R. James offers us a classical example of the nature and burden of such a mixture of the public and the private, the individual and the social when he writes of Gary Sobers:

> The pundits colossally misunderstand Garfield Sobers – perhaps the word should be misinterpret, not misunderstand. Garfield Sobers, I shall show, is a West Indian cricketer, not merely a cricketer from the West Indies. He is the most typical West Indies cricketer that it is possible to imagine. All geniuses are merely people who carry to an extreme definitive the characteristics of the unit of civilization to which they belong and the special act or function which they express or practise. Therefore to misunderstand Sobers is to misunderstand the West Indies, if not in intention, by inherent predisposition.[86]

Sir Garfield Sobers is for James the text of the West Indies writ small. To interpret the individual is to interpret the group. No matter how true or continuing such a view may appear to be, it is impossible to suggest as James appears to, that there is a single unambiguous, natural text of West Indian cricket or society. On the contrary, West Indian selectors must always be careful to balance regional representation. 'Merit' must exist as a factor, indeed the key factor in selection, but a West Indies side made up entirely of players from Barbados, like an Australian Eleven from New South Wales, or an England team made up of Yorkshiremen, is unimaginable. There is also some evidence to suggest that class continues to play a role in selection as well, albeit in a kind of 'reverse discrimination'. Some argue that Carlisle Best failed to retain a Test spot less because of his on-field performance than from a certain public antipathy to his 'superior' academic achievements. The strong antipathy in some quarters to the naming of Carl Hooper to captain the side has something to do with regional animosities as well as with concerns about the individual character of the all-rounder. Once again, Viv Richards' comments about the superiority of cricketers of African descent were not well-received by cricketers in Guyana and Trinidad where Asian-descended West Indians are in a majority.[87] Finally, cricket has come under increasing pressure as a social text and practice as American popular culture infiltrates the Caribbean through television satellite technology and sports like basketball attract young-sters.[88] While it may well be that to interpret Vivian Richards or Gary Sobers is to interpret West Indian society, it now appears equally true that Harold Bloom is correct in his assertion that every reading is necessarily a misreading.[89]

Even the Mother Country, England herself, cannot escape the complexities and contradictions of the power of local communities of interpretation in cricket. The perversity of Yorkshire is well known but other examples can be found adding issues like class and nationalism to the mix of the seemingly pure textualization of English cricket.[90] John Arlott pointed out that in the North, the Midlands and Wales, a radical, working-class political culture surrounds cricket whereas in the South, especially at the MCC, cricket embodies the values of the Establishment.[91] Anyone who knows of the geographic and class-bound dislocations exacerbated by Thatcherism and carried out to tragic levels of inequality in post-Thatcher, New Labour Britain, would hardly be surprised by this analysis, just as anyone who 'knows' cricket could hardly be surprised by the manifest consequences of Thatcher's, Major's and Blair's rule.

Equally important to a proper understanding of 'English' cricket is an appreci-ation of the history of national struggles within the 'United Kingdom', especially in Ireland and Scotland. While cricket is played in both countries, it does not enjoy a high public profile or serve as a locus for national self-identification as it has in other colonies. Perhaps because of geographical proximity to Mother England, cricket in Ireland and Wales has never been able to develop its own 'national' characteristics which were able to emerge in more distant lands. This does not, as could only be expected, prevent the MCC from proclaiming 'its missionary role...to Scotland, Ireland...'.[92] Equally, attempts to foster the game in Scotland are naturally hampered by an inherent national pride and the absurdity of considering Scotland as part of England. David Wilson, then NCA coach in Scotland, summarized:

> ...England should change its name to United Kingdom or Great Britain. How can I enthuse an 11-year-old little Glaswegian tearaway to persist at cricket when his goal is to play for England. 'But sir, I nae want to play for England, I want to beat England'. You see it is incomprehensible to a young Scots would be cricketer, girl or boy that his or her goal is to represent England.[93]

Nowhere, however, has the connection (apparent and real) between nationalism and cricket been more well-documented and thoroughly studied than in Australia.[94] The cricket and nationalism connection there has gone through stages ranging from the imperialist introduction of the game to a sense of national cricketing confidence, even arrogance, that was specifically held up as an example of what federation and cooperation might do and what nationhood had already achieved. As in other cricketing outposts of the Empire, there was from the very beginning an ambivalence in Australian nationalism towards the Mother Country.[95] And this ambivalence continues today. From the public adulation of cricket achievements as cultural icons ('No Australian had written *Paradise Lost*, but Bradman had made 100 before lunch at Lords')[96] to a nearly universal desire to beat the Poms, Australian popular cricket culture has always seen matches against England as the only true test of public and cricket character regardless of either team's ranking in the world order.[97] Despite protests to the contrary about throwing off the Oepidus complex, events since the alleged apex of cricket and nationalism demonstrate a deep and continuing ambivalence in Australian cricket's nationalism. Before a recent defence of the Ashes in England, the Australian side stopped off at Gallipoli in order to experience the true feelings of 'mateship' and the 'Anzac spirit' upon which they would rely to beat the English. For every public celebration, ticker-tape parade and rise in participation after an Ashes victory, there is statement like that of John Curtin during World War II that 'Australians will always fight for those twenty-two yards. Lord's and its traditions belong to Australia just as much as to England.'[98]

None of this really demonstrates or proves anything except once again the point that cricket (and all its social components) is not a single, unitary text, displaying either a linear or an inevitable dialectical tendency. It is, on the contrary, a text open-ended and bounded by the culture in which the interpretive community finds itself.

One more aspect of the cultural heritage of the interpretive community of cricket (at least in Australia, the West Indies, South Africa, New Zealand and England) is the historical 'fact' of the link between cricket and both the traditional values of Christianity and the emerging Victorian ideological practice of muscular Christianity in the English public schools and the tradition of imperialistic missionaries. The Protestant ethic which informed Victorian social and legal practices and norms permeated cricket as well. Erich Geldbach goes so far as to propose a Weberian analysis positing the theory that:

> Both the socio-economic . . . system of capitalism and modern athletics can be traced back to the setting of ascetic Protestantism which acted as a 'cultural catalyst' to bring about modern capitalism and modern sport.[99]

Whatever the final resolution of the Weberian and anti-Weberian chicken and egg debate about Protestantism and capitalism, it is quite clear from our understanding and knowledge of the game that there are obvious parallels between the ethical content of the 'spirit of the game' and certain popular versions of Christian morality. 'It's not cricket' resonates as condemningly as does 'It's not the Christian thing to do', in what many continue to assert are 'our' moral practices.

An interesting example and illustration of this moral interpretative code in cricket practice can be found in Mike Brearley's tribute to former England wicketkeeper Alan Knott upon his retirement.[100] After becoming a Christian in 1979, Knott changed his point of view on life and on cricket and 'came to see his behaviour during the rather ill-tempered series in India in 1972–73 as reprehensible'![101] His conversion did not, however, stop him from going on a rebel tour to apartheid South Africa. For Knott, apartheid apparently fit into an acceptable view of Christian cricket.

Despite the obvious historical and ideological unity of cricket and imperial Christianity, we are faced here again with competing versions of the truth. If such a connection really exists, why did it take Knott's conversion to illustrate for him the error of his ways? Why were the imprecations of those who condemned the events in question as violations of the *moral* code of cricket ineffective? Does this indicate that there is a conflict or that while there may be a practical conjunction one can heed the code only when its source is not human law but God's Law? Can only Christians be true cricketers? Can true cricketers be non-Christians? In the Indian context, can only Hindus be 'Indian' cricketers? What are we to make of the 'Islamic' nature of Pakistan and Pakistani cricket and Yusef Youhana, a Christian Test player? The debates over natural law *versus* human positivism are as central to the understanding of Noonan's jurisprudence as they are to the understanding of cricket. There are, of course, counter-Christian narratives or different Christian narratives in cricket which contradict and enrich the story just as there both secular and competing Hindu or Islamic renderings of the complex texts and practices of Indian and Pakistani cricket. A triumph over one narrow view of Christianity served to 'democratize' the game permitting the playing of the game on Sundays in England by melding capitalism and anti-Puritanism in an interesting and textually complex Weberian interpretive ploy.

Recent revelations about Australian cricket also serve to underline the inherent complexity of the issue of religion (Christianity) in cricket. Bill O'Reilly asserted that a religion-based split tarnished Australian cricket and threatened the careers of several Test and Sheffield Shield players. While Irish-Australians have always played cricket, it would appear that cricket remained, statistically speaking, a Protestant game. However, the deepest split in cricket has occurred historically not between Catholic and Protestant players, but between Catholic players and Protestant administrators who for years ruled the game like feudal landlords. The religious schism was further exacerbated when it became apparent that it was not simply adherence to non-Papist views which was important, but rather membership in the Masonic Lodge.

Membership in the Masons was said to ensure success and in one instance was seen to be a *sine qua non* of the Australian captaincy. In March 2002, Christie's offered for sale a letter in which Don Bradman bitterly attacked his teammates Bill O'Reilly and Jack Fingleton, blaming them for trying to undermine his captaincy on religious grounds.[102] O'Reilly and Fingleton were Irish Catholics, Bradman was a Protestant and a Mason.

Into the semiotic whirl of religion enters the hermeneutic circle of Masonic mysticism and the text of cricket takes on and creates for itself newer meanings and truths.[103] Australian cricket is not the only cricket text to be imbued with religious values and meanings. Indian cricket began and developed on sectarian lines and when one adds ideas of caste into the interpretive framework, Indian cricket becomes even more complex as occidental notions of class and religion dissolve into another cultural matrix. Indian–Pakistani Tests are obviously imbued with all the tensions of the partially religious conflict between those two countries, just as they offer at the same time a potential mode of transcending sectarianism through membership in the seemingly more universal interpretive community of cricket.

Sri Lanka offers the traditional conflict between the predominantly Buddhist Sinhalese population and the Hindu Tamil population. When Sri Lanka met Zimbabwe in late 2001 and early 2002, the first Test was played over six rather than five days. The extra day was allocated as a rest day in order to allow observance of a religious edict that no play could occur on the day of a full moon, which is the day on which Sinhalese Buddhists believe the Buddha was born.[104] Again, one might inquire about the feelings of Tamil players, or fans, when the national team playing the national game is made 'officially' Buddhist, rather than Sri Lankan, and what that says about Tamil claims of institutionalized discrimination. At the same time, it is necessary to be aware that it is not possible even here to reduce Sri Lankan cricket to some one-dimensional idea of 'Buddhism', of Buddhist hegemony, or of cricket. Even 'Buddhism' in this context must be read in subtle and complex ways, including as a legal text. For example, during the recent controversies in that country over the status of the Board, a desate erupted as the chief Buddhist priest criticized the government's Minister for Buddhist Affairs over a contractual dispute concerning the leasing of the stadium at Dambulla for a match against India. The Board was ousted and the government queried the validity of the contract approved by and negotiated with Buddhist authorities.[105]

Finally, in a similar fashion, notions of religion, class and political struggle came together in West Indian cricket in the Leeward Islands Cricket Association's decision to discriminate against Rastafarian cricketers in the 1970s when they passed the following regulation: 'Players will not be allowed on the field with coloured tams or hats, long plaited hair or dreadlocks.'[106] Babylon is everywhere, Jah is great and cricket is complicated.

25 Capitalism and the meaning of cricket

If there is a common juncture at which these disparate and contradictory interpretive elements which inform our understandings of cricket as a social and legal text can join together, it is in the heart of capitalism.[1] Those who bemoan and decry the demise of 'the spirit of the game' identify the ethos which is superseding tradition as 'professionalism'. Greg Chappell ordered his brother to bowl underarm because the spirit of professionalism, of commercial sponsorship, requires winning at all costs. Winning at all costs is not simply the condition precedent to winning the prize money, it is also the ultimate utilitarian bottom-line calculus of commercial capitalism. Homage and obedience to the spirit of the game is one thing, but 'showing the ball' to a batter who goes on to score the winning runs against your side is stupid. 'You can't eat ethics!' No one could dispute, in today's ideological and economic system, that cricket is big business. Yet playing the game well can apparently enter into direct conflict with the profit motive of late modern capitalism. For example, when cricket administrators enter into contracts for a Test series and sell TV rights to broadcasters, there is an interest in ensuring that the game is close, exciting and lasts the full five days; this will guarantee larger attendances and gate receipts and revenues from advertising will be enhanced the more time is spent broadcasting the game. Yet the conflict between bat and ball, the idea of 'winning', the inherent masculine values of 'dominating' and 'destroying' the opposition are all best served in many circumstances in winning as quickly and as devastatingly as possible.[2] At the same time, more fans may tune in to watch or attend matches if 'their' team is winning. Fans like to see good cricket but they also like to see winning cricket and they will pay for and watch both. The interests of sponsors and administrators may or may not be served in playing the game. As always, it all depends.

In modern capitalist society, all elements of culture are open to 'infection' by the ideology of the dominant mode of production. What must be questioned, again, is the tendency to false totalization and unity which informs the debate over the *nexus* between capitalism and sport in our culture. An examination of 'commercialism' and cricket demonstrates the existence of strong historical and current counter-narratives to any one-dimensional ideal type of capitalist cricket.

It is clear, for example, that English cricket, especially English professional cricket has a long history of 'commercialism'.[3] Likewise, commercial interests and the profit motive have always informed international cricket. The first England tour of Australia was a commercial venture, sponsored by Spiers and Pond, 'refreshment contractors'. It repaid the £7,000 outlay with a profit of £11,000 for the sponsors.[4] The 1877–78 Australian tour to England was a cooperative commercial venture where 'Each of the players put in £50 and profits were shared between stockholders according to their investment.'... 'Financially, the tour was extremely successful; stockholders received a return of £750 for their £50 investment.'[5]

It is well known that commercial gambling interests also dominated early Australian and English cricket. In another context, it is clear that without the sponsorship of business enterprises and the practice of providing employment to cricketers, India's cricket could never have survived and flourished.[6]

Still others point to the fact that there exists a happy coincidence between the nature of the game of cricket and sponsor's commercial interests, a coincidence which ensures the continuing viability of world cricket especially as a television product.[7] It seems clear now that if one factor has influenced the interactions between capitalism and cricket in recent years, it is precisely this idea of cricket as a programming product for television. This has become more evident and more serious as global economic phenomena and television and telecommunications technology, combined with the traditional appeal of the game, meet in profit.[8]

Of course, the primary iconic imagery which still resonates through the public consciousness of cricket on the subject of commercialism is the era of World Series Cricket (WSC) or more powerfully still, 'Packer Cricket'. Others have chronicled these events and circumstances and inscribed them in their social and political context.[9] Again, what is important to remember is that the sources of player unrest in the profitability of cricket and the lack of remuneration for the players and the arrogance and autocracy of the national governing bodies, had and have a long and rich history in cricket in every nation and in each country's players' decisions to participate in or stay away from WSC. Players like Clive Lloyd opted into Packer Cricket because of the peculiarly precarious social and financial status of West Indian cricketers.[10] Indians stayed away from WSC because of their unique and remunerative system of sponsorship. Australians who had a long history of dissatisfaction with the policies and practices of the Australian Cricket Board, especially concerning remuneration and player status, flocked to Packer's game.

What Packer Cricket proved in the end is that while the cricket traditionalists could not succeed in their attempted restraint of trade, it was possible to resolve to everyone's satisfaction the apparent conflict between 'the spirit of the game' and capitalist exploitation of the game. Packer's Channel 9 got televised cricket and the ACB reacquired control over international cricket in Australia. The players got more money, more input and more respect, and everyone was happy.

A similar process emerged in the summer months of 2002. With the approaching Champions Trophy tournament in Sri Lanka and with an eye to the lucrative World Cup in South Africa, the ICC sought to impose certain contractual provisions on all international cricketers. The goal of these provisions, which would prevent players from advertising and promoting products and sponsors other than those with official rights for a period preceding and following a particular event, was to stamp out 'ambush advertising'. Here, a company which does not have official sponsorship rights seeks to free ride on a popular sporting event without having paid for the privilege. Similar and related controversies are not unknown in other international sports. The central problem here is that with the rise of cricket as a full-time professional occupation, many international cricketers have lucrative individual sponsorship deals. Sachin Tendulkar, for example, is the most well remunerated and popular advertising figure in India.

The players baulked at the ICC contracts and threatened to boycott the Champions' Trophy series and even the World Cup. In addition to the personal financial stakes of the debates, the players also loudly proclaimed their disappointment that the contractual terms had been imposed without consultation. For many, this harked back to the bad old days of pre-Packer cricket in which players were treated as serfs.[11] An agreement by the ICC that players would be consulted before any new contracts were drawn up in the future averted the boycott. The conflict remains, however, between the commercial contractual interests of 'the game' as embodied by the ICC and the commercial contractual interests of the professional cricketers who earn their livelihood from their status as players, yet who remain bound by the organizational structures of national and international organization within which the game is currently played.

But again, the apparent resolution of the contradiction of cricket reveals still more complexity. While Test players now receive more money for their services, the plight of the ordinary English County professional remains a financially precarious one.[12] Some county clubs continue to struggle with the financial demands of domestic and international obligations.[13] Indian players, once immunized from the pressures which drove others to WSC, later found themselves threatening to strike after demanding a 70 per cent pay increase and continue to fight with authorities over individual sponsorship rights.[14]

Other areas of the actual way in which the game is played highlight the potential for commercial conflict in the sport. Day-night cricket, a Packer innovation, slowly made its way into the sacrosanct arena of first-class cricket as the WACA in Perth became 'the first floodlit venue for first-class cricket in the world'.[15] Now, the Test Match Playing Conditions which govern the highest level of the game permit and encourage play under lights as technology, profit and the best interests of the game become as one.[16]

When controversy around the use of lights in a Test match in Auckland arose, the ICC stated quite simply that while player safety was a major concern at all times: 'International players, however, will understand that whilst the traditional values of our game remain paramount they are in the entertainment business and that demands flexibility and adaptability from them.'[17]

Cricketers are now to be aware of the entertainment value they provide but they must submit themselves to limits on their incomes for the best interests of the game. At the same time, it was pointed out that appeals for the light are often based more in strategic concerns than in safety issues. Players will want to remain on the field or go off depending on the contextualized situation of their team. If the batters are in a position to win the game they will want to stay, if their team is trailing or on the brink of losing they will be more than happy to leave and let time pass. During the Indian innings of over 600 runs at Headingley during the 2002 Test, England were more than happy to claim that bad light made fielding dangerous as Tendulkar smashed their bowling all over the ground.[18] The availability of lighting simply removes one element of tactical decision-making from the game and returns to the essential normative contest between bat and ball. At the same time, the commercial interests of the broadcasters, the sponsors and the home ground are better served as more cricket can be played. In each instance, and in many more, the answer simply raises further questions about the 'real' nature of cricket.

As the commercialization of cricket advances, forms of case-specific anti-commercialism sometimes surface. The ethical correctness of sponsorship from tobacco companies had always been a thorny issue, throwing into contrast considerations of cold hard cash and the nature and image of the sport. The debate surfaced regularly and remains largely unresolved. The New Zealand Cricket Council (NZCC) dropped Rothmans's as its major sponsor. The NZCC quickly pointed out, however, that their decision was a purely commercial, not a moral, one.[19] Commercialism went well with cricket in New Zealand while moralism clearly did not. On the other hand, the Australian Cricket Board, like the New South Wales Rugby League, continued its association with tobacco companies. Here, yet again, we confront the competing world-views of legal formalism and cricket as a higher ethical practice. An ACB spokesperson at the time equated the Board's decision to continue accepting sponsorship from Benson and Hedges with their decision to abide by government bans on links with South Africa. The larger, public issues are to be determined by government and the ACB would operate simply and purely within the bounds of legality. Morality is a non-issue for organized cricket.

> The ACB is there to co-ordinate and run the game of cricket on a national basis in this country. We are not foreign affairs experts. We are not health experts.
> . . .
> You've got to decide whether your sphere of responsibility extends beyond that area of running the game of cricket. The answer is clearly no.[20]

Sounding suspiciously as if it originates from a representative of the asbestos or tobacco industries (after all, they *are* legal products), this statement encapsulates not only a view of cricket but a moral/legal position on the world at large. 'The ACB does not have the expertise in either foreign affairs or health.' This statement carries with it the necessary implication that apartheid and cigarette-caused diseases were not facts on which ordinary citizens can, should, and must make decisions. Rather, they are too complicated, matters for the experts and therefore beyond our capacity to choose. It is a view of the citizen as passive recipient of moral/legal commands from the sovereign. It is Austinianism run rampant.

At the same time of course, the Board had made its own 'private' decision, i.e. that the game is the game and has nothing to do with public, political issues such as apartheid or health. Yet, clearly, its 'private' decision had serious public con-sequences as the blatant effect of the Benson and Hedges boundary signs could not escape even the most naive spectator. Moreover, it was not, has never been, and never will be despite the position of the ACB a logical consequence of anything that the 'game is simply the game'.

For Peter Roebuck the position is as clear as it is for the ACB, yet the conclusion is for him, is quite the opposite: 'Tobacco is legal, right enough, for we live in a relatively free country, yet cricket must see beyond legalisms.'[21]

The same Peter Roebuck who readily leaps to the legal formalist position when Pakistan walks off the pitch against Victoria, can sense no contradiction, or self-loathing, or moment of existential bad faith when he appeals here to the broader spirit of the game. And, of course, he is right. Obedience to the *Laws of Cricket* is synonymous, when faced with the gamesmanship of the Pakistanis, with the preservation of the broader interests of the game, whereas simple-minded reference to governmental regulation has nothing to do with the code of moral and ethical conduct which cricket embodies. His objection to the ACB position here is based on a complete rejection of their ontological world-view. For them, cricket is a game and just a game, for Roebuck, cricket is much more. All other decisions will follow for one or the other from the basic idea/text of what cricket *is* and what it *ought to be*. For some, it must transcend legality and commercial interests, for others, it *cannot* transcend legality and commercial interests. For others, like Roebuck here, it depends.

As government regulations greatly reduced the legal arena in which tobacco companies could advertise, the game found corporate sponsors elsewhere.[22] And as sponsors offered more and more money, they also demanded and received more 'rights' under contract. Stadia are named not after cricketing greats or the location, but after a sponsor's commercial identity.[23] Test and One-Day series, as well as domestic competitions, carry corporate names.[24] Logos appear on the field of play and, with virtual computer technology, on our television screens without needing a physical presence at the match.

Players now carry trademark logos on their uniforms, as do umpires.[25] In the first years of these developments, there was a predictable conflict between ideas of the 'purity' of the game and the reality of commercial life. Sponsorship was permitted but regulation was new and untested. The ICC introduced rules governing the size and placement of sponsor's logos and players tested the limits of legal intervention. In 1995, Greg Blewett, Ricky Ponting and Shane Warne of Australia were fined by the Match Referee for wearing wrist bands featuring commercial logos.[26] The next year Herschelle Gibbs and V.V.S. Laxman were fined for breach of the ICC logo policy and in 1997, Navjot Sidhu was also penalized.[27] The ICC has clarified its policies and practices concerning advertising and its regulations dealing with bat sponsorship after several controversies on the subject.[28] Finally in Jan. 2002, Australian wicketkeeper/batter Adam Gilchrist became the first cricketer at international level to carry commercial advertising on his bat.[29] Gilchrist is still considered by many to be one of the most exciting and best batters in international cricket. He is vice-captain of Australia and a proud wearer of the baggy green cap; he is also an entrepreneur. Capitalism and cricket are each embodied here, and each manages to exist without anyone who watches the game thinking that Gilchrist is playing 'Travelex' cricket.

Nowhere do the interests and issue of cricket and commercialism find a more 'natural' meeting place than in the world of television. It is not accidental that the entire Packer Cricket phenomenon was sparked by Kerry Packer's desire to break the ABC's television monopoly over cricket for the benefit of his Channel 9. Cricket is ideal television and its continuing popularity attests to that.

Indeed in England and Australia televised cricket is of such cultural and national importance that legislation demands that games be shown on free-to-air television. Government policy and broadcasting regulation requires that the 'English' or 'Australian' public have access to cricket on television because cricket on television is somehow part of deeper current understandings of cultural national identity. Pay TV and satellite providers target audiences in the subcontinent with a constant diet of cricket, especially the one-day variety and the Indian, Pakistani, Sri Lankan and Bangladeshi diaspora are all regular consumers of Pay TV cricket. Indeed, the needs of the diaspora sometimes coincide with both commercial and political reality. India and Pakistan can meet in Toronto, in front of an expatriate audience, in a game beamed around the world to still more viewers, and political tensions which make playing games in either country impossible, may sometimes although not always be averted.[30] And the administrations of each country can pocket a tidy profit.[31] But this profit will only subsist as long as the television market remains viable. When India pulled out of the Asian Test championship because of faltering relations with Pakistan over Kashmir, none of the major broadcasters was interested in purchasing the rights to the various games since the largest audience would in effect be lost.[32]

At the same time, there continues to be in cricket, as there is in the globalized capitalist economy in general, a problem of uneven distribution of wealth. The West Indies, in 2002, announced a three-year deficit of US$15 million, while India is the wealthiest nation in the cricketing elite.[33] Boards in various countries, World Cup organizing committees and the ICC are all involved in the commercialization of cricket as pay TV programming.[34] Various controversies erupt over payments, allegations of corruption and breach of contract, and unfair restrictions being placed on players' abilities to seek individual sponsorship deals.[35] Players complain that there is too much One-Day Cricket and not enough Test matches; others assert that the plethora of One-Day Cricket is the cause of cricket's match-fixing scandals. Political unrest in the subcontinent leads to tour cancellations and the loss of revenue for the PCB. India, New Zealand and Sri Lanka cancelled tours to Pakistan because of political and military unrest and the crises in Kashmir and Afghanistan. New Zealand cricketers left Pakistan after an attack on French visitors outside their hotel in early 2002. Both the West Indies and Pakistani authorities sought further compensation as a result of having to shift their 2001/02 series to Sharjah.[36] Australia cancelled a scheduled tour of Zimbabwe following political unrest and international pressure suspending that country from the Commonwealth and desperate efforts to find a suitable neutral venue for matches took place when Australia pulled out of its 2002 tour of Pakistan on security grounds.[37] Contract law, broadcasting regulation, illegal gambling, the war on terrorism, all circulate here as parts to the juridification of the relationships between and among cricket, capital and law. Yet, despite protestations from some that the 'game' is in danger or is already lost, we still watch, sponsors negotiate more and more lucrative contracts for broadcast and other rights, and it is all still cricket.[38]

Cricket is popular not only because of the dramatic content of the 'game itself', e.g. the opposition between batter and bowler, the unfolding story of a five-day Test, like those other popular TV genres, the mini-series or the soap-opera, but because, cricket encapsulates the text of life and law itself. In every ball, every stroke, every catch, every over, we can see, know, understand and give meaning not only 'to the game' but to our lives and our legal relations. Our daily lives are imbued with subtle and not so subtle negotiations with and within global capitalism, from how we get to work, where we work, if we work, to what we eat and watch on TV to the 'choice' of software I use to type this book. We watch cricket partly to escape yet also in part because it allows us not to escape the inescapable but to see some opportunities to negotiate and create different and more complex arrangements and understandings of broader social and political and legal practices.[39]

Some who watch cricket on television 'read' an entirely different text, and given the open-ended picture of both the text and the available possible interpretations, this is hardly surprising. Some see the commercially interrupted Test match broadcast as superficial and trendy, like all popular culture, and they see this as a betrayal of the 'real' game. Others see a deeper meaning in the same surface text. Instead of mere cynicism and pop culture, they see the subliminal advertising impact of the sponsor's messages covering the boundary.

These types of analyses indicate a deep yet at the same time flawed and one-dimensional understanding of the nature of cricket as a social practice. It *is* true that when we watch a ball crash into the boundary, we see an advertising sign, just as it is true that on a close-up of Adam Gilchrist taking strike we see the trademark on his bat and pads. And it is true that comments about 'team-work' and a failing national spirit are 'about' cricket just as they are 'about' values of the corporate capitalist system and a particular vision of patriotism. But those who see nothing but 'capitalism' commit two interpretive errors when they examine the narrative of televised cricket.

First, these questions presuppose a distinction between the surface 'meaning' of the text and its deep structure or 'true meaning'. This is the fundamental failing of all structuralist analysis, and of all analyses of cricket and law which seek to impose or discover an immutable truth in the practice of interpretation. Such interpretive positions cannot see that there is 'truth' in both practices, that our experience of the text is not of a stark contrast of an 'or' but an 'and', or an 'only if', we see and experience and know both that team-work is good cricket and good shopfloor practice. We can live with the conflict, contradiction and values of cricket because we can and do live with conflict, contradiction and values of life on a daily basis and like the legal system and the 'fundamental contradiction' life goes on. The 'spirit of the game' can be, and is, strict adherence to the letter of the law, a supplement but not replacement for the letter of the law, or a transcendent principle which trumps law. It can be any and all of these things at any one time, or at different times, for participants in the construction of the meaning of the *Laws of Cricket* and what it might mean, at a particular time and place to play the game.

Most analysts who pose such queries about sport and capitalism and about cricket and the law, appear to assume that there is not only an 'or' but that the distinction is one between two clear-cut and unambiguous interpretive practices. Cricket (like all other social texts) is a contradictory and ambiguous narrative into which we insert our own extra-textual readings which become part of the new text of cricket. The story of the ball sent crashing to the boundary is not just a text about cricket or advertising, it is a part of a story about race, class, gender, religion, law, ethics etc. The only end to the story is the end we impose on it. The only meaning of the story is the one we impose on it, and in spite of the hegemonic claims of one-dimensional capitalists *and* Marxists to universal interpretive status, our lived experience of cricket is much richer and more complex than such interrogations permit. I do not wish to assert by this, however, that cricket is not imbued with the values of capitalism or class or technology in the new world of globalization. On the contrary, there is little doubt that each of these texts is a sub-text of cricket and that, conversely, cricket is a sub-text of each of them.

Besides giving us a complex text of technological innovation in the postmodern world, televised cricket also raises the fundamental issue of the connection among information, free speech, commerce and democracy. The connection, undiscussed and uncriticized in the UK and Australia between cricket on commercial television and cricket as formative of public, national cultural raises many similar concerns. Are Channel 4's interests in carrying Test match cricket the same as those of the cricket viewing public in cricket as national social text?[40] Why is government policy dealing with the public interest confined in its execution and implementation to commercial corporate interests? Do we care as long as the cricket is on the air and we do not have to pay money to Rupert Murdoch to watch?

Cricket, in fact, does more than promote unquestioning obedience to a one-dimensional view of 'the game' or law, or morality or nation. I will now turn to a brief discussion of 'class' and cricket to show, once more, that critiques of cricket have previously underestimated its interpretive complexity and its function and potential as a social text.

26 Class struggle, old school tie and the meaning of cricket

The chief ideological artifact of the mythological and historical representation of 'true' cricket is the image of the game as one for 'gentlemen'. Besides the obvious appeal to the values of 'the spirit of the game' and 'good sportsmanship', there is in all this an underlying message (and received wisdom) that cricket is, and always has been, an aristocratic or upper-class game. Of course, there is 'truth' to this assertion as can be seen in the origins of the game and its players, where 'professional' cricketers were in fact employed as domestics for the aristocracy when not playing cricket. Indeed, a strong argument can be made that the class-based nature of the sport persisted long after the rest of (English) society had moved forward, not by eliminating class structure, but by making society more complex than the simple gentleman/player dichotomy would indicate. In that sense, at one level, cricket remained an ahistorical relic, a lived experience of the past which ignored the lessons of current society and offered a counter-narrative to the values of the present day. Of course, this does not mean that the counter-narrative was a popular or progressive one. Speaking of the MCC, Ric Sissons paints the following picture of a group which did not differ much from the popular understanding of the make-up of the British judiciary: 'Despite the fundamental changes occurring within the British ruling class and society at large, the MCC Committee remained a bastion of the Conservative, imperialist, landed gentry throughout the inter-war years.'[1]

The MCC, it must be said, did not necessarily stand alone, nor did it appear to be completely out of step with one interpretation of the dominant cricket narrative. The structure of game as played at the first-class level in England, with the absurd distinction between the Gentlemen and the Players, was itself based on class distinctions. And in turn, these class distinctions served to reinforce not only a vision of cricket but of society in a broad sense. At the same time, these divisions were reflective of a conflict in British society between the values of the landed gentry and the urbanized bourgeois class. Cricket, in its class structure, reflected not only the class struggle between worker and capitalist.[2] At the same time, it reflected the struggle for cultural hegemony between competing *factions* of what would historically and ideologically have been considered to be the dominant class.[3] Thus:

The class discrimination in cricket legitimized the class discrimination in society by ranking sportsmanship, individuality and flair, reportedly the qualities of the gentlemanly amateur, higher than competitiveness (defined as an over-eagerness to win), application and consistency, all reportedly the qualities of the professional player.[4]

These attributes, however, were not universally shared by members of each class who played the game, nor were they a universal part of 'cricket', as fact or as myth. While Indian society and West Indian cricket reflected to a greater extent these class values of English cricket, exacerbated under local conditions by considerations of caste, religion and race, Australian cricket, by the 1890s at least, perceived itself to be based on the 'native' Australian cultural characteristics of 'forthrightness' and 'egalitarianism', and Australians did not, for example, hesitate to condemn the absurdity of the English Gentleman/Player distinction. At the same time, Australian cricket continued to be dominated by a hierarchical distinction between the players and the administrators which often played itself out in the stark materialistic terms of inadequate remuneration for those who actually produced value through their labour.

Ironically, it was perhaps the 'egalitarianism' turn of Australian cricket which produced much of the conflict. In the 1890s, along with its egalitarian principles, cricket in Australia was still more sport than business. While rejecting the English class distinctions between cricketers, the Australians adopted the most English of aristocratic values in relationship to their cricket (amateurism of a kind), while at the same time maintaining a class conflict between players and administrators. In each country, 'class', like each other factor or sub-text, operated and continues to operate, in a complex web of interactions with each other individual sub-text to somehow combine to constitute the (in)coherent story of cricket.

At other levels, too, 'class' in cricket operated at different levels within other factors. While sporadic strikes by cricketers in England occurred from 1881, as the labour movement rose in society at large, no real attempt to unionize cricketers ever took place in English cricket.[5] Many possible explanations arise, as applicable here as in many other contexts of labour and legal history. Most cricketers (professionals) had clearly adapted the cult of expertise and merit and saw their remuneration as stemming from their own performance and not from collective efforts; many of the top players earned good money and would perhaps not have benefited from collectivization; cricket, no matter how poorly paid, was a better life than the factory or the pit; business opportunities after cricket were available; and finally, the local County Committee dealt with the workers with an iron fist in a velvet glove. Those who remained loyal were awarded a benefit and often, post-cricket employment, those who breached discipline were summarily dismissed.

In Australia, while 'class' offers itself as a useful analysis in fathoming the players' relationship with the ACB and state boards, and can explain the build-up to Packer cricket, the class factor was, in practice, often overridden in this country by issues of national self-identity, 'civilization' and gender. The historical circumstances of cricket in Australia – the presence of an 'inferior' indigenous culture, the climatological concerns, the 'convict' stain, operated so that cricket became a distinctly 'middle class' game and the Australian middle class became more and more socially amorphous and hegemonic.

And this remains true today. School cricket competitions, for example, are dominated by public schools, 'public' here in the Australian sense, i.e. state schools. In the 1980s and early 1990s, only one private school (that is in English terms, a public school) graduate – spinner Peter Taylor – played Test cricket for Australia. This does not, of course, mean that Australian society or the school system is not class-based. On the contrary, it could indicate that while success in other activities (e.g. university entrance) is virtually assured to private school students, the options of state school graduates may be more limited so that they turn to sport as a channel through which to obtain financial success or a greater sense of self-worth. At the basic level of resources and the ideology of education, it may well be that private school students have been taught to focus on other aspects of education (computers, university entrance exams, for example), while in public schools, limited financial resources and a perception of failure and second-class status as well as an idealized 'working-class culture' so infect the system that students have no choice but to turn to cricket and other sports. Finally, private boys' schools in Australia may be so Anglophile in orientation that only rugby union football is truly important as far as future representative sport is concerned. Whatever the reasons, it is clear that class operates, like other sub-texts, in a complex *matrix* of the social practices which make up cricket. Class analysis is only the beginning, for to understand the role of 'class' in cricket, we must understand everything else that makes up 'class' as well as everything else that makes up 'cricket'.

Yet, just as cricket internationally has been subject to global commercial pressures, so too has the class structure of the game, and the idea of the relationship between players and boards has been changed. A new system of central contracts now governs elite cricket in England.[6] Battles continue to be fought between the national body, the ECB, and the counties over the number of centrally con-tracted players and their availability for county matches.[7] Players attempt to buy out of their contracts to enable them to change employers;[8] county clubs refuse and litigate. In Australia, the newly formed Australian Cricketers' Association brought the game to the brink of its first real strike in 1997 before reaching an agreement with the Board and entering a new era of wealth and security for professional cricketers.[9] Despite, or perhaps because of this newfound wealth, play-ers continue to claim that they are exploited by administrators and sponsors and forced to sign contracts with which they are uncomfortable. Indeed, there is here, as in other sports, great potential for conflict between the player's individual contractual and commercial interests and sponsors and those of the team, Board or competition.[10] Zimbabwean and West Indian players have threatened boycotts and strikes in their effort for better pay and conditions, and Indian, South African, Pakistani and Sri Lankan cricketers have all renegotiated their relationships with the governing authorities.[11] Players in the latest Test-playing country, Bangladesh, have also been involved with contractual disputes with the governing authority.[12] Individuals like South African Daryll Cullinan refuse selection when contract terms are not to their liking.[13] As cricket becomes a truly full-time game, as television deals bring millions into the sport, the producers of value and surplus value demand their fair share. Of course, this gives rise to tension and conflict, just as it gives rise to compromise. Players in England refuse to tour the subcontinent, claiming both exhaustion and fear of danger.[14] Australian cricketers raise concerns over tours scheduled for Zimbabwe and Pakistan. Boards stand firm or agree with the players. Cricketers suffer the consequences or achieve a state of harmony with officials. The Australian players' association and the Board join together in protecting their intellectual property rights in merchandise and memorabilia.[15] Workers and bosses unite under the banner of the struggle over trademark protection. Profits flourish and cricket continues on the field. At the same time, as the Champions Trophy imbroglio demonstrated, the commercial interests of the players and the administrators are not always identical and the potential for important conflict remains.

Finally, it must be noted that cricket is not immune from other factors which have dominated relations between and among labour, management and society as a whole. The Industrial Revolution brought with it mechanization and cricket was not spared.[16] To this day technology and the skill of the curator/artisan combine the modern and the traditional in a perfectly complex combination of contradiction without which cricket could not exist.[17] Other technological innovations and changes have had profound effects on the nature and practice of cricket: the mechanical roller and mowing machine allowed for the construction of better pitches and the fights for ascendancy between bowler and batter; the steam engine and British rail system allowed the game to spread and created a demand which caused the creation of teams of touring professionals; new technology permitted the manufacture of better bats and balls, also making way for better performances by batters and bowlers. At the same time as technology transformed cricket into a modern, urban sport, it also allowed, by way of counter-text, for the privileging of the artisan, with hand-stitched balls and hand-made bats allowing cricket in some way to stop or reverse the flow of time by reference to an outdated manual 'technology' of the artisan. Heavier bats and reduced stitching on balls have become the focus of much debate. Constant debates over 'the white ball' used in One-Day games and the difficulty bowlers have controlling swing with it in the early overs also offer an example of the role of technology in playing the game. The complaint here is that technology in fact lags behind the requirements of the sport. More precisely, the inability of bowlers to control the swing puts them at a distinct disadvantage not just in the direct confrontation with the batter, but it also places them in conflict with the *Laws* and *Playing Conditions* relating to wides.[18] The old is replaced by the new, the new by the newer, yet despite all these changes and innovations, the modern and the traditional somehow continue to co-exist in the text we still 'know' to be cricket.

Nowhere do these elements combine so exquisitely than in one of the most important of cricket's interpretive communities – the crowd.

27 The Hill, the members and others: the crowd as sub-text

If it is correct that cricket informs, and in turn is informed by, the narrative/interpretive structures of society, it should not be surprising that we find, in the sub-text of the crowds who attend cricket matches, the same complex interaction of competing and often contradictory elements.

The role of the crowd is essential in the construction (and deconstruction) of the texts of cricket and law. For some, the idea of 'the crowd' will serve to mask the inequalities and inequities of the society of which they are part by falsely creating an amorphous and homogeneous false image of a group which in reality suffers these inequities. Similarly, constructions of the 'Australian' crowd or of the 'Barmy Army' will always need to be further contextualized, from both the inside and the outside of the phenomenological experience under examination. 'Indian' crowds are seen by Australians and many English fans as riotous assemblies, yet the great Indian Sunil Gavaskar himself spoke of West Indian crowds as barbarians. Bangladeshi crowds may hurl missiles at Pakistani players as a result of frustration at the score or memories of the bitter war of independence.[1] Again, however, any particular vision will itself reveal only part of a very complex picture, imbued with a variety of cultural practices and meanings.

The mythology of 'true' cricket asserts, for example, that English crowds are imbued with, and reflect, the values of that cricket, i.e. that they are sportsman-like and gentlemanly and that cries of 'Well done, old boy!' resound at every fine performance, whether of an English cricketer or some colonial. Cucumber sandwiches are put to one side as the game itself becomes the object of congratu-lation. At the same time, as part of the imperialistic context of a belief in a Denningesque 'true' cricket, there is a widespread interpretive belief that Australian crowds, unlike their English counterparts, are rowdy, jingoistic and just not cricket.[2] There is, of course, some very ample evidence of the rowdy behaviour of Australian cricket crowds, the riot of 1879 in Sydney demonstrating its historical lineage. Both of these visions and versions of the crowd are true and yet at the same time both are equally false. Australians for example have adopted and warmed to the 'Barmy Army' precisely because they, the epitome of the new English crowd, embody the rowdy disrespect for gentlemanly stuffiness which allegedly characterizes Australian cricket fans. The Barmy Army is, in fact, Australian.

But the overarching nature of any such a characterization of traditional fandom, must, like all other overarching interpretations of cricket, be brought into question. For example, no matter how awful crowd behaviour at the SCG may have been in 1879, comments by English cricketers referring to the crowd as 'sons of convicts' must clearly be seen as having contributed to future hostilities by Australian crowds as such comments are fitted into a collective consciousness about cricket, imperialism and national identity.

Nor can we simply treat 'Australian crowds' as an indistinguishable whole. As Cashman clearly points out, Australian crowds from the earliest days have been physically and emotionally segregated on class grounds between the Members' enclosures and the outer, in Sydney historically, the Hill, and more recently in Melbourne, Bay 13, for example.[3] It would appear that the Australian crowd and its behaviour has, in fact, been multifaceted, and determined not in the least by class-based factors in many of its internal sub-texts. Indeed, the bulldozing of the Hill at the SCG and the reconfiguration of Bay 13 at the MCG can be seen as modern attempts to homogenize a heterogeneous agglomeration for the purposes of consumer capitalism. Modern stadium architecture and spatial divisions are employed, along with surveillance techniques and policing practices to create the cricket crowd as passive consumers of spectacle. The 'democratization' of space here becomes a way of ensuring pacification.

It would be necessary to explore more explicitly and in greater detail the historical and contextual environment of 'the Australian crowd' to fully inter- pret its interpretive role and function. So too is it necessary to explore and explode the myth of the English cricket crowd as exemplary of 'true' cricket.[4] Not only are there many historical incidents of ungentlemanly behaviour by English crowds but it is clear that such incidents repeat themselves today. At the fourth Test at Leeds in 1988, 'the West Indian players were the subject of racial abuse from the Yorkshire crowd'.[5] While racism is indeed part of the broad experience of cricket, and of Yorkshire cricket in its very historical structure, it is also true that such a reaction by the crowd was 'not cricket' in the traditional sense of bucolic admiration of the objective skills of all participants. Nor was it 'cricket' to be forced to take measures against crowd 'hooliganism', but English officials have had to restrict licensing laws at grounds and to make special appeals for orderly behaviour.[6]

Thus, the 'English' crowd has, like its counterparts elsewhere in the world of cricket become the target of surveillance and security. Gone are the days when 'hooligans' were associated with the lower class followers of football. Now cricket has become the site of crowd misbehaviour, criminality and criminalization.[7]

English cricketers, officials and commentators have all decried the increasing levels of crowd misbehaviour and violence. Many have issued calls for greater security measures at grounds. Here, as in Australia, fears and concerns about cricket crowds and problems are dealt with through a series of measures, each of which is debated and placed within the appropriate 'public' or 'private' sphere. Ground management and governing bodies, private security consultants and guards are used to render crowd violence a phenomenon outside the traditional discourses of law and order and government concern. The issue again becomes one of occupational health and safety and private liability insurance etc.[8] In England, unlike Australia, or in most other international cricketing countries, the mechanisms for controlling crowd behaviour have remained largely within the private domain. The government in effect has refused, contrary to the usual reaction of New Labour, to give in to the moral panic around cricket crowd management problems. Despite pleas from the game's governing authorities, the official stance has been to refuse to recognize cricket violence as a public crime problem.[9] Instead, 'crime' in the form of unruly crowd behaviour has effectively been privatized and left to local officials and authorities.

Crowd behaviour, including the potential for pitch invasion and physical abuse of players, became a point of concern and controversy at the 1999 World Cup. Australian captain Steve Waugh threatened to boycott matches unless and until security measures were increased and improved.[10] Further controversy erupted during the tournament over concerns raised by a game between India and Pakistan. Not only were the various actors worried about crowd behaviour when the traditional rivals met, but political tensions over Kashmir between the governments threatened to exacerbate the problems.[11] Of course, for many, this issue is not one of 'English' crowds, but of crowds which just happen to be in England. This becomes another version of the Norman Tebbit cricket test.[12] Here the problems are caused by fans of India and Pakistan. They are by definition not 'English' fans regardless of which passport they may carry. As long as old rivalries and tensions inform their choices of which side to support, such fans will never be truly English.[13] For some this will remain a constant truth of the struggle over the nexus between cricket supporters and tests of patriotism and loyalty. At the same time, many administrators, conscious of the bottom line, are engaged in attempts to attract young 'British Asians' to follow the game at all levels.[14]

The problem of racism and racist abuse has long plagued English cricket and English cricket crowds in particular. Of course, they are not alone in the sports' world. Italian and French football are marked by racism and neo-fascism.[15] Yet for several years now, campaigns such as those aiming to 'Hit racism for Six' have struggled with their marginalized status and official indifference to the realities of racism both within the structures of the game and in the stands.[16] The ECB has announced plans to combat racism and government has imposed a charter of racial equality on organized sport, including cricket.[17] At the same time, protest at the presence of depictions of 'Asian' women at the Sir Len Hutton gate at Headingley, claims that Asians are disloyal for supporting visiting teams and racist taunts from 'white' fans continue to inform debate, practice and law on this subject.

In 2001, England captain Nasser Hussain and David Graveney each issued calls for fans to support the 'home' team and to stop cheering for the visitors.[18] At this time, the mythology of a multiracial and multicultural New Britain under New Labour was being contested as 'Asian' youths battled 'English' police and National Front activists in the streets and neighbourhoods of Oldham and

Aylesbury.[19] Vivek Chaudhary put the other view on the politics of cricket spectating in England.

> Hussain has clearly never sat in the stands when England are playing a team from the subcontinent or the West Indies. He has obviously never heard the racist comments coming from some members of the crowd. That's a good enough reason not to support England; its fans hardly endear themselves to the minorities of this country.[20]

It goes without saying that the issues here remain much more complicated than the simplicity implied in the Tebbit cricket test for patriotic belonging. Chaudhary is particularly vociferous in his criticism of Hussain's apparent lack of race consciousness. He accuses the England captain of playing down race and the realities of oppression in favour of a merit-based, all-encompassing Englishness. For Hussain, on the other hand, he does not see himself as a role model for younger Asian cricketers in England they are, English cricketers. Here of course, we encounter all the debates and controversies which surround the politics of identity, the law of affirmative action, ideals and realities of 'equality' and so on. At the very core of these debates are the competing concepts of identity and citizenship, of cricket nationalism and of cricket as nationalism. The struggle here is between a utopian ideal of a colour-blind English identity and one which takes account of race and ethnicity yet finds an inclusive definition and understanding of 'Englishness'. Ian Buruma writes of Arthur Koestler's assertion that there are two kinds of patriotism – the normal variety and football patriotism. For him, the latter was the more firmly entrenched. Buruma goes on to argue that both Chaudhary and Hussain are right, that the issues here at play are complex, they are not black (or brown) and white.[21] Cricket loyalties are not a simple or accurate shorthand for patriotism or even of national identity. Cricket patriotism is not the same as ordinary or constitutional patriotism. Indeed, it might well be asserted that only a country with a truly authentic constitutional patriotism can understand and accept cricket or football patriotism. From the point of view espoused by Buruma, the fact that Australians of Italian heritage are more interested in football than cricket does not make them less Australian. That they support Italy's efforts in the World Cup has nothing to do with their patriotism to Australia. It is only when we fall victim to a limiting, limited and one-dimensional vision of the relationship between sport and nation that the cricket test à la Tebbit can have any relevance. That does not mean that sport, and in this case cricket, can be entirely disassociated from national identity. That would be a complete denial of historical and current reality. But it does mean that there is no single narrative, ideological structure or template which will allow us easy access to the complexities involved.

Of course, one would then wish to point out, in addition to the complexities of any assertion about an 'Asian' propensity to crowd violence, in the context of a multiracial and multicultural Britain, that Australian complaints about crowd violence arose out of games in which neither India not Pakistan featured. They involved games against Scotland and against New Zealand in Cardiff. Again, some might argue that the Scots and the Welsh are not 'English' and so the taxonomy of English cricket crowds cannot be invoked. Yet it seems clear that crowd problems at English grounds also occur during local domestic matches and there is nothing to indicate that when the ICC targeted ground safety concerns that English facilities were somehow exempt.[22]

Instead what operates at one level in England, as elsewhere, is a conflict between two competing notions of what 'cricket' means for the spectator. As Matthew Engel wrote

> There is huge problem about watching cricket. On the one hand, there are those who believe it should be watched either intently or somnolently, according to the mood, but above all quietly. On the other, there are those who see it as an occasion for drinking, dressing up, waving flags, banging drums, blowing bugles and generally letting off steam.[23]

If one adopts the former view of the essential qualities of 'cricket', then it becomes clear that any conflict with supporters of the latter views must be solved by regulation and prohibition. Yet for those of the second persuasion, fundamental rights to the pursuit of happiness and collective intervention in the interpretive practices of cricket, are at some level in play as part of a democratic struggle to participate in 'cricket'.

The most important interpretive function of the crowd is not related to pitch incursions or hooliganism but to its role in providing an ongoing commentary on the game, a reflection of a dominant social ethos and sometimes to affect the outcome of the game itself through the practice of what Australians refer to as barracking. The barracker has long played an important part in the construction of Australian cricket, although that role and the nature of barracking itself has changed.[24] Not only does barracking reflect different historical periods but there are complex sub-texts of barracking, from the polite cheering of the upper-class Members' stand to 'the more basic and earthy barracking which developed in the Outer'.[25] At the same time, to a certain extent, the very nature and function of the barracker as interpreter has been subjected to pressure and change. As cricket becomes more 'commercialized', the game itself can be seen to change from sport to entertainment and from pastime to occupation. The relationship of the spectator to the game becomes less determining, less interactive and more contractual and impersonal. The member of the crowd becomes a 'consumer' of an entertainment product, rather than a participant in a democratically based law-making exercise. Popular spaces are redesigned to be more 'spectator friendly', as cricket as commerce seeks to be a more family entertainment exercise. Similarly, cricketers become more concerned for their safety as the game becomes a full-time professional sport. Their livelihood is now at stake when objects are thrown or pitch invasions occur. Crowd behaviour becomes for the professional cricketer an occupational health and safety issue as it does for the administrators of the game. For sponsors who invest in the sport and in the players, the loss of a Michael Vaughan, Ricky Ponting, Brian Lara or Sachin Tendulkar through injury resulting from crowd violence become matters of commercial importance. For stadium owners, insurance premiums and liability issues for injuries incurred by players or spectators are now questions for police, security officials and legal representatives.[26]

At the same time, cricketers were and remain our national (and international) heroes. Crowds at the Hill in Sydney would taunt visiting West Indies cricketers with racist jibes of 'black monkeys' as they display a sick racist humour by hurling bananas at the deep West Indian fielders as an accompaniment to their insults.[27] They would also rise to cheer a century by Greenidge or Richards, a catch behind by Dujon or a five-wicket innings by Ambrose, Walsh or Marshall. As border conflict, spurred on by factional, ethnic and religious quarrels rages between India and Pakistan,

> Nowhere in the world could Asif Iqbal have got the emotional standing ovation he got on the last day of his last test from 85,000 cricket fans at Eden Gardens in Calcutta. It was particularly noticeable because Iqbal was the captain of Pakistan and India's cricket tests with Pakistan often degenerate into war-like rituals...[28]

Accusations of racism and anti-Asian bias continue to circulate in press reports about Australian cricket crowds. When India and Pakistan toured at the same time, some argued that a common reaction against Australian racism would unite the traditional rivals.[29] During the same season, the Australian crowd at the SCG rose as one to give an ovation for V.V.S. Laxman's 100, his debut century.[30]

Again, crowds do continue to reflect the contradictory myths and conflicting realities of cricket. Nowhere was this better evidenced than in the interpretive community of the Hill at the SCG.[31] From its very origins, the Hill was the site of 'disturbances' and 'rowdy behaviour' and from the very beginning it was the site of the working-class larrikin culture of Australian cricket.[32] From disturbances in the nineteenth century to concerns about 'hooliganism' in the 1960s, to Ray Illingworth's decision to take his English team off the field in 1971 following verbal and physical assaults from the Hill, to mass cries in the 1970s–80s of 'Hadlee's a wanker! Hadlee's a wanker!', there was a popular tendency to see the Hill as simply a site of working-class larrikinism or ocker behaviour. The problems of the Hill were, in short, the problems of the working class. While in the Members' enclosure proper attire is required, on the Hill the crowd sunbathed and engaged in the Mexican Wave.

This, it was argued, demonstrated not only the tendency to rowdiness of the plebeians on the Hill but also provided evidence that the Hill did not reflect, and probably cannot understand, 'true' cricket. The upper-class patrons of the Members' not only kept alive the best traditions of English colonialism and all that it has offered by way of civilizing influence, but they attempted to counter and dissolve the continuing reputation of the Australian crowds as 'not cricket'.

'There is no frivolity in the Members' Stand', one of the untouchables told me. 'And nor should there be. There are certain traditions that we need to uphold in the Members.'[33]

The lower class does not understand nor appreciate the 'truth' of cricket. In Australia, these people would be better off going to a rugby league game, and in England, a soccer match. Cricket is more than a game, it is life itself, it is tradition. So trusted were the Members to fulfil this important social interpretive task of maintaining and re-enforcing tradition that they could be trusted with canned beer, while the rowdy and untrustworthy Hill dwellers could only obtain beer in plastic cups. There are, after all, limits. But even these limits have limits as members are now no longer trusted with glasses of beer. In the end, the descent and disintegration of civilization spread to the Members' stand and the law had to step in to prevent further deterioration of standards of acceptable and civilized behaviour. As a measure for ensuring proper behaviour authorities placed a ban on the sale of full strength beer at the ground following continuing crowd control problems.[34]

And these limits are to be enforced with a typical tool of postmodern capitalism – technology. Technological advances have not only improved the game as it is played, they have changed the way it is viewed, from better facilities for spectators, to radio and especially television, the game has become a transformed high-tech text. But technology has also brought troubles. Radio and television 'massified' cricket. The growth of the One-Day version of the game has exposed the sport to many who may simply not understand 'true' cricket. Seemingly minor technological advances have changed the game for the worse. As Cashman notes, the arrival of the lightweight cooler or 'esky' allowed Australian fans to bring large quantities of alcohol and food with them, saving them from the exorbitant prices charged at grounds by refreshment franchise holders. The game as a result could become more democratic as family entertainment at least to the extent to which family entertainment in Australia is dependent upon the consumption of large quantities of beer. At the same time, the same technological advance led to an apparent increase in rowdy behaviour.[35] This would then mean that families would be reluctant to bring their children to the cricket. Changes in crowd behaviour can be dealt with through *legal* changes. Prohibition and surveillance redefined the role and place of the cricket fan as consumer – banning coolers, limiting the quantity of beer which may be purchased to two per customer at one time, limiting cans to the Members' where they would never be used as projectiles, and finally, by a massive police specialized Tactical Response Group presence. Crowd control techniques can also be dealt with through technology. For every technological problem there is a technological solution as cricket enters the socio-legal state of 1984 and beyond.

As public outrage over 'lawlessness' on the streets leads to the technologization of law enforcement (CCTV on city streets, wiretapping, DNA fingerprinting, videotaping surveillance and statements in police custody, computerized crime profiles and research tools etc.) so too has 'public' outrage about lawlessness at cricket matches led to the introduction of high-tech security solutions to cricket's societal problems. As television and the other media, and cricket officials themselves whip up nationalist feelings for every Test, the same people praised and permitted the introduction of 'the sporting world's largest and most advanced video surveillance system' at the SCG.[36] Like drug testing for the workforce and omnipresent CCTV in our cities and towns, technology will solve the problems it has, in part at least, introduced into the working class. Use technology to create a demand, define the demand as deviant, use technology to combat deviance, a scenario familiar to sociologists and criminologists, now becoming familiar to cricketers.[37]

Yet, the increased use of surveillance technology has not, it would appear, reduced the occurrence of rowdy behaviour and lawlessness at cricket matches. Police in Sydney and Melbourne today conduct pre-game dog- and tactical-team sweeps of pubs near cricket grounds in order to detect, deter and detain troublemakers. Video and computer enhanced surveillance measures have been improved almost yearly and yet there is a consistent history of reports of unruly and unlawful behaviour at Australian cricket grounds.[38] Australian fans retaliate by using laser technology to shine lights in opposing batters' eyes.[39] They throw golf balls at English fielders.[40] They continue to engage in physical battles with police at cricket venues.[41]

Crowd violence can and does pose serious threats to player safety. Flying bottles, golf balls, nails and coins often fly past fielders' heads. In a second team county match, a Gloucestershire bowler was in fact shot with an airgun. The players left the field and the police were called.[42] Again, violence against cricketers either in the form of abuse from the stands or pitch invasions, is perceived to be an increasing problem. It is also a problem which occurs in every country in which the game is played. Overcrowding, traditional rivalry, bad umpiring, the dismissal of a local favourite, alcohol consumption, each of these factors can and does influence crowd behaviour and violence directed at players. Again, as the game becomes professionalized and cricketers are employed full time as cricketers, the stakes are seen to be higher and higher.[43] Crowd troubles which resulted in a pitch invasion in a match between Australia and the West Indies at the Bourda ground meant that the Match Referee was compelled to declare the game a tie. The crowd entered the field of play as Australia were chasing six runs off the last over. As they desperately tried to run between the wickets, the Australians were obstructed by the crowd who thought the match was over since the Australians had not managed to hit a six. The fans removed the stumps, making it impossible for the Windies fielders to finish the game and secure a victory by running out one of the batters (Laws 28 and 38).[44]

Later in the same series in Barbados the crowd hurled bottles onto the field in protest against the run out decision which dismissed Sherwin Campbell. Campbell collided with Australian bowler Brendan Julian and was unable to make his ground as the Australians easily removed the bails. Replays convinced the crowd that Julian had deliberately stepped into Campbell's path. Play was halted, Sir Gary Sobers personally pleaded with the crowd and the Australians recalled Campbell.

Of course, as previous discussion indicates, the legal questions here are fascinating. If Julian deliberately impeded the runner, he has committed clear legal breaches. The Australian decision to recall Campbell was not made, as the provisions of Law 27(8) require, in what would ordinarily and lawfully be considered to have been in a timely fashion, i.e. before the batter leaves the field. Of course, it is possible to argue here that the spirit of the game imposed an obligation to recall the batter even outside the technical limits of the *Law*. Yet if it is permissible to recall a batter at any time after what appears to have been a lawful dismissal, one might wonder what purpose is served by the temporal limit imposed in the *Laws*.

The Match Referee did not indicate that Julian acted maliciously or deliberately. Nonetheless, it may well be argued that in such circumstances, a batter should either not be run out or if he is, the appeal should be withdrawn since he did not make his ground as a result of the 'interference' of the bowler. Yet, we also know as a matter of legal practice that if a batter is forced to go around a bowler who is completing his follow through or is standing his ground, and is run out because he had a bit farther to go and could not run in a straight line, he will not be recalled and no one would expect such an action. Similarly, a batter who falls as he begins his run or slips half way down the pitch will not be allowed to regain his ground. Finally, in the Campbell situation, the opposition are expected, if we agree that there is an ethical obligation to recall him, depending on the facts, to not only give up a wicket which they have lawfully taken, but also to allow a run if Campbell takes up his position at the wicket to which he was running when the collision took place.[45] Not only does the 'spirit of the game' in this case override the clear letter of the *Law*, but it imposes a real disadvantage on the team upon whom the obligation falls. In addition, allowing the batter here to complete his run may well have a broader effect on the bowling side. They might, for example, have had a plan of attack aimed at getting his wicket, a plan which is thwarted by allowing him to avoid the strike. Conversely, the fielding side may have been attempting to keep Campbell at one end in order to concentrate in the next over on the other batter. Again, that tactic is negatived by an obligation imposed by one understanding of the spirit of the game. On the other hand, one might argue that another ethical norm of the spirit of the game would demand that Campbell return to the end from which he was running and 'give up' a run which he did not truly merit.

Furthermore, one needs to make and raise inquiries about the ethical standard and norm at work here. Can the spirit of the game be said to be enforced if compliance is compelled by physical violence and the threat of injury from bottles thrown at players by the crowd? Is this the confirmation of an overarching moral code imposed on the game by the very act of participation or is this anything more complicated than extortion? Is the crowd reaction a democratic reminder to the players of their moral obligations under the normative structures of the spirit of the game or is it mere anarchy? Steve Waugh reported after the Guyana invasion that he feared a 'Monica Seles' type incident, and that he was afraid for his life. He and his teammates were subjected to threats of serious physical injury and required police escorts.[46] Was what the crowd did 'cricket'? Was the decision to recall Campbell 'cricket'? Was this democratic rule-making at its most basic and pure or was it drunken mob behaviour at its worst?

Into the jurisprudential mix of nationalism, imperialism, racism, class and democracy, and the contradictions associated with them, we must add the problems of sexism and homophobia. Cricket spectating has traditionally been a process of male bonding. The SCG and Lords are places where businessmen met other businessmen to watch the cricket, socialize, gossip and deal and working-class men went to drink and enjoy spectating with their 'mates'. Women did not go to the cricket because there were other, more ladylike leisure activities to engage in, or if they did go, they were segregated in the Ladies' Stand and served only as a very minor adornment and sub-text to a hegemonic male interpretive practice. 'Misogyny has been one of the enduring themes of Australian cricket commentary,'[47] and English, New Zealand, South African and subcontinental cricket have been no different. Television cameras continue to pan the crowd for shots of scantily clad females and radio and television commentators interrupt their analyses of the pitch conditions to pass comment on the scene. As a necessary element of the male virility cult and misogyny which inform cricket play and broader spectating practices, homophobic comments have become more and more a part of standard barracking.

Over and over again, cricket reveals itself as a very socialized and socializing interpretive practice which carries with it layer upon layer of meaning. If any one 'event' in the history of cricket serves to illustrate the complex interstices of the interpretive elements of the game and the society of which it is a part, it is the 1932–33 Bodyline series between Douglas Jardine's MCC team and the Australians.

28 Bodyline, postmodernism, law and the meaning of life

No cricket event, not even the infamous underarm bowling incident against New Zealand, has caused more controversy or become such an important part of Australian social history and popular culture as Bodyline.[1] Indeed, it is no exaggeration to say that the series continues to mark cricket relations between England and Australia and to define what is and is not 'cricket' in the minds of supporters in those countries. Bodyline combined at a unique historical juncture almost all of the competing social texts which came together to 'constitute' cricket – nationalism, imperialism, legal formalism, the spirit of the game, racism, class-conflict, rhetorical disputes over language, physical violence and the conflict of strong individual personalities shaped by each of these elements.

Without the individual greatness of Don Bradman there would have been no Bodyline for there would have been no need to develop the 'leg theory' attack to neutralize him as a batter. Without the world-wide economic depression, Bradman could not have emerged as a hero of the popular culture, giving living proof to Australians that their nation could still achieve greatness. Without the individual personality of Douglas Jardine and the passionate hatred which his name still evokes in Australia, the strategy of 'leg theory' and its ruthless physical application would never have occurred and Bodyline would both never have existed or continued to exercise its interpretive dominance today.[2]

The seeds of the fruit reaped in Bodyline were sown long before the 1930s. The very class structure of England, reproduced in the distinction of the Gentlemen and the Players, produced a further class-based division of labour in cricket's practical implementation. Gentlemen batted and produced and reinforced the image of the amateur batter and the Players, the workers, engaged in the plebeian function of fast bowling. Without the inherent class-based hierarchies of cricket and its division of labour, Bodyline would have taken on a very different structure and meaning than the one it continues with today.

The interpretive burden and complexity of Bodyline begins and ends not so much with Larwood's and Voce's assault on Bradman and Woodfull but in the grammatical structures and consequent legal understandings of the event itself. For the English and their Australian native apologists, Jardine adopted 'leg theory', a strategy of bowling legside deliveries (allegedly Bradman's batting weakness) to a packed legside field.[3] For them, this was entirely different from 'Bodyline'.

Indeed, from the English perspective, Bodyline was 'against the interest and spirit of cricket'.[4] In 1932–33 the English simply did not bowl 'Bodyline', a fact the ignorant Australians failed to grasp.[5] 'Leg theory' was a brilliant, ethical and lawful tactical ploy aimed at winning and playing in the spirit of the game. For Australians, 'leg theory' was simply the way the English twisted the language to prettify and neutralize an ugly and mean-spirited strategy. Rather than a gentlemanly idea of 'leg theory' bowling to one side of the wicket, Australians experienced a violent barrage of short-pitched deliveries which continually struck their players on the body and prevented them from playing attacking strokes. Bodyline worked not as a nice 'theory' but as a real, practical physical attack with dire consequences. The legside field placings were effective not as a result of a well-thought out idea, but because in fending off legside bouncers, Australian batters had no choice but to be hit or to play the ball defensively away to leg. In Bodyline, each side has, and continues to have, a completely different interpretive perspective on events, reflected in and re-enforced by the very linguistic/grammatical structures of their 'description' of the 'facts'.

Indeed, English captains continue to practise a particular version of 'leg theory' and to be attacked for doing so. Before the 1998 Ashes series, Australians complained of the English side's negative tactics of using finger spinners (usually left armers) pitching outside a batter's leg stump to a packed leg side field.[6] In the 2002 Test series against India, Sunil Gavaskar and Ian Chappell blasted Nasser Hussain for using a leg theory attack to frustrate Sachin Tendulkar.[7] Some, including Hussain, justified the tactics on the twin bases of their legality and their efficacy. It was boring to watch, but in the end Tendulkar did lose patience and his wicket.[8] In the 2002 Test series, Robert Croft continued his attack outside Tendulkar's leg stump. Again we enter into the debate between legal formalism and legal ethics. For the English, such a tactic is efficacious and legal; for others, it is both boring and 'not cricket'. It is at some level a dishonest containing manoeuvre meant to strangle one of the world's best batters and eliminate any real notion of a confrontation between bat and ball. But events in 1933 had an added dimension, one in which the signifier 'leg theory' and the signified 'Bodyline' created the first postmodern legal crisis of meaning in cricket.

The grammatical differences regarding the sides came to a head at the Adelaide Oval match on 14 Jan. 1933, day two of the third Test, when Woodfull, the Australian captain, was struck over the heart by a delivery from English fast bowler Larwood. Woodfull left the field, and in the next over when Jardine set a legside field, the crowd was outraged and threatened to invade the pitch. After the day's play was terminated, Pelham (later Sir) Warner, the English manager, came to the Australian dressing room to inquire after the health of Woodfull. In words that form part of Australian cricket's Pantheon and which enjoy a status in popular culture equivalent to Gough Whitlam's comments about God and the Governor-General following the 1975 dismissal, Woodfull stated:

> I don't want to speak to you, Mr. Warner. Of two teams out here one is playing cricket, the other is making no effort to play the game of cricket. It is too

great a game for spoiling by the tactics your team is adopting. I don't approve of them and never will. If they are persevered with it may be better if I do not play the game. The matter is in your hands. I have nothing further to say. Good afternoon.[9]

Here we come to the crux of the real issue in the ongoing debate over Bodyline. 'Leg theory' or Bodyline was perfectly within the *Laws of Cricket*. It was legal. In its Bodyline embodiment, assuming there is a difference, even Warner was forced to admit that it violated, without doubt, the spirit of the game. Once again, rule formalism confronts ethical normativity. Jardine stood on his formal legal rights as the Australians invoked a higher order and the issue was, and remains, joined. In reality, however, the issue is not capable of being joined. This is the postmodern jurisprudential crisis of Bodyline.

The issues are not as clear-cut as the 'facts' would indicate. The MCC, for instance, constantly proclaimed throughout the ensuing 'crisis' that not only was Jardine acting legally, but that no MCC team would ever behave in an unsportsmanlike manner. The Australians, who after all were mere colonials, were quite mistaken in accusing a MCC team, the very embodiment of 'cricket', of any kind of illegal *or* immoral behaviour. On the one hand, even those who offer a sympathetic reading of Jardine, describe him as one who '...expected to win by fully and most ruthlessly exploiting the existing rules. Nothing illustrates his attitude better than the ban he imposed on fraternization with the enemy during the bodyline tour...'.[10]

Others continued to insist that he always regarded cricket as 'only a game' and that he had in his personal life a deep concern for philosophical and ethical issues.[11] While the private, post-cricket Jardine saw a reason to think about moral values, the Bodyline captain manifested no such inclination. Rather, he embodied and acted out all of the contradictions of 'true' cricket.

An English gentleman and amateur, he displayed a ruthlessness to which any of those condemned today as bringing too much 'professionalism' to the game could only aspire. A rigid legal formalist, he exploited the *Laws* for his own very personal and public utilitarian ends. His desire to win was both a natural part of cricket as sport and an inevitable result of the times and circumstances. England, too, was in the throes of a depression and required an example of national pride. Her pride as a nation was at stake, but so too was her pride as the Mother Country. Victory was sweet, but victory over a colony, especially the haughty Australians and the prowess of Bradman, would be especially sweet. As the public worlds of Englishness and cricket were brought together, so too was the private world of Douglas Jardine, Oxford Blue and England captain, who personally disliked Australians and was driven by a burning desire to win. And England saw nothing wrong with this, as utilitarian/formalism triumphed over all else.[12]

Australians were more concerned. The text of the cable sent by the ACB to the MCC indicates that Australians were worried that Bodyline created 'intensely bitter feeling between the players, as well as injury'. In addition to being 'not cricket' because it 'menace(d) the best interests of the game', Bodyline was 'not cricket' because it did not allow 'cricket' to be played. 'Protection of the body by the batsman' became 'the main consideration'.[13] The conflict between Jardine's formalism and the Australian's concern about the spirit of the game was more than a disagreement over the 'meaning' of 'leg theory' *versus* Bodyline or about the interpretation of the *Laws* on bowling and field placings. As Woodfull's comments indicate, what was at stake and what continues to be at stake in discussions of Bodyline is the very existence of our 'knowledge' of and about cricket and consequently, the very existence of the game itself. If there is no common understanding about what cricket 'is', about what we 'know' it to be, there can be for many no shared understanding that we are playing or watching or writing about the same game. All of our implied agreements and certainties when we enter the field of play with another team function and are functional because we all agree to be bound by the same rules, both written and unwritten. When the discrepancy between our knowledge of what is occurring and our practical experience is such that we no longer recognize what is going on, then the object of our one shared social understanding no longer exists. When the order of society breaks down and one side takes the law into its own hands, we no longer have a shared practice and experience of 'law'. When one side acts so that the other believes there is only one team 'playing cricket', no one is playing cricket and all the social understandings and local knowledges we have of that activity are threatened with a collapse into meaninglessness. Bodyline exposed cricket to the horror of indeterminacy, even while it upheld an understanding of the letter of the law.

At the same time, it did so by relying on equally 'well known' but indeterminate sub-textual practices we have already seen. The historical origins and acts of the class-based divisions manifested themselves in the very practice of Bodyline. Jardine the amateur ordered Larwood, the professional, to bowl Bodyline. Larwood had no choice under the practices and conventions with which he had been imbued but to comply. Others, like Gubby Allen, an amateur, could refuse, because of his class status, to dirty his hands although he could live with the contradictions of living in an ethical and legal world in which he found himself 'field(ing) close in on the leg side and t(aking) several catches off Larwood's bowling'.[14] He made an apparent existential peace with his own ambiguous moral practice. Several other members of the English team organized a meeting to discuss their opposition to Bodyline and when Jardine barged in, Maurice Tate allegedly dumped a glass of beer over his captain's head. Tate was not selected to play.[15] The attitude of the English side itself was filled with ambiguity and conflicting class interests. Again, however, class solidarity was not necessarily enough to protect one from other socially based considerations and practices. Allen, the amateur, was able to refuse Bodyline and stay in the side, but the Nawab of Pataudi declined to field in a legtrap and was dropped from the side despite having scored a century on debut, after Jardine sarcastically said of him 'I see His Highness is a conscientious objector!'[16]

One could alternatively see this as an utterly racist decision or, as is also possible on the 'facts', one could see Pataudi's removal from the side as a purely utilitarian decision after his batting failure in the second Test. At the same time, the interpretation of Jardine as a racist is fraught with complexity. Jardine was brought up in India, the son of Scottish parents who migrated to the colony. He was sent home for his education. Therefore, his relationship with issues like racism and colonialism was a psychologically complex one. At school he was doubly an outsider, as a Scot and as a boy from the colonies. He would live his life (Oxford Blue, England captain) in cricket as one who epitomized English-ness in the most English of games and at the same time as a man largely without a country. Indeed, in retirement, it was India rather than cricket that dominated his life. Jardine's personal relationship to issues like racism and colonialism was as deep, as complex and as contradictory as the social psychology of cricket itself.

There is an equally ambiguous relationship to issues of class in the attitude of other players. In the fifth Test, Larwood broke a bone in his foot, Jardine would not let him retire until Bradman was out. When that happened, Jardine turned to his great fast bowler and said 'You can go off now, Larwood,' and Bradman and Larwood, in silence, walked off the field together. Larwood never walked on to another Test field,[17] yet until death, Larwood referred to his captain as 'Mr Jardine'.[18] Most Australians now recognize that Larwood was as much a victim of Bodyline as were Woodfull and Bradman. Indeed, this 'knowledge' existed at the time of Bodyline itself. Just as the Australian crowds detested Jardine for Bodyline and the arrogance embodied in his Harlequin cap and silk scarf, they gave Larwood a huge round of applause after he scored 98 as a nightwatchman in the same fifth Test. Such are the complexities of cricket, and the subtleties of our collective construction of meaning in the interpretive practices of cricket.

Bodyline provoked discussions not only about ethics, but about law. In a uniquely cricketing strategy, the MCC, without acknowledging that Jardine had erred, but acting in the spirit and best interests of the game,[19] attempted an ethical solution to Bodyline by leaving matters to the captains to see that the events of the Australian tour were not repeated.[20] Such an appeal failed and a legal solution to the ethical problem was required as the LBW *Law* was modified in 1937, at the recommendation *inter alia* of Harold Larwood, so that a leg-side delivery pitching outside the line of the stumps could not result in a LBW decision. This has in turn resulted in a continuing debate over the demise of leg-spin bowling and the unfairness of denying Shane Warne the possibility of a LBW decision when he is attacking the stumps. The intellectual, ideological and practical legacy of Bodyline infuses many of cricket's sub-texts.

There can be little doubt about the importance of Bodyline as a dominant signifying event not only in cricket but in a broader social context as well. On the other side of the coin, there can be little doubt after even this cursory investigation that the broader social context, not only of the time of Bodyline but of current days also influences our understanding of that signifying event. The popularity in Australia of the Hayes/Schultz film *Bodyline* emphasizes that Bodyline is a part not just of cricket, but of popular culture as well. At the same time, the vigorous and vehement reaction of English cricket writers to the film further underlined the fact that Bodyline may be gone, but it is certainly not forgotten.

John Arlott attacked what he saw as the film's historical and factual inaccuracies and finishes with a rhetorical flourish: 'It has been suggested that the film was made to explain bodyline to those who know nothing about cricket, and that such people enjoyed it. Only they possibly could.'[21]

Over 50 years later, 'Bodyline' still raises the same issues and with the same passions. The English hate *Bodyline* the movie, the Australians adore it. The event is 'bodyline' for the English, Bodyline for Australians and finally, most telling of all, for Arlott only those who know nothing about cricket could enjoy the film. Those who 'know' true cricket also 'know' better. But are we both playing the same game? Is cricket English or Australian? Is it 'known' only by experts or by the broad mass of people who participate in the culture? If Bodyline epitomizes one side of postmodern existence because it opened up and decentred cricket as a 'meaningless' activity, it also continues to epitomize another side of postmodern, globalized existence because such a 'meaningless' activity is so full of meaning for so many people. Bodyline can and should teach us to live with the fact and the law of uncertainty, since uncertainty is the very basis upon which we can and do construct democratically derived legal texts and meanings.

29 Conclusion: on life, law and cricket

Just as law has survived Legal Realism and Critical Legal Studies, just as philosophy has survived the deconstruction of Derrida and Foucault, cricket has survived Bodyline and all the other contradictions of the game. Like all other games, cricket involves a tension between the game as 'game' and the 'game' as an embodiment of cultural lessons and broader messages.[1] This is clearly one of the points I have tried to draw out in this book. I have tried to demonstrate that cricket is a text upon which are inscribed signs and meanings from other texts and experiences (like law) and, at the same time, to show how the lessons we learn from cricket are inscribed in other parts of our lives.

Many might still refuse to accept the validity of the appropriateness of this analysis because they see law as involving something more than what is at stake in cricket. At individual moments (for example child custody hearings) what is at stake in law is clearly more important than what is at stake in cricket (is the batter out LBW?). These individual moments are also often filled with an entire social content (for example male/female relations in the child custody case, or national pride, physical violence in cricket). This complexity of all legal and social practices and moments makes distinguishing between them virtually impossible in a truly meaningful and significant fashion. Indeed this may well on occasion imbue the apparently less important text (cricket) with a much more crucial overall cultural impact.

Others may refuse to recognize the important connections between law and cricket because they suffer from that narrow-mindedness which makes much of what passes for legal scholarship so boring. That disease is an outdated formalism which imbues 'law' with a kind of epistemological hierarchical status which, in practice, it does not deserve. For them, law is a formal and important certainty. Cricket is just a game.

But law is not a formal certainty. It is almost by definition and in practice a combination of uncertainty and certainty. A lawyer sells expertise and knowledge to a client, recognizing that part of that expertise and knowledge lies in identifying the areas of law which are uncertain. Most of what we can know is limited to what we cannot know, in other words the *trace, the unknown* of our knowledge is more vital than any pseudo-epistemology. Medical 'science' can diagnose cancer, but cannot cure the common cold or explain how aspirin works. We watch television and turn off the lights and we can never really explain how electricity functions. We can play cricket or practice law and never really know either law or cricket at any fixed ontico-epistemological point. Bodyline, chucking, ball-tampering and bribery scandals all raise cricket and law to heights of fascinating uncertainty yet we still profess to know and to practise both cricket and law.

Just as a solicitor's advice is always couched in terms of 'it would appear', and just as a barrister or doctor may speak of 'chances' of success, so too is cricket based on a combination of uncertainty and *Laws*.[2] We want umpires to get their decisions and adjudications right while at the same time we know that uncertainty is fair because both sides play on the same pitch and the unexpected, in such circumstances, is to be expected.[3] Cricketers can speak of an expensive missed chance where a batter was dropped on 0 and went on to score a century, while at the same time recognizing there is no statistical or scientific causal connection between the dropped catch and anything specific that happens afterwards. We celebrate the great individuals like Don Bradman or Sachin Tendulkar, and celebrate with equal fervour the great sides whose sum total was often greater than the whole of its parts. What we love in cricket, is '. . . its culture of anarchic individualism and for the peculiar, non-repressive collectivism based on that anarchy'.[4]

Every aspect of cricket contains and competes with its contradiction. We can see it as a formalistic, bourgeois capitalist enterprise or as unveiling possibilities for true human community, or we can see it as both things at once, calling for us to imbue it with meaning through a collective social practice. If we can see this, then perhaps we can see the same thing in law and life; that we are not condemned or restrained except when and if we participate in our own restraint. When we begin to see law and life as cricket, we can begin to take control over the construction of meaning in our daily existence. Cricket and, more particularly, the uncertainty of adjudication under the *Laws of Cricket* can serve as an example of the open-ended possibilities for democratic self-definition.

When we begin to take control over the meaning-machines of our lives, we will realize that the answer to C.L.R. James' vital jurisprudential question, *What do they know of cricket who only cricket know?* is at once nothing and everything. We know nothing of cricket, if we see it as 'only a game' and we know everything of cricket when we know and acknowledge the contexts out of which it is constructed and into which we insert and give meaning to it. James poses the question of postmodern, global existence, of presence and absence, of the *trace*, of erasure, of the possibility of knowing, of knowing the possibility and of the possibility of possibility. He asks us about cricket, law and politics. When we know cricket we will know ourselves.

Notes

Series editor's preface

1 See here particularly texts such as the seminal *Beyond a Boundary* C.L.R. James 1963 and more recently Marqusee, M. *Anyone But England* and Williams, J. (1999) *Cricket and England. A Cultural and Social History of the Inter-war Years.*

2 Down, M. (1985) *Is it Cricket? Power, Money and Politics in Cricket Since 1945* (Queen Anne Press: London). Note that this was written during football's 'dark decade' and before the explosion in football writing post Italia '90, an avalanche precipitated by Nick Hornby's *Fever Pitch.*

3 Greenfield, S. and Osborn, G. (1999) 'The Legal Colonisation of Cricket' *Soundings* Issue 13, 129.

4 p. x.

5 Hutchinson, A. (1994) 'Playing the Game' *Dalhousie Law Journal*, Vol. 17, No. 1, 263.

1 Introduction

1 All references herein will be to the *Laws of Cricket (2000 Code)*, Marylebone Cricket Club, unless otherwise specified.

2 *It's All in the Game: A Nonfoundationalist Account of Law and Adjudication* (Durham and London: Duke University Press, 2000), at p. 190. For further discussion see my, 'Hansie Cronje, Nazi Judges and Other Thoughts on (Not) Playing the Game', 38 *Osgoode Hall L.J.* 563 (2000). For the point at which Hutchinson and I part company (amicably) on the connections between cricket and the law, see *It's All in the Game*, at pp. 27–37.

3 *Wisden, The Laws of Cricket: The 2000 Code and Its Interpretation* (hereafter *Wisden, The Laws of Cricket*) (London: Ebury Press, 2000), at p. 102.

4 Geoff Lawson, 'A victory for the true spirit of the game', *Sun Herald*, 23 Jan. 2000.

5 'Why breaking the law was no sin', *Times*, 19 Jan. 2000.

6 'England triumph in game of forfeit', ibid.

7 Peter Roebuck, 'Historic Test a victory for imagination over introversion', *Sydney Morning Herald*, 20 Jan. 2000.

8 1980 *Code*. See also 3(7) of the 1980 *Code*.

9 'A victory for the true spirit of the game', op. cit.

10 *Law* 21(6).

11 Hutchinson, op. cit., at p. 191.

12 I explore some of the early context of recent cases in, 'Balls, Bribes and Bails: The Jurisprudence of Salim Malik', 3 *Working Papers in Law and Popular Culture*, Manchester Metropolitan University, 1995. More recently, Malik has alleged that both sides in a Pakistan/Australia match had been bribed and that neither knew what the other was doing. According to Malik, batters were trying to get out while bowlers and fielders were at the same time trying to let them score runs. If true, these allegations raise

interesting jurisprudential possibilities about our understanding of what it means to play the game. See Mark Ray, 'Match-fixing: new claims by Malik', *Sydney Morning Herald*, 22 May 2000. For an introduction to the story of cricket corruption and bribery see, Pradeep Magazine, *Not Quite Cricket* (New Delhi and London: Penguin, 2000); Deon Gouws, '...*And Nothing But The Truth'?* (Cape Town: Zebra, 2000); Simon Wilde, *Caught* (London: Aurum Press, 2001).

13   See e.g., Michael Henderson, 'Centurion Test now under the microscope', *Daily Telegraph*, 13 April 2000; Charles Randall, 'Test inquiry upsets Vaughan', *Daily Telegraph*, 15 April 2000; Nasser Hussain, 'Why I'm sure Centurion was no fix', *Daily Telegraph*, 16 April 2000; 'New doubt on Centurion win', *Times*, 16 April 2000. South African sources now assert that Hussain was the initiator of the conversation. This is of some, but not major, jurisprudential import. See Peter Robinson, 'Who initiated the declarations, Cronje or Hussain', *CricInfo*, 23 May 2000; Nasser Hussain, 'How our big moment has been tainted by the manipulators', *Daily Telegraph*, 18 June 2000.

14   Colin Bateman, 'England in South Africa and Zimbabwe, 1999–2000', *Wisden Cricketers' Alamanack* (hereafter *Wisden*) *2001* (Guildford, Surrey: John Wisden & Co. Ltd, 2001), at p. 1051.

15   Owen Slot, 'Money or the Boks', *Sydney Morning Herald*, 17 April 2000.

16   See e.g., 'Gibbs declares his innocence', AFP, 15 April 2000; Owen Slot, 'Revealed: the bribe that split Cronje's team', *Daily Telegraph*, 16 April 2000; Peter Robinson, 'Hansie offered me $15,000 says Gibbs', *CricInfo*, 8 June 2000.

17   Cricket is of course not the only sport in which such questions arise. The controversy surrounding Michael Schumacher's 'victory' in the 2002 Austrian Grand Prix indicates the problematic of knowing what 'playing the game' means. If the game of Grand Prix Formula One racing is man and machine against all the other man and machine combinations, then Ferrari's instruction to its number two driver to make way for Schumacher is the equivalent of match-fixing. If we see Formula One in terms of team driving, leadership points, and Schumacher's place in history then the fact that Rubens Barrichello pulled over and let his teammate pass is part of the game. Similarly, but on the other side of the coin, no one would question a winner of cycling's *Tour de France* for making use of his team's *domestiques* to help him win, or a 1,500-metre runner who benefited from the introduction of a 'rabbit' in the starting field. In these last two cases, contestants enter the sporting event and play the game without any intention of winning, yet they are not 'cheats'.

18   See discussion below, Chapter 14.

19   See e.g., Peter Deeley, 'Australia reduce "cricket carnival" to a dreary crawl', *Daily Telegraph*, 31 May 1999; Phillip Derriman, 'Faint whiff of underarm as Aussies squeeze Kiwis', *Sydney Morning Herald*, 1 June 1999; Andrew Ramsey, 'Go-slow forces re-think', *Australian*, 1 June 1999; 'It's cricket', Editorial, *Sydney Morning Herald*, 2 June 1999.

20   Phil Wilkins, 'What's the point of winning', *Sydney Morning Herald*, 4 Feb. 2002; Michael Koslowski, 'Aussies caught, bowled and gazumped', ibid.; Mike Selvey, 'Underhand payback for that underarm victory', *Guardian*, 5 Feb. 2002; Lynn McConnell, 'Bonus points message will be passed to captains', *CricInfo*, 9 Feb. 2002.

21   See, 'Angry Lara denies collusion over result', *Guardian*, 30 May 1999; '"Bonus point" issue needs to be reconsidered', *Dawn*, 6 Feb. 2002.

22   See, Lynn McConnell, 'Bonus point raises hackles, but all within laws', *CricInfo*, 6 Feb. 2002.

23   It is interesting to note here that when a Pakistani judicial inquiry into cricket corruption found Salim Malik guilty of attempting to fix matches by bribing opposition players, Australian commentators asserted that Malik had now replaced the English captain behind Bodyline, Douglas Jardine as 'cricket's biggest pariah'. Jardine, it should be noted, was guilty 'only' of using the *Laws* of the game to their fullest extent. He was a pure legal formalist who relied on the written text and ignored the spirit of the game. Malik, on the other hand, has been found to be a simple cheat. Australian

moral judgements, which place legality a close second to cheating, demonstrate that 'playing the game', is, as Allan Hutchinson would no doubt agree, a complicated matter. See Greg Baum, 'The man who usurped Jardine as the game's greatest pariah', *Sydney Morning Herald*, 26 May 2000.

24 See e.g., J.T. Noonan, 'The Bribery of Warren Hastings: The Setting of a Standard for Integrity in Administration', 10 *Hofstra L. Rev.* 107 (1082); I. Ayres, 'The Twin Faces of Judicial Corruption: Extortion and Bribery', 74 *Denver U.L. Rev.* 1231 (1997); T.M. DeBiagio, 'Judicial Corruption, The Right to a Fair Trial, and the Application of Plain Error Review: Requiring Clear and Convincing Evidence of Actual Prejudice or Should We Settle For Justice in the Dark?', 25 *Am. J. Crim. L.* 595 (1998).

25 See e.g., 'Umpires tell of approaches', *Sydney Morning Herald*, 21 April 2000; 'Hard word on umpire', *Sydney Morning Herald*, 4 May 2000.

26 'Umpire's legal threat', *Australian*, 14 April 2000; Rupert Guiness, 'Umpire: I'm no cheat', *Australian*, 24 April 2000; Chris Ryan, 'Stewart insists match was clean', *Guardian*, 13 June 2000; Mihir Bose, 'Bacher claims England Test win was tainted', *Daily Telegraph*, 13 June 2000; Neil Manthorp, '"Umpire fixed England test" says Bacher', *Guardian*, 13 June 2000; Mark Jeffreys and Scyld Berry, 'Finger of suspicion raised at umpires', *Daily Telegraph*, 22 April 2001.

27 See e.g., Malcolm Conn, 'Cup final "thrown" by Cronje', *Weekend Australian*, 22–23 April 2000; Mark Fuller, 'Cronje put a dubious spin on Sydney Test tactics, says Mallet', *Sydney Morning Herald*, 24 May 2000; Ingo Gilmour, 'Cronje's decision-making does not make sense: Symcox', *Weekend Australian*, 3–4 June 2000.

28 See e.g., 'Records of Azhar, Cronje and Malik may disappear from Wisden', *CricInfo*, 14 May 2001; S. Santhosh, 'How good be a record that has no honour to it', *CricInfo*, 1 June 2001.

29 See Neil Manthorp, 'Cronje's death leaves his judges stumped', *Guardian*, 3 June 2002; Gerald Shaw, 'Hansie Cronje', *ibid.*; Peter Robinson, 'Cronje lawyer in funeral squabble', *CricInfo*, 3 June 2002.

30 *War Minus the Shooting: A Journey Through South Asia during Cricket's World Cup* (London: Heinemann, 1996), at p. 291.

31 *It's All in the Game*, at p. 191.

2 The legal theory of cricket

1 'Images of Law in Everyday Life: The Lessons of School, Entertainment, and Spectator Sports', 21 *Law & Society Rev.* 185 (1987). One Australian academic based in America has attempted to project cricket and baseball analogies in a comparative legal context. He fails because he treats each text, baseball and cricket, not as a lived social experience, but as a sterile metaphor. See David Partlett, 'The Common Law As Cricket', 43 *Vanderbilt L. Rev.* 1401 (1990). On more technical applications of legal norms to the American pastime, see Roger Abrams, *Legal Bases: Baseball and the Law* (Philadelphia: Temple University Press, 1998). For the idea of sport, ideology and ethics, see generally, Jan Boxill (ed.), *Sports Ethics: An Anthology* (Oxford: Blackwell, 2002).

2 'Dennis Martinez and the Uses of Theory', 96 *Yale L.J.* 1773 (1987). For a detailed analysis of the ways in which we, individually and socially, cope with the existence of such contradictions in our daily lives, see Guido Calabresi and Phillip Bobbitt, *Tragic Choices* (New York and London: W.W. Norton & Co., 1978).

3 I am not asserting here that cricket is the only sport or game to which such analyses can or should be made. I chose it simply out of personal prejudice. For an example of the applicability of this jurisprudential approach to another popular sport, football, see Allan Hutchinson, *It's All in the Game*, op. cit.

4 See Alan Freeman and Elizabeth Mensch, 'The Public/Private Distinction in American Law and Life', 36 *Buffalo L. Rev.* 237 (1987).

5 This is the 'fundamental contradiction' between self and other described by Duncan Kennedy as a key element in the common law tradition. See 'The Structure of Black-stone's Commentaries', 28 *Buffalo L. Rev.* 205 (1979); 'Form and Substance in Private Law Adjudication', 89 *Harvard L. Rev.* 1685 (1976); 'Distributive and Paternalist Motives in Contract and Tort Law, with Special Reference to Compulsory Terms and Unequal Bargaining Power', 41 *Maryland L. Rev.* 563 (1982). But cf., Peter Gabel and Duncan Kennedy, 'Roll Over Beethoven', 36 *Stanford L. Rev.* 1 (1984), renouncing the fundamental contradiction.

6 This echoes the distinctions between realism and formalism. See Gary Peller, 'The Metaphysics of American Law', 73 *Calif. L. Rev.* 1151 (1985).

7 'Taking Law and Popular Culture Seriously: Theorizing Sport and Law', in Steve Greenfield and Guy Osborn (eds.), *Law and Sport in Contemporary Society* (London: Frank Cass, 2000). See J. Neville Turner, 'The Laws of Cricket: A Jurisprudential Minefield', 1 *Baggy Green* (1998). See also, David Jones, 'Bombs stop play', *OSM*, Nov. 2001, at p. 44 on the Afghan cricket teams aborted tour of Pakistan in 2001.

8 Thanks to Vaughan Black and Graeme Coss for discussions on this point. It must be noted that such a discussion can have, in slightly altered circumstances, important legal conse-quences. Thus when the West Indian team was accused, in a newspaper article entitled 'Come On Dollar, Come On' of not trying to win a cricket match, the resulting litigation went to the Privy Council, *Lloyd v. David Syme & Co. Ltd.* (1985) 3 NSWLR 728.

9 For a more detailed discussion of this concept of 'play' and its importance for legal theory, see Francis Mootz, 'The Ontological Basis of Legal Hermeneutics: A Proposed Model of Inquiry Based on the Work of Gadamer, Habermas and Ricoeur', 61 *Boston U.L. Rev.* 523 (1989).

10 J. Huizinga, *Homo Ludens: A Study of the Play-Element in Culture* (Boston: Beacon Press, 1950), at p. 19.

11 *The Poverty of Theory and Other Essays* (New York and London: Monthly Review Press, 1978), at p. 13.

12 On the changing nature, role and function of sport in Britain see e.g., Martin Polley, *Moving the Goalposts: A History of Sport and Society Since 1945* (London and New York: Routledge, 1998).

13 Ashis Nandy, *The Tao of Cricket: On Games of Destiny and the Destiny of Games* (Delhi: Penguin Books, 1989), at p. 8.

14 *Beyond A Boundars* (London: Stanley Paul, 1963), at pp. 13–15. James describes 'The contrast between Matthew's pitiable existence as an individual and the attitude people had towards him' when he played cricket (at p. 14).

15 As described by Sir Len Hutton, the *Observer*, 1986, from *The Book of Cricket Quotations*, op. cit., at p. 3 and Murray Hedgcock, 'Publicity is still intact, if not the man', *Weekend Australian*, 30–31 Dec. 1989.

3 Lord Denning, cricket, law and the meaning of life

1 [1977] 1 QB 966. One may also usefully consult, '*Lacy v. Bingle*: Note of Judgment Delivered on 12th May 1994 by His Honour Judge Hague at Slough County Court'. See Steve Greenfield and Guy Osborn, 'The Sanctity of the Village Green: Preserving Lord Denning's Pastoral Vision' (1994) *Denning L.J.* 53.

2 At p. 976.

3 At p. 981.

4 For an insightful and critical analysis of the underlying historical and ideological position, see generally, Derek Birley, *A Social History of English Cricket* (London: Arum Press, 1999).

5 'Our Village' (1924), in *The Faber Book of Cricket* (Michael Davie and Simon Davie, eds.) (London: Faber & Faber, 1987), at pp. 78–79. The invocative power and appeal

of village cricket is a constant theme. See F. Gale, 'Echoes From Old Cricket Fields' (1871), ibid., at p. 225.

> The first requirement for good village green cricket is that the village itself should be a *bona fide* village, not an outlying colony full of cockney villas inhabited by stuck-up people. There ought to be at least two or three old fogeys who attend every match and declare there never were such days as when Squire A or Squire B, as the case may be, was alive; there must be an inn where the cricketers have met within the memory of all the oldest inhabitants; I prefer a green where the stocks are still standing, and I would rather not play at all if there is no parish beadle.

See also John Ebdon, 'With Bat and Ball in Darkest Surrey' in *The Boundary, Book – Second Innings* (Leslie Frewin ed.) (London: Spring Books, 1986), at p. 86. Michael Parkin offers the following example of an available counter-narrative:

> 'Calder Grove v. Upper Hopton' A cricket club which used the mighty West Indian Test player Collis King to beat a village team – he hit 94, took five wickets, made two catches and ran one man out – has been fined £1 and has had to forfeit the match.
> Collis King was invited to play for the Calder Grove team, of Wakefield, when he was staying with a club member. Mr. Brian Sykes, Calder Grove's representative on the Dewsbury and District League, said: 'We thought his presence would stimulate interest in the club and the league.'
> . . .
> But Upper Hopton was beaten by about 80 runs. On hearing the objection the league executive fined Calder Grove £1 for fielding an ineligible player and reversed the match result. The committee reminded Calder Grove that it had power to deal with questions not provided for in the rules.
> The last word must go to Upper Hopton. Mr. Brook said: 'Calder Grove's ground is a dump, not a patch on ours. It has no gent's lavatory.'

The Guardian Book of Cricket (Matthew Engel ed.) (London: Penguin Books, 1986) at p. 123. As in all stories about cricket, counter-narratives are readily present. This would appear to make cricket much like the common law. See Karl Llewelyn, *The Common Law Tradition: Deciding Appeals* (Boston: Little, Brown, 1960).

6 See Zygmunt Bauman, *Modernity and the Holocaust* (Ithaca and London: Cornell University Press, 1989).
7 See Robert Cover, 'Forward: Nomos and Narrative' 97 *Harv. L. Rev.* 9 (1983) for a rich discussion of the power and function of exclusion in the constitution of community.
8 Simon De Bruxelles, 'Winning side's entry was just not cricket', *Times*, 4 Aug. 2000; Charles Randall, 'Usk go to town in criticism of village contest', *Telegraph*, 5 Aug. 2000.
9 Ibid.

4 Dante, cricket, law and the meaning of life

1 'La Divina Cricketa' in *A La Recherche du Cricket Perdu* (London: Macmillan, 1989), at pp. 25 et. seq.
2 At p. 26.
3 *It's Not Cricket* (London: Faber & Faber, 2001).
4 See Alan Freeman and Elizabeth Mensch, 'The Public/Private Distinction in American Law and Life', op. cit., See also, ECB, 'ECB Chief Executive calls on Chancellor to help clubs', *CricInfo*, 21 Feb. 2002.

5 Laws, not rules or cricket as adjudication

1 *Laws of Cricket* (2000 *Code*) Marylebone Cricket Club (MCC).
2 Eric Midwinter, *Fair Game – Myth and Reality in Sport* (London: Allen & Unwin, 1986), at p. 42.
3 See Jack Pollard, *Australian Cricket – The Game and the Players* (North Ryde: Angus & Robertson, 1988), at p. 12. See also, Jack Pollard, *The Complete History of Australian Cricket, 1803–1995* (Brookvale, NSW: The Book Company, 1995); Eric Midwinter, op. cit., at p. 41. Even then, however, a more specific form of customary law or self-regulation of the market was required. The *Australian Cricketers' Guide* of 1859 contained the following example of industry self-policing.

Rules for cricket betting
1. No bet on any match is payable unless it is played out or given up.
2. If the runs of one player be betted against those of another, the bet depends on the first innings, unless otherwise specified.
3. If a bet be made on both innings, and one party beat the other in one innings, the runs of the first innings shall determine it.
4. If the other party go in a second time, then the bet must be determined by the number on the score.

In *Six and Out!* (Jack Pollard ed.) (Ringwood, Vic.: Penguin, 1990), at p. 96.
4 Midwinter, op. cit., p. 25.
5 *The Laws of Cricket*, Law 42(2), 'The Umpires shall be the sole judges of fair and unfair play.' See also *Law* 3(7), 'The Umpires shall be the sole judges of fair and unfair play.'
6 *Tom Smith's Cricket Umpiring & Scoring: The Essential Guide to the New 2000 Code of the Laws of Cricket*, 5th Edition (London: Weidenfeld & Nicolson, 2000).
7 Pakistan manager Hasib Ahsan, considered by opponents to be an unmitigated cheat, explained this rationale after the Pakistani wicketkeeper Saleem Yousuf claimed to have caught England batter Ian Botham when everyone saw the ball had clearly touched the ground. He said, 'If you get one or two bonus decisions then it can make up for some bad luck which goes against you.' *The Book of Cricket Quotations*, op. cit., at p. 208.
   Levelling out can exist at another level. When the legal system fails, players will resort to a self-help remedy. In a New Zealand tour of Pakistan, Kiwi Manager Ian Taylor admitted that bowler Chris Pringle's performance was enhanced by disfiguring the ball. According to the New Zealanders, they resorted to such tactics only after the umpires refused to take action against Waqar Younis and Wasim Akram for damaging the ball. Arif Abbasi of the Board of Control for Cricket in Pakistan dismissed the New Zealanders' allegations as 'disgraceful' and 'rubbish'. See Phil Wilkins, 'Paradise lost as the bell tolls for dreary England', *Sydney Morning Herald*, 12 Nov. 1990 and 'Pakistanis dismayed by cheating allegation', *Australian*, 14 Nov. 1990. See discussion below in Chapters 18 and 19 on ball-tampering and the law.
8 Law 3(8) 'The Umpires shall be the final judges of the fitness of the ground, weather and light for play.' Although the rest of Law 3(8) contains complex provisions detailing the rights of the players and captains to participate in some decisions on these matters.
9 Law 27(1).
10 Law 27(4).
11 *The Boundary Book – Second Innings*, op. cit., at p. 374.
12 Law 27(3) states that 'For an appeal to be valid it must be made before the bowler begins his run up or, if he has no run up, his bowling action to deliver the next ball, and before Time has been called.'

13 'The "B" in Miandad's Bonnet', *The Cricketer*, Dec. 1990, p. 13.

14 'Unappealing aspects mar what turned out a top test', *Daily Mirror*, 17 Jan. 1990.

15 'Time to blow whistle on dubious umpiring', *Australian*, 17 Jan. 1990.

16 'Alderman's nagging precision presents an appealing case' *Sydney Morning Herald*, 17 Jan. 1990. Roebuck is not, however, a proponent of vigorous appealing in all circumstances. He has denounced over-enthusiastic appeals without hesitation. See 'Tour selection must ignore collywobbles – theirs and ours', *Sydney Morning Herald*, 22 Jan. 1991 criticizing wicketkeepers who 'have been inclined to celebrate rather than appeal, beginning a song and dance reminiscent of Red Indians around a totem pole' and 'Breakdown in discipline must be stemmed', *Sydney Morning Herald*, 1 Feb. 1991 condemning Ian Healy who '... screams appeals for anything and everything, sometimes throws the ball in the air and dances a jig of celebration, conduct calculated to embarrass an umpire who had heard no tickle and accordingly had not raised his finger'.

17 An Indian batter took exception to a leg before wicket appeal by the bowler in a domestic match and 'clubbed' the appellant to death, before the umpire had a chance to give his decision. See, 'Batsman kills bowler for leg-before appeal', AFP, 3 May 1999; 'Out, death before wicket', *Sydney Morning Herald*, 4 May 1999. The batter was arrested by police. Reports do not indicate if he was given out by the umpire.

18 'Skipper Richards denies intimidating umpire with "little jig" ', *Sydney Morning Herald*, 11 April 1990. At other times and in other contexts, intimidating appeals may be necessary. Jack Pollard offers this description of John Gleeson's experience in India in 1969–70.

Indian batsmen prodded, pushed and groped against him without making contact. When he found the edges, catches went down or were denied by local umpires. Finally in a match against North Zone Brian Taber held an edged catch. The entire Australian side appealed. The umpire remained motionless. Two fieldsmen ran in from mid-off and covers and put the question again. Up went the umpire's finger. Thereupon the umpire apologised, saying that with such a strong wind blowing it had taken some time for the sound of the snick to carry to his end. On the South African part of the tour Gleeson took 19 Test wickets in a soundly beaten Australian team.

Australian Cricket – The Game and the Players, p. 476.

19 Id., Respected local cricket commentator Tony Cozier's statements raise doubts however. He offers this description in the *Nation*:

Bailey, taken down the leg-side by Dujon, was startled when he looked up to see umpire Barker moving away and belatedly raising his finger to frantic appeals, led by Vivian Richards, charging forward from first slip, arms waving demandingly. At the instant it appeared an umpiring afterthought and Bailey left, head bowed, indicating it had deflected from his hip not his bat.

20 'Man from BBC stirs up storm in a rum glass', 11 April 1990. In a follow-up, Barnes described the incident as 'a maniacal finger-flicking charge on the umpire...', 'The strange but mortal antics of a demi-god', *Times*, 13 April 1990.

21 'Antics leave bad taste', 15 April 1990. Martin Johnson, writing in *The Cricketer*, 'Nice Guys Come Last' (June 1990, p. 19) described Richards as 'charging from first slip to somewhere in the region of mid-on in a manner that can only normally be accomplished by someone being pursued by a swarm of wasps', while in the same journal (p. 21) ('Reflections from Barbados'), Alan Ross describes 'Richard's disgraceful war dance'.

22 As quoted by Barnes in 'Man from BBC stirs up storm in a rum glass', op. cit.

23 Law 42(13), 1980 *Code*.

24 *Adelaide Advertiser*, 1884, from *The Book of Cricket Quotations*, op. cit., p. 94.
25 *The Book of Cricket Quotations*, op. cit., p. 28.
26 K. Mackay, 'The Barracker and the "Ump" ', in *Six and Out!*, op. cit., p. 370 at 372.

6 Law, codes and the spirit of the game

1 'Cricket ethics – a matter of trust', *Dawn*, 24 Jan. 2000.
2 See e.g., Christopher Martin-Jenkins, 'Benaud extols virtues of fair play', *Times*, 17 July 2001.
3 *Tom Smith's Cricket Umpiring and Scoring*, op. cit., at pp. 26–27.
4 Article 7.
5 Again, there are complex arguments about interpretive technique which might arise here as to the exact status of such a preamble to a *Preamble*, but for present purposes I shall not go into them here.
6 See also Law 3(7).
7 Or Law 3(7).
8 On this subject generally see, Paul McCutcheon, 'Sports Discipline, Natural Justice and Strict Liability', 28 *Anglo-American L. Rev.* 37 (1999); 'Sports Discipline and the Rule of Law', in Steve Greenfield and Guy Osborn (eds.), *Law and Sport in Contemporary Society*, op. cit., at p. 115.
9 I deal with the next stage of proceedings, reporting the offender to other authorities in the next chapter.
10 *Tom Smith's Cricket Umpiring and Scoring*, op. cit., at p. 156.
11 Law 27(2).

7 More law and the spirit of the game

1 'Umpires hope to shame cricket cheats', 15 July 1998.
2 Ibid.
3 See e.g., John Braithwaite, *Crime, Shame and Reintegration* (Cambridge: Cambridge University Press, 1989).
4 A separate *Code of Conduct* is in effect for umpires. This became necessary after a case involving Australian umpire Darrell Hair. Hair was charged under the then general *Code of Conduct* for comments he made concerning the throwing controversy relating to Muttiah Muralitharan. The Commissioner found in that case that the *Code* contained no penalty for breaches by umpires. See discussion below in Chapter 16 and the ICC Media Release, 12 Feb. 1999.
5 E.g., Law 42(4) and (5).
6 See Saadi Thawfeeq, 'When match referees are inconsistent', *Daily News*, 11 Nov. 2001 and discussion below in Chapter 19.
7 See Richard Dwight, 'Hansie's earpiece and Warne's outburst', *Daily News*, 27 May 1999.
8 D.L. Seneviratne, 'A stricter code of conduct for cricket needed', *Daily News*, 17 Feb. 1999.
9 'MacLaurin calls for tougher stance from match referees', *CricInfo*, 18 March 2001. 'Local' authorities have adopted similar attitudes and legal measures in order to stamp out dissent in the game. See e.g., Mark Jeffreys, 'Suspensions set to shake county game', *Daily Telegraph*, 3 Feb. 2002; D.J. Rutnagur, 'Tufnell's rap from dissent', *Daily Telegraph*, 3 June 2002; Rob Steen, 'Kirby in the dock as Leicestershire make their move', *Guardian*, 4 June 2002; ECB, 'Paul Weekes reprimanded under ECB Discipline Code', *CricInfo*, 17 June 2002; 'Mahmud, Mamun disciplined', *Daily Star*, 13 Feb. 2002; Lenin Gani, 'Throw the book at Mahmud', *Daily Star*, 13 Feb. 2002.
10 Loof Lirpa, 'ICC to introduce red card system?', *CricInfo*, 1 April 2001.

11 ICC Media Release, 'ICC targets bad language and behaviour to improve cricket's image', 26 April 2002.

12 David Hopps, 'Speed promises instant justice', *Guardian*, 19 July 2001.

13 ICC, 'Malcolm Speed Letter to Referees', 17 July 2001.

14 See e.g., Partarb Ramchand, 'Curbing players' misbehaviour: ICC chief's commendable move', *CricInfo*, 19 July 2001; V. Ramnarayan, 'It is high-time on-field behaviour was stamped out', *CricInfo*, 11 Aug. 2001.

15 *Sydney Morning Herald*, 14 March 1995.

16 Although the *Code* in force at the time did not contain the same specific provisions as the current version, I am assuming here for the sake of the analysis that the general conduct provisions of the extant *Code* governing for example, bringing the game into disrepute, would have incorporated these traditional criteria.

17 See discussion in Chapter 16.

18 'New Zealand versus Sri Lanka, First Test Match', *Wisden* (1996), at p. 1114.

19 D.J. Cameron, 'The Sri Lankans in New Zealand, 1994–95, ibid., at p. 1109.

20 *Sydney Morning Herald*, 14 March 1995.

21 Simon Briggs, 'The most frenetic one-dayer in history?', *Guardian*, 23 Jan. 1999.

22 Charlie Austin, 'Gough involved in confrontation with Sri Lanka player', *CricInfo*, 3 March 2001.

23 ICC, 'ICC match referee's statement on Akram-Warne incident', 27 Nov. 1999.

24 Peter Roebuck, 'Fleming's pitch battle takes Test fight back a little too far', *Sydney Morning Herald*, 24 Sep. 1999; Mark Ray, 'Batting shows a dead heart', *Sydney Morning Herald*, 25 Sep. 1999.

25 ACB, 'Statement issued by ICC Match Referee', 18 Dec. 2000.

26 Phil Wilkins, 'Waugh confident he will be back for first Test', *Sydney Morning Herald*, 16 Feb. 1998.

27 See e.g., Mark Ray, 'Late collapse ruins openers' century stand', *Sydney Morning Herald*, 24 Sep. 1999, discussing the Vass/Fleming collision, '... in true ICC style nothing was revealed to the cricket public'.

28 Greg Baum, 'Umpire row as Australia go for Ashes victory', *Sydney Morning Herald*, 5 July 1993.

29 Martin Blake, 'Umpire strikes back against players', *Sydney Morning Herald*, 3 Feb. 1994; Linda Peerce, 'The art of appealing: Has it gone too far?', *Sun Herald*, 6 Feb. 1994.

30 Brian Scovell, 'Cut the appeals, captains told', *Daily Mail*, 22 May 1998.

31 Trevor Chesterfield, 'Captains face query over sportsmanship conduct', *CricInfo*, 19 Dec. 1999.

32 'Pakistan's Arshad fined', *Daily News*, 2 July 2000.

33 'Match Referee determined to stamp out excessive appealing', *CricInfo*, 20 Feb. 2001.

34 Paragraph 5.5 of the *Code of Conduct* does indicate however that 'Where there are separate incidents in the course of a match, the umpire should lay separate charges.' I am arguing here that it may be that in some circumstances, the 'incidents' may only constitute an offense when taken together.

35 *It's Not Cricket*, op. cit., at p. 2.

36 'Sri Lankans will carry on appealing, says wicket-keeper Sangkkara', *CricInfo*, 6 March 2001.

37 See Law 36 Leg Before Wicket.

38 Law 27(1) and (2).

39 Law 27(1).

40 Law 27(3) and (4).

41 See *It's All in the Game*, op. cit.

42 For another useful discussion of this in the context of sport and jurisprudence, see Frank Michelman, 'Adjudication as Sport: Rhetoric Astray?', 38 *Osgoode Hall L.J.* 583 (2002).

43 Sean Beynon, 'Sobers: Excessive appealing disgusts and sickens me', *CricInfo*, 17 April 2001. See also Huw Turbevill, 'Marsh throws weight behind attack on excessive appealing', *Telegraph*, 22 April 2001.
44 PTI, 'Match referee cautions Indians', 9 June 2001.
45 See e.g., 'Sportsmanship: Taylor shows what it's all about', *Sydney Morning Herald*, 6 March 1996.
46 'My feud with the Windies Healy', *Sunday Telegraph*, 17 Nov. 1996.
47 See discussion, Chapter 8.
48 *Allan's Australian Cricket Annual* (Busselton, WA: Allan Miller, 1997), at p. 117.
49 'Why Healy winds up the Windies', *Sydney Morning Herald*, 6 Dec. 1996.
50 Martin Blake, 'Waugh slip-up proves costly', *Sydney Morning Herald*, 9 Nov. 1999.
51 'Healy wins praise for Thorpe "no catch" call', *Sun Herald*, 22 June 1997.

8 The man in white is always right: umpires, judges and the rule of law

1   *Tom Smith's Cricket Umpiring and Scoring*, op. cit., at pp. 158–59.
2   Jack Pollard, *Australian Cricket*, op. cit., at p. 1092.
3   'F.A. Tarrant in 1909, A. Ducat in 1921, D.R. Jardine in 1926 and S. Boyes in 1935 are among those who have been recalled after being given out lbw, and congratulations to the umpires concerned for having the courage to alter their verdicts.' Gerald Brodribb, *Next Man In* (London: Souvenir Press, 1995), at p. 184.
4   See 'Ijaz reaches his ton with second chance', *Australian*, 22 April 1997; AFP, 'Double take nets Ijaz century', *Sydney Morning Herald*, 22 April 1997.
5   Id.
6   See, Geoff Longley, 'Snedden takes case to ICC', *Christchurch Press*, 6 Dec. 2001; Nelson Clare, 'Umpire apologises', *Daily Telegraph*, 7 Dec. 2001.
7   Michael Henderson, 'England suffer as umpire fails to stand the test', *Daily Telegraph*, 12 Dec. 2001.
8   See e.g., Lynn McConnell, 'Harper does himself no favours with mistake admission', *CricInfo*, 10 Nov. 2001.
9   Id.
10 Law 27(8). The old Law 27(7) read: 'In exceptional circumstances the Captain of the fielding side may seek permission of the Umpire to withdraw an appeal providing the outgoing batter has not left the playing area. If this is allowed, the Umpire shall cancel his decision.'
11 Brodribb, op. cit., at p. 185.
12 For comments on the Dean Jones dismissal (*infra*) see Greg Growden, 'The bizarre dismissal! Aussies maintain the rage', *Sydney Morning Herald*, 29 March 1991 (N.B. The rhetorical parallel drawn by Growden is with the 1975 constitutional crisis when the Governor-General Sir John Kerr removed the elected government of Labour Prime Minister, Gough Whitlam. The events are known in Australia as the 'dismissal'. For more than 25 years Australian Labour Party supporters have been urged to 'maintain the rage' against Kerr and Malcolm Fraser, the Liberal Party leader asked by Kerr to form the government.); Patrick Smithers, 'Fury at run-out as Aust. faces defeat', *Sydney Morning Herald*, 29 March 1991; 'Answer could be an off-field ref, says top umpire', id.; Patrick Smithers, 'Border: "We probably would have done the same" ', *Sydney Morning Herald*, 30 March 1991; Debbie Spillane, 'Jones' dismissal – it's time to be angry', *Sun Herald*, 31 March 1991.
    'Odd Sportsmanship', *Sydney Morning Herald*, 6 April 1991. He added, somewhat more problematically, to say the least, 'If an Australian or English team had acted in such a manner there would be instant and intensified criticism.'
13 'Foreword', *Cricket Umpiring and Scoring*, op. cit., at pp. ix–x.

14 Wilkins, 'Cricket-Lawson back, but Blues lose Bayliss', *Sydney Morning Herald*, 11 March 1991, and Malcolm Conn, 'Sporting Simon may cost Vics the Shield', *Australian*, 11 March 1991.

15 See discussion below, Chapter 13.

16 On the nature of validity claims in legal and ethical discourse, see Jurgen Habermas, *The Theory of Communicative Action. Vol. 1. Reason and the Rationalization of Society* (Boston: Beacon Press, 1984).

17 See also the discussion of other instances of appeals being withdrawn in Brodribb, op. cit., at pp. 185–86.

18 See PTI, 'Ridley Jacobs suspended for three ODIs', 5 July 2001; Media Release, Zimbabwe Cricket Union, 'Windies wicket-keeper Jacobs banned', 5 July 2001.

19 See ICC, 'Guidelines on the Principles of Natural Justice'.

9 Umpires, decisions and the rule of law

1 A.G. Steel and Hon. R.H. Lyttleton, *Badminton Library – Cricket* (1882) (Shedfield, Hamps: Ashford Press, reprint 1987), p. 218.

2 Id., at p. 222.

3 Id., at p. 223.

4 Jack Pollard, *Australian Cricket – The Game and the Players*, op. cit., at p. 1087.

5 Ibid., pp. 123 and 1088.

6 Gerald Brodribb, *Next Man In*, op. cit., at p. 13.

7 Ibid., at pp. 13–14.

8 See id. and Trevor McDonald, *Clive Lloyd – The Authorised Biography* (London: Granada,1985), at pp. 98 et. seq. for a different perspective on these events.

9 G. Brodribb, op. cit., p. 23.

10 Alan Lee, 'England in New Zealand and Australia, 1987–88', *Wisden* (1989), at p. 924.

11 Id.

12 Martin Johnson, 'England in Pakistan', 1987–88, *Wisden* (1989), at p. 910. In the context of England–Pakistan cricket [*infra*] it is hardly shocking that no more serious disciplinary action was taken. The English interpretation in such cases is that Pakistani umpires are either incompetent or cheats. Broad was 'wrong' in displaying his disagreement because that is simply not done. The fact that he was given out by a Pakistani umpire did, however, serve as a strong mitigating factor in his sentencing.

13 See e.g., Simon Hughes, 'ICC take step in wrong direction', *Daily Telegraph*, 5 March 2002.

14 Malcolm Conn, 'Suspended Sohail to miss first final', *Weekend Australian*, 18–19 Jan. 1997.

15 David Hopps and Oamar Ahmed, 'The Pakistanis in Australia and New Zealand, 1995–96', *Wisden*, at p. 1116.

16 The current provisions which are relevant under the 2000 *Code* are Law 42(11) Damaging the Pitch-Area to be protected and 42(12) Bowler running on the Protected Area after Delivering the Ball.

17 Conn, 'Tour crisis after Pakistani walk-off', *Weekend Australian*, 27–28 Jan. 1990.

18 Under the 2000 *Code*. *Law* 21(3) allows the Umpires to award the match if in their opinion one side 'refuses to play'. They make that determination together. The two umpires then inform the captain that they consider that the team is refusing to play and if the action persists, the match is awarded, Law 21(3) (a) (ii) and (b).

19 'To remain true, cricket needs adjudicators', *Sydney Morning Herald*, 30 Jan. 1990. This position may be explained, in part at least, but the nefarious after-effects of Roebuck's Cambridge legal education and perhaps now to his more recent encounters with the criminal justice system.

20 Conn, op. cit., Bailhache continued to argue the correctness of his actions and the importance of the umpire's role. In a keynote address to the New Zealand

Cricket Umpires Association annual conference, he argued for stronger support from administrators of umpire's decisions and for a reversal in the 'burden of proof', 'We have to get to the position where, if an umpire acts against a player, the player is guilty until he proves himself innocent.' '$1 m cheers to absent friends', *Australian*, 24 Sep. 1990.

21 Martin Blake, 'Mushtaq Ahmed runs on pitch so Pakistan walks off ground', *Sydney Morning Herald*, 27 Jan. 1990.

22 Id.

23 Op. cit.

24 The *Law* is enforced by umpires on this basis. In a Test match between India and Zimbabwe, Indian bowler Ashish Nehra was warned twice by the umpire, after which he changed ends. Australian umpire Daryl Harper then called him for a third infringement and he was removed from the attack. He became the first Indian bowler to be banned in these circumstances. Paul Short, 'Flower power repels the Indian attack', *Sydney Morning Herald*, 10 June 2001. There was some suggestion that the bowler was acting under orders to create a rough area for spinner Harbhajan Singh. See, Anand Vasu, 'Nehra episode an unsavoury controversy', *CricInfo*, 12 June 2001. No further action was taken by the Match Referee.

25 *Cricket Umpiring and Scoring*, op. cit., at p. 228.

26 Conn, op. cit., Phillip Derriman adds to the complexity by pointing out that Pakistan's 'silly' decision to walk off 'was surely the action of a team low in morale and lacking purpose', 'Pakistan Tour of Australia, Dec. 1989–Feb. 1980' in *The ABC Australian Cricket Almanac*, op. cit., p. 127. Thus, the Pakistan action had little or nothing to do with formalist *versus* purposive interpretations of the *Law*. Rather, it was rooted in the complex mass psychology of a team which is not performing as well as expected.

27 Op. cit.

28 For a detailed description of events and the context of this affair, from which my own is drawn, see Martin Johnson, 'England in Pakistan 1987–88', *Wisden* (1989), at pp. 910 et. seq. Again such controversies are constant and continuing. At the first Test, in Karachi in Sep. 1988, Colin Egar, former Australian Test umpire and chair of the Australian Cricket Board, accused the Pakistanis of appointing an incompetent umpire. He, Bob Simpson (Australian coach) and captain Allan Border called for an international inquiry into the standards of Pakistani cricket. See Mike Coward, 'Off-Side?'. See also, Paul Weaver, 'Shakoor renews attack on Gatting', *Guardian*, 13 Oct. 2000; 'The game that changed the face of cricket', *Guardian*, 16 Oct. 2000; Mike Selvey, 'I hadn't a clue what was going on out there', *Guardian*, 16 Oct. 2000; For a broader study of Australian cricket and the subcontinent, see Mike Coward, *Cricket Beyond The Bazaar* (North Sydney: Allen & Unwin, 1990). See also, Raffi Nasim, 'Former Pakistan Umpire Shakoor Rana dies at 65', *CricInfo*, 10 April 2001.

29 Id., at p. 912. It should be noted that Gatting was the apparent first choice to captain England in the Ashes series against Australia in 1989 but Ossie Wheatley, TCCB chairman, exercised his veto power and David Gower was chosen instead (see *Wisden* (1990), pp. 42–43). Wheatley justified his decision by placing Gatting in a category of the ostracized and unforgiven.

> One of the absolutely unbreakable rules of cricket is that no one, but no one, disputes anything with the umpire, least of all, the captain of England. There are no excuses.

The Book of Cricket Quotations, op. cit., p. 169.

Indian captain Sunil Gavaskar, coming from another interpretive standpoint, has a different opinion.

> I am not surprised that the whole of Pakistan is proud of Shakoor. In the history of Pakistan cricket, he will rank along with Hawif, Zaheer, Imran and others for his 'contributions' to Pakistan cricket.

Id., p. 207. In other words, from the perspective of Indian cricket, Shakoor simply carries on a fine Pakistan tradition of cheating.

30 Id., at p. 910. Interestingly, Umpire Constant withdrew from an England–New Zealand Test after a dispute with Kiwi batter Mark Greatbatch in a One-Day game. At first blush, this may lend credence to the Pakistani contentions of his lack of ability. This is not, at least as far as the Greatbatch affair is concerned, the case. Greatbatch argued with Constant over the frequency of bouncers aimed at him. The One-Day rules permitted only *one* bouncer per over. In England, however, a bouncer was defined as passing below head height, while the interpretation in Australia and New Zealand forbade balls *above* shoulder height. In other words, the throat ball was an antipodean bouncer but it was not an English bouncer. On the facts and the law, then, Constant was correct and Greatbatch in error under municipal law. Greatbatch was fined by the New Zealand management for misconduct. Of course, just because Constant was correct here takes nothing away from Imran's position.

31 Id., at p. 909. See also Oamar Ahmed, 'The New Zealanders in Sri Lanka and Pakistan – 1984–85', *Wisden* (1986), p. 926.

32 Id., at p. 910.

33 In the 1990 *Wisden*, John Thicknesse argues that Terry Alderman's success in winning LBW decisions during the 1989 Ashes tour of England can be attributed to 'undue co-operation from the umpires...'. He adds, 'There were times as the series wore on, however, when the response to an Alderman appeal appeared to be almost automatic. It strengthened the impression I had formed over recent home series that, to consolidate their reputation for impartiality, English umpires have tended to favour the opposition, subconsciously or otherwise. What irony if, in probably the only Test-playing country where touring teams might opt for home-based umpires, the England team might think they had a better chance with neutrals.' 'The Australians in England, 1989', pp. 284–85. Australians are quick to point out, however, that English losses to Australian sides are almost always accompanied by much 'whingeing'.

34 See e.g., Rodney Martinesz, 'Interim injunction granted against Cricket Board', *Daily News*, 11 June 1999; Kumar Wethasinghe, 'BCCSL appeals put off for July 1', *Daily News*, 25 June 1999; Rodney Martinesz, 'Allowing Defunct Board to continue would have cost us our ICC status, says AG', *Daily News*, 30 Oct. 1999; 'Probe committee recommends criminal investigation', *CricInfo*, 18 June 2001; Rex Clementine Fernando, 'Recommendations of the Sri Lankan probe committee', *CricInfo*, 19 June 2001; Charlie Austin, 'Interim Committee resigns after request from Sports Minister', *CricInfo*, 22 Dec. 2001; 'Interim committee reappointed to run Sri Lankan cricket board', *CricInfo*, 31 Dec. 2001; Charlie Austin, 'Sri Lankan sports minister intervenes in selection debacle', *CricInfo*, 4 Jan. 2002.

35 See e.g., Sa'aadi Thawfeeq, 'Clouds of uncertainty on cricket TV Deal', *Daily News*, 13 July 1999; 'Legal wrangle continue but BCCSL opens fresh bids', *CricInfo*, 30 Oct. 2001; 'Sri Lanka's Supreme Court Dismisses WSG Nimbus's Action versus the BCCSL', BCCSL, 10 Jan. 2002; 'WSG initiates action against BCCSL', WSG, 12 Jan. 2002.

36 On Sri Lankan cricket in particular see, Mike Marqusee, *War Minus the Shooting* (London: Heinemann, 1996), at pp. 172–88. See also, Ivan Corea, 'The British sports media's witch hunt against Sri Lanka's cricketers', *Daily News*, 8 Feb. 1999; Pat Gibson, 'Ranatunga fires opening shots', *Times*, 5 May 1999; David Hopps, 'Stewart and Ranatunga renew war of words', *Guardian*, 5 May 1999.

37 'The Sri Lankans in Australia, 1995–96', at p. 1124.

38 See Chapter 18.

39 See Chapter 16.

40 See Mike Marqusee, *War Minus the Shooting*, op. cit., at pp. 32–45 and Malcolm Knox, 'At a fever pitch', *Sun Herald*, 31 Jan. 1999.

41 Simon Barnes, 'Loathing bowls flannelled fools', *Sydney Morning Herald*, 26 Feb. 1996. The precipitous return of New Zealand from Pakistan, and threats to the next Australian tour there are in part at least overdetermined by conceptions and constructions of 'terror' and the 'Third World' which politicize cricket while claiming that politics has no role to play in cricket. See 'New Zealand Cricket bring TelstraClear Black Caps home from Pakistan', New Zealand Cricket, 8 May 2002; Martin Blake, 'Suicide bomb blast may cause Australia's tour to Pakistan to be transferred to Sharjah', *Sydney Morning Herald*, 9 May 2002; 'Trauma experts to help Kiwis recover from bomb blast', *Sydney Morning Herald*, 11–12 May 2002; 'Pakistan asks Australia to reconsider', *Sydney Morning Herald*, 16 May 2002; Martin Blake, 'Play it again, Steve, in Casablanca', *Sydney Morning Herald*, 16 May 2002.

42 See generally, Malcolm Knox, 'Sri Lankan joy as ACB moves to no-ball Hair', *Sydney Morning Herald*, 19 Nov. 1998; 'Hair still standing as ACB defers decision', *Sydney Morning Herald*, 20 Nov. 1998; 'Hair affair: ACB wants ICC to make decision', *Sydney Morning Herald*, 27 Nov. 1998; Greg Baum, 'Howzat! Sri Lanka get their Hair out', *Sydney Morning Herald*, 4 Dec. 1998.

43 Law 2(5), 1980 *Code*.

44 Mark Ray, 'Ranatunga is walking a fine line', *Sydney Morning Herald*, 25 Jan. 1999. This was not the first time there had been a legal disagreement between Australia and Sri Lanka over Ranatunga's propensity for injury and need for a runner. See e.g., Michael Koslowski, 'Aussies triumph: Sri Lanka stumble in', *Sun Herald*, 21 Jan. 1996.

45 'Outrageous action must be punished', *Australian*, 25 Jan. 1999; Peter Roebuck, 'Why we need a swift return to the conflict between bat and ball', *Sydney Morning Herald*, 25 Jan. 1999.

46 Andrew Ramsey, 'Ranatunga escapes with suspended sentence', *Australian*, 29 Jan. 1999; 'Not cricket', Editorial, *Sydney Morning Herald*, 30 Jan. 1999; Andrew Ramsey, 'How the legal eagles bailed out Ranatunga', *Weekend Australian*, 30–31 Jan. 1999.

47 Malcolm Conn, 'Lankans quizzed over legal bill', *Australian*, 18 Aug. 1999; Mark Ray, 'ICC "please explain" puts Sri Lankan board on notice', *Sydney Morning Herald*, 18 Aug. 1999.

48 See Jim White, 'Interview: Sanath Jayasuriya', *Guardian*, 13 May 2002.

49 See generally ICC, 'Code of Conduct for Players and Team Officials', 2002. It is important to note that national boards and local authorities have introduced similar and parallel mechanisms for dealing with transgressions at their level as well. For the sake of brevity and concision, I shall limit discussion here to the ICC Code and international cricket.

50 See ICC, '2000 – Penalties imposed on players for breaches of ICC Code of Conduct'.

51 Ibid.

52 *ICC Code of Conduct*, para. 1.3.

53 Op. cit., para. 2.2.

54 Op. cit., paras 3.1 and 4.1.

55 ICC, '1992 – Penalties imposed on players for breaches of ICC Code of Conduct'.

56 In June 2002, my count of the offenders and offences listed by the ICC, indicated 31 breaches each by Pakistan and India, 23 by Australia, 19 by South Africa, Zimbabwe 17, New Zealand 16, Sri Lanka and England 12 each and the West Indies 9.

57 ICC, op. cit., 1993.

58 Op. cit., 1994.

59 Op. cit., 1995.

60 Op. cit., 1996.

61 Op. cit., 1997.

62 Op. cit., 1998.

63 Op. cit., 1999, 2000.

64 Op. cit., 2001.
65 Op. cit., 2002.

10 The man in white is always right (but he is not always neutral)

1 *That's Out!*, op. cit., at p. 72.
2 *The Tao of Cricket*, op. cit., at p. 23 (footnote omitted). It is interesting and important to note, even here, that the Indian umpires were not totally unconstrained in their apparent hometown bias. The *Laws* and their own internalized perceptions of themselves as umpires prevented them from acting completely outside their roles and they did give Indian players out.
3 See 'Test match resumes under shadow of brick throwing incident', *Times*, 2 Jan. 1981, stating:

> Shoaib Mir, one of Pakistan's first-class umpires, said in Lahore he would not officiate in his scheduled match in the Patron Trophy domestic competition as a protest against 'behind the scenes pressure tactics' against umpires. His protest follows the announcement on Saturday by another first-class umpire, Khalid Aziz, that he was retiring from cricket because he had been compelled to make dishonest decisions in matches against the West Indian team now touring Pakistan.

4 See *Badminton Library – Cricket*, op. cit., n. 75, at p. 227. 'Men who are continually wrangling and disputing about the decisions of umpires, and who have earned the reputation of so doing, have in the long run more real cause to complain than their more peaceable *confrères* . . . if, as they allege, they have had to fight an uphill battle on English grounds against the bad decisions of our umpires, we firmly believe they have brought this unfortunate result upon their own heads.' There is here an obvious logical/moral flaw in the gentleman's view of Australian behaviour. On the one hand, they had no cause for complaint because English umpires are unbiased. On the other, if they did have cause for complaint, it is only because the umpires were reacting to unacceptable behaviour by the larrikin colonials.
5 See Richard Cashman, '*Ave a Go, Yer Mug!, Australian Cricket Crowds from Larrikin to Ocker*' (Sydney: Collins, 1984), at pp. 28 et. seq.
6 See Trevor McDonald, *Clive Lloyd – The Authorised Biography*, op. cit., at pp. 98–99.
7 See Ashis Nandy, op. cit., at p. 23. Nandy, while sympathetic to appeals for neutral umpires, feels that the problem is more deep-rooted than that. He explains at p. 113:

> It was the same beggar-thy-neighbour attitude which prompted a section of the audience in some venues in India to heckle and boo Pakistani umpires in Reliance Cup matches, whenever their decisions went against the interests of India. The Reliance Cup matches had neutral umpires. So the Pakistani umpires did not supervise the matches between India and Pakistan; they supervised the matches between India and some other countries. But that did not save them from the wrath of the Indian ultra-nationalists. For, once one accepts the completely interest-based rationality of the modern market and *realpolitik*, all results are interrelated and one operates in a psychological context in which every match seems to have some bearing on the standing of India in world cricket. Messrs Imran Khan, Sunil Gavaskar and the latest hero in the global struggle against the oppression of umpires, Mike Gatting, may feel that neutral umpires or an international panel of umpires will solve controversies on umpiring in international cricket but, in an age of hard nationalism, it is also likely that such controversies will raise their heads again under other guises, once international umpires are introduced and once the spectators get 'sophisticated' in

the strategies of international cricket. Rationally, there can be no end to rational cost-calculation.

 8 'Pakistan's proviso', *Cricket Life International*, May 1990, p. 7.
 9 See e.g., Martin Blake, 'Chappelli: Our umps are the worst', *Sydney Morning Herald*, 3 Feb. 1994; see also 'Umpires "biased"', *Sun Herald*, 19 Sep. 1993.
10 AAP, 'Tests show our umpires score 95 out of 100', *Sydney Morning Herald*, 17 May 2002.
11 See Malcolm Conn, 'Umpiring, batting a disgrace', *Australian*, 11 March 1998.
12 Martin Blake, 'Prasad's dirty dancing', *Sydney Morning Herald*, 28 Dec. 1999; Phil Wilkins, 'Tendulkar almost led walk-off', *Sun Herald*, 16 Jan. 2000; Martin Blake, 'Sachin blasts umpires', 4 Jan. 2001; Phil Wilkins, 'The umpires strike back', *Sydney Morning Herald*, 8 Jan. 2000.
13 See Omar Kureishi, 'Abysmal umpiring by Australians', *Dawn*, 7 Feb. 2000.
14 Phil Wilkins, 'Hair faces ACB rebuke over demand', *Sun Herald*, 23 Jan. 2000; 'Hair pays the penalty', ibid., Andrew Ramsey, 'ACB won't penalise Hair any further', *Australian*, 2 Feb. 2000.
15 Simon Wilde, 'Umpire thrown into firing line again', *Sunday Times*, 22 Oct. 2000.
16 See Charlie Austin, 'Zimbabwean captain left frustrated after poor umpiring in Colombo', *CricInfo*, 30 Dec. 2001.
17 'Pakistan: Five umpires that they have loved to hate', *Sunday Times*, 22 Oct. 2000.
18 G. Viswanath, 'Umpire Dunne in poor light', *Hindu*, 2 Feb. 1999.
19 See e.g., David Hopps, 'Just not cricket', *Guardian*, 10 March 2001.
20 *It's Not Cricket*, op. cit., at p. 3. See also, Christopher Martin-Jenkins, 'Test erupts and pitches cricket to the brink of anarchy', 10 March 2001; Vic Marks, 'Victory beckons – but cricket is the loser', *Observer*, 11 March 2001; Vic Marks, 'Time has come for referral', *Observer*, 11 March 2001.
21 ICC, 'First appointments for new ICC panel umpires and referees', 26 March 2002; ICC, 'ICC Elite Panel of Referees and Umpires', 'ICC announces International panel of Umpires and Referees', 16 May 2002.
22 Tony Becca, 'Elite umpires off to poor start', *Jamaica Gleaner*, 29 April 2002.
23 Ibid.
24 Similar debate continued over decision-making in the Sri Lanka series in India, with umpires being criticized for judicial error.

11 Technology, adjudication and law

 1 ICC, 'ICC Champions Trophy to experiment with technology trial', 18 March 2002. See Geoffrey Dean and Richard Hobson, 'Technology signals end of the umpire', *Times*, 19 March 2002; ICC, 'ICC Elite Umpires support Champions Trophy technology test', 23 March 2002; but cf., Christopher Lyles, 'TV plan turns off Willey', *Daily Telegraph*, 20 March 2002; Martin Blake, 'TV umpires slow the motion', *Sydney Morning Herald*, 11 Sep. 2002.
 2 The introduction of technology and replay adjudication raises similar questions in other sports as well. The Six Nations' rugby union tournament has had to face up to issues of interpretation and allegations of incompetence as well. See, Tim Glover, 'Lies, tries and damned videos', *Independent on Sunday*, 18 Feb. 2001.
 3 See below, Chapter 12.
 4 See 'ECB look into adapting Cyclops technology to solve no-ball problems', *CricInfo*, 11 June 2001.
 5 See e.g., 'New technology brings World Cup into line', *Times*, 7 April 1999; Sa'adi Thawfeeq, 'Too much technology and rules governing cricket says Thomson', *Daily News*, 6 Sep. 1999; Ranjan Anandappa, 'Modern technology will engulf jurisdiction of cricket umpires – Peter Willey', *Daily News*, 10 Oct. 1999; Peter Deeley, 'Snickometer

subject of scrutiny', *Daily Telegraph*, 24 Nov. 1999; Michael Atherton, 'Third umpire is proving second rate', *Daily Telegraph*, 19 Dec. 1999; Geoff Longley, 'Camera glitches solved, says Sky', *Christchurch Press*, 20 Dec. 1999; 'Umpiring decisions: Intikhab Alam for more assistance', *Dawn*, 21 Dec. 1999; Lynn McConnell, 'Snedden wants technology on ICC meeting agenda', *CricInfo*, 16 Jan. 2002; Andrew Ramsey, 'TV trial to give gimmicks flick', *Australian*, 24 July 2002.

6　G. Viswanath, 'Shepherd for optimum use of technology', *Hindu*, 23 Feb. 2000.

7　See 'Shepherd: I almost quit after mistakes', *CricInfo*, 5 April 2002.

8　See Paul Weaver, 'No-ball fiasco clouds Waqar's triumph', *Guardian*, 5 June 2001; 'Graveney sympathetic to umpire's problems', *CricInfo*, 5 June 2001; George Dobell, 'Ray Julian: Umpires were warned they were missing no-balls', *CricInfo*, 6 June 2001; Michael Henderson, 'Technology must not be allowed to threaten game', *Daily Telegraph*, 6 June 2001; ECB, 'ECB fully supports David Shepherd', 6 June 2001.

9　Law 24(15).

10　Law 24(12) and (13).

11　Peter Roebuck, 'How Sth African TV gave Test umpires the finger', *Sydney Morning Herald*, 29 March 1997.

12　ICC, 'Rules and Regulations – Umpires, para. 2 Third Umpire/TV Replays'.

13　See discussion below. Mark Ray, 'Waugh carves out century to steer Australia victory and level the series', *Sydney Morning Herald*, 29 March 2001; 'Ganguly escapes censure over run-out controversy', *Sydney Morning Herald*, 30 March 2001; Mark Ray, 'Waugh wants disciplinary overhaul', *Sydney Morning Herald*, 9 April 2001.

14　See Mark Ray, 'Captain Steve prepares a techno-rap as injured brother Mark bent on early trail home', *Sydney Morning Herald*, 31 March 2001.

15　Rules, para. 2.1 (b).

16　See Peter Deeley, 'ACB place limits on replays', *Daily Telegraph*, 26 Nov. 1999.

17　ICC, *Rules and Regulations*, Umpires, para. 2.1.

18　ICC, 'Penalties imposed on players for breaches of ICC Code of Conduct' (1995).

19　Ibid., 1996.

20　Ibid., 1997.

21　'Umpire's decision is no longer final', *Times*, 6 Jan. 1996. This is the episode for which Cronje was sanctioned, above. The problem here of course is that the illegality of his conduct resulted in a key dismissal on the field, while his punishment affected only him and in an *ex post facto* way. See 'Captain fined as S. Africa triumph', *Weekend Australian*, 6–7 Jan. 1996; Mike Selvey, 'England's dismal roll-over', *Guardian Weekly*, 14 Jan. 1996.

22　See e.g., Brian Burke, 'Third umpire sparks controversy', *Australian*, 28 March 2001.

23　See AFP, 'Windies launch into run chase', *Sydney Morning Herald*, 17 March 1998 where Philo Wallace was given not out in such circumstances. This is obviously not always the case. The first English Test player to be given out after video replay was Robin Smith of England, stumped by Ian Healy, bowled Tim May at Lord's. Patrick Keane, 'TV ump stumps Smith', *Sun Herald*, 20 June 1993. But Smith was given out run out in more controversial circumstances 'on the flimsiest of evidence' in the 1999 World Cup, see Mike Selvey, 'Gone with the whirlwind', *Guardian Weekly*, 17 March 1996.

24　See Malcolm Knox, 'Slater saves the day but series rests with the bowlers', *Sydney Morning Herald*, 5 Jan. 1999.

25　John Etheridge, 'England in Australia, 1998–99', *Wisden* (2000), at p. 1121.

26　See more broadly here Jean Baudrillard, *The Gulf War Did Not Take Place* (Paul Patton trans.) (Sydney: Power Publications, 1995). Cf., Paul Virilio, *Desert Screen: War at the Speed of Light* (New York: Continuum, 2002).

27　The ICC International Panel of Umpires now includes specialist 'Third Umpires' for Test match and One-Day adjudication. See, 'ICC Elite Panel of Referees and Umpires' and ICC, 'ICC announces International Panel Umpires and Referees', 16 May 2002.

28 See e.g., Mark Ray, 'Ponting's field of vision ignites win', *Sydney Morning Herald*, 28 Aug. 1999; Elmo Rodrigopulle, 'Umpires made a mockery of third umpire concept', *Daily News*, 1 Sep. 1999; Mark Ray, 'Waugh's agony', *Sun Herald*, 12 Sep. 1999; Peter Roebuck, 'History is made in most bizarre match I've seen', *Sydney Morning Herald*, 13 Sep. 1999.

29 See e.g., Phil Wilkins, 'Test turns sour as our luck runs out', *Sun Herald*, 27 March 1994.

30 See, 'Ambrose leaves England in tatters', *Weekend Australian*, 7–8 Feb. 1998.

31 Greg Baum, 'Video replay for run-outs runs into a red light', *Sydney Morning Herald*, 20 Oct. 1994.

32 See e.g., AAP, 'Bushrangers fought the Law, but the Law won', *Sydney Morning Herald*, 28 March 2001.

33 Although some umpires may simply not do so, in which case old debates about judicial incompetence may well resurface. See e.g., Peter Roebuck, 'History is made in most bizarre match I've seen', *Sydney Morning Herald*, 13 Sep. 1999.

34 See Charlie Austin, 'West Indies rue umpiring blunder in Kandy Test', *CricInfo*, 25 Nov. 2001.

35 Phil Wilkins, 'England fury over video ref', *Sun Herald*, 13 Dec. 1998.

36 Ibid. See also, Robert Craddock, 'English forget Taylor's catch', *Daily Telegraph*, 17 Dec. 1998; Phil Wilkins, 'Poms Anger Over "Catch"', *Sun Herald*, 13 Dec. 1998. In 2001, the ACB abandoned the use of replays for catch decisions in domestic cricket after a number of complaints about the uncertainty of the decision-making process. See Matthew Hancock, 'Waugh fights blood clotting', *Guardian*, 4 Oct. 2001.

37 Id.

38 The current version under the 2000 *Code* varies little from this formulation. None of the minor changes to the *Law* would have a material effect on the discussion here.

39 See Malcolm Conn, 'Lara hits form and wicket as Vics suffer', *Weekend Australian*, 21–22 Dec. 1996; Anthony Mithen, 'Luckless Lara strikes trouble', *Sydney Morning Herald*, 21 Dec. 1996.

40 Robert Craddock, 'It's The Rule', *Daily Telegraph*, 4 Feb. 1998.

41 See, Malcolm Conn, 'Why Test hero Waugh broke his stumps: It was a war of nerves', *Australian*, 4 Feb. 1998; Malcolm Knox, 'Mark Waugh rattles the bails and Hansie – and saves the Test', *Sydney Morning Herald*, 4 Feb. 1998; Phillip Derriman, 'Some room for doubt over that crucial Waugh decision', *Sydney Morning Herald*, 5 Feb. 1998. See also, J. Neville Turner, 'Flaws in the Laws Revealed: Time for a Radical Overhaul', 1(2) *Baggy Green* (1999).

42 *Tom Smith's Cricket Umpiring*, op. cit., at p. 185. See also, John MacDonald, 'When two's company but three's a crowd', *Weekend Australian*, 7–8 Feb. 1998, citing former Test umpire Mel Johnson, 'It was absolutely clear-cut. I was surprised Steve Randell didn't give him not out straight away'.

12 Leg before wicket, causation and the rule of law

1 *Wisden: The Laws of Cricket*, op. cit., at p. 152.

2 *Tom Smith's Cricket Umpiring*, op. cit., at p. 187. See also, Ben Craven, 'A psychophysical study of leg-before-wicket judgments in cricket', 89 *British Journal of Psychology* 555 (1998).

3 'England were robbed, says Gavaskar', *CricInfo*, 21 Jan. 2002. The English team agreed with Gavaskar's view. See, 'England complain to ICC about Kolkata umpiring', *CricInfo*, 21 Jan. 2002.

4 See e.g., Spiro Zavos, 'Overseas umpires take heat off lbw furore', *Sydney Morning Herald*, 14 Feb. 1994; Col (Retd) Rafi Nasim, 'LBW – the cause of crisis in cricket', *CricInfo*, 27 Sep. 2000.

5 See e.g., cases below and Michael Koslowski, 'Umpires like the look of tourists' legs', *Sydney Morning Herald*, 6 Dec. 1996; Malcolm Knox, 'Taylor's grit a source of Test solution', *Sydney Morning Herald*, 2 Feb. 1998.

6 BillFrindall, *Guiness Cricket Facts and Feats* (London: Guinness, 1987), p. 11.

7 On the history of the LBW Law, G.O. Allen, 'Treasurer's Report to the MCC Annual General Meeting' (1976) in *Faber Book of Cricket*, op. cit., at pp. 345–46.

8 There has been historical controversy about the correct scoring of a delivery which strikes the pads in such a way as the batter would be dismissed LBW (Law 36) but where the ball then travels on to the stumps (Law 30(1) bowled). Law 30(2) provides that 'The striker is out Bowled if his wicket is put down as in 1 above, even though a decision against him for any other method of dismissal would be justified.' Similarly, Brodribb points out that the 'L' of LBW is not always an accurate appellation.

> In a match between Essex and Middlesex at Leyton in 1924 Capt. P. Ashton . . . tried a sweep to leg off J.W. Hearne and was out lbw though the ball actually hit him on the head as he lay full length on the ground.

Op. cit., at p. 248. Of course, the substantive language of the provision does not refer to 'leg' but 'any part of his person'.

9 For a discussion of these issues, see David Fraser and David Howarth, 'More Concern for Cause', 4 *Leg. Stud.* 131 (1984).

10 In addition to considering analogies between LBW and causation in tort law, it is also useful to turn the legal mind to other matters where the law is concerned with events which did not 'happen'. The most obvious example from the criminal law is the law of attempt in general and particularly the law as it relates to the doctrine of impossibility.

11 Law 24(5) *Fair Delivery – The Feet* which reads:

> For a delivery to be fair in respect of the feet, in the delivery stride,
> (i)   the bowler's back foot must land within and not touching the return crease.
> (ii)   the bowler's front foot must land with some part of the foot, whether grounded or raised, behind the popping crease.
> If the umpire at the bowler's end is not satisfied that both these conditions have been met, he shall call and signal no ball.

See Law 9 for a definition of the return and popping crease.

12 See Law 24(2) and (3) and discussion below in Chapters 15 and 16.

13 It is interesting to note, however, that while all participants – players, commentators and spectators – remain willing to engage in heated debate over the 'legal' nature of the Umpire's LBW decision, an entirely opposite position prevails at the 'ethical' level. While there is an ethical imperative in the eyes of some for a batter to 'walk' when caught off an edge, there is no idea that one should walk when struck on the pads. Only the umpire can 'know' that a batter is out LBW. It is possible, therefore, to be in virtually the same 'interpretive' position as the Umpire for a 'legal' debate and in a different, but equally valid, *locus* when the debate shifts to the moral imperative.

14 For a detailed study of the role of the interpretive community, see Stanley Fish, *Is There a Text in this Class?* (Baltimore and London: Johns Hopkins University Press, 1980).

15 See David Fraser, 'Truth and Hierarchy: Will the Circle Be Unbroken?', 33 *Buffalo L. Rev.* 729 (1985).

16 On the importance of the notions of freedom and constraint in interpretation and their application in law and cricket, see Duncan Kennedy, *A Critique of Adjudication*

(*fin de siècle*) (Cambridge and London: Harvard University Press, 1997) and Allan Hutchinson, *It's All in the Game*, op. cit. For another study of the institutional constraints which inform adjudication see, Guido Calabresi, *A Common Law for the Age of Statutes* (Cambridge and London: Harvard University Press, 1982).

17 'Are Cricket Umpires biased?', *New Scientist*, 2 July 1981. See also, John Sumner, 'Australian umpires are the most lenient', *Sydney Morning Herald*, 28 Nov. 1981.

18 Op. cit., pp. 30–31.

19 *It's Not Cricket*, op. cit., at p. 2.

20 See e.g., Jack Pollard, op. cit., at p. 643.

21 Peter Roebuck, 'Time umpires recognised absolutely plonkers is out', *Sydney Morning Herald*, 13 Jan. 1993.

22 See e.g., 'Scientist plans electronic aid to determine lbws', *Sydney Morning Herald*, 3 Aug. 1998; 'Umpires call for "lbw cam"', *Australian*, 5 Aug. 1998; Lynn McConnell, 'Kiwi scientists have cheaper lbw detector', *CricInfo*, 8 Sep. 2000; Richard Hobson, 'Mat finish gets chance to end lbw arguments', *Times*, 8 Sep. 2000; Sky Sports, 'New technology to analyse lbw decisions', 3 May 2001; Paul Weaver, 'Scope for improving the third umpire's profile', *Guardian*, 9 May 2001; Ivo Tennant, 'Eye test proves umpires both right and wrong', *Sunday Times*, 20 May 2001; Mike Selvey, 'Hawkeye and the last of the lbw-shy umpires', *Guardian*, 26 May 2001.

23 'Hawkeye and the last of the lbw-shy umpires', op. cit.

24 See Jon Henderson, 'Dickie bowled over by Hawkeye', *Observer*, 12 May 2002.

25 David Hopps, 'TV on trial as umpires get extra help', *Guardian*, 12 Sep. 2002.

26 AFP, 'Video umpire gives first ever lbw decision', *Sydney Morning Herald*, 13 Sep. 2002.

27 Peter Krupka, 'Finger points to television replays for lbw decisions', *Australian*, 17 July 2002.

28 Martin Blake, 'ICC's decision is plumb lbw, say players', *Sydney Morning Herald*, 17 July 2002; 'Captains oppose use of technology for making LBW decisions', *Dawn*, 21 July 2002.

13 Mankad, Javed, Hilditch, Sarfraz and the rule of law

1 In addition to the original *Mankading*, other such dismissals are rarely recorded in Test history. In the 1977–78 Test at Christchurch, Ewan Chatfield *Mankaded* Derek Randall of England, and in the 1978–79 Perth Test, Alan Hurst did the same to Indian batter Sikander Bakht. To add insult to injury, Sikander was dismissed for a duck. In 1968–69, Charlie Griffith of the West Indies *Mankaded* Ian Redpath of Australia (see discussion *infra*). Press coverage at the time of the original incident was muted. The *Sydney Morning Herald* reported the incident factually stating: 'Brown who had been similarly dismissed by Mankad on a previous occasion and warned on another, walked out of his crease before the ball was delivered' and appeared to place the moral blame on the batsman. See, 'Brown Well Out of Crease, Bat In Air, When Dismissed', 15 Dec. 1947.

   Bill O'Reilly writing for the same newspaper was willing to attach some blame to the bowler 'I feel sure that if a bowler concentrated on effecting that type of dismissal, it would not be difficult to account for at least half the opponents in any match.' He, too, however, placed the real burden on the batter, 'I hope Brown has made up his mind not to offend again...' 'Brown Must Find Counter', ibid.

2 See Law 38, 'run out' and commentary by Don Oslear, *Wisden: The Laws of Cricket*, at pp. 159–60.

3 See Duncan Kennedy, *A Critique of Adjudication*, op. cit.

4 'The Silent Warrior', *Cricket Life international*, May 1990, p. 46 at p. 47. See also 'Pakistan Salutes Walsh', *Times of India*, 19 Oct. 1987.

5 Mike Marqusee, *War Minus the Shooting*, op. cit., at p. 167.
6 Phil Wilkins, 'Tension hits fever pitch as old foes play hardball in Mankad's shadow', *Sydney Morning Herald*, 12 Jan. 2000.
7 In fact, Mankad's moral culpability is doubly eliminated because he had, prior to the Test, run out Brown in a match against an Australian XI at the SCG. On that occasion as well, he had warned Brown.
8 See generally, Simon Rae, *W.G. Grace: A Life* (London: Faber & Faber, 1998).
9 Derek Birley, *The Willow Wand: Some Cricket Myths Explored* (London: Aurum Press, 2000), at p. 40. But cf. *dubitante*, C.F. Pardon, 'S.P. Jones's Run Out', in *Bat and Pad – Writings on Australian Cricket* (Pat Mullins and Phillip Derriman eds.) (Melbourne and Oxford: Oxford University Press, 1984), at p. 144. In another match, W.G. conspired with his brother E.M. so that when E.M. asked Charles Wright the batter to knock the ball to him, E.M. successfully appealed for 'hit the ball twice' (Law 34). W.G. disingenuously proclaimed: 'Well, I never! Here's Chals come all the way from Nottin'am to 'ave a friendly game with us, and you go and do a thing like that to him' *The Book of Cricket Quotations*, op. cit., p. 39.

It may not be cricket, but it is a wicket. Such actions based on pure legal formalism are not unheard of in cricket to this day. In addition to the Javed, Hurst affair (*infra*), another well-known incident occurred in the 1973–74 Test series between England and the West Indies. West Indian batter Alvin Kallicharran left the crease after playing the ball with a defensive stroke to the last delivery of the day. Tony Greig of England, realizing that 'time' had not been called, ran out the batter. The appeal, although successful, was subsequently withdrawn.

10 'Fingleton's Run-Out', *The Australian Cricketer*, 10 Feb. 1934, reproduced in *Bat and Pad*, op. cit., at p. 146. See also Richard Cashman's description of events of an 1873 match when members of the team which had won such a dismissal were 'hooted as they left the field' and the successful 'appellant' was hit by stones thrown by members of his 'own' crowd.
11 Op. cit., at p. 216.
12 Id., at p. 215.
13 'Early Shocks for New Zealand', *Times*, 1 March 1978, 'When a bowler, sees this happening, it is customary to warn the non-striker that if he does it again he will run him out. In this case Chatfield whipped off the bails without such a warning – to the embarrassment, I think of most New Zealanders present, perhaps even to Chatfield's own regret afterwards', and 'This was a watched episode, but it showed how even a game of cricket can get out of hand when it is less than strictly controlled' in 'Botham puts on a one in a hundred display for England', *Times*, 2 March 1978.
14 'Runout of Randall is Defended in NZ', *Times*, 3 March 1978.
15 Phil Wilkins, 'Thrilling Test End', *Sydney Morning Herald*, 30 Jan. 1969.
16 Phil Wilkins, 'Run Out Angers Test Crowd', id.
17 'Fickle Fortune', id.
18 See, Stanley Fish, 'Working On the Chain Gang! Interpretation in Law and Literature', 9 *Critical Inquiry* 201 (1982) and 60 *Tex. L. Rev.* 551 (1982) for an analysis of this particular issue of the requirement of interpretive loyalty.
19 'Bowler "was right" ', *Sun-Herald*, 2 Feb. 1969.
20 'Lawry critical of runout', *Sydney Morning Herald*, 3 Feb. 1969.
21 'Bowler to rescue in Test Farce', *Sydney Morning Herald*, 19 Feb. 1969.
22 Ashis Nandy, op. cit., at p. 112 (footnote omitted).
23 See discussion in Chapter 18 below.
24 For descriptions, see Anton Rippon, *Cricket Around the World* (Ashbourne, Derbys.: 1982), p. 186; Ashis Nandy, op. cit., pp. 29–30 and see 'Haynes out for Handling ball', *Sydney Morning Herald*, 28 Nov. 1983 and 'Moshin out after handling the ball in Test', *Sydney Morning Herald*, 24 Sep. 1982.

25 Rippon, op. cit. and see 'Pakistanis visit ends in sour note', *Australian*, 30 March 1975.

> Hilditch, at the non-striker's end, obligingly saved Sarfraz the trouble of walking out of his way by picking up the ball and tossing it to him. Sarfraz instead chose to ignore the gesture and sprung around to present Umpire Crafter with his second difficult decision. Crafter at first seemed as stunned as everyone at the ground but when Sarfraz prolonged his appeal he had no alternative but to raise his finger.

26 'Cricket? It is near cheating', *Sydney Morning Herald*, 30 March 1975.
27 Id. Indeed, Out Handled the Ball is an extremely rare form of dismissal. In recent times Graham Gooch and Michael Vaughan of England and Steve Waugh of Australia have been given out handled the ball. Besides Hilditch, Mohsin Khan of Pakistan was dismissed at Karachi against Australia in 1982–83 and Desmond Haynes of the West Indies was dismissed at Bombay against India in 1983–84. Again, the Mohsin incident offers a deeply contextualized social text. It occurred during a series in which ill-feeling between the two sides ran high. Earlier in the day, Lawson showed his displeasure at being turned down on an appeal for caught behind against Mohsin and the Pakistani crowd reciprocated by throwing bricks and stones at the Australian fielders. Even this brief description clearly indicates something more complex than a single 'out-handled the ball' in the scorebook.
28 Gerald Brodribb, *Next Man In*, op. cit., at p. 189.
29 'Umpire's Corner', *Cricket World*, Vol. 4, No. 3, March 1990, p. 13.
30 Omar Kureishi, 'Vaughan dismissal, leg theory legitimate tactics', *Dawn*, 25 Dec. 2001. But cf., S. Santhosh, 'Vaughan: Probably is against the spirit of the game', *CricInfo*, 19 Dec. 2001.
31 Mark Nicholas, 'Vaughan is handed a nasty lesson', *Daily Telegraph*, 20 Dec. 2001.

14 It's not cricket: underarm bowling, legality and the meaning of life

 1 Jack Pollard, *Australian Cricket*, op. cit., at p. 267. The incident continues to haunt Trevor Chappell. He points out, however, that at one level, the incident has a different epistemological status than that attributed to it generally. He says that 'Most people did not realise that you had to tell the umpire, and he tells the batsman, that you were going to bowl underarm . . .'. Thus, the 'active' participants 'knew' what was about to occur. This is confirmed by contemporaneous press accounts which indicate clearly that '. . . the Umpires Don Weser and Peter Cronins, having been told by Greg Chappell of his intention and having in turn advised the batsmen, were powerless.' Rex Mossop, 'One ball dents Australia's image as a sports nation', *Sydney Morning Herald*, 2 Feb. 1981. See also Greg Growden, 'Trevor Chappell reflects: Why I bowled Underarm', *Sydney Morning Herald*, 25 March 1986.
[***]
'I was probably disappointed to the extent that it was against the spirit of the game. That was the most disappointing aspect, particularly as it was such a good game of cricket.' Chappell loses some power in his response however when he continues '. . . it was in the rules anyway'. Greg Growden, 'Face to Face with Trevor Chappell', *Sydney Morning Herald*, 27 Oct. 1990. For the perspective of the other active participant, New Zealand batter Brian McKechnie, see Mike Coward, 'The batsman has forgiven, but is not allowed to forget', *Sydney Morning Herald*, 27 March 1986, 'I don't think I had a grudge against Greg Chappell. It was in the rules at the time and what is in the rules is fair.'
 2 Id., at p. 268.
 3 'The Ins and Outs of Bad Sportsmanship', *Good Weekend*, 9 Dec. 1989. It has also been immortalized by Australian cultural icons Roy and H.G., see John Huxley, 'Face to Face with H.G. and Roy', *Sydney Morning Herald*, 16 Dec. 1989.

Now, I was one of those who thought cricket was bound for a burton. The jig's up. They'd tried everything. Privatisation. One-day games. But within minutes of the decade opening, there was that marvellous incident with the underarm delivery.

4 *Sun Herald*, 30 Dec. 1990. Anthony Hay, 'When the sound of bat and ball is all that's needed for a great day's cricket', *Sydney Morning Herald*, 13 March 1997. The 'case' also continues to influence legal discourse. When describing a position of unfair advantage or dominant position in Section 36A of the Commerce Act (N.Z.) 1986, the authors chose to highlight the issue in the trans-Tasman market by using the title, 'Section 36A: Underarm Bowling?', The Interface Between Amended Section 36 of the Commerce Act 1986 and Intellectual Property Law, Competition Law and Policy Institute of New Zealand (Inc.), Aug. 1990 Workshop, at p. 16.

5 Paul Whelan, *Sydney Morning Herald*, 19 Dec. 1990. References to the incident continue to inform Australian/New Zealand relations and to haunt Greg and Trevor Chappell. See e.g., 'Underarm: Chappell admits he was mental', *Weekend Australian*, 13–14 Jan. 1996; Phillip Derriman, 'The ball that changed NZ', *Sydney Morning Herald*, 1 Feb. 1996; Ray Kershler, 'Under not over', *Daily Telegraph*, 1 Feb. 1996; Phil Wilkins, 'Incident that has echoes in Eden', *Sydney Morning Herald*, 14 Feb. 1998; Don Cameron, 'Trevor Chappell: The pain goes on forever', *CricInfo*, 2 Dec. 2001.

6 'Ashamed to be an Aussie', *Sydney Morning Herald*, 2 Feb. 1981.

7 'Irate New Zealanders had plenty to say', id.

8 'NZ wants Chappell's blood', *Sydney Morning Herald*, 2 Feb. 1982.

9 'Sports Opinion', *Sydney Morning Herald*, 2 Feb. 1981.

10 Letters found in 'The Great Underarm Controversy, Sydney Morning Herald', 4 Feb. 1981. It is interesting to note that on the day following the incident, that newspaper received 111 letters. Superstitious English cricketers and cabalists might find ever greater hermeneutic significance in that number. See Harold Bloom, *Kabbalah and Criticism* (New York: Continuum, 1984) and Umberto Eco, *Foucault's Pendulum* (London: Secker and Warburg, 1989).

11 'As a patriotic Australian, I felt humiliated', *Sydney Morning Herald*, 2 Feb. 1981. Hugh Lunn tried to put events in a broader context by pointing to the public, and therefore *moral* nature of Chappell's actions when compared to other cricketing practices. He wrote:

> Yes Greg Chappell you may be a great man who doesn't sledge, never unnecessarily appeals when bowling and never shows disapproval of the decision of umpires. But in a game surrounded by fine sportsmen intent only on playing the game, you dared to publicly display that you were prepared to win without actually cheating. You should have been more underhanded.

'Greg's critics sniping from glass houses', *Australian*, 3 Feb. 1981.

12 'English Umpire lashes us', *Sydney Morning Herald*, 3 Feb. 1981.

13 Bill Frindall, *Cricket Facts and Feats*, op. cit., at pp. 12–13.

14 Op. cit., p. 192.

15 'How Greg Chappell failed the virility test', *New Statesman*, 13 Feb. 1981. It is interesting to note that while Trevor is still 'famous' as the man who bowled underarm, Greg, as captain, was the one who was singled out for moral disapproval for *ordering* his brother to act in that manner.

16 Id.

17 'Chappell: Skipper whose ship died of shame', *Times*, 3 Feb. 1991.

18 Ashis Nandy, op. cit., at p. 29.

19 Harold Larwood, of Bodyline fame pointed out at the time that it would have been possible to prevent a six simply by bowling the ball up and at the wicket. See 'Chappell's Skipper whose ship died of shame', *Times*, 3 Feb. 1991.

15 The chucker as outlaw – legality, morality and exclusion in cricket

1 See generally, Ian Peebles, *Straight from the Shoulder* (London: Hutchinson & Co., 1968).
2 See Jack Pollard, *Australian Cricket*, op. cit., at p. 1048 et. seq. and p. 144.
3 Ibid.
4 E. Docker, 'He Bowled in Splints', in *Six and Out!*, op. cit., at p. 87.
5 *The Guardian Book of Cricket*, op. cit., at p. 12.
6 ' "Dimboola Jim" Shows the Way', in *Six and Out!*, op. cit., pp. 54 et. seq.
7 See Stanley Fish, 'Dennis Martinez and the Uses of Theory', op. cit.
8 Derek Birley, *The Willow Wand*, op. cit., at p. 33.
9 See Jack Pollard, *Australian Cricket*, at pp. 741 et. seq. and 1049 et. seq. and especially Meckiff's own book *Thrown Out* ('as told to Ian McDonald', London: Stanley Paul, 1961).
10 Id., at p. 1050. Writing in *The Age* (5 Jan. 1989) Percy Beames put the events into context. He said:

> It is a great pity English pressman had to wait until Meckiff's success on Saturday to launch their accusations against the fairness of his bowling. But it is not surprising. It has its precedent in the first match of the tour with West Australian Keith Slater. No exception was taken to Slater's bowling action until he burst into prominence by taking four wickets for 17 in a devastating burst in the second innings. Immediately he was dubbed a 'chucker'.

11 Peter Gabel, 'The Phenomenology of Rights-Consciousness and the Pact of the Withdrawn Selves', op. cit.
12 Jack Pollard, at p. 1050.
13 Id., at p. 745. It is interesting to note that at the time when he was finally no-balled by Egar in Brisbane, Meckiff who had lived with the chucking controversy for some time and knew or suspected what was ahead, accepted the umpire's decision in the 'best traditions of the game'. See Colin Egar, 'Colin Egar's Biggest Decision', *Brisbane Courier Mail*, c. 1969, as reproduced in *Bat and Pad*, op. cit., at pp. 232 et. seq. But he did not quietly accept all the consequences of the event. See *Meckiff v. Simpson* [1968] VR 62.
14 Jack Pollard, op. cit., at p. 744.
15 For a discussion of the concept of bad faith and its relationship to the process of adjudication, see David Fraser, 'The Day the Music Died: The Civil Law Tradition for a Critical Legal Studies Perspective', 37 *Loyola L. Rev.* 861 (1987) and especially, Allan Hutchinson, *It's All in the Game*, op. cit. It is possible, nonetheless, to suggest that umpires, like their judicial counterparts, are subject to both conscious and unconscious pressure to conform to a perceived and internalized vision of what is acceptable. Once an issue like chucking becomes a part of public interpretive discourse about cricket, an umpire must necessarily turn his mind more acutely to it. At some stage, it is possible that the umpire then convinces himself psychologically that a bowler is making an illegal delivery even when 'in fact' he is not. In such a case the umpire may find himself in conflict with other members of the interpretive community. Docker, op. cit., *Six and Out!*, pp. 86–87, gives the following example of one possible solution to the interpretive conflict:

In Australia, argument about whether some bowlers threw was almost as old as intercolonial cricket itself. The captain of the N.S.W. side, Dave Gregory, was no-balled for throwing by umpire Nat Thompson in 1871. Gregory was called four times in four successive deliveries. In the course of his fifth, the N.S.W. captain stopped in full stride feeling certain that the fairness of his action had been unjustly predetermined by the umpire. With his arm upright in arrested motion and the ball still in his hand, Thompson loudly called 'no-ball'. Gregory lowered his arm and glared at Thompson. The crowd hooted. For the first but not the last time in Australian cricket an umpire refused to stay at his post. Thompson walked dramatically from the field and the game was halted until a new umpire could be appointed. Gregory's action was never again questioned.

16 Jack Pollard, op. cit., at p. 1047.
17 Id., at pp. 211, 527, 723 and 1049. On Eddie Gilbert's story, see Judy Dungey, 'Cricket's lost legend', *Good Weekend*, 22 Jan. 2000.
18 Jack Pollard, op. cit., p. 11, argues that Marsh was the most deserving of Test selection.

> He was clearly the best Australian bowler of his time but unfortunately that was a period when the White Australian Policy prevailed. Marsh's name was scratched from the list of players who could practise with the New South Wales squad at the SCG by an official who was simply carrying out the racist customs of the day.

19 Id., at p. 724 and, 'Marsh in Splints' (1902) in *Bat and Pad*, op. cit., at p. 211. The experiment was tried again by a South African bowler in 1960 but without Marsh's success. See 'Miscellany' in *The Guardian Book of Cricket*, op. cit., p. 190. The 'modern' equivalent, as we shall see, is the videotaped action of a bowler subjected to scientific biomechanical analyses.
20 Jack Egan, *The Story of Cricket in Australia* (South Melbourne: Macmillan, 1987), at p. 194. See also, Michael Manley, *The History of West Indies Cricket* (London: Andre Deutsch, 1988), p. 174; Charlie Griffith, *Chucked Around* (London: Pelham, 1970); Bill Bradshaw, 'Chucker Charlie's order of the bath', *Observer*, 11 June 2000.
21 Garfield Sobers, *Twenty Years at the Top* (with Brian Scovell, London: Macmillan, 1988), p. 2 and pp. 89 et. seq. The fates of Griffith and Meckiff cannot, for all the pain, compare with that of Essex fast bowler Fred Bull for when 'the sudden reservations in high places about the legitimacy of his bowling must have had a crushing effect'. Bull joined the long and sad list of cricketing suicides. See David Frith, *Silence of the Heart: Cricket Suicides* (Edinburgh and London: Mainstream Publishing, 2001), at p. 158.
22 Imran Khan has accused Manoj Prabhakar of India of throwing. Lance Cairns of New Zealand responded that Wasim Akram of Pakistan was probably a chucker. See 'New Zealand Notes', *Wisden Cricket Monthly*, April 1990, p. 36.
23 V. Ramnarayan, 'Chucking: It isn't cricket!', *CricInfo*, 15 Nov. 2001,

16 Murali, Shoaib and the jurisprudence of chucking

1 'Kiwis thrown into action', *Sydney Morning Herald*, 15 March 1995.
2 See discussion in Chapter 18.
3 Phil Wilkins, 'Lankan action studied by ICC', *Sydney Morning Herald*, 6 Dec. 1995. In 2002, Murali indicated that he was unwilling to tour Australia after consistent questioning of his action there. See, 'Murali reluctant to return', *Sydney Morning*

Herald, 5 June 2002; 'Gilchrist urges Muralitharan to tour Australia', *CricInfo*, 8 June 2002.

4 Trent Bouts, 'The Sri Lankans in Australia, 1995–96', *Wisden* (1997), at p. 1125; Trent Bouts, 'ICC chucking laws look more like throwaway lines', *Australian*, 28 Dec. 1995; Phil Wilkins, 'How the ICC ambushed the spinner', *Sydney Morning Herald*, 28 Dec. 1995.

5 Phil Wilkins, 'Throwing row: Hair speaks out', *Sydney Morning Herald*, 3 Feb. 1996.

6 Australian wicketkeeper and vice-captain Adam Gilchrist apparently asserted that he believes that Muralitharan is in fact a chucker. He places the blame on domestic cricket authorities who make no effort to correct faults in young bowlers' actions. See, 'Gilly brands Murali a chucker', *Sydney Morning Herald*, 27 May 2002. But cf., Dav Whatmore, 'Arms and the man Murali', *Guardian*, 30 May 2002.

7 See, 'Pressure grows to change throw law', *Australian*, 6 Dec. 1995. See also, Mike Coward, 'Hair sparks more controversy', *Australian*, 27 Dec. 1995; Trent Bouts, '"Thrower" may receive life', *Australian*, 27 Dec. 1995.

8 See discussion below, Chapter 18 on ball-tampering.

9 'Boon finds his form among the doom', *Sydney Morning Herald*, 27 Dec. 1995.

10 ACB, 'Gilchrist charged over Muralitharan comments', 27 May 2002.

11 Ibid.

12 See ACB, 'Adam Gilchrist reprimanded by ACB Code of Behaviour Commission', 30 May 2002; Trevor Marshallsea, 'Gilchrist escapes with reprimand', *Sydney Morning Herald*, 31 May 2002.

13 ACB, op. cit.

14 See the discussion below on the new 'throwing' system. See Mike Selvey, 'Perera bowls on through a bend in the rules', *Guardian*, 22 May 2002.

15 Clive Ellis, 'Abrasive Afzaal ruffles tourists', *Daily Telegraph*, 8 June 2002.

16 David Hopps, 'How to get up English noses: chuck in Perera', *Guardian*, 15 June 2002; Simon Briggs, 'Tourists' tactics blasted', *Daily Telegraph*, 15 June 2002.

17 Trevor Marshallsea, op. cit.

18 See, 'England's Butcher challenges fine', *CricInfo*, 7 June 2002; ECB, 'Mark Butcher disciplinary hearing', *CricInfo*, 27 June 2002; Simon Briggs, 'Butcher accepts his punishment', *Daily Telegraph*, 28 June 2002.

19 Stephen Lamb, 'England batsman accuses Perera of throwing', *CricInfo*, 29 May 2002.

20 Phil Wilkins, op. cit.

21 See Lou Rowan, *The Umpire's Story* (North Sydney, NSW: Jack Pollard, 1973), at pp. 146–49. Rowan was the 'other' umpire on the day Meckiff was branded a chucker.

22 Cf., John Benaud, 'Throw offenders out or chuck it in', *Sun Herald*, 31 Dec. 1995.

23 Phil Wilkins, 'Hair stand set to end Murali's tour', *Sydney Morning Herald*, 28 Dec. 1995.

24 See Darrell Hair, *Decision Maker: An Umpire's Story* (Sydney: Random House, 1998), at p. 4.

25 Ibid., at pp. 7–11.

26 Id., at p. 6.

27 See e.g., Trent Bouts. 'Lankans want Hair stood down', *Australian*, 29 Dec. 1995.

28 'Chucked out: cricket's day of shame', *Sydney Morning Herald*, 27 Dec. 1995; Peter Roebuck, 'Contrary umps throw chucking law into confusion', *Sydney Morning Herald*, 28 Dec. 1995.

29 Ibid.

30 Id.

31 Id.

32 Even Darrell Hair 'only' no-balled Muralitharan on seven out of 18 deliveries. While his action is in the opinion of the first umpire to call him for throwing 'diabolical', it is also true that Hair did not believe he threw every ball. See Robert Craddock, 'Fair warning', *Daily Telegraph*, 12 Nov. 1998.

33 'ICC chucks a wobbly and cricket suffers', *Australian*, 29 Dec. 1995.
34 See e.g., Darren Cartwright, 'Make a change for the better: Benaud', *Telegraph Mirror*, 27 Dec. 1995, for Richie Benaud's plea to Sri Lankan administrators to take remedial action for Murali.
35 Brian Burke, 'Windies captain defends Muttiah', *Australian*, 29 Dec. 1995.
36 Mark Irving, 'Sri Lankan not a chucker: Yardley', *Australian*, 28 Dec. 1995; Phil Wilkins, 'Lankans in spin over no-ball saga', *Sydney Morning Herald*, 27 Dec. 1995; Ron Reed, 'Thrown into exile', *Telegraph Mirror*, 27 Dec. 1995; Trent Bouts, ' "I have done nothing wrong" ', *Weekend Australian*, 30–31 Dec. 1995; ' "I know in my mind I'm not chucking" ', ibid.
37 See Barclay Reid, 'Muralitharan in the clear', *Sunday Telegraph*, 31 Dec. 1995; Alex Mitchell, 'Murali has uni tests on action', *Sun Herald*, 14 Jan. 1996.
38 Mark Irving, 'Sri Lankan not a chucker: Yardley', op. cit.
39 See e.g., Frank Tyson, 'National self-interest makes clear-cut ICC rulings elusive', *Australian*, 3 Jan. 1996.
40 Ron Reed, 'Thrown into exile', op. cit.
41 'Throwers chucked out', Editorial, *Sydney Morning Herald*, 30 Dec. 1995.
42 Ihithisham Kamardeen, 'An innocent man's reputation on the line', *Telegraph Mirror*, 27 Dec. 1995.
43 Phil Wilkins, 'Lankans call Hair's bluff', *Sun Herald*, 31 Dec. 1995.
44 Greg Baum, 'Muttiah, Windies pass searching test', *Sydney Morning Herald*, 4 Jan. 1996; Trent Bouts, 'Muttiah passes umpires' test', *Australian*, 4 Jan. 1996.
45 See Trent Bouts, 'Spinner no balled again for throwing', *Weekend Australian*, 6–7 Jan. 1996; Peter Roebuck, 'Cricket shoots itself in the foot over throwing controversy', *Sydney Morning Herald*, 8 Jan. 1996. McQuillan had already expressed concerns about Murali when he stood in a tour match in Queensland and had reported his doubts to the ACB. See, Michael Koslowski, 'Murali again put under blowtorch', *Sydney Morning Herald*, 5 Jan. 1995.
46 See e.g., Martin Chulov, 'Australian greats outraged by umpire's call', *Sun Herald*, 7 Jan. 1996.
47 Robert Craddock, 'Thrown out for good', *Daily Telegraph*, 6 Jan. 1996.
48 Michael Koslowski, 'Lankan rage as Murali called', *Sydney Morning Herald*, 6 Jan. 1996; Andrew Byrne, 'Sri Lankan fans warn umpires: see you in court', *Sydney Morning Herald*, 8 Jan. 1996. Hair in turn threatened legal action against a Sri Lankan official who publicly accused him of bias. See, 'Umpire deliberates over a hair suit', *Sydney Morning Herald*, 9 Dec. 1998.
49 See Mike Marqusee, *War Minus the Shooting: A journey through South Asia during Cricket's World Cup* (London: Heinemann, 1996).
50 See discussion below.
51 'Murali no chucker, swears Yardley', *Sydney Morning Herald*, 28 Feb. 1997.
52 AAP, 'Yardley Defends Controversial Spinner', 4 June 1998.
53 In the Test at the Oval, Murali took a total of 16 wickets for 220 runs, including nine wickets in an innings.
54 'Lloyd casts doubt on spinner', *Guardian*, 31 Aug. 1998. See also, Peter Deeley, 'New twist in tale of spinner's odd action', *Telegraph*, 31 Aug. 1998.
55 See, Chris Lander, 'Magical Murali's Sweet 16', *Mirror*, 1 Sep. 1998; Peter Deeley, 'Lloyd's comment brings complaint', *Daily Telegraph*, 1 Sep. 1998; Sa'adi Thawfeeq, 'Sri Lanka protest over Lloyd remarks', *Daily News*, 2 Sep. 1998; Peter Deeley, 'Lloyd escapes with severe reprimand', *Daily Telegraph*, 4 Sep. 1998.
56 See Malcolm Knox, 'Spinning, to the top', *Sydney Morning Herald*, 2 Sep. 1998.
57 For events leading up to the Adelaide game, see e.g., Michael Horan, 'Reported', *Daily Telegraph*, 15 Jan. 1999; Andrew Ramsey, 'Referee reports Murali throw action', *Australian*, 15 Jan. 1999; Robert Craddock, 'How officials deserted umpires: Scared to make a call against Muralitharan', ibid., Robert Craddock, 'ICC must act mow to end

farce', *Daily Telegraph*, 16 Jan. 1999; Andrew Ramsey, 'Lankans stick with Murali', *Weekend Australian*, 16–17 Jan. 1999; Alex Brown, 'Umpires "fearing" "no-ball" furore', *Sun Herald*, 17 Jan. 1999; Andrew Ramsey, 'Bowling in the shadow of judgment', *Australian*, 18 Jan. 1999.

58 'Arm surgery for Murali', *Daily Telegraph*, 9 Feb. 1999; Malcolm Knox, 'Experts issue challenge on the "chucking illusion"', *Sydney Morning Herald*, 26 Jan. 1999.

59 'Murali slams crowds', *Australian*, 20 Jan. 1999; Malcolm Conn, 'Murali considers future in wake of hostilities', *Australian*, 21 Jan. 1999.

60 'Fix this mess now before things get ugly', *Sydney Morning Herald*, 4 Feb. 1999.

61 'Arm surgery for Murali', op, cit.

62 See Alex Brown, 'Spinner still not cleared by ICC', *Sun Herald*, 24 Jan. 1999; Phil Wilkins, 'Taylor all for panel to clarify confusion', *Sydney Morning Herald*, 25 Jan. 1999; Michael Horan, 'Sri Lankans seek swift solution', *Daily Telegraph*, 26 Jan. 1999.

63 Compare Peter Roebuck, 'A case of the servant wanting to be master', *Sun Herald*, 24 Jan. 1999; Phillip Derriman, 'Australian umpires support Emerson's throwing call', *Sydney Morning Herald*, 25 Jan. 1999; Phil Wilkins, 'An "honest cop" stands on the courage of his convictions', ibid.

64 See, Andrew Ramsey, 'Stressed umpire retired for series', *Australian*, 27 Jan. 1999; Mark Ray, 'Emerson stood down by ACB over stress leave', *Sydney Morning Herald*, 27 Jan. 1999; Timothy Glover, 'Emerson Dumped from Umpiring Panel', *CricInfo*, 17 July 1999.

65 'Umpires given Murali orders', *Guardian*, 9 March 1999.

66 Trevor Marshallsea, 'I might get 600 but Murali will get 1000, says Warne', *Sydney Morning Herald*, 6 March 2003.

67 'Muralitharan's action compared to javelin thrower by Bedi', *CricInfo*, 2 Feb. 2002; Saadi Thawfeeq, 'In defence of Murali', *Daily News*, 2 March 2002; 'Sri Lankans right behind Muralitharan', *Dawn*, 7 March 2002.

68 'Bob Woolmer and Michael Holding say their comments were misquoted', BCCSL, 19 March 2002.

69 'Imran hits back at Shoaib's critics', BBC, 12 May 1999.

70 See 'Akhtar under chucking scrutiny by Australian umpires', AFP, 1 Nov. 1999; 'PCB Press Release on Shoaib Akhtar "throwing" allegations', 2 Nov. 1999; 'ICC referee regrets Emerson's statement', *Dawn*, 3 Nov. 1999.

71 'No action on unofficial video', ACB, 3 Nov. 1999.

72 'Angry Pakistanis hit out over chucking claims', *Sydney Morning Herald*, 2 Nov. 1999. For similar statements, see Martin Blake, 'Akhtar slams chucker claims', *Sydney Morning Herald*, 1 Dec. 1999.

73 A. Jalil, 'Jones and Richards slam Emerson', *Dawn*, 6 Nov. 1999.

74 Peter Deeley, 'Shoaib's action is called into question', *Daily Telegraph*, 30 Nov. 1999; Samiul Hasan, 'ICC confirms: Shoaib's bowling action under scrutiny', *Dawn*, 10 Dec. 1999.

75 Greg Pritchard, 'Lay off Akhtar, legends warn', *Sun Herald*, 5 Dec. 1999.

76 Peter Deeley, 'Shoaib confident about inquiry', *Daily Telegraph*, 1 Dec. 1999.

77 Scyld Berry, 'How the finger of blame was pointed at Akhtar', *Daily Telegraph*, 2 Jan. 2000.

78 Phil Wilkins, 'Candid camera puts Akhtar at cross roads', *Sydney Morning Herald*, 2 Dec. 1999; Samiul Hasan, 'PCB receives video footage on Shoaib's bowling action', *Dawn*, 22 Dec. 1999; AFP, 'Pakistan receives ICC objection over Shoaib's bowling action', 22 Dec. 1999; Nelson Clare, 'ICC put Akhtar's action on agenda', *Daily Telegraph*, 23 Dec. 1999.

79 AFP, 'ICC bans Akhtar for illegal bowling', 31 Dec. 1999.

80 'PCB to protest ICC: Waqar replaces suspended Shoaib for triangular', *Dawn*, 1 Jan. 2000.

81 Owais Tohid, 'ICC allows Akhtar to play in one-day series in Australia', AFP, 8 Jan. 2000; Media Release, ICC, 8 Jan. 2000. For a brief history of recent events see also,

Trent Bouts, 'ICC pitches in with amnesty on throwing', *Weekend Australian*, 24–25 Aug. 1996; 'ICC Panel to Meet', ICC, 17 Aug. 1999; Malcolm Conn, 'ICC set to rewrite throwing law', *Australian*, 19 Aug. 1999; 'ICC bar advisory panel from banning bowlers with suspect action', AFP, 10 Feb. 2000; 'Throwing is the umpire's call', *Jamaica Gleaner*, 18 Feb. 2000; 'ICC to review panel of illegal deliveries', *Dawn*, 28 Feb. 2000.

82 See e.g., 'Aussies at war over Shoaib reprieve', *Guardian*, 10 Jan. 2000; 'ICC decision on Akhtar shocks many', *Hindu*, 10 Jan. 2000; Charles Randall, 'Greig judges Akhtar's delivery as "legal flick"', *Telegraph*, 11 Jan. 2000; Sa'adi Thawfeeq, 'Action on Akhtar was unfair and unjustifiable', *Daily News*, 11 Jan. 2000; Geoff Longley, 'Akhtar's recall by ICC chief surprises Reid', *Christchurch Press*, 15 Jan. 2000.

83 Paul Newman, 'Shoaib stands down over "throwing"', *Daily Telegraph*, 14 May 2000.

84 Lynn McConnell, 'Akhtar reported by Dunedin umpires, heading home', *CricInfo*, 1 March 2001; ICC, 'ICC match Referee Ranjan Madugalle confirms reporting of Shoaib Akhtar', 1 March 2001.

85 See 'Final Bowling Report – University of Western Australia, Department of Human Movement and Exercise Science', 21 April 2001; 'Shoaib's action gets another all-clear', *Guardian*, 8 April 2001.

86 'Shoaib faces more trouble', *Dawn*, 1 Nov. 2001.

87 ICC, 'Shoaib Akhtar reported in Sharjah', 7 Nov. 2001.

88 ICC, 'Process of review for bowlers reported with suspect bowling actions – Terms of Reference'.

89 ICC, 'ICC Appoints Michael Holding as Bowling Advisor to Shoaib Akhtar', 8 Nov. 2001; Simon Briggs, 'ICC forced to act after Shoaib "throwing" call', *Telegraph*, 8 Nov. 2001.

90 PCB, 'PCB statement on Shoaib Akhtar', 8 Nov. 2001.

91 'Letter from PCB to ICC', 10 Nov. 2001; 'PCB takes ICC head-on', *Dawn*, 10 Nov. 2001.

92 PCB, 'University of Western Australia's review of Sharjah tapes on Shoaib Akhtar', 7 Dec. 2001; Nelson Clare, 'ICC consider Shoaib action', *Daily Telegraph*, 26 Dec. 2001; 'Pakistan wants Shoaib cleared', *Dawn*, 9 March 2001.

93 Tony Cozier, 'Doubts over Shoaib's action', *Barbados Nation*, 6 Feb. 2002; Samiul Hasan, 'PCB boss's ultimatum to ICC on Shoaib', *Dawn*, 15 Feb. 2002; 'Shoaib not reported in Sharjah: ICC', *Dawn*, 20 Feb. 2002.

94 Geoff Longley, 'Steve Dunne defends Akhtar', *Christchurch Press*, 4 May 2002; 'New Zealand coach declines comment on Shoaib's action', *Dawn*, 1 May 2002.

95 See e.g., James Knight and Mark Ray, 'Small goes in to bat for young quick Lee', *Sydney Morning Herald*, 10 Dec. 1999; Mark Ray, 'Lee's action thrown into doubt', *Sydney Morning Herald*, 12 July 2000; Malcolm Conn, 'Long run-up to showdown', *Australian*, 12 July 2000.

96 See Mark Ray, 'Now it's Lee: bowling queried', *Sydney Morning Herald*, 9 Dec. 1999; Michael Horan, 'Leave the kid alone', *Daily Telegraph*, 10 Dec. 1999.

97 Martin Blake, 'ICC action for Akhtar', *Sydney Morning Herald*, 23 Dec. 1999; 'Shoaib's OK, so is Lee, say Pakistanis', *Sydney Morning Herald*, 31 Dec. 1999; Alex Brown and Danny Weidler, 'Chucking tests for Lee after whispers', *Sun Herald*, 2 Jan. 2000; Mark Ray and Phil Wilkins, 'ICC derails Express', *Sydney Morning Herald*, 4 Jan. 2000; WACA, 'Lillee pledges support for Lee', 11 July 2000.

98 Mark Ray and Phil Wilkins, 'ICC derails Express', op. cit.

99 Rick Eyre, 'Brett Lee bowling action under ICC review', *CricInfo*, 11 July 2000; 'Lee to address action', ACB, 11 July 2000; ICC, 'Media Release', 11 July 2000; Richard Hobson, 'Australia to stand by Lee as action comes under scrutiny', *Times*, 12 July 2000; David Hopps, 'Australians to rally to defence of "chucker" Lee', *Guardian*, 12 July 2000; Mark Ray, 'Lillee to back Lee's action at hearing', *Sydney Morning Herald*, 1 Aug. 2000.

100 See e.g., AFP, 'ICC handling of Lee row "unsatisfactory": Australia', 12 July 2000; Anand Vasu, 'Brett Lee and Indians, the doubts resurface', *CricInfo*, 13 July 2000; 'Pakistan supports Lee over illegal bowling', ABC, 14 July 2000.

101 'Lee's action thrown on mercy of deliveries panel', *Daily Telegraph*, 18 July 2000.

102 John Polack, 'Lee's action cleared by ICC panel', *CricInfo*, 2 Aug. 2000.

103 See Phil Wilkins, ' "Throw" claim hits second Test', *Sydney Morning Herald*, 12 May 1995.

104 'Ruling could threaten Lee's future', *Daily Telegraph*, 2 Jan. 2000.

105 'Pakistan retaliate with call for video of Walsh', *Guardian*, 5 Jan. 2001.

106 D.J. Rutnagur, 'ECB called in over Wagh spin', *Daily Telegraph*, 15 Sep. 2000; 'Wagh hopes bowling ban will be lifted', *CricInfo*, 9 Feb. 2001; ECB, 'ECB bowling review group lifts suspension', 2 March 2001.

107 See 'Match referee questions Kirtley's action', *CricInfo*, 4 Oct. 2001; 'Kirtley given full support by Sussex over bowling action', Sussex CCC, 5 Oct. 2001; Gareth Davies, ' "Never complain about Kirtley's action. It's an optical illusion" ', *Daily Telegraph*, 9 Oct. 2001; Paul Bolton, 'Kirtley ordered to change his action', *Daily Telegraph*, 20 Nov. 2001; Ralph Dellor, 'Kirtley seeks to clear remodelled bowling action', *CricInfo*, 25 Feb. 2002; Richard Bright, 'Kirtley's suspect action approved', *Daily Telegraph*, 13 March 2002.

108 Mike Selvey, 'England to take a gamble on Kirtley', *Guardian*, 15 Aug. 2002.

109 See Michael Koslowski, 'Rowell steps down after "chucking" report', *Sydney Morning Herald*, 2 Feb. 1996; 'Rowell back for Bulls', *Sun Herald*, 11 Feb. 1996.

110 Malcolm Conn, 'Hewett named by umpires for throwing', *Australian*, 13 March 1996; Malcolm Conn, 'ACB hamstrung in dealing with tampering allegations', *Australian*, 14 March 1996.

111 *Sydney Morning Herald*, 16 Feb. 1998; *Australian*, 18 Feb. 1998.

112 Jon Geddes, 'Lillee clinic salvaged last thrower's career', *Daily Telegraph*, 28 Dec. 1995.

113 'Media Release on Grant Flower', ZCU, 20 Sep. 2000. This was the first time Flower had been no-balled in international cricket, but he had been called for throwing in domestic competition.

114 Anand Vasu, 'Grant Flower's action under fresh scrutiny', *CricInfo*, 21 Nov. 2000.

115 Ibid.

116 Malcolm Knox, 'Chuck this, let's go after the slingers', *Sydney Morning Herald*, 2 Jan. 1997; 'Afridi cleared by committee', *Dawn*, 28 Jan. 2001.

117 'Speedster thrown out of touring party', *Sun Herald*, 21 Oct. 1999; 'PCB's indifference cause of embarrassment', *Dawn*, 23 Oct. 1999; 'Waqar replaces Shabbir Ahmad', *Dawn*, 23 Oct. 1999; 'ICC tele-conference' 'Shabbir records statement', *Dawn*, 12 Nov. 1999; 'ICC bans Shabbir from playing international cricket', *Dawn*, 13 Nov. 1999; 'Suspect action film throws paceman', *Sun Herald*, 14 Nov. 1999; 'ICC umpire clears action of Shabbir', *Dawn*, 10 Aug. 2000.

118 Agha Akbar, 'Shoaib Malik celebrates', *CricInfo*, 20 April 2001.

119 'Malik's action doubtful', *Dawn*, 12 May 2001; see also 'Paceman Junaid reported on four occasions', *Dawn*, 28 Feb. 2002; 'Junaid disappointed being reported', *Dawn*, 6 March 2002.

120 'Lankan bowlers reported', *Sydney Morning Herald*, 15 Feb. 1996.

121 See Trent Bouts, 'Doubts over second Lankan bowler', *Australian*, 8 Jan. 1996; Phil Wilkins, 'Suspect actions get Simmo's scrutiny', *Sydney Morning Herald*, 28 Feb. 1997; 'Kumara Dharmasena cleared to play international cricket', *CricInfo*, 14 June 2000; 'Sri Lanka: Dharmasena eligible', *Daily News*, 15 June 2000; Sa'adi Thawfeeq, 'Sri Lankan selectors recall Kumar Dharmasena after two years in the wilderness', *Daily News*, 25 June 2000.

122 Sa'adi Thawfeeq, 'Sri Lankan fast bowler reported for suspect action', *CricInfo*, 18 Aug. 2001; 'ICC to look at Perera's action', *Times*, 20 Aug. 2001; 'BCCSL to send report on Suresh Perera to ICC', *Daily News*, 22 Oct. 2001.

123 Mike Selvey, 'Sri Lanka agree to play by ICC's book of anomalies', *Guardian*, 22 May 2002; Angus Fraser, 'Dilemma for Sri Lanka as Perera is reported', *Independent*, 22 May 2002; 'Sri Lankan response to Perera report', ECB, 22 May 2002.

124 ICC, 'Process of review for bowlers reported with suspect bowling actions – Terms of Reference'.

125 Ibid., Section D (2).

126 I am using this real case here as a hypothetical example. I am not suggesting that umpires Harper and Venkat acted in this way in the game in question.

127 Malcolm Knox, 'Warne likely to miss Sharjah', *Sydney Morning Herald*, 12 March 1998; John Benaud, 'Bent elbow band plays on', *Sun Herald*, 15 March 1998.

128 'Harbhajan Singh omitted for Wills Cup', *Hindu*, 19 Oct. 1998.

129 Anand Vasu, 'Harbhajan makes history as India restrict Aussies', *CricInfo*, 11 March 2001.

130 England also suffered at the hands of the bowler known as the 'Turbanator'. See, Andy Wilson, 'Falling for the trick of the Turbanator', *Guardian*, 4 Dec. 2001.

131 'Indian spinners throw suspect styles into spotlight', *Observer*, 23 Sep. 2001.

132 'Muralitharan's action compared to javelin thrower by Bishen Bedi', *CricInfo*, 2 Feb. 2002.

133 See Geoff Longley, 'Drumm mum on chucking', *Christchurch Press*, 11 Dec. 2000; New Zealand Cricket, 'Umpires report a second Indian player for suspect bowling action', 11 Dec. 2000.

17 Bouncers: terror and the rule of law in cricket

1 'Ambition and the Almighty', *Cricket Life international*, Feb. 1990, p. 29 at 30.

2 See Mark Nicholas, 'The Great Fast Bowler', *Wisden* (2000), at p. 77.

3 On the apparent contradiction of the outlaw as hero, see Paul F. Angiolillo, *A Criminal as Hero – Angelo Duca* (Lawrence: The Regents Press of Kansas, 1979). The issue of the outlaw as hero is, of course, a highly problematic one, particularly in these days of a return to the value of law and order. Popular culture has a long history of the outlaw hero, Robin Hood, Ned Kelly etc. as well as one of 'glamorizing' the criminal lifestyle. Debates about the appropriateness of either and about the distinction between them are problematic and heated. Were Pretty Boy Floyd and Joey Gallo (praised in song by Woody Guthrie and Bob Dylan) heroes like Robin Hood, fighting for the oppressed, or were they simply thugs? Are bouncers 'good' even if illegal or is fast, short-pitched bowling a slight on the game?

4 At the same time, there may have been a conflict between the various factors of Law 42(8). For example, a bowler may 'attempt' or indeed 'intend' to intimidate a batter without at the same time 'intending' to inflict injury. Does this mean that 'intimidation' means only an attempt to inflict personal injury or can it be given a different meaning? On the other hand, it is clear that all bouncers, not to mention the presence of several fast bowlers in an attack, are meant, in part at least, to 'intimidate' opposing strikers, yet it was clear that not all 'intimidation' in practice or by convention, was meant to fall under the provision of Law 42(8).

5 'Keeping matters under control', *Cricket Life International*, March 1990, p. 40.

6 *That's Out!*, op. cit., at p. 55.

7 Patrick Smithers, 'McDermott warned as bumpers put helmets to the Test', *Sydney Morning Herald*, 6 March 1991.

8 *The Guardian Book of Cricket*, op. cit., p. 181 describing the first Test, 25 Feb. 1975.

9 The account is taken from the following newspaper accounts of the incident, 'I Thought It Was A Joke', *Sun Herald*, 28 Dec. 1980; Bill O'Reilly, 'Intimidatory bowling-bounce it out of the rules', id. and Mungo MacCallum, 'It's our moments like these . . . you need Frisbees', id.

10 Geoff Lawson, after his jaw was broken by a Curtly Ambrose bouncer. *The Book of Cricket Quotations*, op. cit., p. 81. No doubt the cult of virility overlays and underpins the interpretive matrix here.

11 Op. cit., at p. 50 and 'keeping matters under control', op. cit. As an example of the *Law* in action he offers the following:

> In 1989 at the Foster's Oval, I had occasion to warn Mervyn Hughes, the Australian fast bowler, when I thought he was overdoing it. I started with an unofficial warning and Mervyn pretended not to hear it. He bounced the very next one which did not amuse me at all and so I had to have a serious word with him. He ignored that as well and bounced the third one on the trot. I called 'no ball' and, as per the provisions of the law, informed my colleague at square leg and the Australian captain Allan Border. I cannot say Border applauded my decision but to be fair, he came to me after the day's play to express his agreement with my decision, adding that he thought that I had applied the law very well.

Warnings were issued only rarely. In addition to Bird's admonition of Hughes (see also *Wisden* (1990), at p. 310), warnings were given by umpire Tony Crafter to West Indian bowlers Ambrose and Patterson during the Melbourne Test in 1988–89 and the English bowler Capel during the 1990 fifth Test at St John's. See *Wisden* (1990), p. 972 and Christopher Martin-Jenkins, 'Déjà vu: Battered England Succumb in Familiar Fashion', *The Cricketer*, June 1990, p. 14. As Martin-Jenkins points out, however, warnings appear to have been issued in a seemingly arbitrary fashion. In the same Test, Robin Smith of England received 10 bouncers in 12 deliveries and no warning was given. While it may be argued that Smith was a recognized batter and Capel was warned for bouncing Patrick Patterson, a bowler, it could be argued that 10 out of 12 is illegal in anyone's book and that such inconsistency did little to instil confidence in the judicial system.

12 Dickie Bird (with Keith Lodge), *My Autobiography* (London: Hodder and Stoughton, 1997), at p. 107.

13 See Mike Coward, 'Off-Side?' op. cit., Phil Wilkins, 'Pakistan want intimidatory bowling stopped', *Sydney Morning Herald*, 18 Jan. 1990; John Benaud, 'Unappealing aspects mar what turned out a top test', *Daily Mirror*, 17 Jan. 1990. Such debates are not limited to Australia as the England tour of the West Indies demonstrates.

> It was the first time on the tour the intimidation of batsmen has been a factor, in itself a surprise, but its reintroduction produced a depressing lack of reaction from the umpires who watched impassively before tea as Smith received six bouncers in seven balls from Ian Bishop and Courtney Walsh.

Alan Lee, 'Lamb's men to the bouncer slaughter', *Weekend Australian*, 14–15 April 1990.

14 As quoted in Phil Wilkins, 'Pakistan want intimidatory bowling stopped', op. cit.

15 Op. cit.

16 Jeff Wells, 'Nobody is halting cricket's headlong slide into the slime', *Australian*, 10 Jan. 1990.

17 Henry Blofeld, 'A violent decade with cricket to match', *Weekend Australian*, 30–31 Dec. 1989; Peter Roebuck, 'For cricket's sake, let's hope this isn't another flat track', *Sydney Morning Herald*, 19 Jan. 1990. Roebuck put it this way:

> Do you know what happens to umpires who take decisive action? Do you imagine they are thanked for their trouble? To the contrary, they are condemned by one captain or another and so sent to cricket's equivalent of a Siberian labour camp.

See also Phillip Derriman, 'Can cricket salvage victory from a follow-on?', *Sydney Morning Herald*, 30 Aug. 1990; Christopher Martin-Jenkins, 'Editorial – ICC: The World Expects…', *The Cricketer*, July 1990, p. 3 and Jack Bannister, 'Ban the bouncer!', *Wisden Cricket Monthly*, July 1990, p. 21.

18 Dickie Bird, *My Autobiography*, op. cit., at p. 107.

19 'What Intimidation?', *Cricket Life international*, March 1990, p. 41; Ian Chappell, 'Lions *v.* Christians', id., p. 36.

20 For example, some argue that the change to the LBW Law in 1935 which permits the interception of the ball with the front pad outside the line of the stumps has led to a change in batting techniques. With the changed technique, players of the modern era have become 'front foot players' and have lost the ability to 'play back'. Because the hook is a back foot shot, some argue that today's players are not technically competent to play the bouncer. Added to the rest of this technical sub-plot is the fact that Wyatt was Douglas Jardine's vice-captain during Bodyline (*infra*). It was as a result of Bodyline that the LBW *Law* was changed. Wyatt's interpretation of the connection between the 1935 amendments, the lack of modern skilled back foot play and the dominance of fast bowlers may perhaps be influenced by his part in Bodyline, although he was not uncritical of Jardine's tactics. For some bouncers were ruining the game. From another perspective, one might argue in defence of bouncers as part of the game and both teams use them. One might further contextualize things and see both positions as not only representing each side's view in fact but see these statements as part of a pre-trial publicity campaign meant to influence by subtle psychology the interpretive mind set of the adjudicator (umpire).

21 'Unfair victims', *Cricket Life International*, March 1990, p. 37.

22 Ashis Nandy, op. cit., n. 20, p. 119.

23 'But what a West Indian, brought up on hard wickets and used to the chest-high delivery calls a bouncer and what an English player says is a bouncer are two different deliveries. A good player should be able to move behind the line of a chest-high delivery and play it down in front of him', Garfield Sobers, *Twenty Years at the Top*, op. cit., at p. 3.

24 John Byrell, *Thommo Declares* (Cammeray, NSW: Horwitz Grahame, 1986), at p. 53. For the Australian penchant for short, fast bowling see also, Christopher Martin-Jenkins, 'New laws crack down on aggressors', *Times*, 7 May 2000.

25 Dennis Lillee, 'Back to the Dark' (1974) as found in *The Book of Cricket Quotations*, op. cit., at p. 82.

26 Tony Greig said of Geoffrey Boycott, 'His ability to be where the fast bowlers aren't has long been a talking point amount cricketers.' Id., p. 7.

27 Op. cit., p. 132.

28 ICC, 'Test Match Playing Conditions', para. 33.

29 Trevor Marshallsea, 'Waugh backs fiery Lee after another tail attack', *Sydney Morning Herald*, 19 Dec. 2001.

30 Ibid.

31 Mike Selvey, 'Defeat leaves England bruised', *Guardian Weekly*, 6 March 1994; Phil Rothfield, 'I'd send off bullies: Gooch', *Sunday Telegraph*, 6 March 1994.

32 John Thirsk, 'Ducking for cover', *Sunday Telegraph*, 23 Dec. 2001.

33 'If you're not up to it – then don't bat', *Sunday Telegraph*, 23 Dec. 2001.

34 'Hey, Brett, here's a New Year's resolution: give up the demented rabbit-hunting', *Sydney Morning Herald*, 20 Dec. 2001.

35 See, 'Walking wounded: Kumble does a McCosker and returns to the battlefield', *Sydney Morning Herald*, 14 May 2002.

18 Ball-tampering and the rule of law

1 Wisden, The Laws of Cricket, op. cit., at p. 187.

2 Ibid., at pp. 187–90.

3　See Alan Lee, 'Umpire's protests rejected by TCCB', *Australian*, 24 Nov. 1995.

4　I reproduce both the 1980 *Code* and the 2000 *Code* provisions since much of the controversy relating to ball-tampering predates the current version of the *Laws*. Indeed, as I hope to show, many of the interpretive difficulties which arose in the most well-known cases involving ball-tampering allegations have in fact led to the legislative reforms embodied in the new version of the *Laws*.

5　Para. 8 and para. 9 respectively.

6　Naturally, for left arm bowlers the issue remains the same, only opposite.

7　Wasim also manages to sow doubt in the batter's mind by gripping the ball during his run up to the crease in such a way that the ball, the seam and the shine remain hidden until the last possible moment. He clearly adopts a position that the bowler owes no duty of disclosure to the batter.

8　See e.g., Jennie Brookman, 'Pakistani speed bowls ball testers over', *Times Higher Education Supplement*, 2 July 1993; Wanda Jamrozik, 'Swing Low, Sweet Cricket Ball', *Independent Monthly*, March 1994; Philip Derriman, 'Here's the dirt on the secrets of swing', *Sydney Morning Herald*, 30 July 1994.

9　See 'Nawaz sues Lamb for libel', *Australian*, 17 Nov. 1993; 'Lamb stands by "cheat" claim', *Sydney Morning Herald*, 18 Nov. 1993; 'Video evidence used to back Lamb's defense', *Sydney Morning Herald*, 19 Nov. 1993.

10　See 'Controversy rages on', *Weekend Australian*, 20–21 Nov. 1993; 'Ball-tampering case takes surprise swing', *Sydney Morning Herald*, 20 Nov. 1993.

11　See e.g., 'Botham was "the greatest all-rounder"', *Sydney Morning Herald*, 26 July 1996; 'Miller tampered with the ball, says Imran', *Sydney Morning Herald*, 27 July 1996; 'Botham takes on Imran again', *Sydney Morning Herald*, 11 Sep. 1996; Caroline Davies, 'Owzat? Botham bowled over as libel jury delivers verdict to Imran', *Sydney Morning Herald*, 2 Aug. 1996; Tim Jones, 'Sundries in libel case to cost Lamb, Beefy dearly', *Australian*, 2 Aug. 1996.

12　'Miller tampered with the ball, says Imran', op. cit.

13　Norman Harris, 'Inside Edge – Ball-tampering dampener', *Observer*, 4 Aug. 2002.

14　The 2000 *Code* appears to have dealt with this by the inclusion of more general language in the substantive text prohibiting '... any other action whatsoever which is likely to alter the condition of the ball...', 42(3) (b).

15　'Tamperer nabbed', *Sydney Morning Herald*, 17 Nov. 1994.

16　See Ivo Tennant, *Imran Khan* (London: H.F. & G. Witherby, 1994).

17　Ibid., at pp. 11–12.

18　See Alex Mitchell, 'We're all cheats: Imran's shock admission over ball-tampering', *Sun Herald*, 21 Nov. 1993; 'Imran admits he cheated: report', *Sydney Morning Herald*, 9 May 1994; 'Imran quits ICC over tamper row', *Sydney Morning Herald*, 17 May 1995.

19　'Ball row an issue of class – Imran', *Sydney Morning Herald*, 3 Sep. 1994.

20　Mike Coward, 'Ball-tampering's ugly implications transcend the boundary', *Weekend Australian*, 27–28 Nov. 1993.

21　See 'Ball row an issue of class', op. cit.; Robert Craddock, 'Crackdown on Trickers', *Telegraph Mirror*, 12 Dec. 1995.

22　See e.g., Derek Pringle's confession immediately following his retirement from cricket and Geoff Lawson's similar admission, *Sydney Morning Herald*, 29 Nov. 1993; Geoff Lawson, 'Ball-tampering? I'll let you in on a dark secret', *Sydney Morning Herald*, 1 Dec. 1993.

23　See Terry Smith, 'Blues centre of ball storm', *Daily Telegraph*, 12 March 1996; Phil Wilkins, 'Victorians accuse Stuart of tampering', *Sydney Morning Herald*, 12 March 1996.

24　Another possible explanation for this is that the England pace attack has been so pitiful over the last few years that they couldn't possibly be cheating. Yet another explanation, in response, could be that not only are they not very good bowlers, they aren't very good cheats. It should be noted however that at least Don Oslear is consistent in his condemnation of ball-tamperers, wherever they may be found.

25 This does not mean however that suspicions about the Pakistanis have also disappeared. See below.

26 'Atherton cleared of ball tampering', *Sydney Morning Herald*, 25 July 1994.

27 See Martin Johnson, 'Some dirt will stick to Atherton', *Sydney Morning Herald*, 26 July 1994; Martin Johnson, 'Now the dirt is following Atherton', *Sydney Morning Herald*, 27 July 1994 (questioning whether Burge 'put the question'). See also, Alan Lee, 'Pressure mounts for resignation', *Australian*, 27 July 1994; Martin Johnson, 'Brief flashes of hope in a besieged skipper's agony', *Sydney Morning Herald*, 22 June 1995 (asserting that the question was in fact put to Atherton who lied).

28 Mike Atherton, *Opening Up* (London: Hodder and Stoughton, 2002), at pp. 107–22.

29 Brian Scovell, 'How Atherton got dirt on his hands', *UK Mail*, 25–31 July 1994.

30 'Test Referee's Statement', *Telegraph Mirror*, 27 July 1994.

31 Id.

32 See ' "Dismay bordering on anger" inside ICC', *Sydney Morning Herald*, 27 July 1994; 'England hierarchy stands by its man', *Australian*, 27 July 1994; Bruce Wilson, 'Atherton told he must go', *Telegraph Mirror*, 27 July 1994; Brian Scovell, 'Lord's meeting to decide Mike's fate', *Telegraph Mirror*, 27 July 1994; Mike Quirk, 'Press united in quit chorus', *Telegraph Mirror*, 27 July 1994; Martin Johnson, 'Media lynching party has Atherton in its sights', *Sydney Morning Herald*, 28 July 1994; Martin Johnson, 'Be careful where you scratch, Mr. Atherton', *Sydney Morning Herald*, 29 July 1994; Peter Roebuck, 'Atherton must not capitulate to reptiles of the press', *Sydney Morning Herald*, 29 July 1994; Tim De Lisle, 'Cricket and the Media in 1994', *Wisden*, op. cit., at 1359.

33 Quoted in ' "Dismay bordering on anger" inside ICC', op. cit.

34 See for example the case of Pat Symcox of South Africa who was permitted to remove both dirt and perhaps 'the remnants of greasy deodorant' from a ball which had habitually rubbed in his armpit. Malcolm Knox, 'Taylor's grit a source of Test salvation', *Sydney Morning Herald*, 2 Feb. 1998.

35 *Opening Up*, op. cit., at p. 109.

36 See Christopher Martin-Jenkins, 'ICC must change laws on ball tampering', *Weekly Telegraph*, 27 July–2 Aug. 1994.

37 See Martin Johnson, 'Some dirt will stick to Atherton', op. cit. stating that 'If, however, Burge did not ask this question, it hardly places him in the Perry Mason class of cross-examination'; and see Martin Johnson, 'Now the dirt is following Atherton', op. cit. 'On the other hand, it was such an obvious question to have asked, that Burge can be assured not to have an ancestral bloodline to the Spanish Inquisition'.

38 'Test Referee's Statement', op. cit.

39 *ICC Code of Conduct*, para. 2. As I shall argue below, the literalist reading of the idea/ text of 'play' is put to rest by the extension of the Match Referee's jurisdiction to the 'precincts of the Ground'.

40 *Opening Up*, op. cit., at p. 108.

41 Peter Roebuck, 'Atherton must not capitulate to the reptiles of the press', op. cit.

42 Although Roebuck does confusingly refer to Atherton's offence having been committed in the course of his duties. On one reading, he can be seen to be asserting that it is the England captain's role and duty to lie and cheat. This is a view confirmed as asserting a more general duty in English cricket in Stephen Fry's novel *The Liar* (1991, at 285), where we find the following exchange: 'You won't cheat will you sir?' 'Cheat? Good heavens. This is an amateur cricket match amongst leading prep schools, I'm an Englishman and a schoolmaster supposedly setting an example to his young charges. We are playing the most artistic and beautiful game man ever devised. Of course I'll cunting well cheat'.

43 *Tom Smith's Cricket Umpiring and Scoring*, op. cit., at p. 224.

44 'Atherton's finest hours', *Sydney Morning Herald*, 6 Dec. 1995.

45 'Captain defiant saves the day', 10 Dec. 1995.

46 'Controversy rages on', *Weekend Australian*, 20–21 Nov. 1993; 'Ball-tampering case takes surprise swing', *Sydney Morning Herald*, 20 Nov. 1993.

47 See Alan Lee, 'Umpire's protests rejected by TCCB', *Australian*, 24 Nov. 1993; 'Cover-up over ball-tampering-umpire', *Sydney Morning Herald*, 25 Nov. 1993.

48 See Alan Lee, op. cit.

49 Id.

50 Although it is important to signal that Oslear equally condemns all ball-tamperers, regardless of national origin.

51 'Cover-up over ball-tampering-umpire', *Sydney Morning Herald*, 25 Nov. 1993.

52 See Trent Bouts, 'Gagging of Test referees renders ICC out of touch', *Australian*, 18 Oct. 1995.

53 As if, by definition, they weren't already disadvantaged.

54 Cricket's judicial branch has not learned from its mistakes, however. See below.

55 *ICC Code of Conduct*, para. 3 (b) (iii), Oct. 1995.

56 Trent Bouts, *Weekend Australian*, 4–5 Nov. 1995; Phil Wilkins, *Sun Herald*, 5 Nov. 1995; Robert Craddock, *Sunday Telegraph*, 5 Nov. 1995.

57 Bouts, op. cit.

58 Wilkins, op. cit.

59 Playing Condition 7. See discussion below. Bouts, op. cit., Craddock, op. cit.

60 See Phil Wilkins, 'Umpires said nothing – manager', *Sydney Morning Herald*, 6 Nov. 1995.

61 See Trent Bouts, 'Leading umpires suspended by ACB' *Weekend Australian*, 18–19 Nov. 1995.

62 Id., Phil Wilkins puts the umpires' error down to their 'striving to be as diplomatic as possible'. 'Umpires act on tampering', *Sun Herald*, 10 Dec. 1995 as if their function were ambassadorial rather than judicial and as if Australian umpires have a reputation for a soft approach where 'Pakistani law-breaking' is concerned.

63 Phil Wilkins, 'Upset tourists gagged over tampering claims', *Sydney Morning Herald*, 11 Dec. 1995.

64 See 'Guilty', *Sunday Telegraph*, 10 Dec. 1995; Robert Craddock, 'Sri Lanka in disgrace', *Sunday Telegraph*, 10 Dec. 1995; Phil Wilkins, 'Umpires act on tampering', *Sun Herald*, 10 Dec. 1995.

65 Phil Wilkins, 'Upset tourists gagged over tampering claims', *Sydney Morning Herald*, 11 Dec. 1995.

66 Robert Craddock, 'Sri Lankans in disgrace' op. cit.; Wilkins, op. cit.

67 Id.

68 It has been noted here that Muralitharan's action has been the object of much speculation, including allegations that he is in fact a 'chucker'. This has meant that the attention of the umpires and of the television has been quite seriously focused on him. To engage in ball-tampering during his bowling spell would have been the height of foolishness or bravery. See Phil Wilkins, 'Lankan action studied by ICC', *Sydney Morning Herald*, 6 Dec. 1995; 'Pressure grows to change throw law', *Australian*, 6 Dec. 1995; Jeff Wells, 'Time for some real action on suspect actions', *Sydney Morning Herald*, 14 Dec. 1995. Indeed, in the Boxing Day Test at the MCG, umpire Darrell Hair no-balled Muralitharan for 'chucking' on the first day. *ABC Radio* and *Channel 9* TV commentators were stunned by Hair's decision and speculated for several minutes as to whether the no-ball call was for a popping crease infringement before coming to the conclusion that 'chucking' was indeed the issue. The case caused a sensation. See, Malcolm Conn and Trent Bouts, 'Umpire accuses Sri Lankan of throwing 7 times', *Australian*, 27 Dec. 1995; Trent Bouts, '"Thrower" may receive life', id.; Mike Coward, 'Hair sparks more controversy', id.; Robert Craddock, 'Thrown Into Exile', *Daily Telegraph Mirror*, 27 Dec. 1995; Darren Cartwright, 'Make a change for the better: Benaud', id.; Ron Reed, 'Hair raised by 7 deadly spins', id.; Ithithisham Kamardeen, 'An innocent man's reputation on the line', id.; Ron Reed, 'Distraught Meckiff relives nightmare',

id.; Robert Craddock, 'Muralitharan is not the only culprit', id.; Phil Wilkins, 'Lankans in a spin over no-ball saga', *Sydney Morning Herald*, 27 Dec. 1995; Wilkins, 'Now a ninth Test "chucker"', id.; Peter Roebuck, 'Chucked out: cricket's day of shame', id. He was again no-balled in the One-Day International at the Gabba on 5 Jan. 1996. The controversy continues.

69 Wilkins, op. cit.

70 See Mike Coward, 'ICC outrage is rough justice for Lankans', *Australian*, 11 Dec. 1995; Trent Bouts, 'Umpires blunder over ball – Sri Lankan guilt now in doubt', *Australian*, id.; Bouts, 'Sri Lanka to fight tamper finding', *Australian*, 12 Dec. 1995; Ron Reed, 'Sri Lankans have a right to be angry', *Telegraph Mirror*, 12 Dec. 1995; 'Just not cricket', Editorial, *Telegraph Mirror*, 12 Dec. 1995; Peter Roebuck, 'Ball-tampering conviction unsafe and unfair', *Sydney Morning Herald*, 15 Dec. 1995; Trent Bouts, 'Sri Lankan board official calls for public apology', *Weekend Australian*, 16–17 Dec. 1995.

71 Although it now appears that a major source of disagreement between the umpires was whether to allow the ball to remain in play.

72 Para. 2.4.

73 Unless of course, one seeks to invoke an extra-cricket, but legal set of norms like the laws of defamation. See, 'SL threat to sue', *Sun Herald*, 24 Dec. 1995.

74 *ICC Code of Conduct, Standard Playing Conditions and Regulations*, Oct. 1995.

75 Id. The current *Code* also imposes obligations of notice and procedural fairness in the conduct of hearings. See Part E, 'The Reporting/Notification Procedure; Part G, 'The Disciplinary Procedure'; Part H, 'The Referee's Decision' and *Guidelines on the Principles of Natural Justice*.

76 'The Sri Lankans in Australia', *Wisden*, 1997, at p. 1125.

77 Similar allegations were made against Hayat when he stood as the local umpire in the first Test between Australia and Pakistan in Karachi in 1994 (below) and refused an LBW appeal which would have won the Test for Australia. See 'Non-local Test umpires needed', Editorial, *Sydney Morning Herald*, 4 Oct. 1994. In relation to Ponting's dismissal, see, Trent Bouts, 'Ponting "robbed" of century on debut', *Australian*, 11 Dec. 1995; Phil Wilkins, 'Sri Lanka led to the slaughter', *Sydney Morning Herald*, 11 Dec. 1995.

78 'ICC outrage is rough justice for Lankans', op. cit.

79 Trent Bouts, 'Sri Lankan board official calls for public apology', op. cit.

80 'SL threat to sue', *Sun Herald*, 24 Dec. 1995. 'ICC tampering', *Sydney Morning Herald*, 27 Dec. 1995.

81 *ICC Code of Conduct*, **Match Referee**, para. 4 (c) (I) '*The Referee's decision is final*'.

82 See, on the availability of judicial review, *Maloney v. New South Wales National Coursing Association Ltd.* [1978] 1 NSWLR 161; *Dale v. New South Wales Trotting Club Ltd.* [1978] 1 NSWLR 551; *Forbes v. New South Wales Trotting Club Ltd.* [1978–79] 143 CLR 242. The case does raise interesting jurisdictional issues however since the Match Referee operates as the representative of the London-based ICC. The question of the legal and jurisdictional relationship between the ACB and the ICC would have to be resolved in order to determine, for example, the identity of the appropriate defendant.

83 David Richards, Chief Executive, International Cricket Council, 'Statement', 24 Dec. 1995, *Telegraph Mirror*, 26 Dec. 1995. See also, Phil Wilkins, 'Lankans cleared over ball damage', *Sydney Morning Herald*, 26 Dec. 1995; Ron Reed, 'Row leaves no winners', *Telegraph Mirror*, 26 Dec. 1995; Tony Harper and Robert Craddock, 'Not Guilty: ICC clears Sri Lanka of ball tampering', id.; Trent Bouts, 'Sorry ICC overturns conviction', *Australian*, 26 Dec. 1995.

84 Reed and Bouts in particular point out that the Sri Lankans were not completely clear of suspicion (Bouts) or that '. . . the suspicion remains that the Sri Lankans have been cleared on a technicality rather than unequivocally found not guilty'; (Reed) op. cit. See also 'ICC Tampering', Editorial, *Sydney Morning Herald*, 27 Dec. 1995.

85 Although it appears that it was umpire Hayat who refused to 'confiscate' the ball despite umpire Parker's express wish that he do so and despite the imprecations of Referee Dowling. See Wilkins, op. cit. and Reed, op. cit.

86 See ICC *Test Match Playing Conditions*, para. 4, Appointment of Umpires, Oct. 1995.

87 See again Allan Hutchinson's insightful observations in *It's All in the Game*, op. cit.

88 *ICC Regulations*, ICC Match Referee, para. 1 (a), ICC Oct. 1995.

89 Id., para. 2 (b).

90 Id., para. 3 (b) (i).

91 ICC Code of Conduct for Players and Team Officials, Para. D (5). Para. D (8) repeats the Referee's obligation to uphold Law 42.1 – fair play.

92 It could of course be argued that if he refused to 'act' this would be tantamount to a slap in the face to the umpires and a possible violation of his express duty to support them.

93 See Wilkins op. cit., 'The Sri Lankans are gentlemen of the game, not artful dodgers. It is for the best that the slur has been erased.'

94 'Salim Malik fined for umpire accusation', *Sydney Morning Herald*, 18 Feb. 1995; 'Umpire accused of tampering', *Sunday Telegraph*, 19 Feb. 1995.

95 *It's Not Cricket*, op. cit., at pp. 5–6. But cf., Mike Marqusee, *Anyone But England* (London: Verso, 1994), at pp. 247–50.

96 Malcolm Knox, 'I'm no ball tamperer, says Cronje', *Sydney Morning Herald*, 17 Dec. 1997; Malcolm Conn, 'Cronje victim of Test ploy: Woolmer', *Australian*, 18 Dec. 1997. This is the reason umpires now take possession of the ball during breaks in play.

97 'I'm no ball tamperer, says Cronje'.

98 Ibid.

99 Malcolm Knox, 'Cronje's lesson in composure', *Sydney Morning Herald*, 20 Dec. 1997.

100 *Wisden: The Laws of Cricket*, op. cit., at p. 192.

101 Simon Wilde, 'Ball-tampering allegations against Pakistan', *Sunday Times*, 31 May 1999.

102 'Pakistan hit by fresh ball-tampering allegations at World Cup', AFP, 9 June 1999.

103 'Ball-tampering allegations against Pakistan', op. cit.

104 A.C. Ganesh, 'Waqar caught by TV, bowled by John Reid', *CricInfo*, 9 July 2000; Rehan Siddiqui, 'Waqar first to be fined for ball tampering', *Dawn*, 11 July 2000.

105 'Waqar to be fined for bringing country's name into disrepute', *Dawn*, 14 July 2000.

106 Para. D 5 (c).

107 See Samiul Hasan, 'John Reid not acceptable, ICC told', *Dawn*, 8 Dec. 1999; 'ICC withdraws nomination of John Reid', *Dawn*, 25 Dec. 1999.

108 'Umpire biased, says Pakistan', *Sydney Morning Herald*, 11 July 2000; Col (Ret'd) Rafi Nasim, 'Pakistan players victims of justice?', *CricInfo*, 9 July 2000.

109 See *inter alia*, 'Defends action: Reid says everyone knows who is guilty', *Dawn*, 14 July 2000; Sa'adi Thawfeeq, 'Waqar banned, Mahmood fined, Moin warned', *Daily News*, 10 July 2000; 'Reid unfazed at claims of bias', *Christchurch Press*, 18 July 2000.

19 The little master, ball-tampering and the rule of law

1 See Partab Ramchand, 'Pak charges dismissed but Indians are angry', *CricInfo*, 27 Jan. 2001; 'Indians upset by Pakistan charge', *CricInfo*, 27 Jan. 2001; Martin Blake, 'Pakistan accuse Sachin', *Sydney Morning Herald*, 27 Jan. 2001.

2 'Pakistan accuse Sachin', op. cit.

3 'Pak charges dismissed but Indians are angry', op. cit.

4 'Indians upset by Pakistan charge', op. cit.

5 Ibid.

6 Telford Vice, 'Tendulkar awaits verdict in ball-tampering inquiry', *Guardian*, 20 Nov. 2001.

7 Ibid.

8 See D.J. Rutnagur, 'Tendulkar on tampering charge', *Telegraph*, 20 Nov. 2001.

9 ICC, 'ICC Match Referee confirms disciplinary action for Indian cricketers', 20 Nov. 2001.

10 Richard Hobson, 'England's Test schedule at risk as India seeks shorter series', *Times*, 20 Nov. 2001; David Hopps, 'Fury over India Test threat', *Guardian*, 20 Nov. 2001.

11 'BCCI call for Denness's removal', *CricInfo*, 20 Nov. 2001; David Hopps, 'Sack referee, demands Dalmiya', *Guardian*, 21 Nov. 2001.

12 ICC, 'ICC statement on penalties imposed during India's second test match in South Africa', 21 Nov. 2001; 'ICC will not overrule Denness decision', *CricInfo*, 21 Nov. 2001.

13 'Ball tampering controversy aired in Indian parliament', *CricInfo*, 22 Nov. 2001. Peter Roebuck, 'Ball-tampering farce latest example of the game's old-world inconsistencies', *Sydney Morning Herald*, 22 Nov. 2001.

14 See e.g., Paul McGregor, 'The Denness controversy: why critics are missing the point', *CricInfo*, 21 Nov. 2001; Lynn McConnell, 'Denness decisions clearest sign yet of cricket clean-up', *CricInfo*, 21 Nov. 2001.

15 See Anand Vasu, 'Former cricketers express anger at Denness' decision', *CricInfo*, 20 Nov. 2001.

16 Peter Hanlon, 'Tendulkar penalty soft, says Waugh', *Sydney Morning Herald*, 22 Nov. 2001.

17 AFP, 'Indian fans furious with Steve Waugh', 22 Nov. 2001.

18 'Pakistan monitoring controversy', *Dawn*, 21 Nov. 2001.

19 'The seamy underbelly of Port Elizabeth', *CricInfo*, 20 Nov. 2001.

20 See, *inter alia*, UCB, 'UCB response to ICC statement on match referee', 21 Nov. 2001; Anand Vasu, 'Cricket takes a body blow in ICC clash with cricket boards', *CricInfo*, 22 Nov. 2001.

21 Tony Connelly, 'ICC denies appeal to replace Denness', *Independent*, 22 Nov. 2001; Mike Selvey, Neil Manthorp and David Hopps, 'India and South Africa face ban', *Guardian*, 23 Nov. 2001; Neil Manthorp, 'Mbeki's move puts game in a spin', *Guardian*, 23 Nov. 2001.

22 'Pakistan supports BCCI stand', *Dawn*, 24 Nov. 2001.

23 D.J. Rutnagur, 'England back ICC as row puts tour at risk', *Telegraph*, 24 Nov. 2001; 'Sri Lankan board back ICC actions in Denness controversy', *CricInfo*, 23 Nov. 2001.

24 UCB, 'UCBSA issues statement regarding third Castle Lager/MTN Test', 22 Nov. 2001; ICC, 'ICC stands by Denness as match referee for third Test', 22 Nov. 2001.

25 See e.g., 'Dalmiya may have Packer-style breakaway in mind', *Guardian*, 24 Nov. 2001; Scyld Berry, 'Dalmiya's sights are on new world order', *Telegraph*, 25 Nov. 2001; Mihir Bose, 'Dalmiya thrives in role as king of the jungle', *Telegraph*, 27 Nov. 2001.

26 Mihir Bose, 'Indian board may round on Dalmiya', *Telegraph*, 28 Nov. 2001.

27 See e.g., Mark Lawson, 'A test of the old, white cricket world', *Guardian*, 24 Nov. 2001.

28 Anand Vasu, 'Former cricketers express anger at Denness' decision', op. cit.

29 Ibid.

30 'Sri Lankan board back ICC actions in Denness controversy', op. cit.

31 See 'ICC postpones referees' commission on Denness affair', *CricInfo*, 19 Feb. 2002; David Hopps, 'Dalmiya stops play', *Guardian*, 20 Feb. 2002; the ICC has readjusted its adjudication procedures and named an elite panel of umpires and an 'elite' panel of Match Referees, in part at least to raise standards in the judicial branch of the game, ICC, 'ICC recruits former Test stars for match Referees Panel', *CricInfo*, 1 March 2002.

32 See, 'Time to declare: keep the contest on the field, not off it', *Guardian*, 26 Nov. 2001.

20 Delay and over-rates: temporality and the meaning of cricket

1 *Tom Smith's Cricket Umpiring and Scoring*, op. cit., at pp. 227–28.

2 Alan Lee, 'Heroism in vain by Smith and Hussain', *Australian*, 18 April 1990.

3 'England's April Fool', *Cricket Life international*, May 1990, p. 24. See also 'England undone by rains and Haynes', *Cricket Life international*, May 1990, p. 12.

4 'The Equalizer', *Cricket Life international*, May 1990, p. 19 at p. 20. England were subjected to heavy fines for slow over rates during the 1990–91 Ashes series in Australia. While some slow play might be attributed to such external, 'objective' factors like hot weather, law reform is still seen as the appropriate solution. See Phillip Derriman, 'Time and motion cricket', *Sydney Morning Herald*, 6 Feb. 1991.

    The debate continued. During the 1991 Australian tour of the West Indies, Patrick Smithers criticized the situation in the first innings of the second Test at Georgetown Guyana as follows: 'The West Indies applied the water-torture technique at Bourda yesterday with such precision it would have made a secret policeman proud.' Smithers then called for the ICC to take steps by 'impos(ing) a penalty that has a direct bearing on the outcome of the game', but added, that, of course, Australia, according to Bob Simpson 'have never played that way, I don't think we ever will.' Only the bad guys exploit the *Laws*. While Smithers' desire for legal change has in fact taken place, it is hard to assert that the amendments to the *Laws of Cricket* have in reality had any impact on the way the game is played. See 'Marsh repels stalling tactics', *Sydney Morning Herald*, 25 March 1991.

5 Mike Selvey, 'Antics leave bad taste', *Guardian Weekly*, 15 April 1990. See also Christopher Martin-Jenkins, 'Leadership, Inspiration and Slow Progress', *The Cricketer*, May 1990, p. 3 accusing both sides of 'manipulating the regulations and abusing the game'. Christopher Martin-Jenkins, 'Devastating Malcolm, Then England Cruelly Denied', id., p. 11 describing the third Test at Port-of-Spain and accusing the West Indies of having 'behaved like an Italian football team defending a one-nil lead with ten minutes of a Cup Final to go' and declaring his 'firm suspicion that [England] would not have behaved much better had the roles been reversed'. Finally, it should be noted that the Indian team committed similar offences – 'desultory field changes and general dawdling' during a Test at Old Trafford, despite the fact that spinners bowled two thirds of all their overs. See, 'Now, Smith joins the run feast', *Weekend Australian*, 11–12 Aug. 1990. The 1991 Australian tour of the West Indies also raised the issue of time-wasting by the Windies side. Their tactics were described as '(t)he cynicism which masquerades as Caribbean professionalism' by Terry Brindle, 'Aussies outgun exploiting Windies', *Australian*, 11 March 1991 and an urgent meeting was held between the sides to avoid further controversy id and 'Sides meet on slow overs', *Sydney Morning Herald*, 11 March 1991. Again, some evidence of a deeper, more nefarious sub-text has crept into the discussion. Allan Border referred to the concerns of the Australian side 'because of situations we've run into before, especially when you're in India or Pakistan', id. Apparently, only dark-skinned cricketers engage in time-wasting tactics.

6 See Duncan Kennedy, *A Critique of Adjudication*, op. cit.

7 Of course, some batters can be simply boring in their lengthy occupation of the crease. Geoff Boycott was once dropped from the England side for taking six hours to score 106 runs against India. The difference between the two cases is one of the existential subtleties and joys of cricket.

8 *Tom Smith's Cricket Umpiring*, op. cit., at p. 228.

9 Op. cit.

10 Sir Garfield Sobers, for instance, clearly sees the problem as having its source in English touring sides, op. cit., at p. 9. Brodribb takes a more 'balanced' view, blaming it on everybody, op. cit., at pp. 294–96. Michael Manley echoes (op. cit.) Gary Sobers' contention that the English introduced delaying tactics into the game and that current attacks on slow over rates are cynical indirect complaints about the success of the West Indies all-pace battery. Australians, too, blame the English, especially Sir Leonard Hutton.

11 See Section 3 – 'Minimum Over Rates' 3.1 et. seq. See also, 'India's players fined by match referee', *Times*, 14 Aug. 1997.

12 See Section 3.6.
13 ICC – 'Test Match Playing Conditions', Para. 3 – 'Hours of Play, Intervals and Minimum Overs in the Day', Para. 3.1 (Minimum overs), 3.2 (Extra Time), 3.3 (Use of Lights).
14 Phillip Derriman, 'A concentrated pace attack that's slowing down the game of cricket', *Sydney Morning Herald*, 12 Dec. 1989. At the same time, yet another reversal occurs in the temporal matrix. While slow bowlers bowl more quickly than fast bowlers, good slow bowlers, especially leg spinners, take more time to develop their skills.
15 *Lillywhite's Cricketer's Companion*, as reported in *The Book of Cricket Quotations*, op. cit., p. 86.
16 *The Book of Cricket Quotations*, op. cit., p. 87.
17 See AFP, 'Wis players apologised for time wasting in tense test says Pollock', *CricInfo*, 3 April 2001.
18 See, ibid.; 'Tactics "not spirit of the game"', *Barbados Nation*, 7 April 2001; Derrick Nicholas, 'West Indies players reprimanded by Board', *CricInfo*, 29 April 2001.
19 'Tactic "not spirit of the game"', op. cit.

21 Ethical discourse, legal narrative and the meaning of cricket

1 See Duncan Kennedy, 'The Structure of Blackstone's Commentaries', op. cit.
2 Ashis Nandy, op. cit., at p. 115. For more traditional views on the value of cricket in providing a good liberal education, see G. Orwell, 'Raffles and Miss Blandish', cited in *The Faber Book of Cricket*, op. cit., at p. 131 and A. Lang, 'A Liberal Education', id., pp. 4 et. seq.
3 Johann Huizinga, *Homo Ludens*, op. cit., at pp. 30–31 argues that the cheat, who on the surface, accepts the rules of the game is dealt with less harshly than the spoil-sport who rejects the game (and its moral vision) *per se*. This may not obtain in cricket where both types of 'outsider' are treated as morally inferior. Lord Denning's newcomer is a spoil-sport and the object of moral opprobrium. Ian Meckiff was branded a cheat for throwing and subjected to more serious moral opprobrium. It would appear that while the Other/Outsider (spoil-sport/newcomer) is immoral, or perhaps amoral for failing to acknowledge the inherent and superior ethos of the game, the Other/Insider is morally *more* culpable because of his betrayal. He has acted as a *traitor* by denouncing what he had once accepted whereas the newcomer has never accepted the code and can perhaps be forgiven for his ignorance. He is not a heretic but an unsaved savage for whom there is still hope of redemption.
4 Factors such as gender, for example, might well figure in the construction of a possible counter-counter-narrative. While the practical wisdom of boys who participate in sports indicates that with participation their 'knowledge' of the acceptability of rule-violative behaviour increases, female participants may gain the 'knowledge' as their participation grows that breaking the rules is *not* acceptable. This could appear to confirm Carol Gilligan's thesis (*In a Different Voice* (Cambridge: Harvard University Press, 1982)) that male and female children have different moral values and experiences. At the same time, however, we must be careful not to fall into a form of ontological reductionism. Many questions about the inculcation of moral values in children remain unanswered and it would be a grave mistake to assume that there is an irreducible and essential 'male' or 'female' morality of cricket.
5 'Cheating, biting, kicking; it's all in the game', *Sydney Morning Herald*, 11 June 1990.
6 'William Gilbert Grace' in *The Great Victorians* (1932) reproduced in *The Faber Book of Cricket*, op. cit., at pp. 94 and 92. For a much harsher view on Grace's ethics and the ethics of cricket, see Derek Birley, *The Willow Wand*, op. cit. See also, Simon Rae, *It's Not Cricket* op. cit., *passim*.
7 Op. cit., at pp. 125–26.

8 Law 35, Hit Wicket. See Richard Cashman, 'Ave A Go, Yer Mug, op. cit., at p. 110, even though, as Cashman points out 'The appeal, however, was a legitimate one as it occurred after Benaud had surprised Solomon by a wrong 'un and had forced him into hurried shot.' This incident again points to the fact that 'cricket' consists of more than one 'interpretive community', each of which contributes its own hermeneutic vision and practices to the 'text'. From Benaud's perspective, the appeal was a good one, a dismissal brought about through skill. For the crowd, a dismissal which occurs when a cap strikes the stumps smacks of narrow positivism and is 'not cricket'.

22 You ... – sledging and cricket as ethical discourse

1 The *ICC Code of Conduct* adds that it is a Level 2 offence to engage in 'Deliberate or malicious distraction on the field of play' (this supplements and does not replace ICC *Playing Condition* clause 32), Art. 2.7. *Playing Condition* 32 requires that the umpire report such actions which breach Law 42(4) to the Match Referee and replaces the reference 'Governing Body' with 'ICC match referee'.
2 In Oct. 2001, England wicketkeeper James Foster became the first international cricketer to be convicted for deliberately disturbing a batter at the crease. He was found guilty of bringing the game into disrepute and given a severe reprimand and warning about future conduct. See ICC, '2001: Penalties imposed on players for breaches of ICC Code of Conduct', 7 Oct. 2001, Harare.
3 See e.g., Michael Henderson, 'Waugh's masterful display', *Daily Telegraph*, 14 June 1999; Mark Nicholas, 'Gibbs' horror opens door to great escape', ibid.
4 Ibid.
5 *ICC Code of Conduct*, Art. 1.4.
6 Ibid., Art. 1.6.
7 Ibid., Art. 2.9.
8 Ibid., Arts 3.4 and 4.5.
9 An example from British domestic cricket indicates that 'acceptance standards' may differ according to the level of play, elite *versus* lower grades, and according to local norms. A visiting Australian player was banned for four months from a local competition in Wales for swearing. David Lovell, who averaged 199.6 with the bat might well have used language which would not raise any objections in a game in Australia but which offended the more delicate Welsh players. See, 'Language ban', *Sydney Morning Herald*, 3 May 2002.
10 For example, Mark Taylor as captain of Australia is credited by many for forbidding his players to sledge Salim Malik of Pakistan about match-fixing and bribery while the controversy raged off the field. See, Scyld Berry, 'Taylor: His Place in the Pantheon', *Wisden* (2000), p. 73 at pp. 74–75.
11 See Charlie Austin, 'Hussain calls for ICC to look at consistency of umpires', *CricInfo*, 26 Feb. 2001.
12 Again, see generally Allan Hutchinson, *It's All in the Game*, op. cit., passim.
13 See Peter Deeley, 'The Pakistani's in Australia, 1999–2000', *Wisden*, 2001, at pp. 1123 et. seq.; 'Pakistan shows concern over Aussie sledging', *Dawn*, 1 Dec. 1999; 'Aussie team reprimanded over sledging', *Dawn*, 3 Dec. 1999.
14 Martin Blake, 'ACB says no truth in Pakistan boycott', *Sydney Morning Herald*, 4 Dec. 1999.
15 But cf., Hugh Mackay, 'Sledging is just not cricket', *Sydney Morning Herald*, 4 Dec. 1999.
16 See Trevor Marshallsea, 'Bucket tipped on Australian sledgers', *Sydney Morning Herald*, 30 May 2002. Smith had made the same allegations in an earlier interview published in South Africa, see John Townsend and AAP, 'Below the belt: Smith slams Warne and McGrath as worst of Australian sledgers', *Sydney Morning Herald*, 12 April 2002.
17 Ibid.

18 Ibid.
19 See, Trevor Marshallsea, 'Waugh backs players in sledging row', *Sydney Morning Herald*, 31 May 2002.
20 'McGrath fires bumper at sledger Smith', *Sydney Morning Herald*, 17 June 2002.
21 Mike Behr, 'Australians can't take what they give: Smith', *Sydney Morning Herald*, 8–9 June 2002.
22 'Now Bevan has his say: we play by the rules, OK?', *Sydney Morning Herald*, 10 June 2002.
23 See, Mark Fuller, 'Ponting draws his line on sledging', *Sydney Morning* Herald, 6 June 2002; Malcolm Conn, 'Ponting's sledging admission', *Australian*, 12 June 2002; 'Sledging: Ponting admits there's a long way to go', *Sydney Morning Herald*, 12 June 2002.
24 'McGrath fires bumper at sledger Smith', op. cit.
25 'Hughes and Warne face sledging fines', *Sydney Morning Herald*, 7 March 1994; 'Bowler's fines signal warning against future bad behaviour', ibid., 8 March 1994.
26 ICC, '1995 – Penalties imposed on players for breaches of ICC Code of Conduct'.
27 Ibid.
28 1996, ibid.
29 1997, ibid.
30 1998, ibid.
31 1999, ibid.
32 2000, ibid.
33 See e.g., ' "Sledging" complaint due to be settled', *Lancashire Evening Telegraph*, 13 June 2000.
34 'Shoaib apologizes over gesture', *Dawn*, 15 Nov. 2001.
35 Ian Chappell, 'Sorry Robin, old . . . but it's the thin edge of the Sledge', *Sun Herald*, 21 Oct. 1990.
36 Mike Atherton describes Australian sledging in this context and argues that in some cases, for example that of Graeme Hick, it had the desired effect. See, *Opening Up*, op. cit., at p. 138.
37 See e.g., 'Waugh lets rip in protest at new sledging penalty', *Sun Herald*, 20 Aug. 2000; 'Sledging should be handled by cricket boards', *Dawn*, 30 Aug. 2000.
38 Neil Manthorp, 'South Africa hit by verbal bouncers', *Daily Telegraph*, 9 Dec. 2001.
39 Although sledging is also an apparent element of 'women's cricket' as well. See David Harrison, 'Ugliness in the slips – Australian women cricketers accused of being world's worst sledgers', *Sydney Morning Herald*, 25 June 2001.
40 On the other side of the coin, lawyers should note that public accusations of sledging can lead to legal action for defamation. While the practice may be accepted, public and open discourse of the practice is not. See *Chappell v. Mirror Newspapers Ltd.* (NSWCA) (1984) *Aust. Torts Reports* 80–691 involving published reports that Ian Chappell had sledged Len Pascoe in a Sheffield Shield match. Off field criticism can also result in litigation or threats to sue, see e.g., Malcolm Conn, 'Simpson, Jones deny legal action', *Australian*, 19 Jan. 1994; 'Intikhab Alam threatens legal action over King Richards' remarks', AFP, 9 May 2000; 'Defamation case against Bedi adjourned to Aug. 11', PTI, 28 April 2001.
41 Richard Cashman, 'Ave a Go Yer Mug', op. cit., at p. 142.
42 There are occasional 'attempts' to overcome this idea, but the centrality of sledging to Australian cricket practice and mythology seems well-established. See e.g., John Huxley, 'Taylor's first command: cut the sledging', *Sydney Morning Herald*, 20 May 1994; Peter Roebuck, 'Waugh's winning band needs to discover merits of good manners', *Sydney Morning Herald*, 23–25 Dec. 2000; Richard Hinds, 'Pretty good tactic as Indians show some Australian-style ugliness', *Sydney Morning Herald*, 24 March 2001. In 1979–80, Dennis Lillee was censured by his friend and former Australian teammate, Lennie Pascoe, the NSW fast bowler and recognized as the first player of non-English-speaking background to play Test cricket for Australia, because of the

'rudeness of Lillee's "sledging" which included references to Pascoe's ancestry'. Jack Pollard, op. cit., at p. 272.

> When, last Christmas, Ian Chappell, now a seriously competent operator for Channel Nine, was asked to have a talk with the young man who had been appointed to captain the Australian Under-19 side against their English counter-parts he urged him most strongly not to allow his players to waste their time sledging.

43 See Mike Selvey, 'England object to overboard sledge', *Guardian*, 19 Feb. 2001.
44 The quotations are taken from televised interviews and the following newspaper and magazine articles: Phil Wilkins, 'Sri Lanka claims racial jibes in Test', *Sydney Morning Herald*, 21 Dec. 1989; Mike Coward, 'Accepting victory with grace', *Cricket Life international*, Feb. 1990, p. 21; Phil Wilkins, ' "Sledgers" must be sent off, says Sri Lankan boss', *Sydney Morning Herald*, 22 Dec. 1989; Jeff Wells, 'Nobody is halting cricket's headlong slide into the slime', *Australian*, 10 Jan. 1989; Peter Roebuck, 'Gulf in expected etiquette may explain "unsavory" utterings'; Imran Khan, 'Editorial', *Cricket Life international*, Feb. 1990, p. 1.
45 Phil Wilkins, ' "Sledgers" must be sent off, says Sri Lankan boss', op. cit.
46 Op. cit.
47 Id.
48 Phil Wilkins, 'Sri Lanka claims racial jibes in Test', op. cit.
49 Khan, op. cit.

> The Sri Lankans' anger about racist remarks by the Australians is something I fail to understand. Unless one has an inferiority complex about one's race, why should it worry anyone if he is called black or brown? If someone called me a brown man or a Paki, I would accept it as an indisputable fact.

50 See Peter Roebuck, op. cit.
51 Phil Wilkins, ' "Sledgers" must be sent off, says Sri Lankan boss', op. cit. On the damaging effect of racial slurs and their legal status, see Richard Delgado, 'Words That Wound: A Tort Action for Racial Insults, Epithets and Name-Calling', 17 *Harv. C.R.–C.L.L.Rev.* 133 (1982) and Mari Matsuda, 'Public Response to Racist Speech: Considering the Victim's Story', 87 *Mich. L. Rev.* 2320 (1989). On racial vilification and codes of practice in sport, see Lawrence McNamara, 'Tackling Racial Hatred: Conciliation, Reconciliation and Football', 6 *Australian Journal of Human Rights*, 5 (2001).
52 See Alan Freeman and Elizabeth Mensch, 'The Public-Private Distinction in American Law and Life', op. cit., for a study of the mutability and contextuality of these norms. At the same time, of course, neither the public nor the private realm of male cricketing interpretive practices is troubled by the phallocentric referent.
53 Phil Wilkins, 'Sri Lanka claims racial jibes in Test', op. cit.
54 See Peter Roebuck, 'Gulf in expected etiquette may explain "unsavory" utterings', op. cit.
55 Malcolm Conn, 'Lara outburst disgraceful: Warne', *Australian*, 11 Feb. 1997.
56 'Waugh blasts Lara over McGrath spit', *Guardian*, 9 April 1999.
57 It must be said however that only an Australian is likely to find such an interpretation in any way appealing or persuasive. McGrath was universally condemned for bringing the game into disrepute. No other remedy than a public sanction would or could be acceptable in such circumstances. See, e.g., Paul Weaver, 'McGrath fined for spitting incident', *Guardian*, 8 April 1999; Sambo, 'Spitting isn't cricket', *Googler's Gazette*, *CricInfo*, 9 April 1999.
58 Patrick Smithers, 'Windies abuse – it's making Border happy', *Sydney Morning Herald*, 22 March 1991.

59 Robert Grant, 'McGrath denies racism claim', *CricInfo*, 8 May 2001.
60 Ihithisham Kamardeen, 'Captain Jayasuriya backs former teammate in monkey business', *Sun Herald*, 13 May 2001.
61 However, it should be noted that at the time the comments are alleged to have been made, the *Code of Conduct* merely prohibited 'sledging' and not racial abuse more specifically.
62 *ICC Code of Conduct*, Art. 2.9.
63 Mark Fuller, 'McGrath plays straight bat to Sri Lankan claims of uncouth delivery – and seeks legal advice', *Sydney Morning Herald*, 9 May 2001.

23 Walking, the judicial function and the meaning of law

1 For example under Law 2(9), 'A Batsman may retire at any time during his innings.'
2 *Twenty Years at the Top*, op. cit., at p. 126. Trevor Bailey notes, in addition, that besides walking, Sobers was known to, in the appropriate circumstances, give up his wicket. 'Sir Gary' as reported in *The Faber Book of Cricket*, op. cit., at p. 109. For other instances of giving up a wicket, see Gerald Brodribb, op. cit., at pp. 154–55.
3 Id., pp. 127 et. seq. Michael Manley (op. cit., p. 312) notes that in the 1983–84 series with India, Gavaskar hit 236 not out to break Sir Donald Bradman's record in scoring his thirtieth Test century. The West Indians, however, felt that Gavaskar had been caught at slip for a second ball duck. They 'were unofficially convinced that he was out and embittered by the action of the umpire that they declined to congratulate him when he completed the hundred that gave him the world record. This is not the most sporting moment in the history of the team'.
4 On the use and role of shaming in criminological theory and practice, see John Braithwaite, *Crime, shame and reintegration*, op. cit. See also Robert Cover, 'Nomos and Narrative', op. cit.
5 Op. cit., p. 128.
6 Again this raises, but leaves unanswered, the question raised in relation to the Ian Meckiff affair. What was it about throwing which made the sin so terrible that the public/private split could not protect him?
7 Op. cit., at p. 127.
8 Ashis Nandy, op. cit., at p. 40.
9 Jack Pollard, *Australian Cricket*, op. cit., at p. 114. There was an equally infamous incident in which Sir Donald Bradman refused to 'walk', was given not out and went from his 21 runs at the time to score 187 to lead Australia to victory at home against the English. Bradman insists the ball hit the ground, the English side disagreed. Id., p. 30.
10 Quoted in Derek Birley, op. cit., at p. 37 (footnote omitted).
11 Ibid.
12 Ashis Nandy, op. cit., at p. 40.
13 Op. cit., at p. 127. Indeed it was in such circumstances that his sledging of d'Oliveira (*supra*) took place.
14 Vic Marks, *The Wisden Illustrated History of Cricket* (London: Macdonald Queen Anne Press, 1988), p. 192.
15 Terry Brindle, *Australian*, 16 July 1989.
16 It should also be noted that the Australian outburst of anger over Hemmings' refusal to walk threatened to manifest itself not against Hemmings but against the umpires, thereby violating another ethical 'imperative', unquestioning obedience and recognition of the umpires' absolute authority. Here, yet another ethico-legal norm came into play as Allan Border fulfilled his obligations as captain to quell his team's anger.
17 Greg Growden, 'Dyer's straits', *Sydney Morning Herald*, 27 Oct. 1990.
18 Neil Manthorp, *CricInfo*, 25 March 2001.
19 'Atherton right not to walk', *Australian*, 29 July 1998.

20 Patrick Compton, 'Uncertain Boucher would not walk', *Star*, 17 Jan. 2002.
21 Simon Barnes, *Phil Edmonds – A Singular Man* (1986), p. 67. One can again identify the use of the 'c' word to invoke disgust and exclusion in the manly world of cricket.
22 'Early shocks for New Zealand', 1 March 1978.
23 See, Jon Culley, 'Stewart's stubbornness sours England's day of batting brilliance', *Independent*, 12 Aug. 2002; Mark Nicholas, 'ICC take a step too far', *Daily Telegraph*, 14 Aug. 2002.
24 Mark Tallentire, 'India batsmen play hardball with the rules, says Gough', *Guardian*, 16 July 2002.
25 Mike Selvey, 'Fired-up Ganguly puts India on front foot', *Guardian*, 10 Aug. 2002.

24 Other stories about cricket, law and the meaning of life

1 'The Week in Britain', *Guardian Weekly*, 29 April 1990. That was not the first time Tebbit resorted to cricket analogies in the political sphere. Speaking of the Conservative's defeat in the European Parliamentary elections of 1989 he had opined: 'The Conservatives played like England cricketers – too many rash strokes and run-outs, dropped catches and bowling anywhere but the stumps.' *The Book of Cricket Quotations*, op. cit., p. 130.
2 Id.
3 'Wisden report angers players', *Sydney Morning Herald*, 4 July 1995; David Frith, 'Batting for free speech when all I wanted was a visceral view', *Weekend Australian* 8–9 July 1995; 'Wisden editor apologises for race article', *Guardian Weekly*, 16 July 1995;
4 See e.g., Paul Vallely, 'Asians reject Blunkett's "British test"', *Independent on Sunday*, 10 Feb. 2002.
5 See Robert Cover, 'Violence and the Word', 95 *Yale L.J.* 1601 (1986).
6 B. Boothroyd, 'Keep the Game at Home', in *The Boundary Book*, op. cit., at p. 268.
7 Eric Midwinter, *Fair Game – Myth and Reality in Sport*, op. cit., at p. 31. Nor do written accounts purvey a different, more sensitive ideology. The 1990 *Wisden* (p. 302) account of the third One-Day match between England and Australia includes an irrelevant description of '... the longest and easily the most stylish 'streak' on an English cricket ground, by a shapely young lady ...'.
8 Christopher Niesche, 'Second XI earn their selection to play elite role', *Australian*, 25 Nov. 2002.
9 See Rod Marsh, *Gloves, Sweat and Tears* (Ringwood, Vic: Penguin, 1984), at p. 45:

> I think the idea of setting world drinking records on aeroplanes was born in 1973 when I was lucky (or unlucky) enough to be seated next to Doug Walters on the way back from the West Indies.

See also 'Record 58 not out is no boon for the body', *Sydney Morning Herald*, 11 Dec. 1989 and John Huxley, 'Face to Face with H.G. and Roy', *Sydney Morning Herald*, 16 Dec. 1989, where the social analysts comment:

> At the end of the decade, cricket is in safe hands again, thanks to the blokes, like, well Stumpy Boon who now holds the world record (footnote omitted) for drinking cans between Mascot and Heathrow. We can be proud.

10 'Off The Beat', *Sydney Morning Herald*, 3 March 1990. At the same time, 'drugs' are *not acceptable*. See *The Book of Cricket Quotations*, op. cit., p. 112, although association with breweries and tobacco companies (*infra*) seems to be unproblematic for cricket administrators in Australia.
11 'Crowe's "promotion" of beer criticised', *The Press*, 6 Feb. 1991.

12 See David Beresford, 'Ntini found guilty of rape', *Guardian*, 24 April 1999; Ray Kennedy, 'Pioneer cricketer sentenced for rape', *Times*, 29 May 1999; Christopher Munnion, 'Cricketer cleared of rape to rejoin South African squad', *Daily Telegraph*, 30 Oct. 1999.

13 See 'Conservative New Zealand not stumped for a good sex scandal', *Sydney Morning Herald*, 16 Dec. 1989 and 'Life for sex killings', *Sydney Morning Herald*, 22 Dec. 1989; 'Retrial for bondage pair', *Sydney Morning Herald*, 4 Aug. 1990.

   The New Zealand criminal justice system continued to be troubled by this sex and cricket case. The second trial again failed to reach a result, and a third trial took place. See 'Jury ponders sex death case', *Sydney Morning Herald*, 23 Feb. 1991 and 'Jury dilemma in bondage death', *Sun Herald*, 24 Feb. 1991 and 'Third bondage trial', *Sydney Morning Herald*, 25 Feb. 1991. One of the accused, dominatrix Renee Chignell was acquitted but later convicted on drugs charges. See, 'Chignell case', *Sunday Star-Times*, 20 Feb. 2000.

14 See, Andrew Darby, 'Top umpire in court over assaults', *Sydney Morning Herald*, 25 May 1998; 'Sex charges against umpire increase to 26', *Sydney Morning Herald*, 17 July 1998; Bruce Montgomery, 'Guilty verdict brings disgrace', *Australian*, 12 Aug. 1999; Andrew Darby, 'Randell sent to jail for four years for assaults', *Sydney Morning Herald*, 14 Aug. 1999; 'Child molesting ex-umpire set to be freed', *Sydney Morning Herald*, 1 Aug. 2001; John Polack, 'Former Test umpire Randell granted parole', *CricInfo*, 3 April 2002.

15 See Colin Randall, 'From woman to woman-beater', *Daily Telegraph*, 22 Jan. 1998; 'Boycott on front foot as press steams in', *Daily Telegraph*, 24 Jan. 1998; Peter Wilmouth, 'Law, lies and dangerous liaisons', *Sun Herald*, 1 March 1998; Andrew Lee, 'Boycott stumped by French conviction', *Times*, 11 Nov. 1998; Jon Henley, 'French court throws out Boycott appeal', *Guardian*, 4 May 2000.

16 'Cricketer gets suspended term for caning youths', *Guardian*, 20 Oct. 2001.

17 See generally, Steve Greenfield and Guy Osborn, *Contract and Control in the Entertainment Industry* (Aldershot: Ashgate, 1998), esp. at pp. 135–74; 'The Legal Regulation of Football and Cricket: 'England's Dreaming', in *Sport, Popular Culture and Identity* (Maurice Roche ed.) (Aachen: Meyer & Meyer Verlag, 1998), at p. 193; 'Artist or Artisan? The Legal and Extra Legal Influence on Cricketers' Terms and Conditions', 2 *Culture, Sport, Society* 56 (1999).

18 See, 'Pakis arrested on drug charges', *Sun Herald*, 11 April 1993; 'Pakistan drug charges dropped', *Australian*, 14 April 1993; 'Drugs debacle may prompt Pakistan to cancel tour', *Sydney Morning Herald*, 15 April 1993; Bronwyn Wilkinson, 'South African players fined for smoking marijuana', *UCB*, 11 May 2001; Peter Robinson, 'Gibbs in hot water again after dope smoking incident', *CricInfo*, 11 May 2001.

19 See, Christopher Martin-Jenkins, 'Giddins banned for 20 months for cocaine use', *Daily Telegraph*, 21 Aug. 1996; 'Hollioake censured over drug claim', *Sydney Morning Herald*, 4 May 1998; Graham Otway, 'Drug-test loophole exposed by illness', *Times*, 28 June 1998; Nelson Clare, 'Spencer banned after failed test', *Daily Telegraph*, 20 April 2001; Partab Ramchand, 'After match fixing, a drugs scandal now hits Indian cricket', *CricInfo*, 5 July 2001; Mihir Bose, 'ICC to discuss drug abuse by cricketers', *Daily Telegraph*, 12 Oct. 2001; ACB, 'ACB Anti-Doping Policy', 21 Feb. 2002; David Sygall, 'Senior QC slams "grossly unfair" doping ban', *Sun Herald*, 3 March 2002.

20 See Giles Whittell, 'US court rules Imran is father of love child', *Times*, 14 Aug. 1997.

21 'Lara's model girlfriend accuses him of physical abuse', *Sun Herald*, 30 Dec. 2001; Charles Randall, 'Lara quick to dismiss incident as lovers' tiff', *Daily Telegraph*, 31 Dec. 2001.

22 *The Book of Cricket Quotations*, op. cit., p. 97.

23 'News Round' – Equal Rights in *Cricket Life international*, Feb. 1990, p. 7.

24 See Andrew Sharpe, *Transgender Jurisprudence: Dysphoric Bodies of Law* (London: Cavendish, 2002).

25 'Middlesex ballot on women', *Times*, 20 April 1990 and Simon Barnes, 'Lord's stands firm', *Times*, 12 May 1990.

26 Barnes, id.

27 'Men remain the Lords at Lord's', *Sydney Morning Herald*, 25 Feb. 1998; Alan Lee and Claudia Joseph, 'MCC ends 200-year ban on women members', *Times*, 29 Sep. 1998.

28 *Australian*, 16 April 1997.

29 Vaneisa Baksh, 'Good news for female fans in the Caribbean', *Guardian*, 6 June 2000.

30 See e.g., 'Muslim Bangladesh to have women's cricket team', AFP, *CricInfo*, 28 June 2000; 'Women's cricket in India has not come a long way: Shubangi', *CricInfo*, 1 July 2000; but cf., Lynn McConnell, 'Overseas players keen to catch women's cricket wave in NZ', *CricInfo*, 4 Sep. 2001.

31 See Steve Connelly, 'Abortion shame for cricket chiefs', *Sydney Morning Herald*, 13 March 1998; Amelia Gentelman, 'Cricket board pressured woman to have abortion', *Guardian Weekly*, 22 March 1998.

32 See, Vivek Chaudhary, 'Yorkshire ex-players erupt as "southerner" Major asked to unveil gates', *Guardian*, 4 Aug. 2001; Yorkshire did issue an apology to former county player Bob Appleyard for any implication that Appleyard's objections to the gate as historically inaccurate were informed by racial bias. See Richard Bright, 'Appleyard secures Yorkshire apology', *Daily Telegraph*, 8 Aug. 2001.

33 Tanya Aldred, 'Only Yorkshire's old guard could bar women at the gate', *Guardian*, 6 Aug. 2001. For another manifestation of Yorkshire parochialism, see Martin Searby, 'Gough prefers Yorkshire-born captain' *Daily Telegraph*, 3 Oct. 2001. More generally see, Ben Carrington and Ian McDonald, 'Whose game is it anyway? Racism in local league cricket', in *Race, Sport and British Society* (Ben Carrington and Ian McDonald eds.) (London and New York: Routledge, 2001), at p. 49.

34 See generally, Susan Cahn, *Coming On Strong: Gender and Sexuality in Twentieth Century Women's Sport* (Cambridge: Harvard University Press, 1994).

35 See, Bronwen Gora, 'Sex rights for all', *Sunday Telegraph*, 17 April 1994; 'Women tackle taboos', *Sydney Morning Herald*, 18 Nov. 1995; Matthew Fynes-Clinton, 'Cricket image hit for a six', *Sunday Telegraph*, 22 Dec. 1996; Rhonda Bushby, 'Women turning sexuality scandal into success story', *Australian*, 22 Jan. 1997.

36 Amanda Weaver, 'Australian captain blasts "boring" NZ cricket', *Sydney Morning Herald*, 13 Nov. 1996.

37 David Harrison, 'Ugliness in the slips – Australian women cricketers accused of being world's worst sledgers', *Sydney Morning Herald*, 25 June 2001.

38 I develop this in more detail in 'What's Love Got To Do With It? Critical Legal Studies, Feminist Discourse and the Ethic of Solidarity', 11 *Harvard Women's L.J.* 53 (1988).

39 Op. cit., p. 128.

40 For the problems associated with the status and role of 'minor literature', see 'What's Love Got To Do With It?', op. cit., at pp. 78–79 and works cited.

41 See Bill Frindall, 'Unveiling the Ladies' in *The Boundary Book*, op. cit., at pp. 214 et. seq.

42 Bill Frindall, *Guinness Cricket Facts and Feats*, op. cit., at p. 192.

43 'England Captain Jane Powell explains some of the problems' in 'Cricket Equipment Preview', *The Cricketer* 1990, p. 53. 'Only six women players have any form of contract from the manufacturers.' The problem and imagery are also exacerbated by the tendency for women cricketers to wear skirts. This sets them apart in a significant and signifying way in the image they present on the field of play and identifies the game as not 'cricket'. Former England captain, Rachel Heyhoe Flint supports 'the wearing of trousers if we are to be fully recognized as cricketers. No longer will we gather headlines such as 'Skirts at the Wicket', 'Fashion in the Field' in *The Boundary Book*, op. cit., at p. 199.

44 For example, in a story on cricket in the *Sydney Morning Herald* of 5 Dec. 1989, Phil Wilkins, 'NSW triumph but Qld cry it's not cricket', 30 paragraphs of text are dedicated to the 'cricket' story and two paragraphs at the end tell about the fitness of 'World class batter Lindsay Reeler' for the forthcoming national women's championship.

In another brief story of only a few paragraphs, the same newspaper, 'No ticker tape welcome for this Test side', *Sydney Morning Herald*, 16 Jan. 1990 points out that the world's best women's cricket team, the Australian side, have received no public attention or adulation. 'Even though we have had three times as much success as the men, no one knows who we are. There certainly haven't been any ticker tape parades...'. The same newspaper dedicated a multi-page colour 'Ashes souvenir' to the Ashes winning (male) Australian team, *Sydney Morning Herald*, 28 Sept. 1989. Coverage of a women's Test series against India was given greater coverage although complaints about the gender disparity in the media continue to be voiced. See Amanda Weaver, 'Testing times for women's cricket', *Sydney Morning Herald*, 26 Jan. 1991 but cf. Phillip Derriman, 'Howzat! Women settle a sore point', *Sydney Morning Herald*, 25 March 1991, pointing to increased mainstream media courage of women's cricket.

45 Op. cit., at p. 200. Women are also making inroads into other male interpretive sub-communities. Stevenie Harman became the first woman in Australia named to umpire an interstate cricket match. See Greg Growden, 'Harman set to make first-class decisions', *Sydney Morning Herald*, 11 Oct. 1990. As in the case of her judicial counterparts, however, the real questions of sex and gender remain unanswered. Is there a 'female' interpretation of the LBW Law or is Law so inherently patriarchal that the idea of a female judge is an oxymoron?

46 Perhaps again, the analysis of H.G. and Roy is appropriate.

> Not long after, (the beginning of the decade) there was that clash when Javed Miandad took on Dennis Lillee. It was mano to mano – head to head – toe to toe. Just a couple of big blokes, with nobody but themselves involved. Cricket had turned the corner.

Nor would they be disappointed with subsequent developments in cricket. In a domestic game, 'Indian test bowler Rashid Patel used a stump to beat up a batsman after softening him up with a bouncer...', 'New-style Stumping all the rage in India', *Sydney Morning Herald*, 31 Jan. 1991. See also 'A sport smeared by shock and shame', *Times*, 1 Feb. 1991.

A photograph in the same newspaper two days later showed the incident and its caption described how the bowler 'lost his cool and went on the warpath'. There can be little doubt about the universal condemnation which followed the event, although one must nonetheless wonder whether subtle racist images are not conveyed by the headline and photograph.

Even such a clearly outrageous event nonetheless occurs in a particular context. The match in question was apparently characterized by 'acrimony' between the two sides and the Indian Cricket Board has widened its investigation of the 'incident' to include the conduct of other players. See 'Board follows on Stump attack', *Australian*, 6 Feb. 1991. A court order subsequently prevented a replay of the match. This judicial intervention in cricket's internal adjudicatory ethos halted the Ranji Trophy for the first time in its history. See 'Trophy stumped', *Australian*, 6 March 1991, 'The bowler, Rashid Patel, was suspended from first class cricket for 13 months. The batsman, Raman Lamba, suffered a 10 month bar for using abusive language to Patel.' See, *Cricketer*, April 1991, p. 7.

47 See Mark Fuller and Shahid A. Hashmi, 'Australia cry off Pakistan', *Guardian*, 10 Aug. 2002; Stephen Brenkley, 'Pakistan fears take Tests into the neutral zone', *Independent on Sunday*, 11 Aug. 2002; 'Millionaire's plan to save Pakistan', *Guardian*, 19 Aug. 2002.

48 'Angry Richards late for Test after press box row', *Sydney Morning Herald*, 16 April 1990.

49 'Running the gauntlet', *Cricket Life International*, June 1990, p. 28. Richards was subsequently censured by the West Indian cricket authorities. See 'In the News', *The Cricketer*, July 1990, p. 4 and id.; Tony Cozier, 'West Indies: The Board's Displeasure', p. 62.

50 For one English journalist who is aware of these issues, see 'Man from BBC stirs up storm in a rum glass', *Times*, 11 April 1990; Simon Barnes, 'The importance of being too earnest', *Times*, 12 April 1990 and 'The strange but mental antics of a demi-god', *Times*, 13 April 1990. In the aftermath, Richards, who later flew to the UK to join his new team Glamorgan was escorted from the airport by guards, who according to first reports (later denied), were armed police officers. See 'Armed guards, but Richards not fazed', *Sydney Morning Herald*, 25 April 1990:

> The policemen who escorted Vivian Richards, the West Indies captain, through Heathrow last week were, contrary to reports, not armed, the junior Home Office minister, Mr. Peter Lloyd, said on Monday. Glamorgan, which Richards was joining for his first season, had requested an escort for their new star.

Times, 3 May 1990.

51 See Michael Manley, op.cit., at p. 62. Such concerns operate on a daily basis in the West Indies and resonate with deep meaning in everyday experience. Thus, when the Barbados Cricket Association sought to ban musical instruments from the Kensington Oval during the 1991 Australian tour, fans protested vehemently and engaged in acts of civil disobedience by smuggling instruments into the ground. One fan voiced the interpretive sub-text of racism and its historical legacy in the West Indies when he '...drew a comparison with the banning by white plantation owners of Afro-style drumming in the days of slavery, and said it was appalling the BCA had shown such insensitivity'. See Patrick Smithers, 'Calypso fans get the drum on noise', *Sydney Morning Herald*, 14 March 1991.

52 Although one might bring perjured libel actions and still, perhaps, maintain one's place as a member of the established hierarchy, or not. See, Ivo Tennant and Andrew Norfolk, 'MCC may expel disgraced peer', *Times*, 5 Sep. 2002; Ivo Tennant, 'MCC considers Archer's membership', ibid.

53 Op. cit., at p. 57. Such contradictory manifestations of English racist attitudes to cricketers of colour later had a direct legal impact when Leary Constantine, the great West Indian cricketer and black rights activist, successfully sued a hotel which refused accommodation to him and his family. See *Constantine v. Imperial Hotels Limited* [1944] 1 K.B. 693. Constantine is described in the case as 'the well-known West Indian cricketer'. We are left to wonder whether an 'ordinary' black victim would have had the means or opportunity to bring such an action or to succeed if he had.

54 As reported in 'Brixton *v.* Police' in *Cricket on the Air*, op. cit., at p. 34.

55 David Hopps, 'Run-out triggers red alert', *Guardian*, 17 Sep. 2002.

56 Mike Marqusee, *War Minus the Shooting*, op. cit., at pp. 100–21.

57 See David O'Reilly, 'Cricket's keeper pulls up stumps', *Bulletin*, 9 April 1996, at p. 23.

58 Geoffrey Dean, 'Zimbabwe crisis too close to home for players', *Times*, 23 May 2000.

59 Ian Woolridge, 'Why cricket must shun this tyrant's killing fields', *Daily Mail*, 11 Aug. 2001; 'MP calls for cancellation of England's tour of Zimbabwe', *CricInfo*, 14 Aug. 2001; Donald Trelford, 'Tour Cancellation would do more harm than good', *Daily Telegraph*, 25 Aug. 2001; 'Zimbabwe tour will go ahead, says ECB Chief Executive', *CricInfo*, 28 Aug. 2001; Charles Randall, 'England urged by MPs to abort tour', *Daily Telegraph*, 25 Sep. 2001.

60 ZCU, 'Integration Task Force within the ZCU', 26 March 2001.

61 ZCU, 'Zimbabwe Cricket Union's Integration Task Force unveils its goals and recommendations', 24 May 2001.

62 Tony Cozier, 'Racial tension on Zimbabwe board', *Barbados Nation*, 18 July 2001; Larry Moyo, 'Zimbabwe players' association speaks out', *CricInfo*, 21 July 2001; ZCU, 'Media reports concerning racism in cricket', 20 Oct. 2001.

63 Neil Manthorp, 'Campbell given suspended ban', *Daily Telegraph*, 3 Nov. 2001; ZCU, 'Report of Disciplinary Board of Inquiry into comments made by Alistair Campbell', 15 Nov. 2001.

64 See Rob Steen, 'Schoolboy warms the heart of Zimbabwe', *Guardian*, 31 July 2001; Andrew Meldrum, 'Masakadza is great hope for change', *Guardian*, 25 Sep. 2001.

65 See 'South Africa's sporting breakdown', *Guardian*, 26 Feb. 1999.

66 See e.g., Vivek Chaudhary, 'End of lilywhite rainbow', *Guardian*, 25 Feb. 1999; Scyld Berry, 'Row over race quotas offers England hope', *Daily Telegraph*, 12 Sep. 1999; Christopher Martin-Jenkins, 'South Africa divided over pace of change', *Times*, 25 Nov. 1999; Nelson Clare, 'Board warned over selection', *Daily Telegraph*, 1 Dec. 1999; Ken Borland, 'Ex UCB president Ray White lashes out – cricket and politics in South Africa', *CricInfo*, 23 Feb. 2000; UCB, 'Sports Minister addresses SA selection committee', 13 Aug. 2001.

67 'Balfour concerned over Ntini's axing', *Mercury*, 26 Dec. 2001.

68 Mark Fuller, 'Chief vetoes selection on race grounds', *Sydney Morning Herald*, 3 Jan. 2002.

69 'Why Justin Ontong deserves better than a helping hand from the board', *Sydney Morning Herald*, 3 Jan. 2002; 'No place for racial quotas in cricket', Editorial, *Weekend Australian*, 5–6 Jan. 2002; but cf., Richard Hinds, 'Some white Proteas have yet to bloom in the new South Africa', *Sydney Morning Herald*, 5 Jan. 2002; 'South African cricket still seeing arguments in black and white', *Guardian*, 7 Jan. 2002; UCB, 'United Cricket Board Media Statement', 8 Jan. 2002.

70 'South Africa board ends race quotas', *Guardian*, 8 July 2002.

71 'That Jack Marsh would have been one of the world's greatest bowlers if he had been a white man I have always believed. If he had been able to win a place in Test match cricket, I believe his bowling would have established a fresh standard of hard-wicket excellence and created a new type, differing altogether from anything ever known before', J.C. Davis, 'Jack Marsh' in *The Referee*, 9 June 1916, as reproduced in *Bat and Pad*, op. cit., at p. 212.

72 Jack Egan, op. cit., at p. 55. One black, born in Jamaica of West Indian parents, has in fact played Test cricket for Australia. Samuel Morris played in one Test against England at Melbourne in 1885. He scored 14 runs in two innings (4 and 10 not out) and took 2 wickets for 73. See Jack Pollard, *Australian Cricket*, op. cit., pp. 764–65. Andrew Symonds, a non-Aboriginal 'black' cricketer has played for Australia in the One-Day game.

73 See id., pp. 52 et. seq.; D. MacDonald, 'The 1868 Tour' in *Bat and Pad*, op. cit., at p. 209.

74 Jack Pollard, op. cit., at p. 4.

75 At p. 238.

76 Ashis Nandy, op. cit., at p. 50.

77 Eric Midwinter, *Fair Game*, op. cit., at p. 30.

78 F. Thompson, 'Selected Essays' (1927) reproduced in *The Faber Book of Cricket*, op. cit., at p. 102.

79 See David Fraser, 'What's Love Got To Do With It?' op. cit., and Jessica Benjamin, *The Bonds of Love* (New York: Pantheon, 1988).

80 For more detailed studies of various aspects of Indian cricket and culture, see Ashis Nandy, op. cit., Richard Cashman, *Patrons, Players and the Crowd – The Phenomenon of Indian Cricket* (Delhi and London: Sangam Books, 1980) and Mihir Bose, *A History of Indian Cricket* (London: Andre Deutsch, 2002).

81 Op. cit., p. 7.

82 Id., p. 43.

83 Id., p. 122.

84 For detailed accounts of the cricket struggle, see C.L.R. James, *Beyond A Boundary* (London: Stanley Paul, 1963) and C.L.R. James, *Cricket* (London: Alison & Busby,

1986) (Anna Grimshaw ed.); Michael Manley, *The History of West Indian Cricket*, op. cit.; Hilary Beckles, *The Development of West Indies Cricket, vol. 1, The Age of Nationalism; vol. 2, The Age of Globalization* (London: Pluto Press, 1998).

85 See e.g., Hubert Devonish, 'African and Indian consciousness at play: a study in West Indies cricket and nationalism', in Hilary Beckles and Brian Stoddart (eds.), *Liberation Cricket: West Indies Cricket Culture* (Manchester and New York: Manchester University Press, 1995), at p. 179.

86 From 'The Great All-Rounders' (J. Arlott ed.) (1969) as reproduced in *Cricket*, op. cit. For a similar analysis of the juncture of the public and the private in the career of Sir Gary Sobers, see Brian Stoddart, 'Gary Sobers and Cultural Identity in the Caribbean', 5 *Sporting Traditions* 131 (1988) and Michael Manley, op. cit. For the threat to such cultural identity posed by the technological innovation of satellite dishes capable of disseminating American spectator sports and images to the impoverished youth of the West Indies, see, Patrick Smithers, 'Even at cricket, the Yanks can dish it out', *Sydney Morning Herald*, 13 March 1991.

87 Alan Lee, 'Viv under fire after "African descent" claim', *Australian*, 15 March 1990.

88 Patrick Smithers, 'Even at cricket, the Yanks can dish it out', op. cit.

89 *Agon* (Oxford: Oxford University Press, 1982). See my 'Truth and Hierarchy: Will the Circle Be Unbroken?', op. cit., for a discussion of the relevance of this idea to legal interpretive practice.

90 See Mike Marqusee, 'In search of the unequivocal Englishman: The conundrum of race and nation in English cricket', in Ben Carrington and Ian McDonald (eds.), *'Race', Sport and British Society*, op. cit., at p. 121.

91 *The Guardian Book of Cricket*, op. cit., p. 169.

92 *Wisden* (1990), at p. 330.

93 'Interview', *Cricket World*, Vol. 4, No. 6, June 1990, p. 11.

94 See Ric Sissons and Brian Stoddart, *Cricket and Empire: The 1932–33 Bodyline Tour of Australia* (Sydney and London: George Allen & Unwin, 1984) and Jack Egan, op. cit., and P. Derriman, *Bodyline* (Sydney: Fontana, 1986).

95 For another example of the function of sport and national ambivalence to collective self-identity, see David Fraser and Alan Freeman, 'What's Hockey Got To Do With It, Anyway? Comparative Canadian-American Perspectives on Constitutional Law and Rights', 36 *Buffalo L. Rev.* 259 (1987).

96 Award-winning Australian author Tom Kenneally (also a rugby league fan) in 'The Cyclical Supremacy of Australia in World Cricket' in *Summer Days* (1981), as reproduced in *The Faber Book of Cricket*, op. cit., at pp. 274–75.

97   Australia's national flag and anthem reformers are about 75 years behind the times. Well before the turn of the century and the achievement of Federation, Australia had already shed its Oedipus complex towards the mother country through the unlikely medium of the cricket field.

'Sport as jingo juice – how cricket sparked Australian nationalism', *National Times*, 2–7 July 1973.

98 As quoted in *Bat and Pad*, op. cit., at p. 154.

99 'Protestantism – capitalism – sports', 1977 *North American Society for Sport History – Proceedings and Newsletter* 11, at p. 12.

100 'Alan Knott – A Thorough Genius' in *Wisden* (1986), at pp. 69 et. seq.

101 Id., p. 72.

102 See AAP, 'Sir Donald's bigots – tour letter for sale', *Sydney Morning Herald*, 8 March 2002.

103 For a fuller treatment, see Umberto Eco, *Foucault's Pendulum*, op. cit.

104 'Six-day Test? Once in a full moon', *Sydney Morning Herald*, 27 Dec. 2001.

105 See Rex Clementine Fernando, 'Chief priest slams authorities over Dambulla Stadium controversy', *CricInfo*, 16 June 2001.

106 *The Book of Cricket Quotations*, op. cit., p. 108.

25 Capitalism and the meaning of cricket

1 See Nigel Kerner, 'Money Money Money: Sport and Cricket', *CricInfo*, 28 May 2001.

2 See e.g., 'Quick finishes short change ECB', *CricInfo*, 2 July 2000.

3 See generally, Ric Sissons, *The Players: A Social History of the Professional Cricketer* (Sydney: Pluto, 1988). As early as 1852 there was sufficient demand in England to justify in market terms the existence of two touring professional teams (pp. 29–30).

4 Jack Egan, op. cit., at pp. 42 et. seq. Even local cricket in Australia, as in England, operated under a form of entrepreneurial sponsorship, usually from the local taverns, as 'The publicans acted as entrepreneurs and offered other attractions on match days to retain a drinking clientele.' John Daly, *Elysian Fields: Sports, Class and Community in Colonial South Australia 1836–1890* (Adelaide: J.A. Daly, 1982), at pp. 39–40.

5 Id., pp. 78 and 81.

6 See especially Richard Cashman, *Patrons, Players and the Crowd*, op. cit.

7 See Ralph Dellor, 'ICC harnesses the power of television to extend cricket's boundaries', *CricInfo*, 18 Feb. 2002.

8 See e.g., Vijay Lokapally, 'Globalisation, at what cost!', *CricInfo*, 17 Sep. 1999. See also, Simon Barnes, 'Programme Notes: Television made in heaven as Sky falls in on Sri Lanka', *Times*, 19 March 2001.

9 For a good discussion of the issues and events, see Peter McFarline, *A Game Divided* (Richmond, Vic: Marlin, 1977); Steve Greenfield and Guy Osborn, 'Circus Games: Contract and control in cricket', in *Contract and Control in the Entertainment Industry*, op. cit., at pp. 135 et. seq.

10 John McDonald, *Clive Lloyd – The Authorised Biography*, op. cit., at p. 90:

> The careers of West Indian cricketers have always been precarious. Because there is no fulltime professional cricket in the islands, cricketers must come to England 'to make a living' playing the game. At the end of their playing days West Indian cricketers had to keep on trying to find some other form of work, since the financial rewards from cricket had never afforded a comfortable retirement. That fact has always haunted West Indian players, many of whom return to their countries of origin, where employment possibilities have always been at a premium.

11 See Reuters, Greg Buckle, 'Australia players reject Champions Trophy contracts', *CricInfo*, 14 Aug. 2002; David Hopps and Rahul Bhattacharya, 'England in sponsor conflict', *Guardian*, 15 Aug. 2002; Angus Fraser, 'ICC marketing dispute looms for England', *Independent*, 16 Aug. 2002; Reuters, N. Ananthanarayanan, 'ICC row brings focus on India's endorsement-rich players', *CricInfo*, 20 Aug. 2002; Stephen Brenkley, 'Dalmiya the key as Indian players dig in over contracts', *Independent on Sunday*, 25 Aug. 2002; Michael Peters, 'When the brand becomes bigger than the team', *Guardian*, 21 Aug. 2001; AAP, 'Leading players sign up for Champions Trophy', *Sydney Morning Herald*, 23 Aug. 2002; Rahul Bhattacharya, 'Quick fix leaves Indians isolated', *Guardian*, 23 Aug. 2002; Rahul Bhattacharya, 'India players close to agreeing peace deal', *Guardian*, 28 Aug. 2002; Reuters, 'South African players delay signing ICC contracts', *CricInfo*, 30 Aug. 2002; 'Sri Lankan players agree to sign ICC contract', *CricInfo*, 30 Aug. 2002; Mihir Bose, 'ICC contract row rumbles on as Dalmiya rejects deadline', *Telegraph*, 30 Aug. 2002; Tony Cozier, 'West Indies in for Mo' Money, *Nation*, 31 Aug. 2002; Rahul Bhattacharya, 'India dig in on sponsors', *Guardian*, 3 Sep. 2002; Reuters, 'Champions Trophy row recedes as SAfricans sign', *CricInfo*, 3 Sep. 2; Rahul Bhattacharya, 'India settle sponsorship row', *Guardian*, 10 Sep. 2002; ICC, 'BCCI Removes Commercial Logo from Indian Team Shirts', *CricInfo*, 14 Sep. 2002; Saadi Thawfeeq, 'More problems for the ICC', *Daily News*, 14 Sep. 2002.

12 An interesting question arising from the plight of professional cricketers in both England and Australia stems from the tax law perspective as to the status of benefit years and other payments received. Are such payments *ex gratia* and non-taxable or are they professional income? Cf. *Moorhouse v. Dooland* [1955] 1 All ER 93 and *Seymour v. Reed* (1927) 11 TC 625. The Inland Revenue continued its pursuit of 'benefit' proceeds. This intriguing question also arises during consideration of an Australia–West Indies Test match at the Bourda Oval in Georgetown, Guyana. Following local practice, fans poured on to the field to congratulate Richie Richardson on his century. As part of this congratulation, Richardson received cash from the crowd. Are such payments part of cricketer's taxable income as a normal incident of employment or are they tax-free gifts?

13 John Collis, 'Yorkshire struggle to pay players' wages', *Guardian*, 10 Aug. 2002.

14 'News Register', *Wisden Cricket Monthly*, Dec. 1989, p. 4.

15 'News Round', *Cricket Life International*, June 1990, p. 7. See also *Sun Herald*, 16 Sep. 1990.

16 See Mark Nicholas, 'ICC are justified in restricting players' self-interest', *Daily Telegraph*, 3 April 2002; ICC, 'Test lights here to Stay!', 3 April 2002.

17 Ibid.

18 Despite the provisions of Law 3(9), play was halted after Nasser Hussain's intervention with the umpires. See Stephen Brenkley, 'The hour that will live forever', *Independent on Sunday*, 25 Aug. 2002.

19 'The Benson and Hedges Connection', *Cricketer*, April 1977, p. 4; *Wisden Cricketers' Almanack* (1986), p. 53. 'The whole business of tobacco sponsorship is fast becoming a vexed question', *Times*, 3 May 1990.

20 Malcolm Conn, 'Storm blowing away smokescreen of bias', *Weekend Australian*, 22–23 Dec. 1990.

21 'When smoke gets in your eyes, it gives the game away', *Sydney Morning Herald*, 14 Dec. 1990.

22 Controversy continued to emerge as a result of conflicts in international norms. Advertising of a tobacco company's logo on Pakistani bats created tension during a tour. See, Simon Chapman, 'Cricket's new ashes battle', *Sydney Morning Herald*, 7 Jan. 1997; Justine Ferrari, 'AMA hits tobacco bat cover-up for six', *Australian*, 8 Jan. 1997. Nonetheless, changes in public attitudes and tougher regulatory standards 'imposed' some kind of solution on the issue of cricket sponsorship. See, Robin Marler, 'Last gasp for posterity', *Sunday Times*, 12 July 1998; Malcolm Knox, 'One by one, sporting venues decide to butt out', *Sydney Morning Herald*, 24 July 1998.

23 Surrey CCC, 'Lucrative deal sees The Oval become The AMP Oval', 20 June 2001.

24 See e.g., 'PCB makes new terms for deal with IMG', *Dawn*, 18 Aug. 2000; ECB, 'CricInfo to sponsor County Championship', 19 April 2001; ACB, 'CUB and ACB renew One-Day International Partnership', 12 June 2001; Lynn McConnell, 'New sponsorship sets up domestic game', *CricInfo*, 4 Oct. 2001; ACB, 'Hutchinson wins Test cricket rights', 11 Oct. 2001; PCB, 'PCB clarifies agreement with sponsors', 10 Dec. 2001; ACB, 'Travelex and ACB sign multi-million dollar agreement', *CricInfo*, 30 Jan. 2002; 'ICC chief executive requests compromise on Dilmah–Pepsi sponsorship clash', *CricInfo*, 18 March 2002.

25 See e.g., ICC, 'ICC and Emirates Airline sign partnership for Elite Panels of Umpires and Referees', *CricInfo*, 12 July 2002.

26 ICC, 'Penalties imposed on players for breaches of ICC Code of Conduct', 1995.

27 Ibid., 1996 and 1997.

28 See e.g., 'Singer sponsorship for Arjuna's bat', *Daily News*, 27 May 1999; George Dobell, 'Lara's bat logo provokes legal wrangle', *CricInfo*, 2 April 2001; Derrick Nicholas, 'Lara allowed to use his new bat after ICC retracts ban', *CricInfo*, 7 April 2001; Simon Hart, 'Waugh goes in to bat for sponsorship deal', *Daily Telegraph*, 24 June 2001; ICC, 'Advertising on Clothing and Equipment'.

29 John Polack, 'Gilchrist creates first with bat sponsorship deal', *CricInfo*, 11 Jan. 2002.

30 See, 'India and Pakistan to discuss resuming cricket ties', *CricInfo*, 25 March 2001; 'PCB policy on India unchanged', *Dawn*, 21 Jan. 2002.
31 See e.g., 'PCB to earn $2 m form one-dayers in Dubai', *Dawn*, 1 June 2000; 'TWI bags Indian team sponsorship rights', *CricInfo*, 22 May 2001.
32 'TV channels snub Asian Test Championship', *Dawn*, 5 March 2002; 'Sri Lankans face television blackout in ATC final', *CricInfo*, 5 March 2002.
33 Derrick Nicholas, 'West Indies to raise financial problems with ICC', *CricInfo*, 29 May 2002.
34 Qamar Ahmed, 'ICC to make $600 million from next World Cup TV rights', *Dawn*, 24 June 2000; Peter Robinson, 'TV bonanza for 2003 World Cup', *CricInfo*, 4 Aug. 2000; Derrick Nicholas, 'World Cup rights sold for US $230 million', *CricInfo*, 28 June 2000; ICC, 'World Cup 2003 will be one of the World's great sporting events says ICC CEO', 1 Nov. 2001; 2003 Cricket World Cup, '$2-million jackpot for World Cup winners', 13 April 2002.
35 See e.g., Nizamuddin Ahmed, 'Veetee – Coming to a boil', *Daily Star*, 2 June 1999; 'WorldTel, BCB reach agreement', *Daily Star*, 19 Sep. 2000; 'CBI team in Monaco to probe award of telecast rights', *CricInfo*, 26 July 2001; BCCSL, 'Wrangle over TV rights continues in Sri Lanka', 7 Nov. 2001; 'BCCSL clarifies position regarding sponsors', 22 Nov. 2001; Sa'adi Thawfeeq, 'Board chairman defends Taj television deal after newspaper allegations', *Daily News*, 26 Jan. 2002; BCCSL, 'BCCSL Chairman explains why WSG Nimbus deal was cancelled', *CricInfo*, 24 Feb. 2002; BCCSL, 'BCCSL signs USD 13.9 million television contract with Taj television', *CricInfo*, 25 March 2002.
36 See 'Pakistan seek compensation for lost tour funds', *CricInfo*, 18 Jan. 2002.
37 Trevor Marshallsea, 'Skipper worried by player safety', *Sydney Morning Herald*, 22 March 2002; Craig Skehan, 'PM's aide: cricket tour backs terror', *Sydney Morning Herald*, 22 March 2002; ACB, 'ACB withdraws from 2002 Travelex Tour of Zimbabwe', 27 March 2002; ICC, 'ICC responds to cancellation of Australian tour of Zimbabwe', 27 March 2002; cf., Omar Kureishi, 'Shame on Australia, shame on ICC', *Dawn*, 3 April 2002.
38 See Mike Selvey, 'Online bonanza sparks rift', *Guardian*, 14 May 2001.
39 See also, Rod Brookes, *Representing Sport* (London: Arnold, 2002).
40 See Paul McCann, 'Last stand for BBC's ball-by-ball coverage', *Times*, 24 Feb. 2000; John Goodbody, 'Channel 4 shares in England's triumph', *Times*, 4 July 2000; ECB, 'ECB extends TV contracts with Channel 4 and Sky Sports', 22 May 2001.

26 Class struggle, old school tie and the meaning of cricket

1 *The Players*, op. cit., at p. 252.
2 For a list of the practical reflections of this struggle at the petty but ideologically important level, see id., pp. 167 et. seq.
3 See Nicos Poulantzas, *Classes in Contemporary Capitalism* (London: Verso, 1975).
4 Ashis Nandy, op. cit., at p. 19.
5 See Ric Sissons, *The Players*, op. cit., at pp. 167 et. seq., pp. 226 et. seq. But recent attempts by the ICC to impose limits on players' contractual freedoms have resulted in a burgeoning international trade union movement among cricketers. See, David Hopps, 'Players unite to take on ICC', *Guardian*, 21 Sep. 2002.
6 An entire book on the socio-legal aspects of player contracts, sponsorship and broadcasting rights awaits. In the meantime, I refer to the work of my colleagues Steve Greenfield and Guy Osborn, op. cit., passim; see also, 'England awards twelve players central contracts', *CricInfo*, 29 March 2001; Mark Nicholas, 'Contracts work, at least on paper', *Daily Telegraph*, 11 May 2000; ECB, 'ECB announces rest periods for contracted players', 28 Aug. 2001; 'ECB announces increased funding for Professional

Cricketers' Association', 18 Dec. 2001; Charles Randall, 'Increase in central contracts agreed', *Daily Telegraph*, 7 March 2002.

7 ECB, 'FCF approve new structure for central contracts', *CricInfo*, 12 Aug. 2002; Paul Weaver, 'Extra contracts agreed', *Guardian*, 13 Aug. 2002; but cf., Mike Selvey, 'MacLaurin hits the wall', *Guardian*, 1 Aug. 2002.

8 See e.g., Ralph Dellor, 'What price a transfer system', *CricInfo*, 7 Dec. 2001; Christopher Martin-Jenkins, 'Lancashire make late bid to keep Crawley', *Times*, 8 Jan. 2002; Ralph Dellor, 'Crawley and Habib cases open up new possibilities for cricket transfer market', *CricInfo*, 16 Feb. 2002; 'Habib pays to leave county', *Observer*, 17 Feb. 2002; Charles Randall, 'ECB stand off in Crawley case', *Daily Telegraph*, 8 March 2002.

9 See e.g., Alan Kennedy, 'Cricket's strike rate hits $1 million', *Sydney Morning Herald*, 10 Nov. 2001.

10 Malcolm Conn, 'Boycott looming over sponsorship rights', *Australian*, 5 June 2002; Mark Jeffreys, 'Contract row poses threat to World Cup', *Daily Telegraph*, 9 June 2002.

11 See e.g., Trevor Chesterfield, 'Contract squabble hits Zimbabwe', *CricInfo*, 26 Oct. 1999; ZCU, 'Zimbabwe Cricket Union Media Release on players' remuneration for England tour', 20 May 2000; Dingi Ntuli, 'Zimbabwe Test cricketers engage lawyer in quest for pay hike', *Zimbabwe Herald*, 23 May 2000, 'ZCU statement on players' remuneration', 26 Sep. 2000; 'The craze for contracts', *Sunday Times*, 20 Feb. 2000; Trevor Chesterfield, 'British pound more lucrative than South Africa A team', *Pretoria News*, 29 Feb. 2000; PTI, 'Indian cricketers want system of graded payment', *CricInfo*, 18 May 2001.

12 See e.g., 'Cricketers to pull punches', *Daily Star*, 8 Nov. 1999; 'Irate cricketers to meet today', ibid., 9 Nov. 1999; Syedur Rahman, 'Dispute puts Bangladesh cricket in jeopardy', *CricInfo*, 19 Nov. 1999; 'CWAB sticks to its guns', *Daily Star*, 23 Nov. 1999.

13 Peter Robinson, 'Cullinan snubs South African Test team, Pollock extremely doubtful starter', *CricInfo*, 5 March 2002; Statement issued by Daryll Cullinan, ibid.; UCB, 'Cullinan withdraws after demands are not met', ibid.

14 See e.g., 'Atherton, Stewart and Gough likely to miss India tour', *CricInfo*, 26 Aug. 2001; ECB, 'ECB issues statement regarding availability for winter tours', 26 Aug. 2001.

15 ACB, 'ACB and ACA issue warning over unofficial, unlicensed merchandise & memorabilia', 20 March 2000.

16 It should also be noted that such technology changes had profound effects on general rules of legal liability. For example, the invention of barbed wire had serious effects on vital issues of trespass by cattle in the American West and on legislative decisions to impose liability to 'fence in' or to 'fence out'! See *Delaney v. Erickson* 10 Neb. 492, 6 NW 600 (1880).

17 Jeff Wells, 'Rare delight from an unsung hero' (Peter Stowe, curator at Hobart's Bellerive Oval), *Australian*, 20 Feb. 1990. Compare the introduction of computer technology in the art of law practice and the decision by the ICC to give elite umpires and referees computers to allow them to share information and communicate about legal and adjudication issues, 'Top cricket officials given computers to improve consistency', *CricInfo*, 25 March 2002.

18 See Law 25 and 'One Day International Playing Conditions', para. 8.

27 The hill, the members and others: the crowd as sub-text

1 See e.g., Shahryar Khan, 'Pakistan looking for clean sweep after crowd trouble mars second win in Dhaka', *CricInfo*, 24 Jan. 2002.

2 Richard Cashman, *Ave a Go*, op. cit., at p. 34. See also, Martin Sharp, '"A Degenerate Race": Cricket and Rugby Crowds in Sydney, 1890–1912', 4 *Sporting Traditions* 134 (1988).

3 Ibid., e.g., n. 11 and p. 135.

4 Id., at p. 58, 'Australia had no monopoly on cricket unrest.' Nor are the upper classes of England immune. A letter to the editor of the Guardian on June 16, 1948 contains the following:

> Sir, – As one who loves cricket, I would like to give expression to my feelings of disgust at the unseemly conduct of many of the spectators of the cricket at Trent Bridge in the closing stages of the play on Saturday.
> I was listening to the commentator on the wireless, and unless I had heard the booing of the Australian bowler I should not have thought that such a thing could take place on any English cricket ground; also, and this is a dreadful thing, much of it appeared to come from the occupants of the pavilion stand.

The Guardian Book of Cricket, op. cit., p. 193.
5 *Wisden* (1989), p. 306.
6 *Wisden* (1986), p. 54. It should be noted, as Norman Tebbit points out, it is also inaccurate to speak of a homogeneous English cricket crowd. Since 1963, a large West Indian contingent has been 'settled into its own niche of tradition on English grounds' (Michael Manley, op. cit., p. 167). Similarly, large Indian crowds have made a noisy contribution to 'English' cricket, although this ended after an edict from the MCC. See Gideon Haigh, 'Larger than life and a lot quieter', *Sydney Morning Herald*, 2 Aug. 1990. This has been echoed in moves by Barbadian cricket authorities. Indeed, it is equally inaccurate to speak of the West Indian crowd as homogeneous. Traditional issues of class and race which have informed cricket in the Caribbean also have a direct impact on the crowd. Thus, recent statements by Viv Richards (*q.v.*) on the superiority of Afro-Caribbean cricketers, combined with the population dynamics of different countries in the West Indies, have meant that on occasion the crowd at the Bourda Oval in Georgetown, Guyana have given vocal support to the touring Australian side. See also, Frank Manning, 'Celebrating Cricket: The Symbolic Construction of Caribbean Politics', *American Ethnologist* 616 (1981).
7 See, Peter Deeley, 'Chants and security men raise hackles', *Daily Telegraph*, 9 June 1998.
8 See e.g., 'PCA demands tighter security for players', 8 June 2001; 'ECB takes action after Edgbaston pitch invasion', 8 June 2001; Simon Briggs, 'Waugh pitches into ECB over players' safety', *Daily Telegraph*, 9 June 2001; 'Trescothick and Graveney call for tougher penalties for pitch invaders', *CricInfo*, 10 June 2001; David Lloyd, 'Unruly crowds could end up wrecking game', *Daily Telegraph*, 11 June 2001; Michael Henderson, 'Pitch invasions: time to act', *Daily Telegraph*, 18 June 2001.
9 See, 'ECB requests government intervention as Lord's considers fencing', 20 June 2001; Mike Selvey, 'No change in crowd laws before India and Sri Lanka tour in 2002', *Guardian*, 20 June 2001; Vivek Chaudhary, 'Review rules out new laws on crowds', *Guardian*, 28 Sep. 2001.
10 BBC, 'Australians threatening walkout', 24 May 1999. See also, Maurice Chittenden and Graham Otway, 'MCC in secret move to stump cricket louts', *Sunday Times*, 9 May 1999. South Africa, hosts of the 2003 World Cup announced strict measures to prevent pitch invasions, see Peter Robinson, 'Zero tolerance for 2003 CWC pitch invasions', *CricInfo*, 23 June 2001 but cf., Michael Crutcher, 'Australians demand extra security from South African fans', *CricInfo*, 23 Feb. 2002; Trevor Marshallsea, 'Aussies angry as fans turn on them', *Sydney Morning Herald*, 24 Feb. 2002.
11 BBC, 'India and Pakistan pledge to play on', 28 May 1999; 'Rival captains united on fan fears', *Guardian*, 1 June 1999; Nasir Malick, 'Pakistan-India match: British police taking foolproof security steps', *Dawn*, 2 June 1999; 'Cricket clash drowns out Kashmir fighting', *Times*, 9 June 1999.
12 See Steve Greenfield and Gut Osborn, 'Oh to be in England? Mythology and Identity in English Cricket', 2 *Social Identities* 271 (1996). Indeed, during the preparations for the 1999 World Cup, British immigration officials initiated a regulatory policy of

setting cricket questions to be asked of visitors from 'Asia' claiming to be entering the country to watch the tournament. Here, in an interesting twist on Tebbit's original test, a 'genuine' entrant would be a real cricket fan and supporter of an Asian team. See Tim Reid, 'Cricket test for Asian visitors', *Times*, 18 May 1999.

13 See, Tim Reid, 'English cricket fans have team to support', *Times*, 5 June 1999. Cf. Mike Marqusee, *Anyone But England: Cricket and the National Malaise* (London: Verso, 1994).

14 See e.g., Norman Harris, 'Inside Edge' – 'A gap between the markets', *Observer*, 4 Aug. 2002.

15 See e.g., Dino Dimeo, 'Rome au stade du fascisme', *Le Monde*, 17 Dec. 2000; Phillippe Broussard, 'Le football italien miné par la violence et le racisme de certains supporteurs', *Le Monde*, 26 March 2001.

16 See e.g., Steve Greenfield and Guy Osborn, 'Enough is Enough: Race, Cricket and Protest in the UK', 30 *Sociological Focus* 373 (1997).

17 See John Duncan, 'Fear of cricket "apartheid"', *Guardian Weekly*, 17 May 1998; 'ECB step up anti-racism plans', 25 Jan. 1999; 'ECB welcomes plans to improve racial equality', 16 Nov. 1999; Donald Trelford, 'ECB get to grips with racism in cricket', *Daily Telegraph*, 16 Nov. 1999; John Goodbody, 'Sport charter aims to stamp out racism', *Times*, 22 March 2000; Michael Henderson, 'Why bigots have no place in our game', *Daily Telegraph*, 11 Sep. 2000.

18 Richard Hobson, 'Home fixture that is away for England cricketers', *Times*, 27 April 2001; 'Graveney calls for England support at Old Trafford', *CricInfo*, 28 May 2001. But cf., Brough Scott, '"To have my son captain England in India. It couldn't get any better"', *Daily Telegraph*, 11 Nov. 2001.

19 See the Parekh Report, *The Future of Multicultural Britain: The Parekh Report* (London: Profile Books, 2000). See also, Tanya Aldred, '"Nationality is a thing of the past"', *Guardian*, 21 June 2002.

20 'A question of support', *Guardian*, 29 May 2001.

21 See 'Why the cricket test fails', *Guardian*, 4 June 2001; but cf., Michael Henderson, 'English game all the better for "Anglicised" players', *Daily Telegraph*, 4 June 2001.

22 ICC, 'ICC Plan for Improved Safety Conditions at Grounds', 12 Oct. 1999; Nelson Clare, 'ICC act on grounds', *Daily Telegraph*, 13 Oct. 1999.

23 'Oh no, don't stop the carnival', *Guardian*, 27 May 1999; 'Windies now reggae boys', *Barbados Nation*, 14 June 2000.

24 See Richard Cashman, 'Ave a Go, op. cit., for a detailed discussion of the different types of barracking.

25 Ibid., p. 21.

26 See ECB, 'Pitch invader prosecuted', *CricInfo*, 27 June 2002.

27 What used to be 'joke' has become a serious ethical and legal problem and in some cases an offence. For an introduction to the important issues of crowd-based racist abuse, see Lawrence McNamara, 'Sport, Spectators and Traditions of Hatred: Responding to Racist Abuse', 10 *Griffith L.R.* 99 (2001). As the Eric Cantona case indicates, such abuse can sometimes result in the player taking 'self-remedies' against abusive fans. During a Sahara Cup match against India in Toronto in Sep. 1997, Inzamam Ul-Haq of Pakistan went after an abusive fan by leaping into the grandstand with his bat. Match Referee Jackie Hendricks found Inzamam guilty of bringing the game into disrepute and suspended him for two matches.

28 Ashis Nandy, op. cit., p. 4.

29 Malcolm Knox, 'Try telling Indian cricket fans it's just a bit of fun', *Sydney Morning Herald*, 5 Jan. 2000.

30 Mark Ray, 'McGrath strikes just in time as overtime request pays off', *Sydney Morning Herald*, 5 Jan. 2000.

31 See, Jack Pollard, 'The Hill at Sydney', *The Boundary Book*, op. cit., at pp. 286 et. seq.

32 Similarly, the patrons of Bay 13 at the MCC have developed a 'cult of personality' with certain players like Dennis Lillee, Max Walker and Merv Hughes. It would oversimplify (incorrectly) matters however, to imply that all practices of Australia crowds are homogeneous. As Cashman points out, there are distinctive local characteristics of crowd behaviour and traditions at each ground. '*Ave a Go*, op. cit., at p. 116.

33 It must also be noted that the interpretive practice of the 'crowd' as it imbues the text of cricket with meaning is not limited to what occurs on the field of play. At the SCG, for example, as the Mexican wave ripples from stand to stand, those seated in the Members do not, of course, participate. Their failure to do so is greeted time after time with a chorus of boos emanating not only from the Hill but from every other stand as well. All members of 'the crowd' rise in hermeneutic solidarity against the snobs and upper-class humourless twits in the Members' stand.

34 Ardyn Bernoth, 'SCG's drinkers' low blow', *Sydney Morning Herald*, 9 Dec. 1997.

35 '*Ave a Go*, op. cit., at pp. 118–19.

36 *Sunday Telegraph*, 21 Jan. 1990.

37 And law. Criticism of crowd control techniques or the lack thereof by police can also result in the issuance of defamation writs. See 'Bajan cop sues Waugh', *Trinidad Express*, 1 May 1999 and discussion below.

38 See e.g., Phillip Derriman, 'SCG crowd troubles being eliminated', 14 Jan. 1994; Phil Wilkins, 'Boredom blamed for SCG shame', *Sydney Morning Herald*, 10 Dec. 1996; Malcolm Knox, 'Better than bad old days, but still not cricket', *Sydney Morning Herald*, 11 Dec. 1996; Michael Evans, 'Authorities move to prevent SCG pitch invasions', *Sydney Morning Herald*, 3 Jan. 1997; Mike Coward, 'Australian limited overs crowds worst in world', *Weekend Australian*, 4–5 Jan. 1997; Greg Bearup, 'War on louts: pitch invaders face $5000 fines', 9 Jan. 1997; John Larkin, 'SCG gets tough on hooligans', *Sunday Telegraph*, 6 April 1997; 'Legless fans face early dismissal in SCG crackdown', *Sydney Morning Herald*, 4 Dec. 1997; Stefanie Balogh, 'Pitch invasion a $1000 "stupidity"', *Australian*, 7 Jan. 1998; 'SCG Trust fires warning' *Sydney Morning Herald*, 17 Sep. 1998; Peter Kogoy and Daniel Dasey, 'Trust vows to best thugs', *Sun Herald*, 17 Jan. 1999; Stephen Gibbs, 'Cricket yob caught and bowled', *Sydney Morning Herald*, 4 March 1999; 'Police shake up security to put stopper on beer boors', *Sydney Morning Herald*, 17 Jan. 2002; Anthony Dennis, 'Flanneletted fools absent from view in SCG crackdown on louts', *Sydney Morning Herald*, 18 Jan. 2002.

39 Heather Gallagher, 'Cricket laser jammers face jail', *Daily Telegraph*, 15 Jan. 1999.

40 Michael Horan, 'Peacemaker', *Daily Telegraph*, 16 Jan. 1999.

41 John Salvado, 'Waugh, Fleming and officials condemn crowd', AAP, *CricInfo*, 11 Jan. 2002; 'Fleming threatens to take New Zealand off the field if bottles fly', *CricInfo*, 14 Jan. 2002; Ben Mitchell, 'Inquiry called on cricket punch-up', *Weekend Australian*, 15–16 Jan. 2000; Mark Fuller, '"We'll walk off MCG", Gilchrist warns', *Sun Herald*, 13 Jan. 2002.

42 Sean Beyon, *CricInfo*, 31 Aug. 2001.

43 See e.g., Michael Henderson, 'ECB must adopt ruthless streak on pitch invaders', *Daily Telegraph*, 7 Aug. 2000.

44 AFP, 'Referee rules tie as Australian batsmen saved from mob', *CricInfo*, 22 April 1999; 'Australian cricketers' union calls for improved safety', 22 April 1999; 'Tie verdict resolves final-ball chaos', *Times*, 22 April 1999.

45 See 'Angry crowd brings series to chaotic close', *Times*, 26 April 1999.

46 AFP, 'Waugh feared for his life', *CricInfo*, 22 April 1999; Mike Selvey, 'Guyana set to carry the can for riots', *Guardian*, 27 April 1999; 'Diplomatic official helps Aussies leave Barbados', *CricInfo*, 2 May 1999; 'Barbados: Curb drinking at cricket', *Barbados Nation*, 11 May 1999.

47 Richard Cashman, '*Ave A Go*, op. cit., p. 123.

28   Bodyline, postmodernism, law and the meaning of life

1   Bodyline has also spawned an incredibly rich cricket literature. For an example, see Ric Sissons and Brian Stoddart, *Cricket and Empire: 1932–33 Bodyline Tour of Australia* (Sydney and London: George Allen & Unwin, 1984); Phillip Derriman, *Bodyline* (Sydney: Fontana, 1984); Gilbert Mant, *A Cuckoo in the Bodyline Nest* (Kenthurt, NSW: 1992). Bodyline continues as part of the popular consciousness of both England and Australia. In June 1990, the ball struck for the winning runs of the series sold at auction for a significant sum, *Sunday Telegraph*, 3 June 1990. See also, Nick Richardson, 'Still Keeping Score', *Bulletin*, 26 July 1996, at pp. 26 et. seq., on the donation of Jack Fingleton's Bodyline letters to the New South Wales Library.

2   Jack Fingleton, former Test cricketer and author, writing in 1968 referred to the English captain in the following terms: 'Jardine was 130 years after his time. He should have gone to Australia in charge of a convict hulk.' From *Bodyline Remembered*, reproduced in *Bat and Pad*, op. cit., at p. 48.

3   Sydney Smith, *History of the Tests*, op. cit., at p. 235 'Jardine, one of the ablest skippers England ever sent to Australia adopted a policy of leg theory…'

4   Sir Pelham Warner, *Lord's, 1787–1945* (London: Pavilion, 1987), at p. 214.

5   'Much confusion has been caused by a very large number of people who thought that Body Line was another form for Leg Theory, and this fact was not at first generally recognized over here.' Id.

6   Malcolm Knox, 'Positive view on negative balls', *Sydney Morning Herald*, 5 Aug. 1998.

7   S. Santhosh, 'Gavaskar's not-so-Sunny side', *CricInfo*, 4 Jan. 2002; 'Chappelli blasts negative Poms', *Daily Telegraph*, 4 Jan. 2002; See also, Ralph Dellor, 'Dexter condemns Hussain's leg theory in India', *CricInfo*, 6 March 2002.

8   Omar Kureishi, 'Vaughan dismissal, leg theory legitimate tactics', *Dawn*, 25 Dec. 2001.

9   As quoted in *The Faber Book of Cricket*, op. cit., at p. 220.

10   Ashis Nandy, op. cit., at p. 16.

11   Sir Lawrence Jones, 'An appreciation in *The Times*' (24 June 1958), in *The Faber Book of Cricket*, op. cit., at p. 222.

12   See Derek Birley, *The Willow Wand*, op. cit., at pp. 97–113.

13   As reproduced in Jack Pollard, *Australian Cricket*, op. cit., at p. 154.

14   Jack Egan, op. cit., at p. 146.

15   Id., p. 137.

16   Ashis Nandy, op. cit., at pp. 140–41.

17   Jack Fingleton, 'Bodyline Remembered', op. cit., at p. 49.

18   Peter Roebuck, 'Larwood's awesome legacy lives', *Sydney Morning Herald*, 17 Feb. 1990. See also David Frith, 'The Last of the Line', *Wisden* (1996), at p. 31.

19   'Admitting it is within the law – there are many things in cricket which by the laws of the game are right, but which are "not done". Is it worth while if, as a result of bodyline, England and her greatest cricketing Dominion are to "fight" each other? It was not thus that cricket gained its great name, a name synonymous with all that is fair, and kindly, noble and upright.' P.F. Warner, 'Letter to the *Daily Telegraph*', June 1933, in *The Faber Book of Cricket*, op. cit., at p. 245.

20   See Jack Egan, op. cit., at p. 154; Jack Fingleton, op. cit., at p. 51 and Donald Bradman, *The Art of Cricket*, op. cit., at pp. 198 et. seq.

21   *Guardian*, 8 June 1985, as reproduced in the *Guardian Book of Cricket*, op. cit.

29   Conclusion: on life, law and cricket

1   See Johan Huizinga, *Homo Ludens*, op. cit., at p. 29 on the role of this tension in sport.

2   See especially, Ashis Nandy, op. cit.

3   'Pitched Battle', *Cricket Life international*, June 1990, p. 5.

4   Ashis Nandy, op. cit., p. 20.

Index